SPAC
BASTARDS

VOLUME 2: THE COST OF DOING BUSINESS

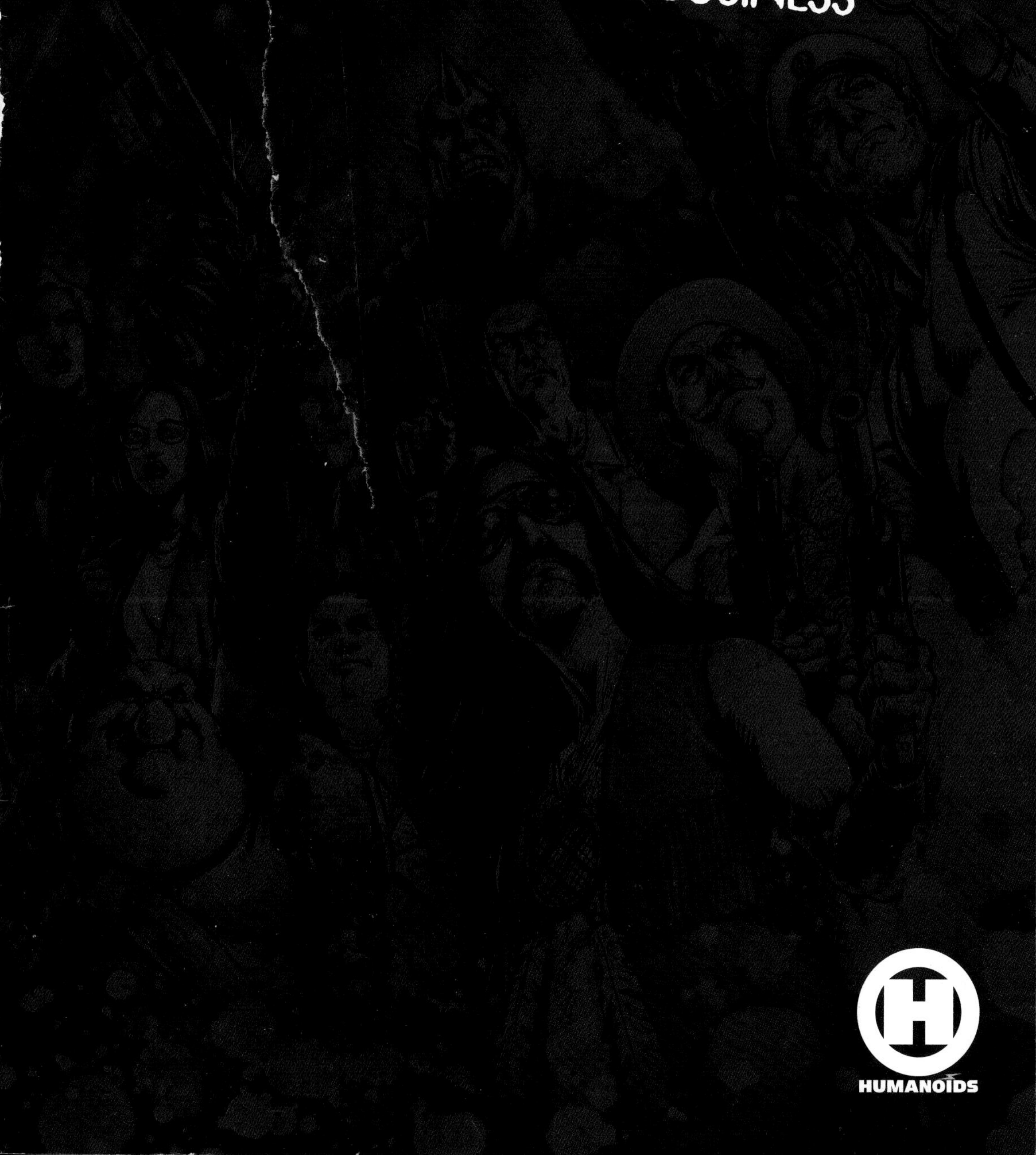

HUMANOIDS

SPACE BASTARDS

VOLUME TWO - THE COST OF DOING BUSINESS

ERIC PETERSON & JOE AUBREY | Writers

DARICK ROBERTSON (EP. 6-7), SIMON BISLEY (MANNY CORNS, ZUNA),

CLINT LANGLEY (CALTO FREMIS, NOBODY BEATS THE MANICORN),

GABO (THE BROWN BUFFALO MEETS THE AVOCADO KID, FAILED FIRST DAYS),

BOO COOK (COLLATERAL DAMAGE) & COLIN MACNEIL (RESURRECTION MARY) | Artists

PETE PANTAZIS (EP. 6-7, ZUNA, RESURRECTION MARY) & PAUSCORPI (MANNY CORNS) | Colorists

TAYLOR ESPOSITO | Letterer

DARICK ROBERTSON with PETE PANTAZIS | Cover

SPACE BASTARDS created by ERIC PETERSON,
JOE AUBREY & DARICK ROBERTSON

MARK WAID | Publisher
ROB LEVIN & JAKE THOMAS | Editors
JERRY FRISSEN | Art Director
RYAN LEWIS | Designer

FABRICE GIGER | CEO
MATTHIEU COPPET | GROUP COO
ALEX DONOGHUE | COO, U.S. Operations
GUILLAUME NOUGARET | CFO
JERRY FRISSEN | Senior Art Director
JAKE THOMAS | Executive Editor
AMANDA LUCIDO | Operations Coordinator
BETH YORK | Development Director, Film & TV
EDMOND LEE | Director, Licensing
BRUNO BARBERI | CTO
licensing@humanoids.com | Rights and Licensing
PR@humanoids.com | Press and Social Media

WWW.SPACEBASTARDS.COM | The Official Site for Limited Edition Hardcovers

To E and J.
—Joe

To Joe, for making me sit up straighter
amidst everything else you do and are. To
Darick for plucking visuals from our brains
and making them better than we imagined.
To Simon, Clint, Boo, Colin, Glenn and
Karen, Gabo— the Space Bastards.

—Eric

To Marc Greenberg, for always having my
back. Special thanks to Jeff Johnson and
Stephen J.B. Jones.

—Darick

HUMANOIDS

SPACE BASTARDS VOL. 2: THE COST OF DOING BUSINESS. First Printing. This book is a publication of Humanoids, Inc. 8033 Sunset Blvd. #628, Los Angeles, CA 90046. Copyright Eric Peterson & Joe Aubrey & Humanoids, Inc., Los Angeles (USA). All rights reserved. Humanoids® and the Humanoids logo are registered trademarks of Humanoids, Inc. in the U.S. and other countries. LCCN: 2021935216

This volume collects Space Bastards: Tooth & Mail Issues 7-9, Space Bastards: Special Delivery, and Bonus Stories "Calto Fremis," "Resurrection Mary," & "Failed First Days."

The story and characters presented in this publication are fictional. Any similarities to events or persons living or dead are purely coincidental. No portion of this book may be reproduced by any means without the express written consent of the copyright holder except for artwork used for review purposes. Printed in **Lithuania.**

(CO-)AUTHOR FOREWORD

So this is it. You hold in your hands the end of the arc started last year through Humanoids' killer run. The culmination of seven years of comic book work and 15 years since the idea of Davey Proton, Roy Sharpton, Manny, and the rest first entered our heads.

This whole experience has been mind-shattering in the best way. We wrote the material enclosed in this, in the volume one trade paperback, and in the four spacebastards.com hardcovers between the hours of 10pm and 5am across clumps of months from 2014-2020. The bulk of the *Tooth and Mail* episodes happened over a six month period. Years of getting pages back from Darick Robertson and laughing and then immediately begging for the next page. And then the itch. The Space Bastards universe gives us an itch. It hurts when we spend too long not actively writing in that space, and living in it.

"Well, what else can we write?"

"There's a lot of characters here that we haven't explored. But if we open that box..."

"I kind of want to open that box..."

"Alright, let's just do one. With Colin MacNeil from *2000AD*'s America."

"That was stupendously fun. What if we worked with Simon Bisley and Clint Langley and Boo Cook?"

We opened the box. The body of work (before we even landed a publisher) doubled. We walked into Humanoids with (mostly) everything you see here and more, with no promise of anyone ever even liking it.

And then the pandemic. No shows, anywhere. Issues came out. There were reviews that we are eternally grateful for. Podcasts, interviews. We weren't totally in a vacuum but, in recent months when we've gotten a chance to meet readers in person, it has been completely surreal. It's been years and years of us two jokers just trying to make each other laugh over scripts and then laughing over art that is way better than we have a right to be associated with. But there is nothing like a new reader coming up and asking about Leroy Palestine or Calto Fremis. Knowing they love it enough to remember the last names of these characters.

Spawning *Space Bastards* from our brains into the cosmos was something that we probably just had to do with our lives. However, knowing that people love it as much as we do is more valuable than the ticket it cost to take this ride.

Thank you, all. And welcome to the service.

—**Eric Peterson**

PREVIOUSLY IN SPACE BASTARDS: TOOTH & MAIL

The Intergalactic Postal Service, a collection of violent brigands known as "Space Bastards," controls the transport of mail throughout the cosmos. They are crude. They are dangerous. They are also, oddly, heroes of the rough and tumble space frontier.

But not to everyone.

Wayne Powers, CEO of Powers Industries, wants them destroyed. He has developed a teleportation technology that will render the Space Bastards obsolete. That still wasn't quite enough for Wayne Powers, though.

So he blew them all up.

TOOTH & MAIL:
EPISODE 6

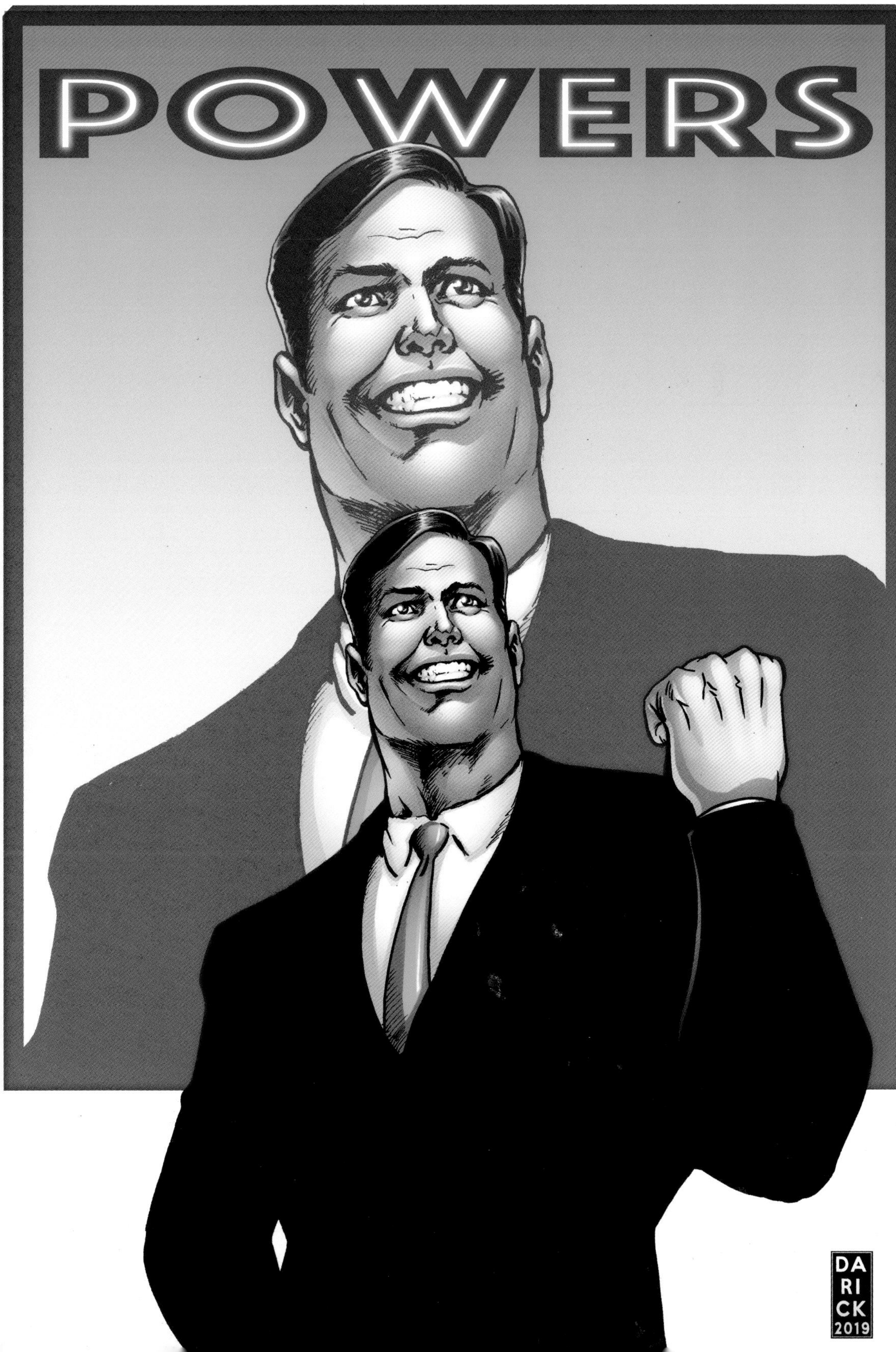
POWERS
DA
RI
CK
2019

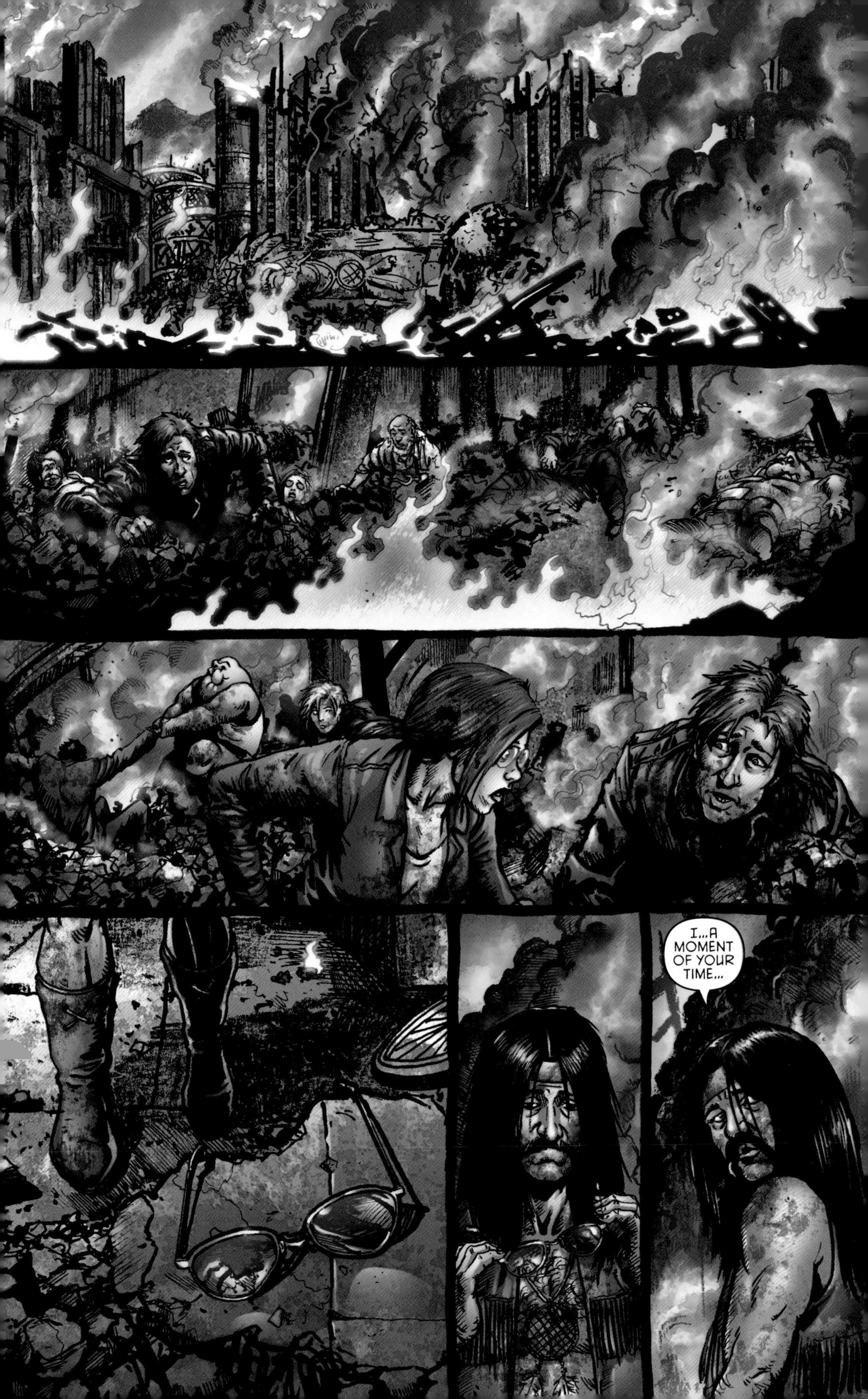
I...A MOMENT OF YOUR TIME...

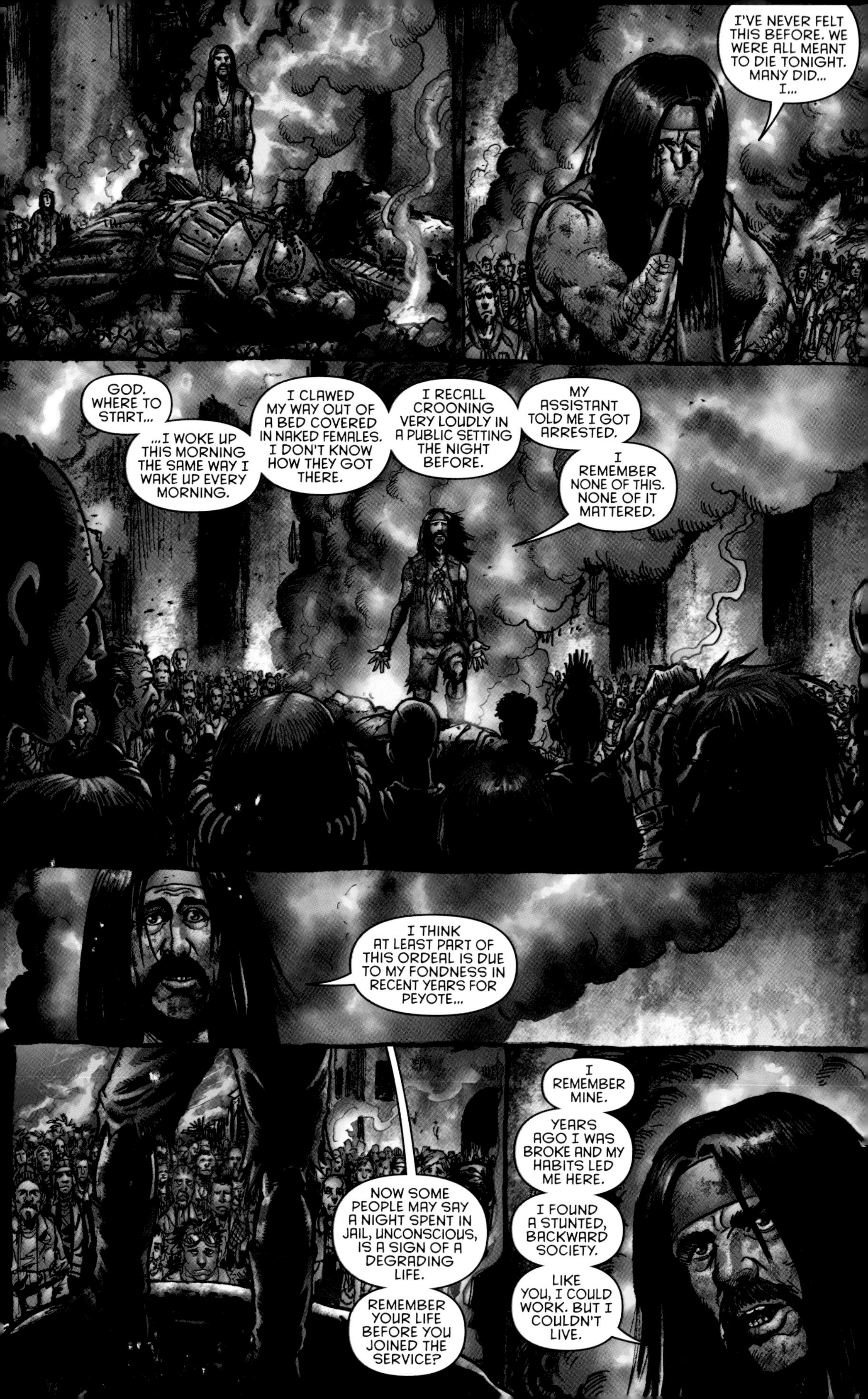
I'VE NEVER FELT THIS BEFORE. WE WERE ALL MEANT TO DIE TONIGHT. MANY DID... I...
GOD. WHERE TO START...
...I WOKE UP THIS MORNING THE SAME WAY I WAKE UP EVERY MORNING.
I CLAWED MY WAY OUT OF A BED COVERED IN NAKED FEMALES. I DON'T KNOW HOW THEY GOT THERE.
I RECALL CROONING VERY LOUDLY IN A PUBLIC SETTING THE NIGHT BEFORE.
MY ASSISTANT TOLD ME I GOT ARRESTED.
I REMEMBER NONE OF THIS. NONE OF IT MATTERED.
I THINK AT LEAST PART OF THIS ORDEAL IS DUE TO MY FONDNESS IN RECENT YEARS FOR PEYOTE...
NOW SOME PEOPLE MAY SAY A NIGHT SPENT IN JAIL, UNCONSCIOUS, IS A SIGN OF A DEGRADING LIFE.
REMEMBER YOUR LIFE BEFORE YOU JOINED THE SERVICE?
I REMEMBER MINE.
YEARS AGO I WAS BROKE AND MY HABITS LED ME HERE.
I FOUND A STUNTED, BACKWARD SOCIETY.
LIKE YOU, I COULD WORK. BUT I COULDN'T LIVE.

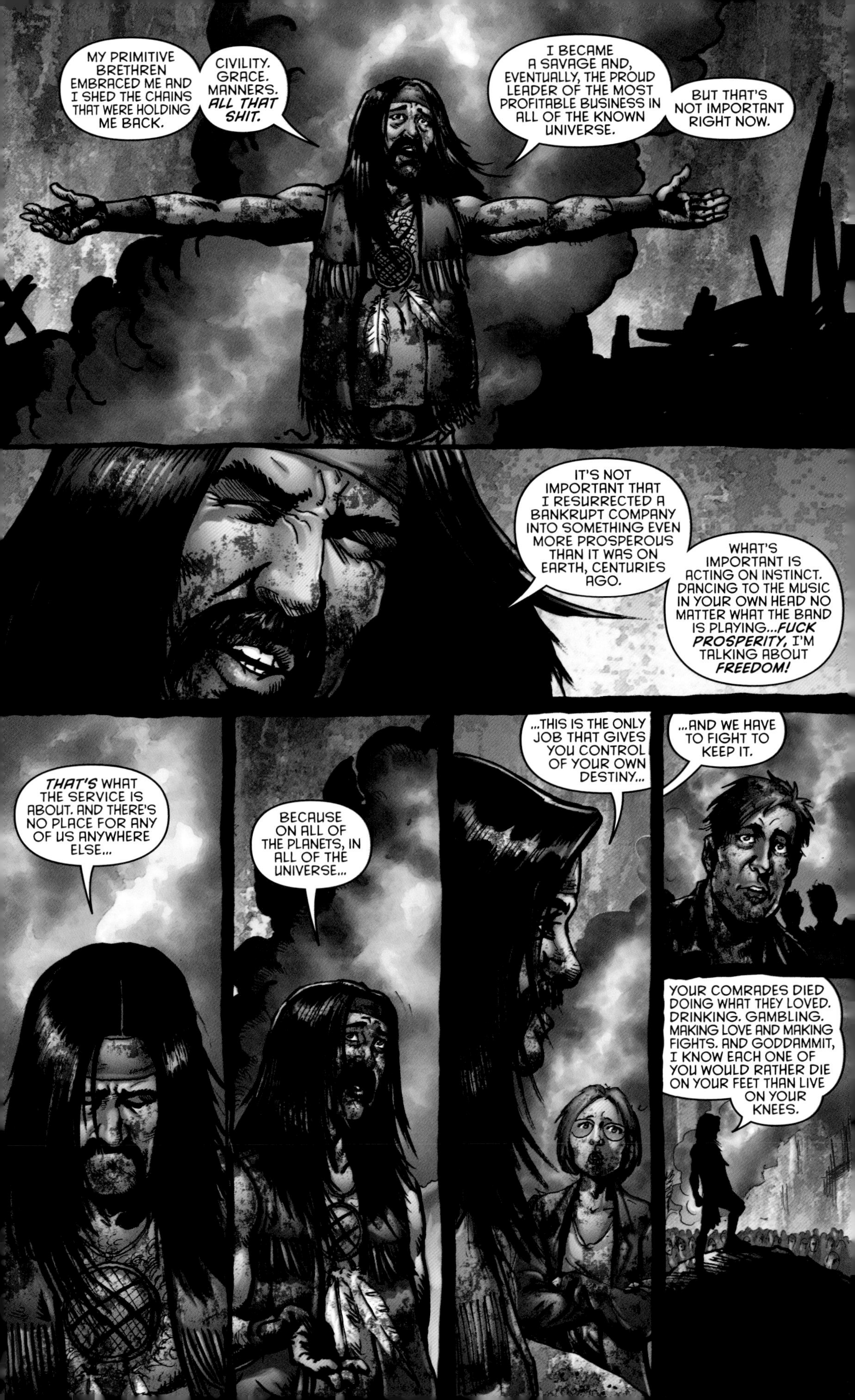
MY PRIMITIVE BRETHREN EMBRACED ME AND I SHED THE CHAINS THAT WERE HOLDING ME BACK.
CIVILITY. GRACE. MANNERS. ALL THAT SHIT.
I BECAME A SAVAGE AND, EVENTUALLY, THE PROUD LEADER OF THE MOST PROFITABLE BUSINESS IN ALL OF THE KNOWN UNIVERSE.
BUT THAT'S NOT IMPORTANT RIGHT NOW.
IT'S NOT IMPORTANT THAT I RESURRECTED A BANKRUPT COMPANY INTO SOMETHING EVEN MORE PROSPEROUS THAN IT WAS ON EARTH, CENTURIES AGO.
WHAT'S IMPORTANT IS ACTING ON INSTINCT. DANCING TO THE MUSIC IN YOUR OWN HEAD NO MATTER WHAT THE BAND IS PLAYING...FUCK PROSPERITY, I'M TALKING ABOUT FREEDOM!
THAT'S WHAT THE SERVICE IS ABOUT. AND THERE'S NO PLACE FOR ANY OF US ANYWHERE ELSE...
BECAUSE ON ALL OF THE PLANETS, IN ALL OF THE UNIVERSE...
...THIS IS THE ONLY JOB THAT GIVES YOU CONTROL OF YOUR OWN DESTINY...
...AND WE HAVE TO FIGHT TO KEEP IT.
YOUR COMRADES DIED DOING WHAT THEY LOVED. DRINKING. GAMBLING. MAKING LOVE AND MAKING FIGHTS. AND GODDAMMIT, I KNOW EACH ONE OF YOU WOULD RATHER DIE ON YOUR FEET THAN LIVE ON YOUR KNEES.

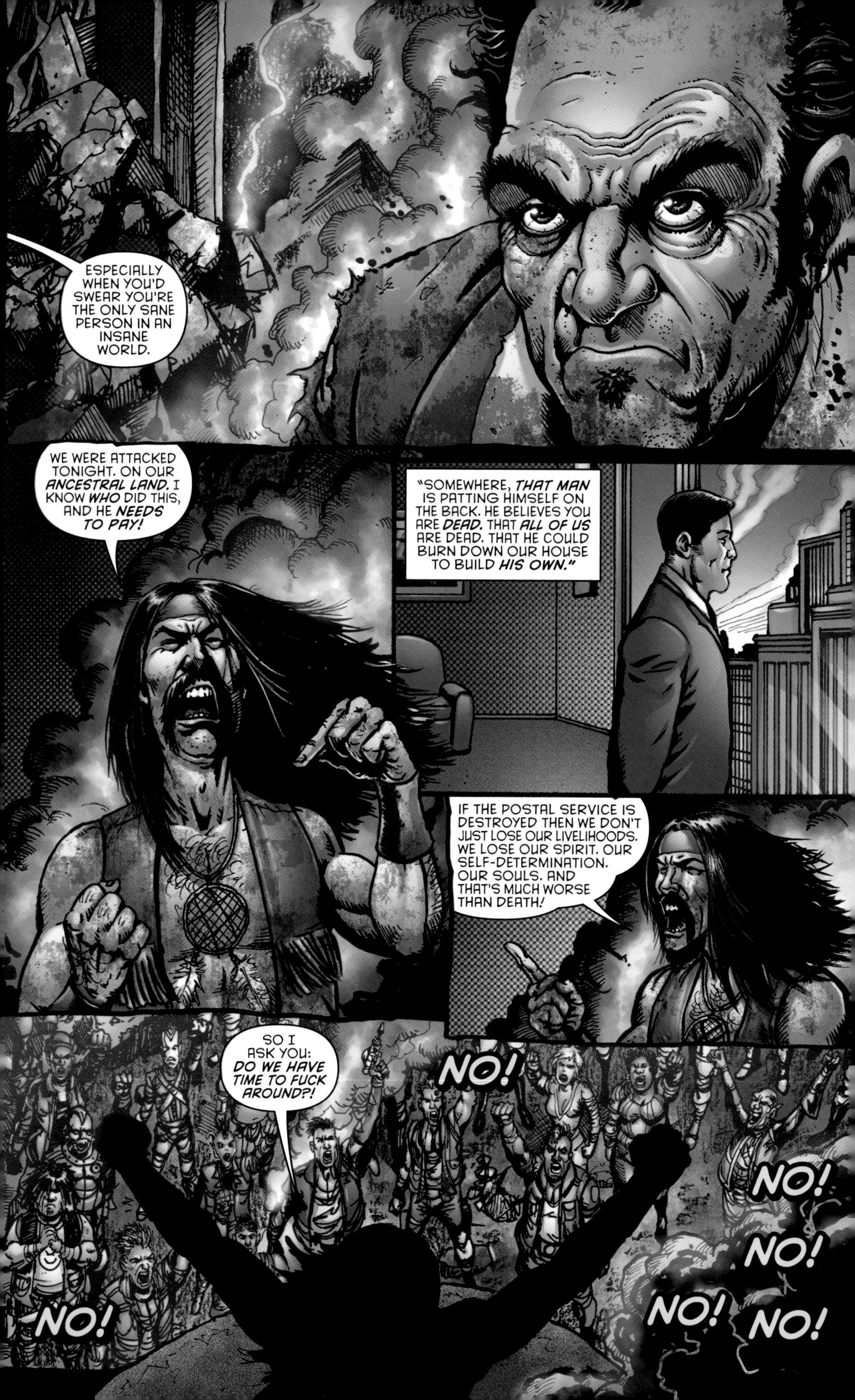

ESPECIALLY WHEN YOU'D SWEAR YOU'RE THE ONLY SANE PERSON IN AN INSANE WORLD.
WE WERE ATTACKED TONIGHT. ON OUR *ANCESTRAL LAND.* I KNOW *WHO* DID THIS, AND HE *NEEDS TO PAY!*
"SOMEWHERE, *THAT MAN* IS PATTING HIMSELF ON THE BACK. HE BELIEVES YOU ARE *DEAD.* THAT *ALL OF US* ARE DEAD. THAT HE COULD BURN DOWN OUR HOUSE TO BUILD *HIS OWN.*"
IF THE POSTAL SERVICE IS DESTROYED THEN WE DON'T JUST LOSE OUR LIVELIHOODS. WE LOSE OUR SPIRIT. OUR SELF-DETERMINATION. OUR SOULS. AND THAT'S MUCH WORSE THAN DEATH!
SO I ASK YOU: *DO WE HAVE TIME TO FUCK AROUND?!*
NO!
NO!
NO!
NO!
NO!
NO!

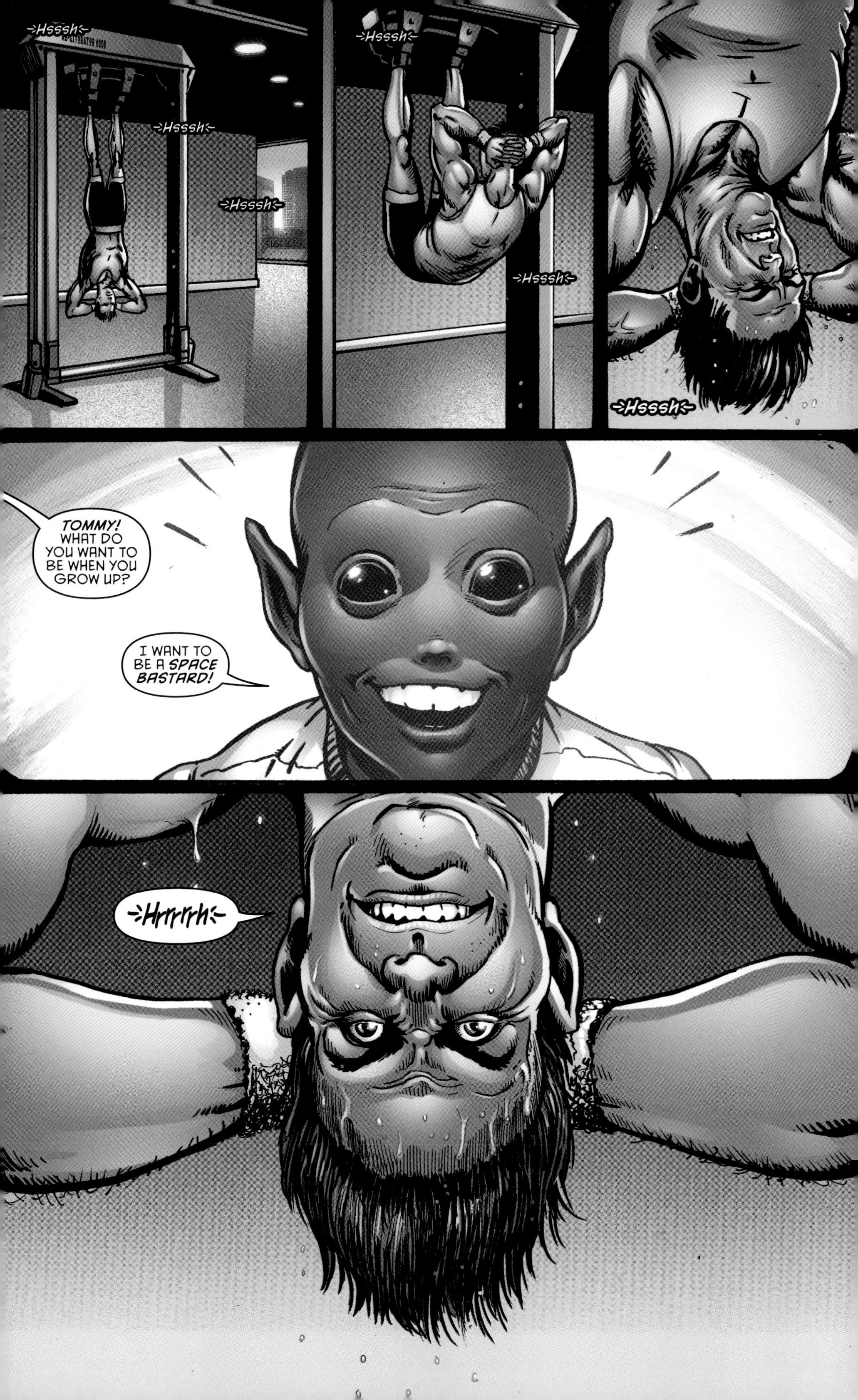

-Hsssh-
-Hsssh-
-Hsssh-
-Hsssh-
-Hsssh-
-Hsssh-
TOMMY! WHAT DO YOU WANT TO BE WHEN YOU GROW UP?
I WANT TO BE A SPACE BASTARD!
-Hrrrrh-

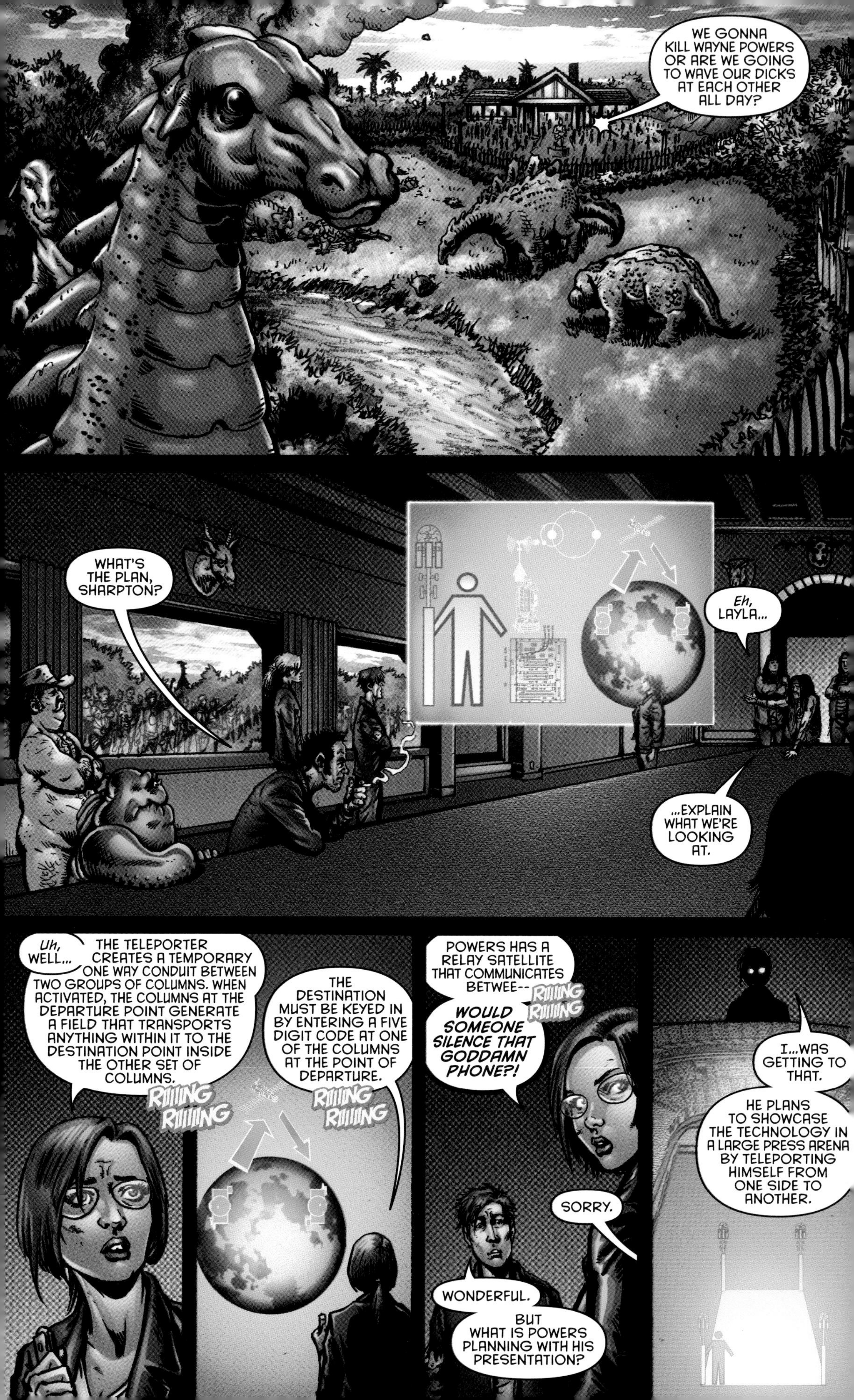
WE GONNA KILL WAYNE POWERS OR ARE WE GOING TO WAVE OUR DICKS AT EACH OTHER ALL DAY?
WHAT'S THE PLAN, SHARPTON?
Eh, LAYLA...
...EXPLAIN WHAT WE'RE LOOKING AT.
Uh, WELL...
THE TELEPORTER CREATES A TEMPORARY ONE WAY CONDUIT BETWEEN TWO GROUPS OF COLUMNS. WHEN ACTIVATED, THE COLUMNS AT THE DEPARTURE POINT GENERATE A FIELD THAT TRANSPORTS ANYTHING WITHIN IT TO THE DESTINATION POINT INSIDE THE OTHER SET OF COLUMNS.
RIIIING RIIIING
THE DESTINATION MUST BE KEYED IN BY ENTERING A FIVE DIGIT CODE AT ONE OF THE COLUMNS AT THE POINT OF DEPARTURE.
RIIIING RIIIING
POWERS HAS A RELAY SATELLITE THAT COMMUNICATES BETWEE--
RIIIING RIIIING
WOULD SOMEONE SILENCE THAT GODDAMN PHONE?!
SORRY.
WONDERFUL.
BUT WHAT IS POWERS PLANNING WITH HIS PRESENTATION?
I...WAS GETTING TO THAT.
HE PLANS TO SHOWCASE THE TECHNOLOGY IN A LARGE PRESS ARENA BY TELEPORTING HIMSELF FROM ONE SIDE TO ANOTHER.

SO I THINK OUR **BEST CHANCE** OF SUCC... IS--

HERE'S THE **PLAN,** GUYS.

KLIK

THE PLAN

WE BREAK INTO THE SATELLITE AND CHANGE THE CODES. WAYNE CAN'T TELEPORT AND HE URINATES ON HIMSELF.

KLIK

WE NEED TO DO **MORE** THAN **SABOTAGE** THE DEMONSTRATION. WE HAVE TO ELIMINATE **ALL TRACES** OF THIS TECHNOLOGY.

ACCORDING TO THE FILES, POWERS HAD A PROTOTYPE STORED HERE, ON MAMMET IV.

OKAY, NEW PLAN GUYS. WE TAKE THAT PROTOTYPE AND TELEPORT A STEAMING STACK OF HUMAN SHIT INTO THE MID... HIS BIG SHO...

RIIIING RIIIING

CHRIST ALMIGHTY.

SORRY. MY FUCKING EX-WIFE...THE GIFT THAT KEEPS ON TAKING.

YOU CAN CHAT WITH HER ON THE WAY.

Aw, MAN, I--

ENOUGH. THIS IS **NOT THE DAY.** YOU WILL GO GET THE PROTOTYPE. AND YOU **WILL SHIT IN IT.**

SOMEONE ELSE GO TO THE SATELLITE AND ENSURE THAT LEROY'S SHIT GETS THROUGH. LEROY, EAT BUFFALO WINGS ON THE WAY.

A LOT OF THEM.

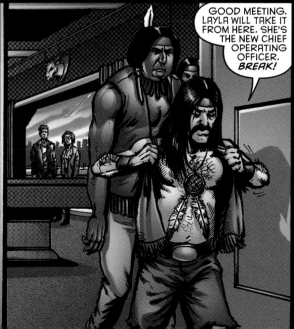

GOOD MEETING. LAYLA WILL TAKE IT FROM HERE. SHE'S THE NEW CHIEF OPERATING OFFICER. **BREAK!**

OKAY...LET ME COME UP WITH SOMETHING THAT ACTUALLY **MAKES SENSE.**

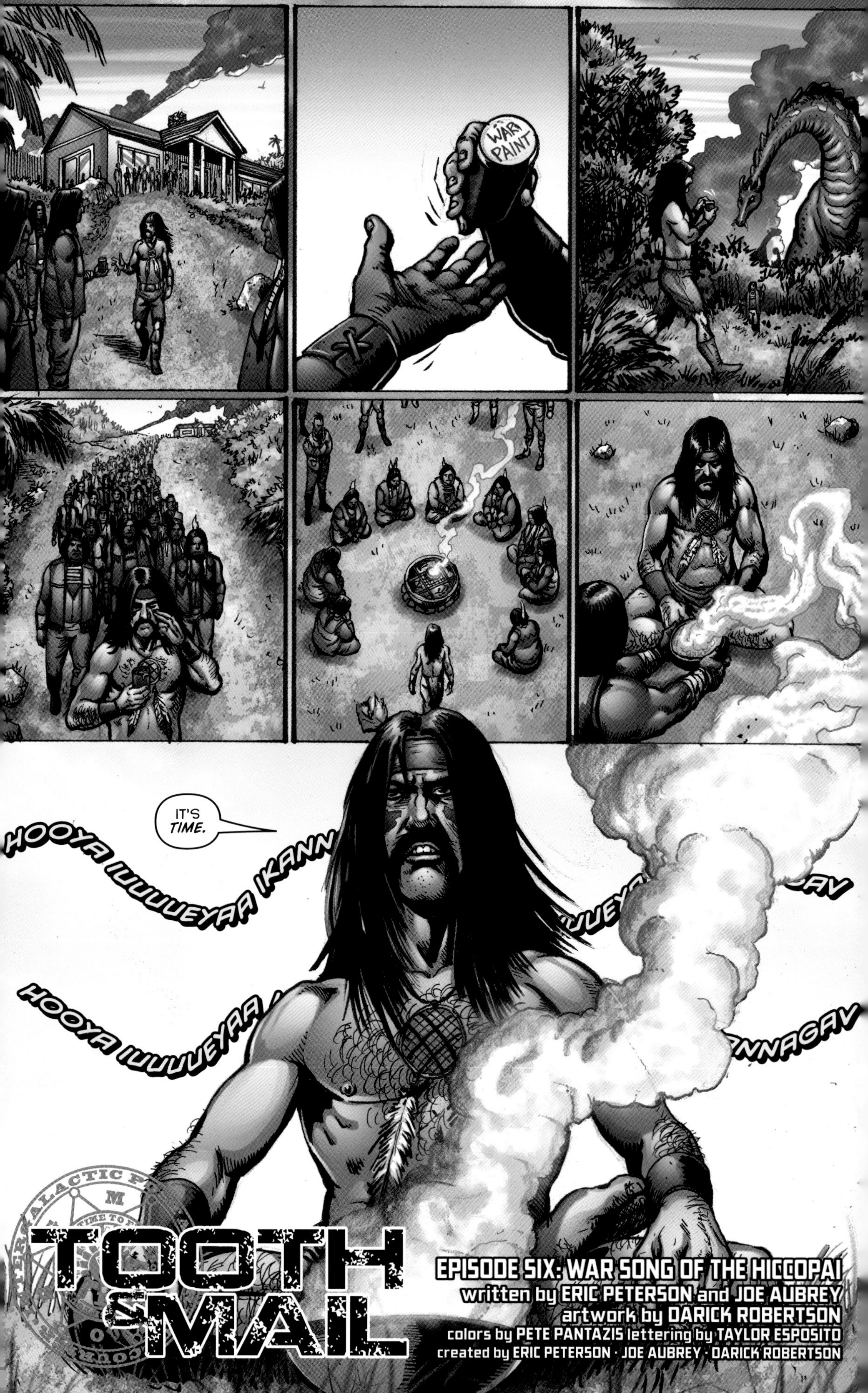
WAR PAINT
IT'S TIME.
HOOYA IUUUUEYAA IKANN
HOOYA IUUUUEYAA
NNAGAV
TOOTH & MAIL
EPISODE SIX: WAR SONG OF THE HICCOPAI
written by ERIC PETERSON and JOE AUBREY
artwork by DARICK ROBERTSON
colors by PETE PANTAZIS lettering by TAYLOR ESPOSITO
created by ERIC PETERSON · JOE AUBREY · DARICK ROBERTSON

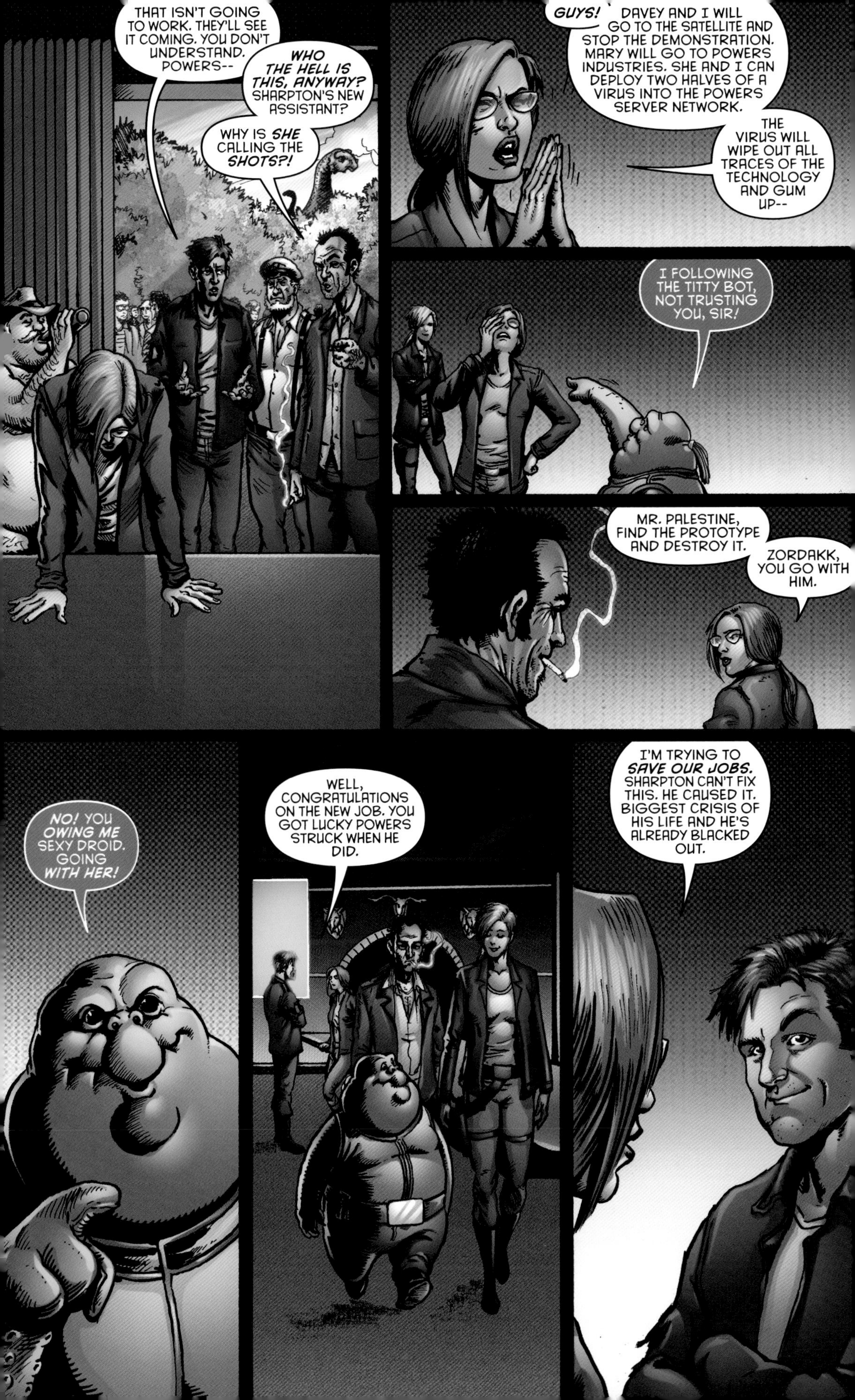
THAT ISN'T GOING TO WORK. THEY'LL SEE IT COMING. YOU DON'T UNDERSTAND. POWERS--
WHO THE HELL IS THIS, ANYWAY? SHARPTON'S NEW ASSISTANT?
WHY IS SHE CALLING THE SHOTS?!
GUYS!
DAVEY AND I WILL GO TO THE SATELLITE AND STOP THE DEMONSTRATION. MARY WILL GO TO POWERS INDUSTRIES. SHE AND I CAN DEPLOY TWO HALVES OF A VIRUS INTO THE POWERS SERVER NETWORK.
THE VIRUS WILL WIPE OUT ALL TRACES OF THE TECHNOLOGY AND GUM UP--
I FOLLOWING THE TITTY BOT, NOT TRUSTING YOU, SIR!
MR. PALESTINE, FIND THE PROTOTYPE AND DESTROY IT.
ZORDAKK, YOU GO WITH HIM.
NO! YOU OWING ME SEXY DROID. GOING WITH HER!
WELL, CONGRATULATIONS ON THE NEW JOB. YOU GOT LUCKY POWERS STRUCK WHEN HE DID.
I'M TRYING TO SAVE OUR JOBS. SHARPTON CAN'T FIX THIS. HE CAUSED IT. BIGGEST CRISIS OF HIS LIFE AND HE'S ALREADY BLACKED OUT.

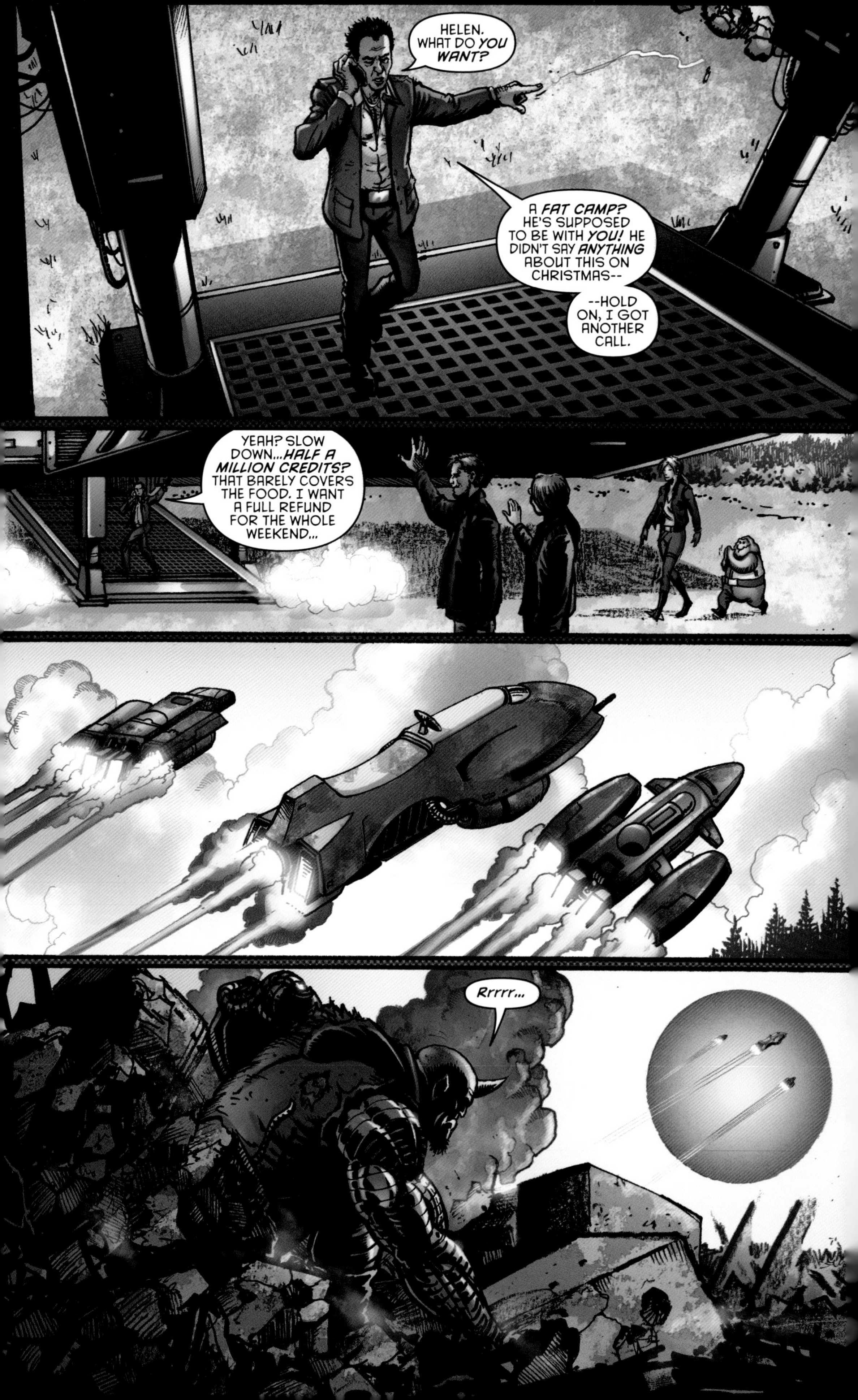
HELEN. WHAT DO YOU WANT?
A FAT CAMP? HE'S SUPPOSED TO BE WITH YOU! HE DIDN'T SAY ANYTHING ABOUT THIS ON CHRISTMAS--
--HOLD ON, I GOT ANOTHER CALL.
YEAH? SLOW DOWN...HALF A MILLION CREDITS? THAT BARELY COVERS THE FOOD. I WANT A FULL REFUND FOR THE WHOLE WEEKEND...
Rrrrr...

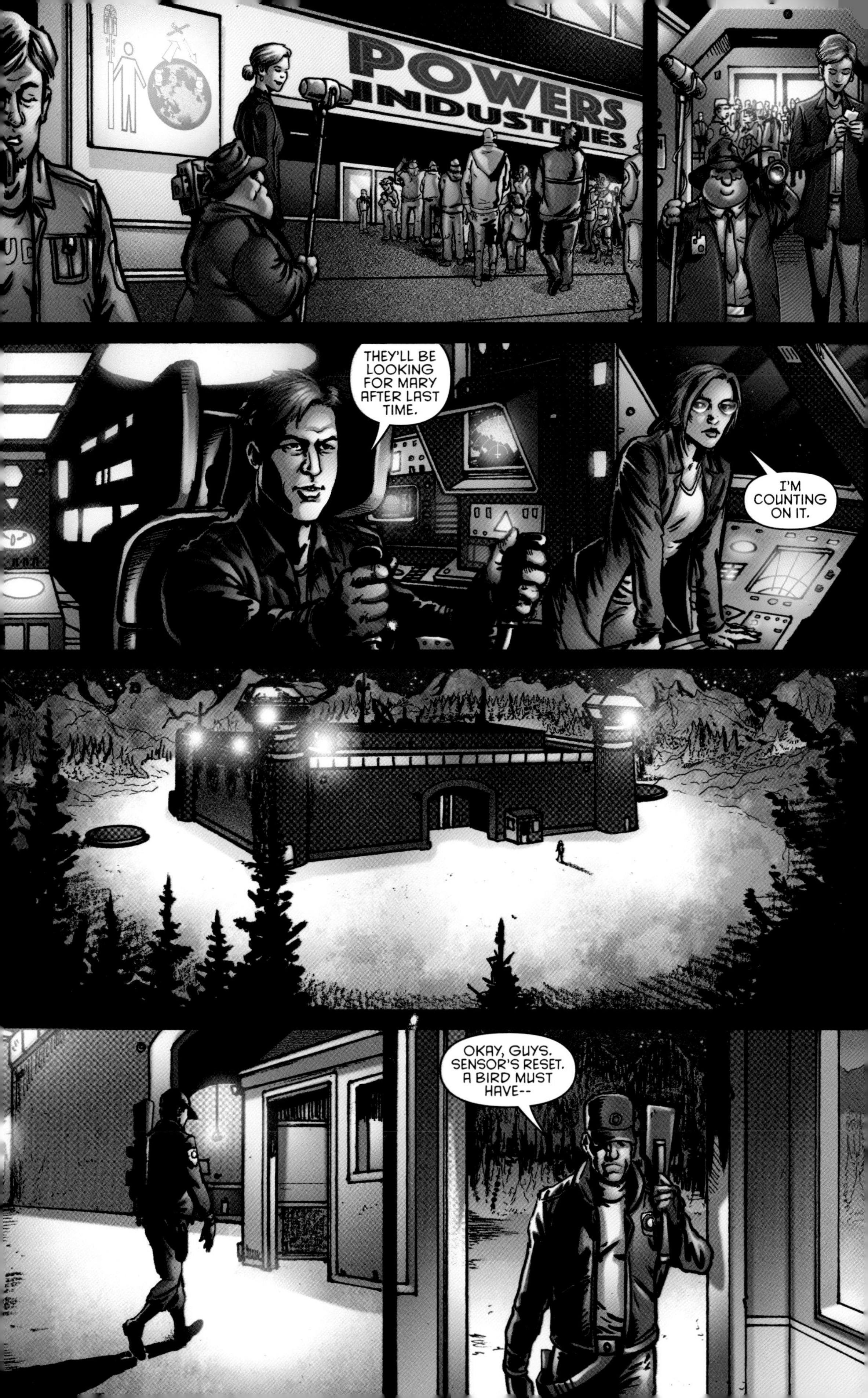
POWERS INDUSTRIES
THEY'LL BE LOOKING FOR MARY AFTER LAST TIME.
I'M COUNTING ON IT.
OKAY, GUYS. SENSOR'S RESET. A BIRD MUST HAVE--

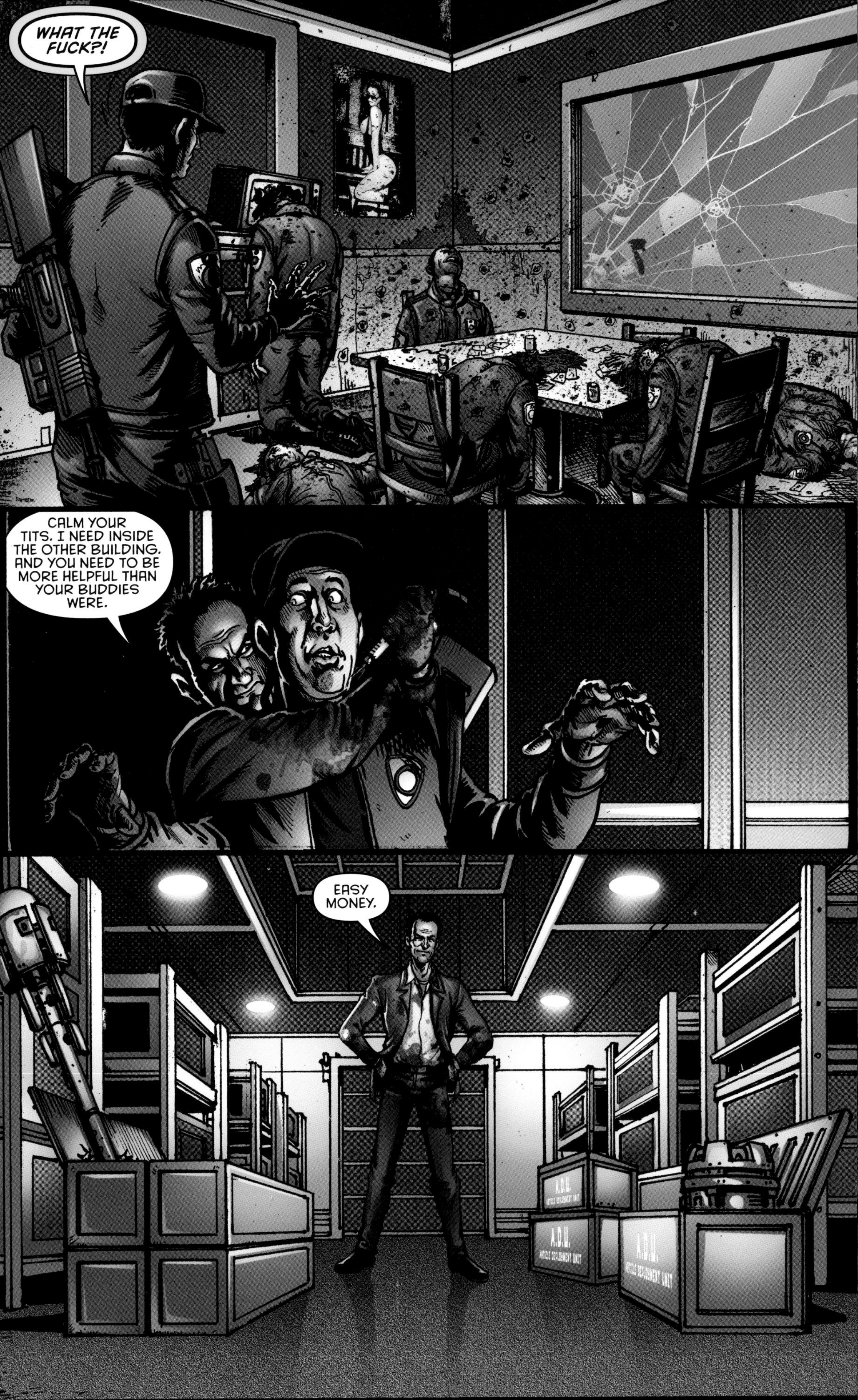
WHAT THE FUCK?!
CALM YOUR TITS. I NEED INSIDE THE OTHER BUILDING. AND YOU NEED TO BE MORE HELPFUL THAN YOUR BUDDIES WERE.
EASY MONEY.
A.D.U.
A.D.U.
A.D.U.

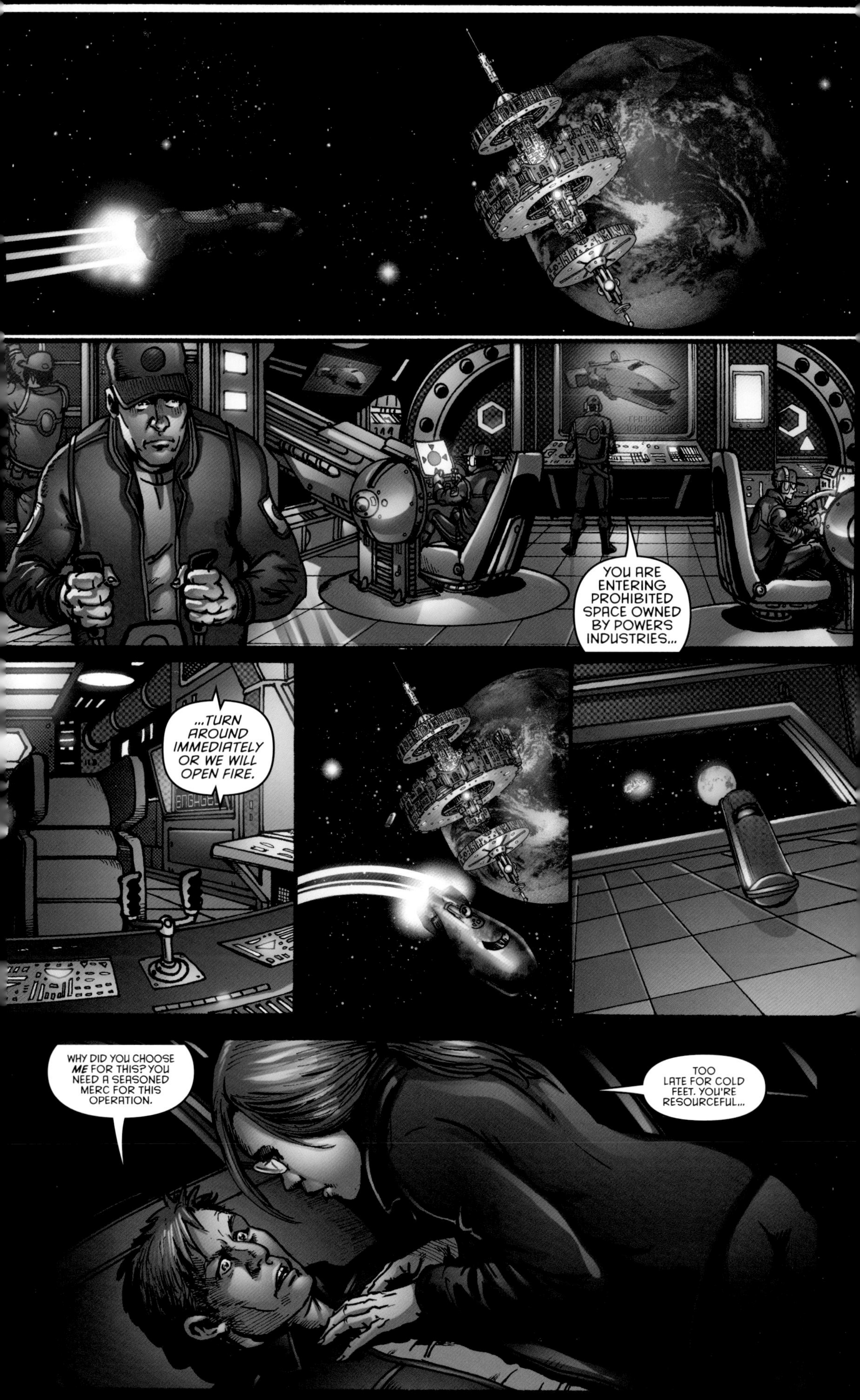
YOU ARE ENTERING PROHIBITED SPACE OWNED BY POWERS INDUSTRIES...
...TURN AROUND IMMEDIATELY OR WE WILL OPEN FIRE.
WHY DID YOU CHOOSE ME FOR THIS? YOU NEED A SEASONED MERC FOR THIS OPERATION.
TOO LATE FOR COLD FEET. YOU'RE RESOURCEFUL...

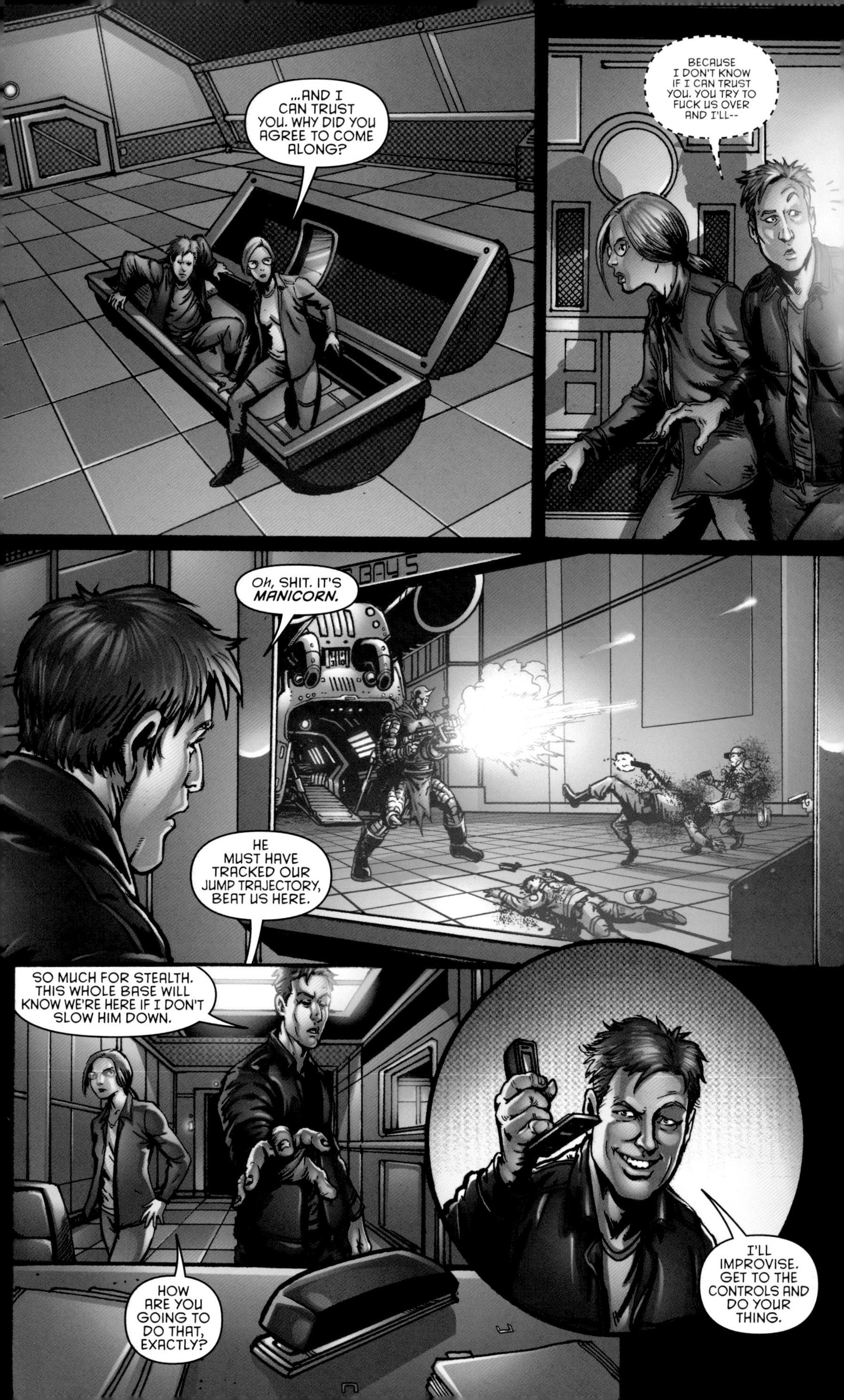
...AND I CAN TRUST YOU. WHY DID YOU AGREE TO COME ALONG?
BECAUSE I DON'T KNOW IF I CAN TRUST YOU. YOU TRY TO FUCK US OVER AND I'LL--
BAY 5
Oh, SHIT. IT'S ***MANICORN.***
HE MUST HAVE TRACKED OUR JUMP TRAJECTORY, BEAT US HERE.
SO MUCH FOR STEALTH. THIS WHOLE BASE WILL KNOW WE'RE HERE IF I DON'T SLOW HIM DOWN.
HOW ARE YOU GOING TO DO THAT, EXACTLY?
I'LL IMPROVISE. GET TO THE CONTROLS AND DO YOUR THING.

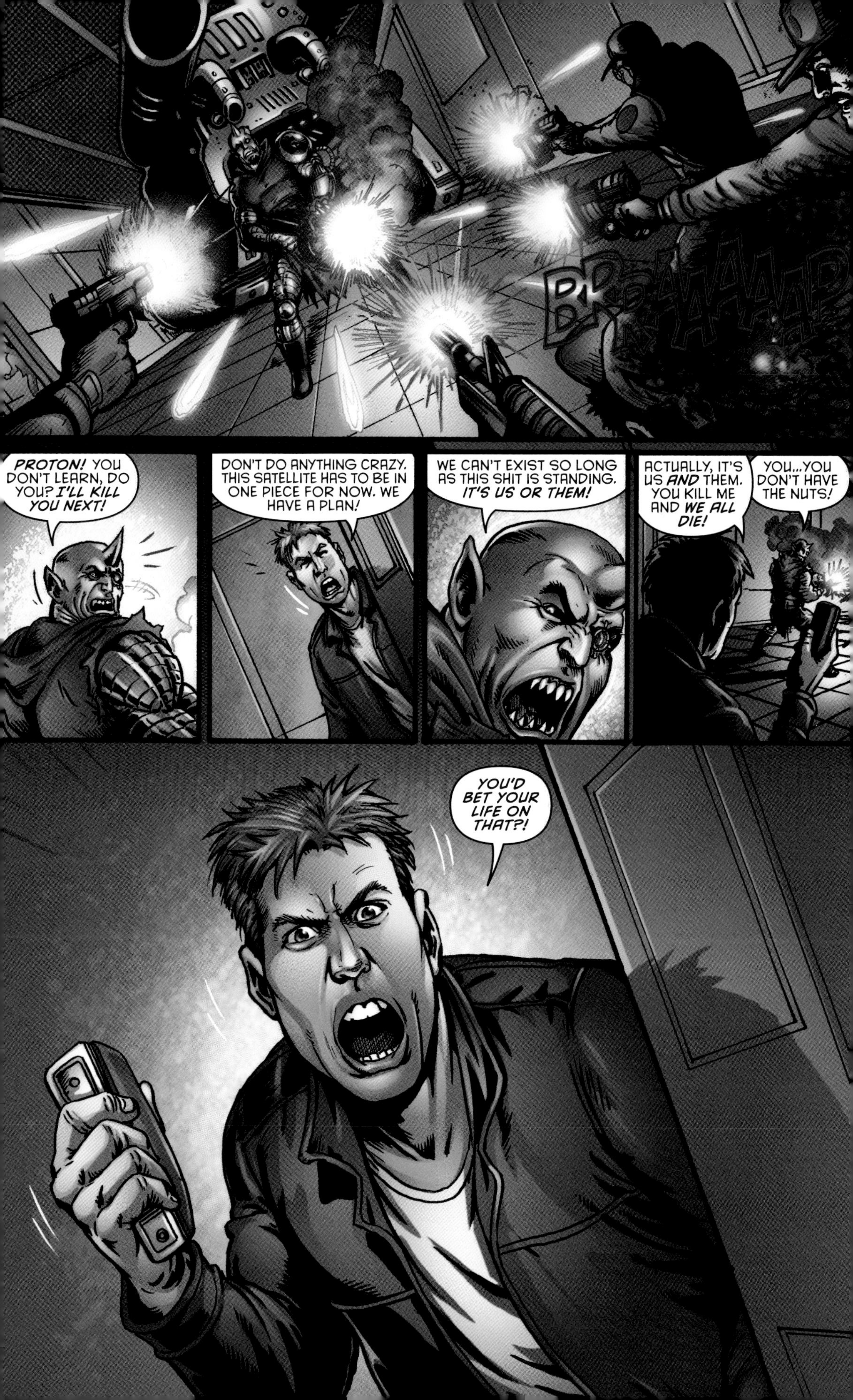
PROTON! YOU DON'T LEARN, DO YOU? I'LL KILL YOU NEXT!
DON'T DO ANYTHING CRAZY. THIS SATELLITE HAS TO BE IN ONE PIECE FOR NOW. WE HAVE A PLAN!
WE CAN'T EXIST SO LONG AS THIS SHIT IS STANDING. IT'S US OR THEM!
ACTUALLY, IT'S US AND THEM. YOU KILL ME AND WE ALL DIE!
YOU...YOU DON'T HAVE THE NUTS!
YOU'D BET YOUR LIFE ON THAT?!

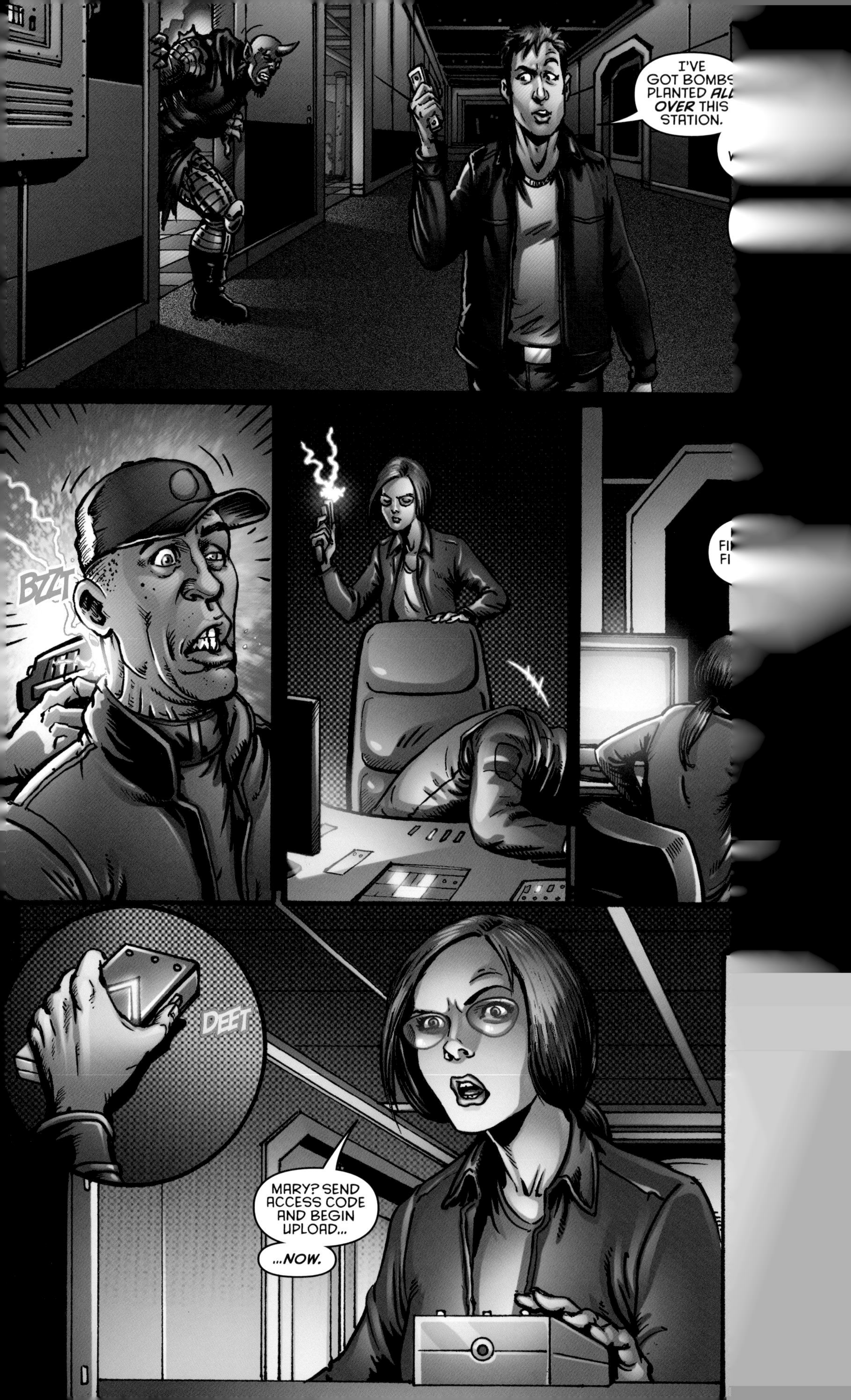
I'VE GOT BOMBS PLANTED ALL OVER THIS STATION.
BZZT
DEET
MARY? SEND ACCESS CODE AND BEGIN UPLOAD...
...NOW.

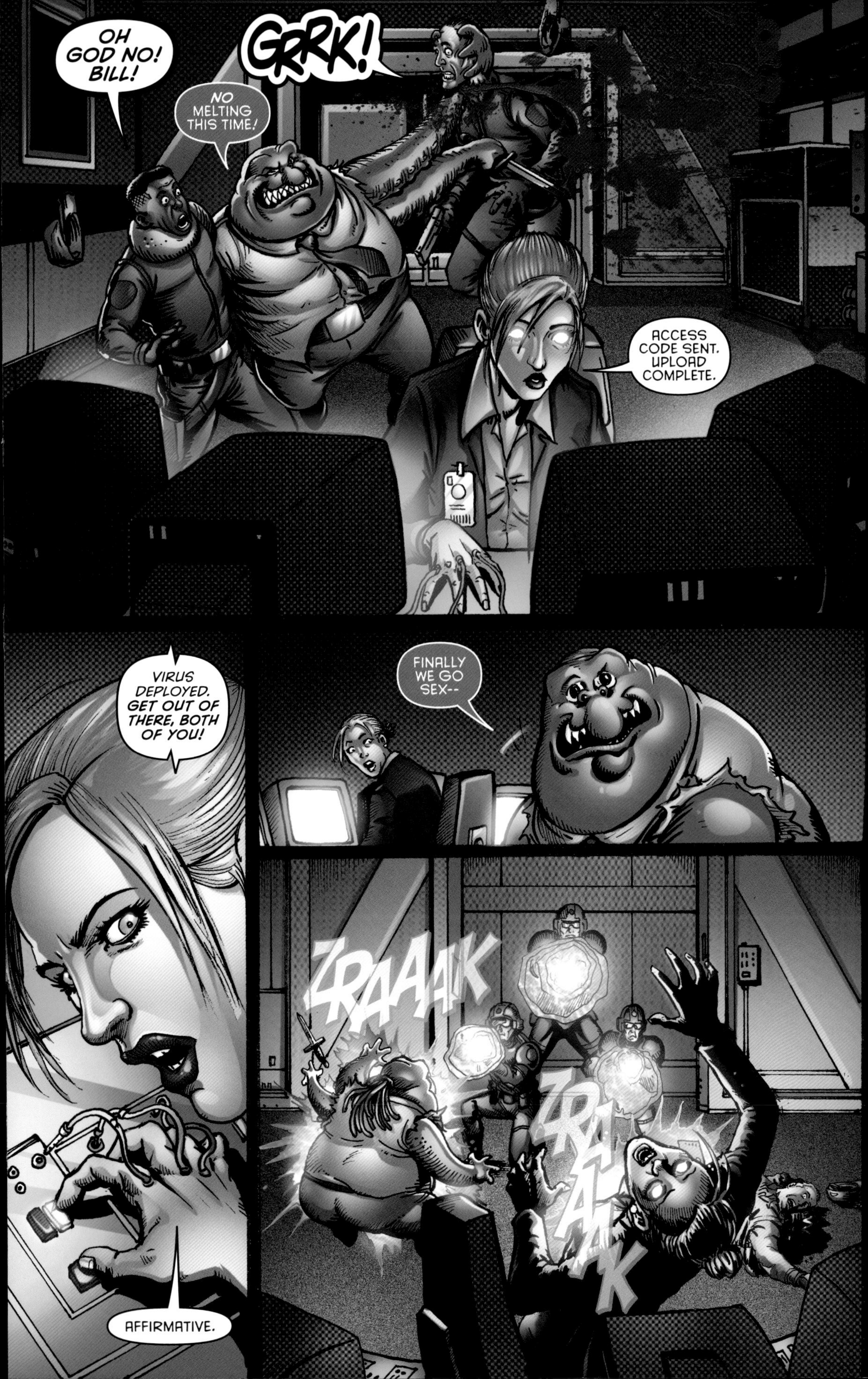
OH GOD NO! BILL!
GRRK!
NO MELTING THIS TIME!
ACCESS CODE SENT. UPLOAD COMPLETE.
VIRUS DEPLOYED. GET OUT OF THERE, BOTH OF YOU!
FINALLY WE GO SEX--
ZRAAAAK
ZRAAAK
AFFIRMATIVE.

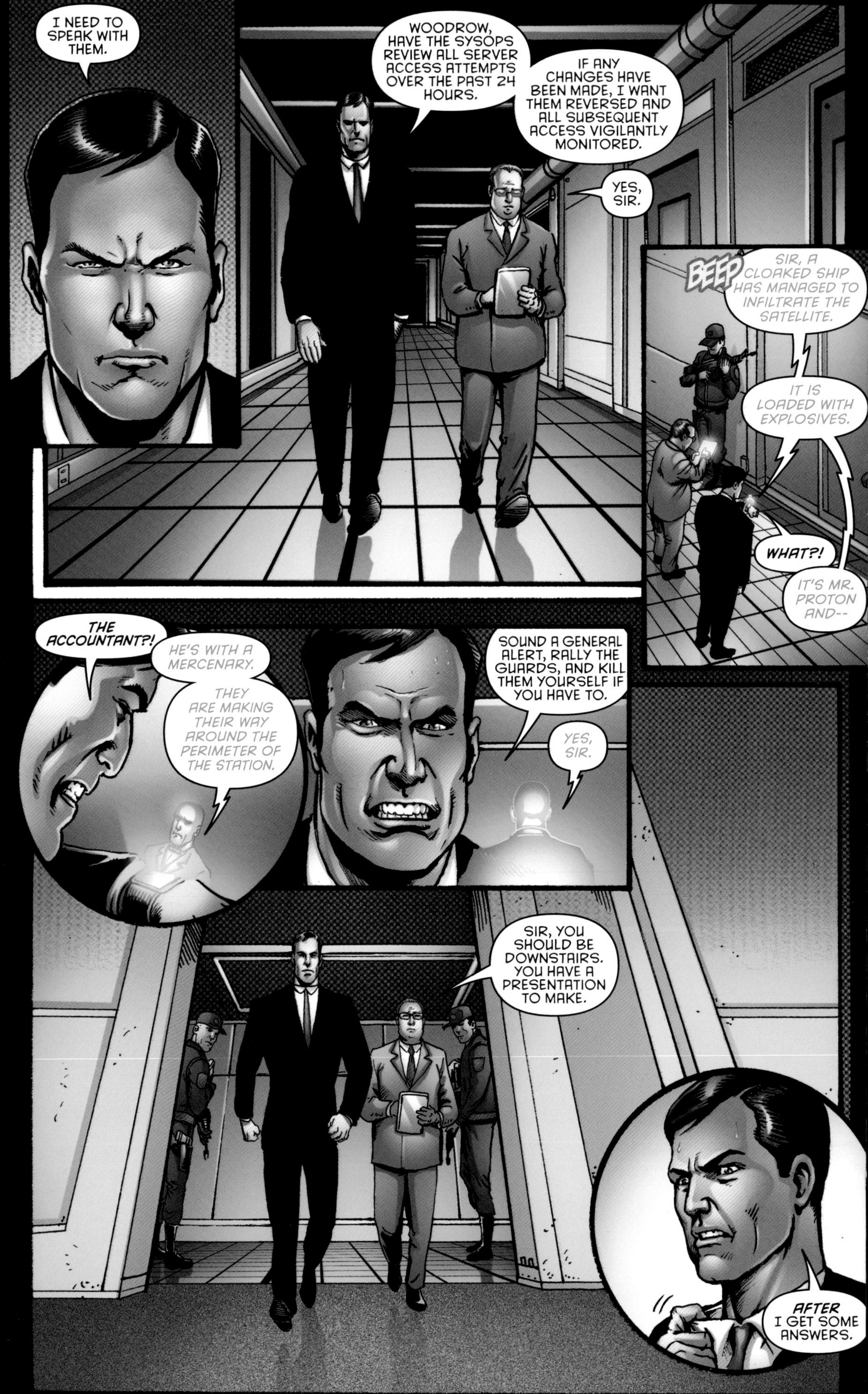
I NEED TO SPEAK WITH THEM.
WOODROW, HAVE THE SYSOPS REVIEW ALL SERVER ACCESS ATTEMPTS OVER THE PAST 24 HOURS.
IF ANY CHANGES HAVE BEEN MADE, I WANT THEM REVERSED AND ALL SUBSEQUENT ACCESS VIGILANTLY MONITORED.
YES, SIR.
BEEP
SIR, A CLOAKED SHIP HAS MANAGED TO INFILTRATE THE SATELLITE.
IT IS LOADED WITH EXPLOSIVES.
WHAT?!
IT'S MR. PROTON AND--
THE ACCOUNTANT?!
HE'S WITH A MERCENARY.
THEY ARE MAKING THEIR WAY AROUND THE PERIMETER OF THE STATION.
SOUND A GENERAL ALERT, RALLY THE GUARDS, AND KILL THEM YOURSELF IF YOU HAVE TO.
YES, SIR.
SIR, YOU SHOULD BE DOWNSTAIRS. YOU HAVE A PRESENTATION TO MAKE.
AFTER I GET SOME ANSWERS.

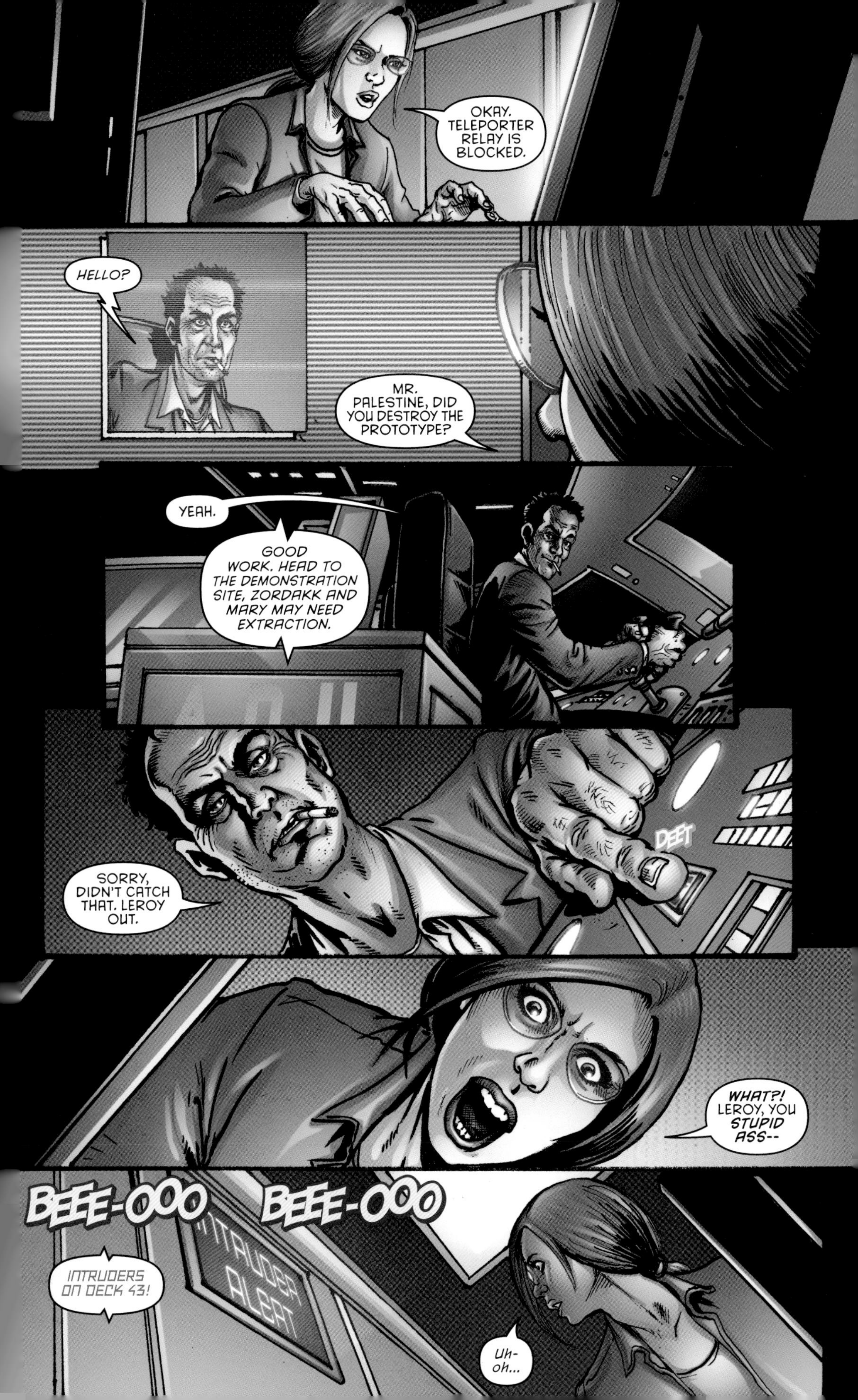
OKAY. TELEPORTER RELAY IS BLOCKED.
HELLO?
MR. PALESTINE, DID YOU DESTROY THE PROTOTYPE?
YEAH.
GOOD WORK. HEAD TO THE DEMONSTRATION SITE, ZORDAKK AND MARY MAY NEED EXTRACTION.
DEET
SORRY, DIDN'T CATCH THAT. LEROY OUT.
WHAT?! LEROY, YOU STUPID ASS--
BEEE-OOO BEEE-OOO
INTRUDER ALERT
INTRUDERS ON DECK 43!
Uh-oh...

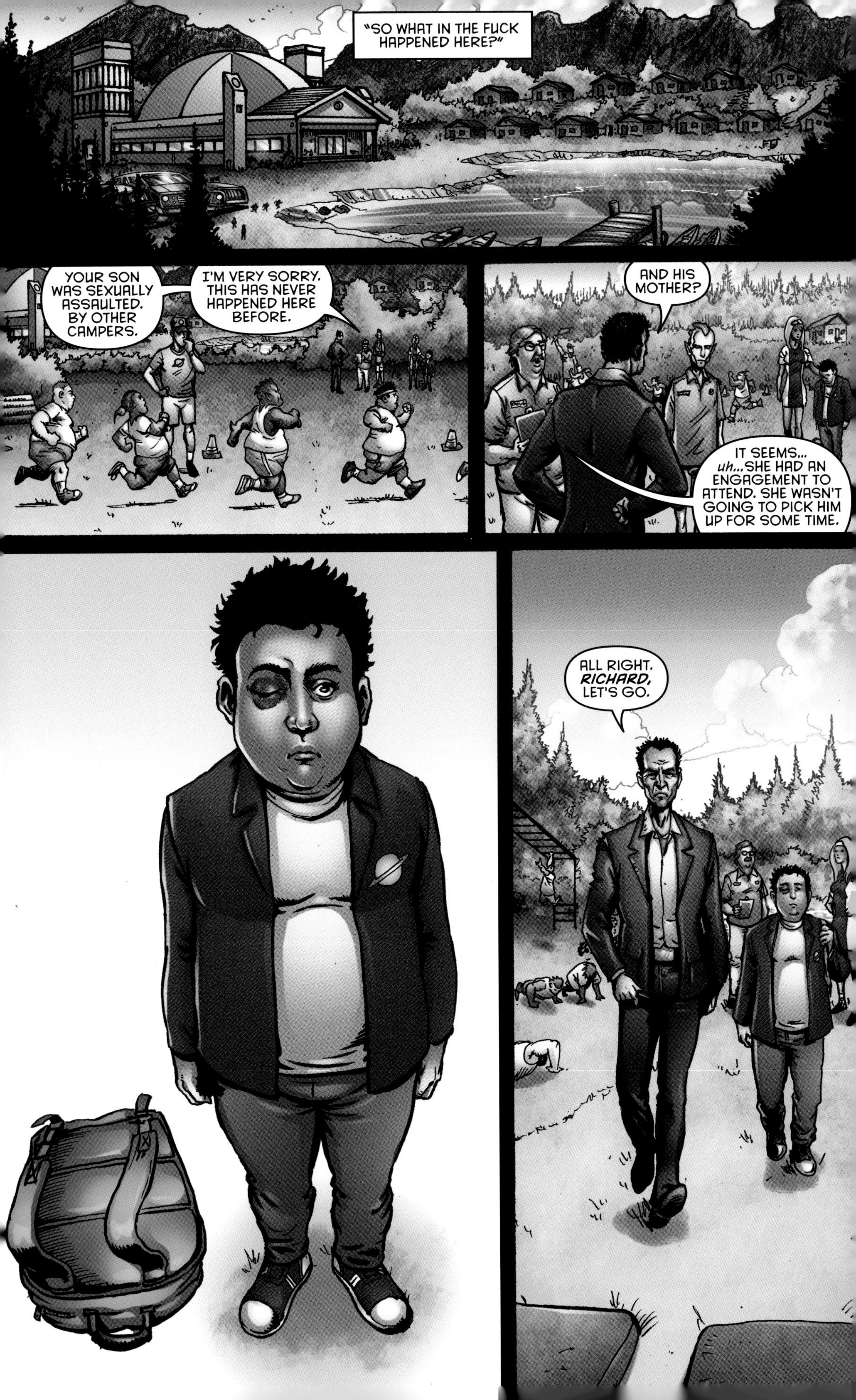
"SO WHAT IN THE FUCK HAPPENED HERE?"
YOUR SON WAS SEXUALLY ASSAULTED. BY OTHER CAMPERS.
I'M VERY SORRY. THIS HAS NEVER HAPPENED HERE BEFORE.
AND HIS MOTHER?
IT SEEMS... uh...SHE HAD AN ENGAGEMENT TO ATTEND. SHE WASN'T GOING TO PICK HIM UP FOR SOME TIME.
ALL RIGHT. RICHARD, LET'S GO.

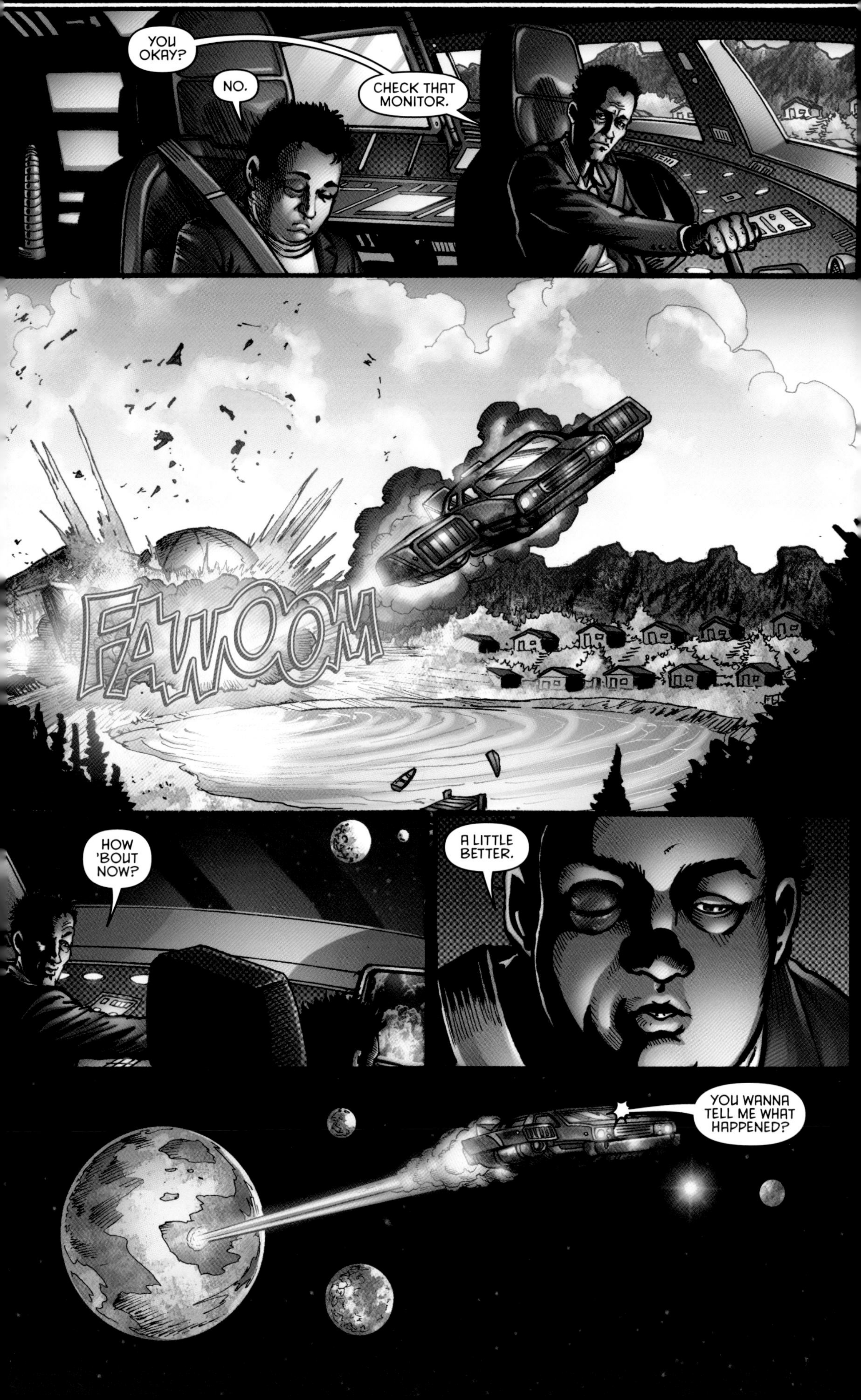
YOU OKAY?
NO.
CHECK THAT MONITOR.
FAWOOM
HOW 'BOUT NOW?
A LITTLE BETTER.
YOU WANNA TELL ME WHAT HAPPENED?

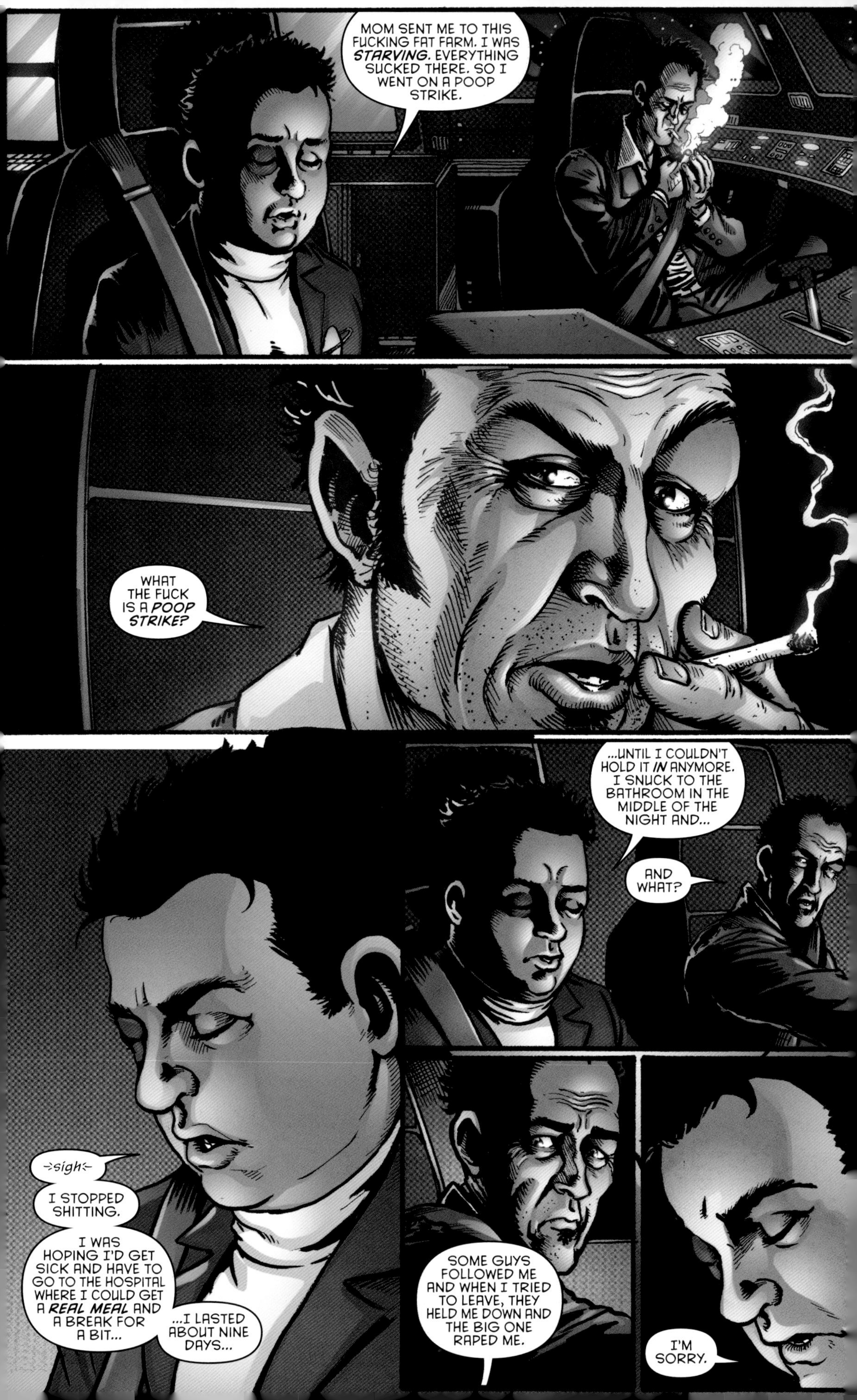
MOM SENT ME TO THIS FUCKING FAT FARM. I WAS STARVING. EVERYTHING SUCKED THERE. SO I WENT ON A POOP STRIKE.
WHAT THE FUCK IS A POOP STRIKE?
-sigh-
I STOPPED SHITTING.
I WAS HOPING I'D GET SICK AND HAVE TO GO TO THE HOSPITAL WHERE I COULD GET A REAL MEAL AND A BREAK FOR A BIT...
...I LASTED ABOUT NINE DAYS...
...UNTIL I COULDN'T HOLD IT IN ANYMORE. I SNUCK TO THE BATHROOM IN THE MIDDLE OF THE NIGHT AND...
AND WHAT?
SOME GUYS FOLLOWED ME AND WHEN I TRIED TO LEAVE, THEY HELD ME DOWN AND THE BIG ONE RAPED ME.
I'M SORRY.

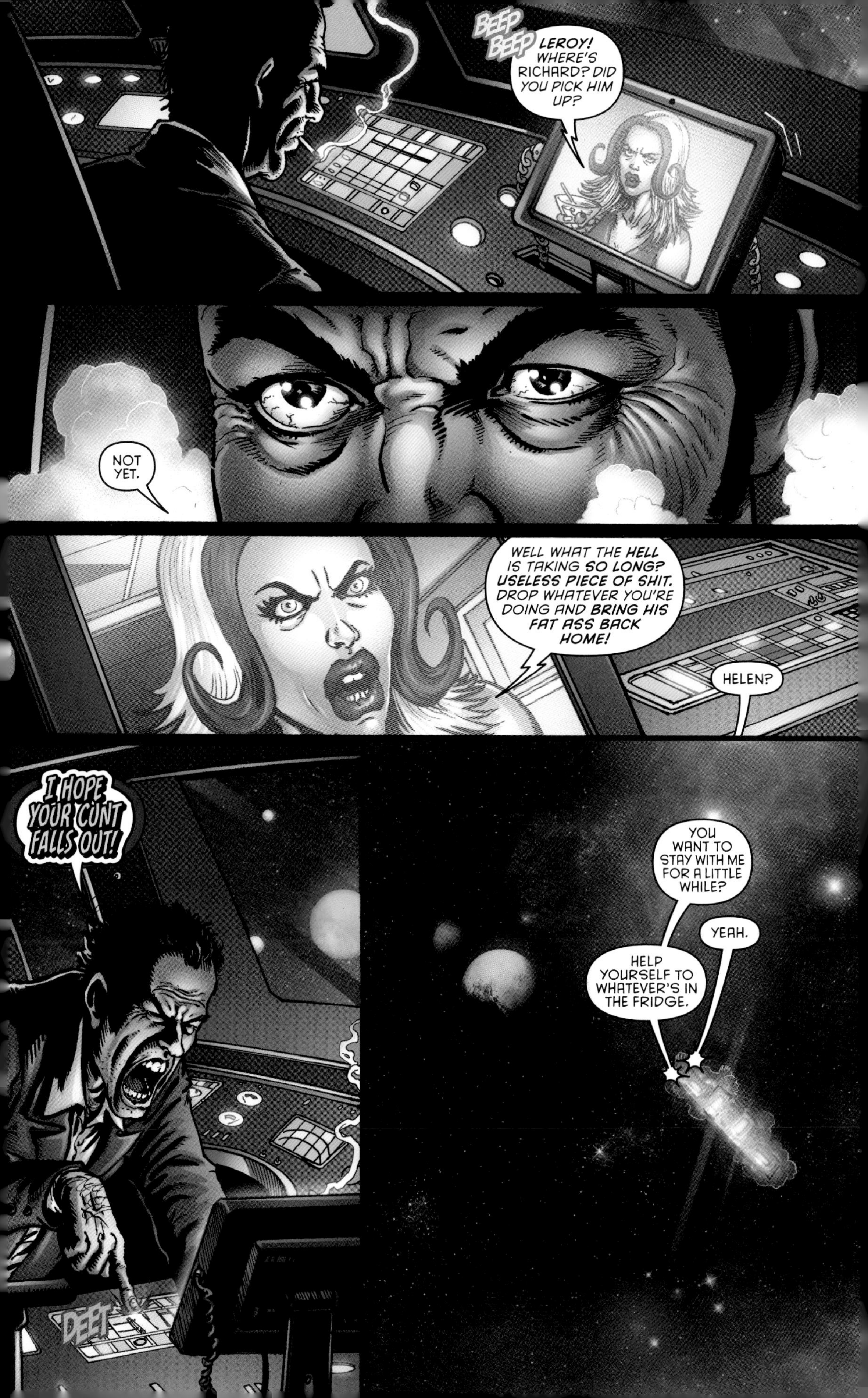
BEEP BEEP
LEROY! WHERE'S RICHARD? DID YOU PICK HIM UP?
NOT YET.
WELL WHAT THE HELL IS TAKING SO LONG? USELESS PIECE OF SHIT. DROP WHATEVER YOU'RE DOING AND BRING HIS FAT ASS BACK HOME!
HELEN?
I HOPE YOUR CUNT FALLS OUT!
DEET
YOU WANT TO STAY WITH ME FOR A LITTLE WHILE?
YEAH.
HELP YOURSELF TO WHATEVER'S IN THE FRIDGE.

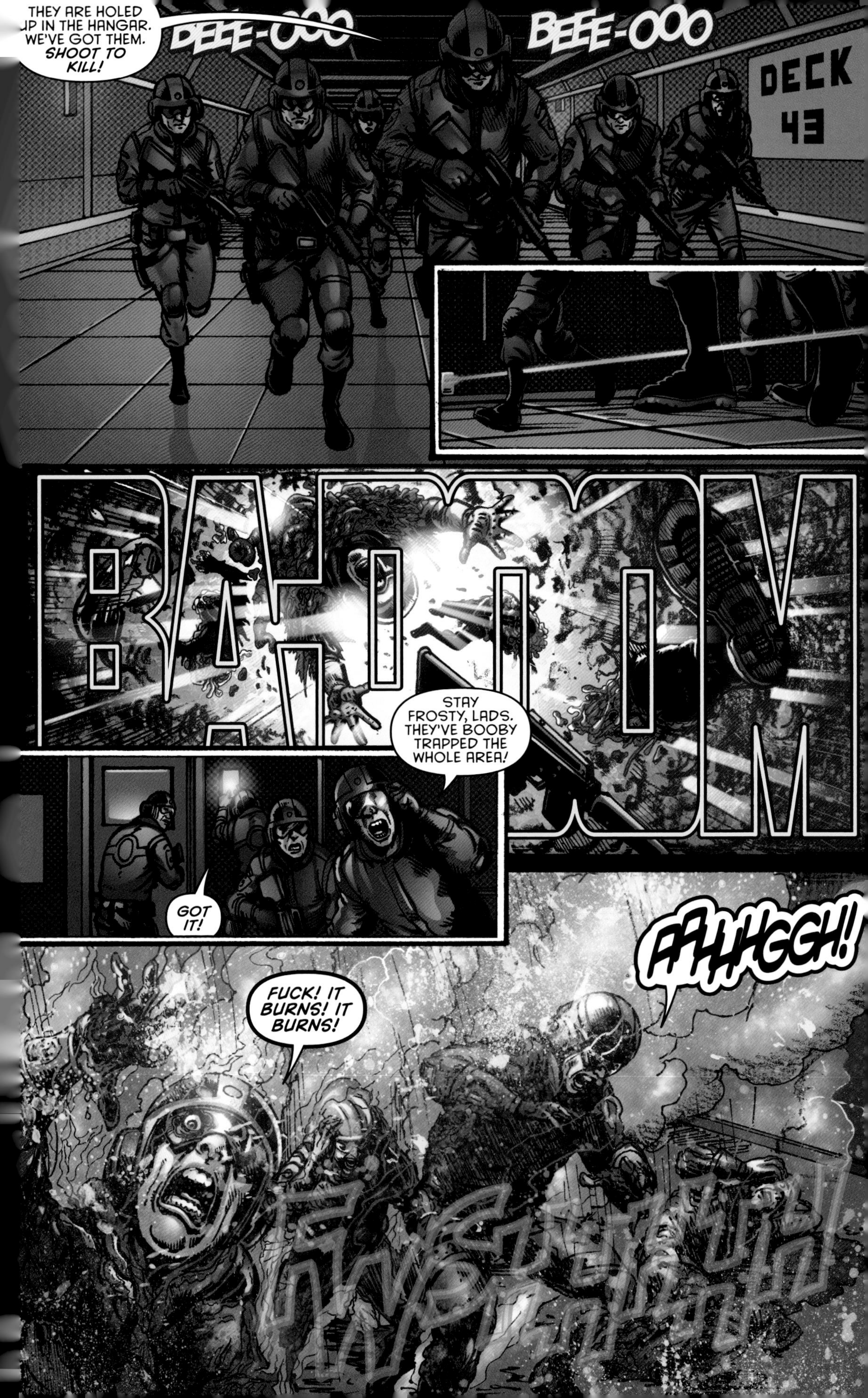
THEY ARE HOLED UP IN THE HANGAR. WE'VE GOT THEM. *SHOOT TO KILL!*
BEEE-OOO
BEEE-OOO
DECK 43
STAY FROSTY, LADS. THEY'VE BOOBY TRAPPED THE WHOLE AREA!
GOT IT!
FUCK! IT BURNS! IT BURNS!

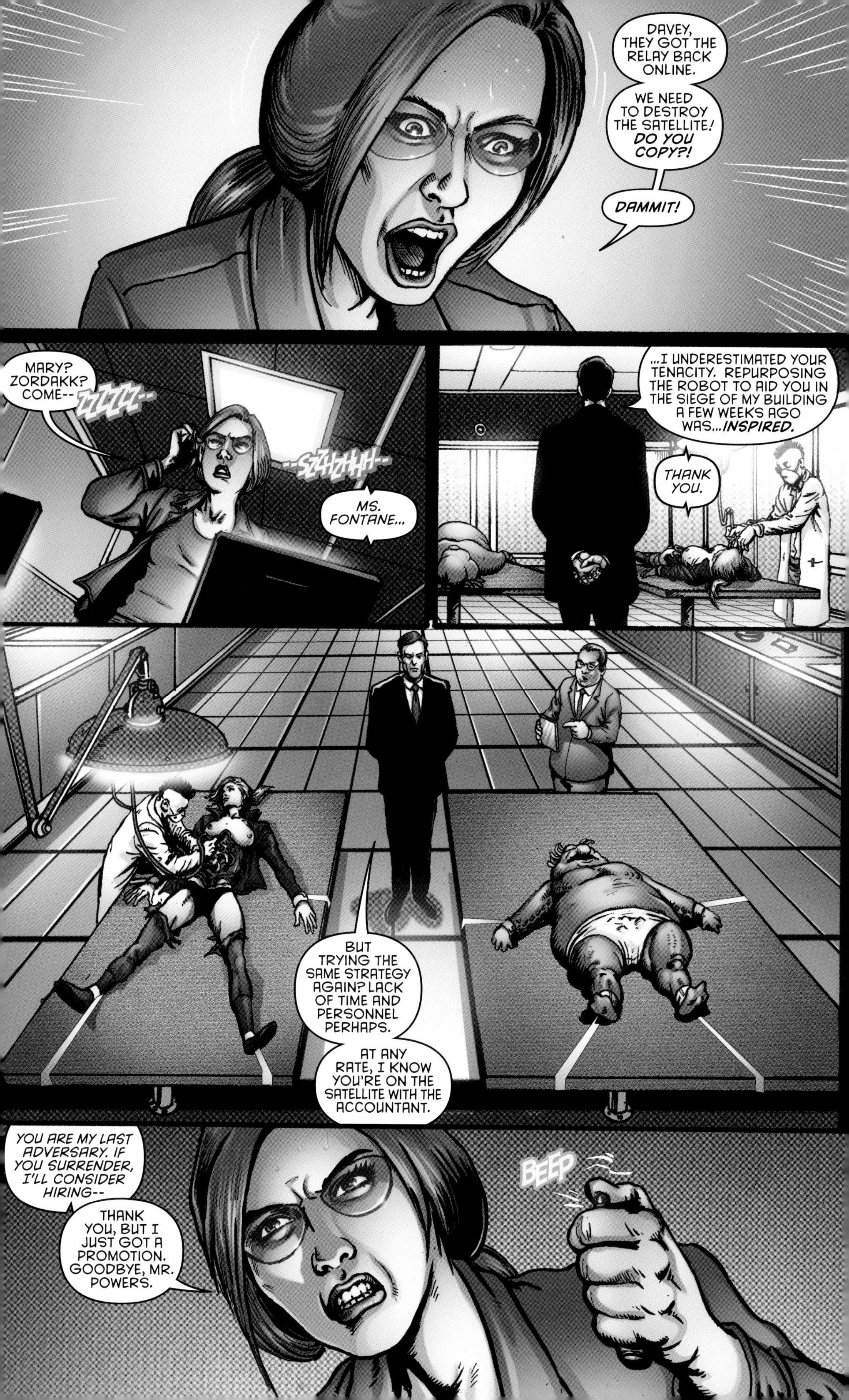
DAVEY, THEY GOT THE RELAY BACK ONLINE.
WE NEED TO DESTROY THE SATELLITE! DO YOU COPY?!
DAMMIT!
MARY? ZORDAKK? COME--
ZZZZZ--
--SZZHZHHH--
MS. FONTANE...
...I UNDERESTIMATED YOUR TENACITY. REPURPOSING THE ROBOT TO AID YOU IN THE SIEGE OF MY BUILDING A FEW WEEKS AGO WAS...INSPIRED.
THANK YOU.
BUT TRYING THE SAME STRATEGY AGAIN? LACK OF TIME AND PERSONNEL PERHAPS.
AT ANY RATE, I KNOW YOU'RE ON THE SATELLITE WITH THE ACCOUNTANT.
YOU ARE MY LAST ADVERSARY. IF YOU SURRENDER, I'LL CONSIDER HIRING--
THANK YOU, BUT I JUST GOT A PROMOTION. GOODBYE, MR. POWERS.
BEEP

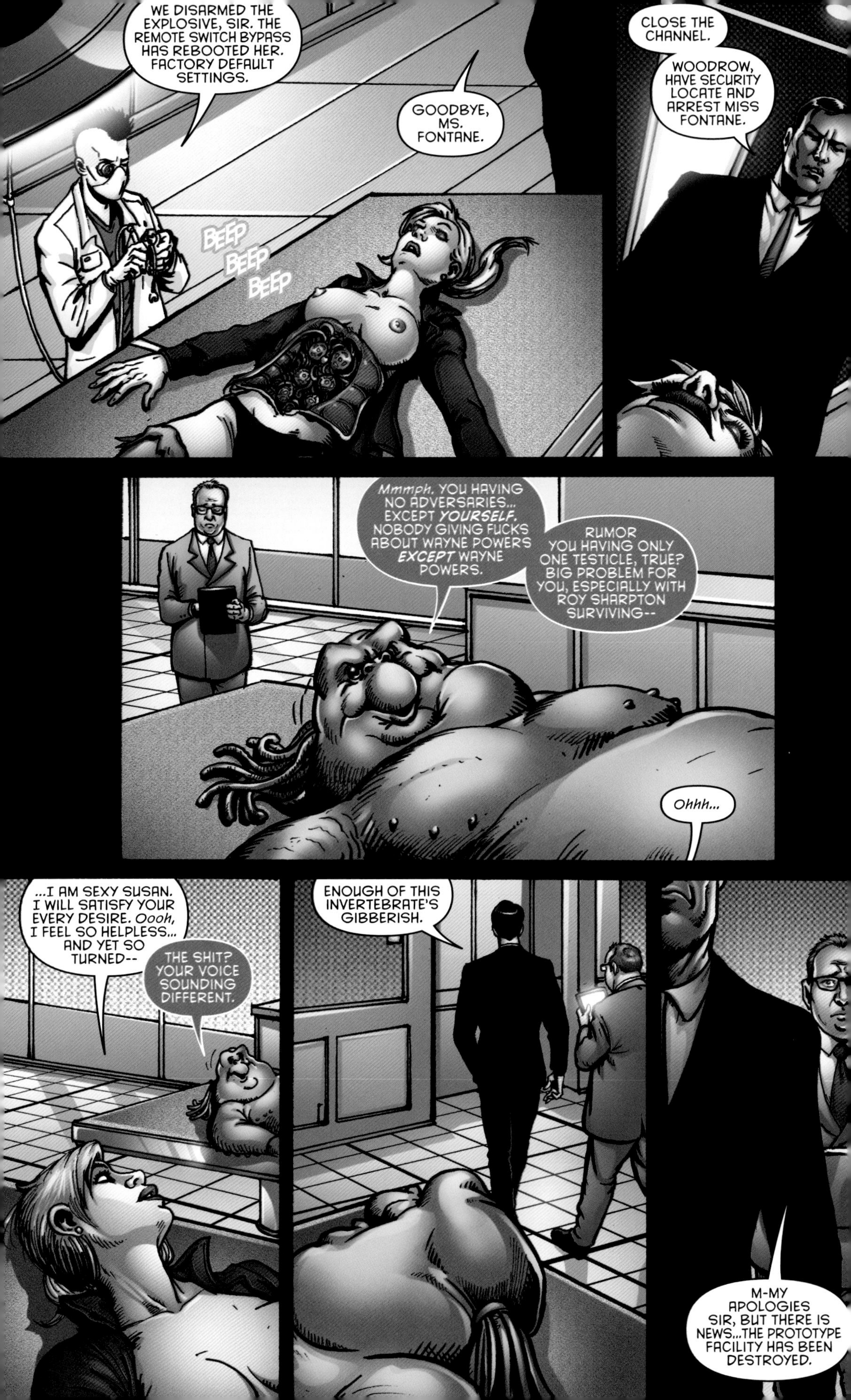
WE DISARMED THE EXPLOSIVE, SIR. THE REMOTE SWITCH BYPASS HAS REBOOTED HER. FACTORY DEFAULT SETTINGS.
GOODBYE, MS. FONTANE.
BEEP BEEP BEEP
CLOSE THE CHANNEL.
WOODROW, HAVE SECURITY LOCATE AND ARREST MISS FONTANE.
Mmmph. YOU HAVING NO ADVERSARIES... EXCEPT *YOURSELF.* NOBODY GIVING FUCKS ABOUT WAYNE POWERS *EXCEPT* WAYNE POWERS.
RUMOR YOU HAVING ONLY ONE TESTICLE, TRUE? BIG PROBLEM FOR YOU, ESPECIALLY WITH ROY SHARPTON SURVIVING--
Ohhh...
...I AM SEXY SUSAN. I WILL SATISFY YOUR EVERY DESIRE. *Oooh,* I FEEL SO HELPLESS... AND YET SO TURNED--
THE SHIT? YOUR VOICE SOUNDING DIFFERENT.
ENOUGH OF THIS INVERTEBRATE'S GIBBERISH.
M-MY APOLOGIES SIR, BUT THERE IS NEWS...THE PROTOTYPE FACILITY HAS BEEN DESTROYED.

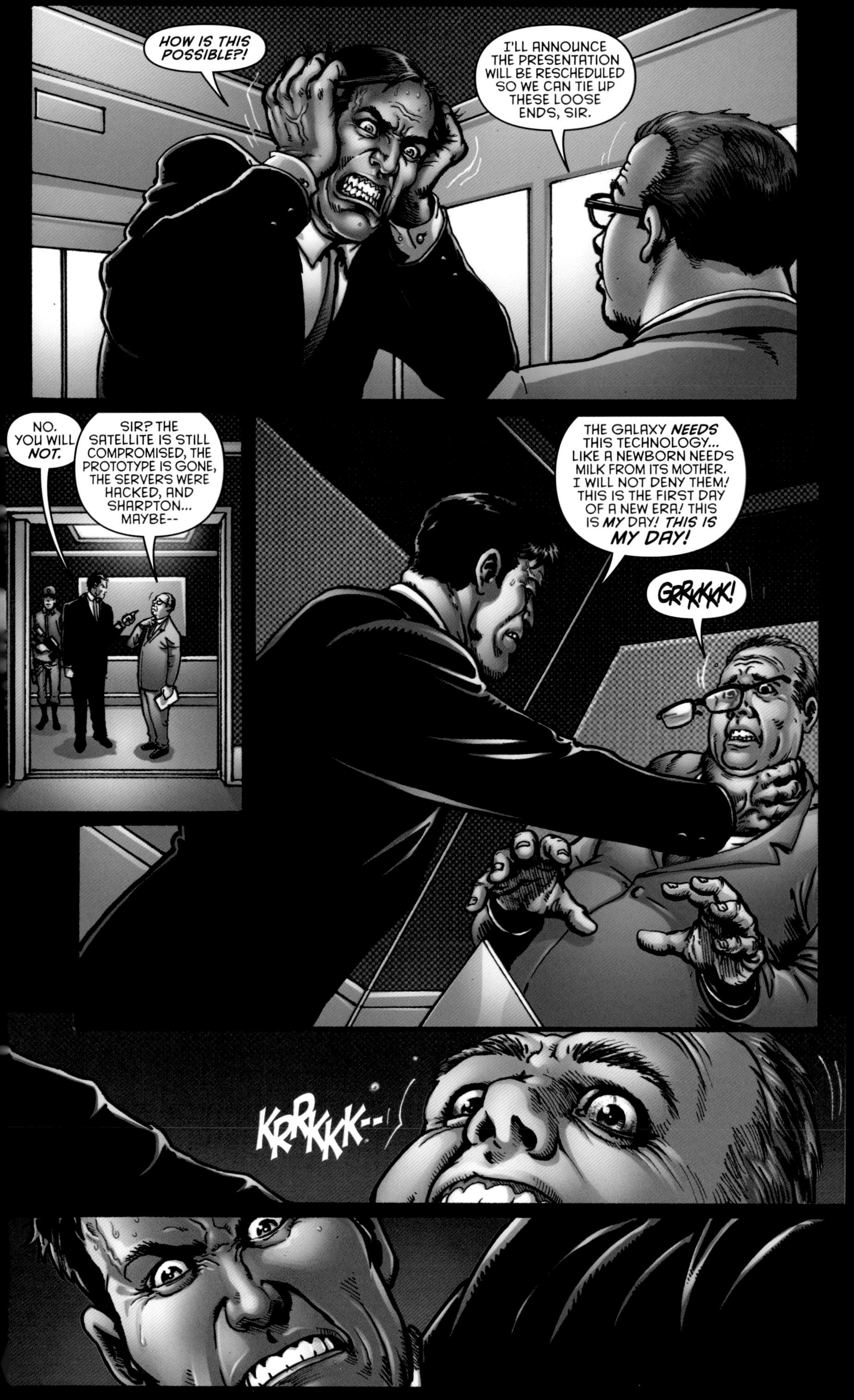
HOW IS THIS POSSIBLE?!
I'LL ANNOUNCE THE PRESENTATION WILL BE RESCHEDULED SO WE CAN TIE UP THESE LOOSE ENDS, SIR.
SIR? THE SATELLITE IS STILL COMPROMISED, THE PROTOTYPE IS GONE, THE SERVERS WERE HACKED, AND SHARPTON... MAYBE--
NO. YOU WILL NOT.
THE GALAXY NEEDS THIS TECHNOLOGY... LIKE A NEWBORN NEEDS MILK FROM ITS MOTHER. I WILL NOT DENY THEM! THIS IS THE FIRST DAY OF A NEW ERA! THIS IS MY DAY! THIS IS MY DAY!
GRRKKKK!
KRRKKK--

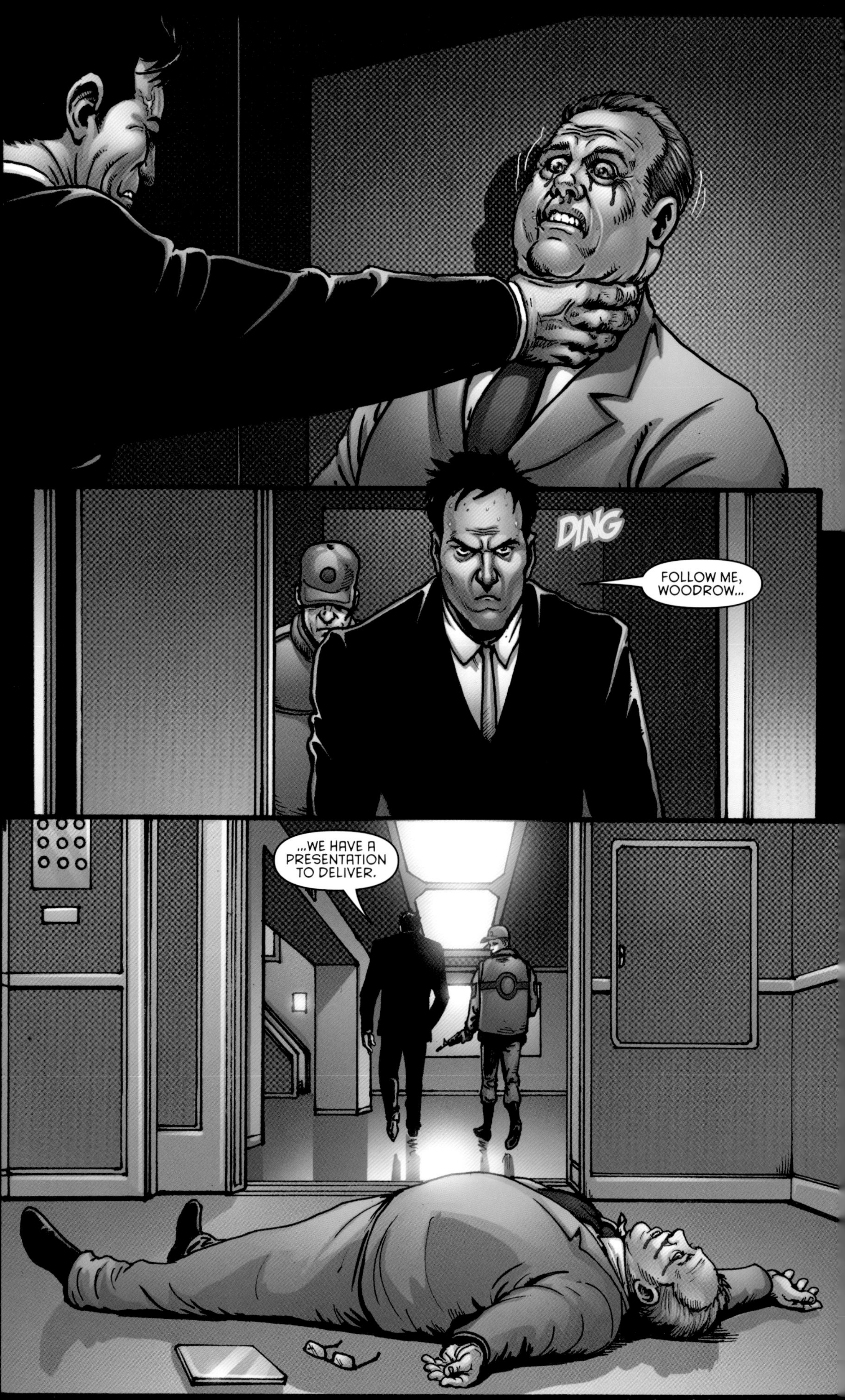
DING
FOLLOW ME, WOODROW...
...WE HAVE A PRESENTATION TO DELIVER.

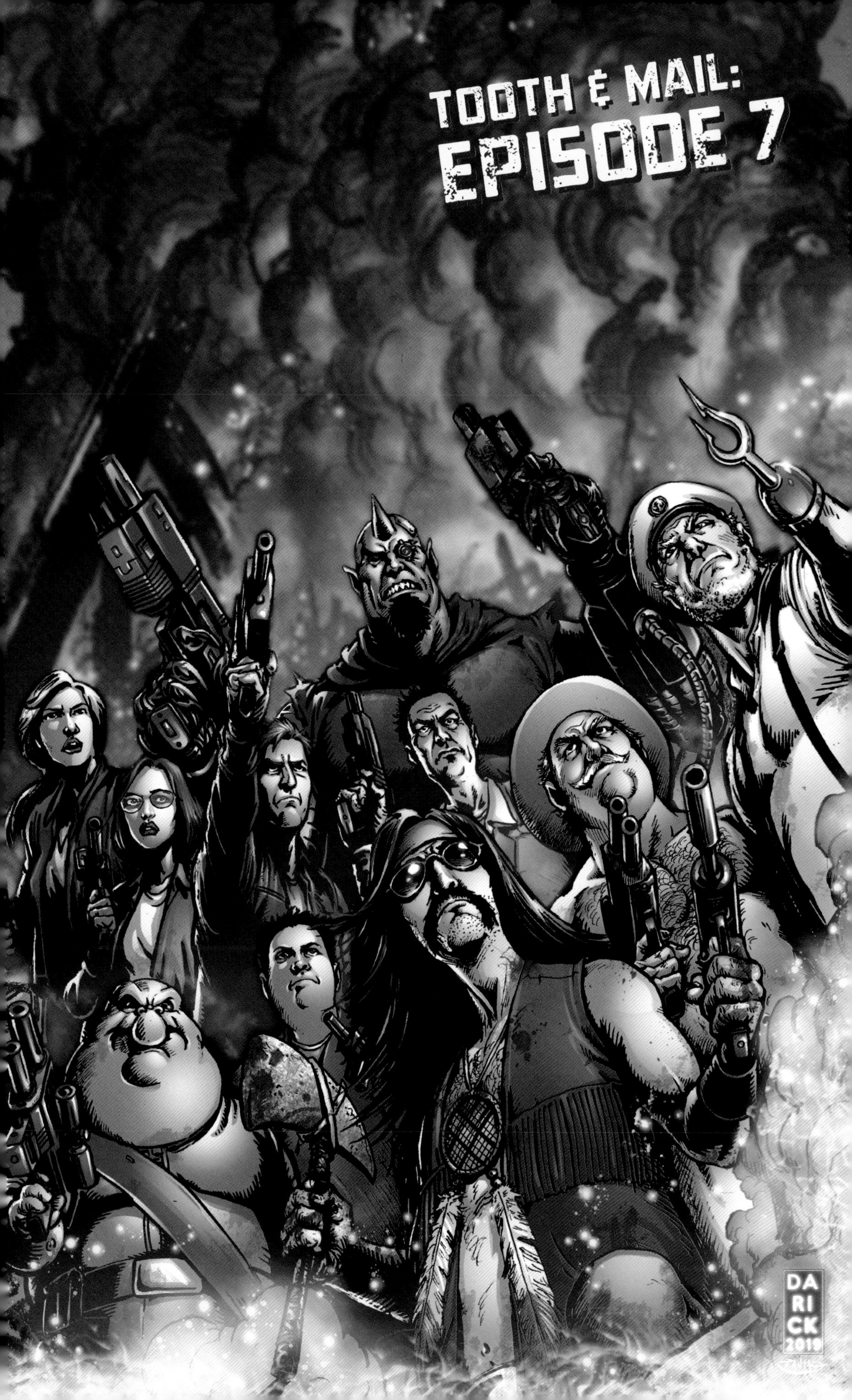
TOOTH & MAIL:
EPISODE 7
DA RI CK 2019

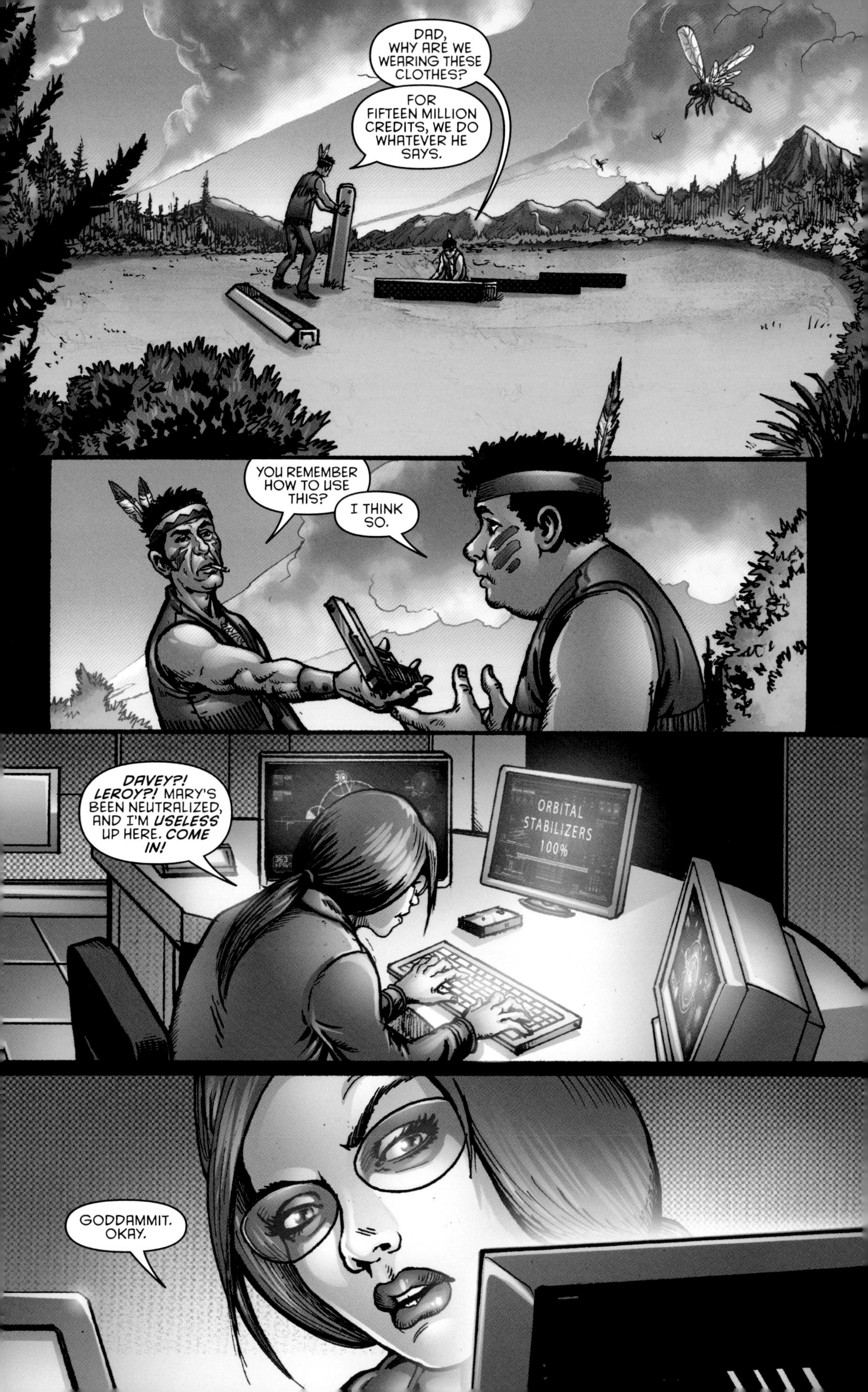
DAD, WHY ARE WE WEARING THESE CLOTHES?
FOR FIFTEEN MILLION CREDITS, WE DO WHATEVER HE SAYS.
YOU REMEMBER HOW TO USE THIS?
I THINK SO.
DAVEY?! LEROY?! MARY'S BEEN NEUTRALIZED, AND I'M USELESS UP HERE. COME IN!
ORBITAL STABILIZERS 100%
GODDAMMIT. OKAY.

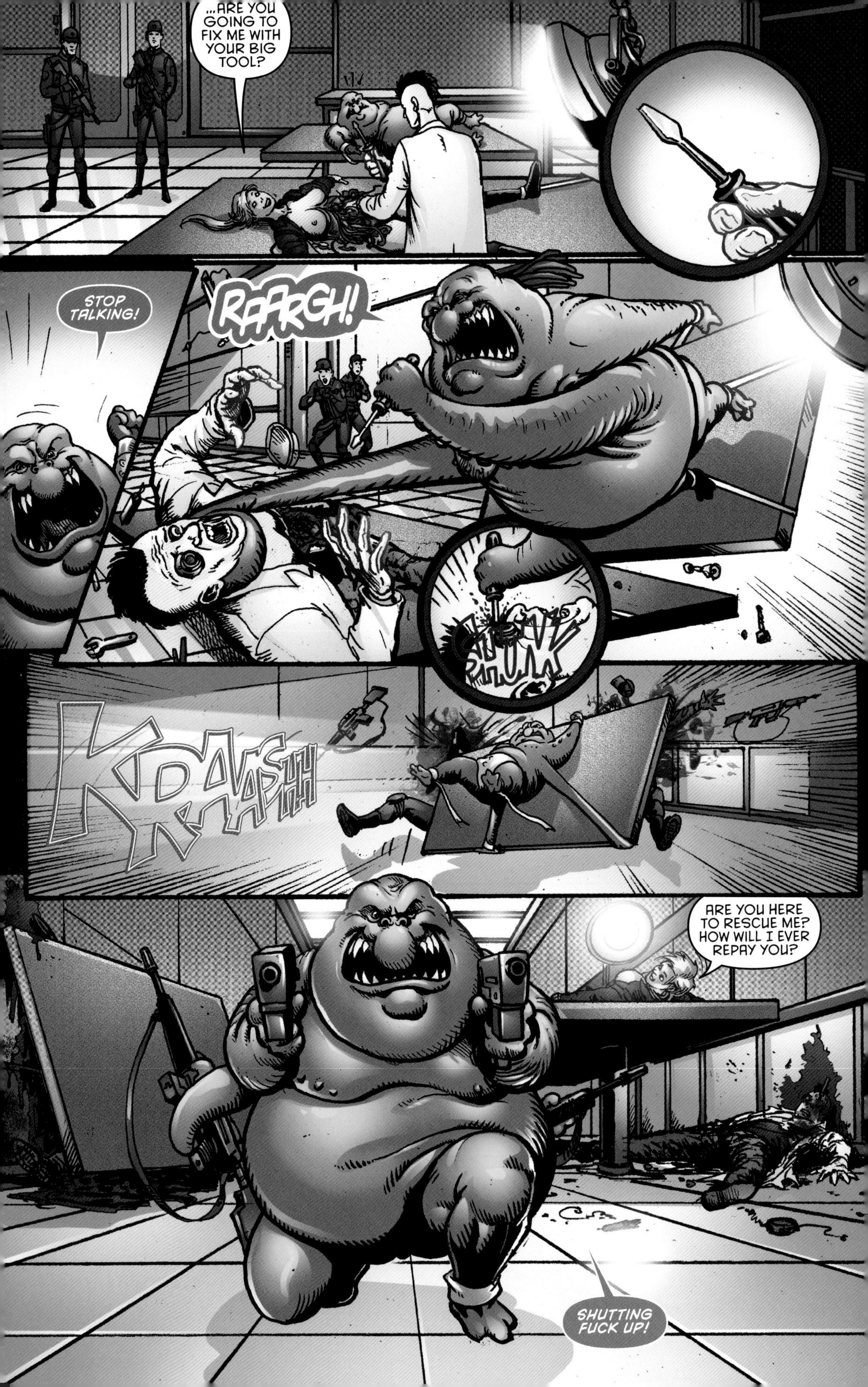
...ARE YOU GOING TO FIX ME WITH YOUR BIG TOOL?
STOP TALKING!
RAARGH!
SHUNK
KRAASHHH
ARE YOU HERE TO RESCUE ME? HOW WILL I EVER REPAY YOU?
SHUTTING FUCK UP!

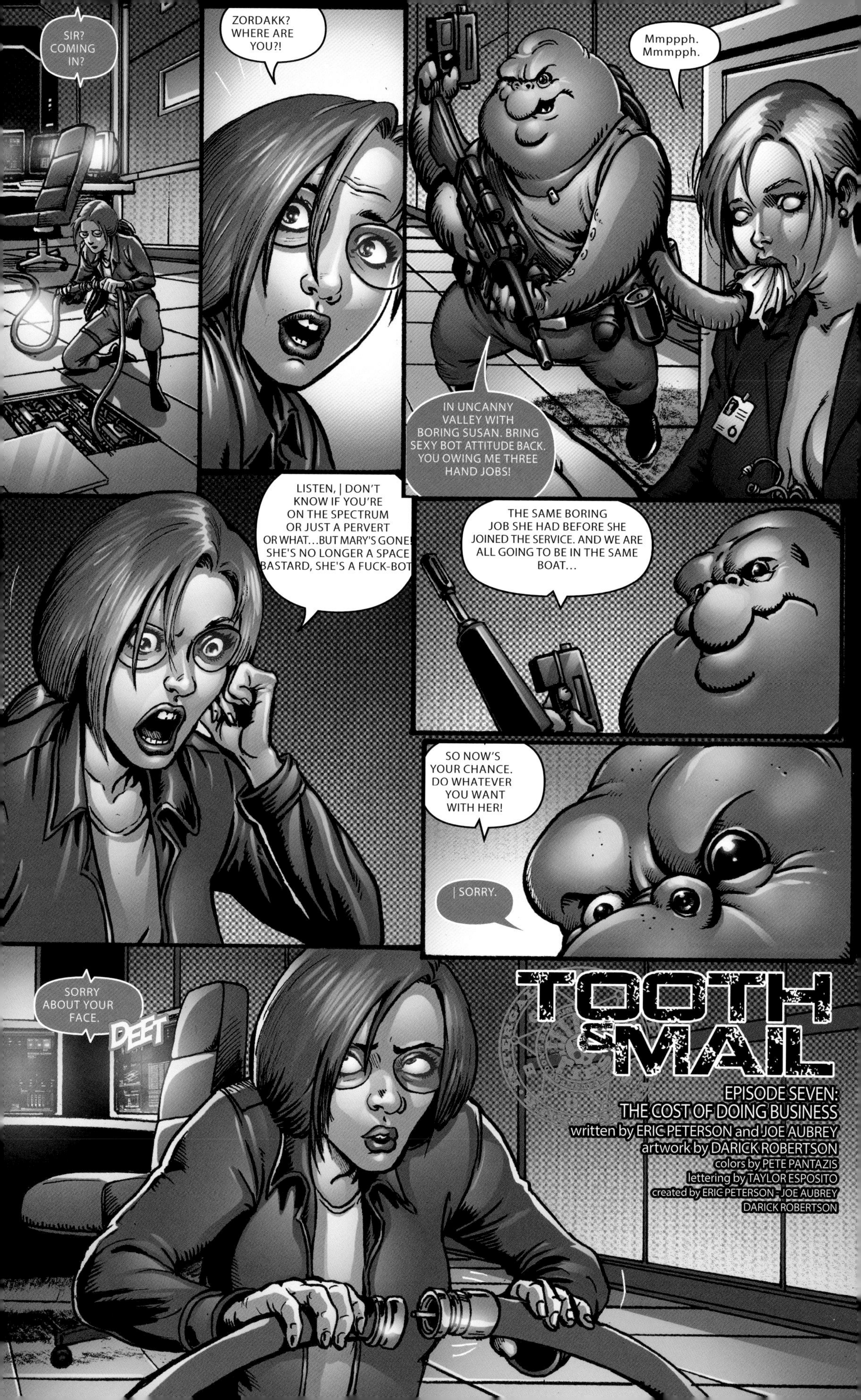
SIR? COMING IN?
ZORDAKK? WHERE ARE YOU?!
Mmppph. Mmmpph.
IN UNCANNY VALLEY WITH BORING SUSAN. BRING SEXY BOT ATTITUDE BACK. YOU OWING ME THREE HAND JOBS!
LISTEN, I DON'T KNOW IF YOU'RE ON THE SPECTRUM OR JUST A PERVERT OR WHAT…BUT MARY'S GONE! SHE'S NO LONGER A SPACE BASTARD, SHE'S A FUCK-BOT
THE SAME BORING JOB SHE HAD BEFORE SHE JOINED THE SERVICE. AND WE ARE ALL GOING TO BE IN THE SAME BOAT…
SO NOW'S YOUR CHANCE. DO WHATEVER YOU WANT WITH HER!
I SORRY.
SORRY ABOUT YOUR FACE.
DEET
TOOTH & MAIL
EPISODE SEVEN: THE COST OF DOING BUSINESS
written by ERIC PETERSON and JOE AUBREY
artwork by DARICK ROBERTSON
colors by PETE PANTAZIS
lettering by TAYLOR ESPOSITO
created by ERIC PETERSON - JOE AUBREY
DARICK ROBERTSON

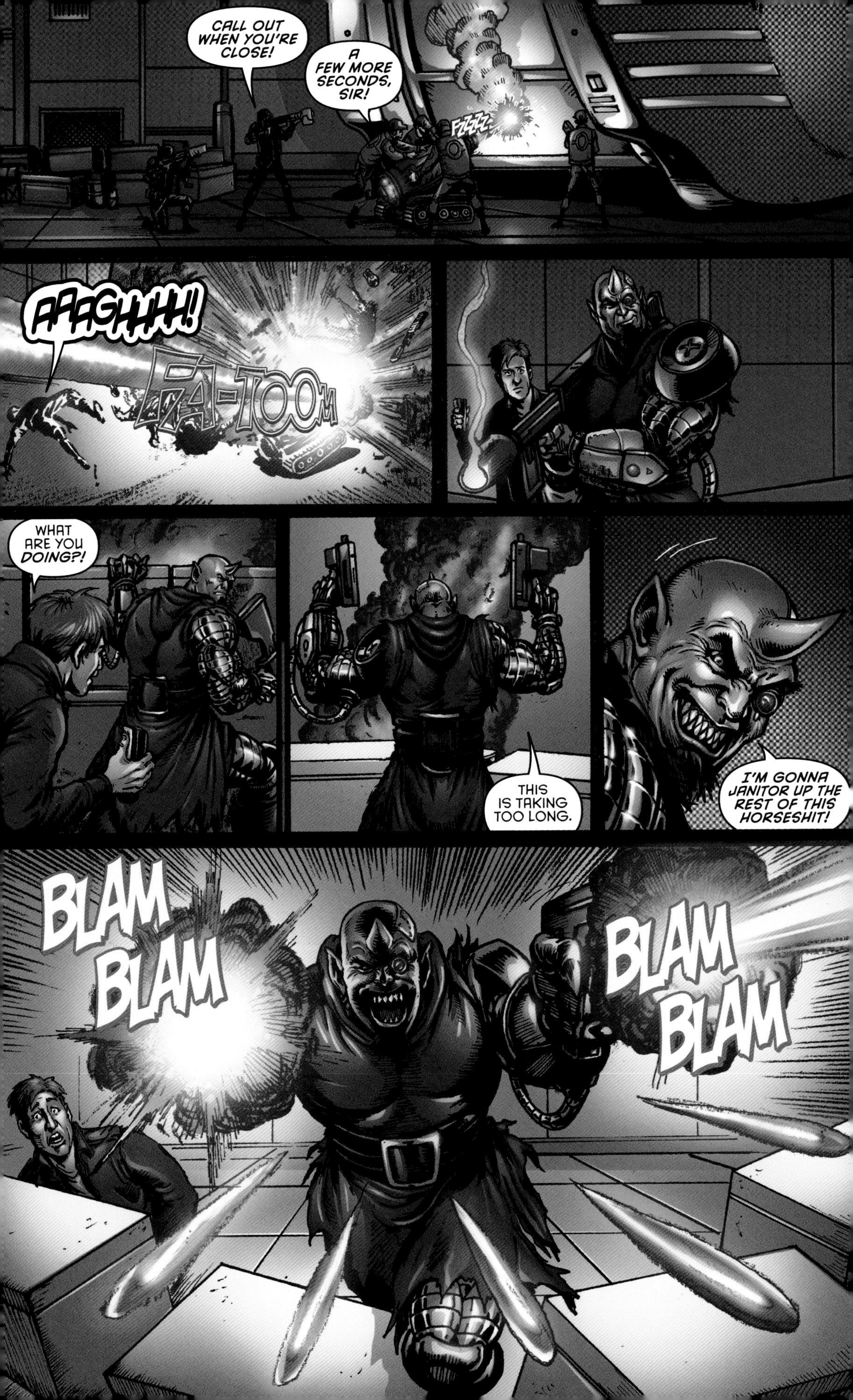
CALL OUT WHEN YOU'RE CLOSE!
A FEW MORE SECONDS, SIR!
FZZZZ
AAAGHHH!
FA-TOOM
WHAT ARE YOU DOING?!
THIS IS TAKING TOO LONG.
I'M GONNA JANITOR UP THE REST OF THIS HORSESHIT!
BLAM BLAM
BLAM BLAM

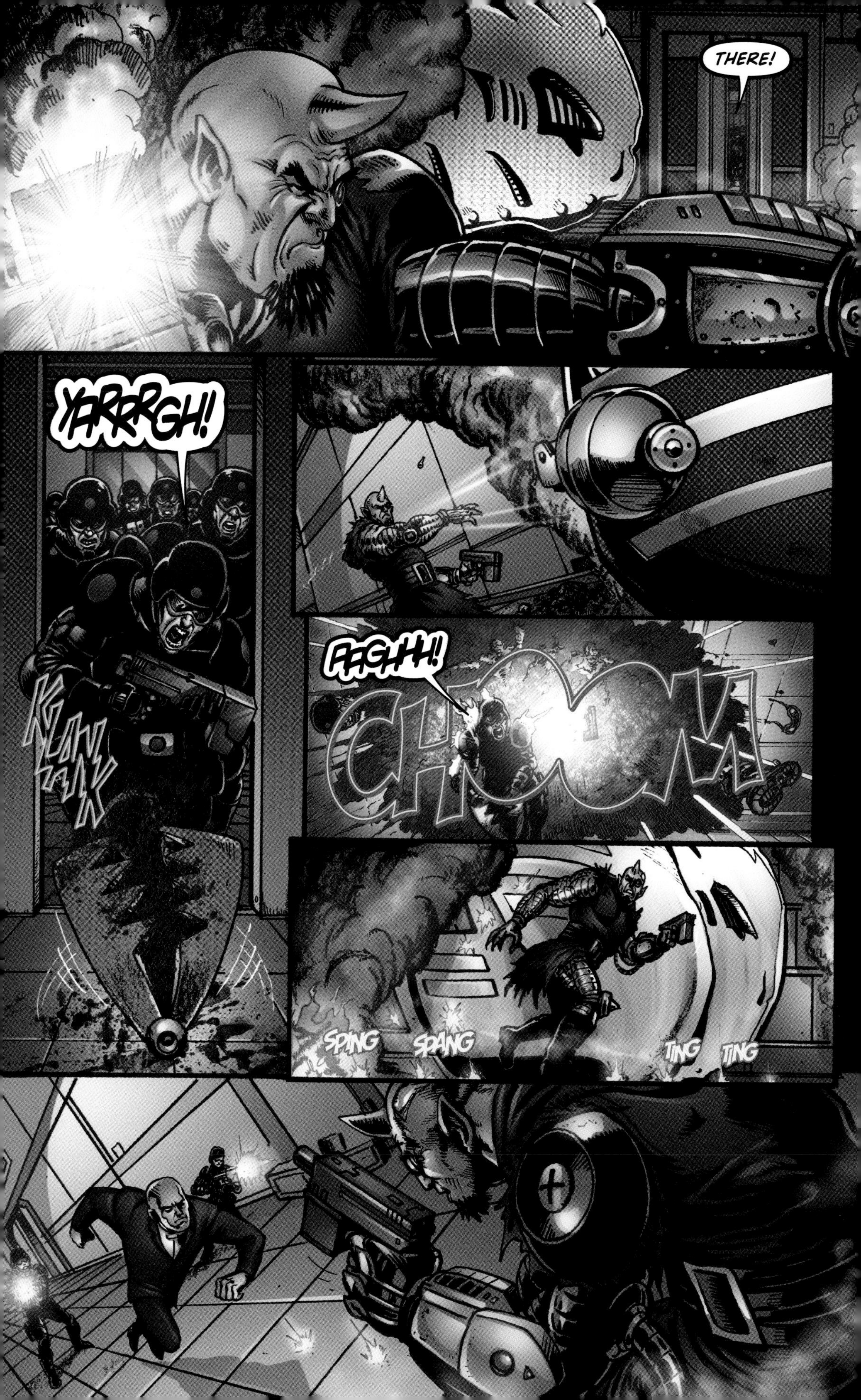
THERE!
YARRRGH!
KLAK KLAK
PAGHH!
CHOOOM
SPING
SPANG
TING
TING

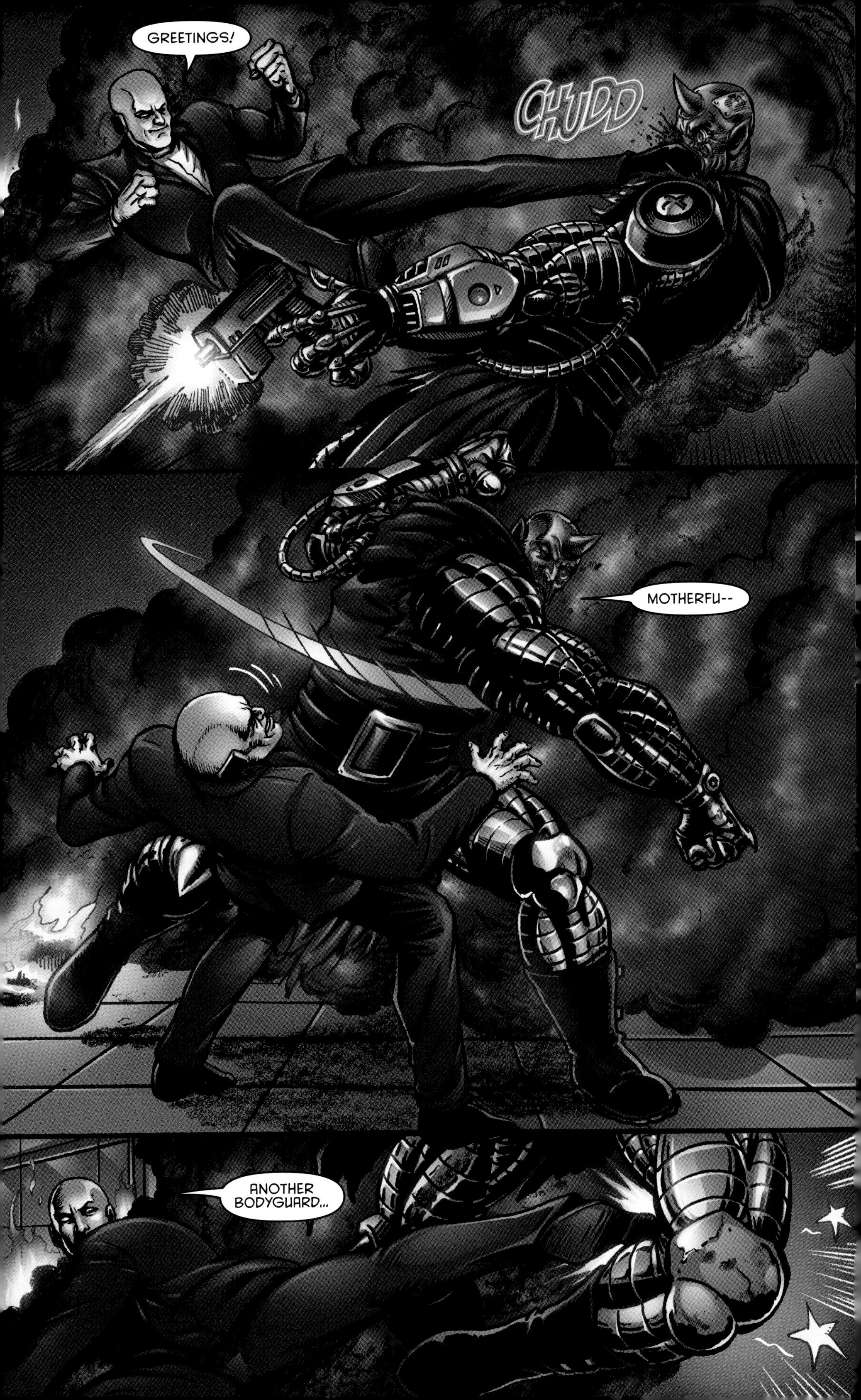
GREETINGS!
CHUDD
MOTHERFU--
ANOTHER BODYGUARD...

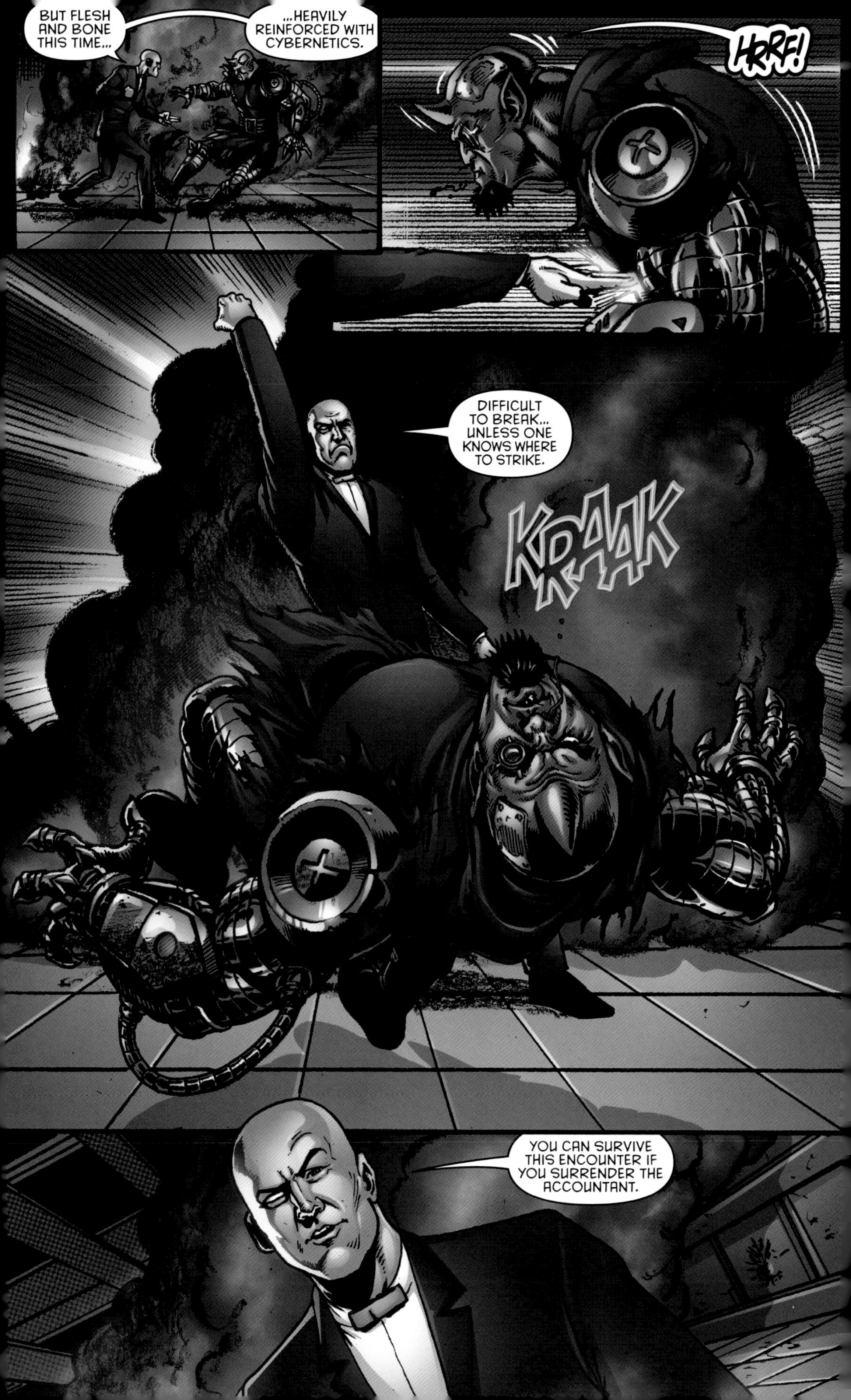
BUT FLESH AND BONE THIS TIME...
...HEAVILY REINFORCED WITH CYBERNETICS.
HRRF!
DIFFICULT TO BREAK... UNLESS ONE KNOWS WHERE TO STRIKE.
KRAAK
YOU CAN SURVIVE THIS ENCOUNTER IF YOU SURRENDER THE ACCOUNTANT.

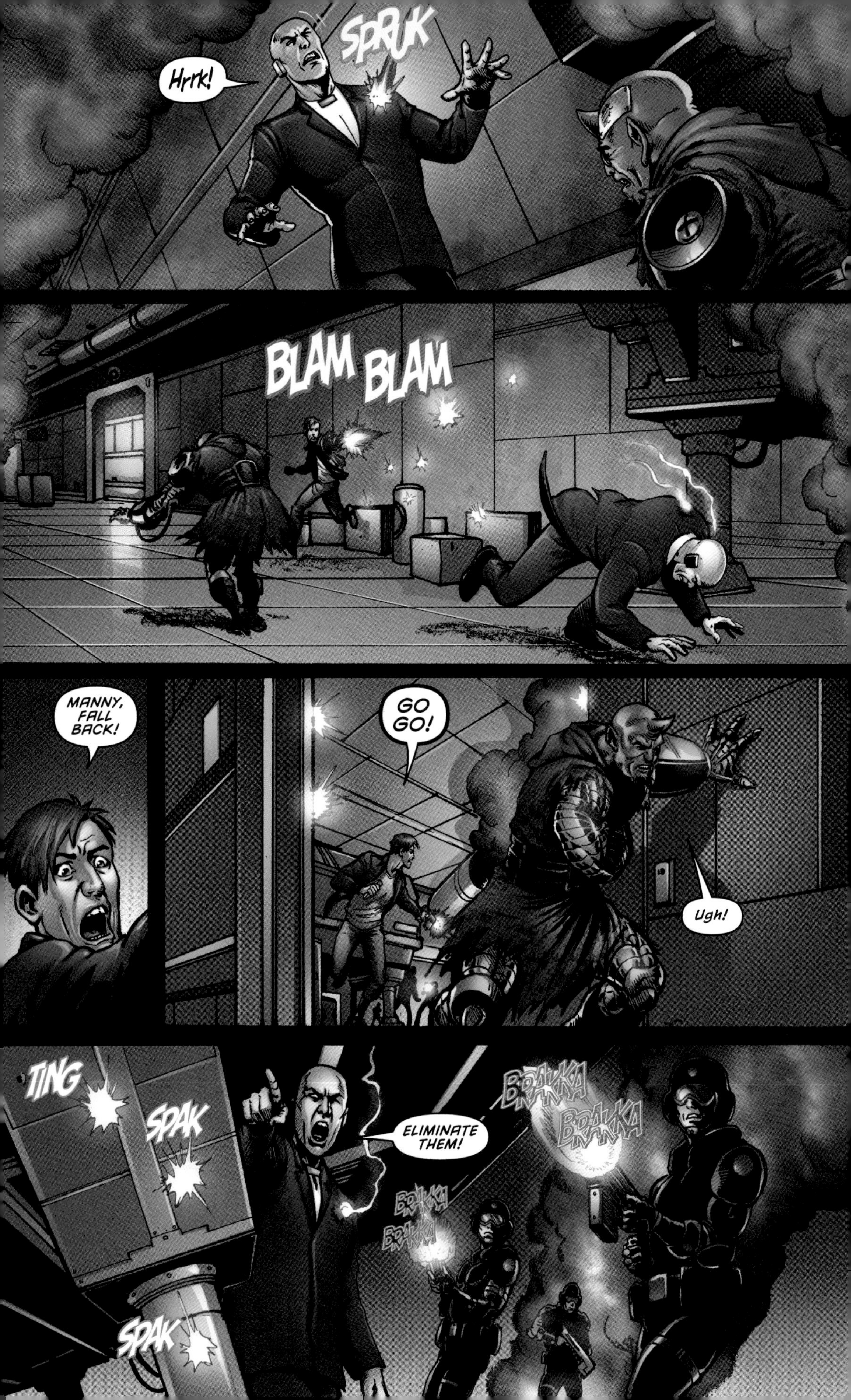

Hrrk!
SPRUK
BLAM BLAM
MANNY, FALL BACK!
GO GO!
Ugh!
TING
SPAK
ELIMINATE THEM!
BRAKKA
BRAKKA
BRAKKA
BRAKKA
SPAK

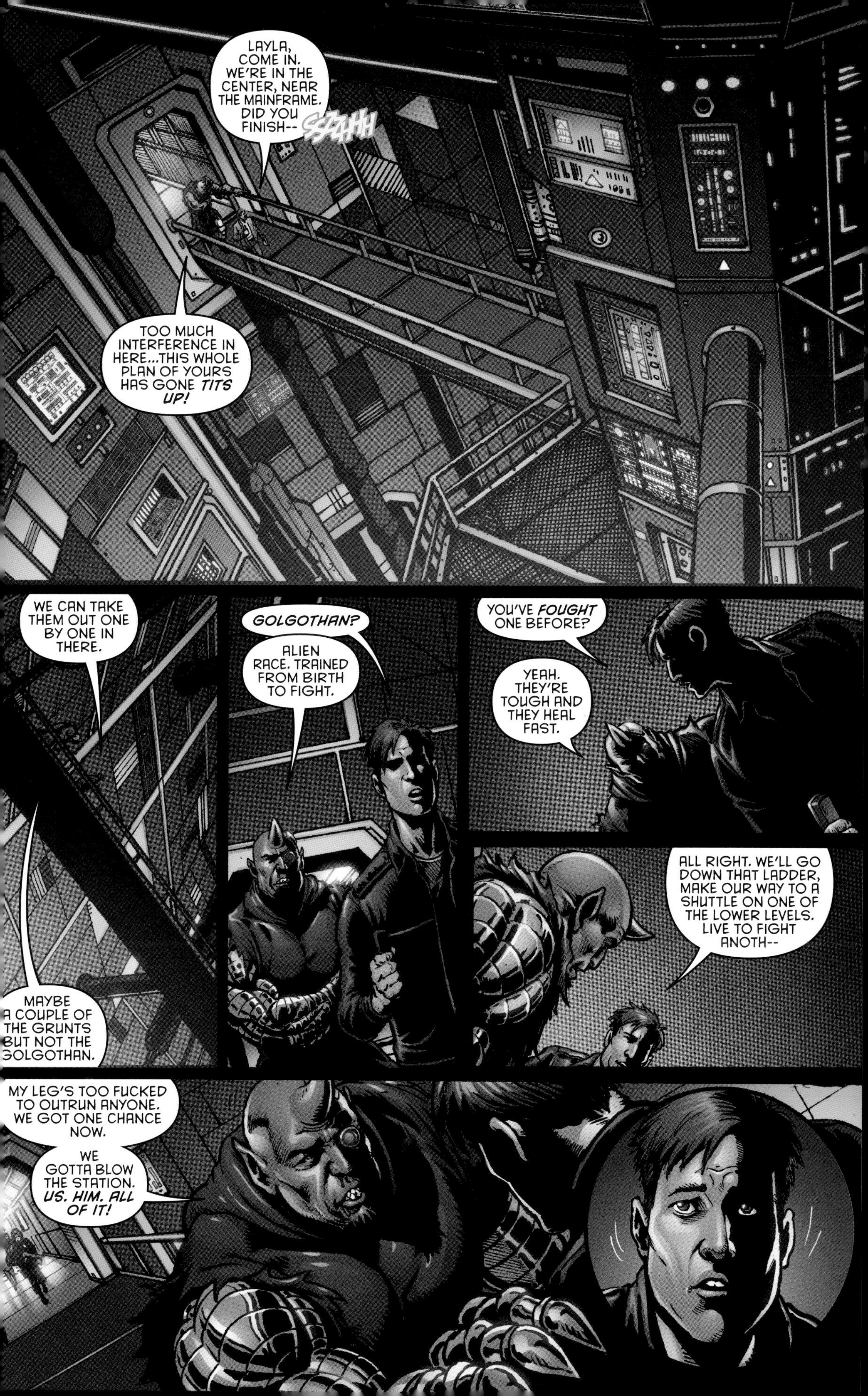
LAYLA, COME IN. WE'RE IN THE CENTER, NEAR THE MAINFRAME. DID YOU FINISH--
SSSZZHHH
TOO MUCH INTERFERENCE IN HERE...THIS WHOLE PLAN OF YOURS HAS GONE *TITS UP!*
WE CAN TAKE THEM OUT ONE BY ONE IN THERE.
MAYBE A COUPLE OF THE GRUNTS BUT NOT THE GOLGOTHAN.
GOLGOTHAN?
ALIEN RACE. TRAINED FROM BIRTH TO FIGHT.
YOU'VE *FOUGHT* ONE BEFORE?
YEAH. THEY'RE TOUGH AND THEY HEAL FAST.
ALL RIGHT. WE'LL GO DOWN THAT LADDER, MAKE OUR WAY TO A SHUTTLE ON ONE OF THE LOWER LEVELS. LIVE TO FIGHT ANOTH--
MY LEG'S TOO FUCKED TO OUTRUN ANYONE. WE GOT ONE CHANCE NOW.
WE GOTTA BLOW THE STATION. *US. HIM. ALL OF IT!*

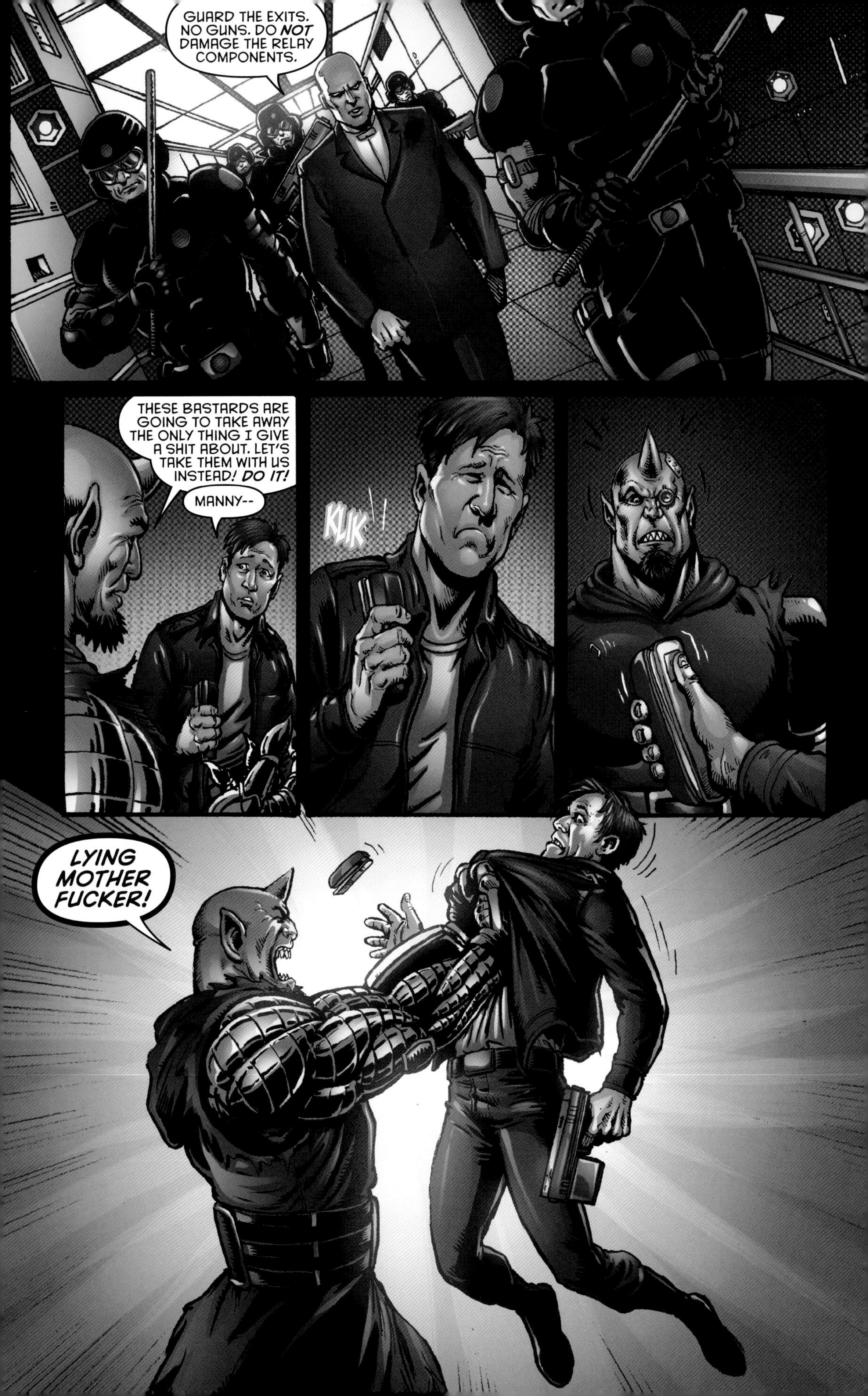
GUARD THE EXITS. NO GUNS. DO NOT DAMAGE THE RELAY COMPONENTS.
THESE BASTARDS ARE GOING TO TAKE AWAY THE ONLY THING I GIVE A SHIT ABOUT. LET'S TAKE THEM WITH US INSTEAD! DO IT!
MANNY--
KLIK
LYING MOTHER FUCKER!

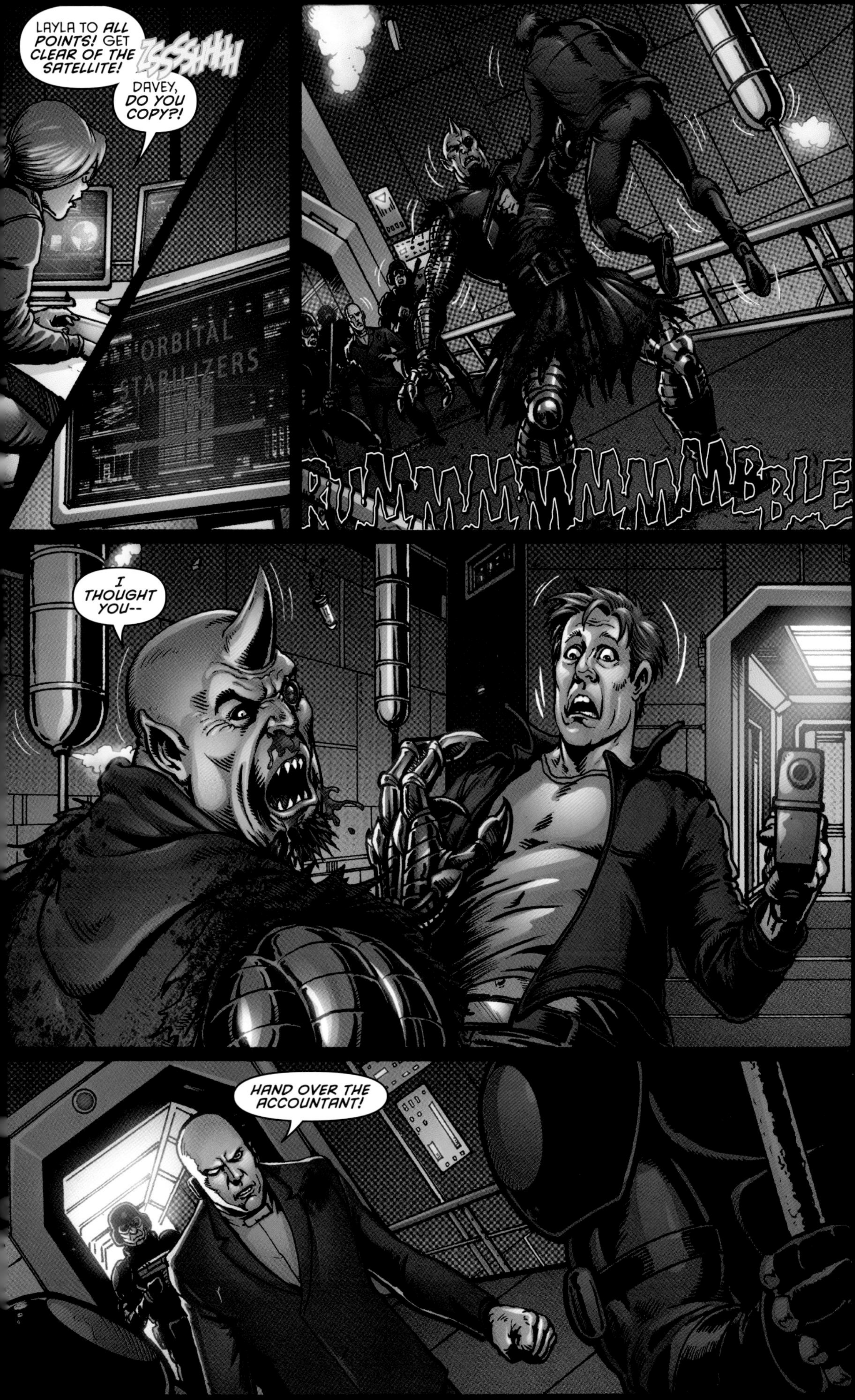
LAYLA TO ALL POINTS! GET CLEAR OF THE SATELLITE!
ZSSSHHH
DAVEY, DO YOU COPY?!
ORBITAL STABILIZERS
RUMMMMMMMMMBBLE
I THOUGHT YOU--
HAND OVER THE ACCOUNTANT!

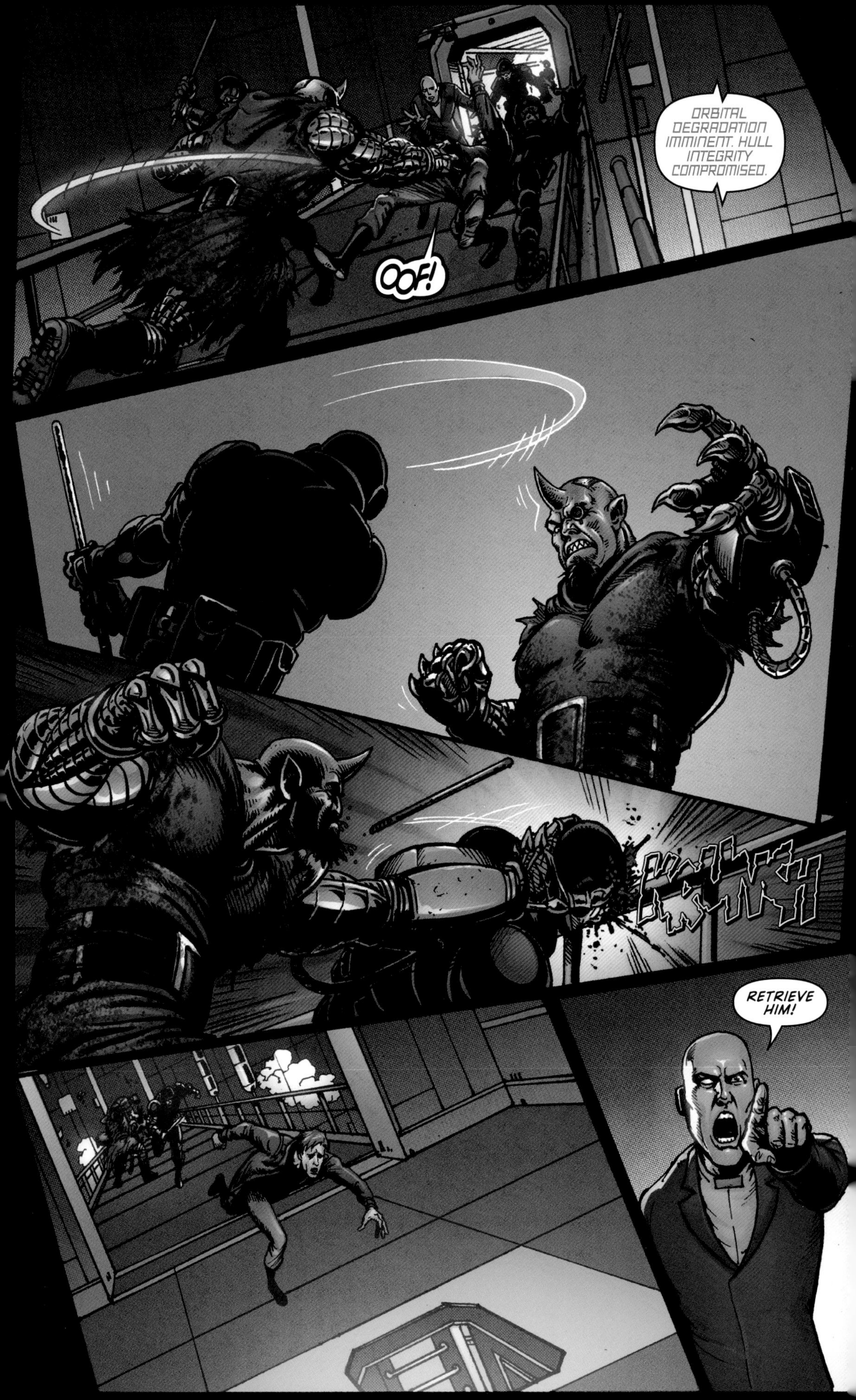
ORBITAL DEGRADATION IMMINENT. HULL INTEGRITY COMPROMISED.
OOF!
RETRIEVE HIM!

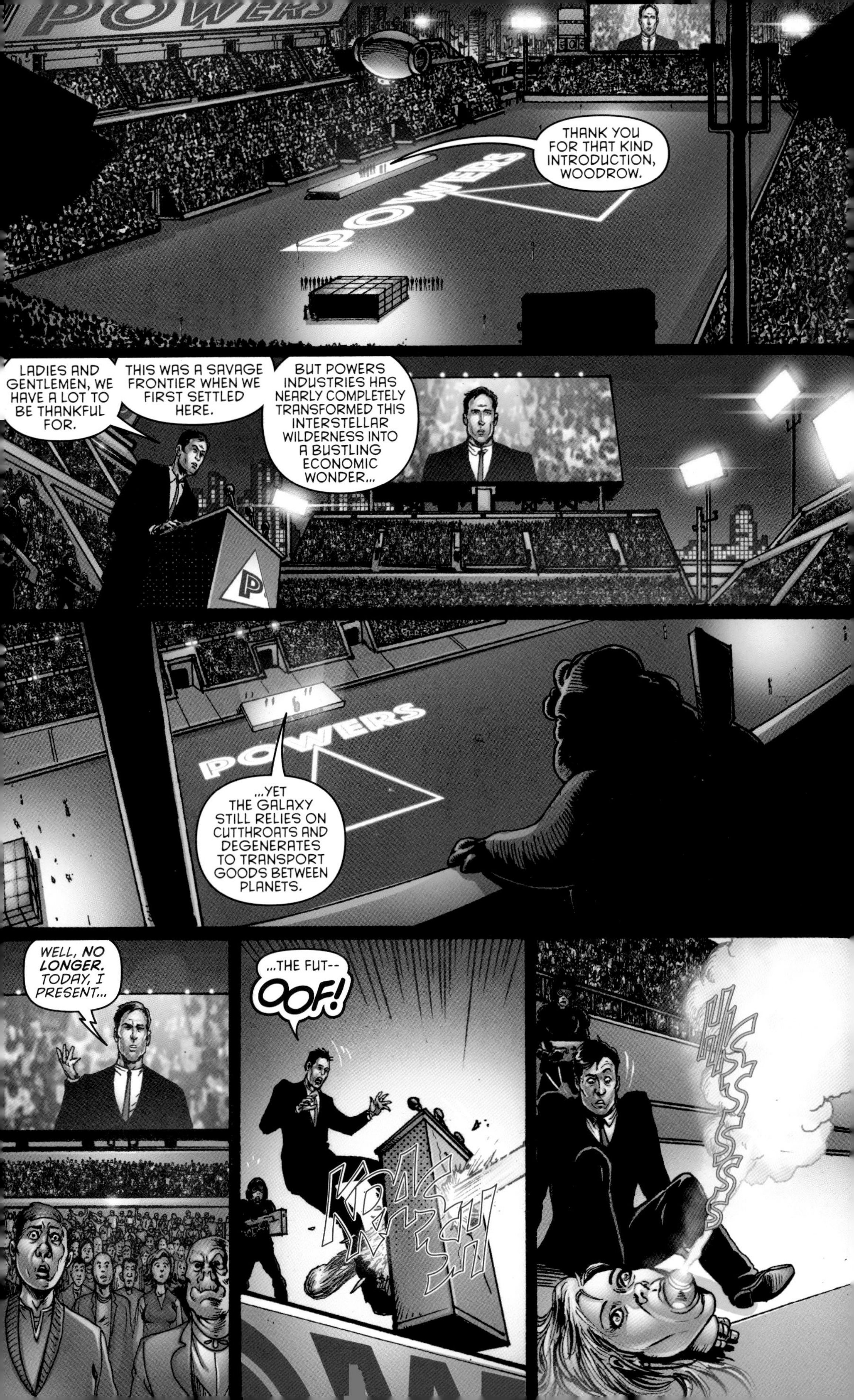
POWERS
THANK YOU FOR THAT KIND INTRODUCTION, WOODROW.
POWERS
LADIES AND GENTLEMEN, WE HAVE A LOT TO BE THANKFUL FOR.
THIS WAS A SAVAGE FRONTIER WHEN WE FIRST SETTLED HERE.
BUT POWERS INDUSTRIES HAS NEARLY COMPLETELY TRANSFORMED THIS INTERSTELLAR WILDERNESS INTO A BUSTLING ECONOMIC WONDER...
POWERS
...YET THE GALAXY STILL RELIES ON CUTTHROATS AND DEGENERATES TO TRANSPORT GOODS BETWEEN PLANETS.
WELL, NO LONGER. TODAY, I PRESENT...
...THE FUT--
OOF!

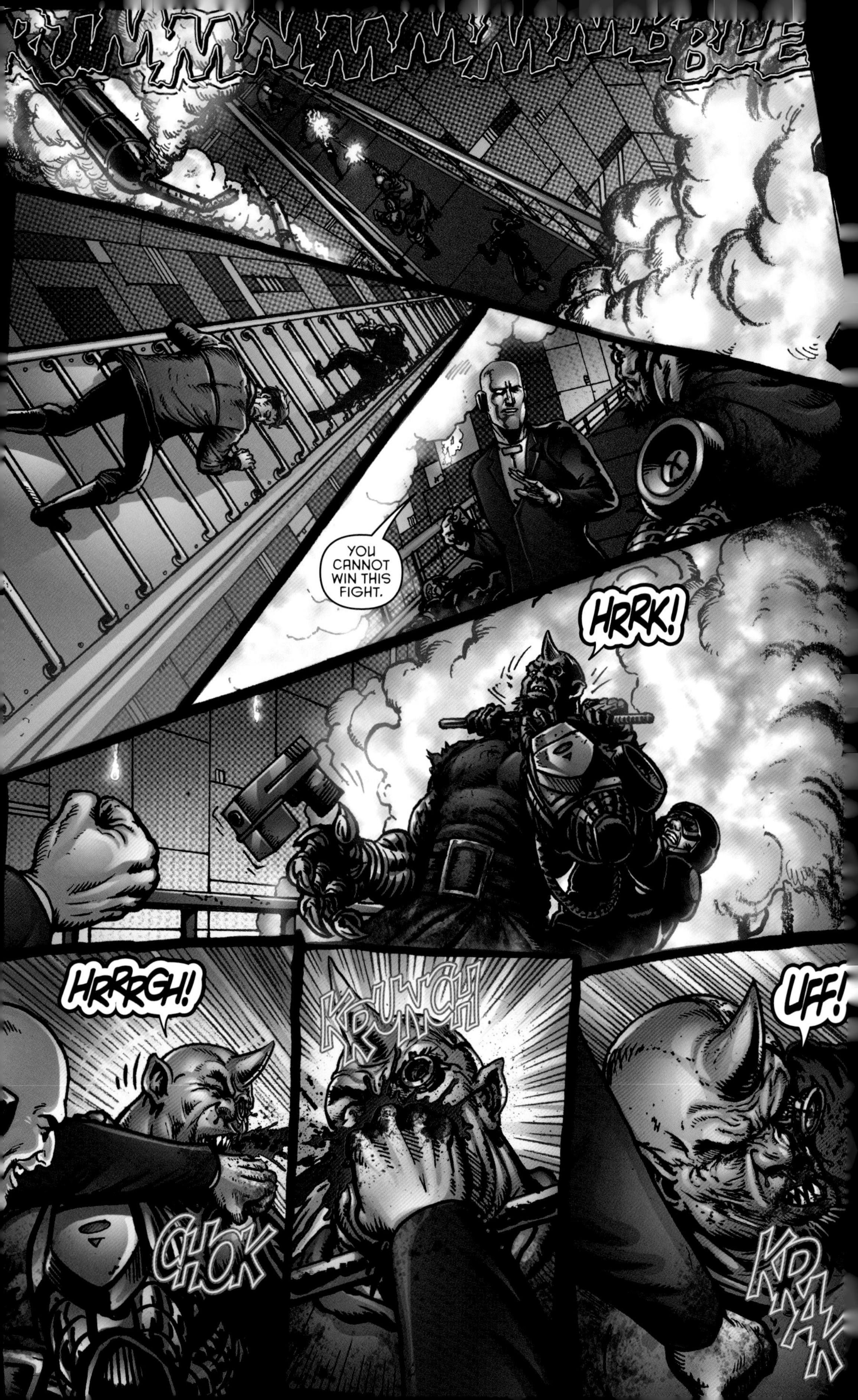
RUMMMMMMMMMBBLE
YOU CANNOT WIN THIS FIGHT.
HRRK!
HRRRGH!
CHOK
KRUNCH
UFF!
KRAK

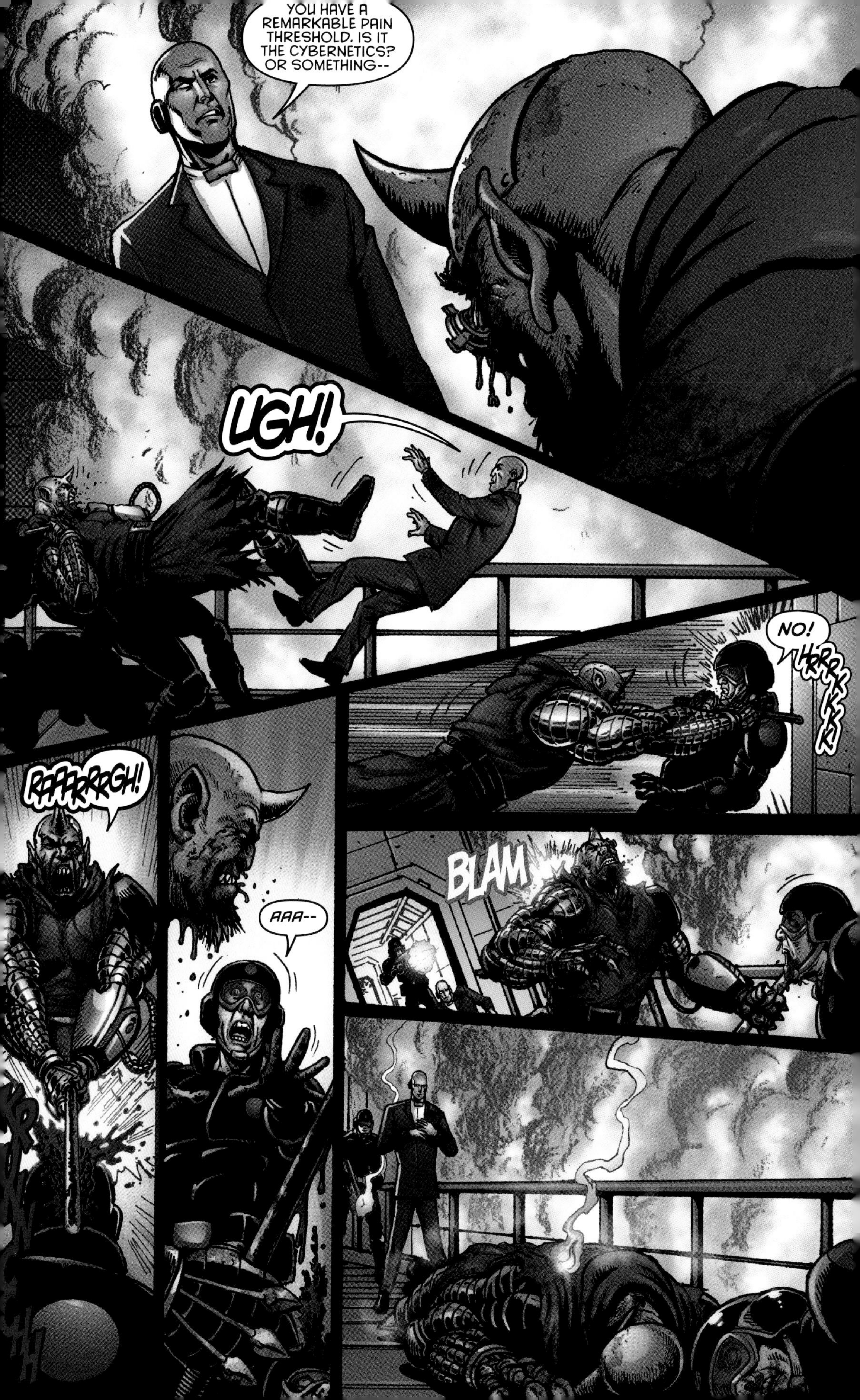
YOU HAVE A REMARKABLE PAIN THRESHOLD. IS IT THE CYBERNETICS? OR SOMETHING--
UGH!
NO!
HRRKKKK!
RAAARRRGH!
AAA--
BLAM

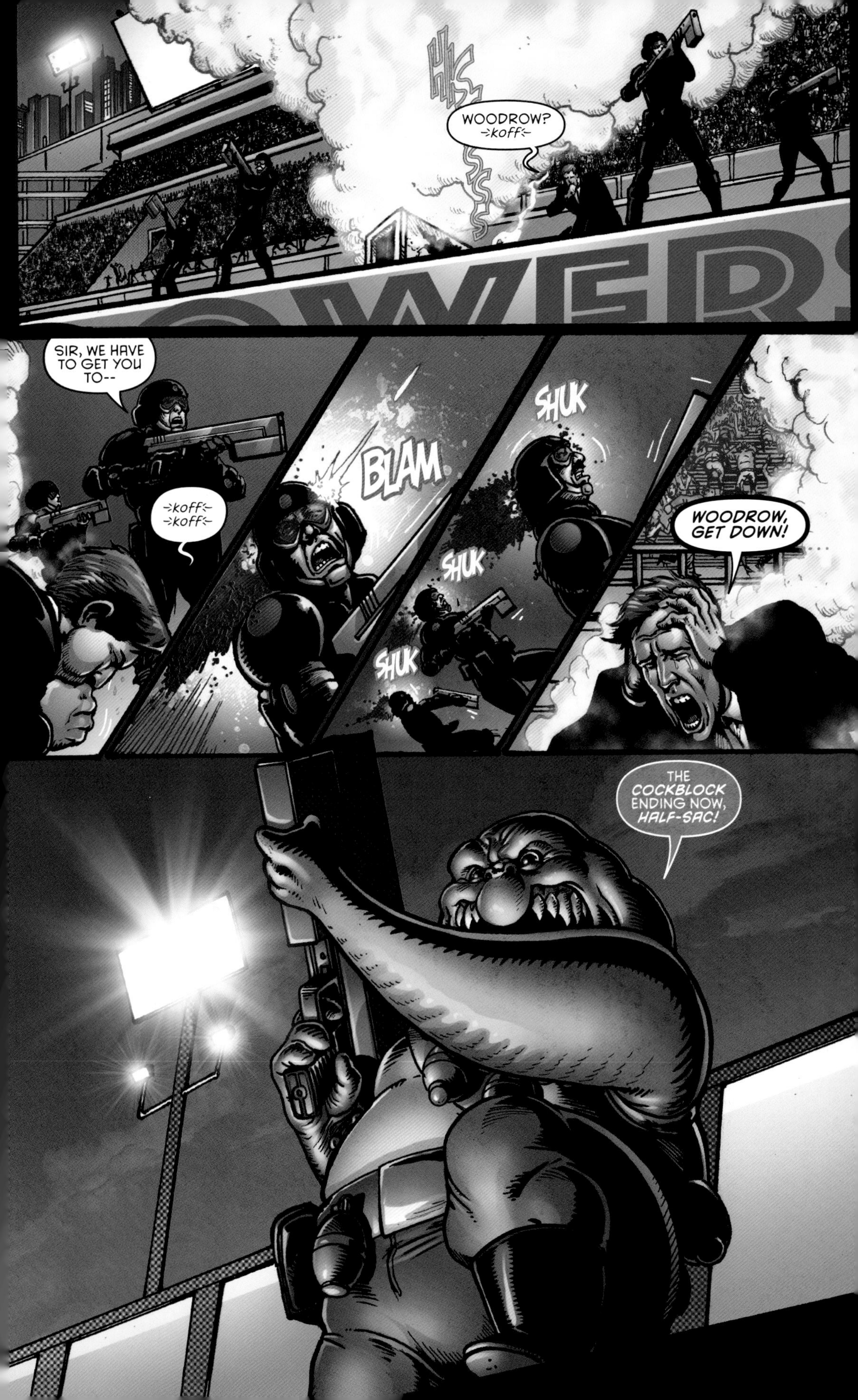
HISSSSS
WOODROW? -koff-
SIR, WE HAVE TO GET YOU TO--
-koff- -koff-
BLAM
SHUK
SHUK
SHUK
WOODROW, GET DOWN!
THE COCKBLOCK ENDING NOW, HALF-SAC!

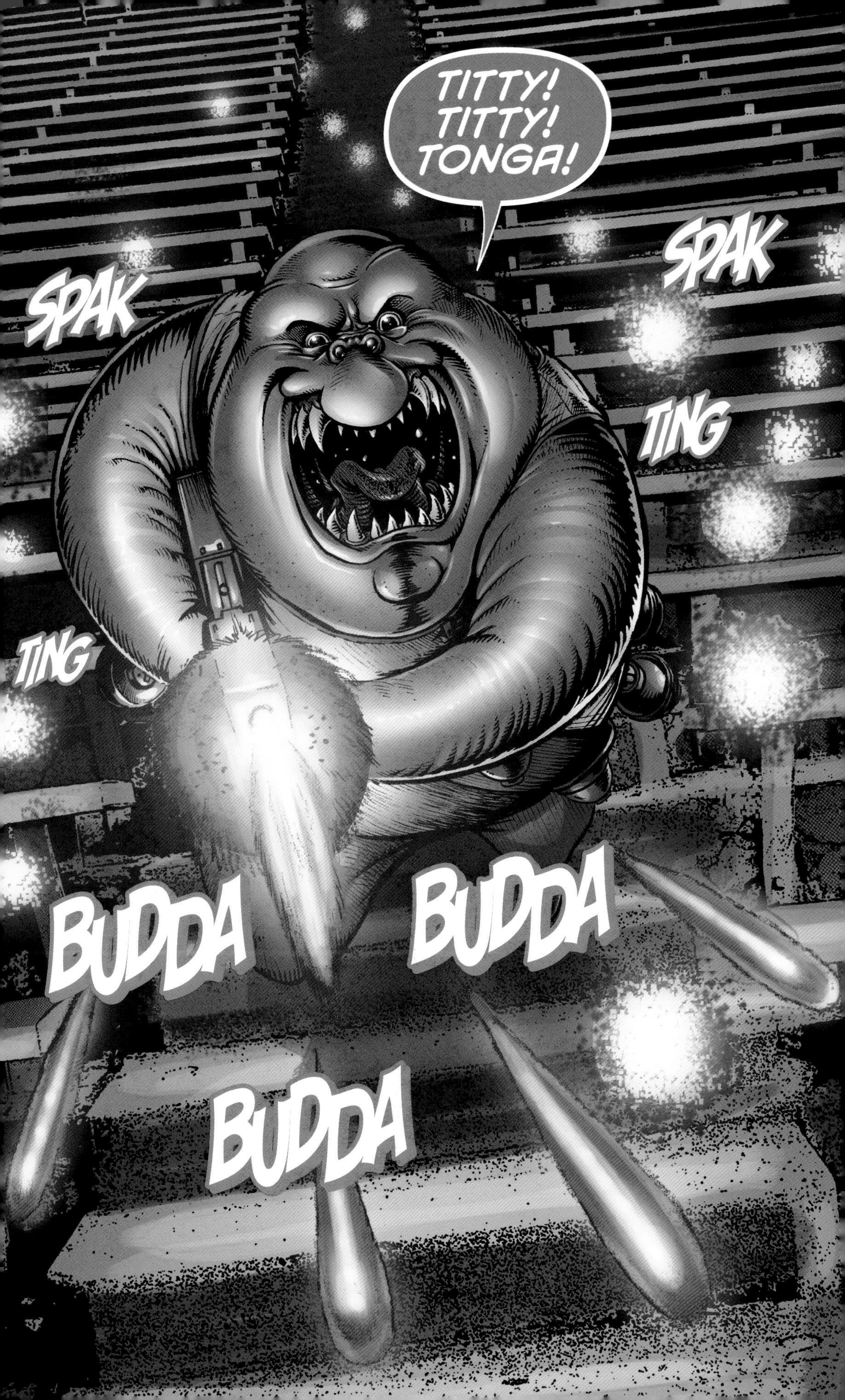
TITTY! TITTY! TONGA!
SPAK
SPAK
TING
TING
BUDDA
BUDDA
BUDDA

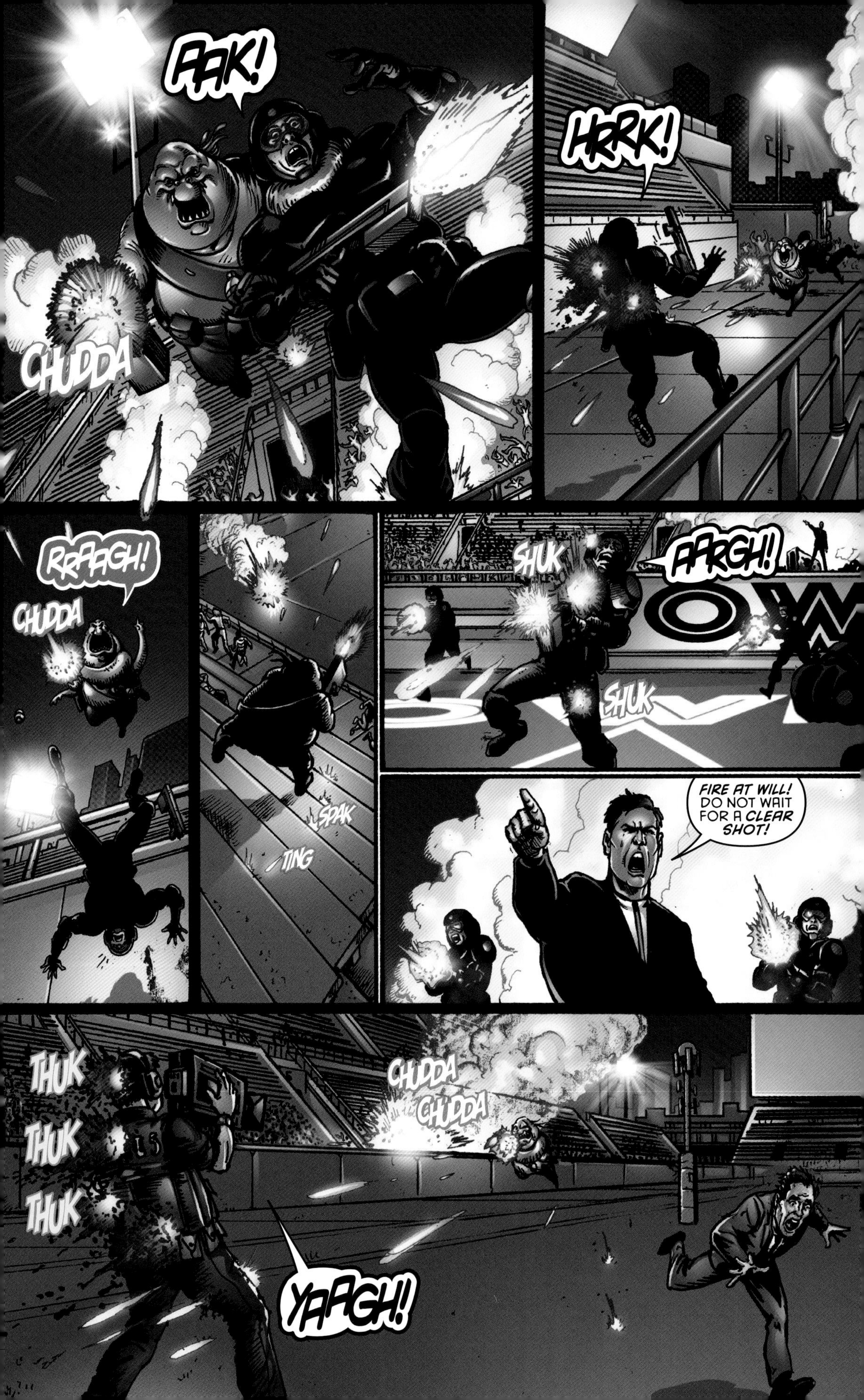
AAK!
CHUDDA
HRRK!
RRAAGH!
CHUDDA
SPAK
TING
SHUK
AARGH!
SHUK
FIRE AT WILL! DO NOT WAIT FOR A CLEAR SHOT!
THUK
THUK
THUK
CHUDDA
CHUDDA
YAAGH!

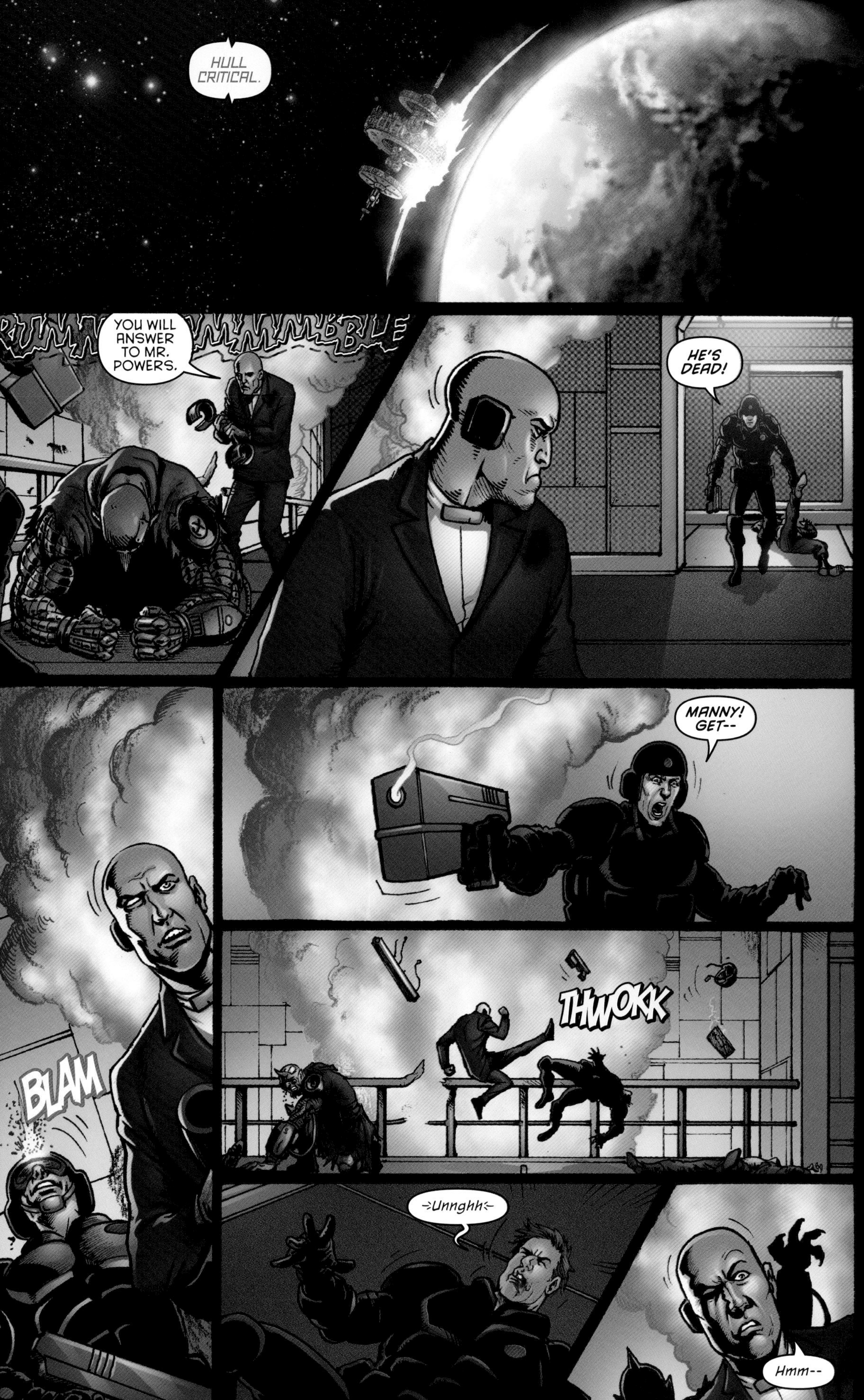
HULL CRITICAL.
YOU WILL ANSWER TO MR. POWERS.
HE'S DEAD!
MANNY! GET--
BLAM
THWOKK
Unnghh
Hmm--

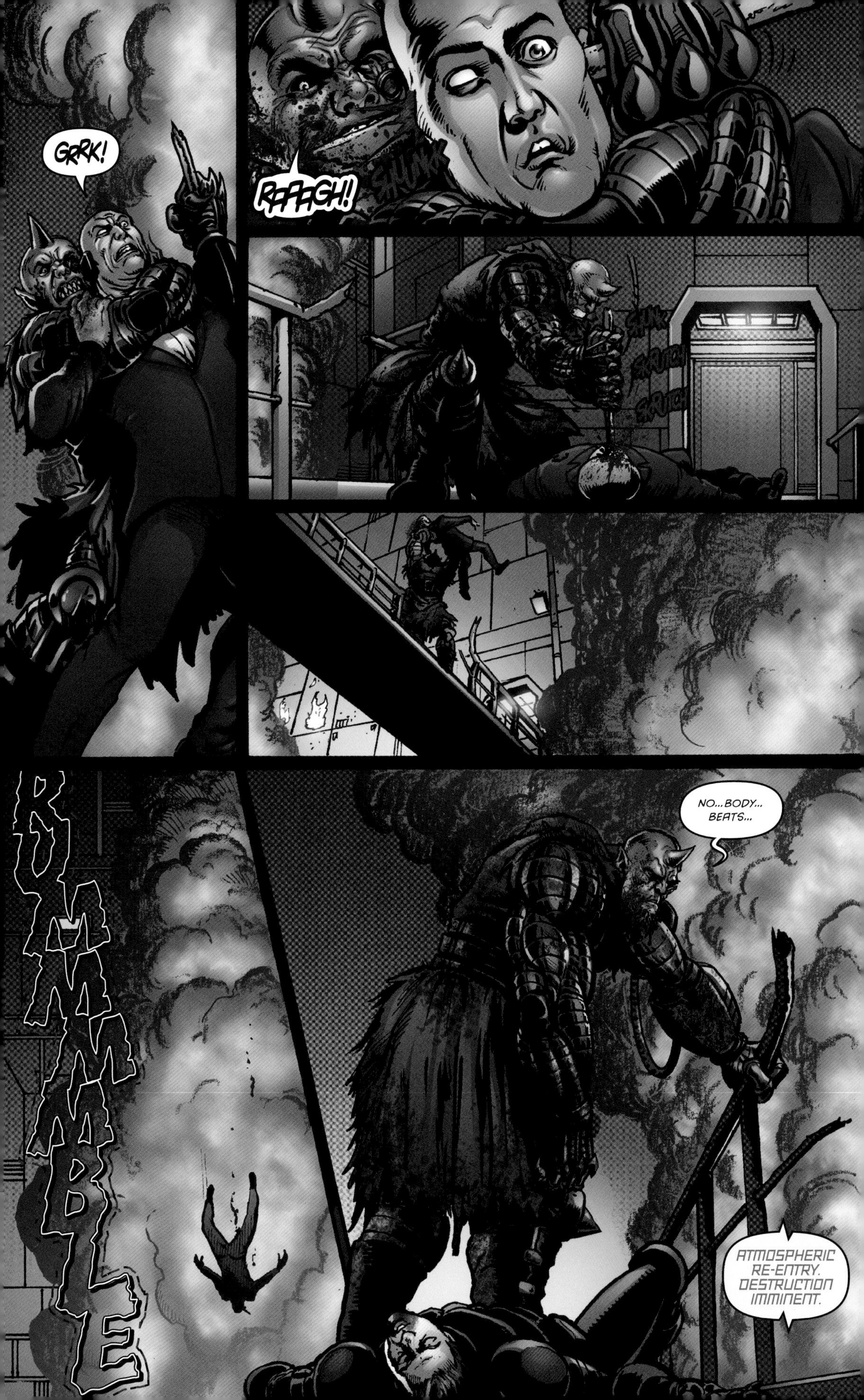
GRRK!
RAAAGH!
SHUNK
SHUNK
SKRUTCH
SKRUTCH
RUMMMBLE
NO... BODY... BEATS...
ATMOSPHERIC RE-ENTRY. DESTRUCTION IMMINENT.

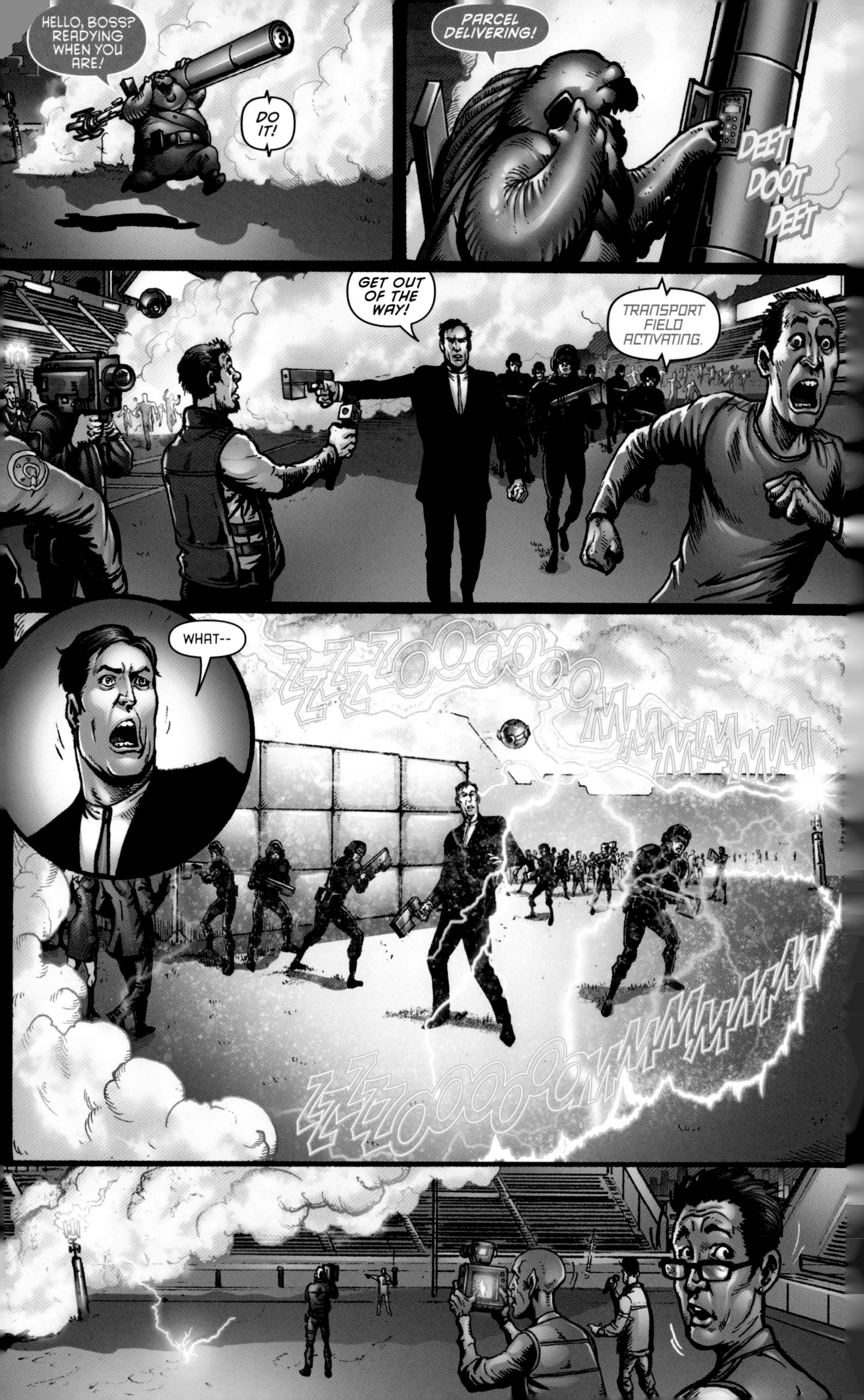
HELLO, BOSS? READYING WHEN YOU ARE!
DO IT!
PARCEL DELIVERING!
DEET DOOT DEET
GET OUT OF THE WAY!
TRANSPORT FIELD ACTIVATING.
WHAT--
ZZZZOOOOOOOOMMMMMMMMM
ZZZZOOOOOOOMMMMMMMMM

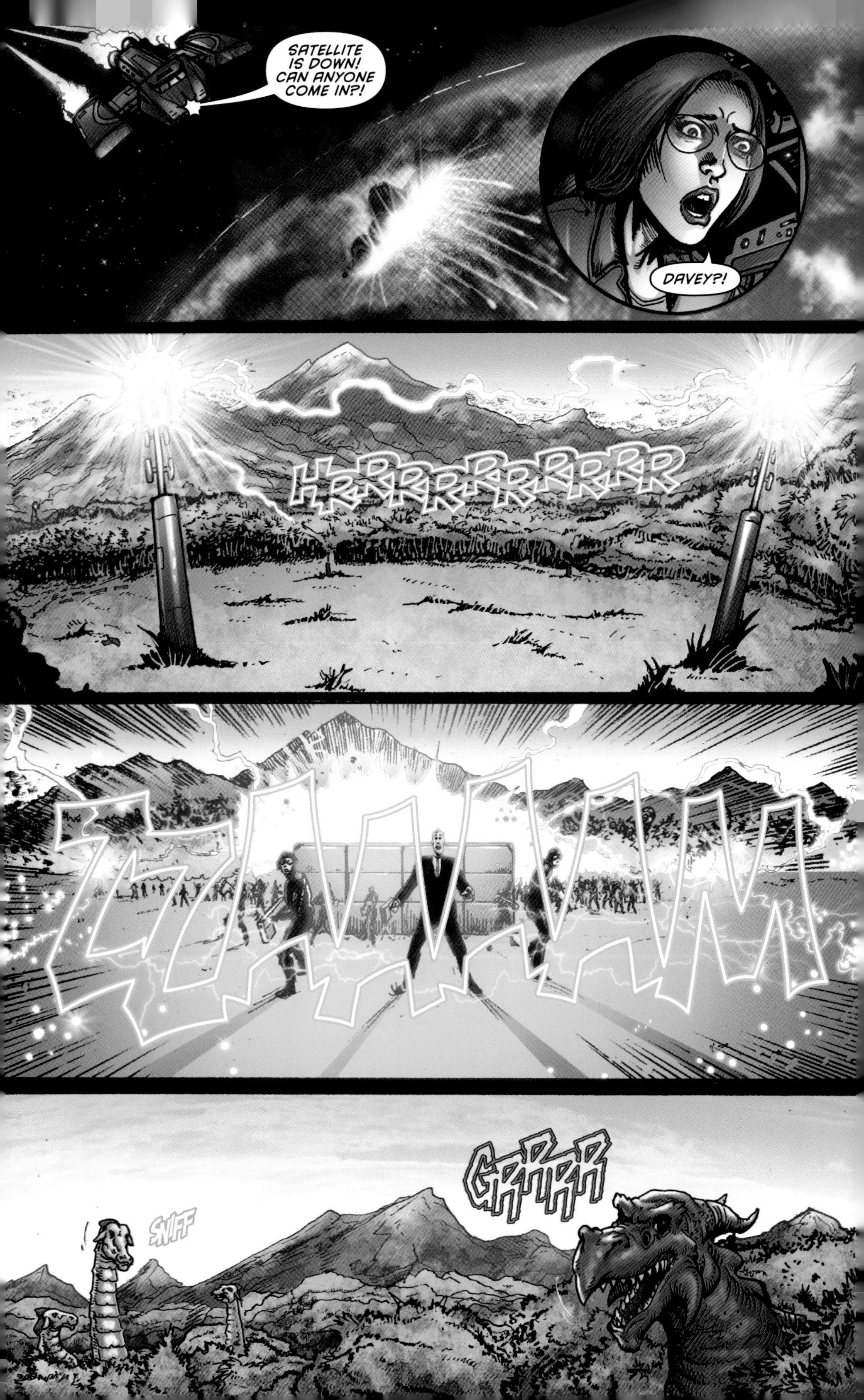
SATELLITE IS DOWN! CAN ANYONE COME IN?!
DAVEY?!
HRRRRRRRRRRR
ZZVVVAM
GRRRR
SNIFF

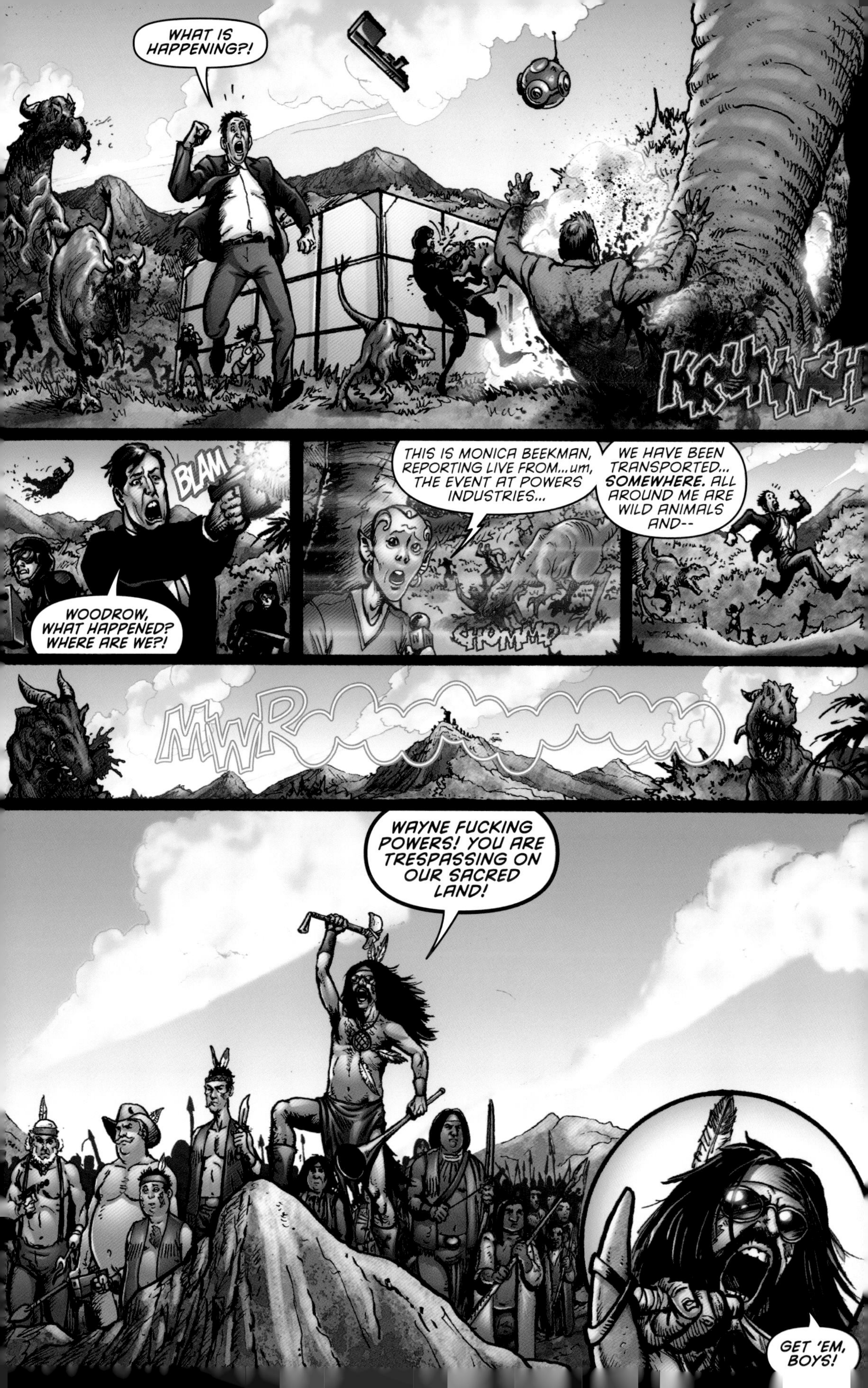
WHAT IS HAPPENING?!
KRUNCH
BLAM
WOODROW, WHAT HAPPENED? WHERE ARE WE?!
THIS IS MONICA BEEKMAN, REPORTING LIVE FROM...um, THE EVENT AT POWERS INDUSTRIES...
WE HAVE BEEN TRANSPORTED... SOMEWHERE. ALL AROUND ME ARE WILD ANIMALS AND--
MWROOOOOOOOOOO
WAYNE FUCKING POWERS! YOU ARE TRESPASSING ON OUR SACRED LAND!
GET 'EM, BOYS!

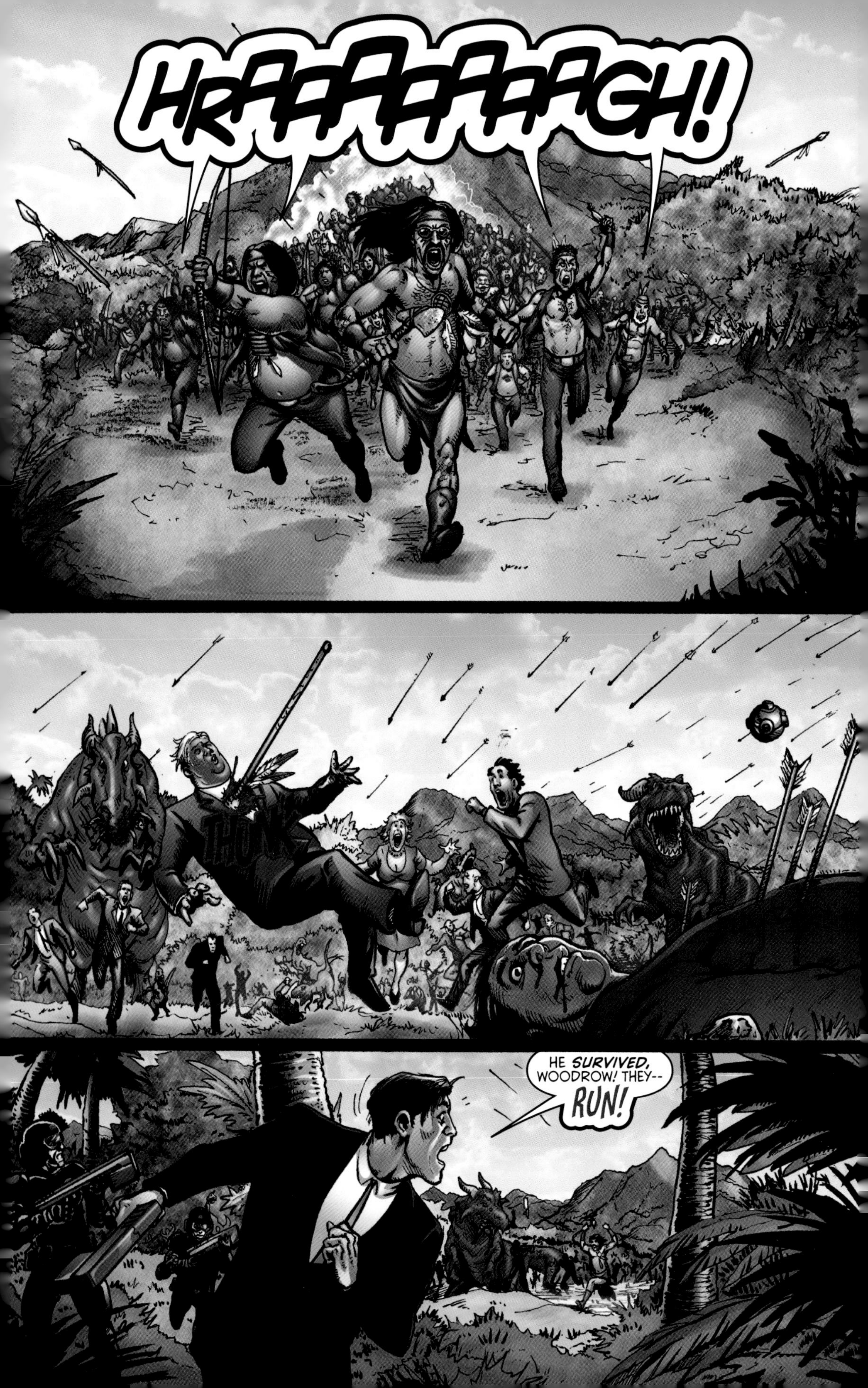
HRAAAAAAAGH!
THUNK
HE SURVIVED, WOODROW! THEY-- RUN!

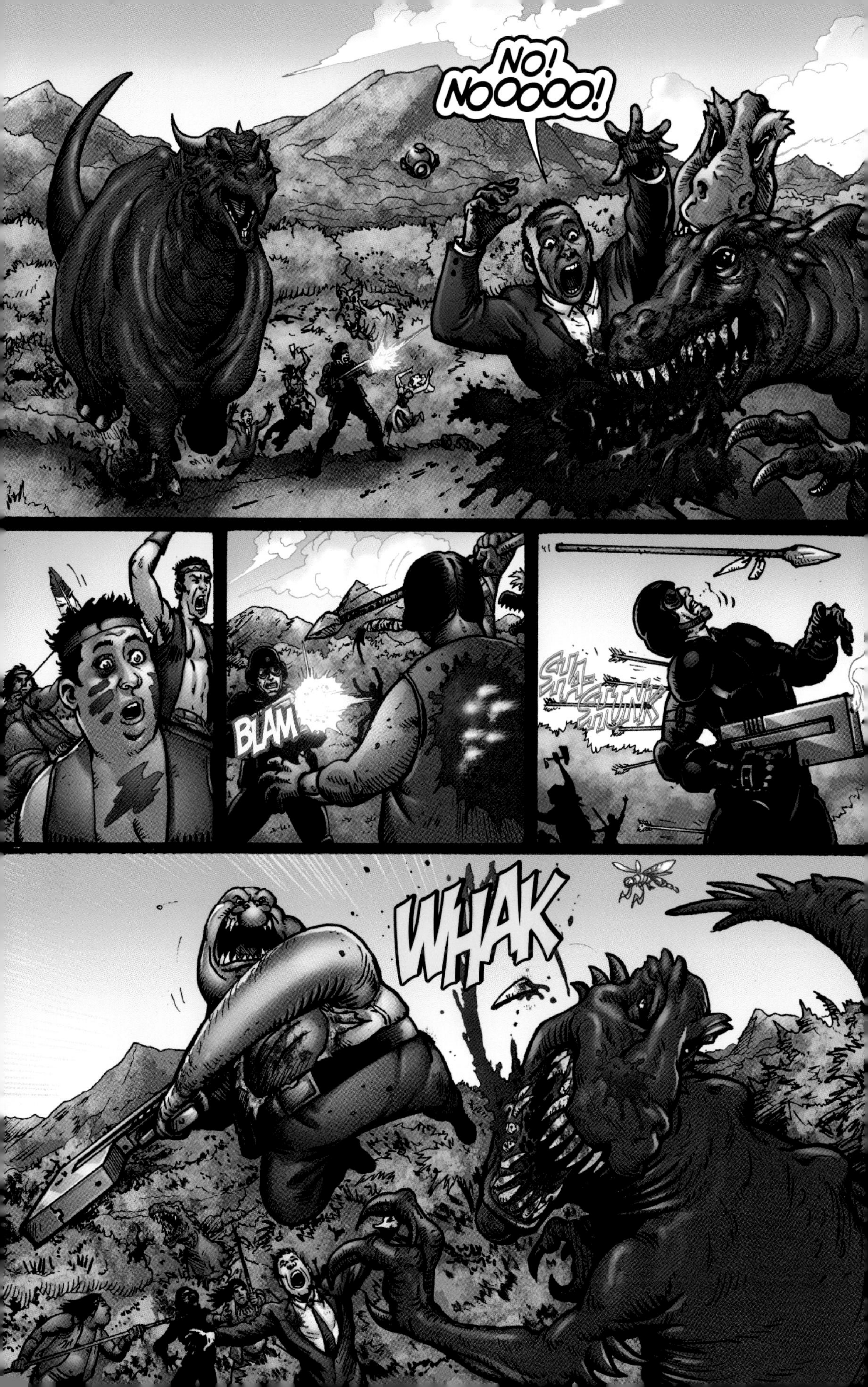

NO! NOOOOO!
BLAM
SHA-SHUNK
SHUNK
WHAK

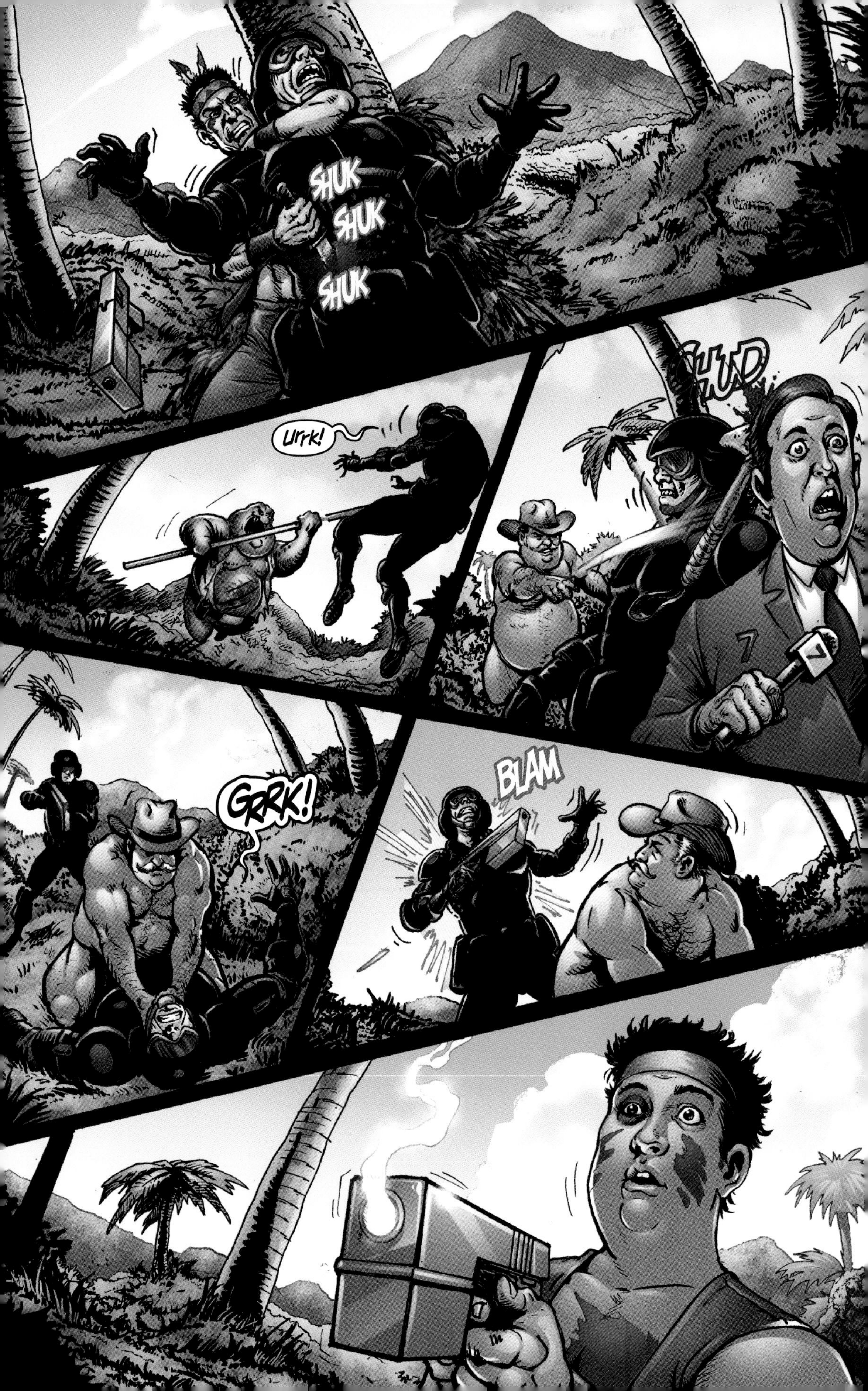
SHUK
SHUK
SHUK
Urrk!
GRRK!
BLAM

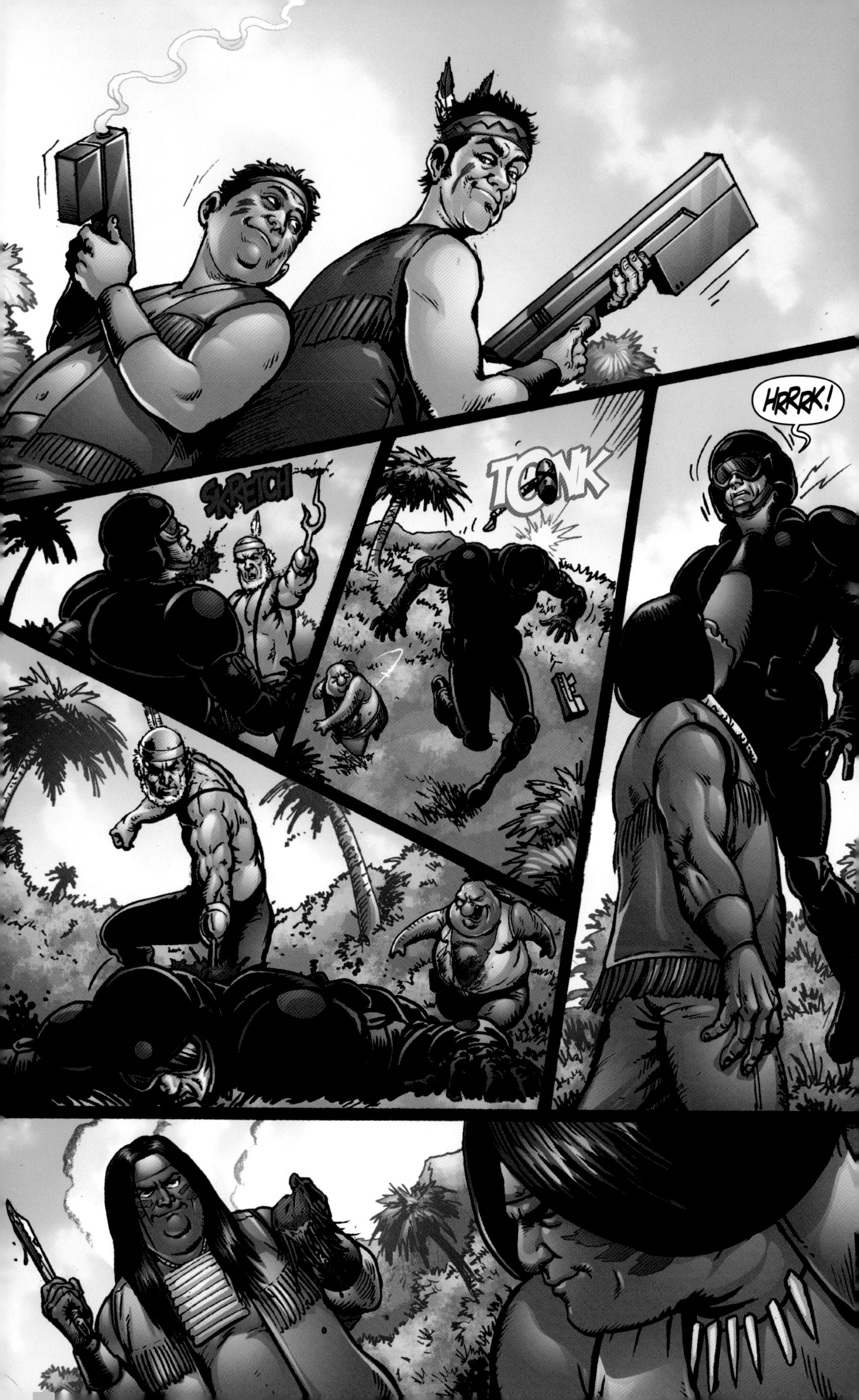
SKRETCH
TONK
HRRRK!

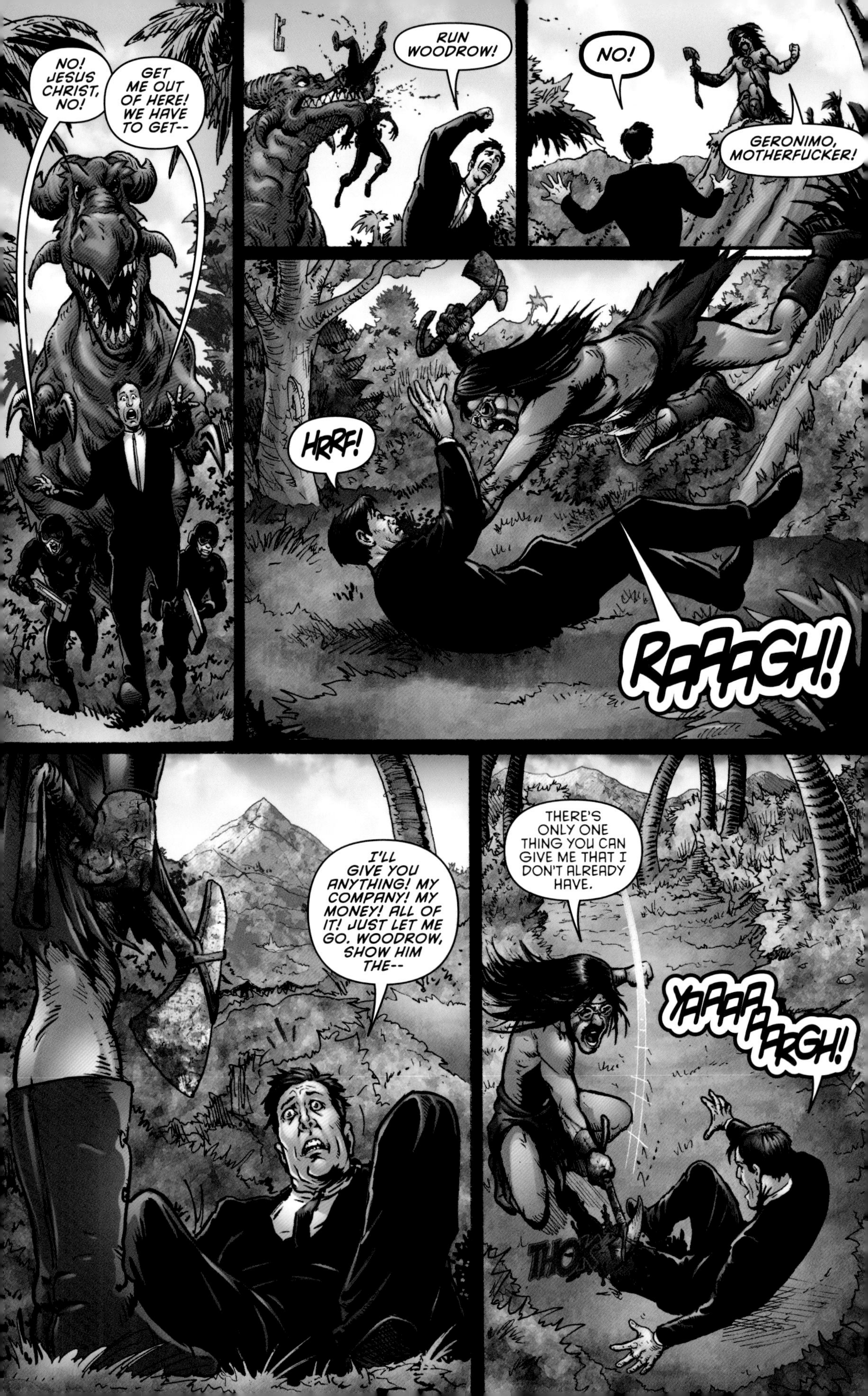
NO! JESUS CHRIST, NO!
GET ME OUT OF HERE! WE HAVE TO GET--
RUN WOODROW!
NO!
GERONIMO, MOTHERFUCKER!
HRRF!
RAAAGH!
I'LL GIVE YOU ANYTHING! MY COMPANY! MY MONEY! ALL OF IT! JUST LET ME GO. WOODROW, SHOW HIM THE--
THERE'S ONLY ONE THING YOU CAN GIVE ME THAT I DON'T ALREADY HAVE.
YAAAAAARGH!
THOK

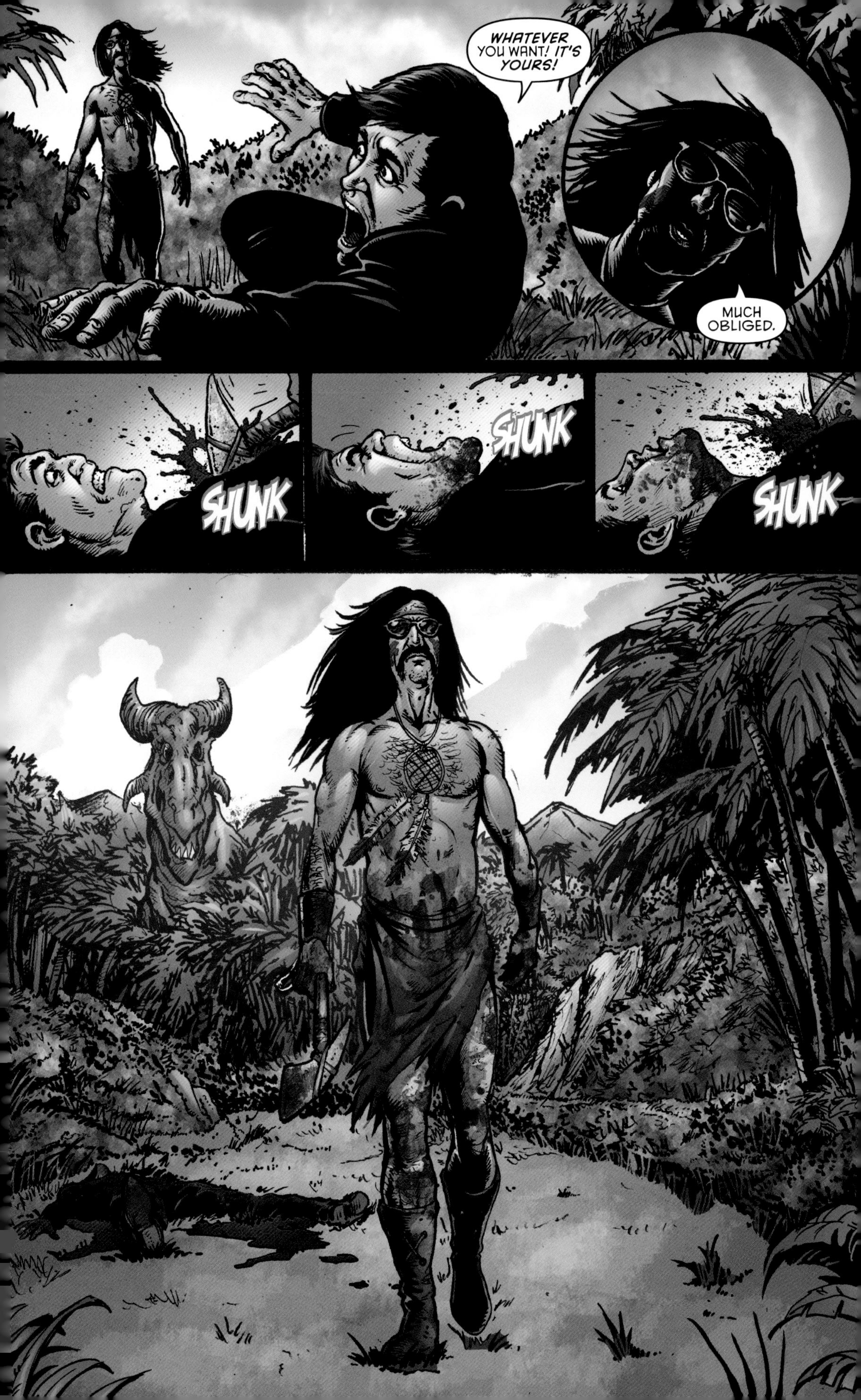
WHATEVER YOU WANT! IT'S YOURS!
MUCH OBLIGED.
SHUNK
SHUNK
SHUNK

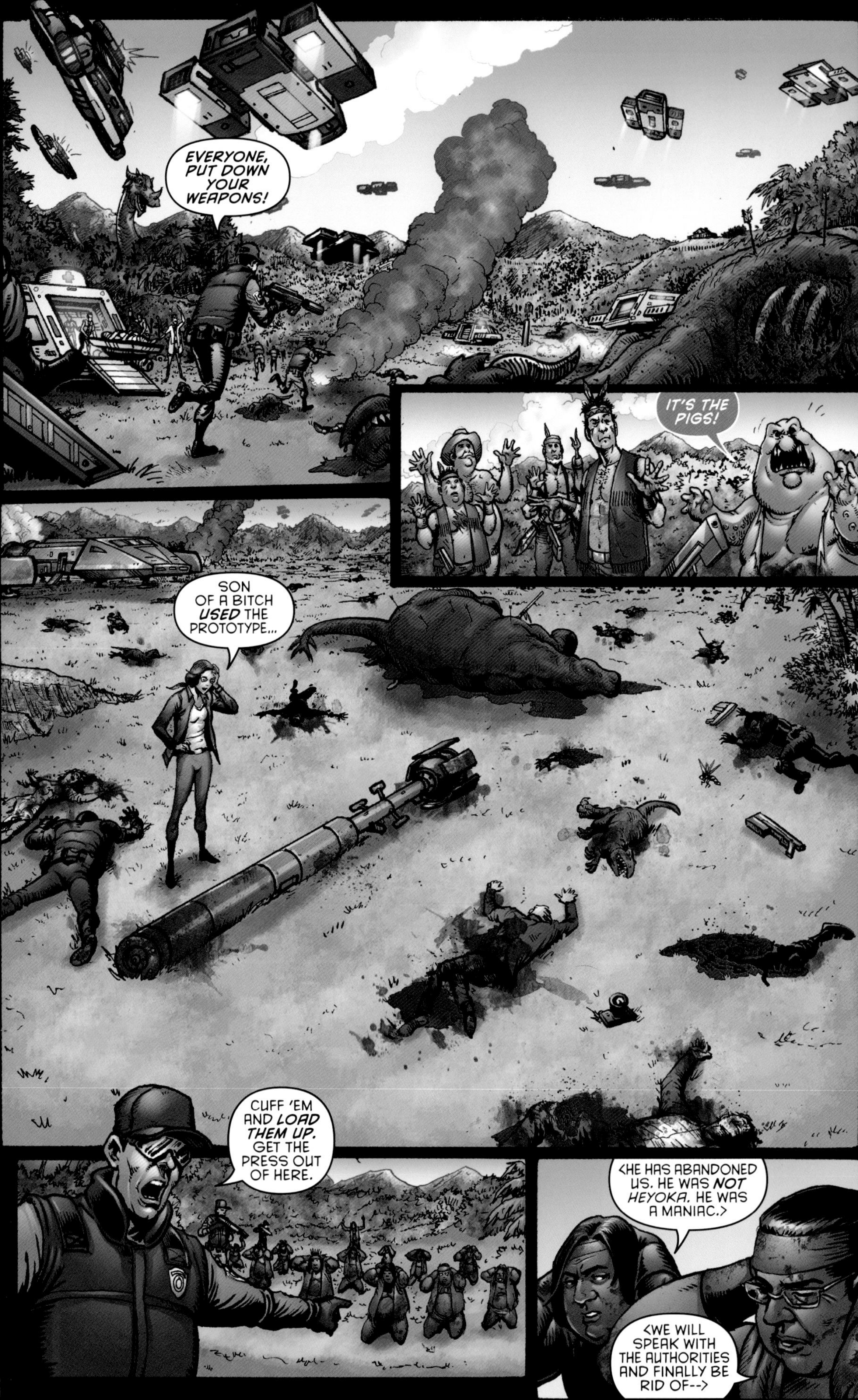
EVERYONE, PUT DOWN YOUR WEAPONS!
IT'S THE PIGS!
SON OF A BITCH USED THE PROTOTYPE...
CUFF 'EM AND LOAD THEM UP. GET THE PRESS OUT OF HERE.
<HE HAS ABANDONED US. HE WAS NOT HEYOKA. HE WAS A MANIAC.>
<WE WILL SPEAK WITH THE AUTHORITIES AND FINALLY BE RID OF-->

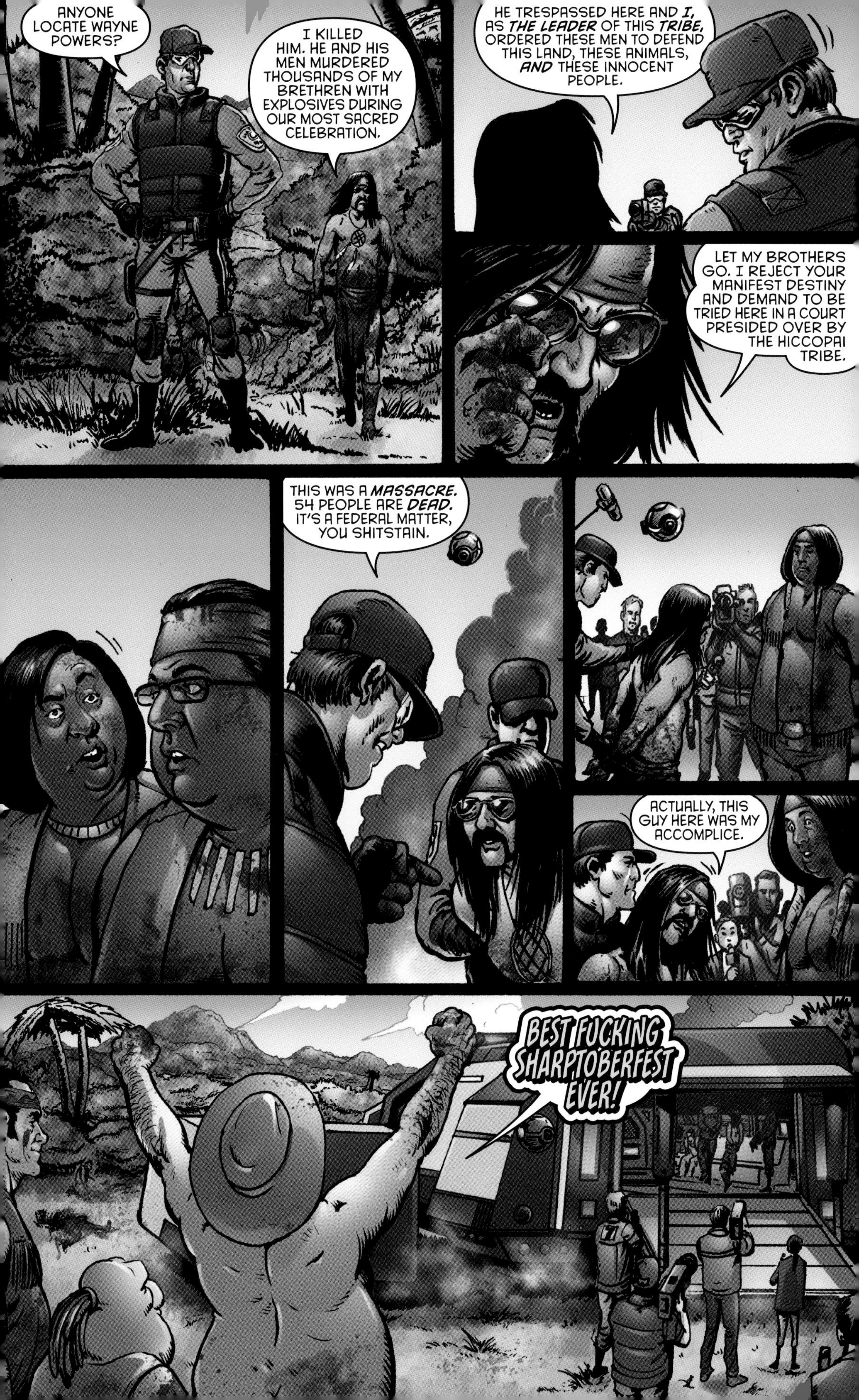
ANYONE LOCATE WAYNE POWERS?
I KILLED HIM. HE AND HIS MEN MURDERED THOUSANDS OF MY BRETHREN WITH EXPLOSIVES DURING OUR MOST SACRED CELEBRATION.
HE TRESPASSED HERE AND *I*, AS *THE LEADER* OF THIS *TRIBE*, ORDERED THESE MEN TO DEFEND THIS LAND, THESE ANIMALS, *AND* THESE INNOCENT PEOPLE.
LET MY BROTHERS GO. I REJECT YOUR MANIFEST DESTINY AND DEMAND TO BE TRIED HERE IN A COURT PRESIDED OVER BY THE HICCOPAI TRIBE.
THIS WAS A *MASSACRE.* 54 PEOPLE ARE *DEAD.* IT'S A FEDERAL MATTER, YOU SHITSTAIN.
ACTUALLY, THIS GUY HERE WAS MY ACCOMPLICE.
BEST FUCKING SHARPTOBERFEST EVER!

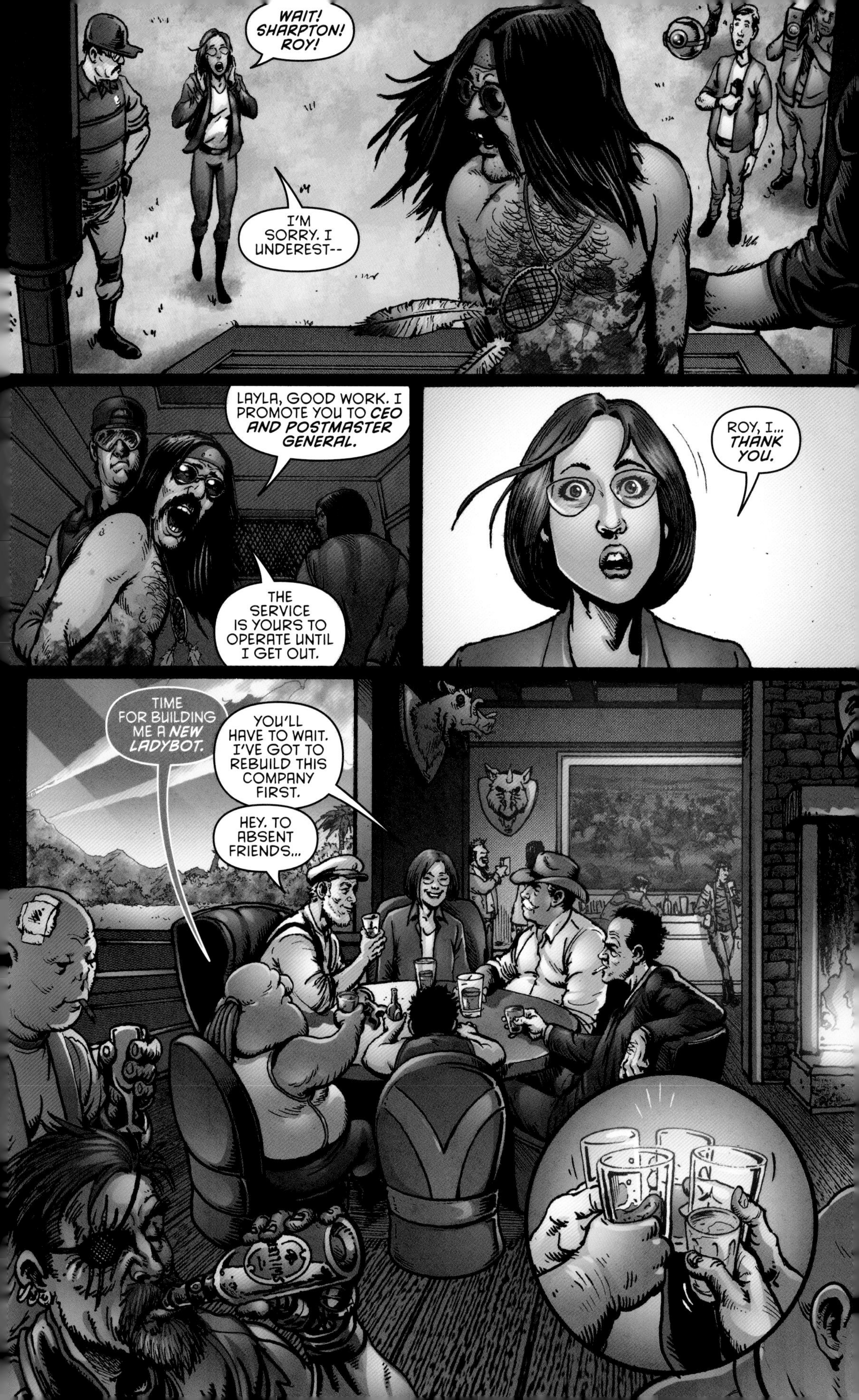
WAIT! SHARPTON! ROY!
I'M SORRY. I UNDEREST--
LAYLA, GOOD WORK. I PROMOTE YOU TO CEO AND POSTMASTER GENERAL.
THE SERVICE IS YOURS TO OPERATE UNTIL I GET OUT.
ROY, I... THANK YOU.
TIME FOR BUILDING ME A NEW LADYBOT.
YOU'LL HAVE TO WAIT. I'VE GOT TO REBUILD THIS COMPANY FIRST.
HEY. TO ABSENT FRIENDS...

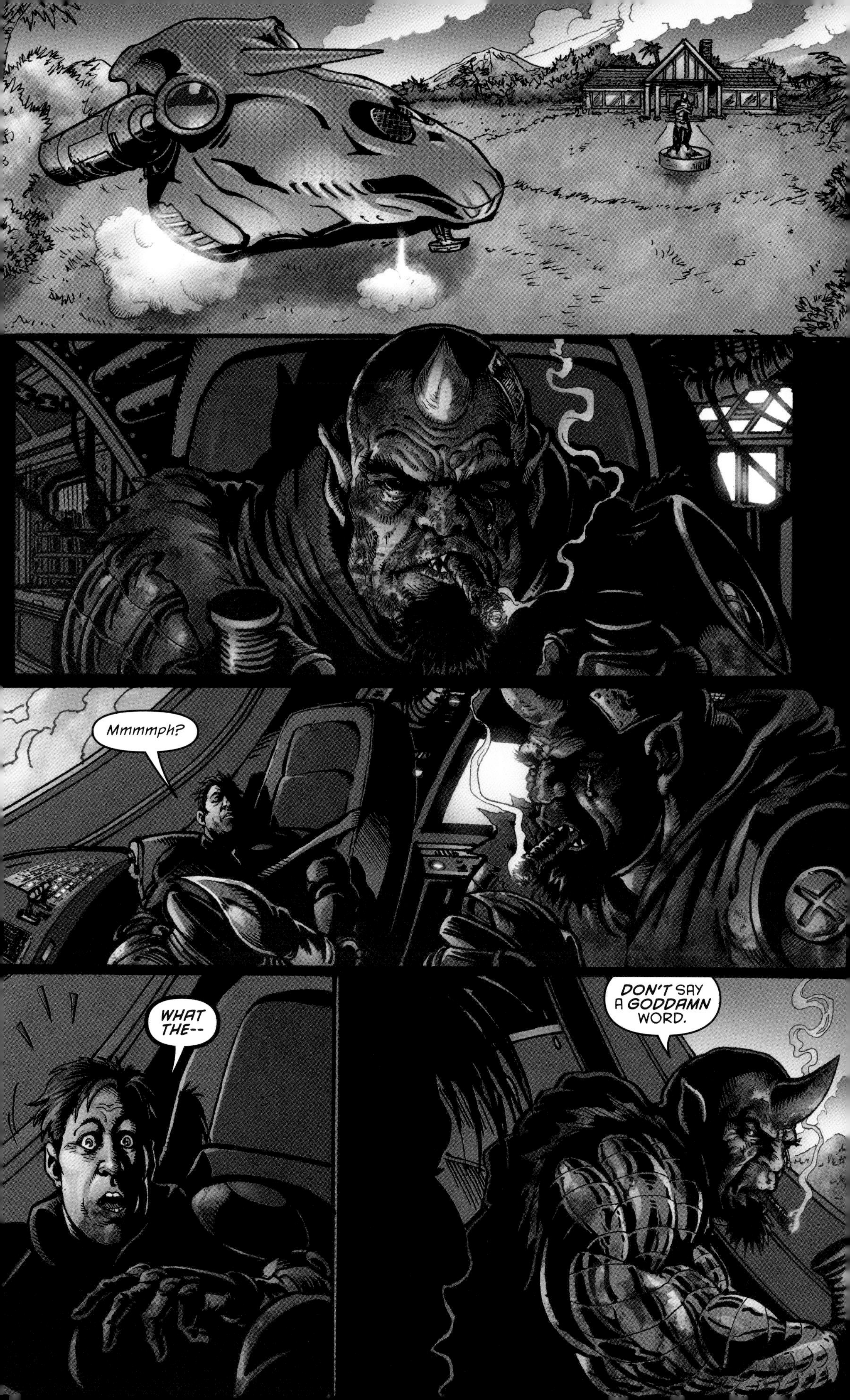
Mmmmph?
WHAT THE--
DON'T SAY A GODDAMN WORD.

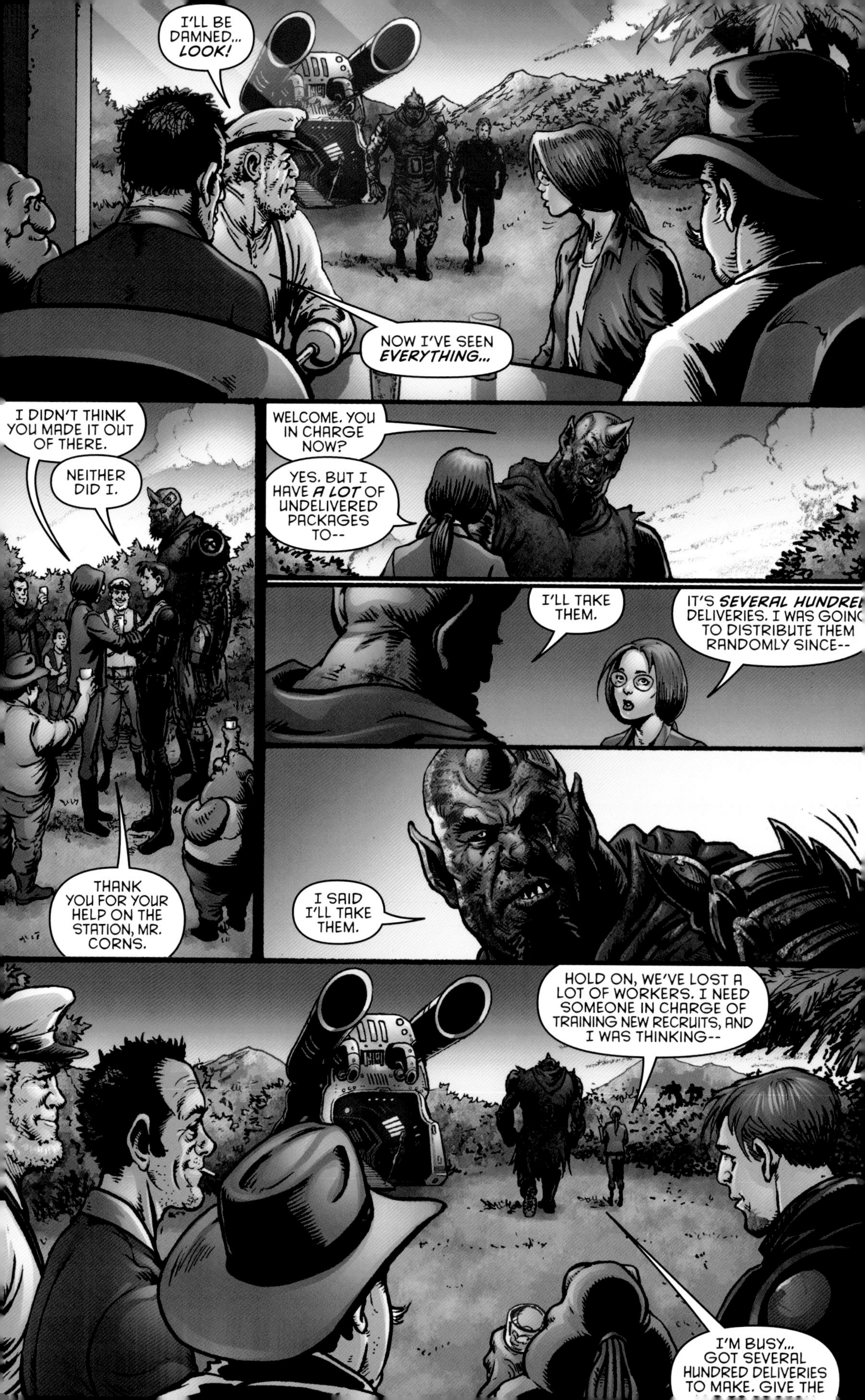
I'LL BE DAMNED... LOOK!
NOW I'VE SEEN EVERYTHING...
I DIDN'T THINK YOU MADE IT OUT OF THERE.
NEITHER DID I.
THANK YOU FOR YOUR HELP ON THE STATION, MR. CORNS.
WELCOME. YOU IN CHARGE NOW?
YES. BUT I HAVE A LOT OF UNDELIVERED PACKAGES TO--
I'LL TAKE THEM.
IT'S SEVERAL HUNDRE
DELIVERIES. I WAS GOIN
TO DISTRIBUTE THEM RANDOMLY SINCE--
I SAID I'LL TAKE THEM.
HOLD ON, WE'VE LOST A LOT OF WORKERS. I NEED SOMEONE IN CHARGE OF TRAINING NEW RECRUITS, AND I WAS THINKING--
I'M BUSY... GOT SEVERAL HUNDRED DELIVERIES TO MAKE. GIVE THE

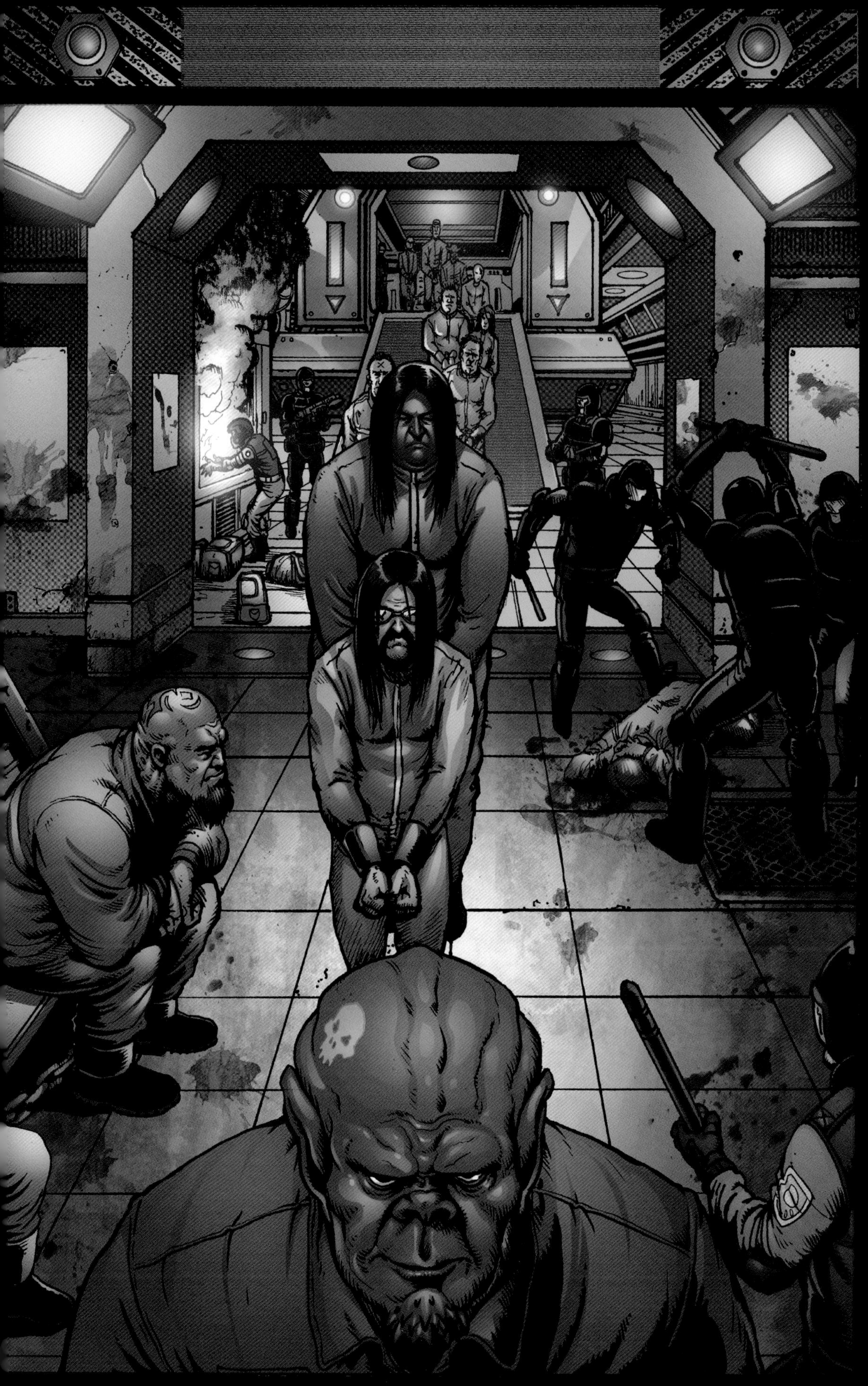

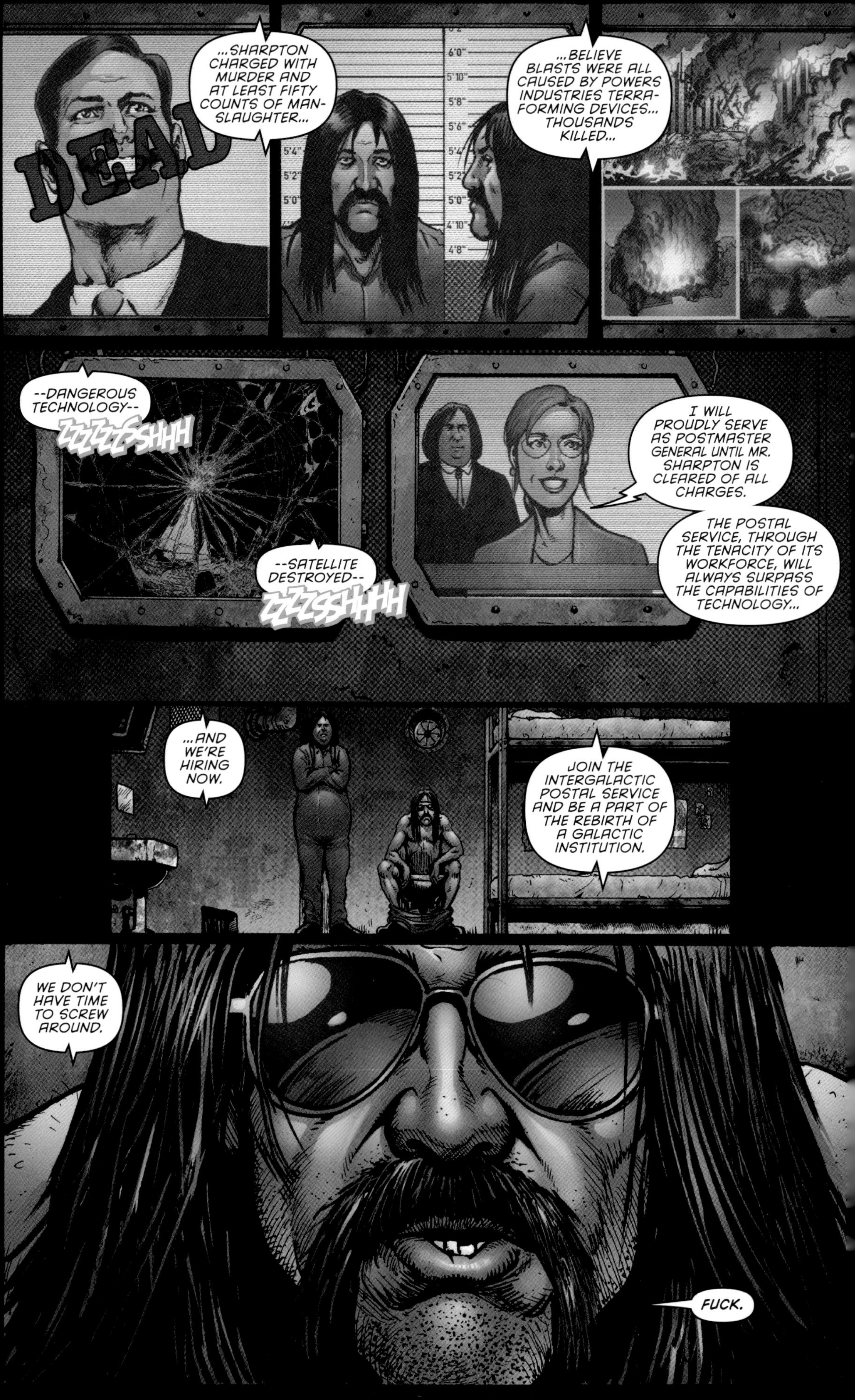
DEAD
...SHARPTON CHARGED WITH MURDER AND AT LEAST FIFTY COUNTS OF MAN-SLAUGHTER...
...BELIEVE BLASTS WERE ALL CAUSED BY POWERS INDUSTRIES TERRA-FORMING DEVICES... THOUSANDS KILLED...
--DANGEROUS TECHNOLOGY--
ZZZZZSHHH
I WILL PROUDLY SERVE AS POSTMASTER GENERAL UNTIL MR. SHARPTON IS CLEARED OF ALL CHARGES.
THE POSTAL SERVICE, THROUGH THE TENACITY OF ITS WORKFORCE, WILL ALWAYS SURPASS THE CAPABILITIES OF TECHNOLOGY...
--SATELLITE DESTROYED--
ZZZZSHHHH
...AND WE'RE HIRING NOW.
JOIN THE INTERGALACTIC POSTAL SERVICE AND BE A PART OF THE REBIRTH OF A GALACTIC INSTITUTION.
WE DON'T HAVE TIME TO SCREW AROUND.
FUCK.

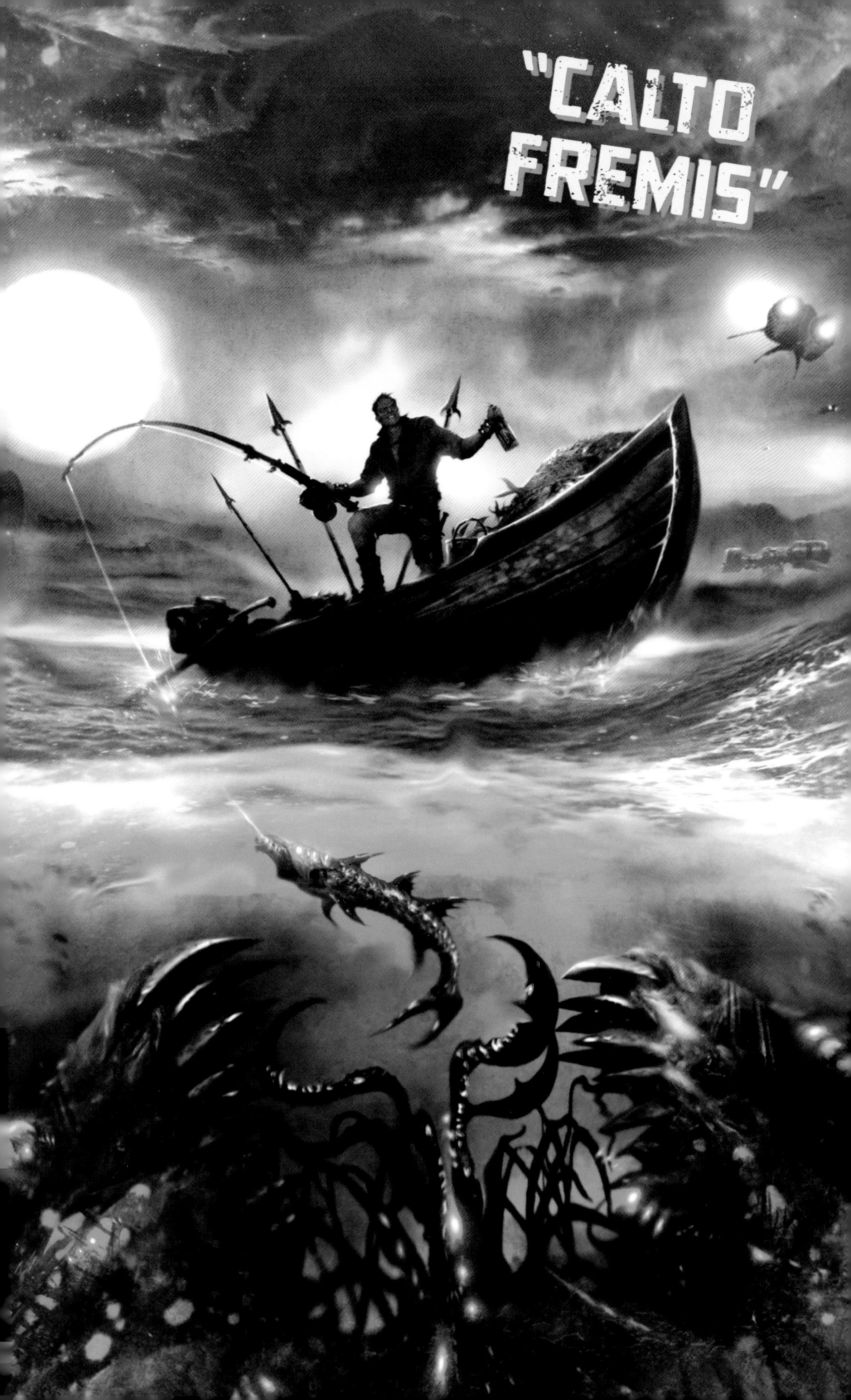
"CALTO FREMIS"

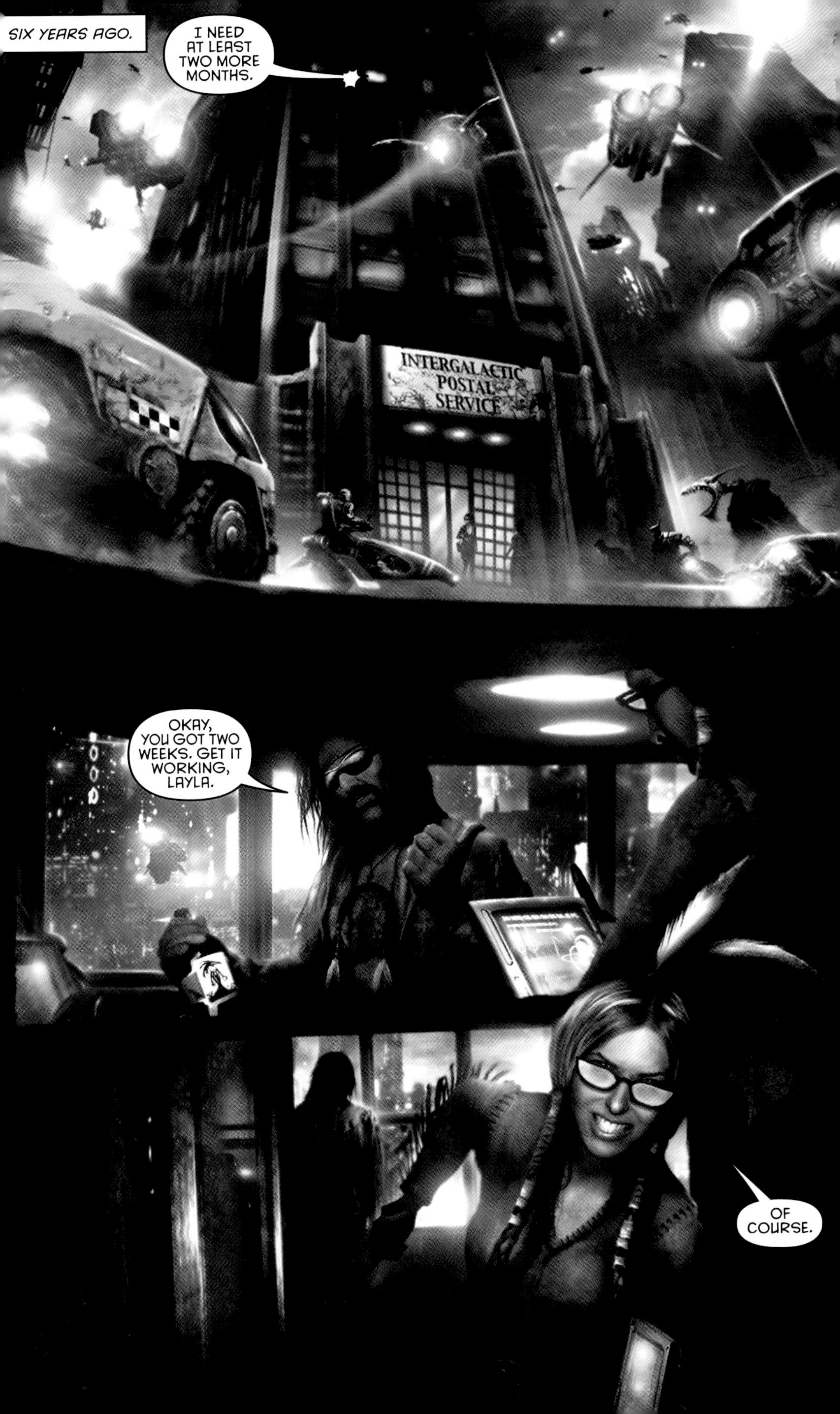
SIX YEARS AGO.
I NEED AT LEAST TWO MORE MONTHS.
INTERGALACTIC POSTAL SERVICE
OKAY, YOU GOT TWO WEEKS. GET IT WORKING, LAYLA.
OF COURSE.

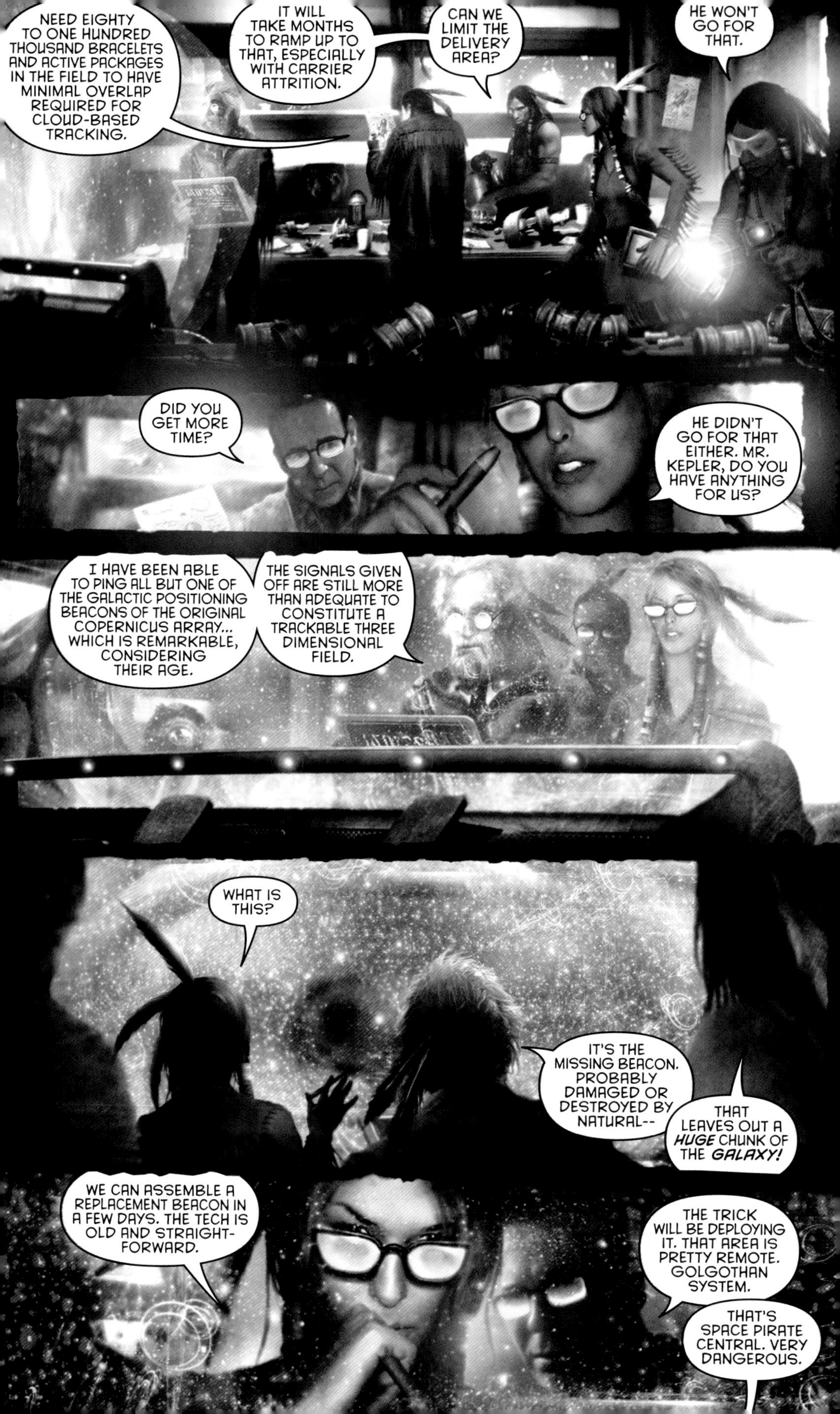
NEED EIGHTY TO ONE HUNDRED THOUSAND BRACELETS AND ACTIVE PACKAGES IN THE FIELD TO HAVE MINIMAL OVERLAP REQUIRED FOR CLOUD-BASED TRACKING.
IT WILL TAKE MONTHS TO RAMP UP TO THAT, ESPECIALLY WITH CARRIER ATTRITION.
CAN WE LIMIT THE DELIVERY AREA?
HE WON'T GO FOR THAT.
DID YOU GET MORE TIME?
HE DIDN'T GO FOR THAT EITHER. MR. KEPLER, DO YOU HAVE ANYTHING FOR US?
I HAVE BEEN ABLE TO PING ALL BUT ONE OF THE GALACTIC POSITIONING BEACONS OF THE ORIGINAL COPERNICUS ARRAY... WHICH IS REMARKABLE, CONSIDERING THEIR AGE.
THE SIGNALS GIVEN OFF ARE STILL MORE THAN ADEQUATE TO CONSTITUTE A TRACKABLE THREE DIMENSIONAL FIELD.
WHAT IS THIS?
IT'S THE MISSING BEACON. PROBABLY DAMAGED OR DESTROYED BY NATURAL--
THAT LEAVES OUT A *HUGE* CHUNK OF THE *GALAXY!*
WE CAN ASSEMBLE A REPLACEMENT BEACON IN A FEW DAYS. THE TECH IS OLD AND STRAIGHT-FORWARD.
THE TRICK WILL BE DEPLOYING IT. THAT AREA IS PRETTY REMOTE. GOLGOTHAN SYSTEM.
THAT'S SPACE PIRATE CENTRAL. VERY DANGEROUS.

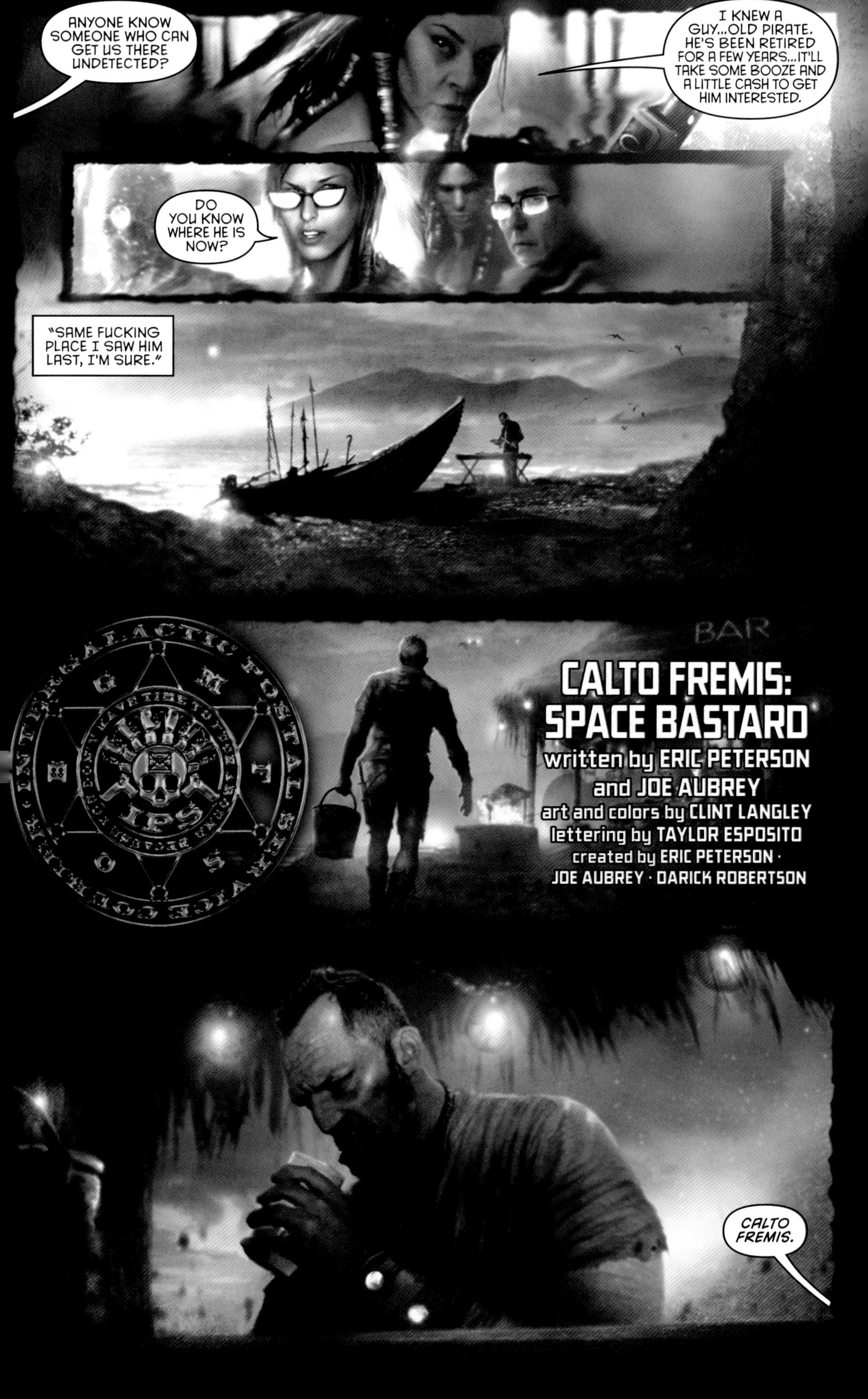
ANYONE KNOW SOMEONE WHO CAN GET US THERE UNDETECTED?
I KNEW A GUY...OLD PIRATE. HE'S BEEN RETIRED FOR A FEW YEARS...IT'LL TAKE SOME BOOZE AND A LITTLE CASH TO GET HIM INTERESTED.
DO YOU KNOW WHERE HE IS NOW?
"SAME FUCKING PLACE I SAW HIM LAST, I'M SURE."
BAR
INTERGALACTIC POSTAL SERVICE COURIER
IPS
CALTO FREMIS: SPACE BASTARD
written by ERIC PETERSON and JOE AUBREY
art and colors by CLINT LANGLEY
lettering by TAYLOR ESPOSITO
created by ERIC PETERSON · JOE AUBREY · DARICK ROBERTSON
CALTO FREMIS.

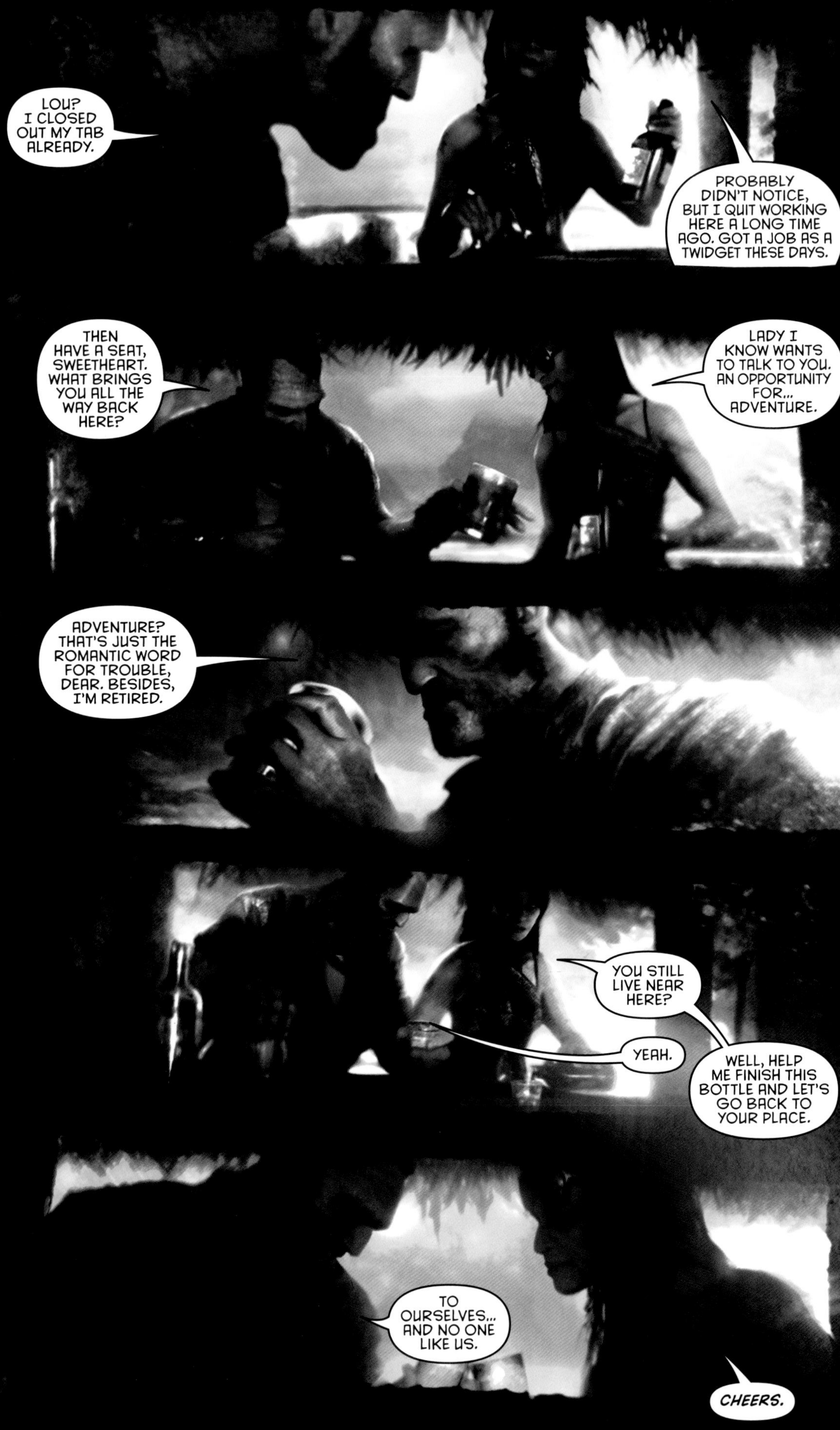

LOU? I CLOSED OUT MY TAB ALREADY.
PROBABLY DIDN'T NOTICE, BUT I QUIT WORKING HERE A LONG TIME AGO. GOT A JOB AS A TWIDGET THESE DAYS.
THEN HAVE A SEAT, SWEETHEART. WHAT BRINGS YOU ALL THE WAY BACK HERE?
LADY I KNOW WANTS TO TALK TO YOU. AN OPPORTUNITY FOR... ADVENTURE.
ADVENTURE? THAT'S JUST THE ROMANTIC WORD FOR TROUBLE, DEAR. BESIDES, I'M RETIRED.
YOU STILL LIVE NEAR HERE?
YEAH.
WELL, HELP ME FINISH THIS BOTTLE AND LET'S GO BACK TO YOUR PLACE.
TO OURSELVES... AND NO ONE LIKE US.
CHEERS.

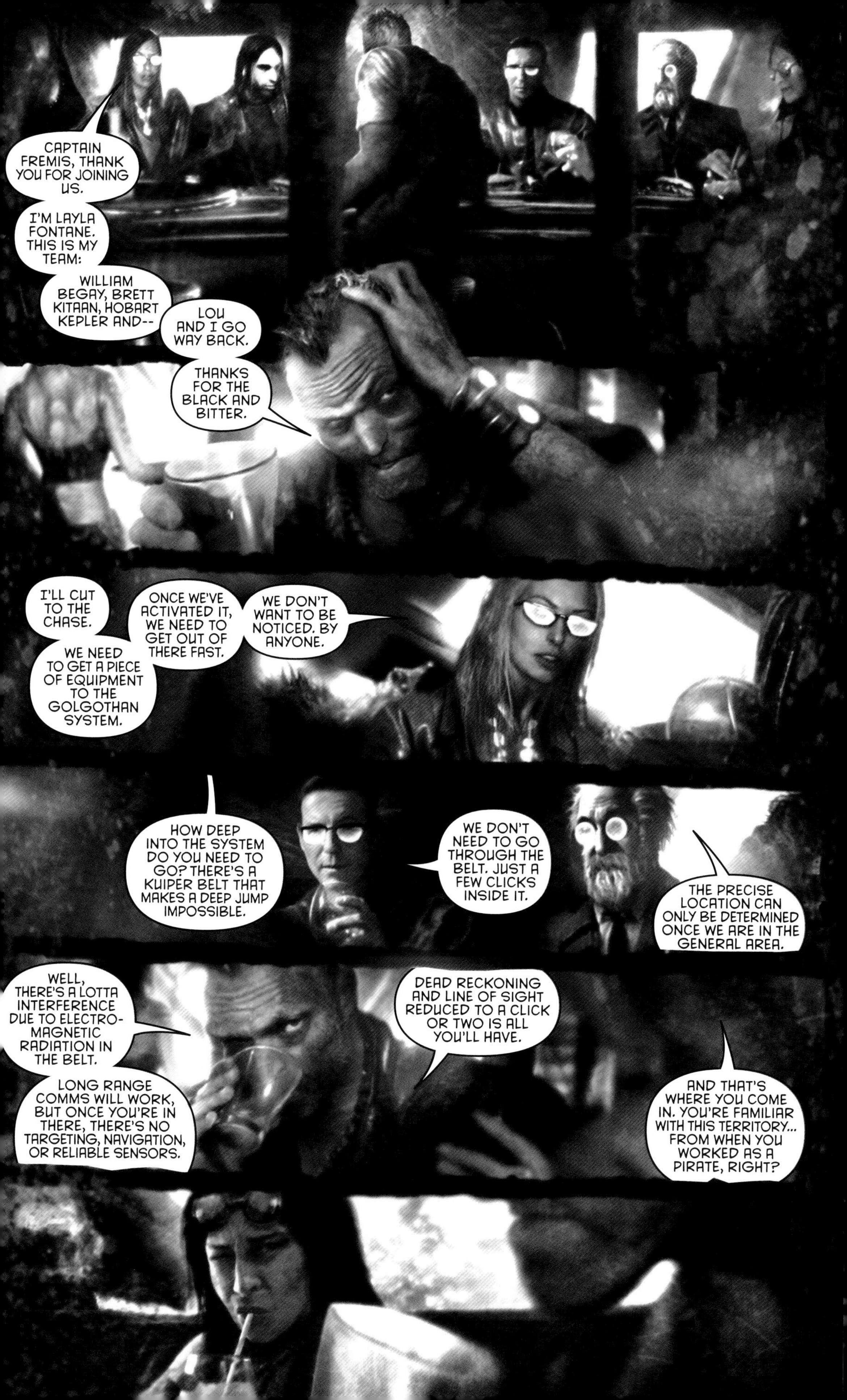
CAPTAIN FREMIS, THANK YOU FOR JOINING US.
I'M LAYLA FONTANE. THIS IS MY TEAM:
WILLIAM BEGAY, BRETT KITAAN, HOBART KEPLER AND--
LOU AND I GO WAY BACK.
THANKS FOR THE BLACK AND BITTER.
I'LL CUT TO THE CHASE.
WE NEED TO GET A PIECE OF EQUIPMENT TO THE GOLGOTHAN SYSTEM.
ONCE WE'VE ACTIVATED IT, WE NEED TO GET OUT OF THERE FAST.
WE DON'T WANT TO BE NOTICED. BY ANYONE.
HOW DEEP INTO THE SYSTEM DO YOU NEED TO GO? THERE'S A KUIPER BELT THAT MAKES A DEEP JUMP IMPOSSIBLE.
WE DON'T NEED TO GO THROUGH THE BELT. JUST A FEW CLICKS INSIDE IT.
THE PRECISE LOCATION CAN ONLY BE DETERMINED ONCE WE ARE IN THE GENERAL AREA.
WELL, THERE'S A LOTTA INTERFERENCE DUE TO ELECTRO-MAGNETIC RADIATION IN THE BELT.
LONG RANGE COMMS WILL WORK, BUT ONCE YOU'RE IN THERE, THERE'S NO TARGETING, NAVIGATION, OR RELIABLE SENSORS.
DEAD RECKONING AND LINE OF SIGHT REDUCED TO A CLICK OR TWO IS ALL YOU'LL HAVE.
AND THAT'S WHERE YOU COME IN. YOU'RE FAMILIAR WITH THIS TERRITORY... FROM WHEN YOU WORKED AS A PIRATE, RIGHT?

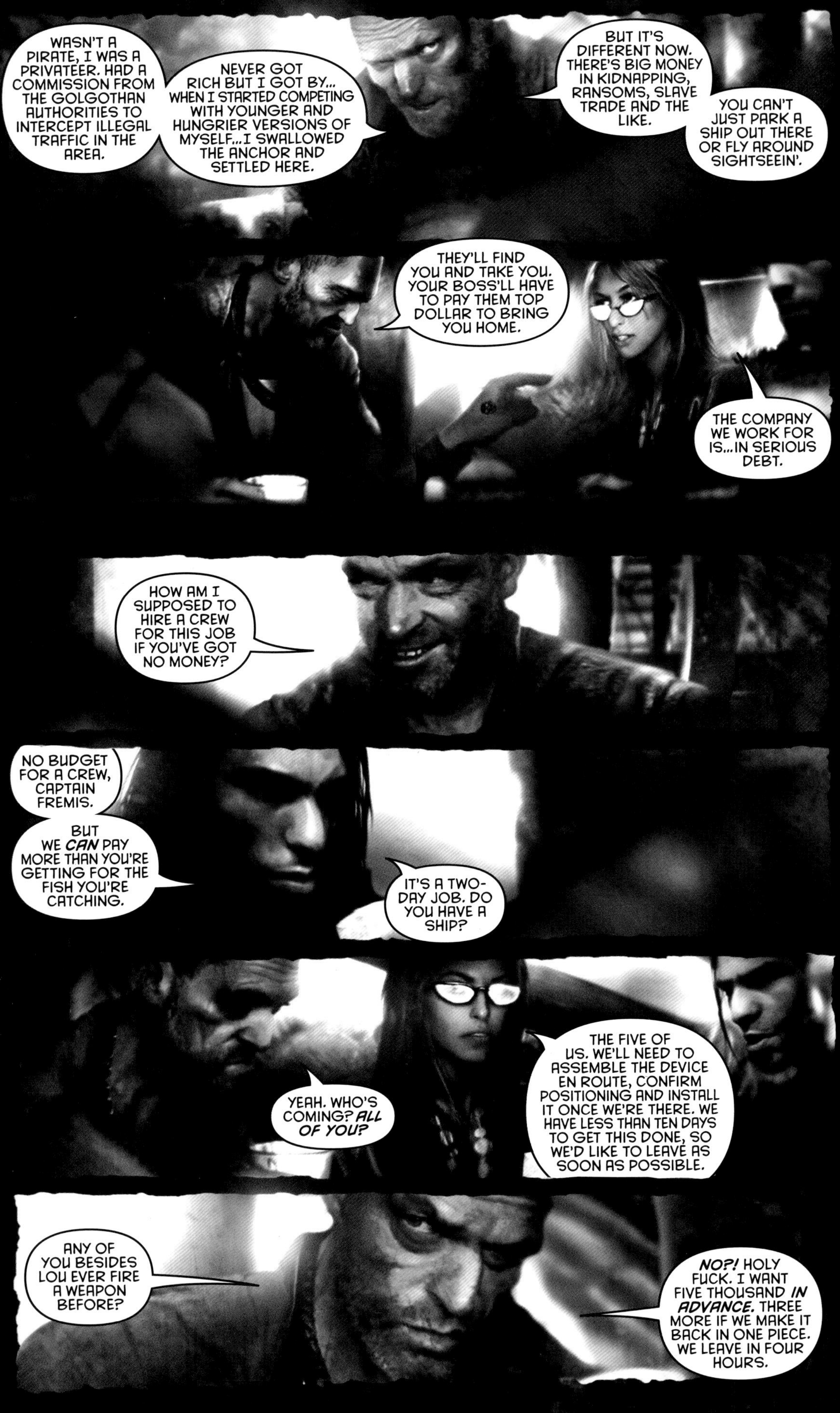

WASN'T A PIRATE, I WAS A PRIVATEER. HAD A COMMISSION FROM THE GOLGOTHAN AUTHORITIES TO INTERCEPT ILLEGAL TRAFFIC IN THE AREA.
NEVER GOT RICH BUT I GOT BY... WHEN I STARTED COMPETING WITH YOUNGER AND HUNGRIER VERSIONS OF MYSELF...I SWALLOWED THE ANCHOR AND SETTLED HERE.
BUT IT'S DIFFERENT NOW. THERE'S BIG MONEY IN KIDNAPPING, RANSOMS, SLAVE TRADE AND THE LIKE.
YOU CAN'T JUST PARK A SHIP OUT THERE OR FLY AROUND SIGHTSEEIN'.
THEY'LL FIND YOU AND TAKE YOU. YOUR BOSS'LL HAVE TO PAY THEM TOP DOLLAR TO BRING YOU HOME.
THE COMPANY WE WORK FOR IS...IN SERIOUS DEBT.
HOW AM I SUPPOSED TO HIRE A CREW FOR THIS JOB IF YOU'VE GOT NO MONEY?
NO BUDGET FOR A CREW, CAPTAIN FREMIS.
BUT WE *CAN* PAY MORE THAN YOU'RE GETTING FOR THE FISH YOU'RE CATCHING.
IT'S A TWO-DAY JOB. DO YOU HAVE A SHIP?
YEAH. WHO'S COMING? *ALL OF YOU?*
THE FIVE OF US. WE'LL NEED TO ASSEMBLE THE DEVICE EN ROUTE, CONFIRM POSITIONING AND INSTALL IT ONCE WE'RE THERE. WE HAVE LESS THAN TEN DAYS TO GET THIS DONE, SO WE'D LIKE TO LEAVE AS SOON AS POSSIBLE.
ANY OF YOU BESIDES LOU EVER FIRE A WEAPON BEFORE?
NO?! HOLY FUCK. I WANT FIVE THOUSAND *IN ADVANCE.* THREE MORE IF WE MAKE IT BACK IN ONE PIECE. WE LEAVE IN FOUR HOURS.

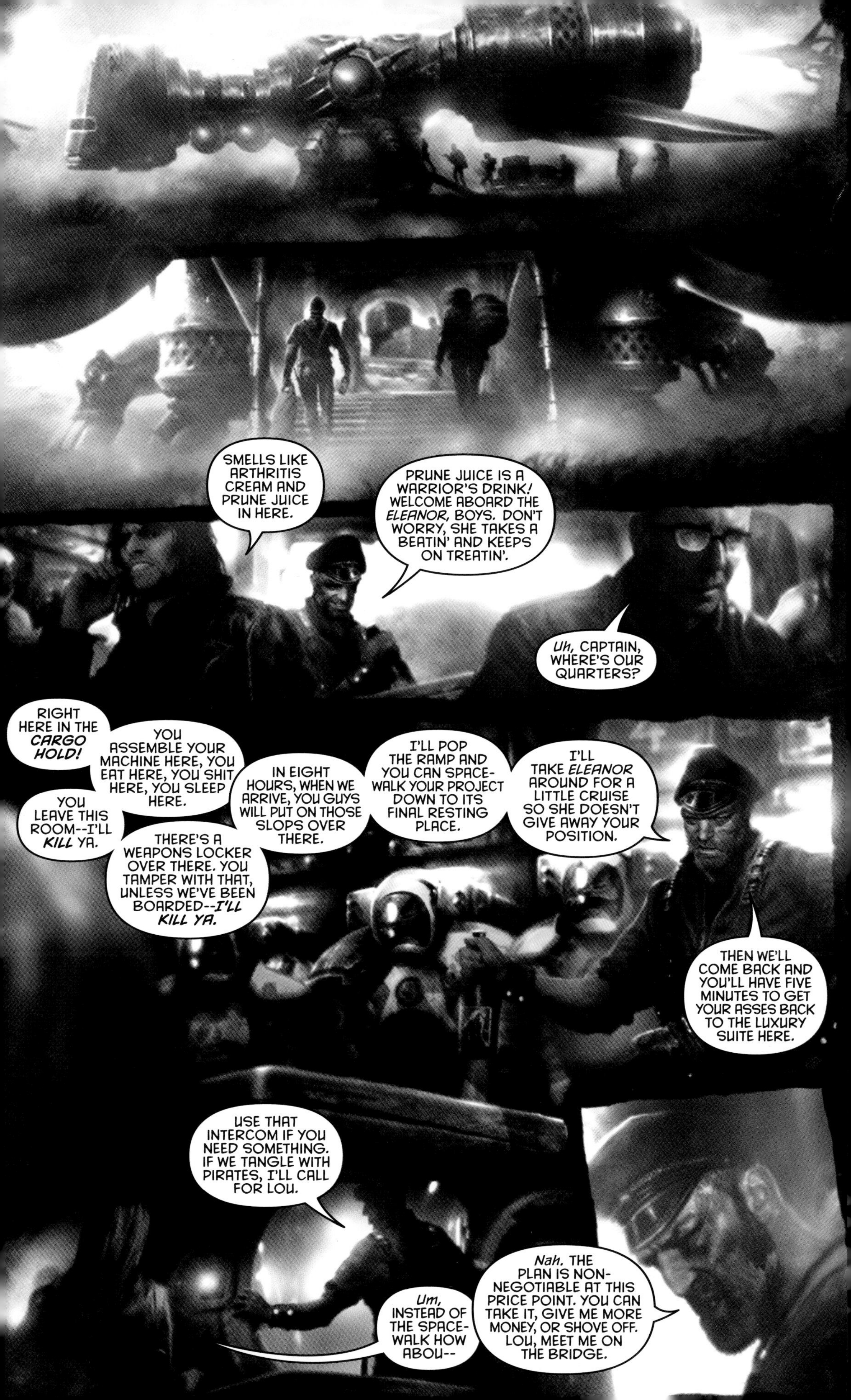
SMELLS LIKE ARTHRITIS CREAM AND PRUNE JUICE IN HERE.
PRUNE JUICE IS A WARRIOR'S DRINK! WELCOME ABOARD THE *ELEANOR*, BOYS. DON'T WORRY, SHE TAKES A BEATIN' AND KEEPS ON TREATIN'.
UH, CAPTAIN, WHERE'S OUR QUARTERS?
RIGHT HERE IN THE ***CARGO HOLD!***
YOU ASSEMBLE YOUR MACHINE HERE, YOU EAT HERE, YOU SHIT HERE, YOU SLEEP HERE.
YOU LEAVE THIS ROOM--I'LL ***KILL*** YA.
THERE'S A WEAPONS LOCKER OVER THERE. YOU TAMPER WITH THAT, UNLESS WE'VE BEEN BOARDED--***I'LL KILL YA.***
IN EIGHT HOURS, WHEN WE ARRIVE, YOU GUYS WILL PUT ON THOSE SLOPS OVER THERE.
I'LL POP THE RAMP AND YOU CAN SPACE-WALK YOUR PROJECT DOWN TO ITS FINAL RESTING PLACE.
I'LL TAKE *ELEANOR* AROUND FOR A LITTLE CRUISE SO SHE DOESN'T GIVE AWAY YOUR POSITION.
THEN WE'LL COME BACK AND YOU'LL HAVE FIVE MINUTES TO GET YOUR ASSES BACK TO THE LUXURY SUITE HERE.
USE THAT INTERCOM IF YOU NEED SOMETHING. IF WE TANGLE WITH PIRATES, I'LL CALL FOR LOU.
UM, INSTEAD OF THE SPACE-WALK HOW ABOU--
NAH. THE PLAN IS NON-NEGOTIABLE AT THIS PRICE POINT. YOU CAN TAKE IT, GIVE ME MORE MONEY, OR SHOVE OFF. LOU, MEET ME ON THE BRIDGE.

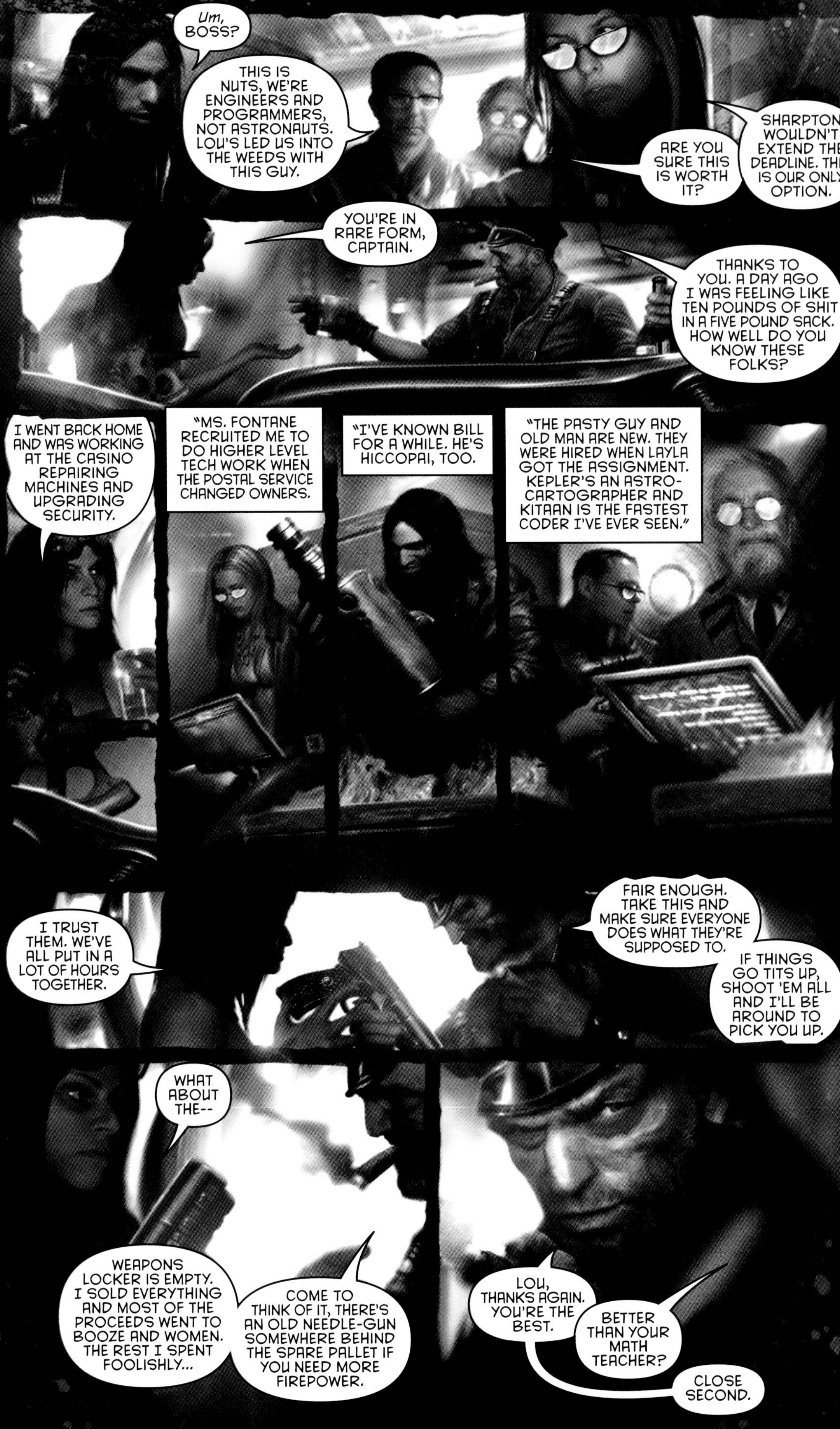
UM, BOSS?
THIS IS NUTS, WE'RE ENGINEERS AND PROGRAMMERS, NOT ASTRONAUTS. LOU'S LED US INTO THE WEEDS WITH THIS GUY.
ARE YOU SURE THIS IS WORTH IT?
SHARPTON WOULDN'T EXTEND THE DEADLINE. THIS IS OUR ONLY OPTION.
YOU'RE IN RARE FORM, CAPTAIN.
THANKS TO YOU. A DAY AGO I WAS FEELING LIKE TEN POUNDS OF SHIT IN A FIVE POUND SACK. HOW WELL DO YOU KNOW THESE FOLKS?
I WENT BACK HOME AND WAS WORKING AT THE CASINO REPAIRING MACHINES AND UPGRADING SECURITY.
"MS. FONTANE RECRUITED ME TO DO HIGHER LEVEL TECH WORK WHEN THE POSTAL SERVICE CHANGED OWNERS.
"I'VE KNOWN BILL FOR A WHILE. HE'S HICCOPAI, TOO.
"THE PASTY GUY AND OLD MAN ARE NEW. THEY WERE HIRED WHEN LAYLA GOT THE ASSIGNMENT. KEPLER'S AN ASTRO-CARTOGRAPHER AND KITAAN IS THE FASTEST CODER I'VE EVER SEEN."
I TRUST THEM. WE'VE ALL PUT IN A LOT OF HOURS TOGETHER.
FAIR ENOUGH. TAKE THIS AND MAKE SURE EVERYONE DOES WHAT THEY'RE SUPPOSED TO.
IF THINGS GO TITS UP, SHOOT 'EM ALL AND I'LL BE AROUND TO PICK YOU UP.
WHAT ABOUT THE--
WEAPONS LOCKER IS EMPTY. I SOLD EVERYTHING AND MOST OF THE PROCEEDS WENT TO BOOZE AND WOMEN. THE REST I SPENT FOOLISHLY...
COME TO THINK OF IT, THERE'S AN OLD NEEDLE-GUN SOMEWHERE BEHIND THE SPARE PALLET IF YOU NEED MORE FIREPOWER.
LOU, THANKS AGAIN. YOU'RE THE BEST.
BETTER THAN YOUR MATH TEACHER?
CLOSE SECOND.

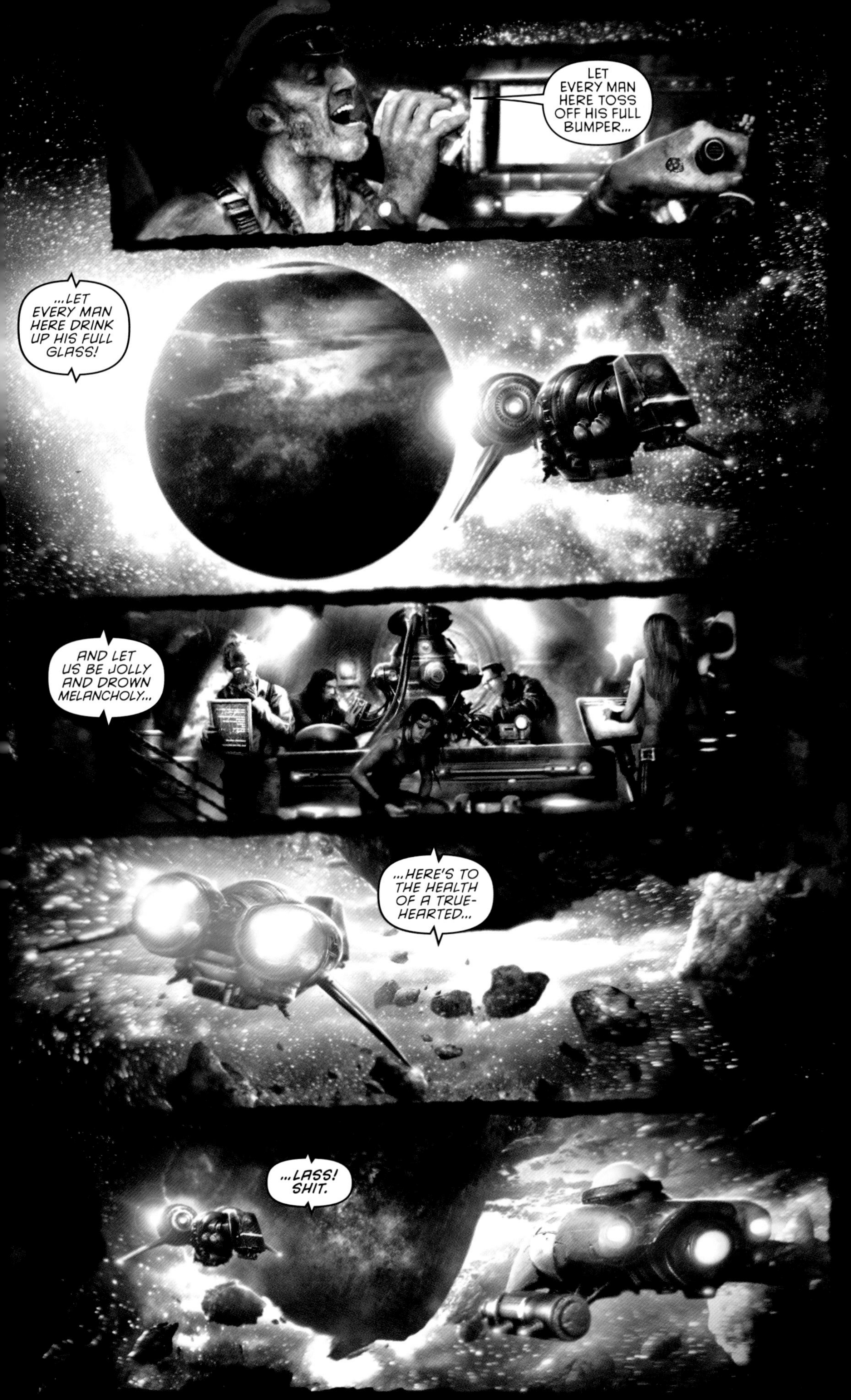
LET EVERY MAN HERE TOSS OFF HIS FULL BUMPER...
...LET EVERY MAN HERE DRINK UP HIS FULL GLASS!
AND LET US BE JOLLY AND DROWN MELANCHOLY...
...HERE'S TO THE HEALTH OF A TRUE-HEARTED...
...LASS! SHIT.

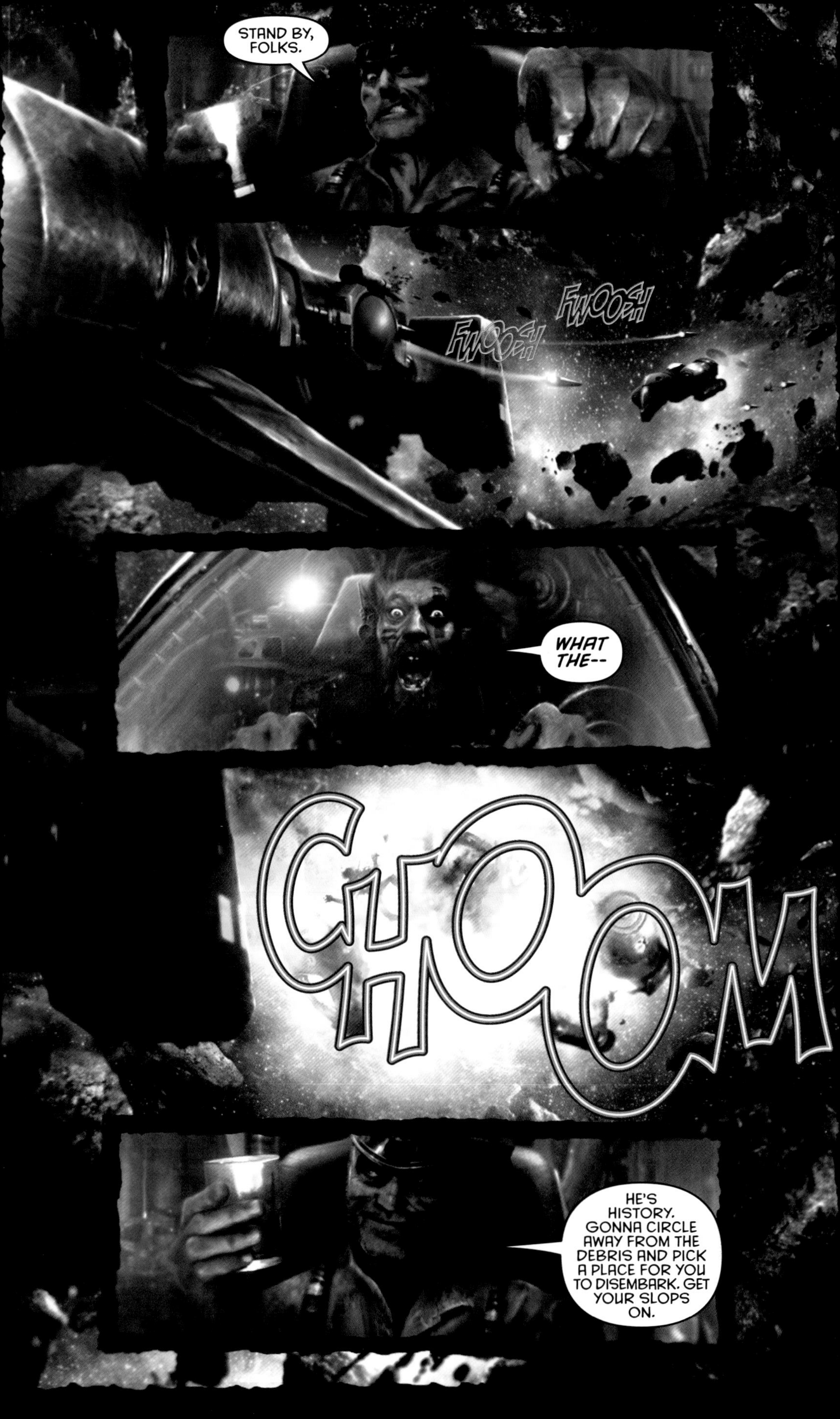
STAND BY, FOLKS.
FWOOSH
FWOOSH
WHAT THE--
CHOOOM
HE'S HISTORY. GONNA CIRCLE AWAY FROM THE DEBRIS AND PICK A PLACE FOR YOU TO DISEMBARK. GET YOUR SLOPS ON.

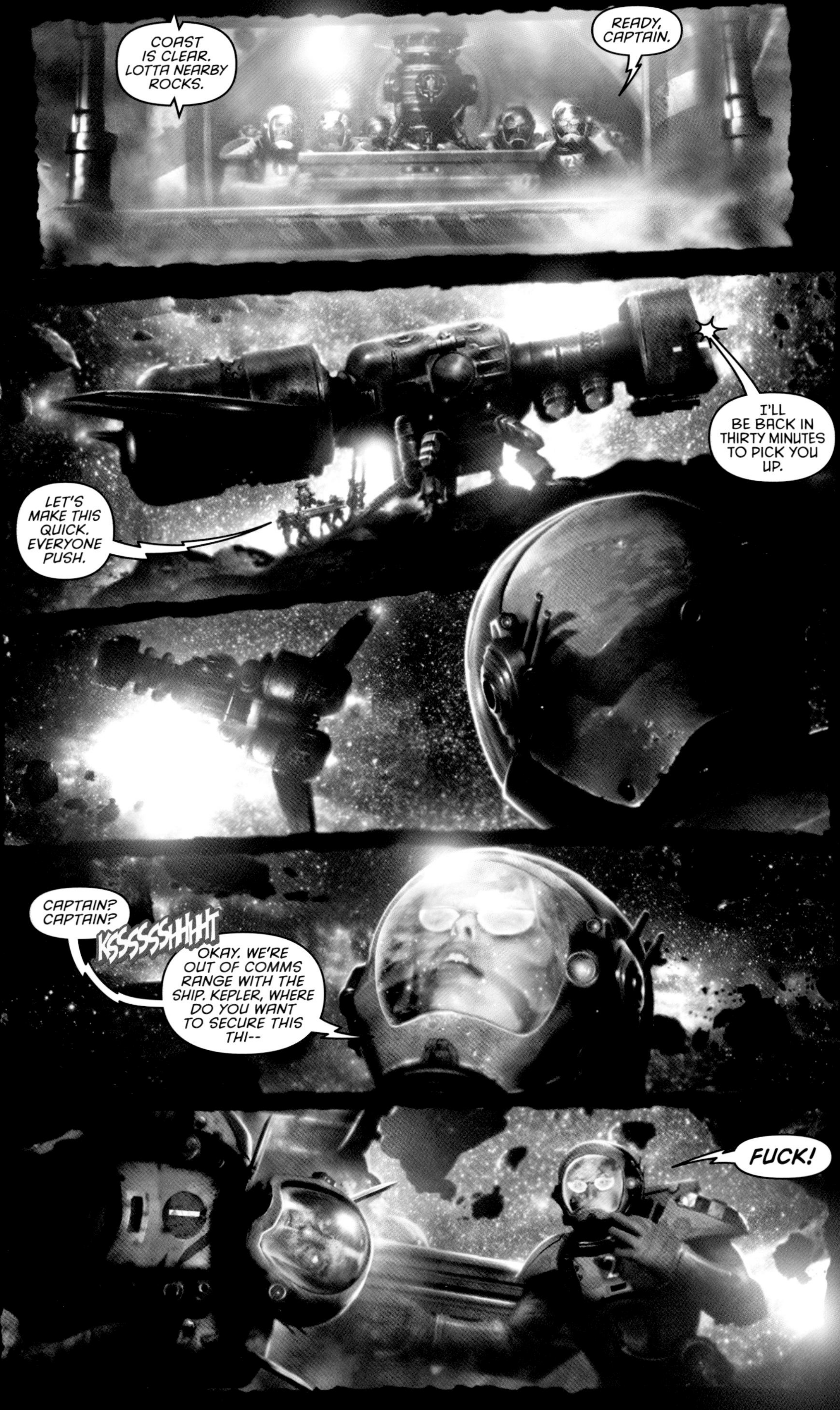

COAST IS CLEAR. LOTTA NEARBY ROCKS.
READY, CAPTAIN.
I'LL BE BACK IN THIRTY MINUTES TO PICK YOU UP.
LET'S MAKE THIS QUICK. EVERYONE PUSH.
CAPTAIN? CAPTAIN?
KSSSSSSHHHHT
OKAY. WE'RE OUT OF COMMS RANGE WITH THE SHIP. KEPLER, WHERE DO YOU WANT TO SECURE THIS THI--
FUCK!

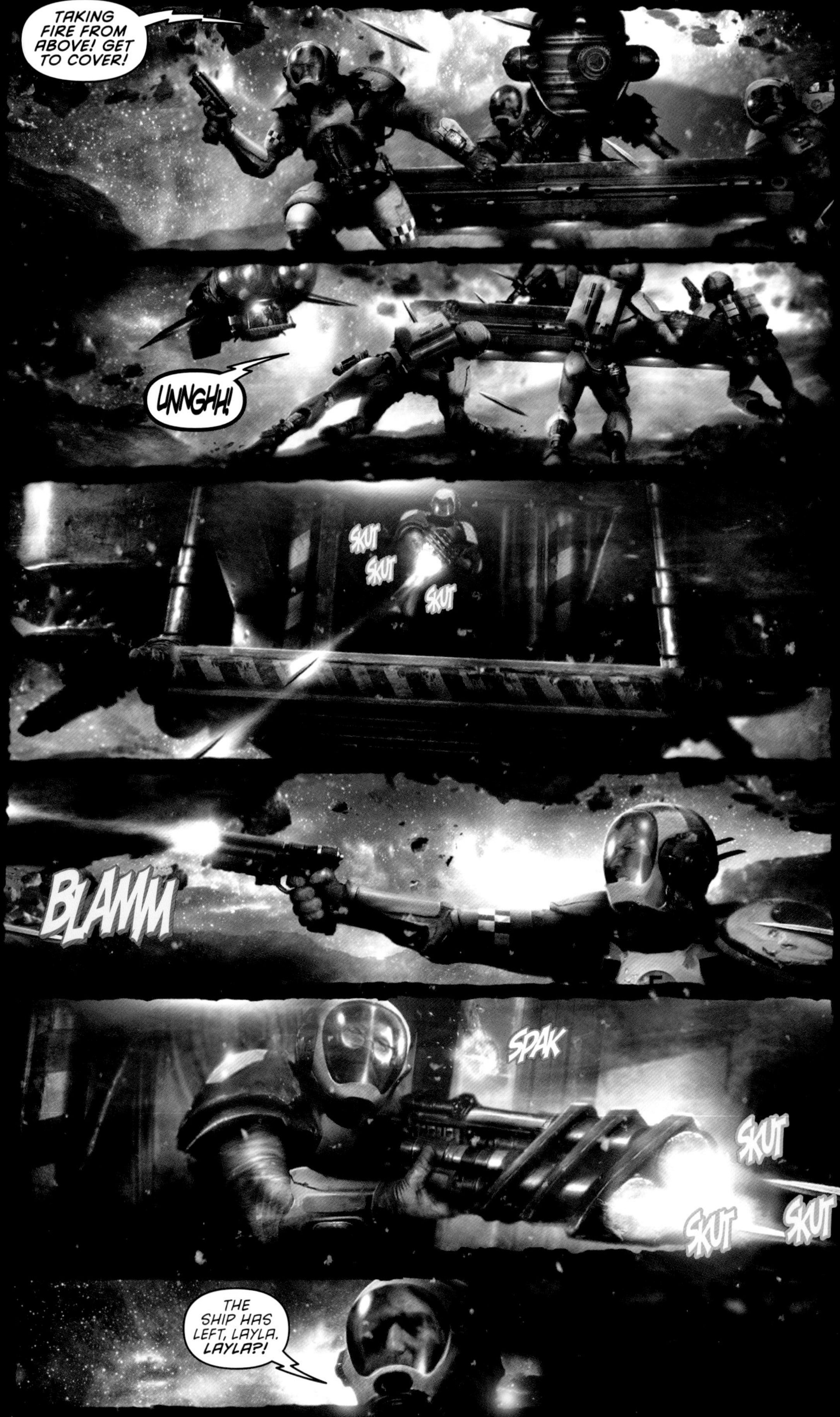
TAKING FIRE FROM ABOVE! GET TO COVER!
UNNGHH!
SKUT
SKUT
SKUT
BLAMM
SPAK
SKUT
SKUT
SKUT
THE SHIP HAS LEFT, LAYLA. LAYLA?!

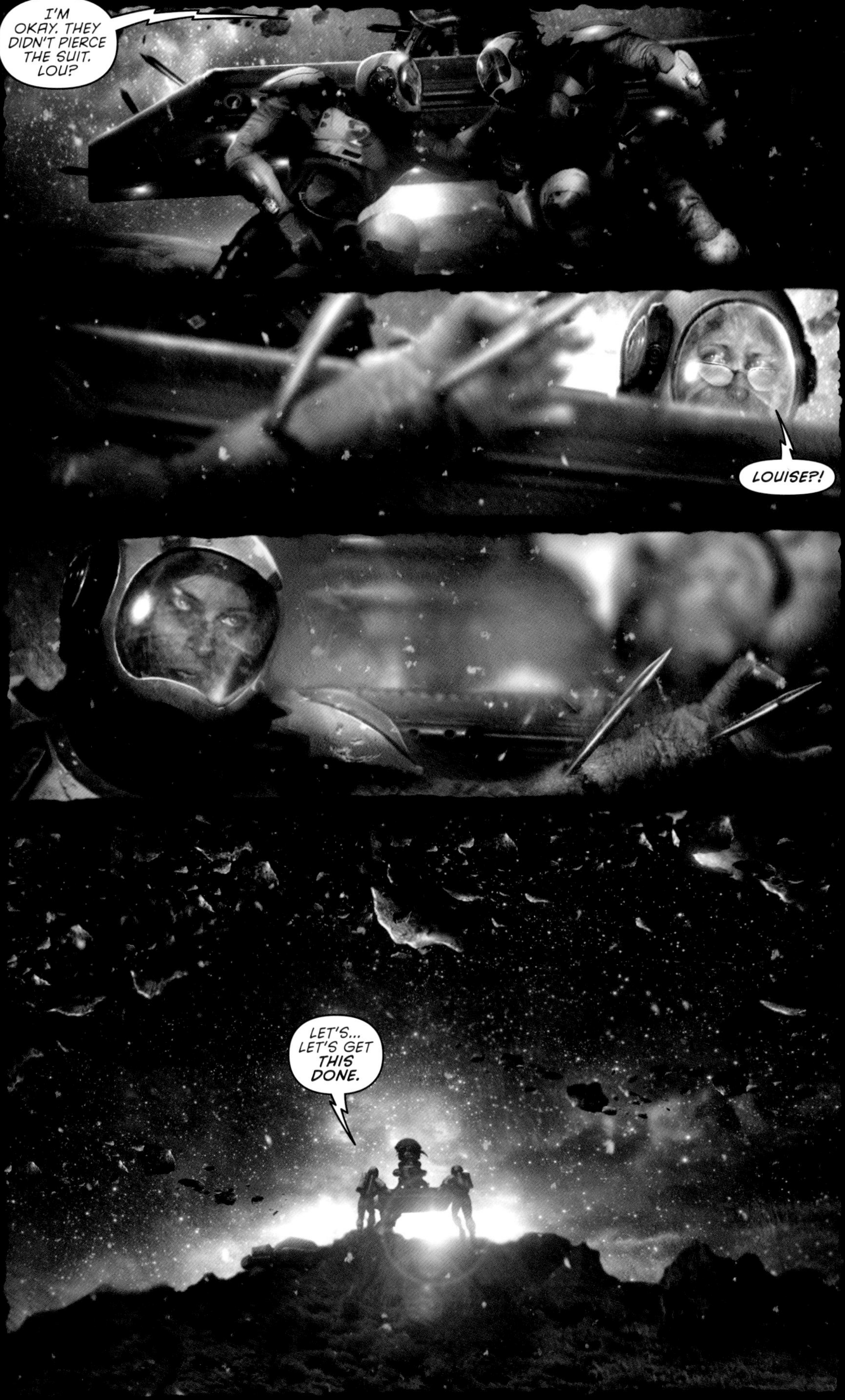
I'M OKAY. THEY DIDN'T PIERCE THE SUIT. LOU?
LOUISE?!
LET'S... LET'S GET THIS DONE.

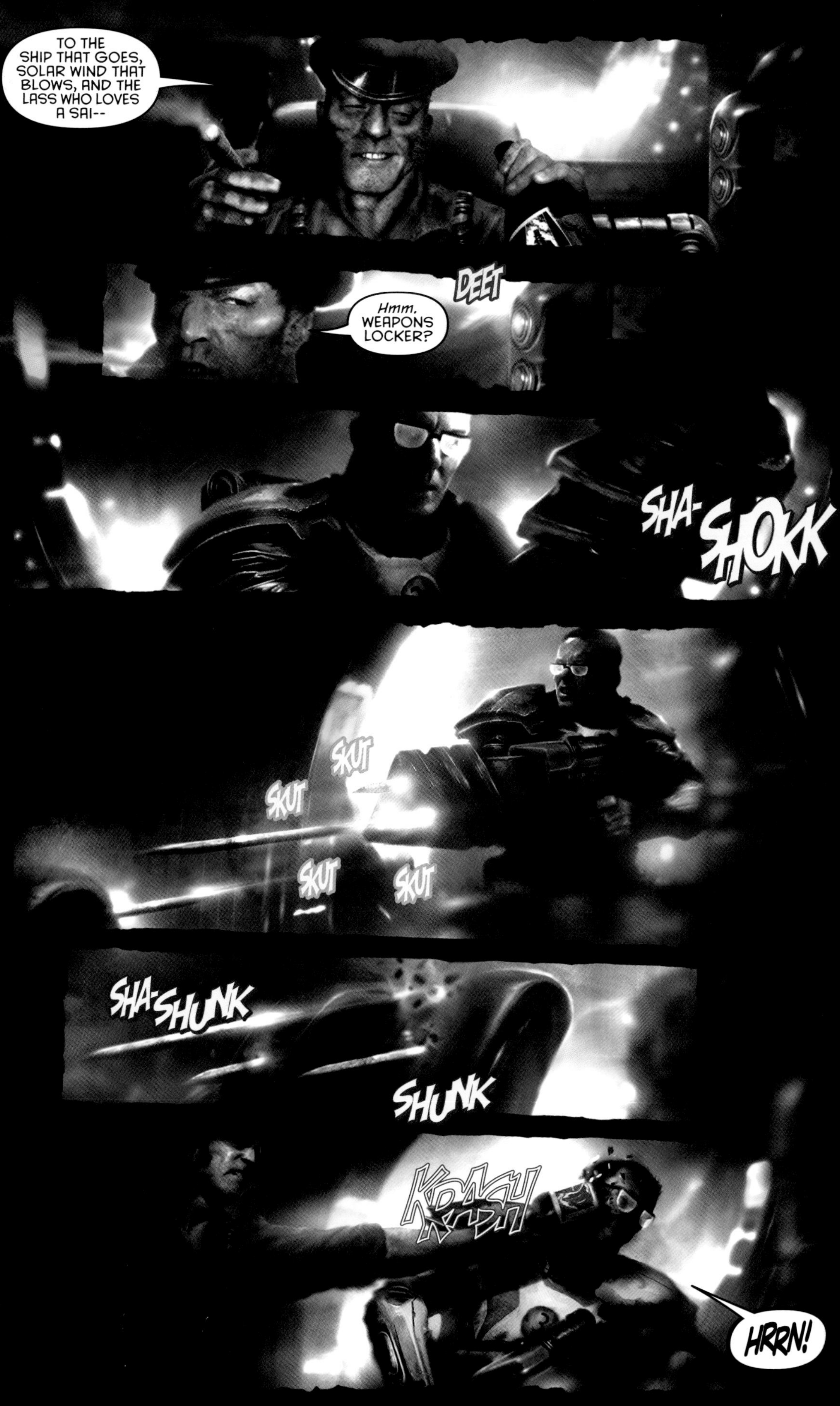
TO THE SHIP THAT GOES, SOLAR WIND THAT BLOWS, AND THE LASS WHO LOVES A SAI--
DEET
Hmm. WEAPONS LOCKER?
SHA-SHOKK
SKUT
SKUT
SKUT
SKUT
SHA-SHUNK
SHUNK
KRASH
HRRN!

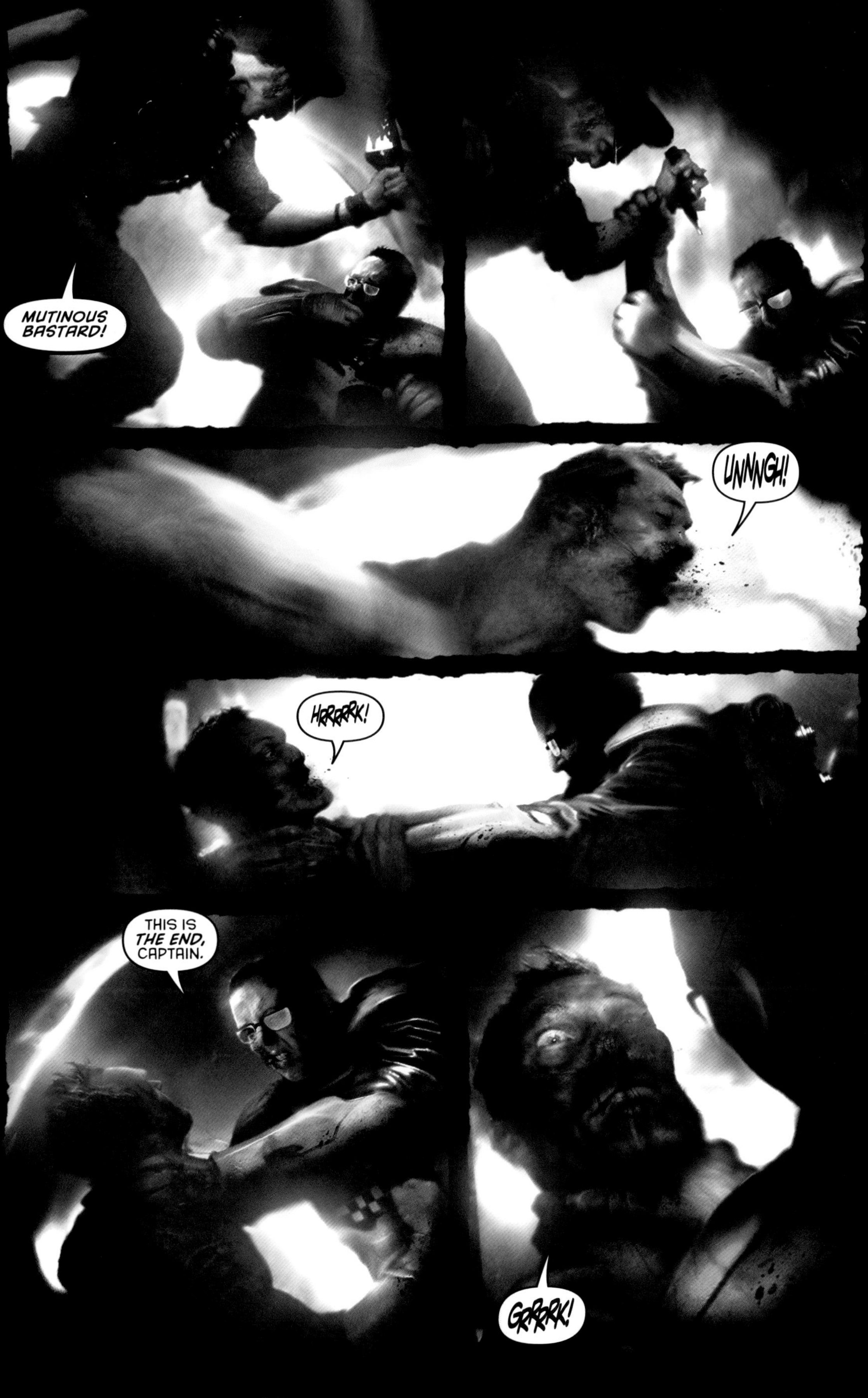
MUTINOUS BASTARD!
UNNNGH!
HRRRRRK!
THIS IS THE END, CAPTAIN.
GRRRRK!

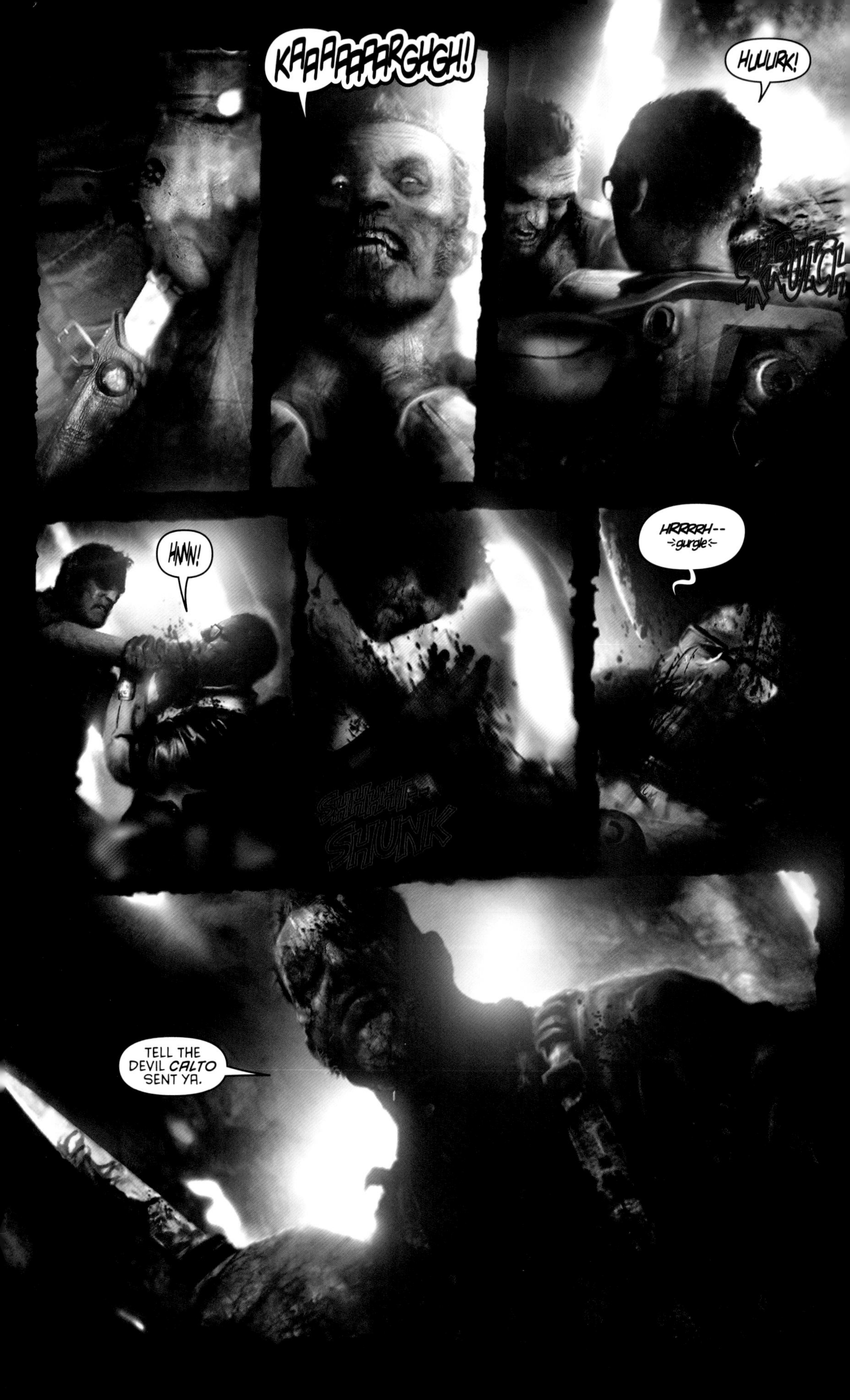
KAAAAAAARGHGH!
HUUURK!
HNN!
SHUNK
HRRRRH--
gurgle
TELL THE DEVIL CALTO SENT YA.

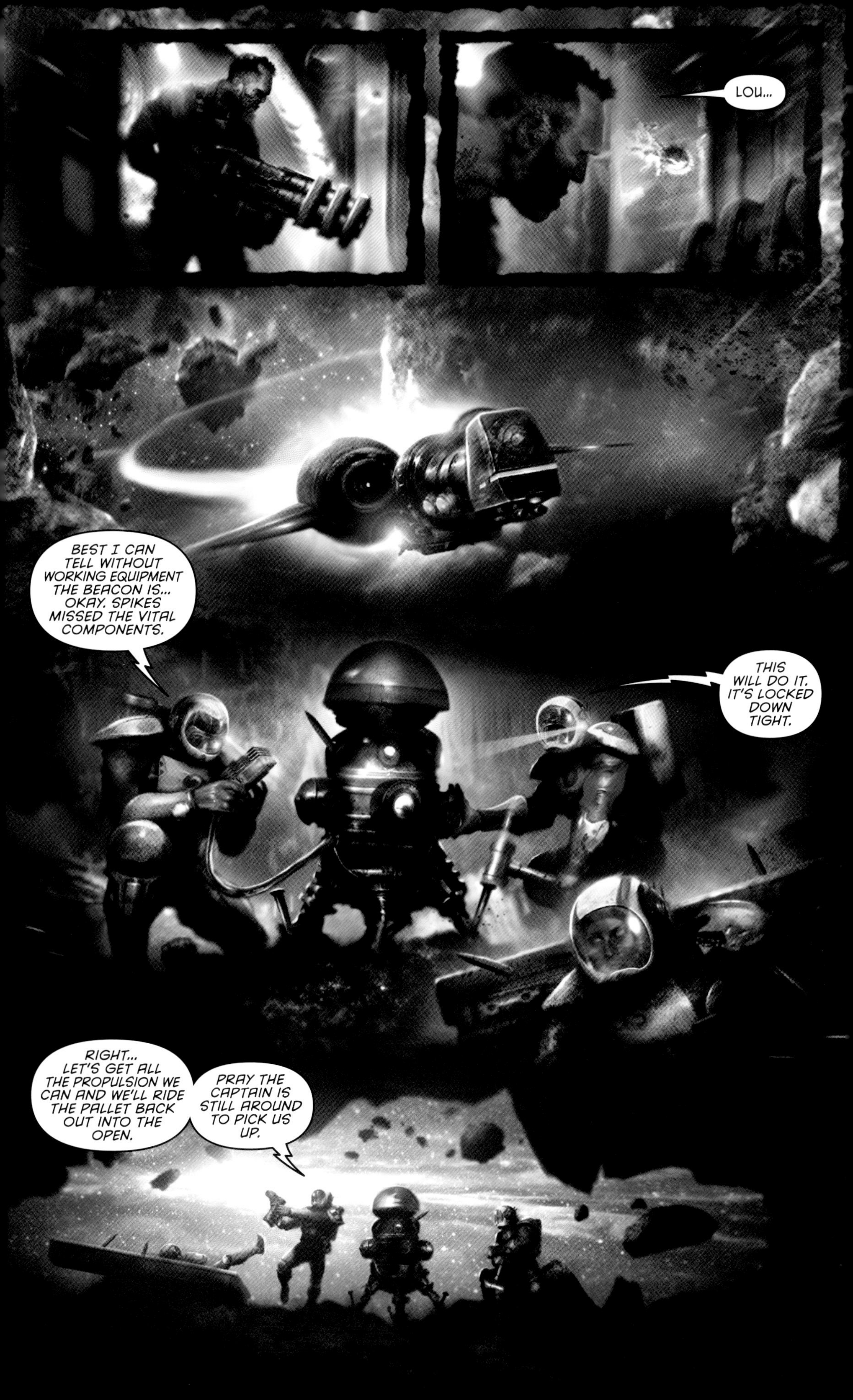
LOU...
BEST I CAN TELL WITHOUT WORKING EQUIPMENT THE BEACON IS... OKAY. SPIKES MISSED THE VITAL COMPONENTS.
THIS WILL DO IT. IT'S LOCKED DOWN TIGHT.
RIGHT... LET'S GET ALL THE PROPULSION WE CAN AND WE'LL RIDE THE PALLET BACK OUT INTO THE OPEN.
PRAY THE CAPTAIN IS STILL AROUND TO PICK US UP.

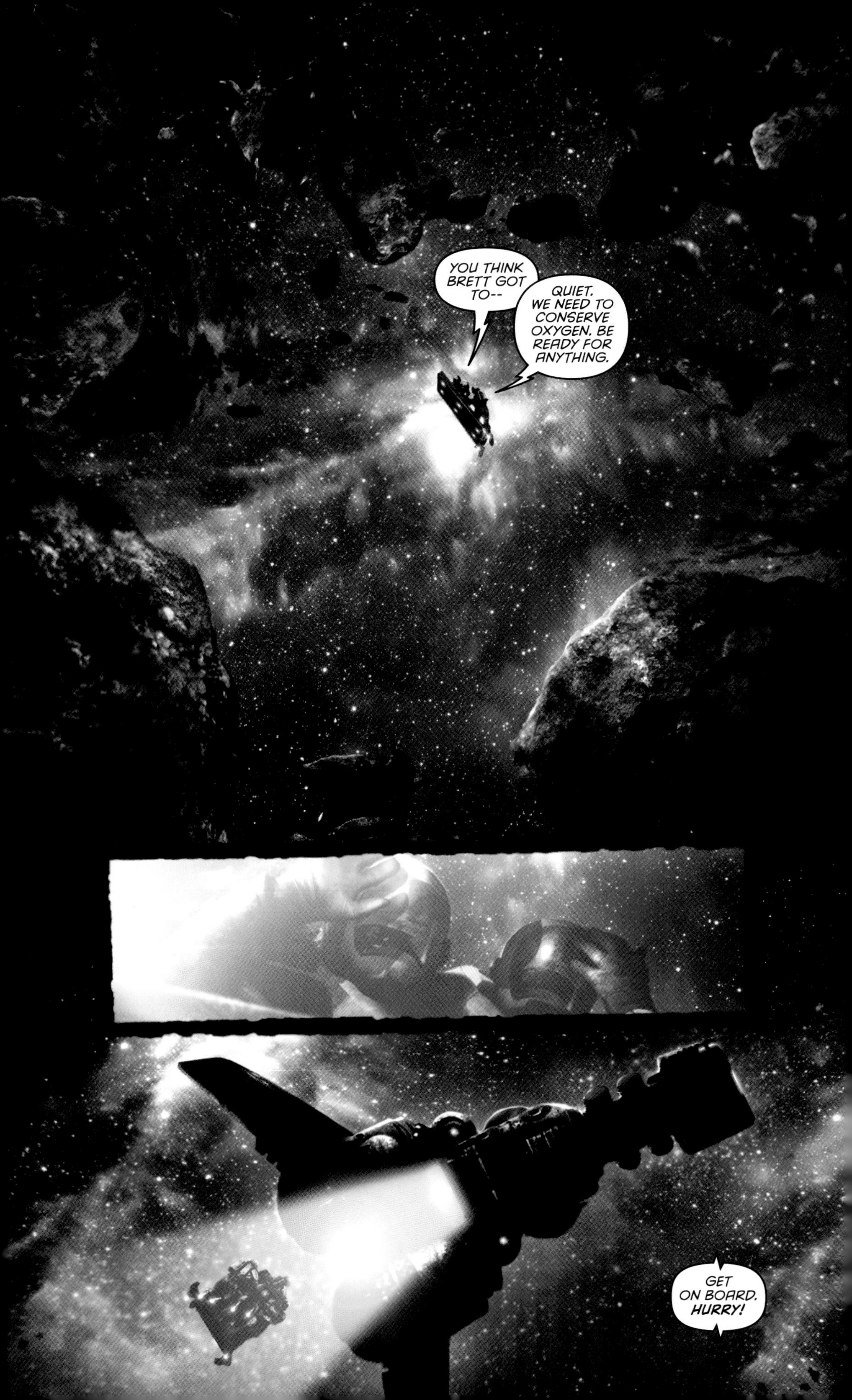
YOU THINK BRETT GOT TO--
QUIET. WE NEED TO CONSERVE OXYGEN. BE READY FOR ANYTHING.
GET ON BOARD. HURRY!

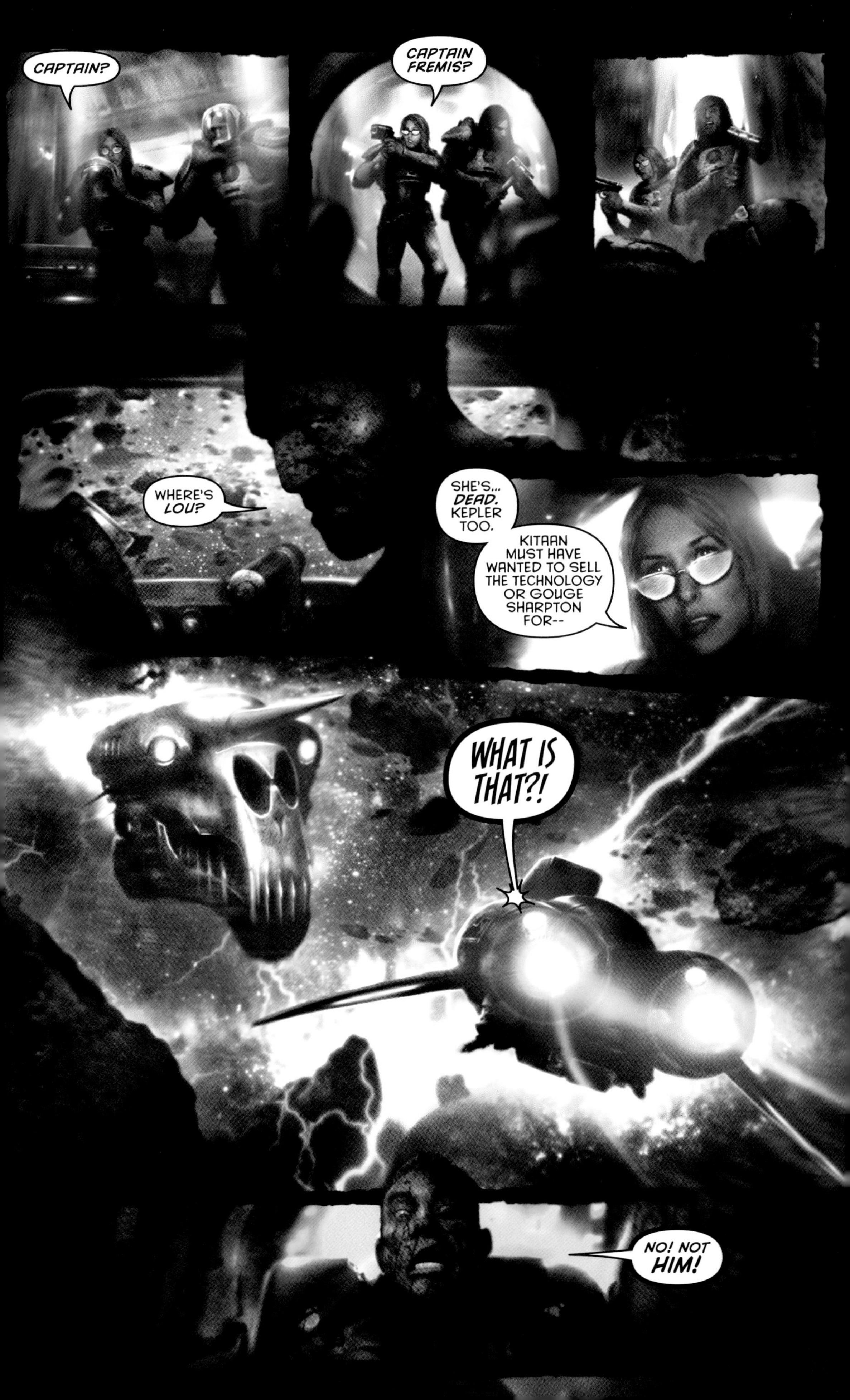
CAPTAIN?
CAPTAIN FREMIS?
WHERE'S LOU?
SHE'S... DEAD. KEPLER TOO.
KITAAN MUST HAVE WANTED TO SELL THE TECHNOLOGY OR GOUGE SHARPTON FOR--
WHAT IS THAT?!
NO! NOT HIM!

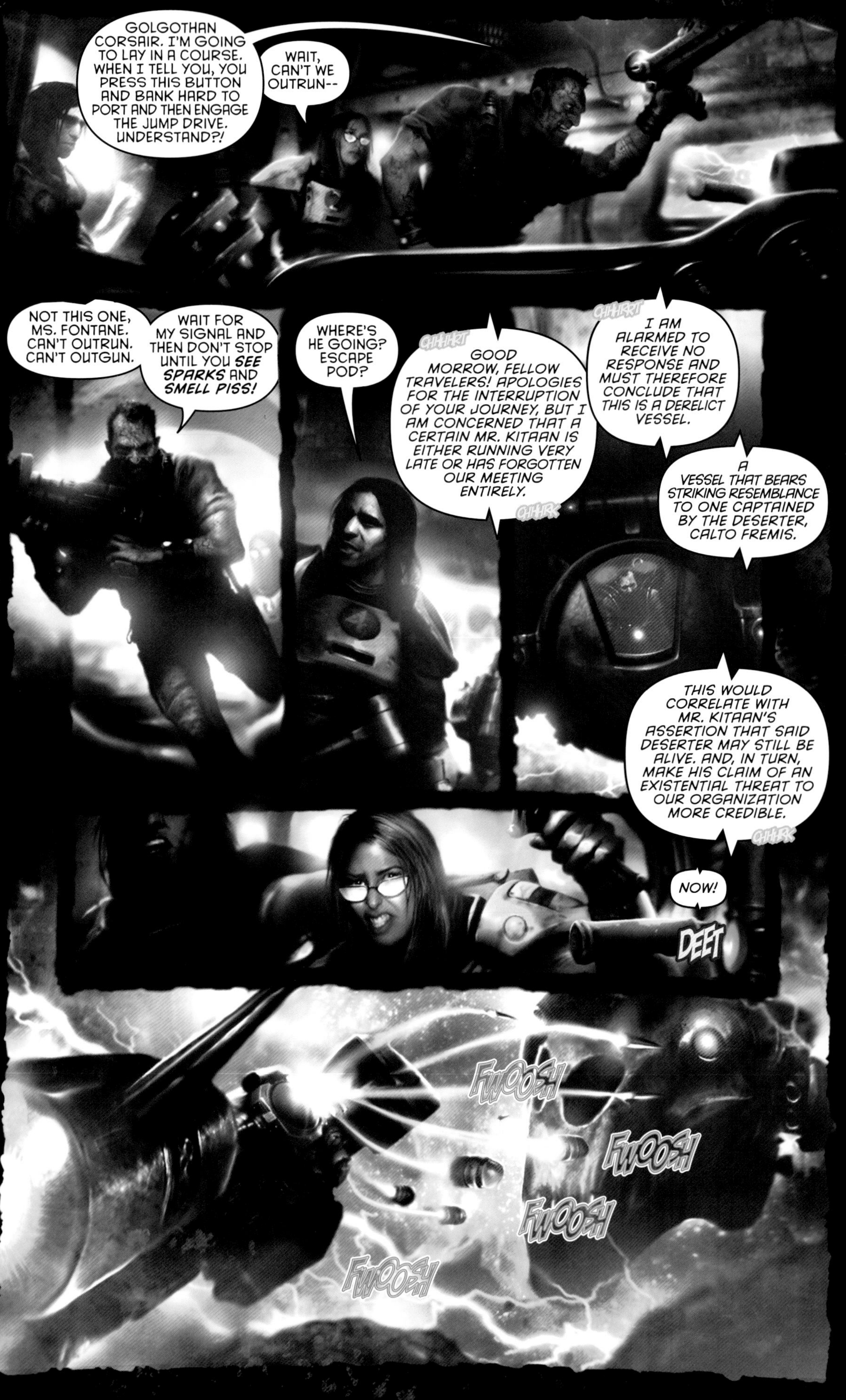
GOLGOTHAN CORSAIR. I'M GOING TO LAY IN A COURSE. WHEN I TELL YOU, YOU PRESS THIS BUTTON AND BANK HARD TO PORT AND THEN ENGAGE THE JUMP DRIVE. UNDERSTAND?!
WAIT, CAN'T WE OUTRUN--
NOT THIS ONE, MS. FONTANE. CAN'T OUTRUN. CAN'T OUTGUN.
WAIT FOR MY SIGNAL AND THEN DON'T STOP UNTIL YOU ***SEE SPARKS*** AND ***SMELL PISS!***
WHERE'S HE GOING? ESCAPE POD?
CHHHRRT
GOOD MORROW, FELLOW TRAVELERS! APOLOGIES FOR THE INTERRUPTION OF YOUR JOURNEY, BUT I AM CONCERNED THAT A CERTAIN MR. KITAAN IS EITHER RUNNING VERY LATE OR HAS FORGOTTEN OUR MEETING ENTIRELY.
CHHHRK
CHHHRRT
I AM ALARMED TO RECEIVE NO RESPONSE AND MUST THEREFORE CONCLUDE THAT THIS IS A DERELICT VESSEL.
A VESSEL THAT BEARS STRIKING RESEMBLANCE TO ONE CAPTAINED BY THE DESERTER, CALTO FREMIS.
THIS WOULD CORRELATE WITH MR. KITAAN'S ASSERTION THAT SAID DESERTER MAY STILL BE ALIVE. AND, IN TURN, MAKE HIS CLAIM OF AN EXISTENTIAL THREAT TO OUR ORGANIZATION MORE CREDIBLE.
CHHHRK
NOW!
DEET
FWOOSH
FWOOSH
FWOOSH
FWOOSH

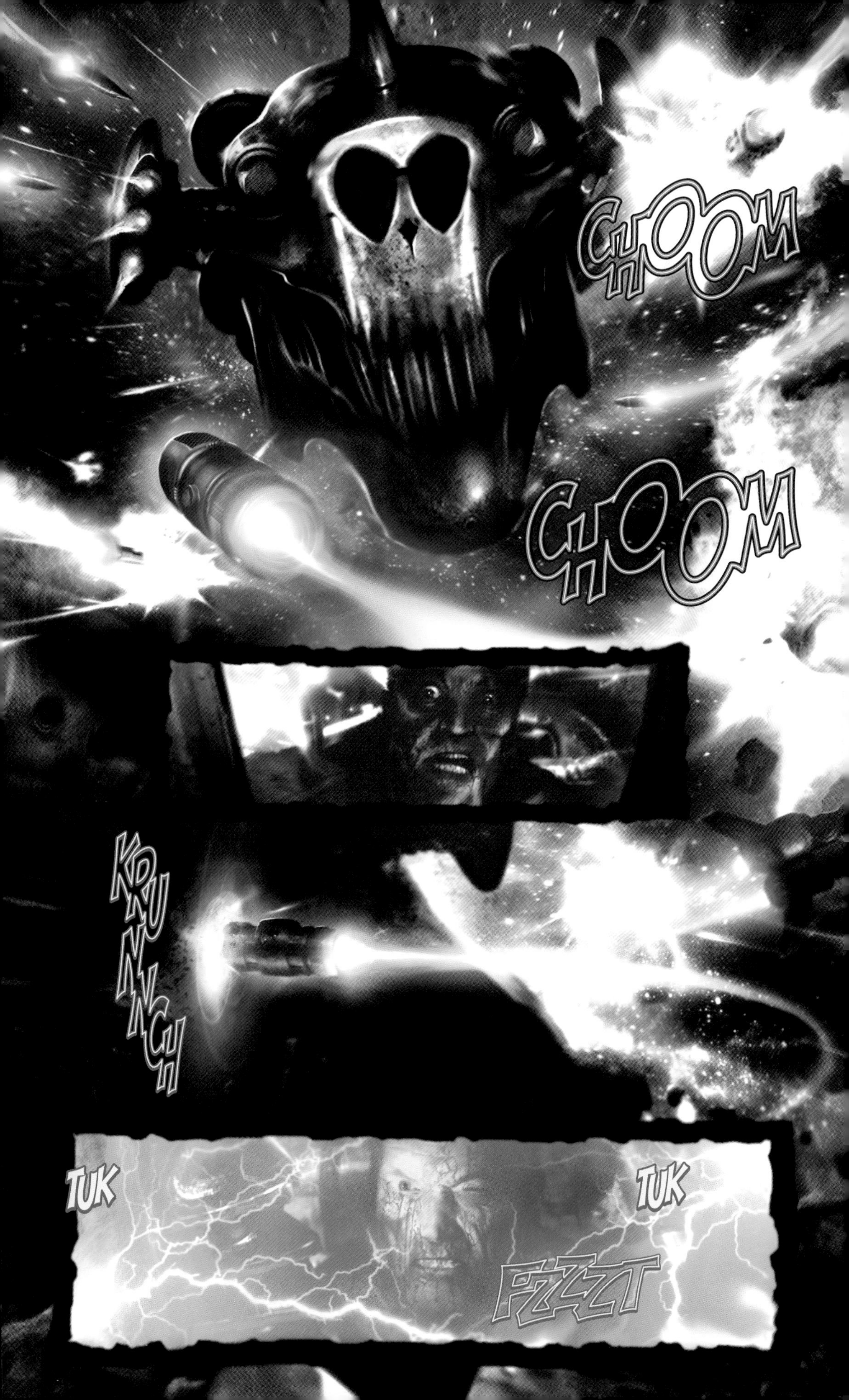
CHOOOM
CHOOOM
KRUNNCH
TUK
TUK
FZZZT

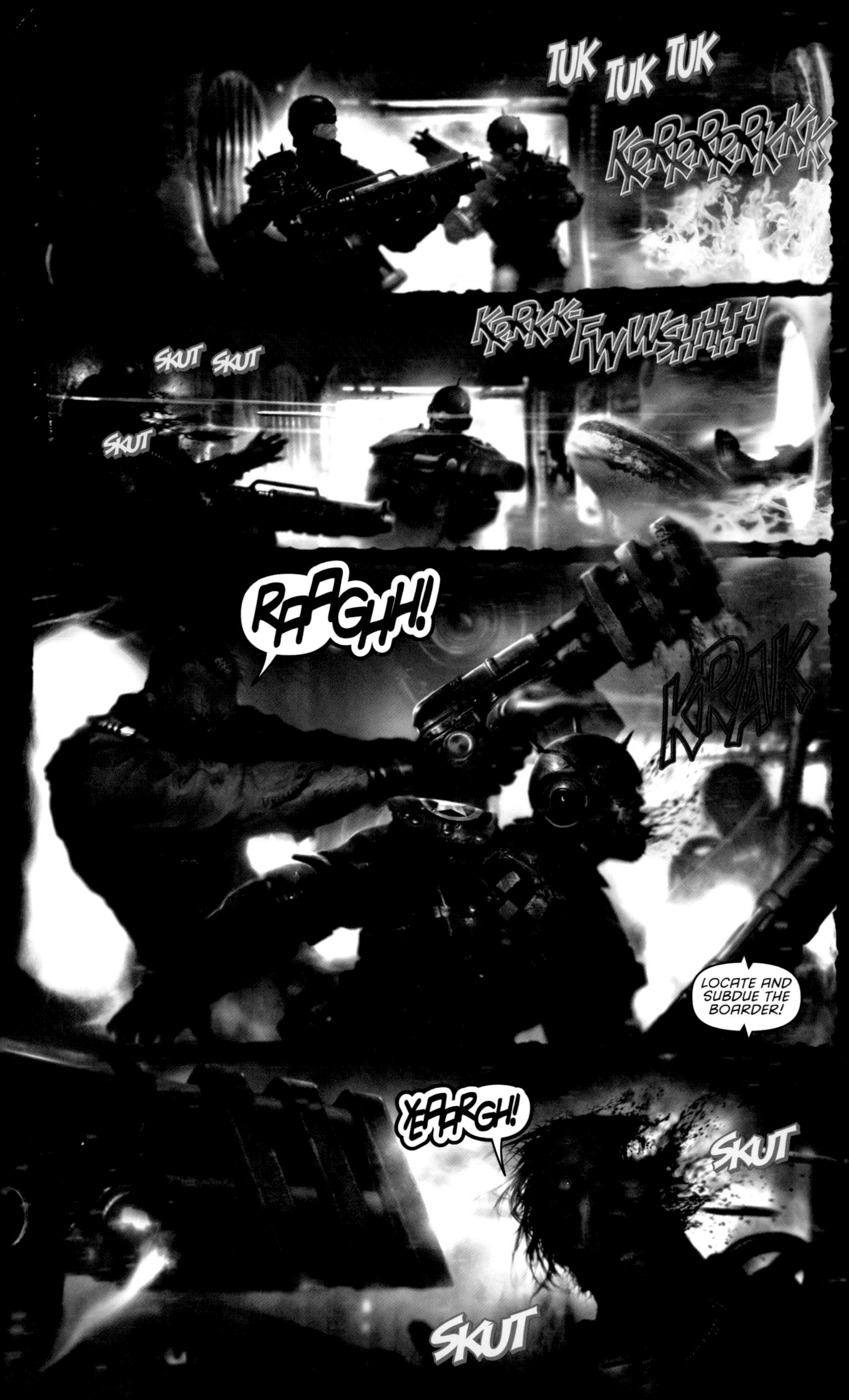
TUK TUK TUK
SKUT SKUT
SKUT
RAAGHH!
LOCATE AND SUBDUE THE BOARDER!
YEAARGH!
SKUT
SKUT

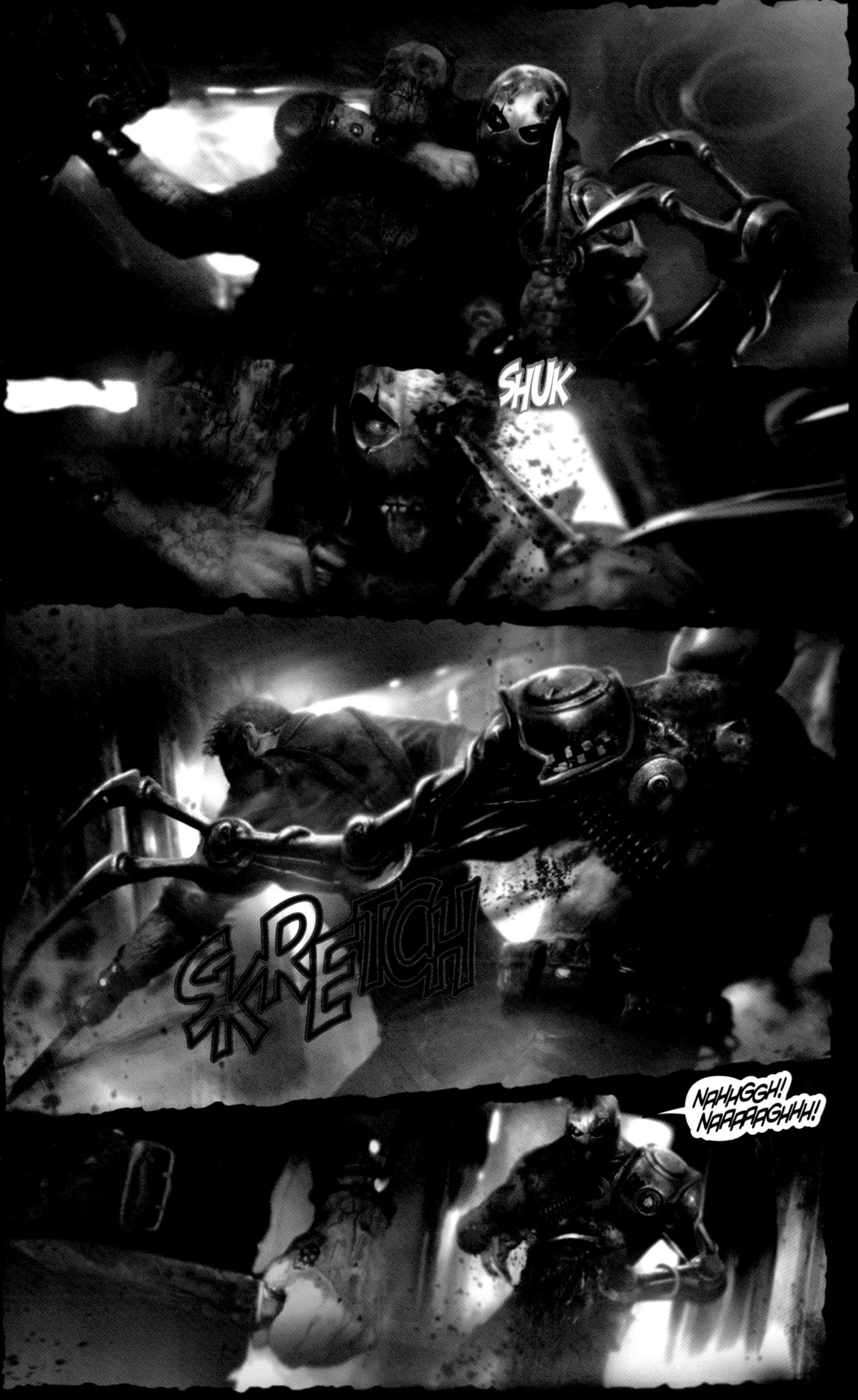
SHUK
SKRETCH
NAHHGGH!
NAAAAAGHHH!

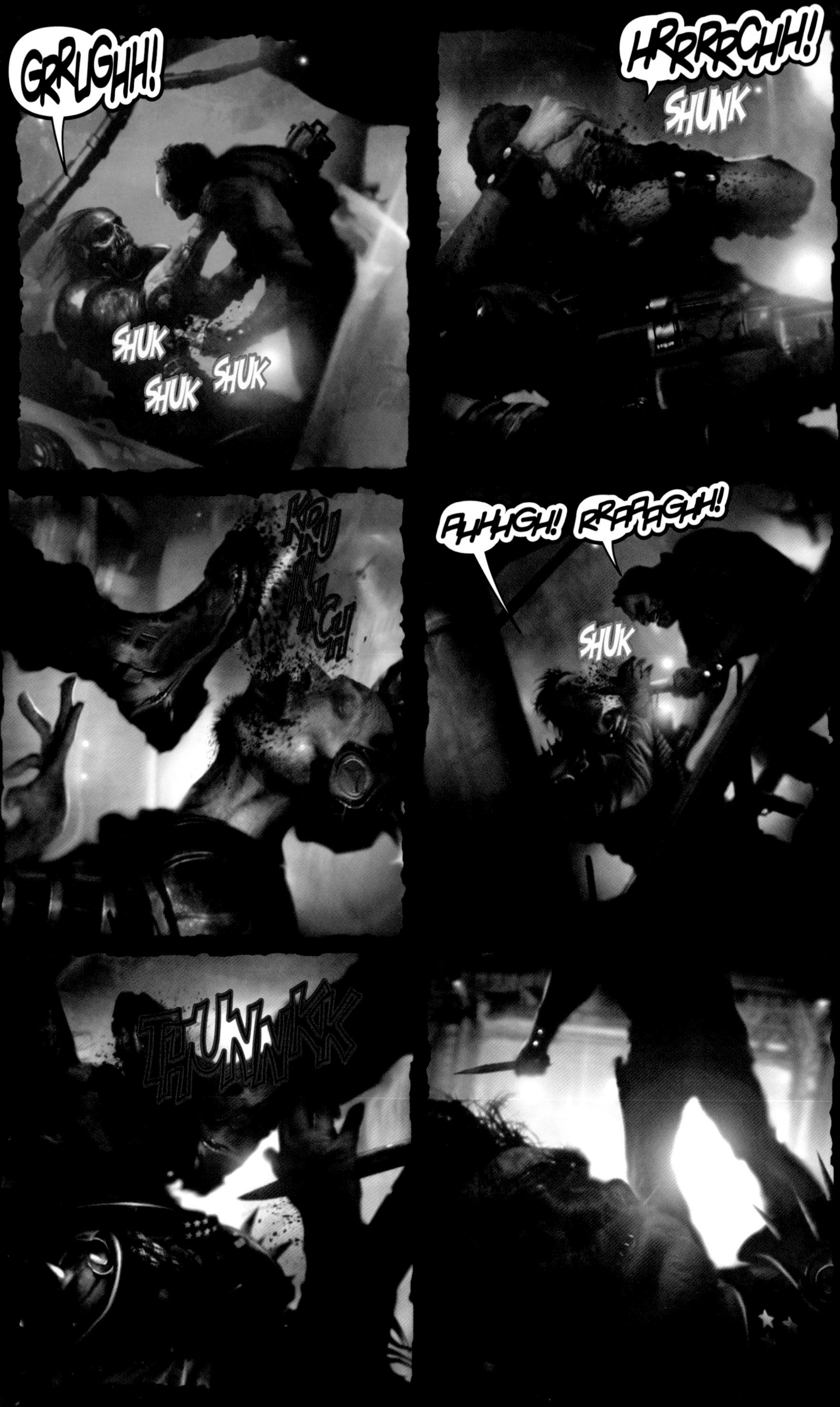
GRRLGHH!
SHUK
SHUK
SHUK
HRRRRCHH!
SHUNK
KRUNNNCH
AHHGH!
RRAAAGH!
SHUK
THUNKK

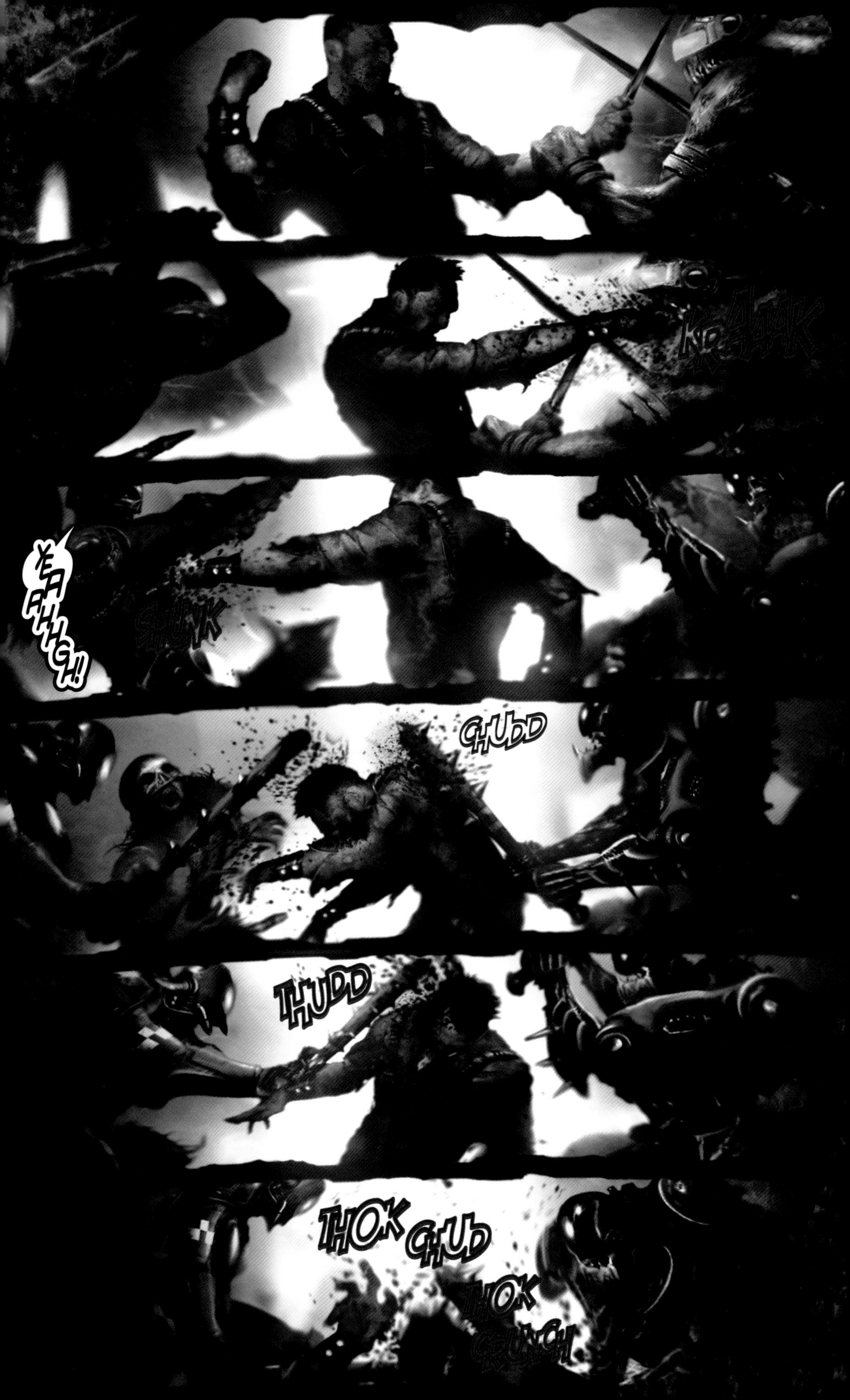
KRAAAK
YEAAHHGH!
CHUDD
THUDD
THOK CHUD
THOK
CRUNCH

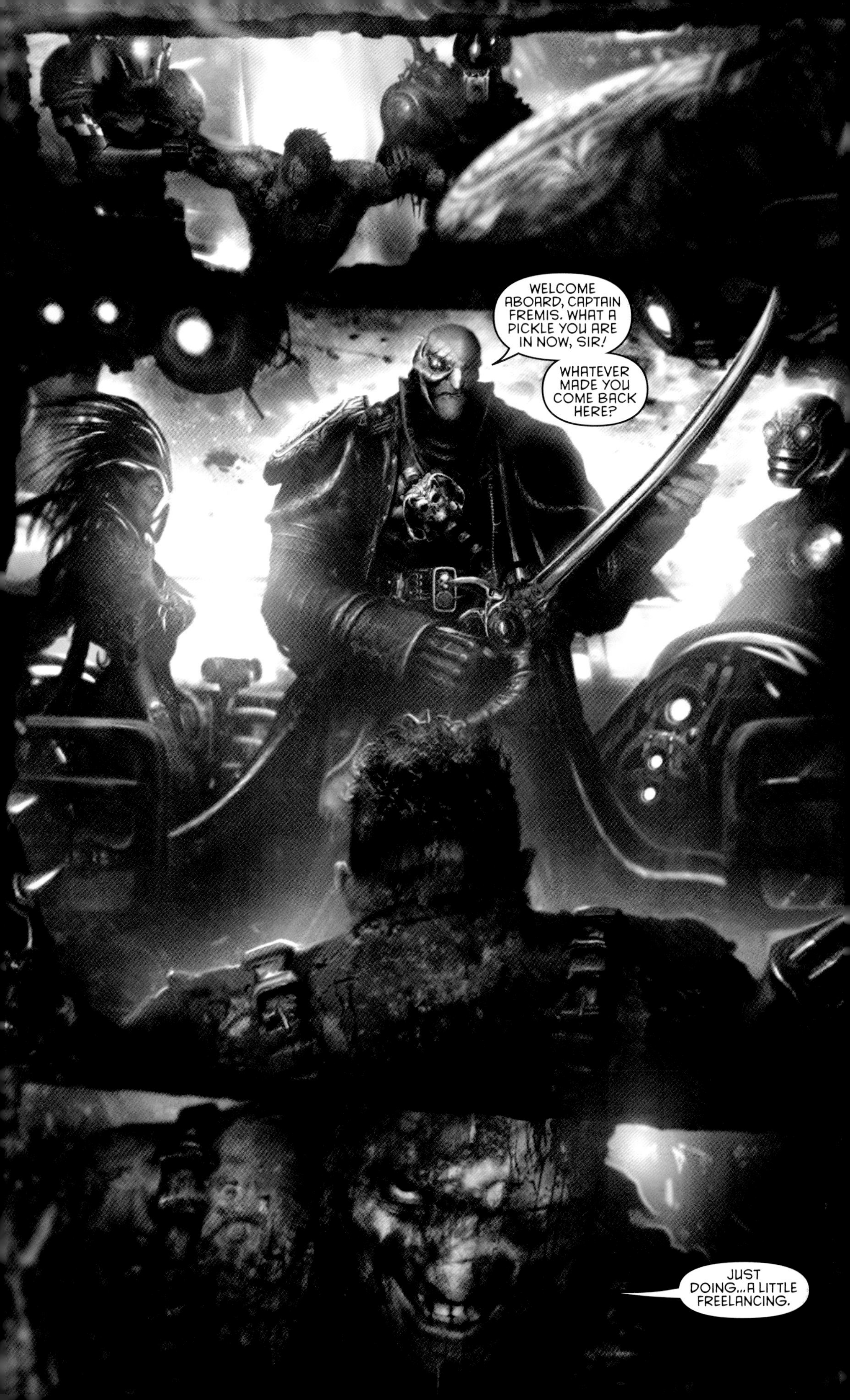
WELCOME ABOARD, CAPTAIN FREMIS. WHAT A PICKLE YOU ARE IN NOW, SIR!
WHATEVER MADE YOU COME BACK HERE?
JUST DOING... A LITTLE FREELANCING.

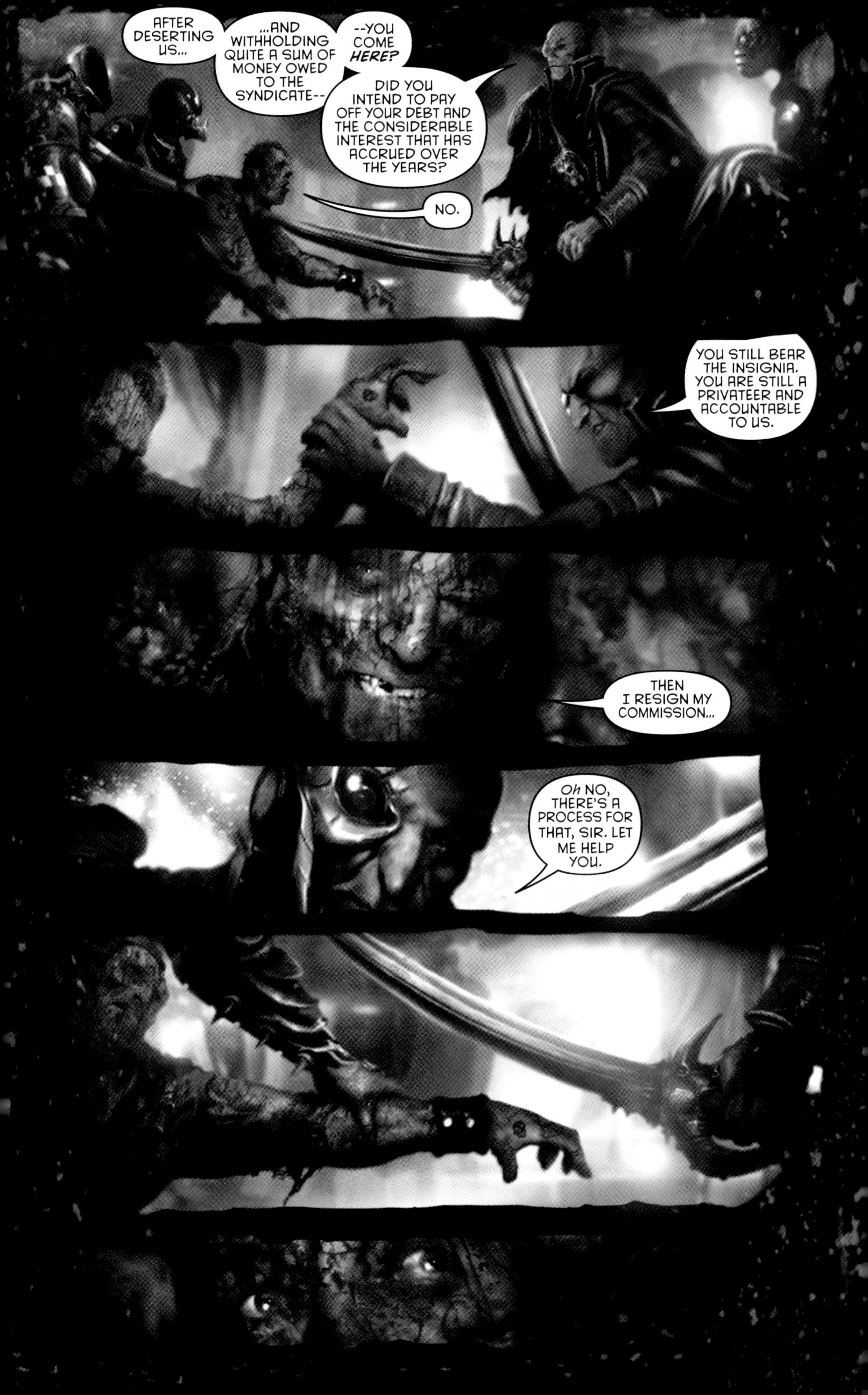

AFTER DESERTING US...
...AND WITHHOLDING QUITE A SUM OF MONEY OWED TO THE SYNDICATE--
--YOU COME *HERE?*
DID YOU INTEND TO PAY OFF YOUR DEBT AND THE CONSIDERABLE INTEREST THAT HAS ACCRUED OVER THE YEARS?
NO.
YOU STILL BEAR THE INSIGNIA. YOU ARE STILL A PRIVATEER AND ACCOUNTABLE TO US.
THEN I RESIGN MY COMMISSION...
Oh NO, THERE'S A PROCESS FOR THAT, SIR. LET ME HELP YOU.

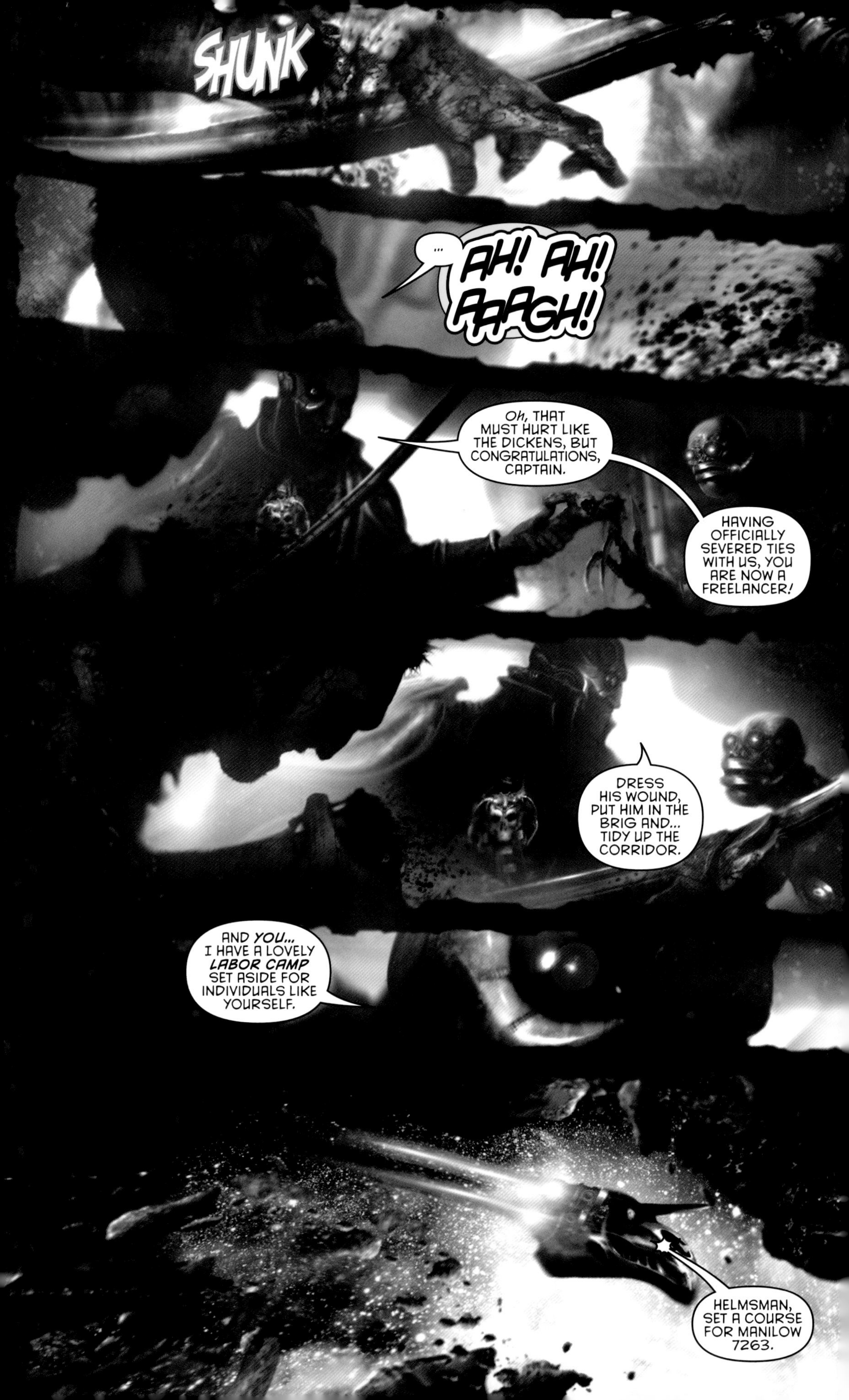
SHUNK
...AH! AH! AAAGH!
Oh, THAT MUST HURT LIKE THE DICKENS, BUT CONGRATULATIONS, CAPTAIN.
HAVING OFFICIALLY SEVERED TIES WITH US, YOU ARE NOW A FREELANCER!
DRESS HIS WOUND, PUT HIM IN THE BRIG AND... TIDY UP THE CORRIDOR.
AND YOU... I HAVE A LOVELY LABOR CAMP SET ASIDE FOR INDIVIDUALS LIKE YOURSELF.
HELMSMAN, SET A COURSE FOR MANILOW 7263.

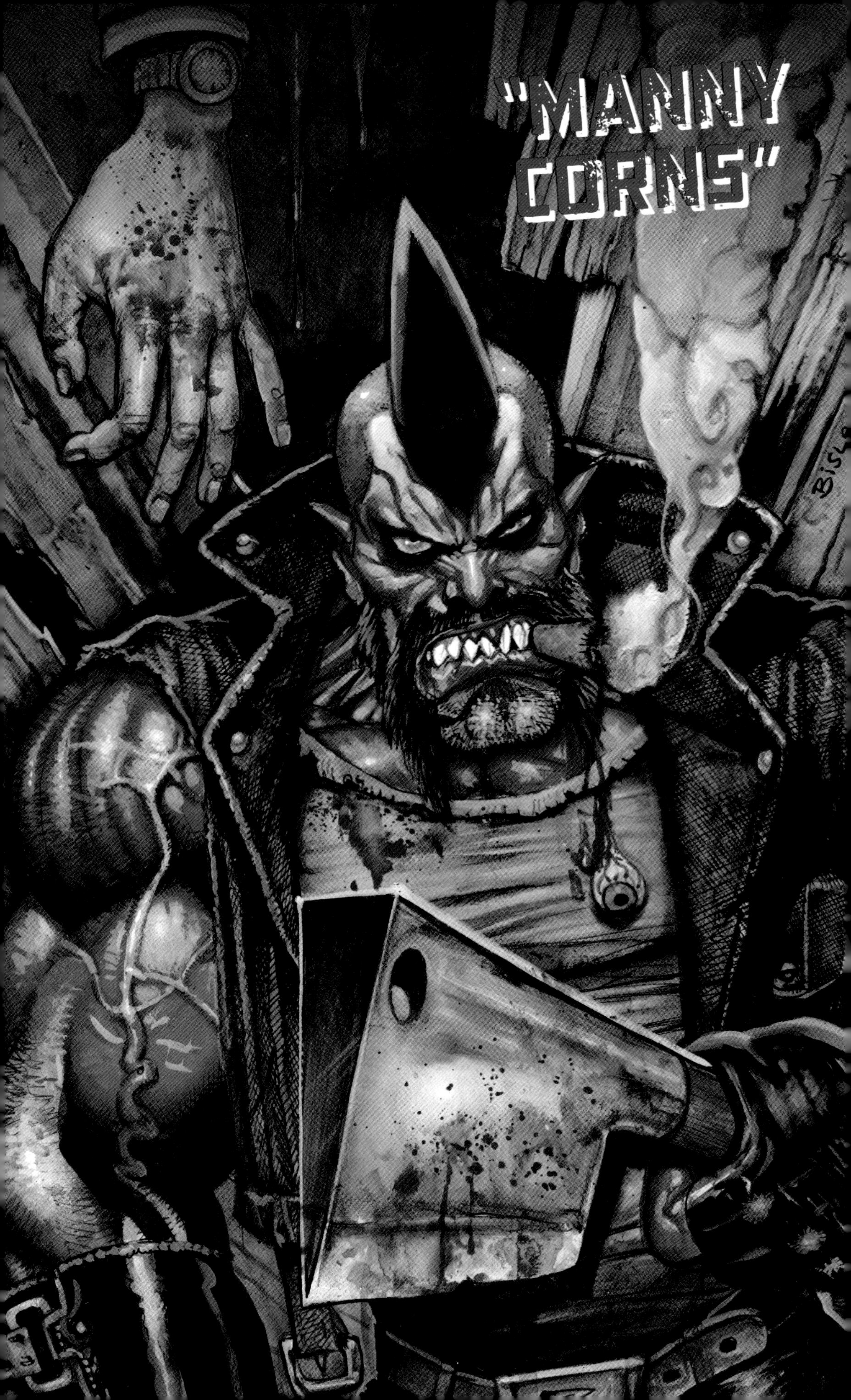
"MANNY
CORNS"

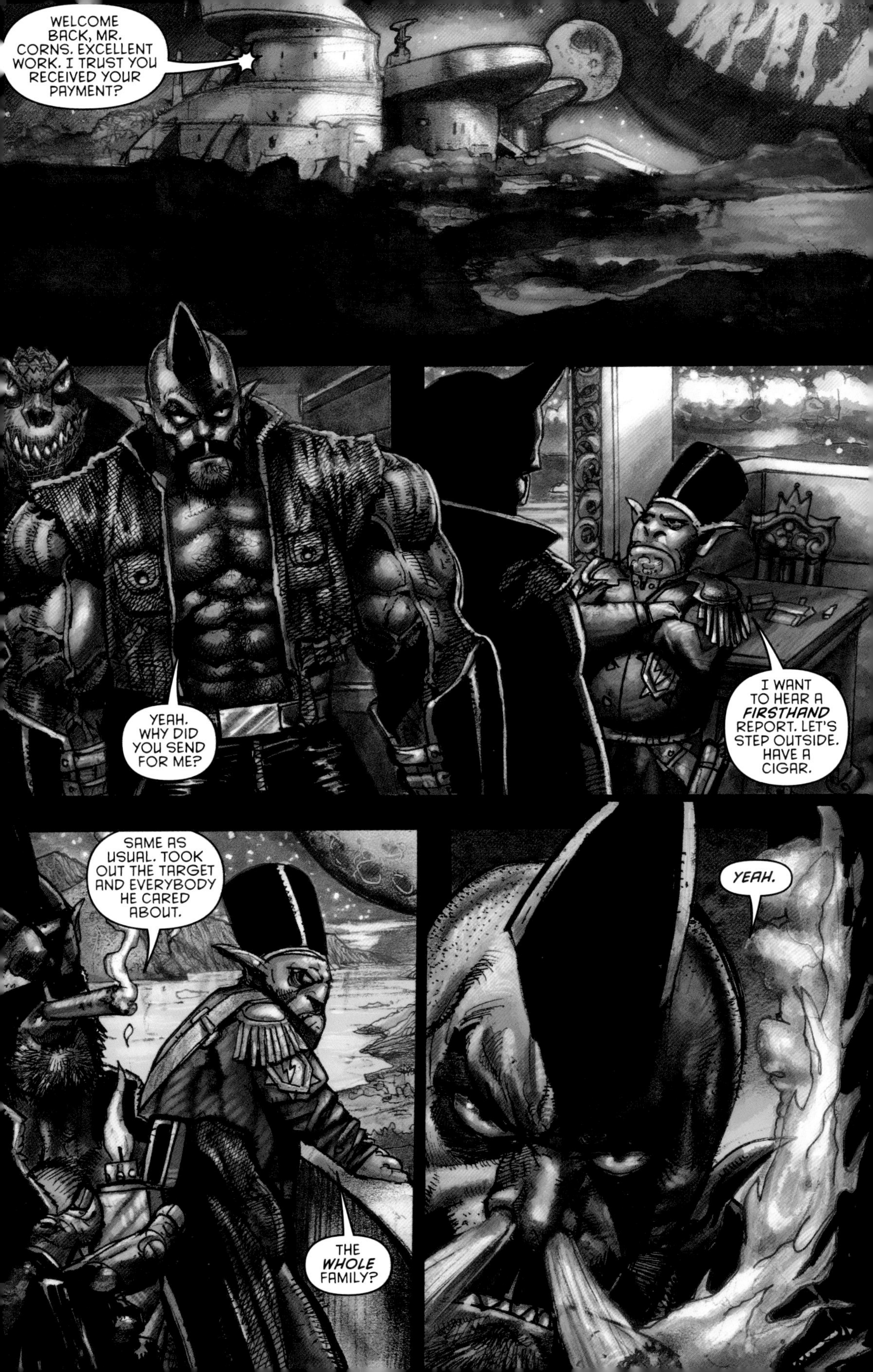
WELCOME BACK, MR. CORNS. EXCELLENT WORK. I TRUST YOU RECEIVED YOUR PAYMENT?
YEAH. WHY DID YOU SEND FOR ME?
I WANT TO HEAR A *FIRSTHAND* REPORT. LET'S STEP OUTSIDE. HAVE A CIGAR.
SAME AS USUAL. TOOK OUT THE TARGET AND EVERYBODY HE CARED ABOUT.
THE *WHOLE* FAMILY?
YEAH.

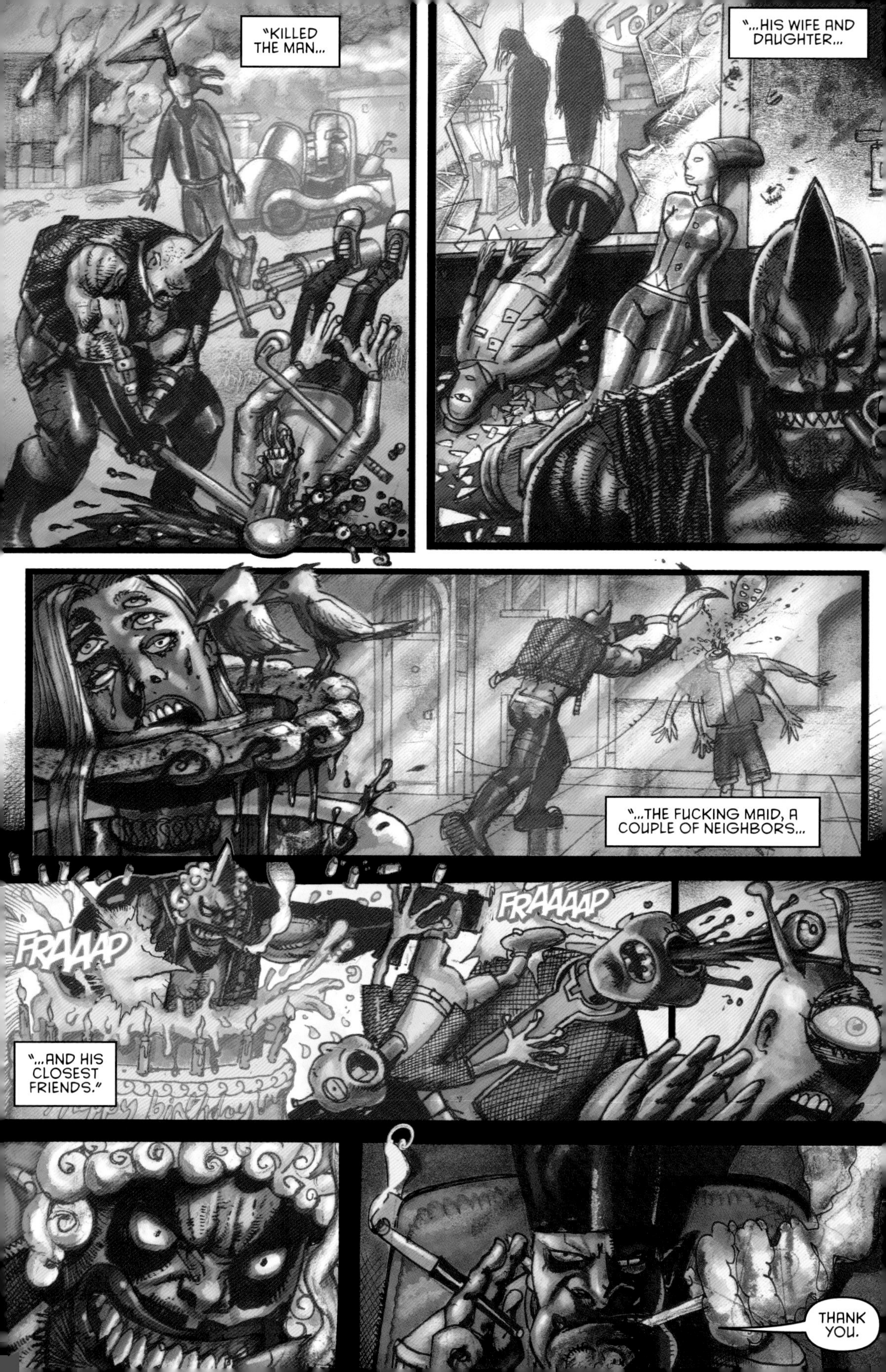
"KILLED THE MAN...
"...HIS WIFE AND DAUGHTER...
"...THE FUCKING MAID, A COUPLE OF NEIGHBORS...
FRAAAP
FRAAAAP
"...AND HIS CLOSEST FRIENDS."
THANK YOU.

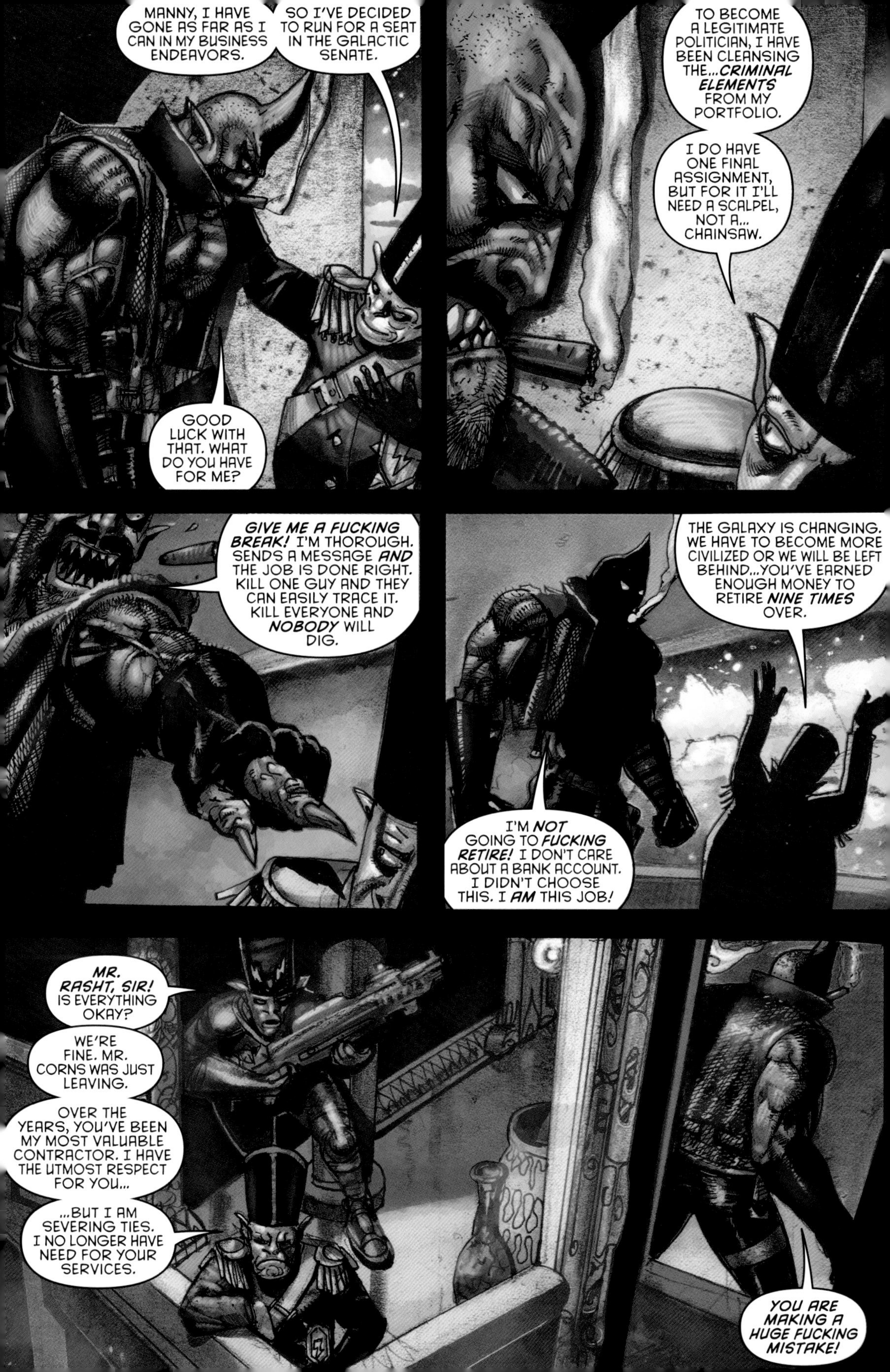
MANNY, I HAVE GONE AS FAR AS I CAN IN MY BUSINESS ENDEAVORS.
SO I'VE DECIDED TO RUN FOR A SEAT IN THE GALACTIC SENATE.
GOOD LUCK WITH THAT. WHAT DO YOU HAVE FOR ME?
TO BECOME A LEGITIMATE POLITICIAN, I HAVE BEEN CLEANSING THE...*CRIMINAL ELEMENTS* FROM MY PORTFOLIO.
I DO HAVE ONE FINAL ASSIGNMENT, BUT FOR IT I'LL NEED A SCALPEL, NOT A... CHAINSAW.
GIVE ME A FUCKING BREAK! I'M THOROUGH. SENDS A MESSAGE *AND* THE JOB IS DONE RIGHT. KILL ONE GUY AND THEY CAN EASILY TRACE IT. KILL EVERYONE AND *NOBODY* WILL DIG.
THE GALAXY IS CHANGING. WE HAVE TO BECOME MORE CIVILIZED OR WE WILL BE LEFT BEHIND...YOU'VE EARNED ENOUGH MONEY TO RETIRE *NINE TIMES* OVER.
I'M *NOT* GOING TO *FUCKING RETIRE!* I DON'T CARE ABOUT A BANK ACCOUNT. I DIDN'T CHOOSE THIS. I *AM* THIS JOB!
MR. RASHT, SIR! IS EVERYTHING OKAY?
WE'RE FINE. MR. CORNS WAS JUST LEAVING.
OVER THE YEARS, YOU'VE BEEN MY MOST VALUABLE CONTRACTOR. I HAVE THE UTMOST RESPECT FOR YOU...
...BUT I AM SEVERING TIES. I NO LONGER HAVE NEED FOR YOUR SERVICES.
YOU ARE MAKING A HUGE FUCKING MISTAKE!

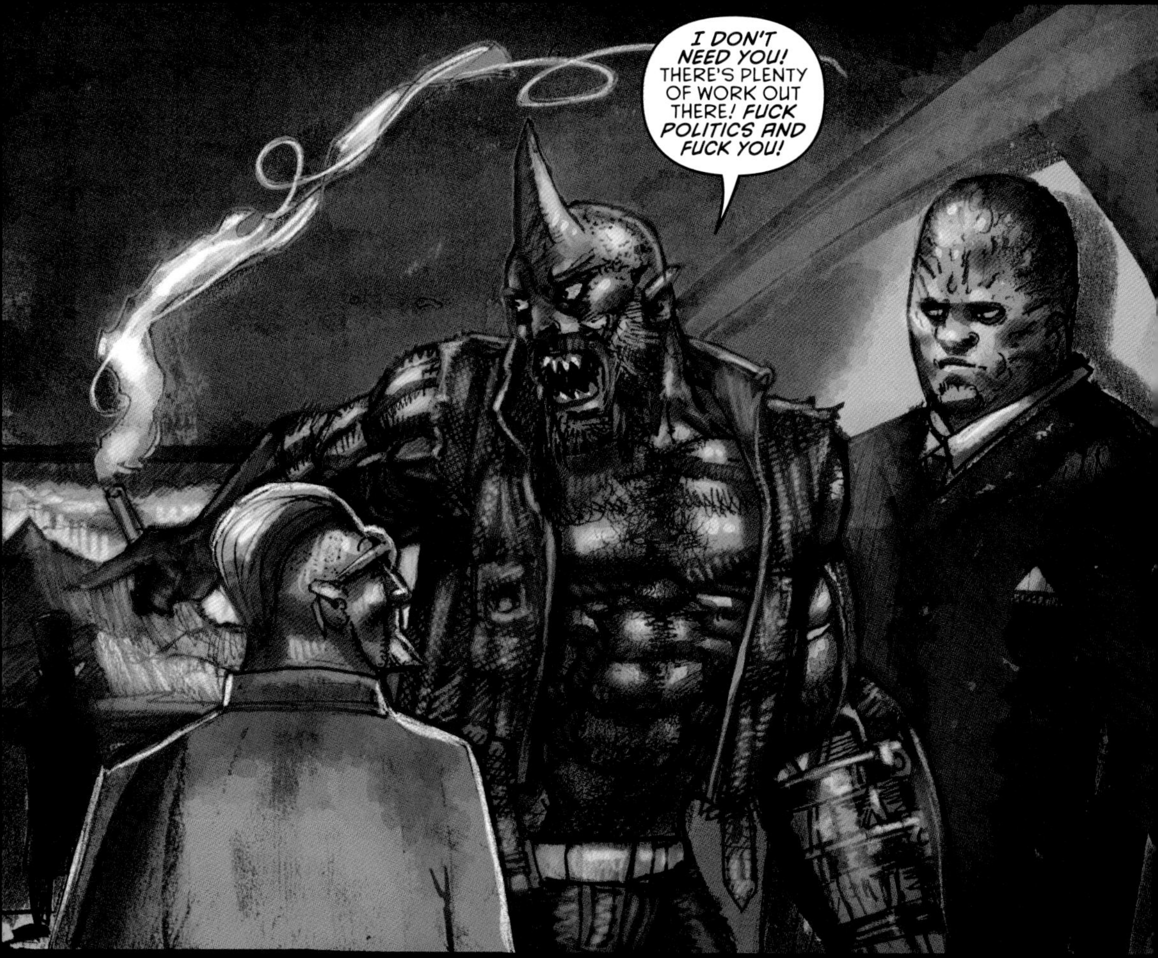
I DON'T NEED YOU! THERE'S PLENTY OF WORK OUT THERE! FUCK POLITICS AND FUCK YOU!

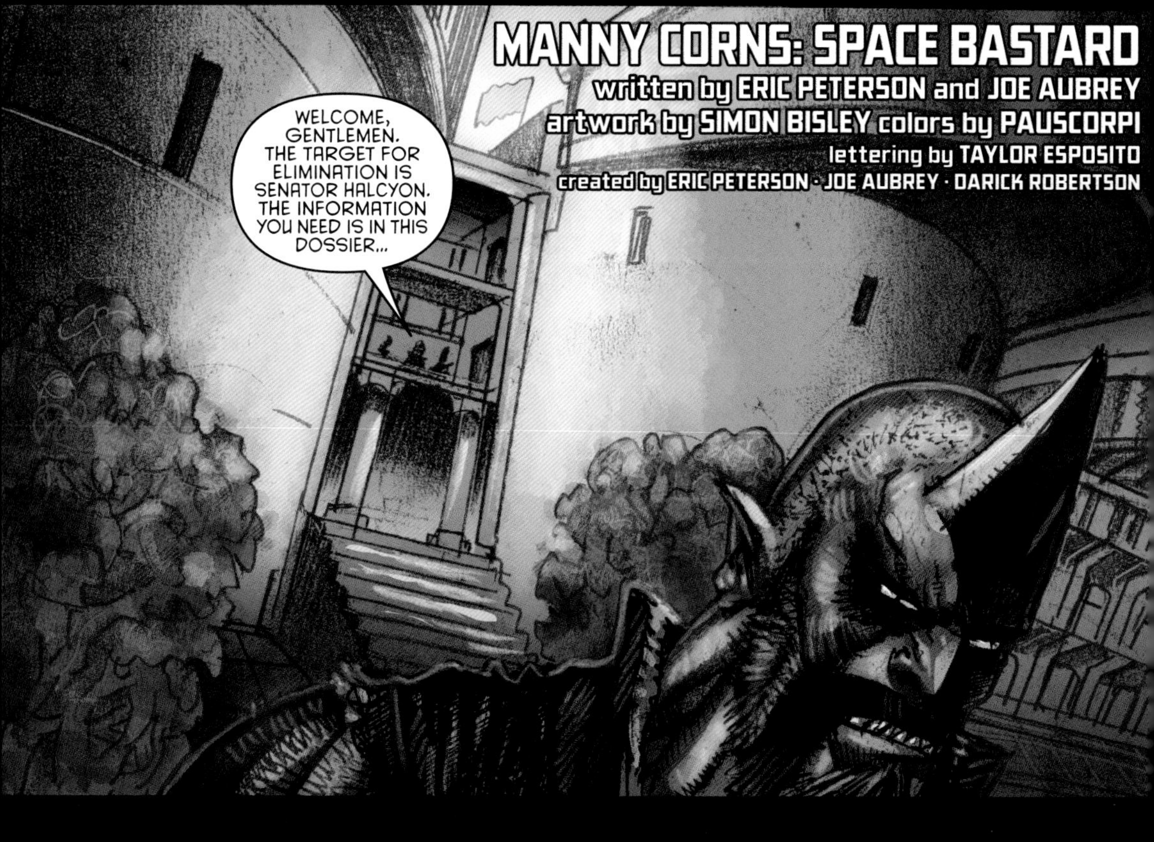
MANNY CORNS: SPACE BASTARD
written by ERIC PETERSON and JOE AUBREY
artwork by SIMON BISLEY colors by PAUSCORPI
lettering by TAYLOR ESPOSITO
created by ERIC PETERSON · JOE AUBREY · DARICK ROBERTSON
WELCOME, GENTLEMEN. THE TARGET FOR ELIMINATION IS SENATOR HALCYON. THE INFORMATION YOU NEED IS IN THIS DOSSIER...

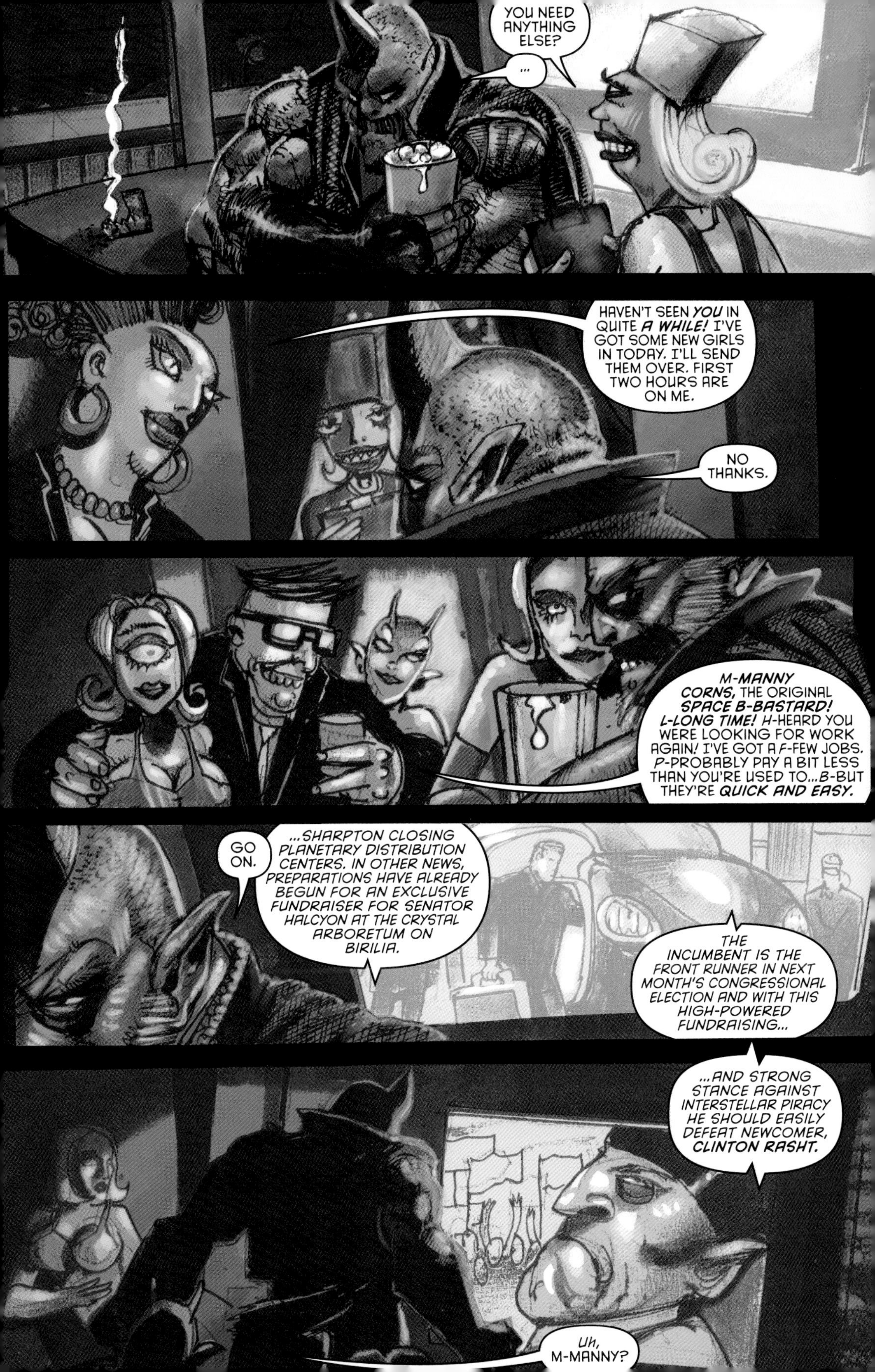
YOU NEED ANYTHING ELSE?
...
HAVEN'T SEEN YOU IN QUITE A WHILE! I'VE GOT SOME NEW GIRLS IN TODAY. I'LL SEND THEM OVER. FIRST TWO HOURS ARE ON ME.
NO THANKS.
M-MANNY CORNS, THE ORIGINAL SPACE B-BASTARD! L-LONG TIME! H-HEARD YOU WERE LOOKING FOR WORK AGAIN! I'VE GOT A F-FEW JOBS. P-PROBABLY PAY A BIT LESS THAN YOU'RE USED TO...B-BUT THEY'RE QUICK AND EASY.
GO ON.
...SHARPTON CLOSING PLANETARY DISTRIBUTION CENTERS. IN OTHER NEWS, PREPARATIONS HAVE ALREADY BEGUN FOR AN EXCLUSIVE FUNDRAISER FOR SENATOR HALCYON AT THE CRYSTAL ARBORETUM ON BIRILIA.
THE INCUMBENT IS THE FRONT RUNNER IN NEXT MONTH'S CONGRESSIONAL ELECTION AND WITH THIS HIGH-POWERED FUNDRAISING...
...AND STRONG STANCE AGAINST INTERSTELLAR PIRACY HE SHOULD EASILY DEFEAT NEWCOMER, CLINTON RASHT.
UH, M-MANNY?

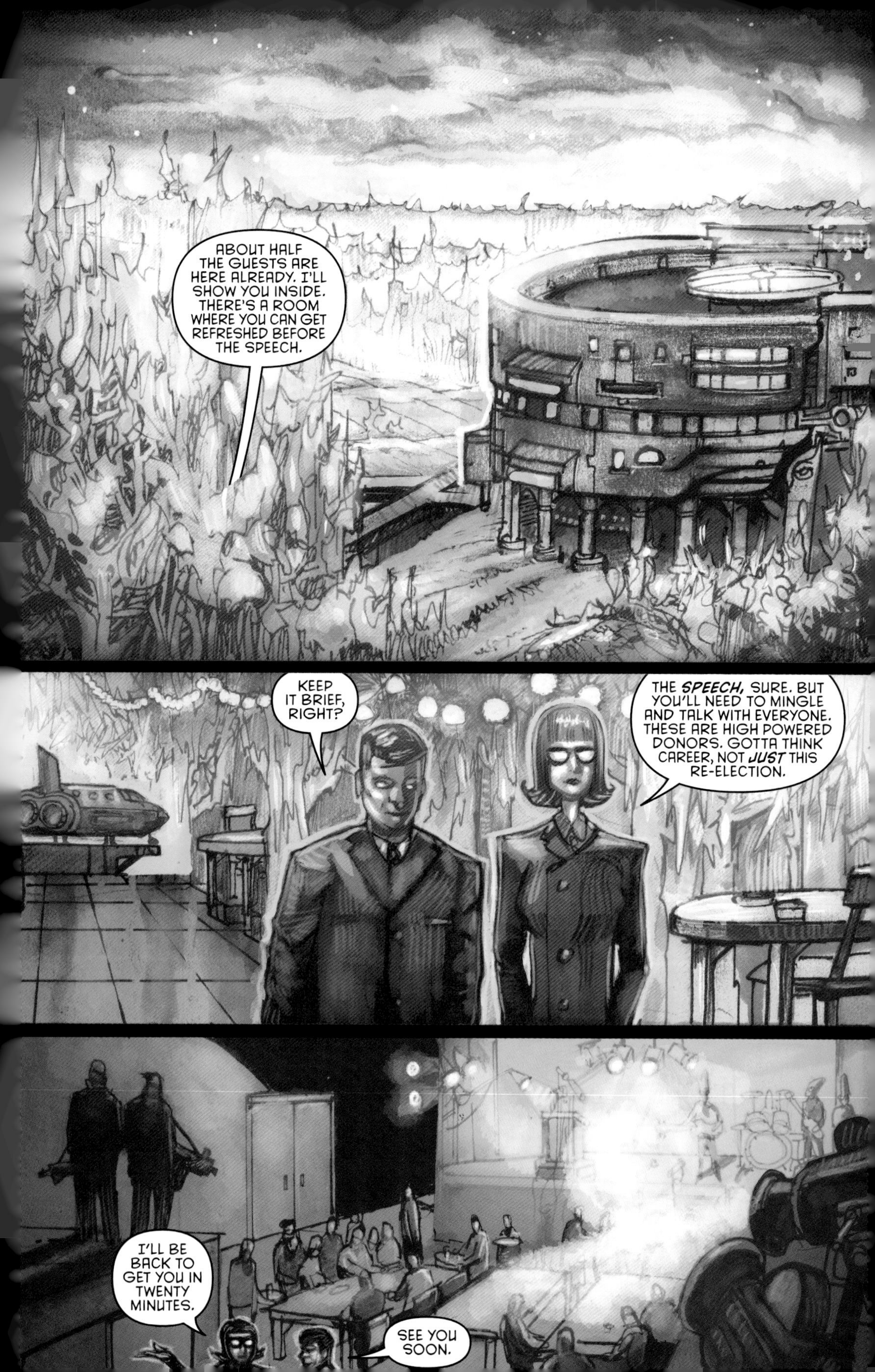
ABOUT HALF THE GUESTS ARE HERE ALREADY. I'LL SHOW YOU INSIDE. THERE'S A ROOM WHERE YOU CAN GET REFRESHED BEFORE THE SPEECH.
KEEP IT BRIEF, RIGHT?
THE *SPEECH,* SURE. BUT YOU'LL NEED TO MINGLE AND TALK WITH EVERYONE. THESE ARE HIGH POWERED DONORS. GOTTA THINK CAREER, NOT *JUST* THIS RE-ELECTION.
I'LL BE BACK TO GET YOU IN TWENTY MINUTES.
SEE YOU SOON.

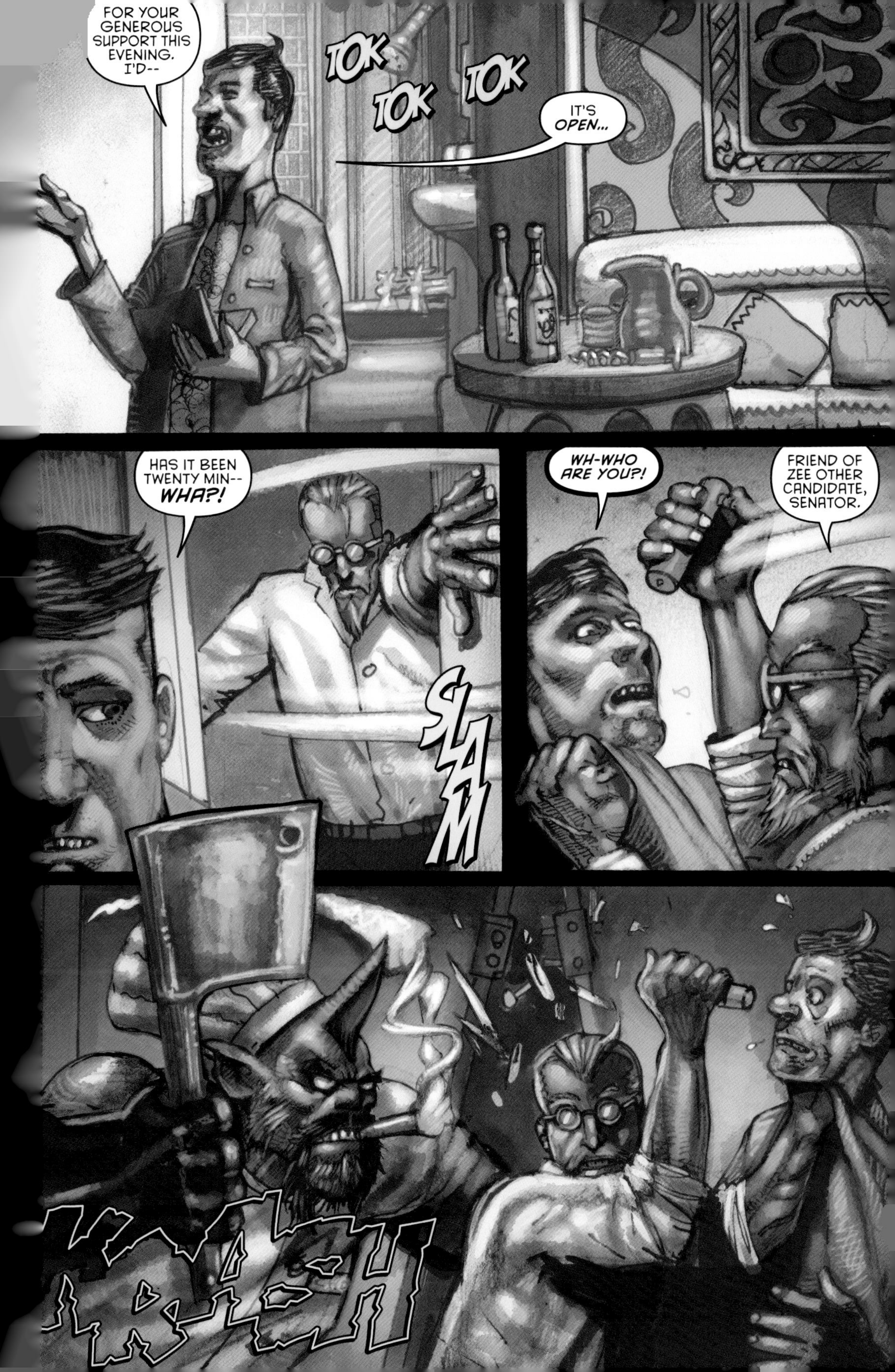

FOR YOUR GENEROUS SUPPORT THIS EVENING. I'D--
TOK
TOK
TOK
IT'S OPEN...
HAS IT BEEN TWENTY MIN-- WHA?!
SLAM
WH-WHO ARE YOU?!
FRIEND OF ZEE OTHER CANDIDATE, SENATOR.

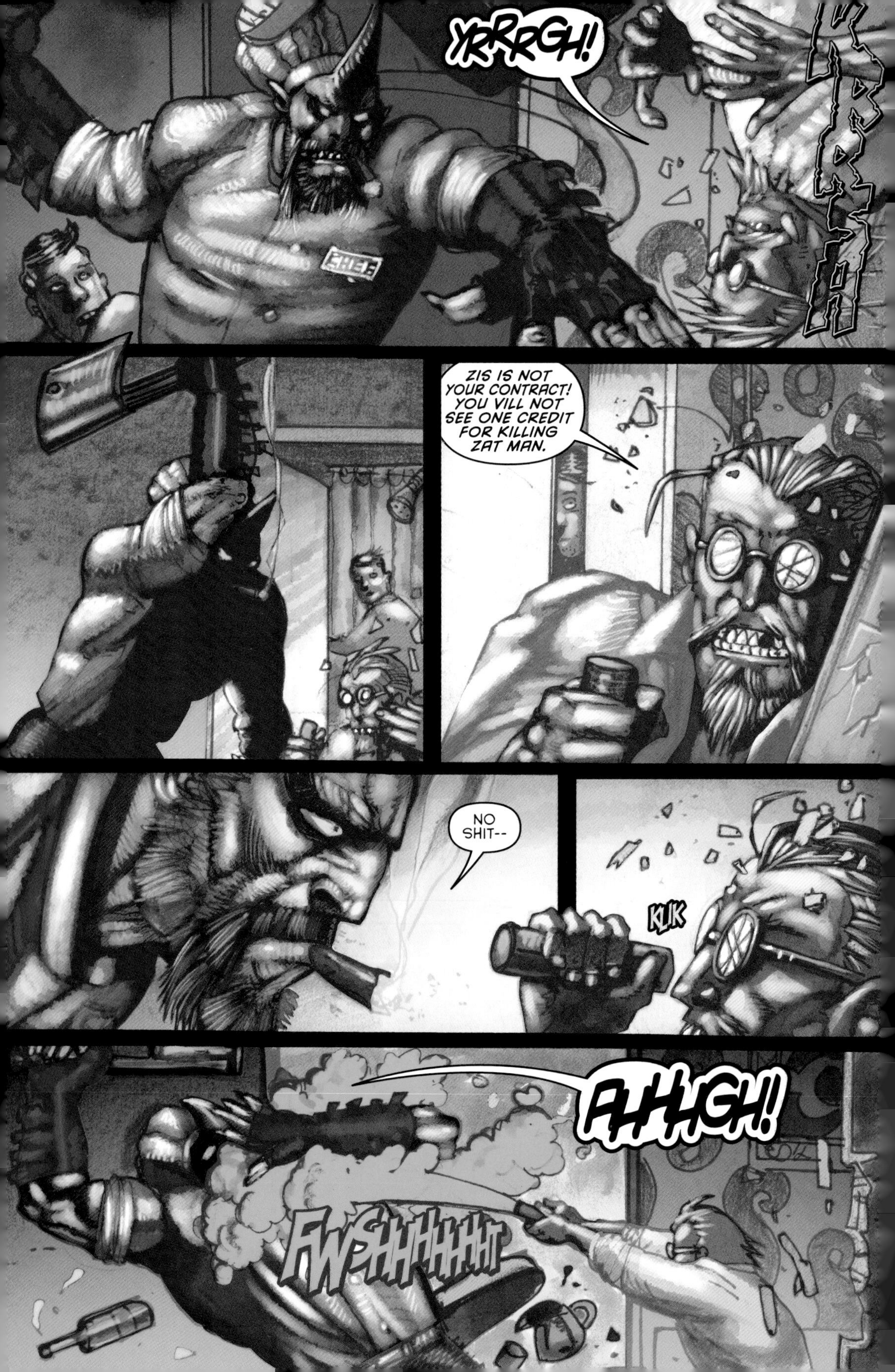
YRRRGH!
ZIS IS NOT YOUR CONTRACT! YOU VILL NOT SEE ONE CREDIT FOR KILLING ZAT MAN.
NO SHIT--
KLIK
AHHUGH!
FWSHHHHHHT

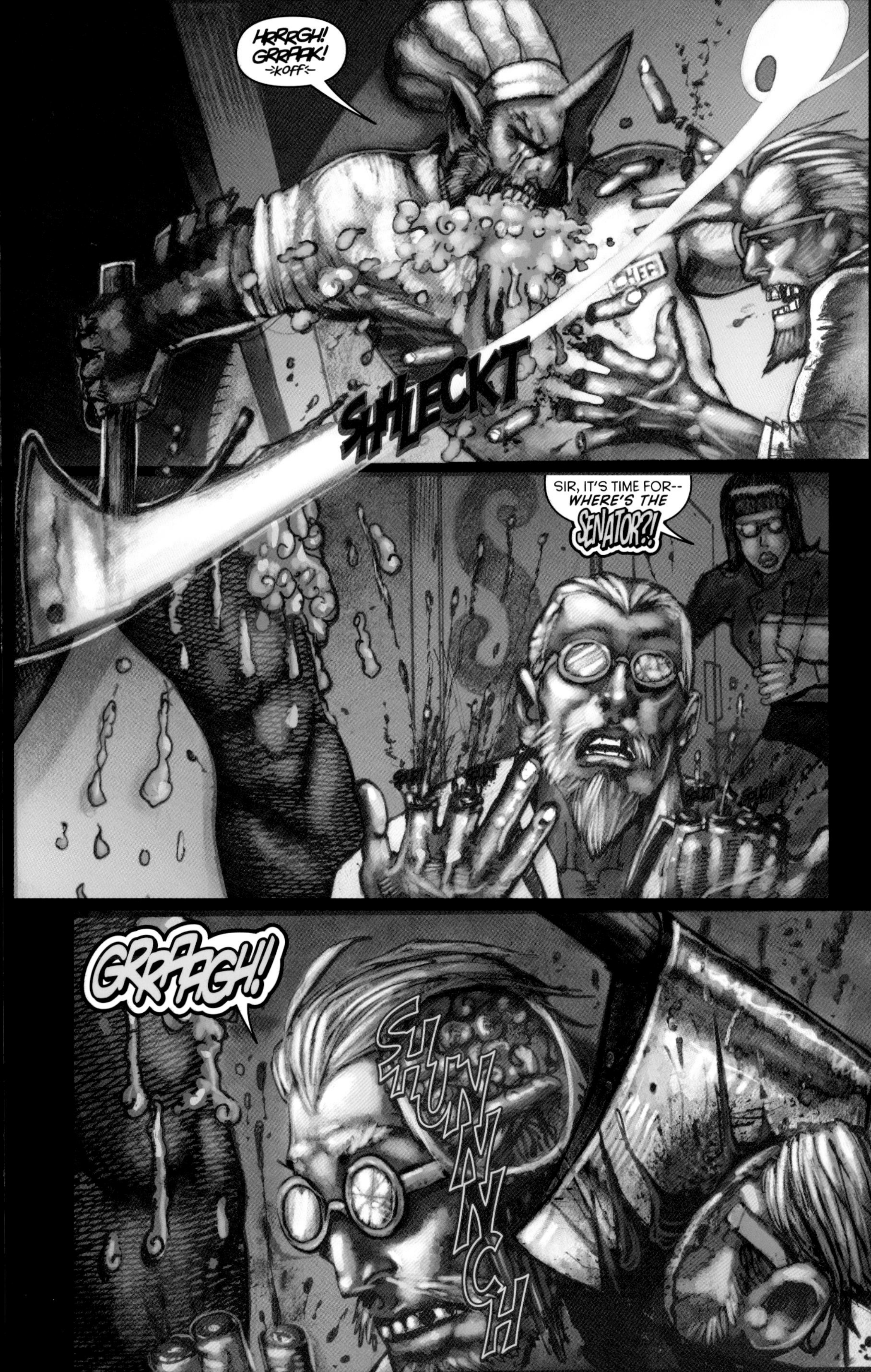
HRRRGH! GRRAAK!
KOFF
CHEF
SHLECKT
SIR, IT'S TIME FOR-- WHERE'S THE SENATOR?!
GRRAAGH!
SHUNNCH

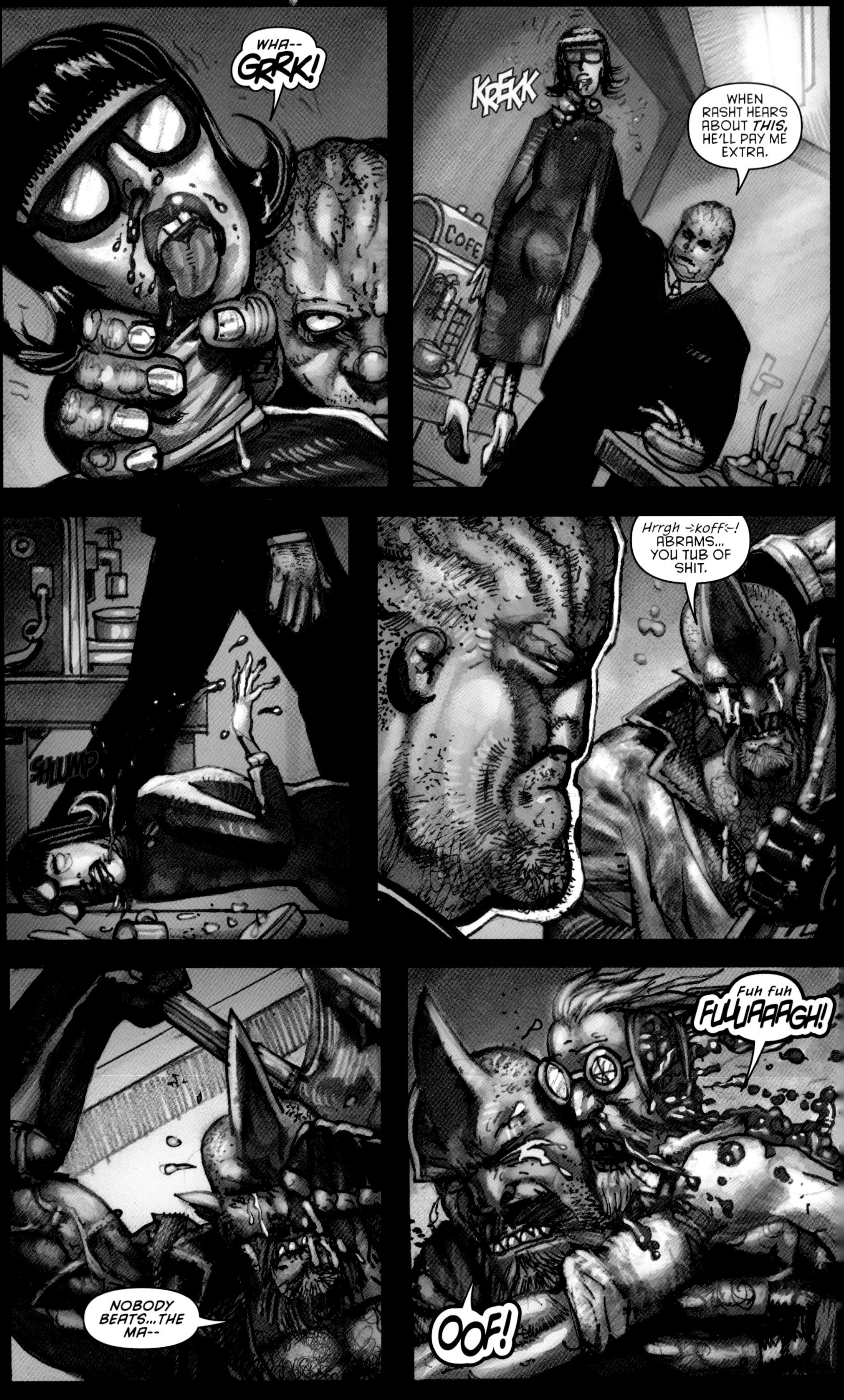
WHA-- GRRK!
KREKK
WHEN RASHT HEARS ABOUT THIS, HE'LL PAY ME EXTRA.
SHLUMP
Hrrgh -koff-! ABRAMS... YOU TUB OF SHIT.
NOBODY BEATS...THE MA--
Fuh fuh FUUUAAAGH!
OOF!

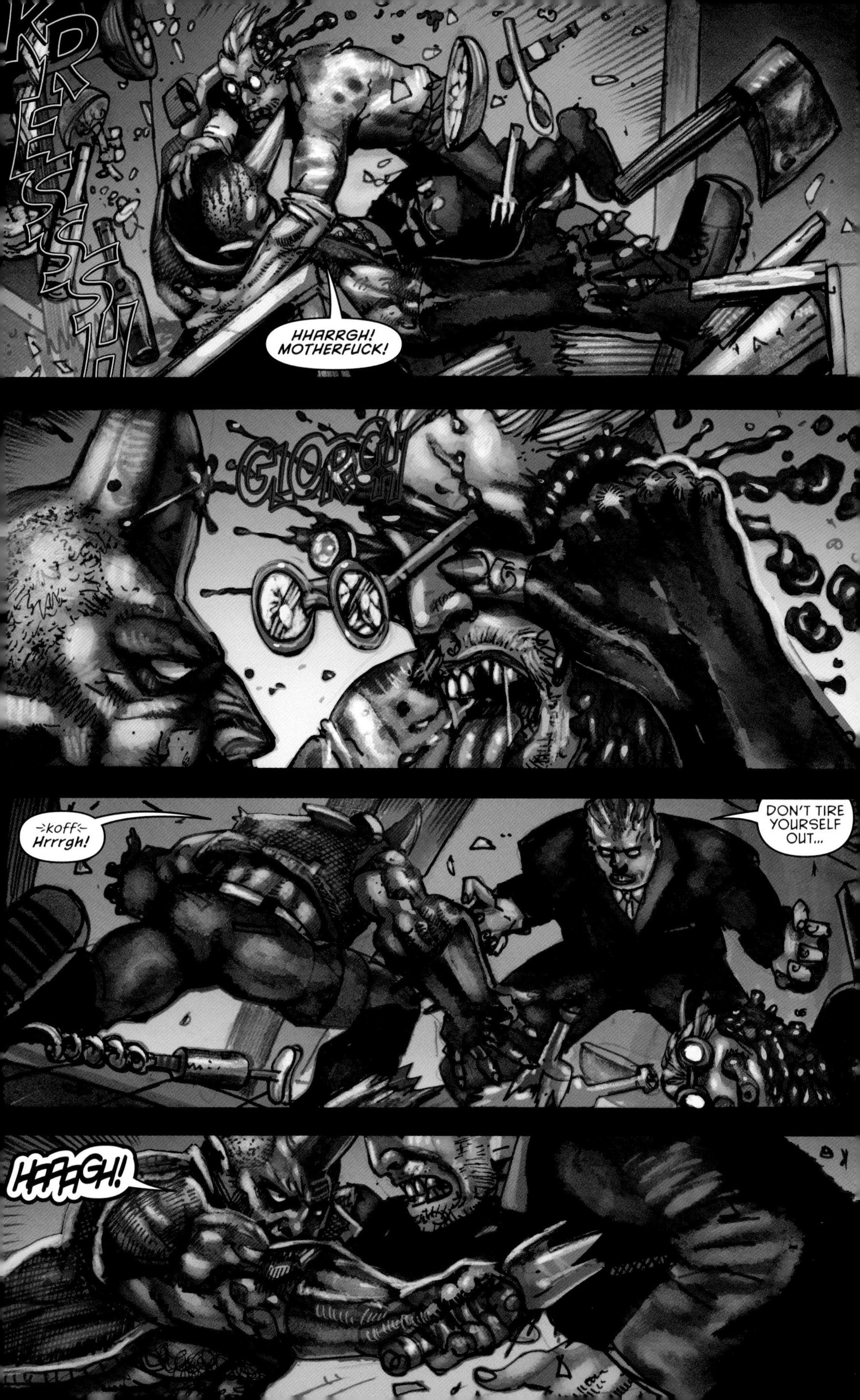
HHARRGH! MOTHERFUCK!
GLORGH
-koff- Hrrrgh!
DON'T TIRE YOURSELF OUT...
HRRGH!

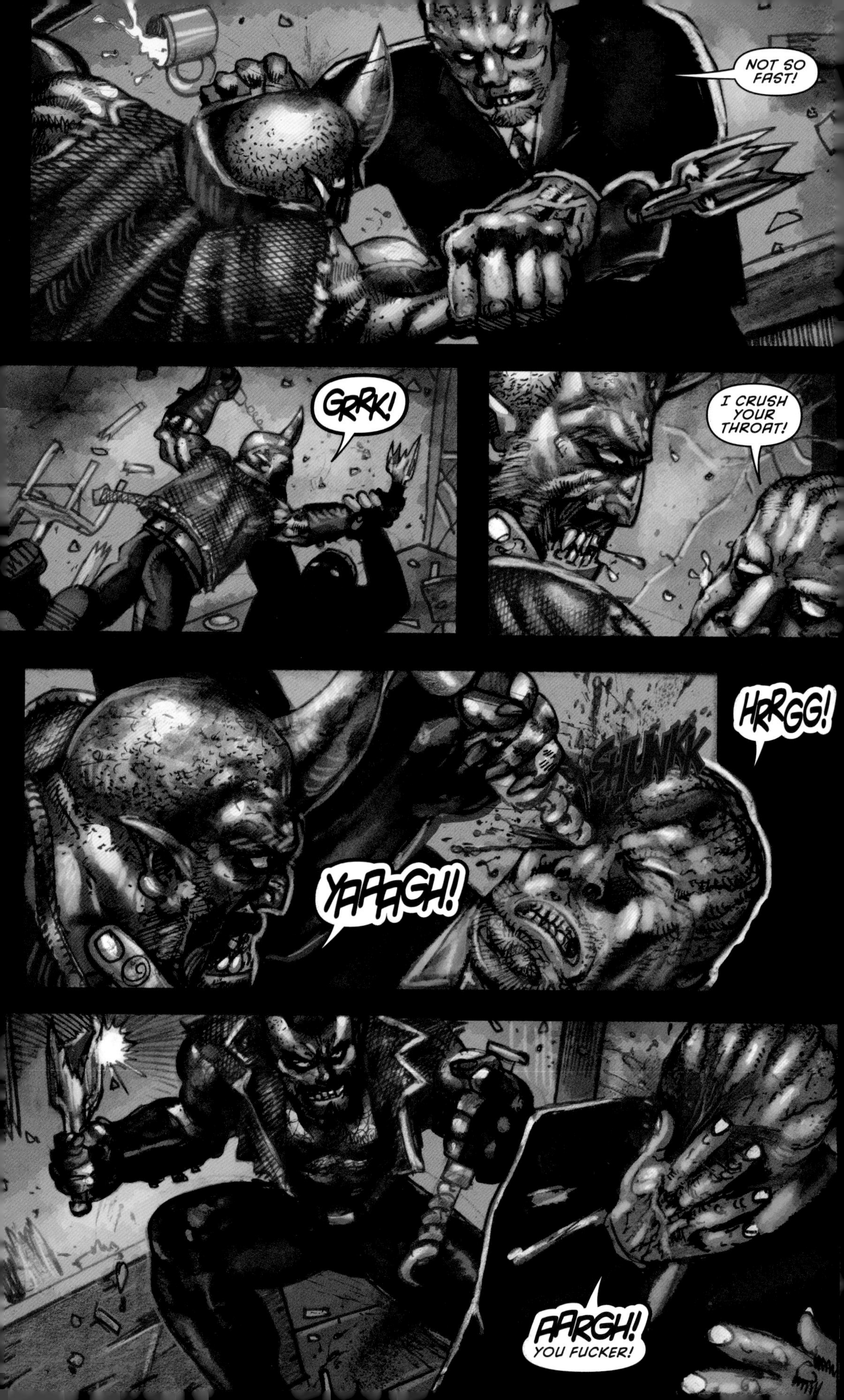
NOT SO FAST!
GRRK!
I CRUSH YOUR THROAT!
SHUNKK
HRRGG!
YAAAGH!
AARGH! YOU FUCKER!

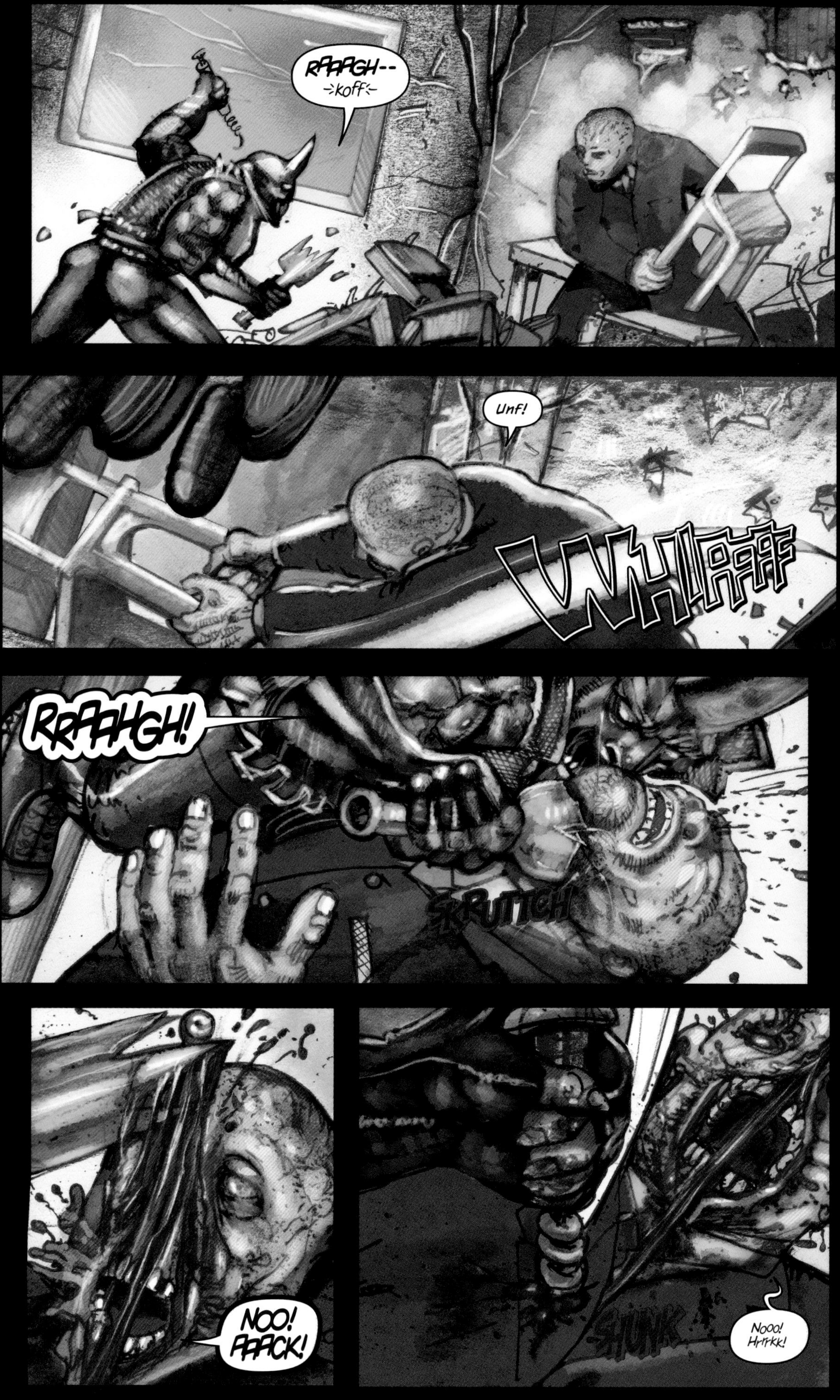
RAAAGH--
koff
Unf!
RRAAAGH!
SKRUTTCH
NOO! AAACK!
SHUNK
Nooo! Hrrrkk!

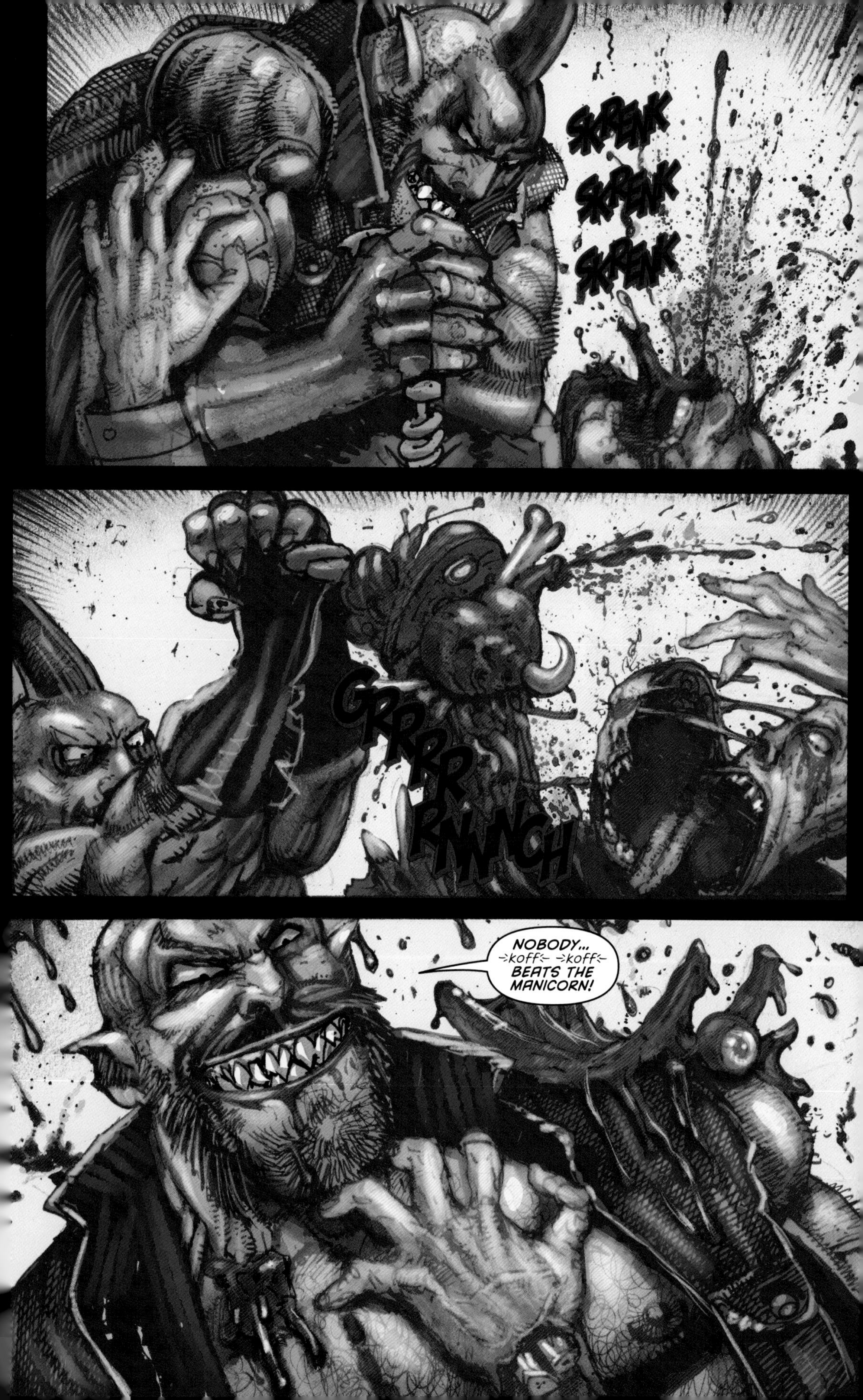
SKRENK
SKRENK
SKRENK
GRRRR
RNNNCH
NOBODY... koff koff BEATS THE MANICORN!

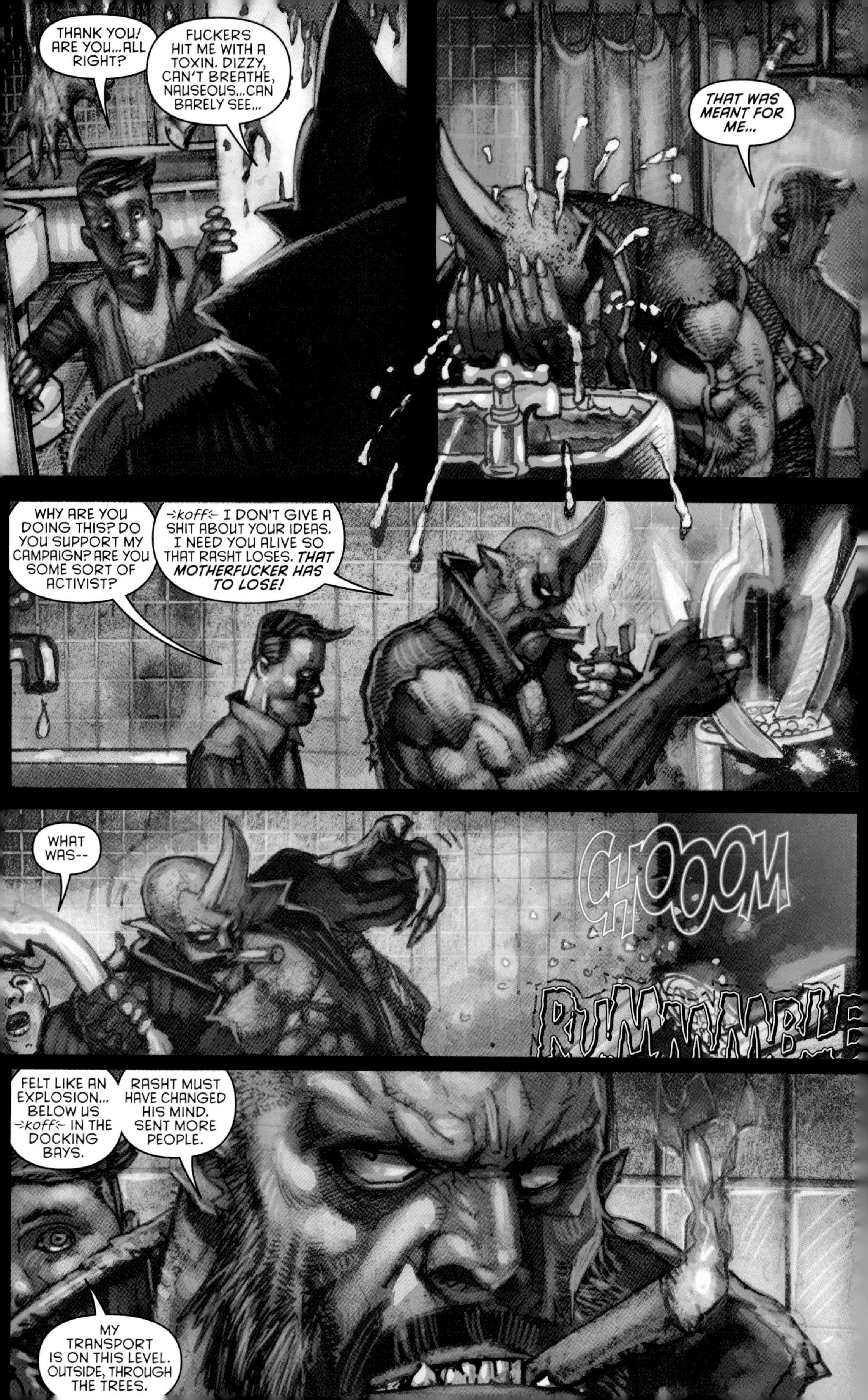
THANK YOU! ARE YOU...ALL RIGHT?
FUCKERS HIT ME WITH A TOXIN. DIZZY, CAN'T BREATHE, NAUSEOUS...CAN BARELY SEE...
THAT WAS MEANT FOR ME...
WHY ARE YOU DOING THIS? DO YOU SUPPORT MY CAMPAIGN? ARE YOU SOME SORT OF ACTIVIST?
=>koff<= I DON'T GIVE A SHIT ABOUT YOUR IDEAS. I NEED YOU ALIVE SO THAT RASHT LOSES. THAT MOTHERFUCKER HAS TO LOSE!
WHAT WAS--
CHOOOM
RUMMMMBLE
FELT LIKE AN EXPLOSION... BELOW US =>koff<= IN THE DOCKING BAYS.
RASHT MUST HAVE CHANGED HIS MIND. SENT MORE PEOPLE.
MY TRANSPORT IS ON THIS LEVEL. OUTSIDE, THROUGH THE TREES.

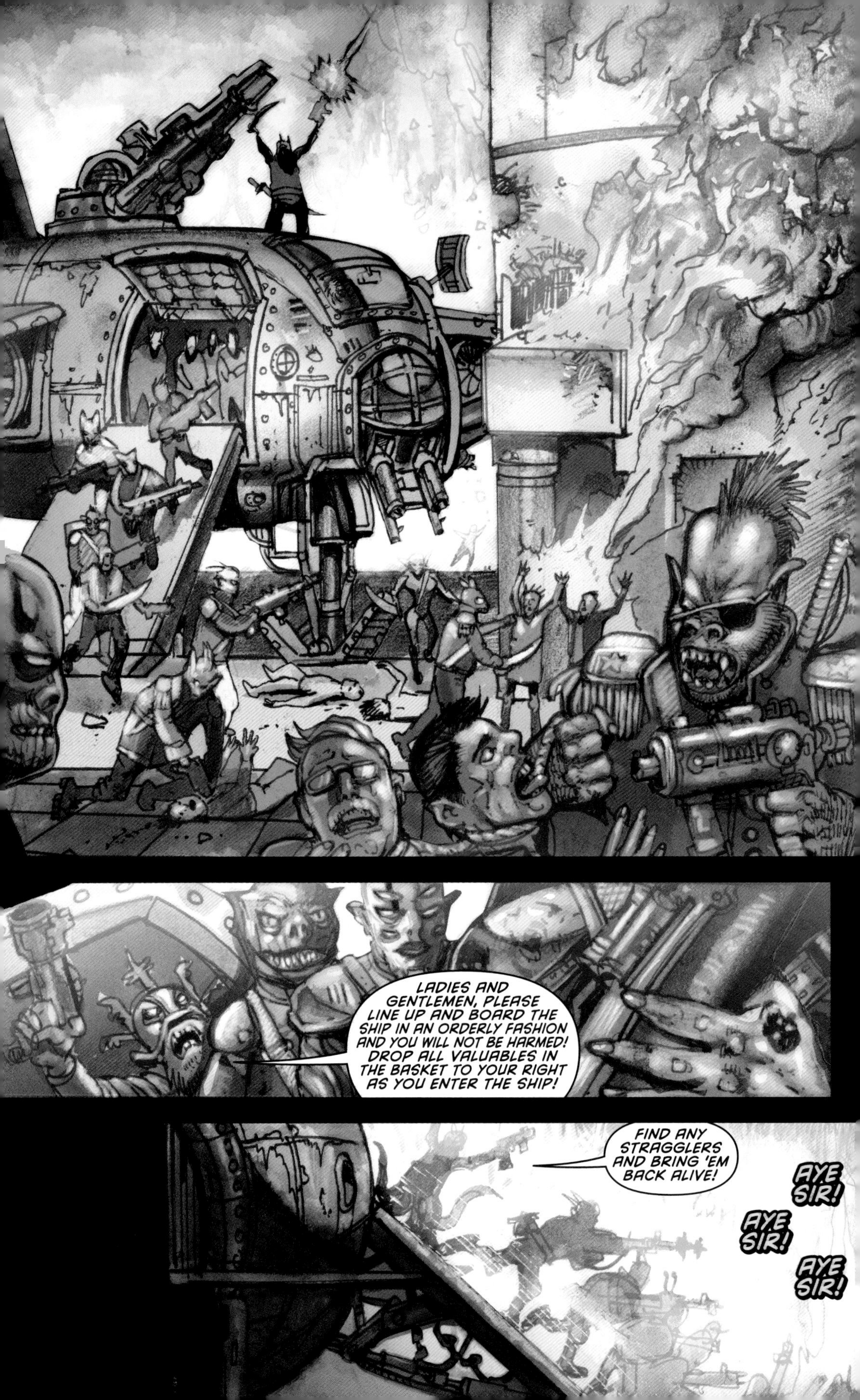
LADIES AND GENTLEMEN, PLEASE LINE UP AND BOARD THE SHIP IN AN ORDERLY FASHION AND YOU WILL NOT BE HARMED! DROP ALL VALUABLES IN THE BASKET TO YOUR RIGHT AS YOU ENTER THE SHIP!
FIND ANY STRAGGLERS AND BRING 'EM BACK ALIVE!
AYE SIR!
AYE SIR!
AYE SIR!

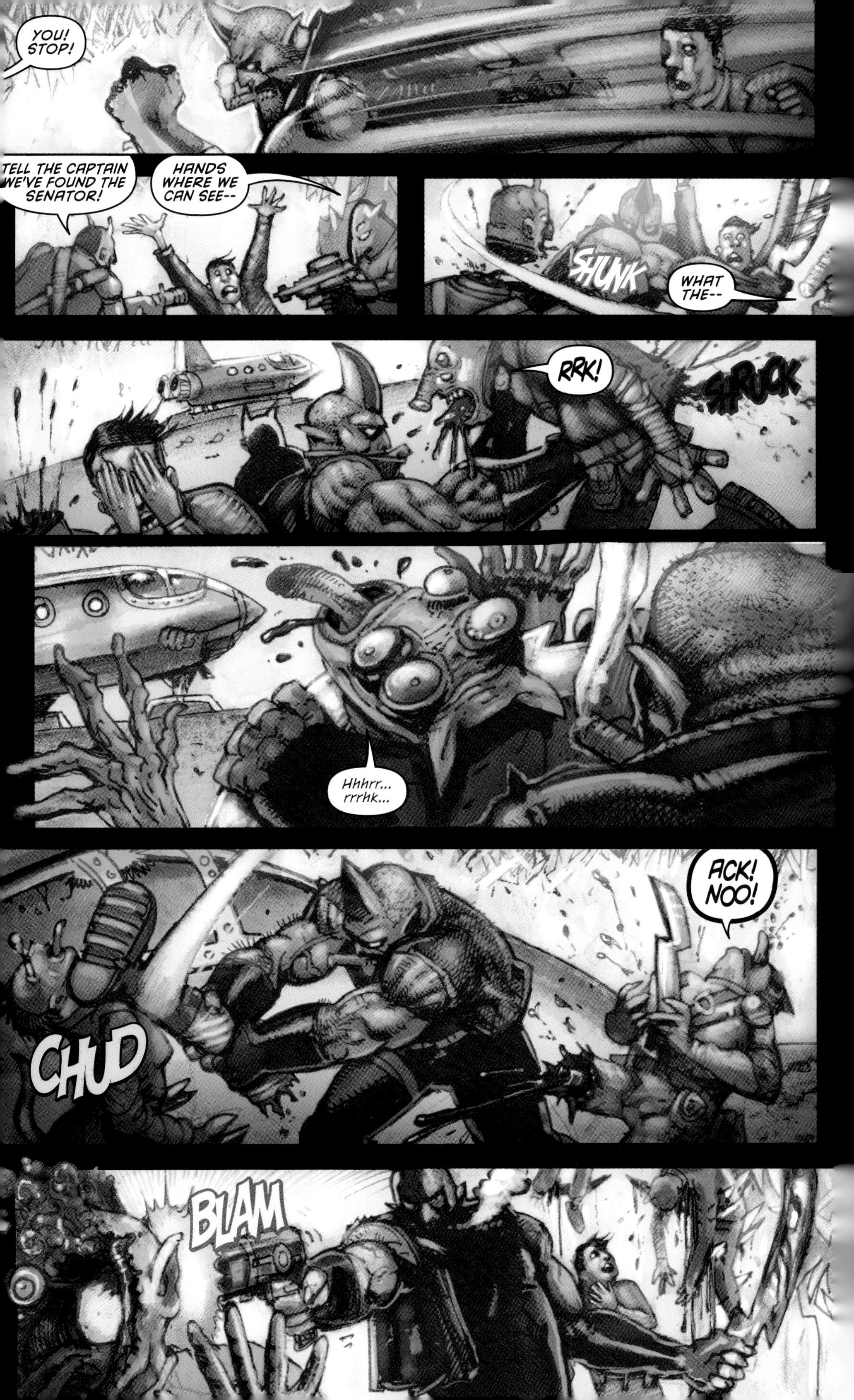
YOU! STOP!
TELL THE CAPTAIN WE'VE FOUND THE SENATOR!
HANDS WHERE WE CAN SEE--
SHUNK
WHAT THE--
RRK!
SHRUCK
Hhhrr... rrrhk...
ACK! NOO!
CHUD
BLAM

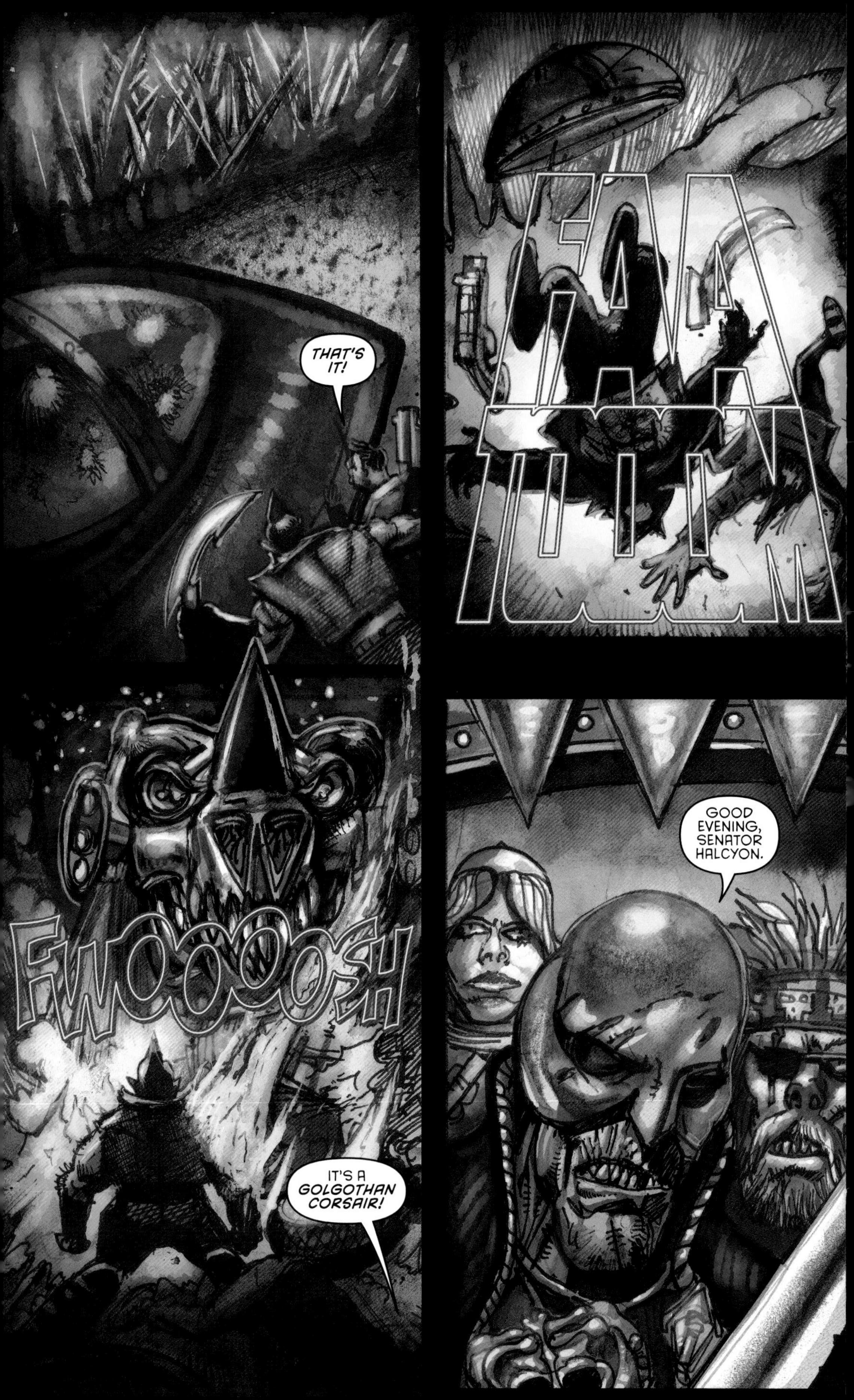
THAT'S IT!
FAAA
TOOOM
FWOOOOSH
IT'S A GOLGOTHAN CORSAIR!
GOOD EVENING, SENATOR HALCYON.

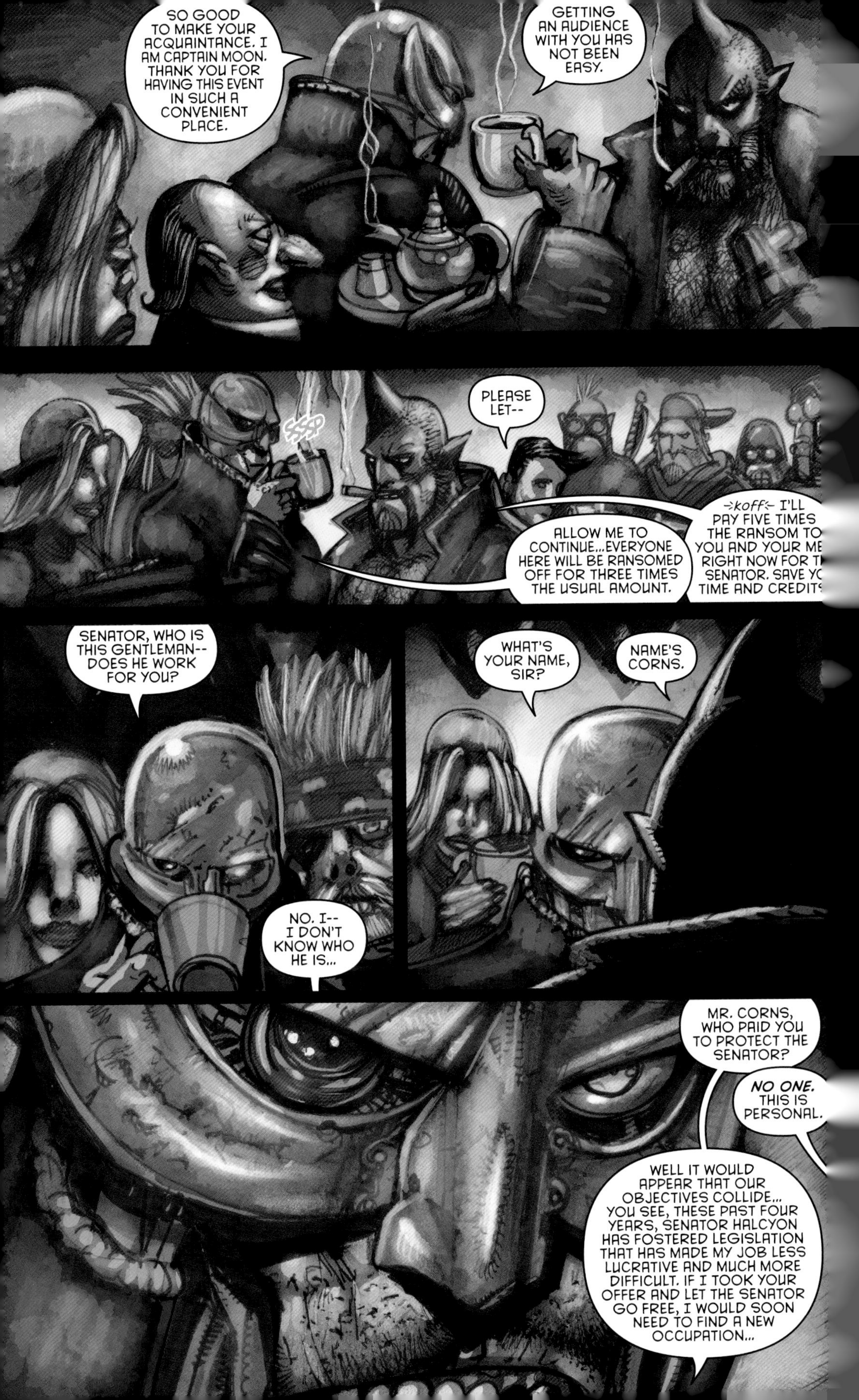
SO GOOD TO MAKE YOUR ACQUAINTANCE. I AM CAPTAIN MOON. THANK YOU FOR HAVING THIS EVENT IN SUCH A CONVENIENT PLACE.
GETTING AN AUDIENCE WITH YOU HAS NOT BEEN EASY.
SSSP
PLEASE LET--
ALLOW ME TO CONTINUE...EVERYONE HERE WILL BE RANSOMED OFF FOR THREE TIMES THE USUAL AMOUNT.
koff I'LL PAY FIVE TIMES THE RANSOM TO YOU AND YOUR ME RIGHT NOW FOR T SENATOR. SAVE YO TIME AND CREDITS
SENATOR, WHO IS THIS GENTLEMAN-- DOES HE WORK FOR YOU?
NO. I-- I DON'T KNOW WHO HE IS...
WHAT'S YOUR NAME, SIR?
NAME'S CORNS.
MR. CORNS, WHO PAID YOU TO PROTECT THE SENATOR?
NO ONE. THIS IS PERSONAL.
WELL IT WOULD APPEAR THAT OUR OBJECTIVES COLLIDE... YOU SEE, THESE PAST FOUR YEARS, SENATOR HALCYON HAS FOSTERED LEGISLATION THAT HAS MADE MY JOB LESS LUCRATIVE AND MUCH MORE DIFFICULT. IF I TOOK YOUR OFFER AND LET THE SENATOR GO FREE, I WOULD SOON NEED TO FIND A NEW OCCUPATION...

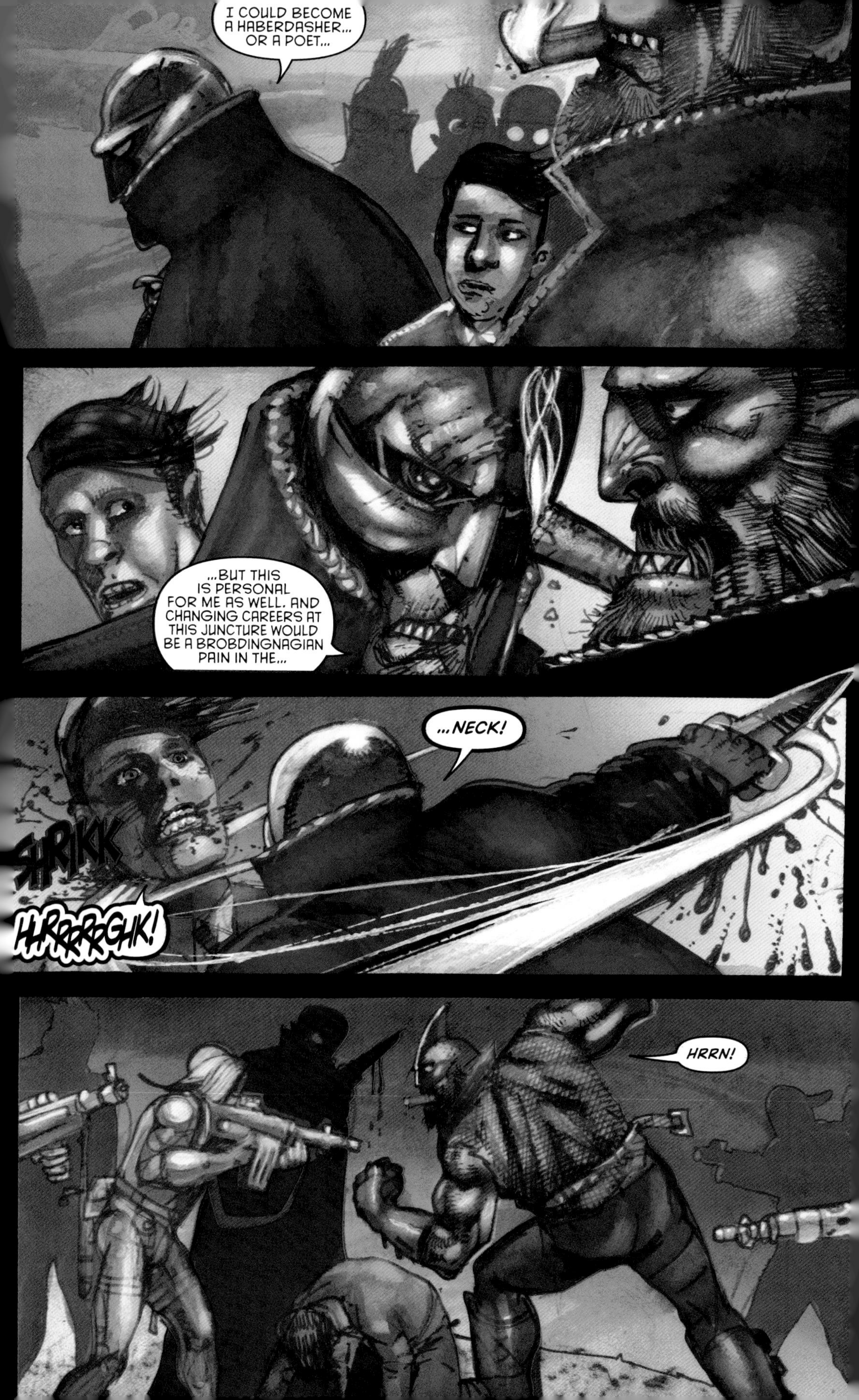
I COULD BECOME A HABERDASHER... OR A POET...
...BUT THIS IS PERSONAL FOR ME AS WELL. AND CHANGING CAREERS AT THIS JUNCTURE WOULD BE A BROBDINGNAGIAN PAIN IN THE...
...NECK!
SHRIKK
HURRRRRGHK!
HRRN!

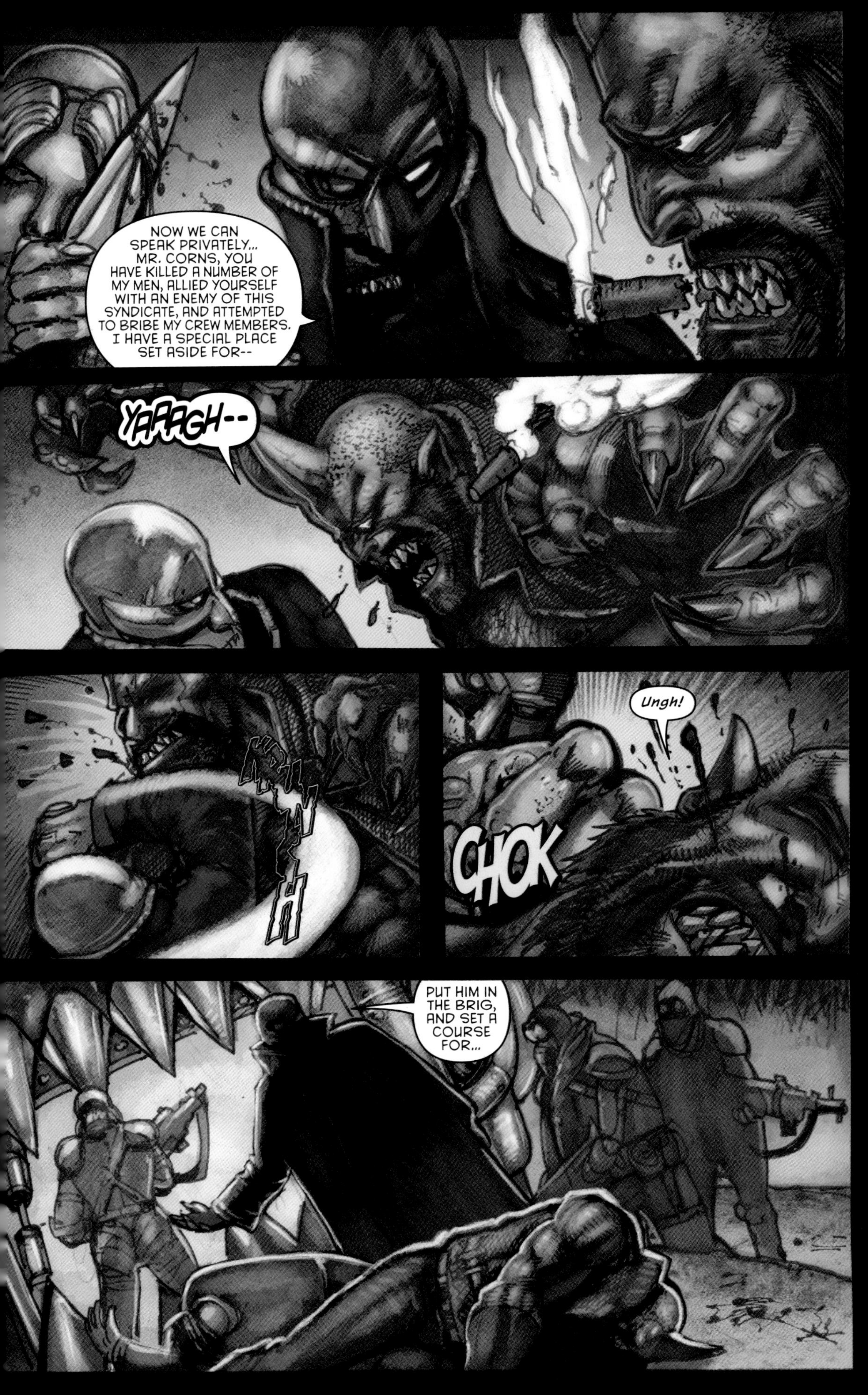
NOW WE CAN SPEAK PRIVATELY... MR. CORNS, YOU HAVE KILLED A NUMBER OF MY MEN, ALLIED YOURSELF WITH AN ENEMY OF THIS SYNDICATE, AND ATTEMPTED TO BRIBE MY CREW MEMBERS. I HAVE A SPECIAL PLACE SET ASIDE FOR--
YAAAGH--
Ungh!
CHOK
PUT HIM IN THE BRIG, AND SET A COURSE FOR...

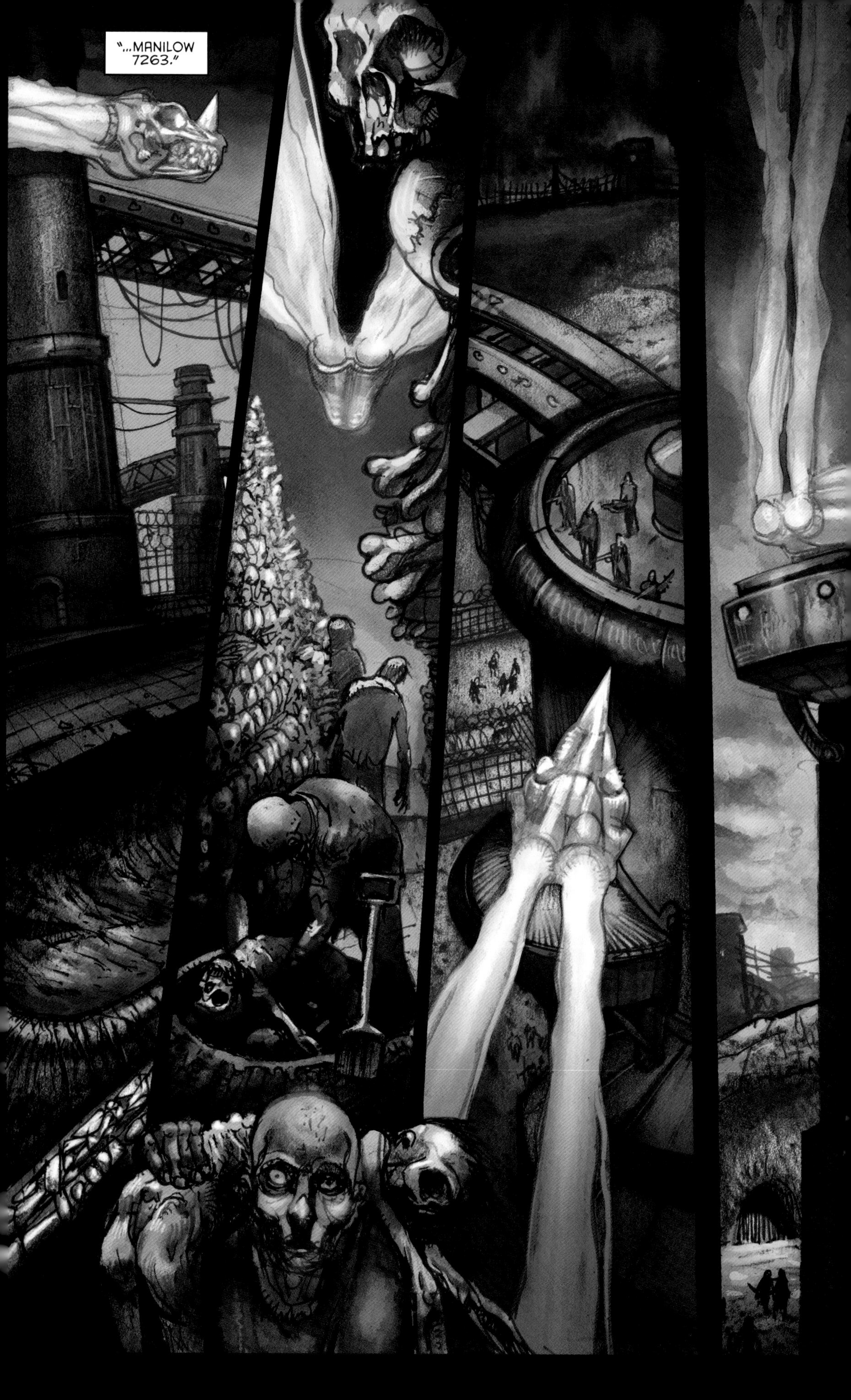
"...MANILOW 7263."

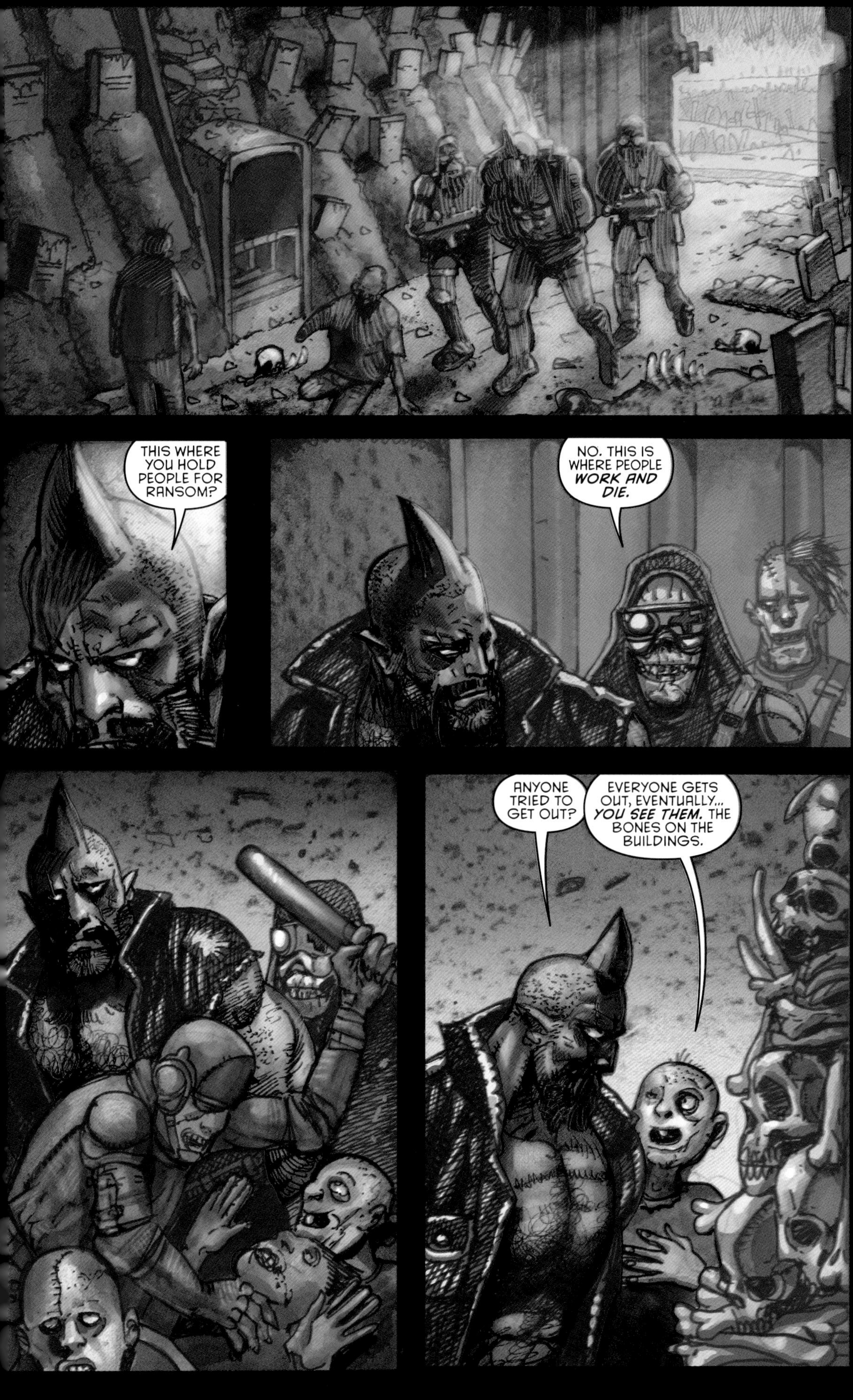
THIS WHERE YOU HOLD PEOPLE FOR RANSOM?
NO. THIS IS WHERE PEOPLE *WORK AND DIE.*
ANYONE TRIED TO GET OUT?
EVERYONE GETS OUT, EVENTUALLY... *YOU SEE THEM.* THE BONES ON THE BUILDINGS.

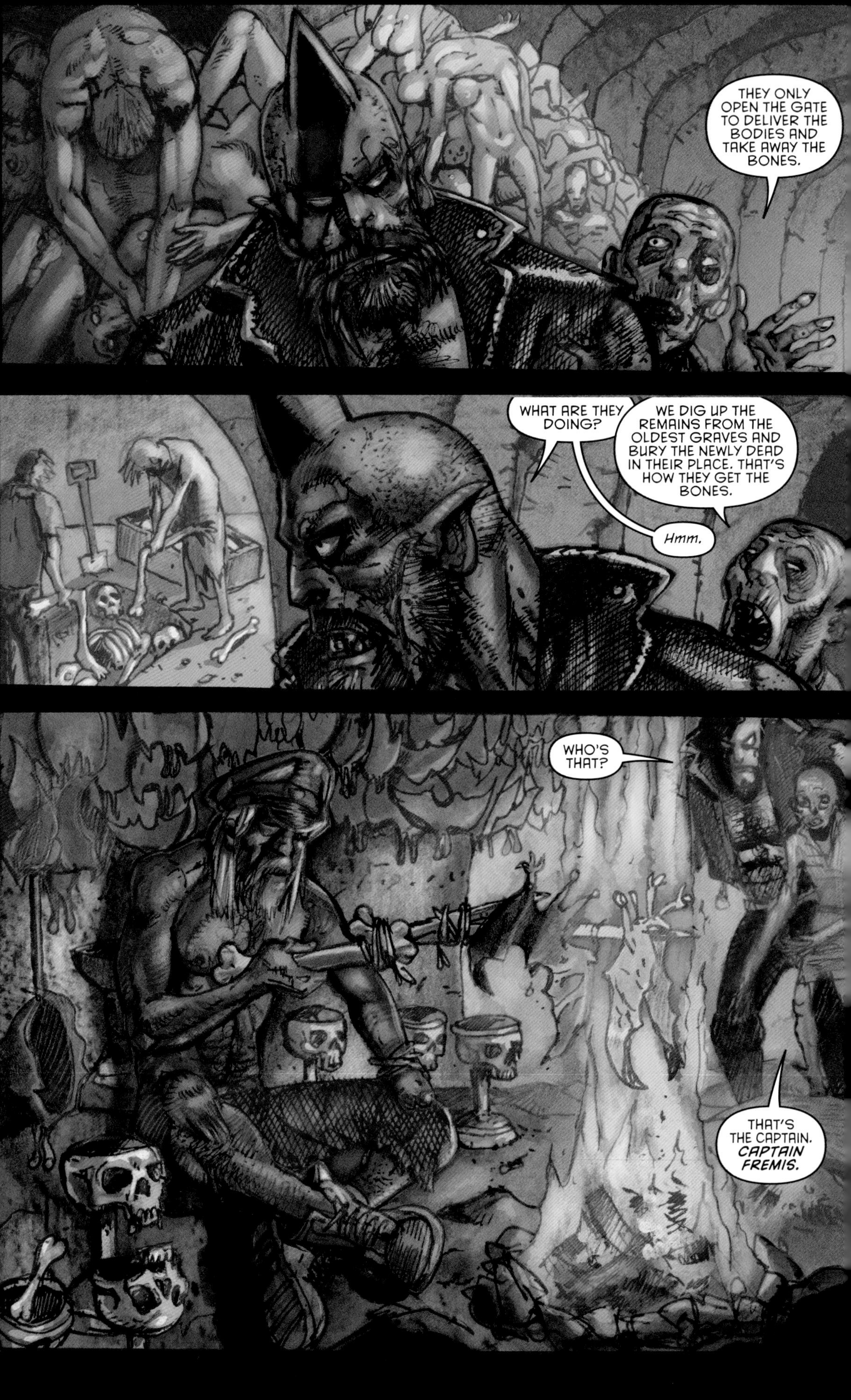
THEY ONLY OPEN THE GATE TO DELIVER THE BODIES AND TAKE AWAY THE BONES.
WHAT ARE THEY DOING?
WE DIG UP THE REMAINS FROM THE OLDEST GRAVES AND BURY THE NEWLY DEAD IN THEIR PLACE. THAT'S HOW THEY GET THE BONES.
Hmm.
WHO'S THAT?
THAT'S THE CAPTAIN. CAPTAIN FREMIS.

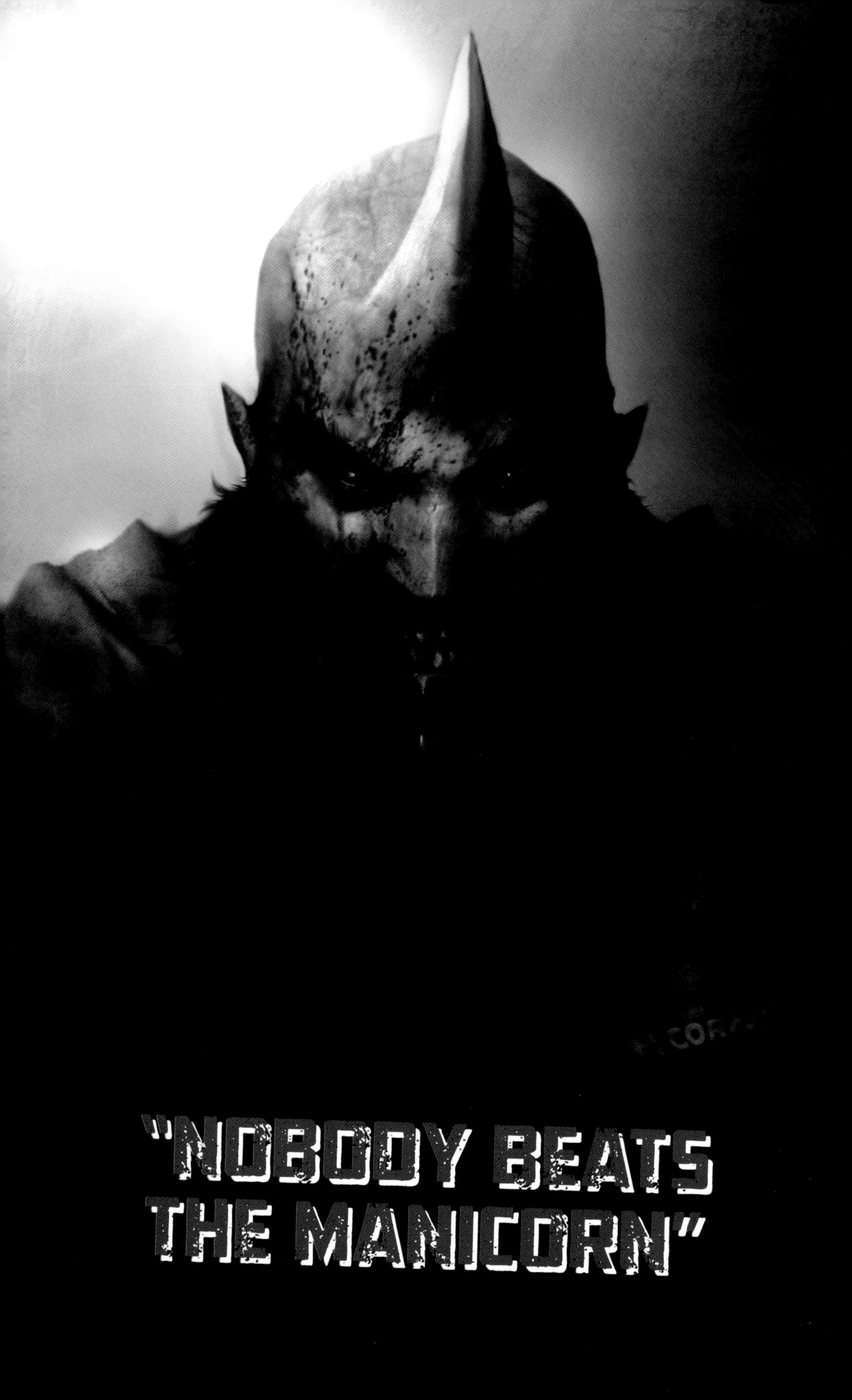
"NOBODY BEATS
THE MANICORN"

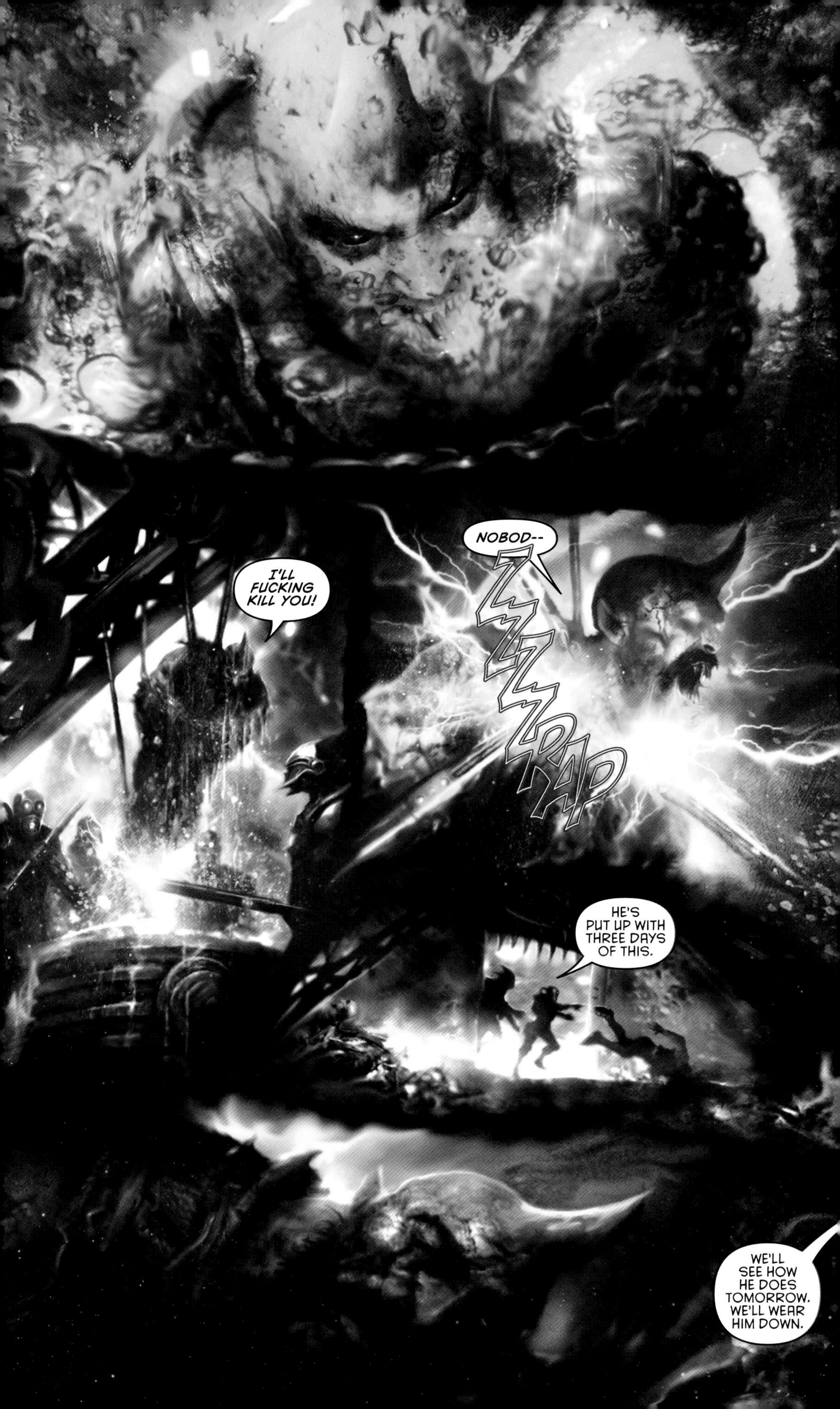
I'LL FUCKING KILL YOU!
NOBOD--
ZZZRAP
HE'S PUT UP WITH THREE DAYS OF THIS.
WE'LL SEE HOW HE DOES TOMORROW. WE'LL WEAR HIM DOWN.

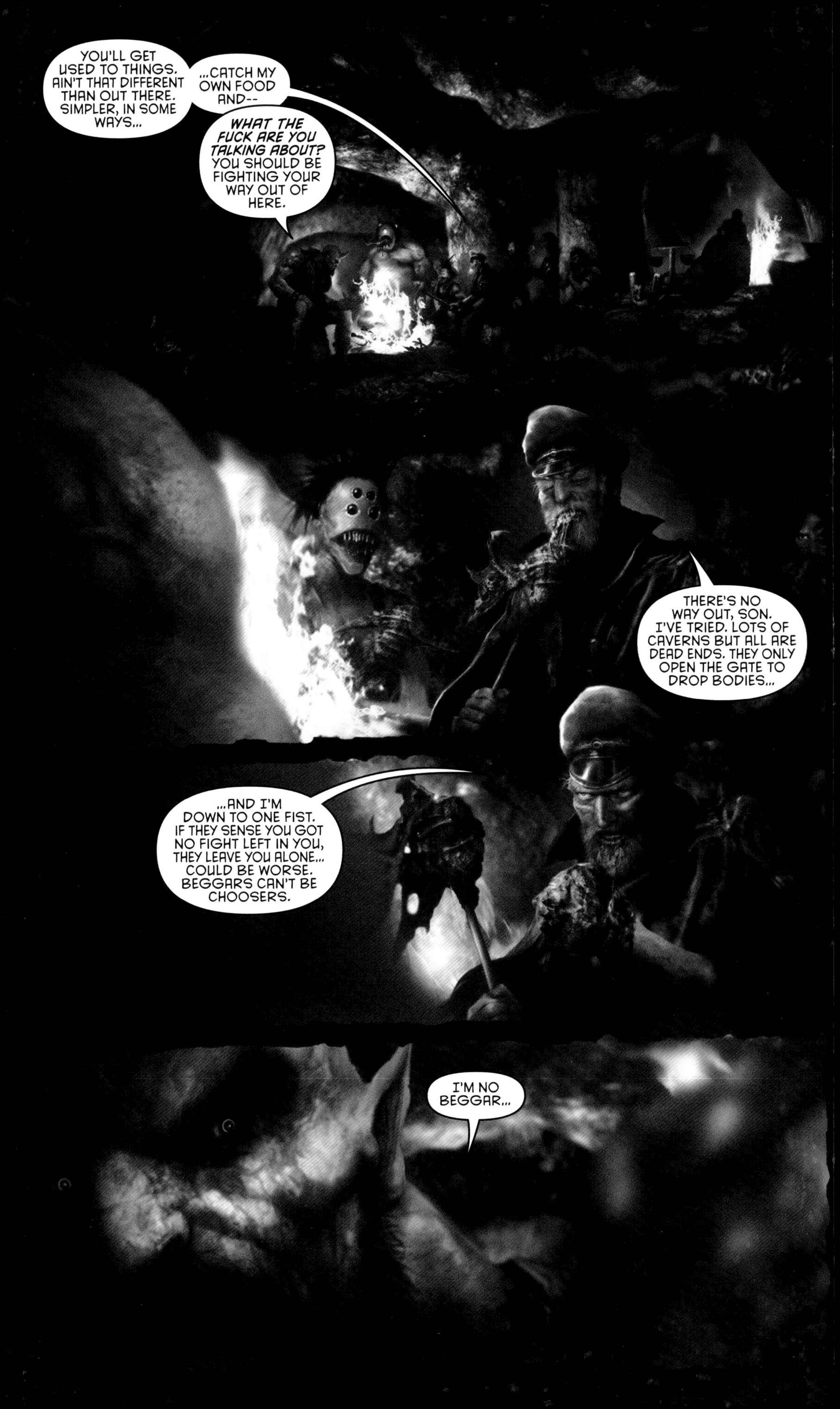
YOU'LL GET USED TO THINGS. AIN'T THAT DIFFERENT THAN OUT THERE. SIMPLER, IN SOME WAYS...
...CATCH MY OWN FOOD AND--
WHAT THE FUCK ARE YOU TALKING ABOUT? YOU SHOULD BE FIGHTING YOUR WAY OUT OF HERE.
THERE'S NO WAY OUT, SON. I'VE TRIED. LOTS OF CAVERNS BUT ALL ARE DEAD ENDS. THEY ONLY OPEN THE GATE TO DROP BODIES...
...AND I'M DOWN TO ONE FIST. IF THEY SENSE YOU GOT NO FIGHT LEFT IN YOU, THEY LEAVE YOU ALONE... COULD BE WORSE. BEGGARS CAN'T BE CHOOSERS.
I'M NO BEGGAR...

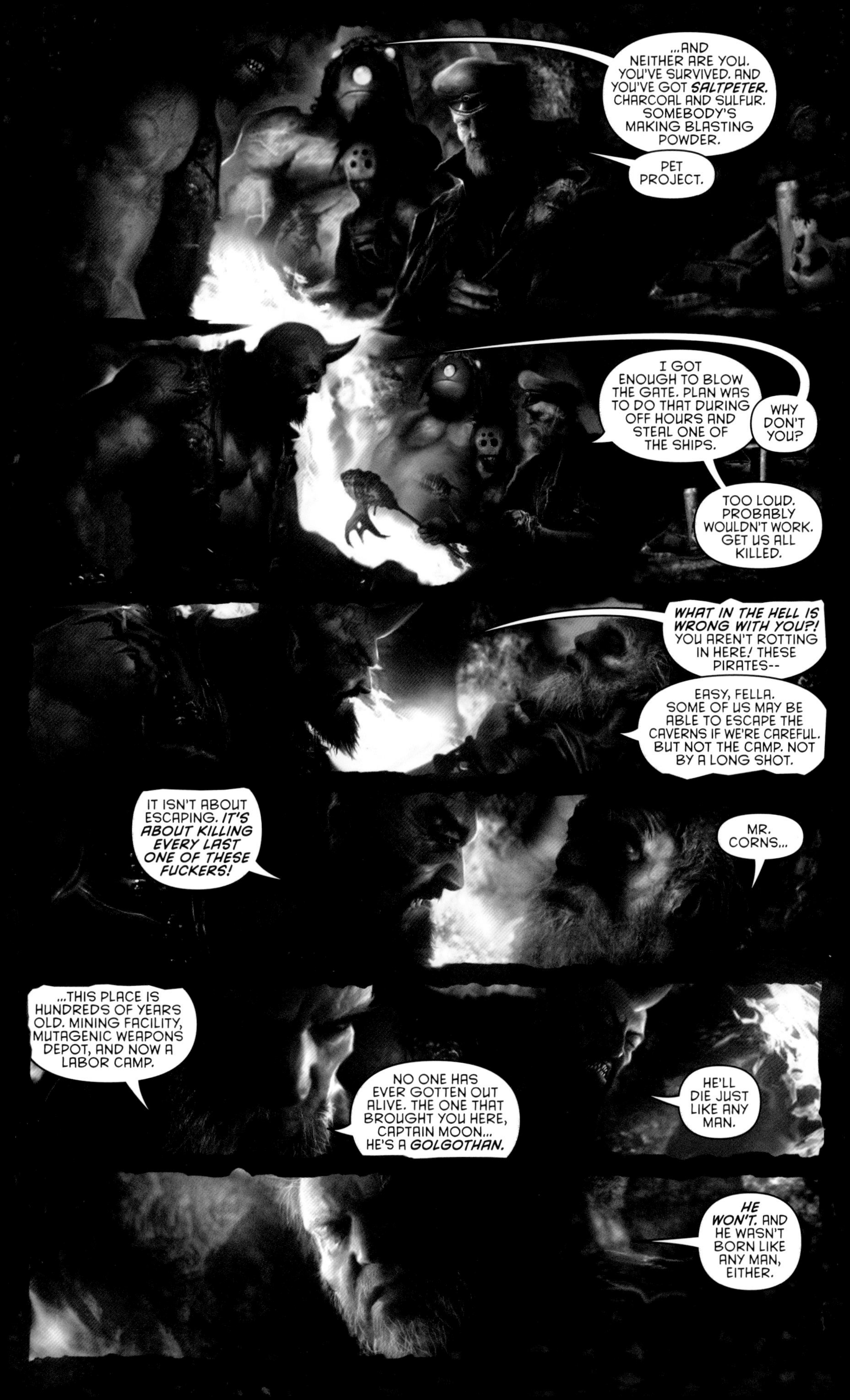
...AND NEITHER ARE YOU. YOU'VE SURVIVED. AND YOU'VE GOT *SALTPETER.* CHARCOAL AND SULFUR. SOMEBODY'S MAKING BLASTING POWDER.
PET PROJECT.
I GOT ENOUGH TO BLOW THE GATE. PLAN WAS TO DO THAT DURING OFF HOURS AND STEAL ONE OF THE SHIPS.
WHY DON'T YOU?
TOO LOUD. PROBABLY WOULDN'T WORK. GET US ALL KILLED.
WHAT IN THE HELL IS WRONG WITH YOU?! YOU AREN'T ROTTING IN HERE! THESE PIRATES--
EASY, FELLA. SOME OF US MAY BE ABLE TO ESCAPE THE CAVERNS IF WE'RE CAREFUL. BUT NOT THE CAMP. NOT BY A LONG SHOT.
IT ISN'T ABOUT ESCAPING. *IT'S ABOUT KILLING EVERY LAST ONE OF THESE FUCKERS!*
MR. CORNS...
...THIS PLACE IS HUNDREDS OF YEARS OLD. MINING FACILITY, MUTAGENIC WEAPONS DEPOT, AND NOW A LABOR CAMP.
NO ONE HAS EVER GOTTEN OUT ALIVE. THE ONE THAT BROUGHT YOU HERE, CAPTAIN MOON... HE'S A *GOLGOTHAN.*
HE'LL DIE JUST LIKE ANY MAN.
HE WON'T. AND HE WASN'T BORN LIKE ANY MAN, EITHER.

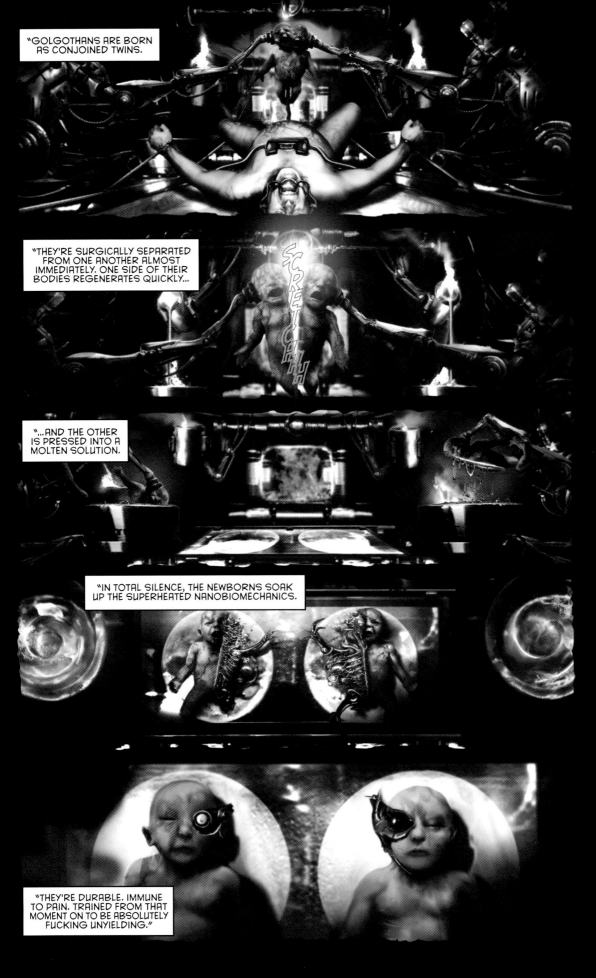

"GOLGOTHANS ARE BORN AS CONJOINED TWINS.

"THEY'RE SURGICALLY SEPARATED FROM ONE ANOTHER ALMOST IMMEDIATELY. ONE SIDE OF THEIR BODIES REGENERATES QUICKLY...

SCRETCHH

"...AND THE OTHER IS PRESSED INTO A MOLTEN SOLUTION.

"IN TOTAL SILENCE, THE NEWBORNS SOAK UP THE SUPERHEATED NANOBIOMECHANICS.

"THEY'RE DURABLE. IMMUNE TO PAIN. TRAINED FROM THAT MOMENT ON TO BE ABSOLUTELY FUCKING UNYIELDING."

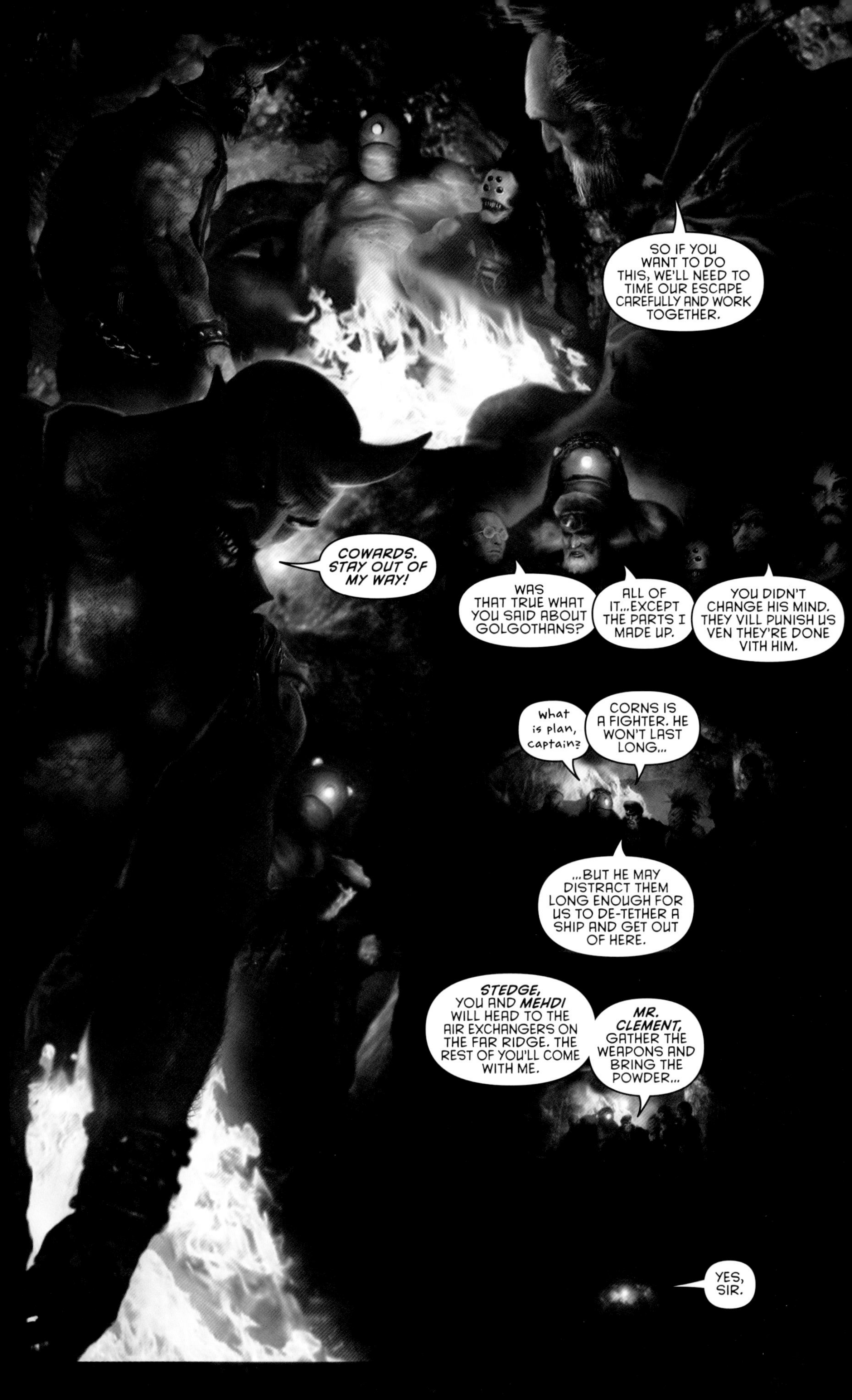
SO IF YOU WANT TO DO THIS, WE'LL NEED TO TIME OUR ESCAPE CAREFULLY AND WORK TOGETHER.
COWARDS. STAY OUT OF MY WAY!
WAS THAT TRUE WHAT YOU SAID ABOUT GOLGOTHANS?
ALL OF IT...EXCEPT THE PARTS I MADE UP.
YOU DIDN'T CHANGE HIS MIND. THEY VILL PUNISH US VEN THEY'RE DONE VITH HIM.
What is plan, captain?
CORNS IS A FIGHTER. HE WON'T LAST LONG...
...BUT HE MAY DISTRACT THEM LONG ENOUGH FOR US TO DE-TETHER A SHIP AND GET OUT OF HERE.
STEDGE, YOU AND MEHDI WILL HEAD TO THE AIR EXCHANGERS ON THE FAR RIDGE. THE REST OF YOU'LL COME WITH ME.
MR. CLEMENT, GATHER THE WEAPONS AND BRING THE POWDER...
YES, SIR.

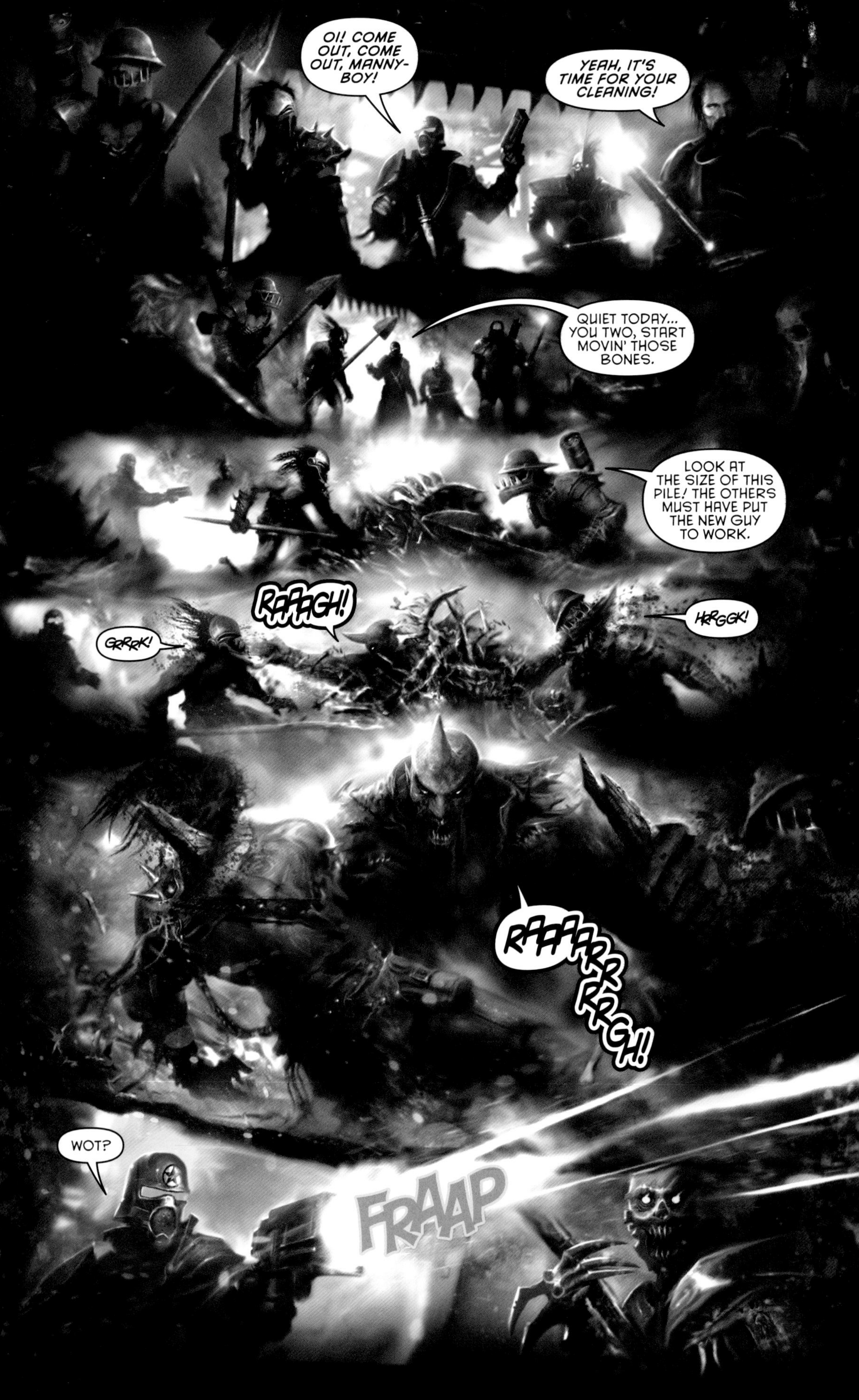
OI! COME OUT, COME OUT, MANNY-BOY!
YEAH, IT'S TIME FOR YOUR CLEANING!
QUIET TODAY... YOU TWO, START MOVIN' THOSE BONES.
LOOK AT THE SIZE OF THIS PILE! THE OTHERS MUST HAVE PUT THE NEW GUY TO WORK.
GRRRK!
RAAAGH!
HRRGGK!
RAAARRRRGH!
WOT?
FRAAP

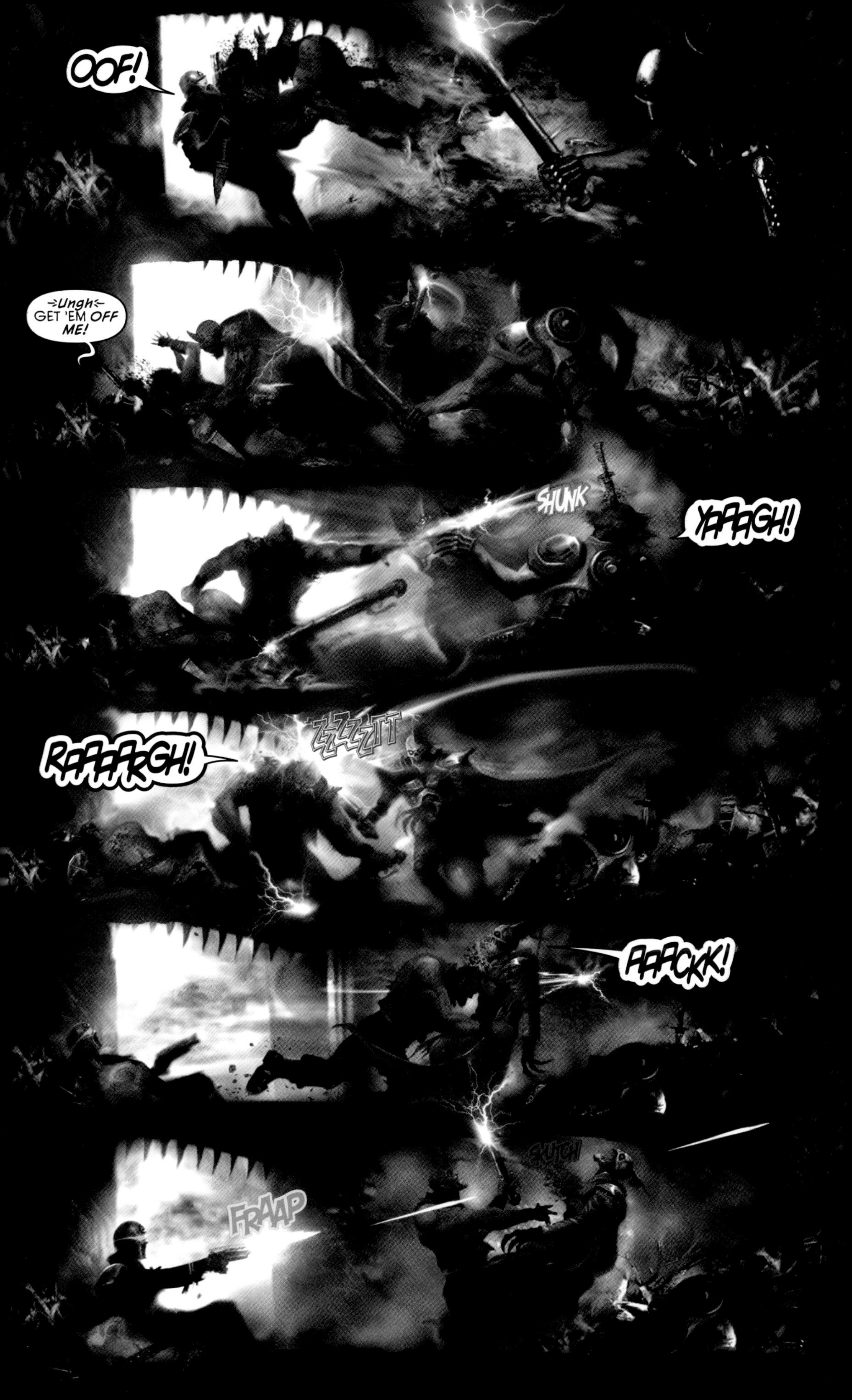
OOF!
Ungh GET 'EM OFF ME!
SHUNK
YAAAGH!
RAAAARGH!
ZZZZZTT
AAACKK!
SKUTCH
FRAAP

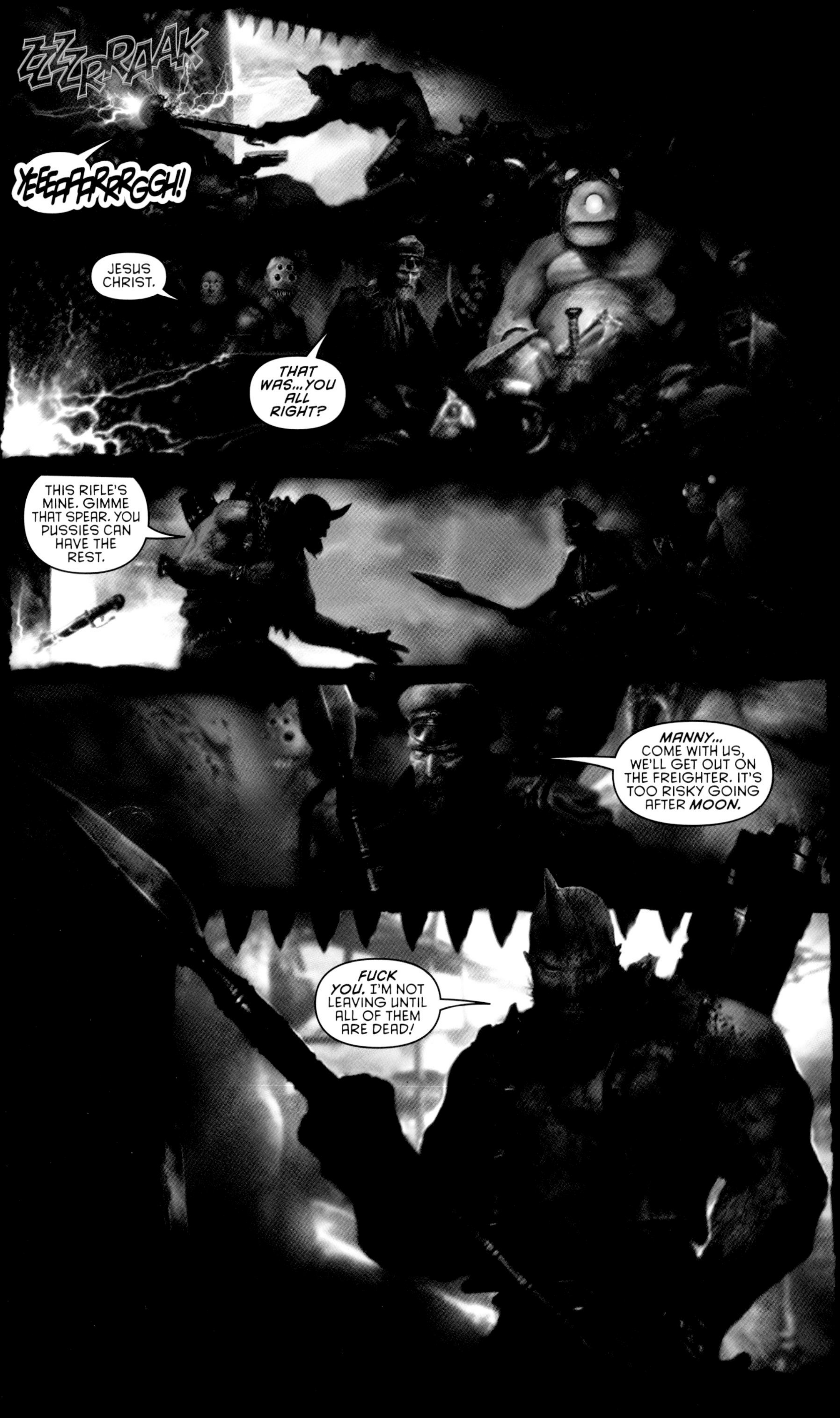
ZZZZRRAAK
YEEEFFRRRGGH!
JESUS CHRIST.
THAT WAS...YOU ALL RIGHT?
THIS RIFLE'S MINE. GIMME THAT SPEAR. YOU PUSSIES CAN HAVE THE REST.
MANNY... COME WITH US, WE'LL GET OUT ON THE FREIGHTER. IT'S TOO RISKY GOING AFTER MOON.
FUCK YOU. I'M NOT LEAVING UNTIL ALL OF THEM ARE DEAD!

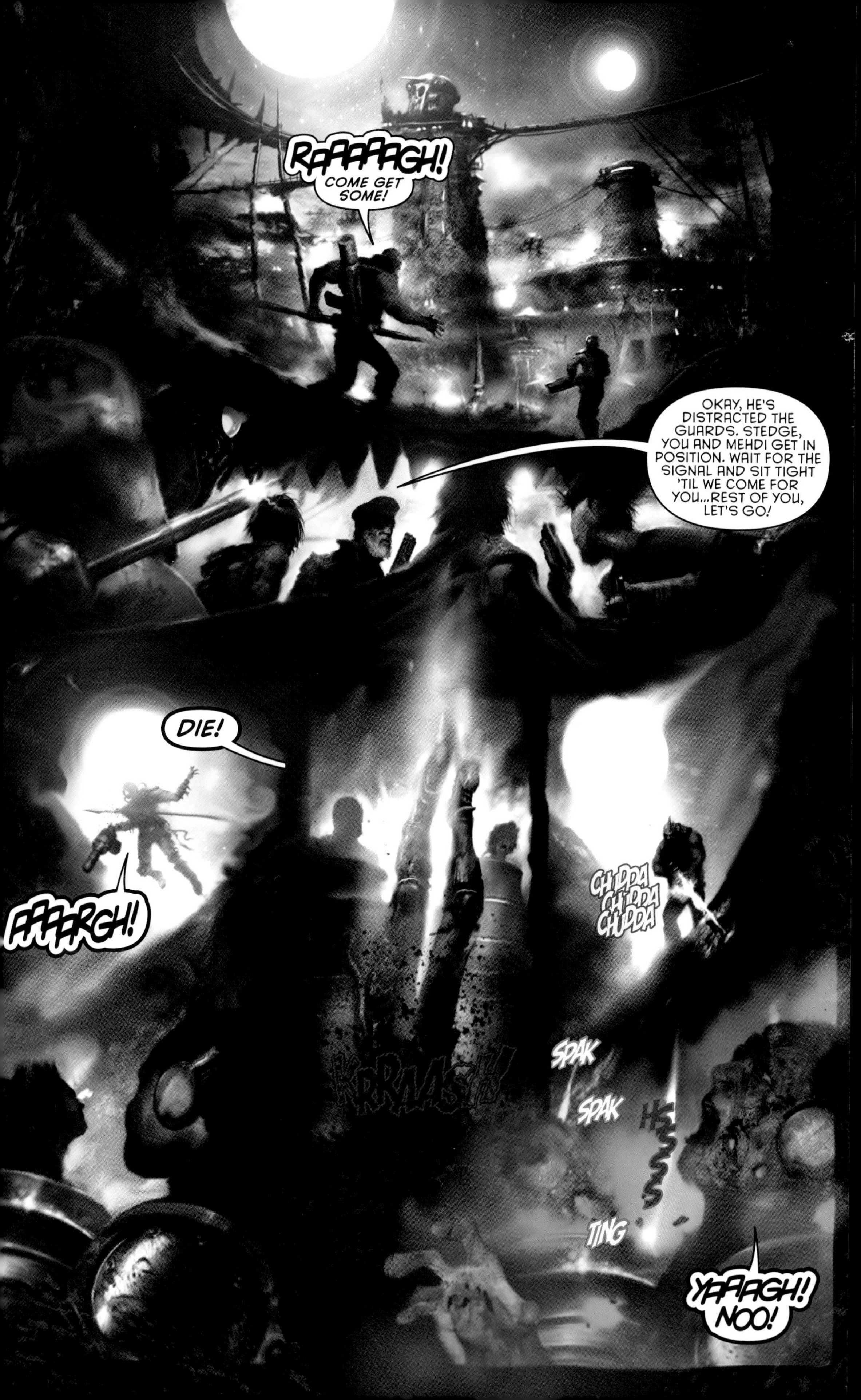
RAAAAAGH!
COME GET SOME!
OKAY, HE'S DISTRACTED THE GUARDS. STEDGE, YOU AND MEHDI GET IN POSITION. WAIT FOR THE SIGNAL AND SIT TIGHT 'TIL WE COME FOR YOU...REST OF YOU, LET'S GO!
DIE!
AAAARGH!
CHUDDA CHUDDA CHUDDA
KRRAAASH!!
SPAK
SPAK
HSSSSS
TING
YAAAGH! NOO!

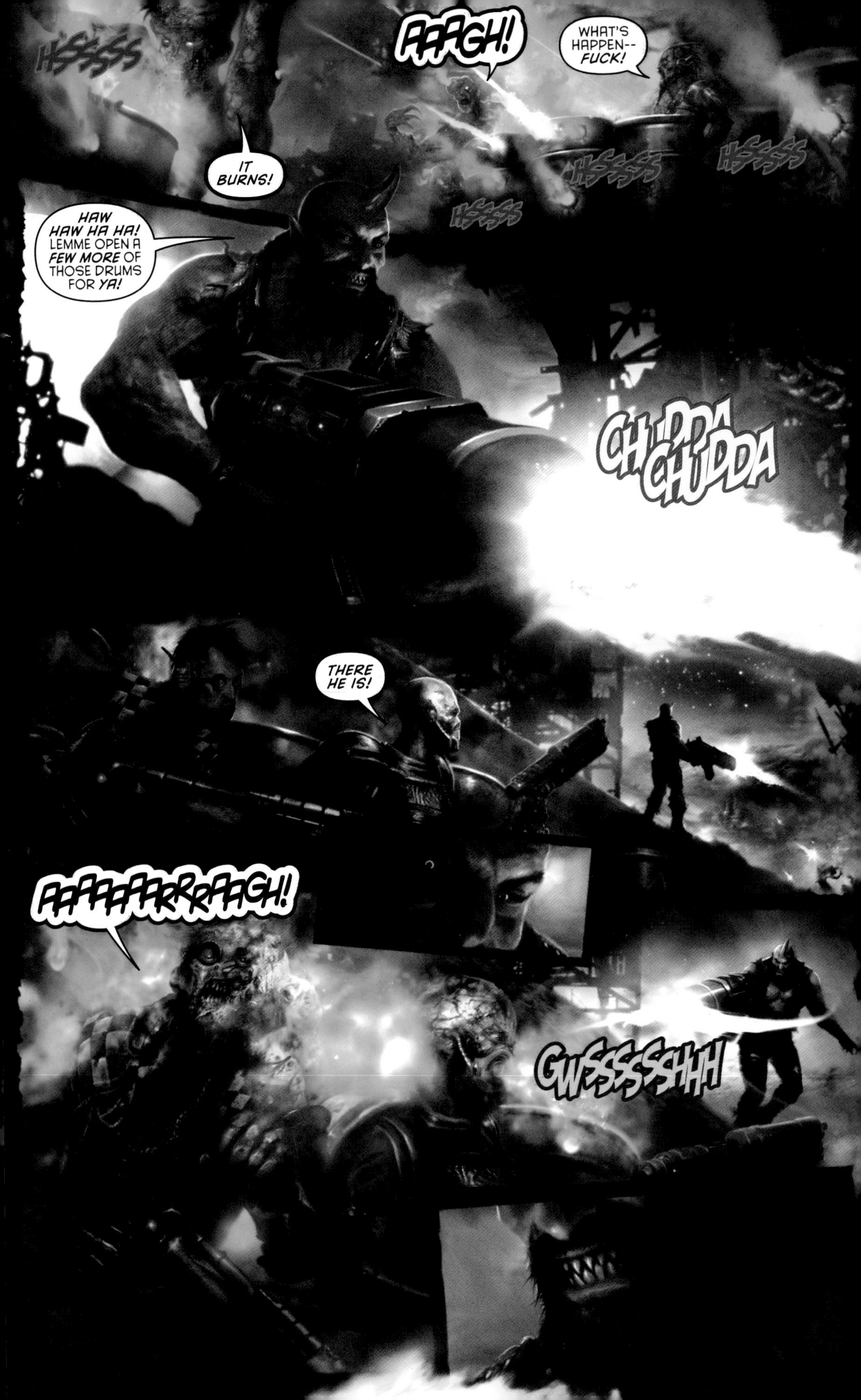
HSSSSSS
AAAGH!
WHAT'S HAPPEN-- FUCK!
IT BURNS!
HSSSSS
HSSSSS
HSSSS
HAW HAW HA HA! LEMME OPEN A FEW MORE OF THOSE DRUMS FOR YA!
CHUDDA CHUDDA
THERE HE IS!
AAAAAARRRAAGH!
GWSSSSSHHH

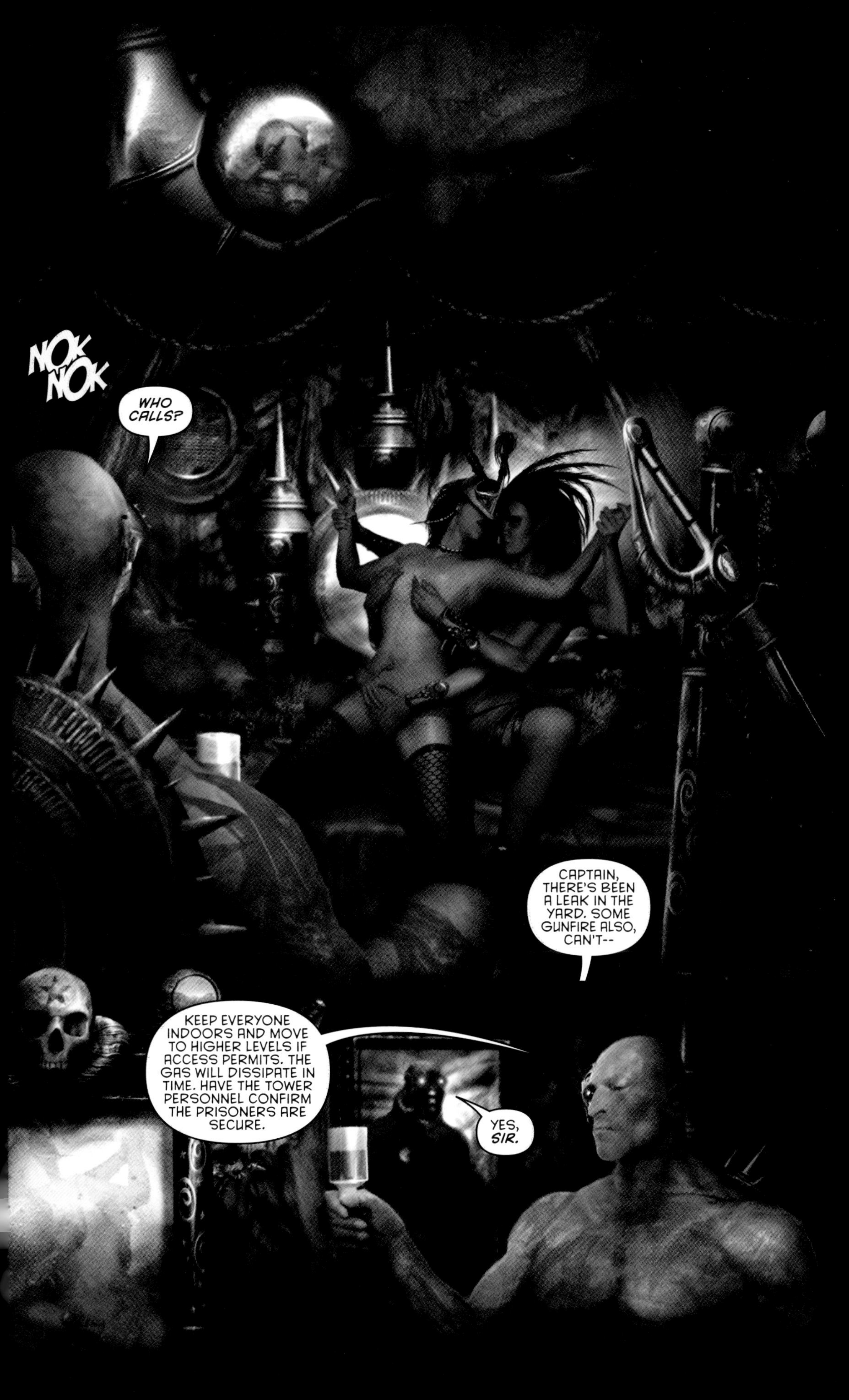
NOK NOK
WHO CALLS?
CAPTAIN, THERE'S BEEN A LEAK IN THE YARD. SOME GUNFIRE ALSO, CAN'T--
KEEP EVERYONE INDOORS AND MOVE TO HIGHER LEVELS IF ACCESS PERMITS. THE GAS WILL DISSIPATE IN TIME. HAVE THE TOWER PERSONNEL CONFIRM THE PRISONERS ARE SECURE.
YES, SIR.

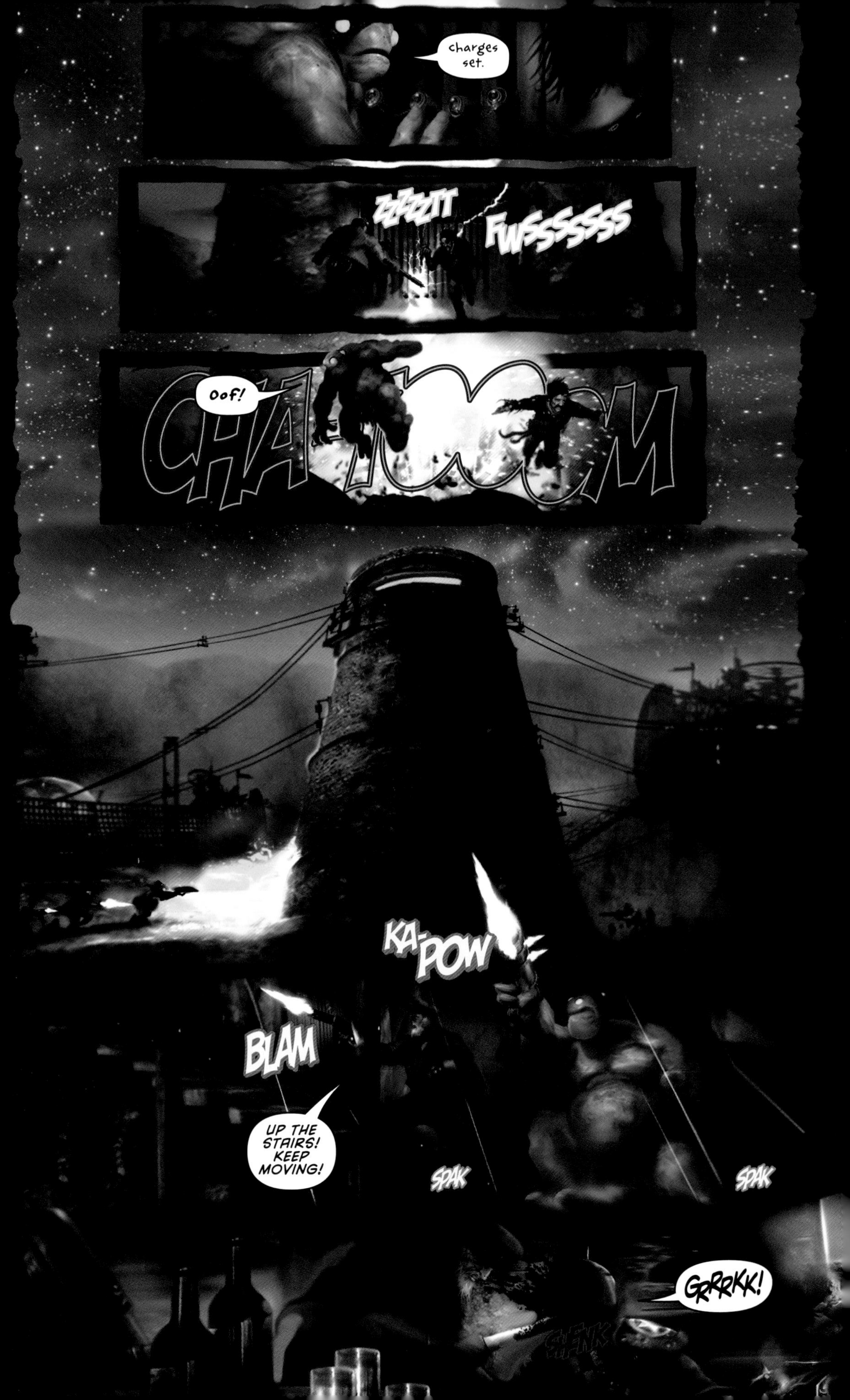

charges set.
ZZZZZITT
FWSSSSSS
Oof!
CHA-TOOOM
KA-POW
BLAM
UP THE STAIRS! KEEP MOVING!
SPAK
SPAK
GRRRKK!

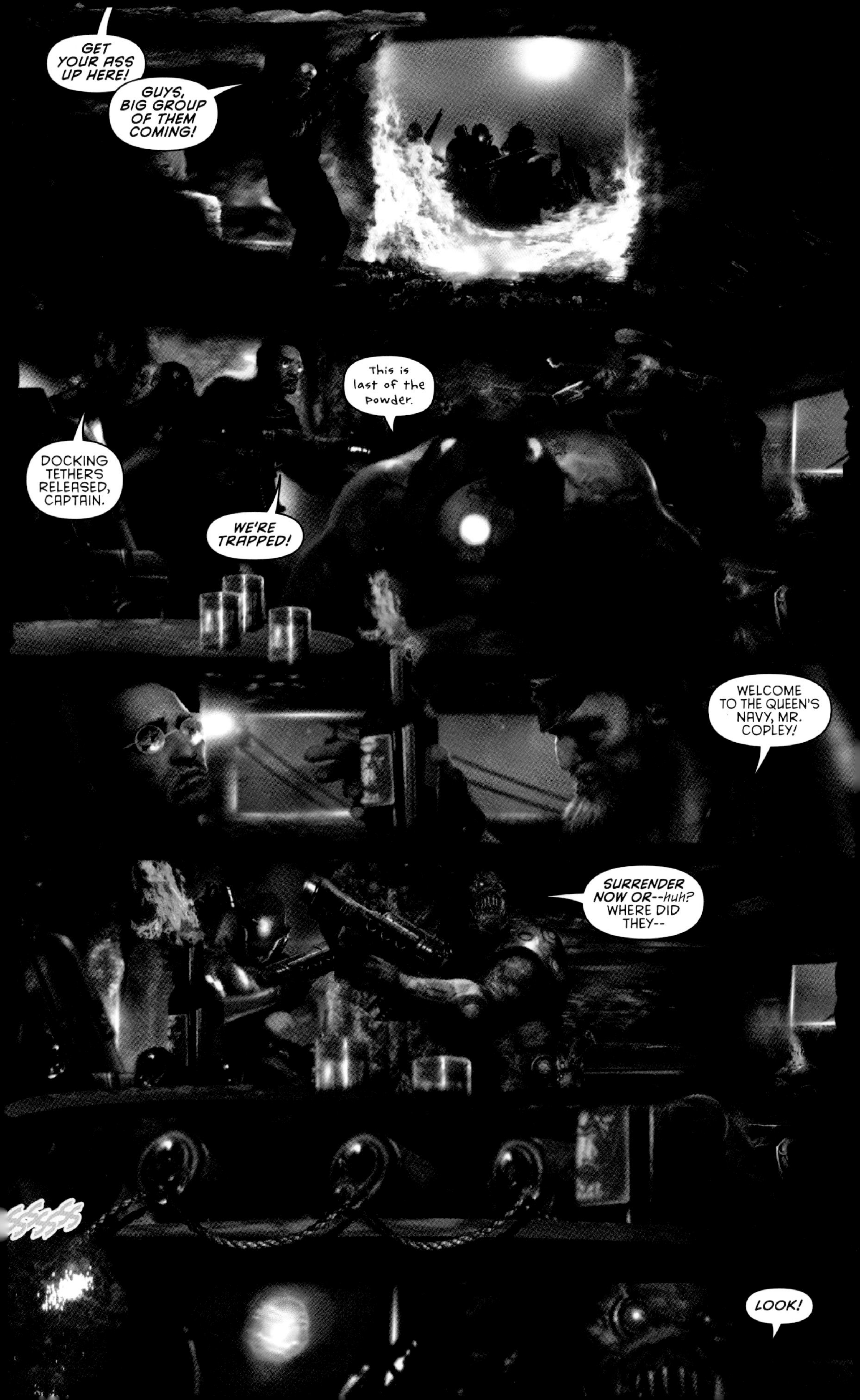
GET YOUR ASS UP HERE!
GUYS, BIG GROUP OF THEM COMING!
This is last of the powder.
DOCKING TETHERS RELEASED, CAPTAIN.
WE'RE TRAPPED!
WELCOME TO THE QUEEN'S NAVY, MR. COPLEY!
SURRENDER NOW OR--*huh?* WHERE DID THEY--
LOOK!

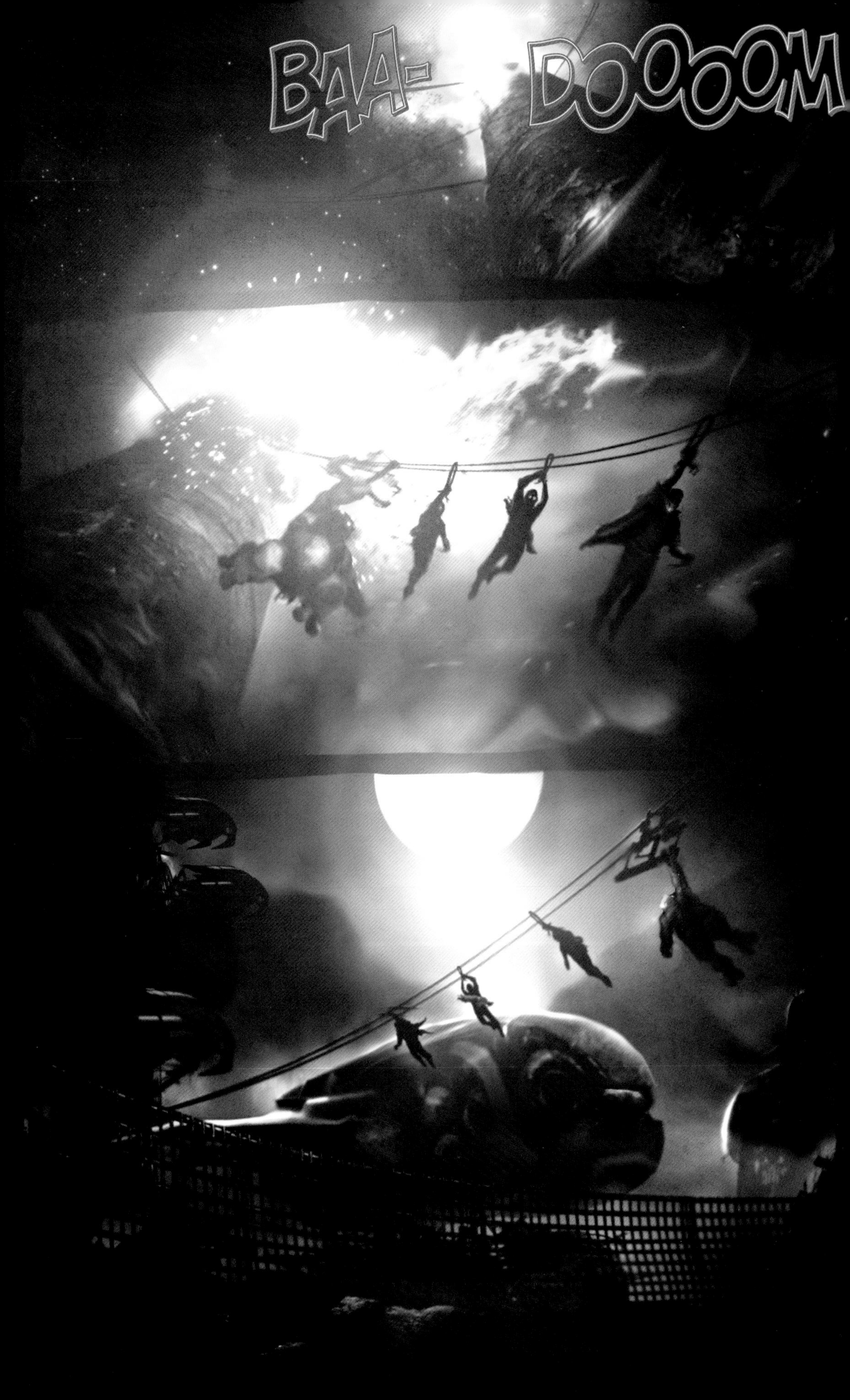
BAA-
DOOOOOM

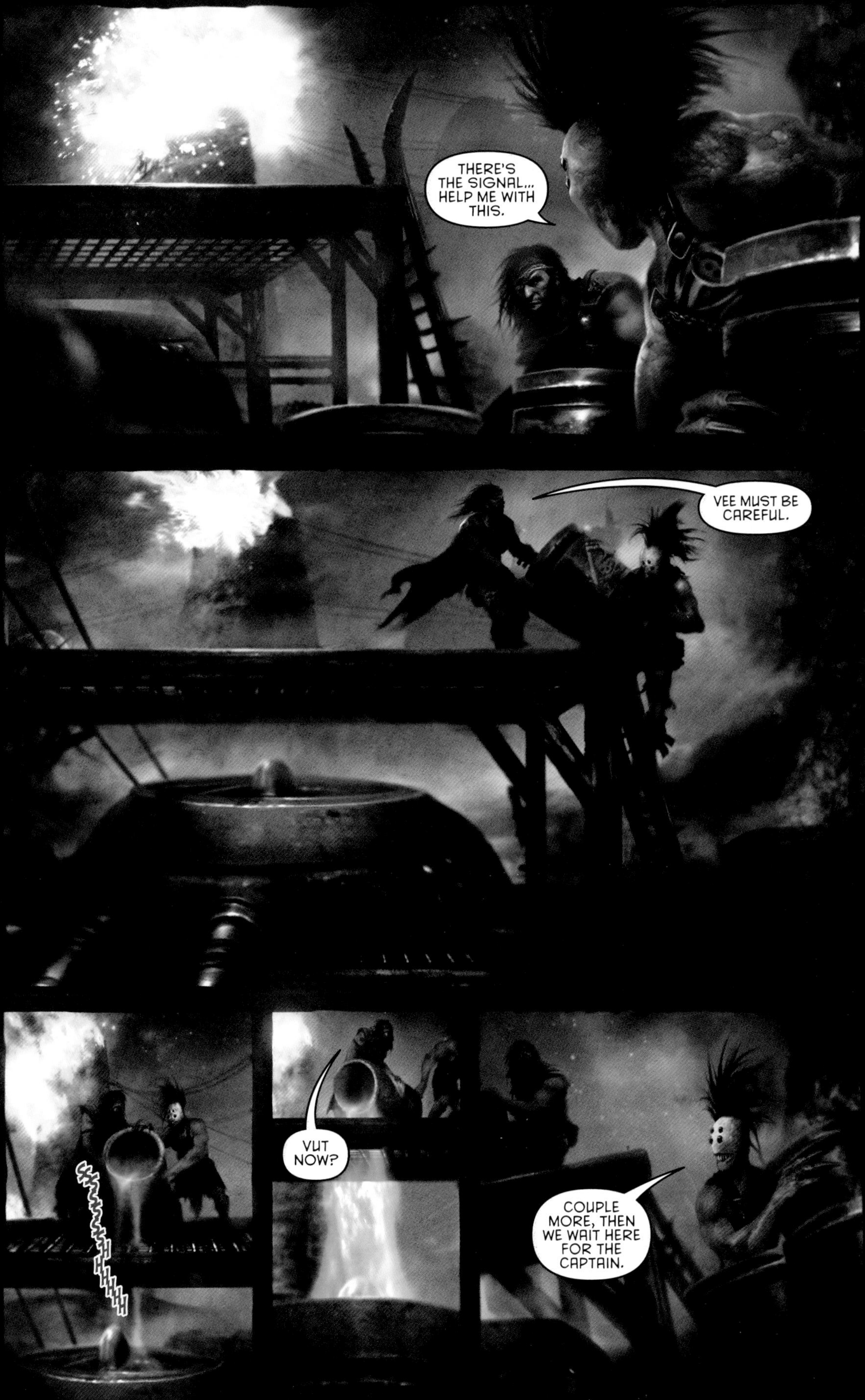
THERE'S THE SIGNAL... HELP ME WITH THIS.
VEE MUST BE CAREFUL.
VUT NOW?
COUPLE MORE, THEN WE WAIT HERE FOR THE CAPTAIN.

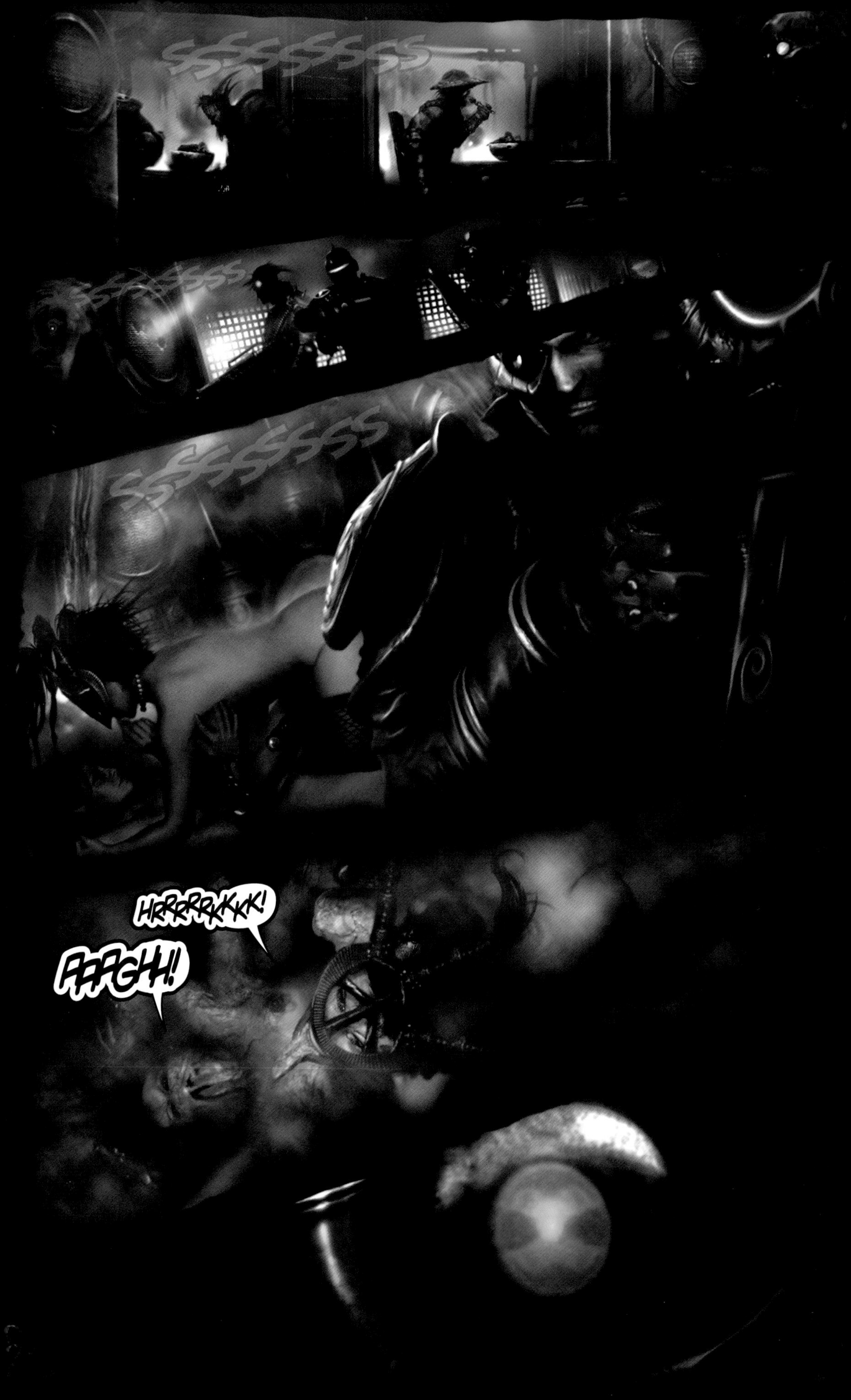
HRRRRRKKKK!
AAAGH!

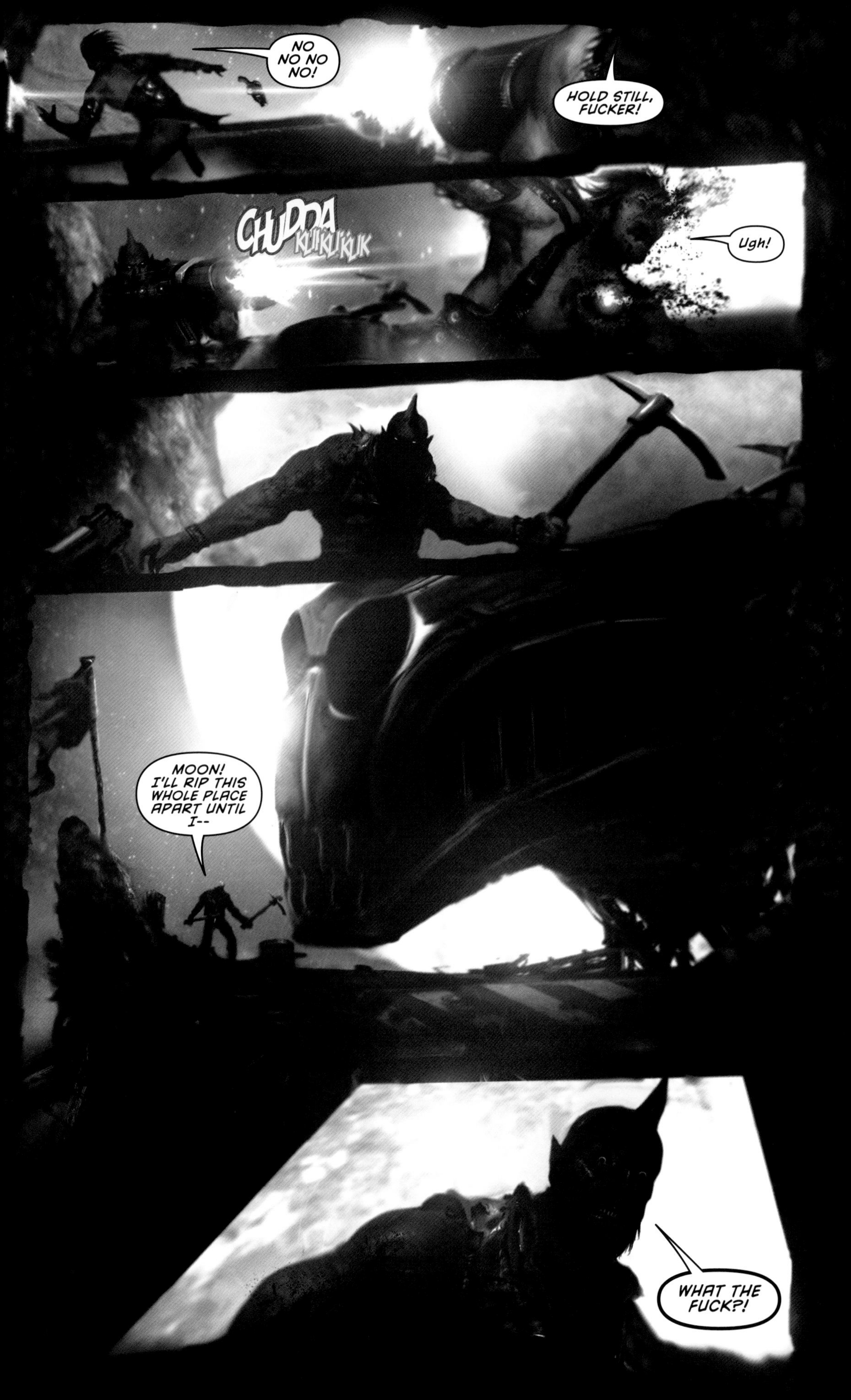
NO NO NO NO!
HOLD STILL, FUCKER!
CHUDDA KUKUKUK
Ugh!
MOON! I'LL RIP THIS WHOLE PLACE APART UNTIL I--
WHAT THE FUCK?!

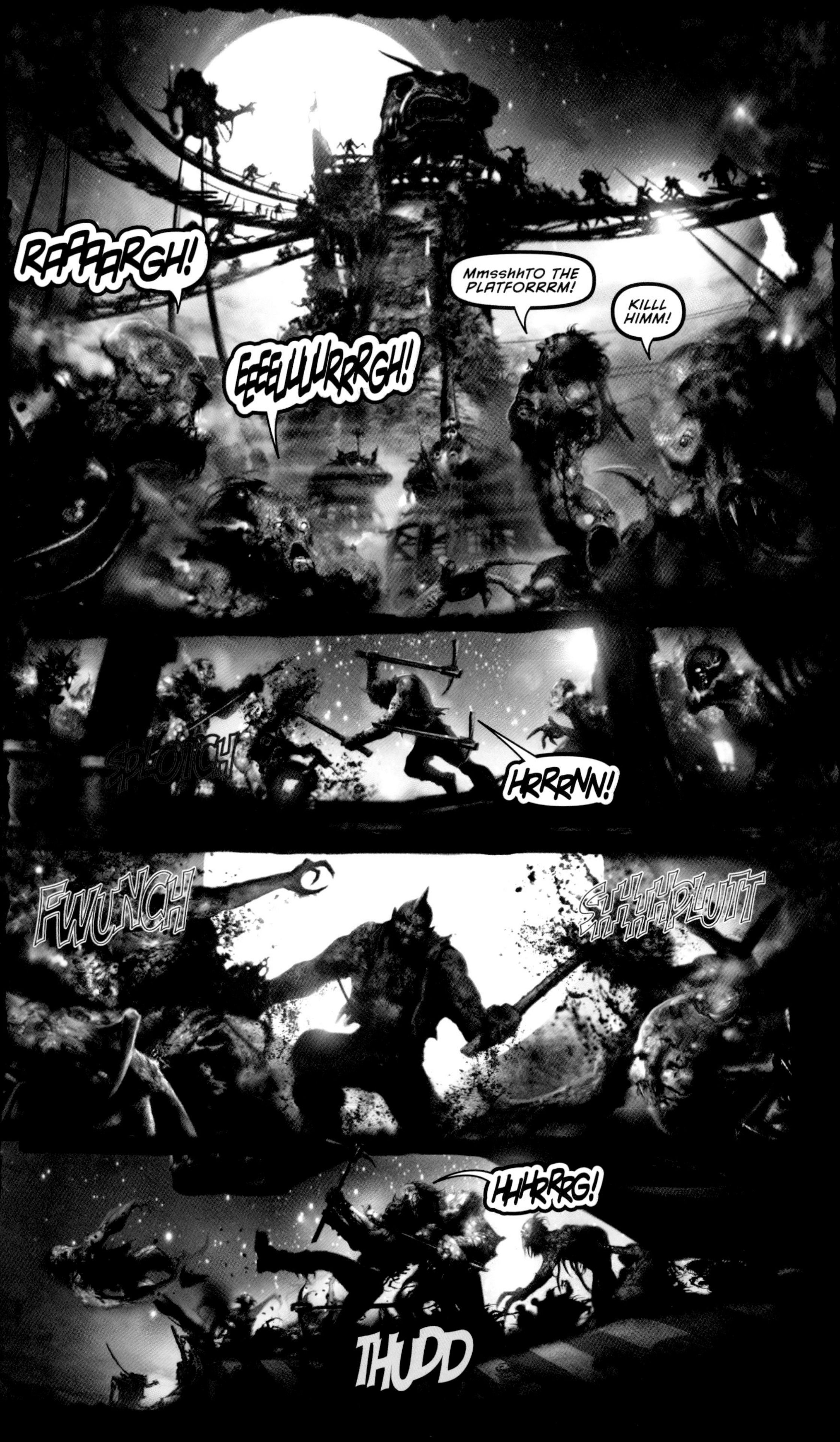

RAAAARGH!
MmsshhTO THE PLATFORRRM!
KILLL HIMM!
EEEELLLURRRGH!
SPLOTCH
HRRRNN!
FWUNCH
SHHHPLUTT
HHHRRRG!
THUDD

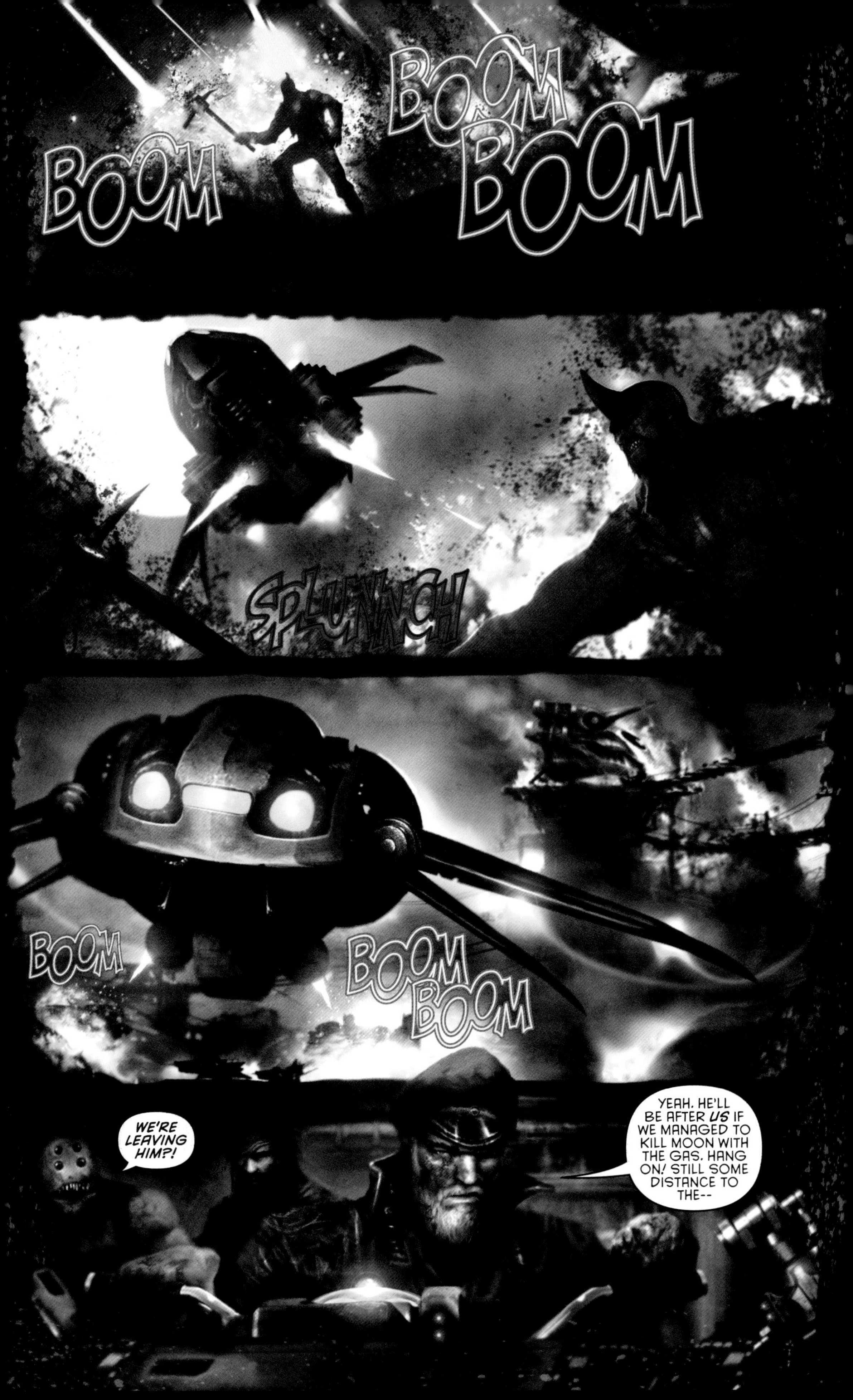
BOOM
BOOM
BOOM
BOOM
SPLUNNCH
BOOM
BOOM
BOOM
WE'RE LEAVING HIM?!
YEAH. HE'LL BE AFTER *US* IF WE MANAGED TO KILL MOON WITH THE GAS. HANG ON! STILL SOME DISTANCE TO THE--

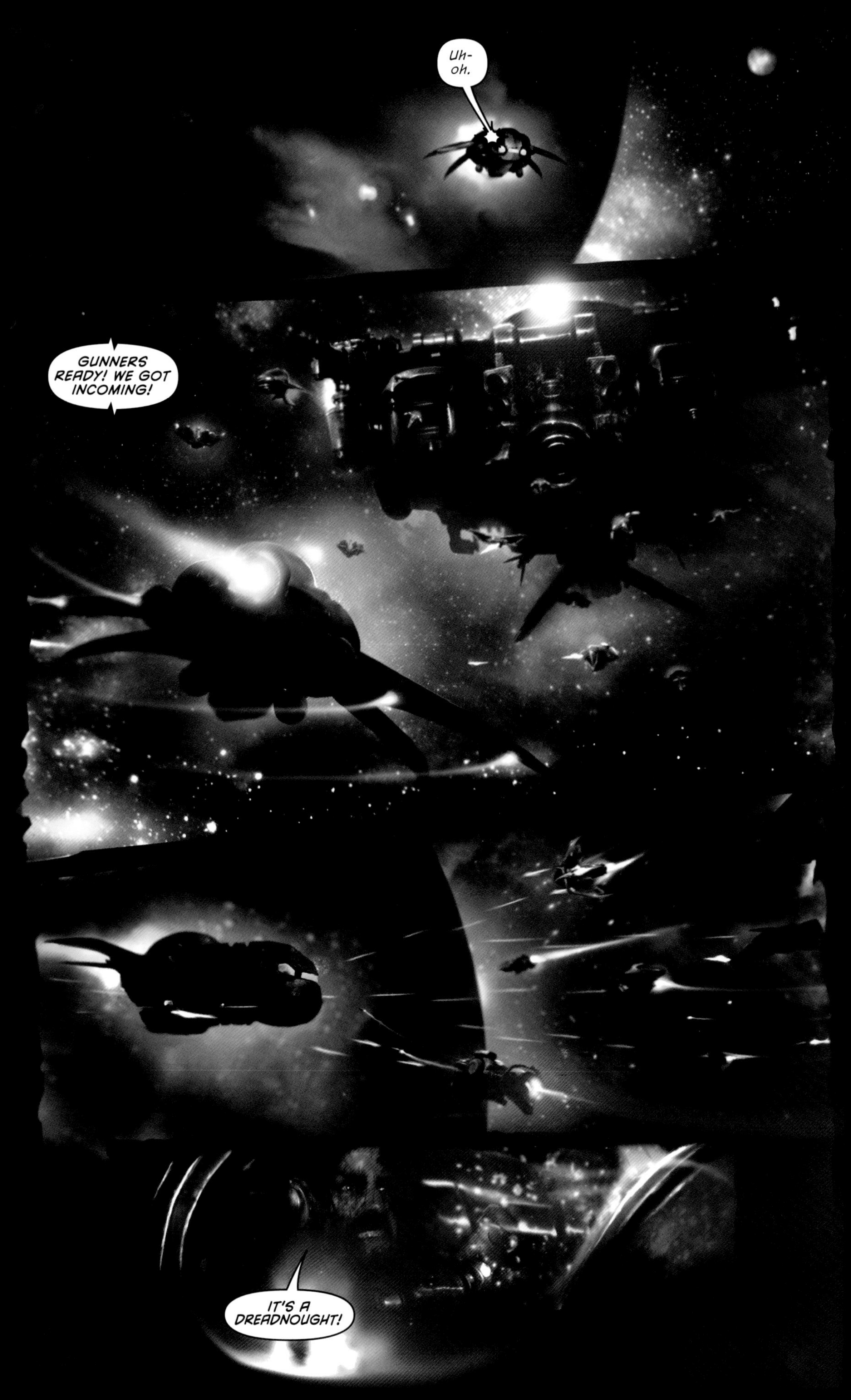
Uh-oh.
GUNNERS READY! WE GOT INCOMING!
IT'S A DREADNOUGHT!

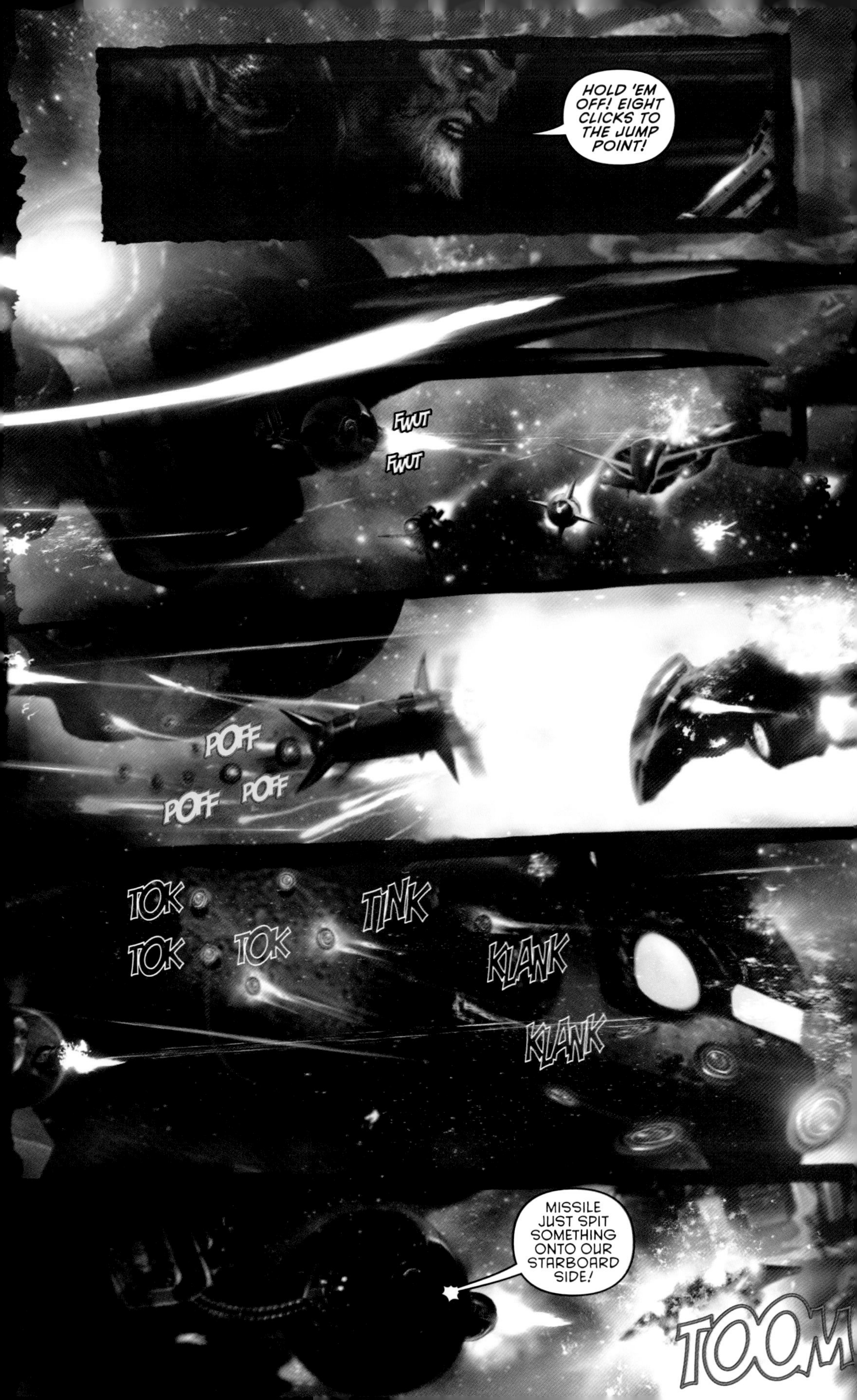
HOLD 'EM OFF! EIGHT CLICKS TO THE JUMP POINT!
FWUT
FWUT
POFF
POFF
POFF
TOK
TOK
TOK
TINK
KLANK
KLANK
MISSILE JUST SPIT SOMETHING ONTO OUR STARBOARD SIDE!
TOOM

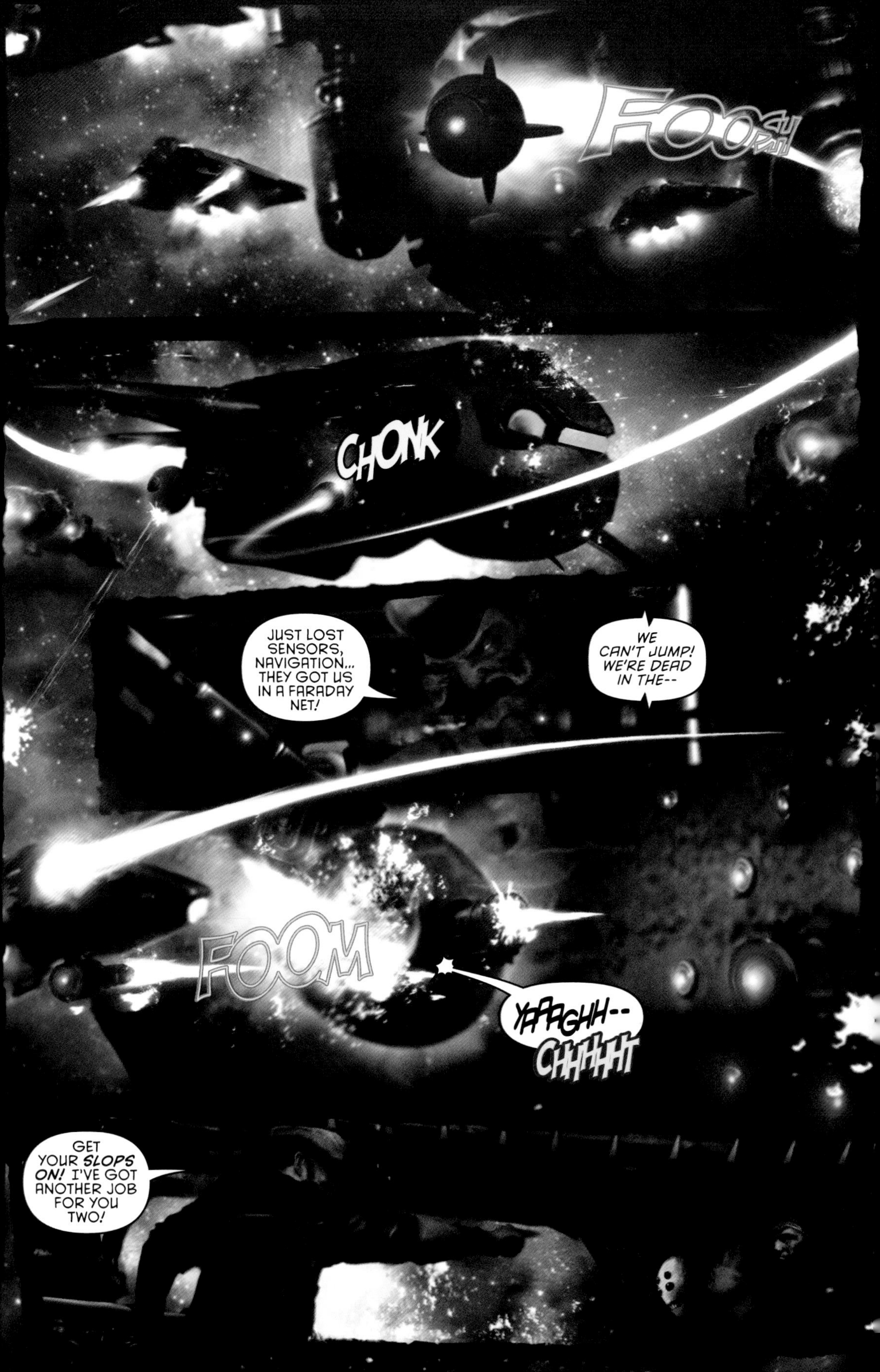
FOOSH
CHONK
JUST LOST SENSORS, NAVIGATION... THEY GOT US IN A FARADAY NET!
WE CAN'T JUMP! WE'RE DEAD IN THE--
FOOM
YEAAGHH--
CHHHHT
GET YOUR SLOPS ON! I'VE GOT ANOTHER JOB FOR YOU TWO!

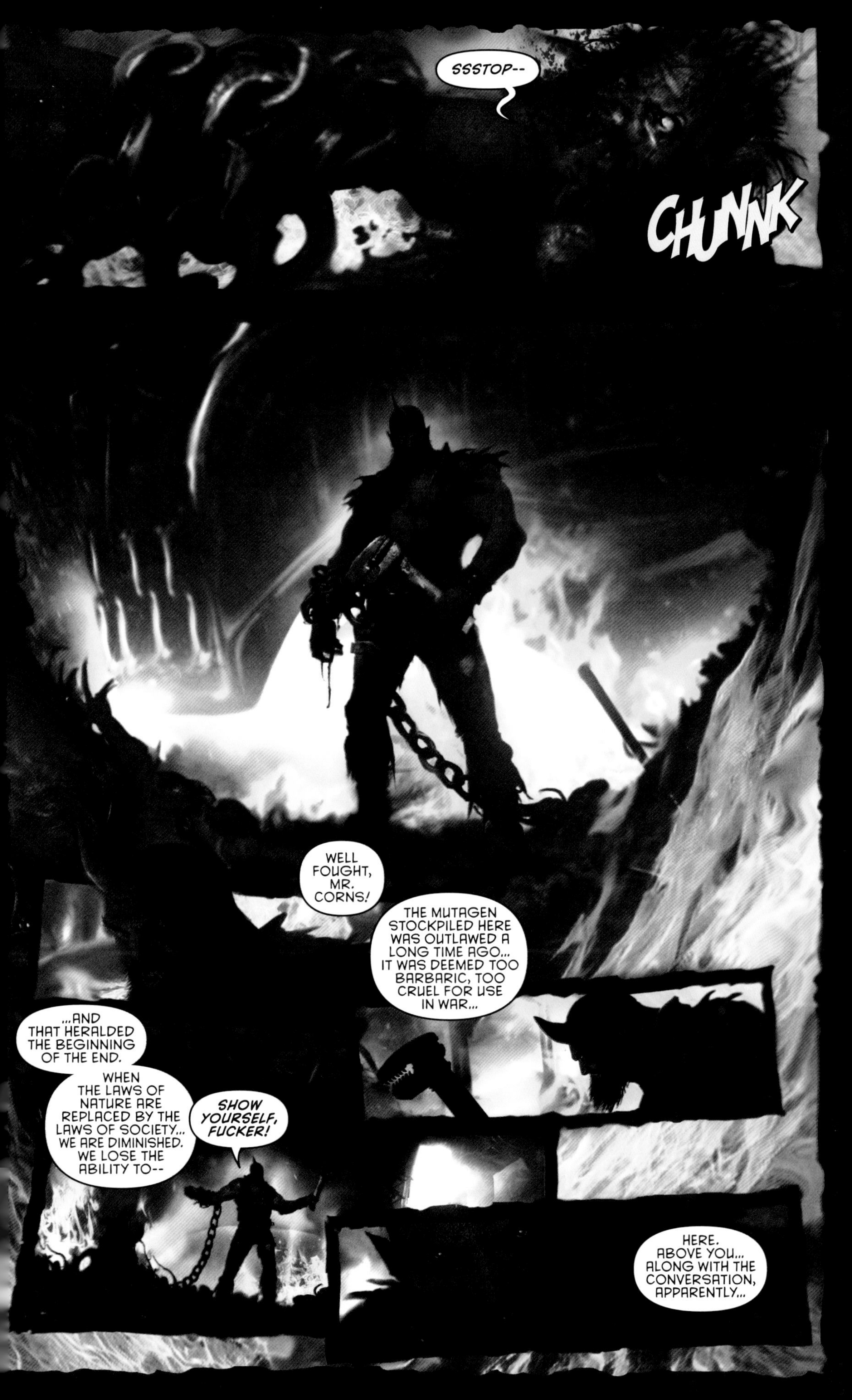
SSSTOP--
CHUNNK
WELL FOUGHT, MR. CORNS!
THE MUTAGEN STOCKPILED HERE WAS OUTLAWED A LONG TIME AGO... IT WAS DEEMED TOO BARBARIC, TOO CRUEL FOR USE IN WAR...
...AND THAT HERALDED THE BEGINNING OF THE END.
WHEN THE LAWS OF NATURE ARE REPLACED BY THE LAWS OF SOCIETY... WE ARE DIMINISHED. WE LOSE THE ABILITY TO--
SHOW YOURSELF, FUCKER!
HERE. ABOVE YOU... ALONG WITH THE CONVERSATION, APPARENTLY...

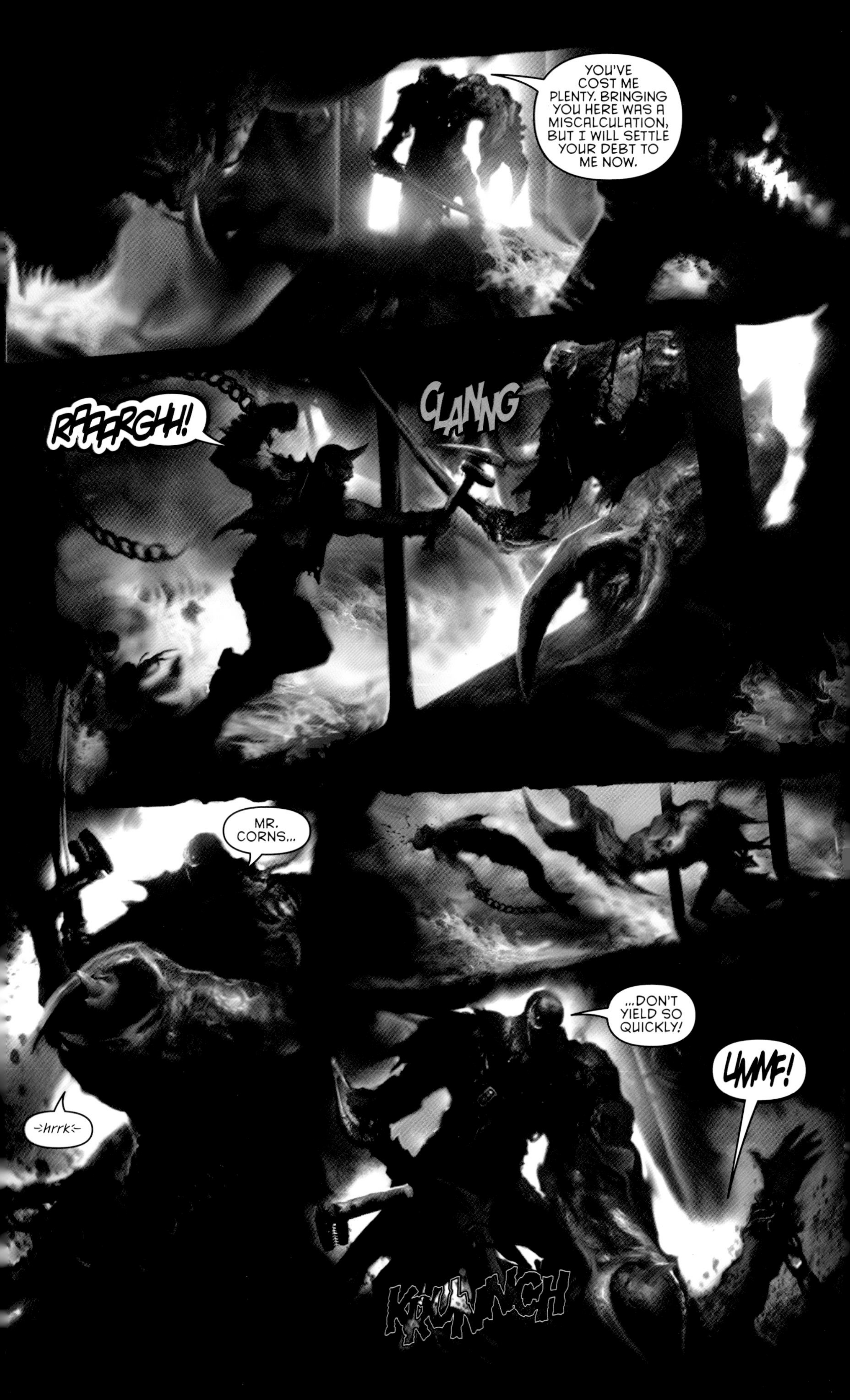
YOU'VE COST ME PLENTY. BRINGING YOU HERE WAS A MISCALCULATION, BUT I WILL SETTLE YOUR DEBT TO ME NOW.
RAAARGH!
CLANNG
MR. CORNS...
...DON'T YIELD SO QUICKLY!
UMMF!
hrrk
KRUNNCH

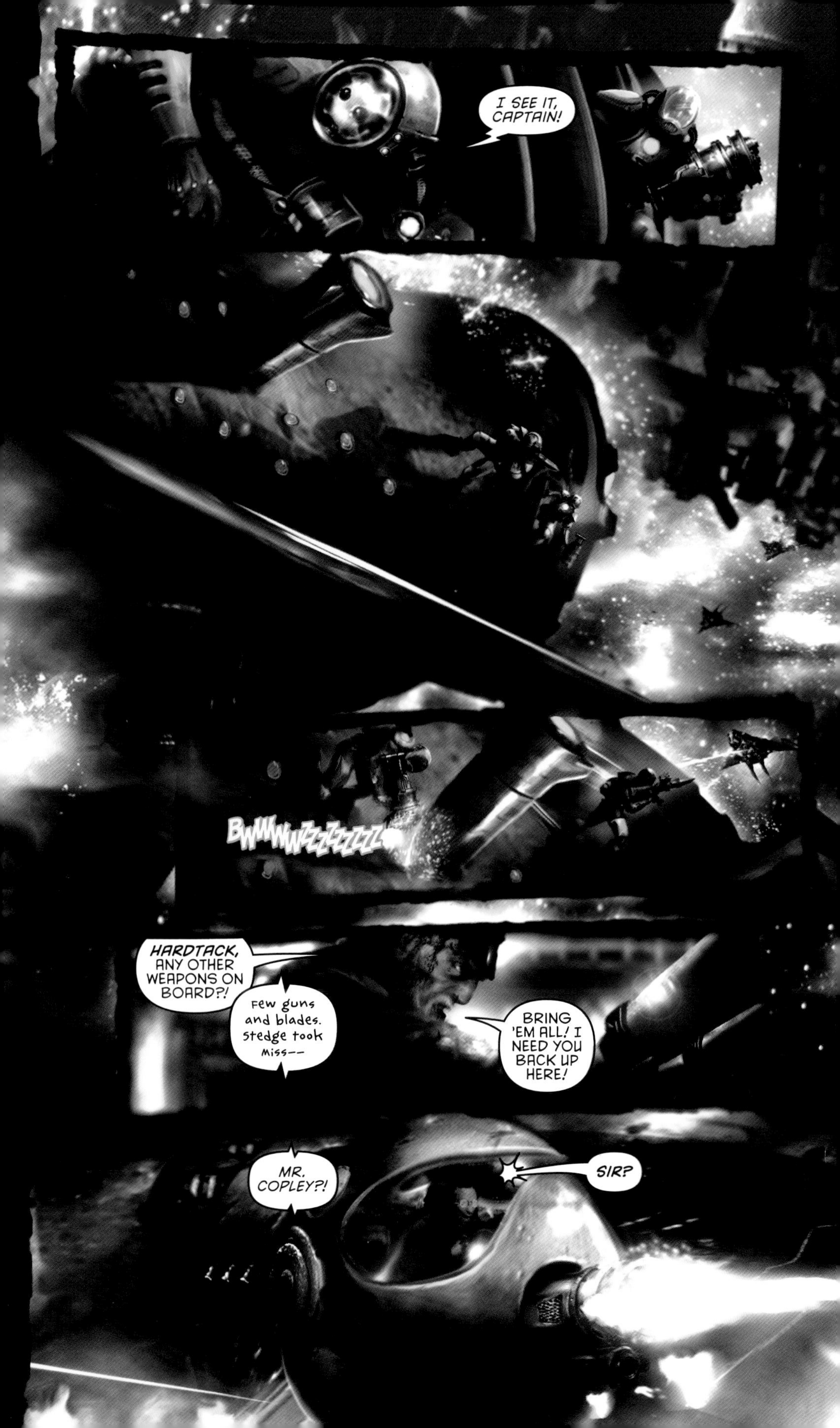
I SEE IT, CAPTAIN!
BWWWWWZZZZZZZZ
HARDTACK, ANY OTHER WEAPONS ON BOARD?!
Few guns and blades. Stedge took miss--
BRING 'EM ALL! I NEED YOU BACK UP HERE!
MR. COPLEY?!
SIR?

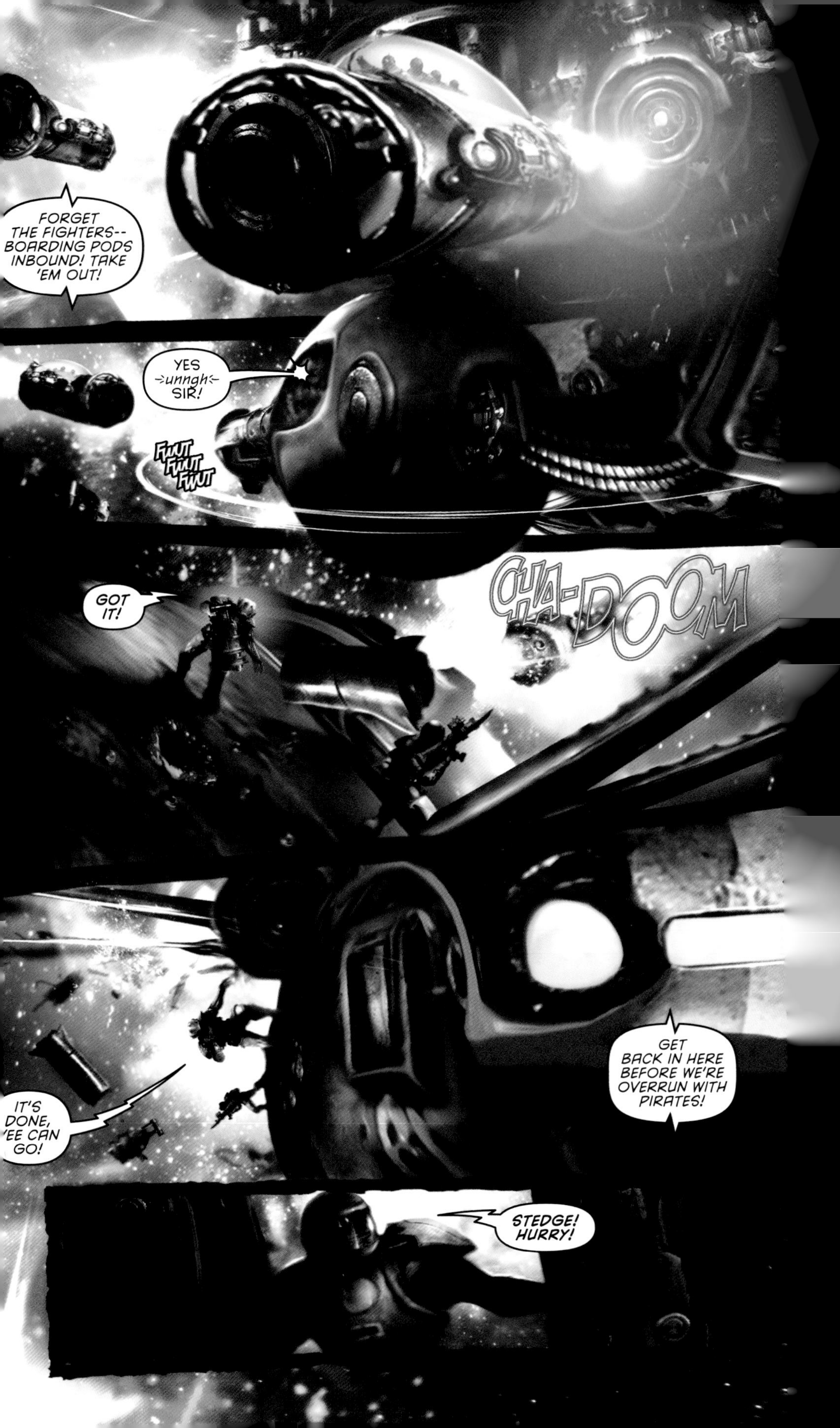
FORGET THE FIGHTERS-- BOARDING PODS INBOUND! TAKE 'EM OUT!
YES -unngh- SIR!
FWUT FWUT FWUT
GOT IT!
CHA-DOOM
IT'S DONE, 'EE CAN GO!
GET BACK IN HERE BEFORE WE'RE OVERRUN WITH PIRATES!
STEDGE! HURRY!

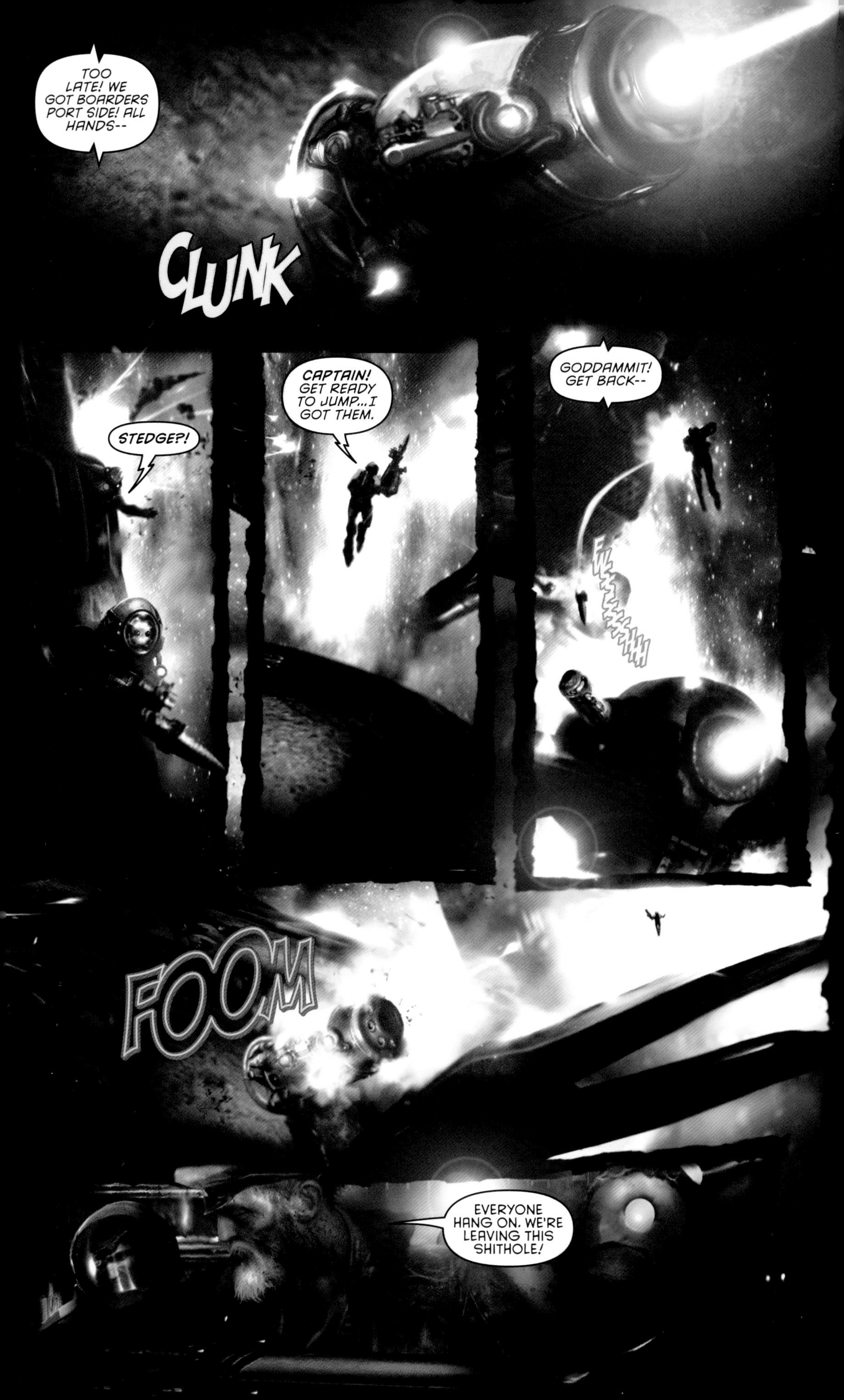
TOO LATE! WE GOT BOARDERS PORT SIDE! ALL HANDS--
CLUNK
STEDGE?!
CAPTAIN! GET READY TO JUMP...I GOT THEM.
GODDAMMIT! GET BACK--
FOOM
EVERYONE HANG ON. WE'RE LEAVING THIS SHITHOLE!

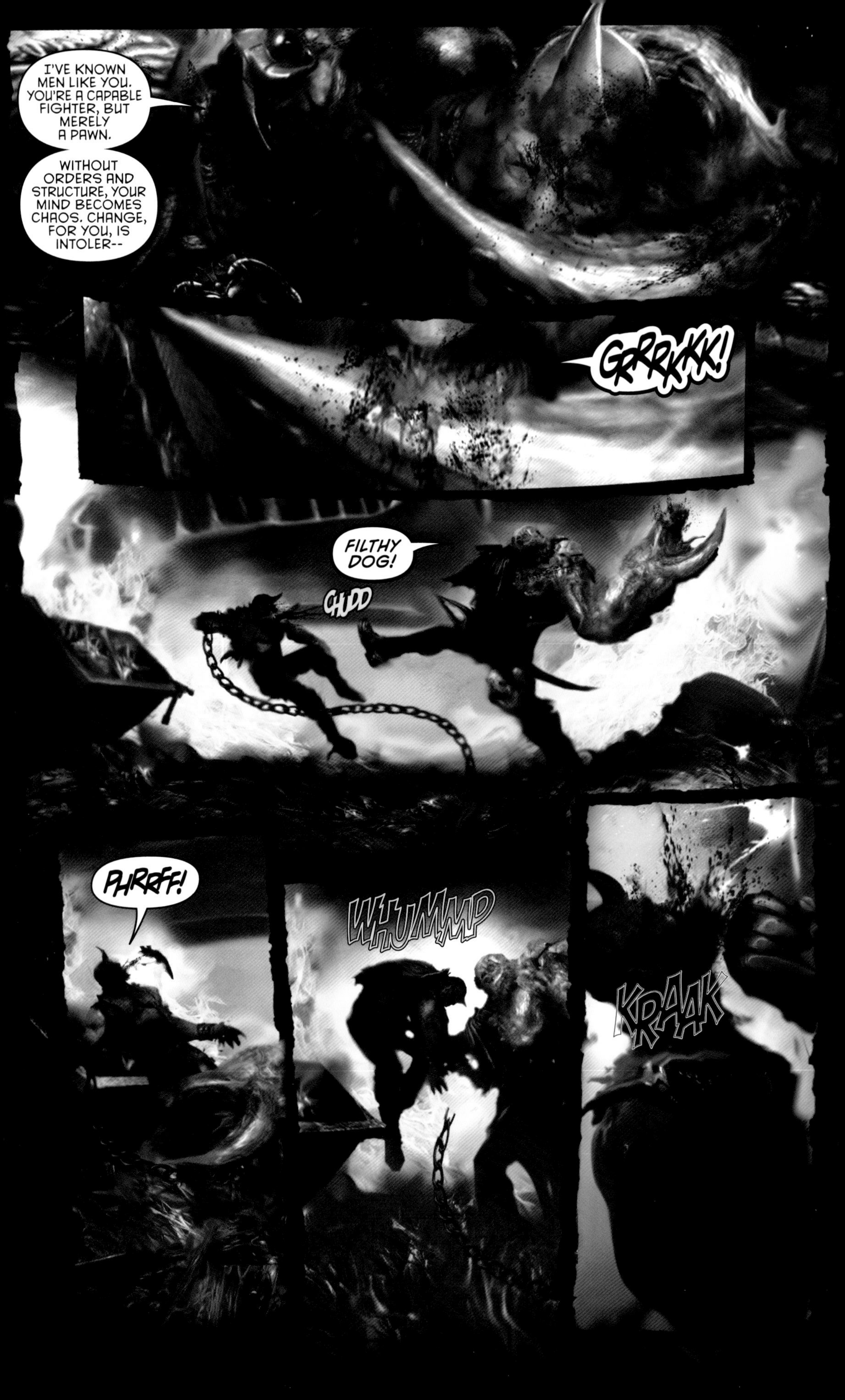
I'VE KNOWN MEN LIKE YOU. YOU'RE A CAPABLE FIGHTER, BUT MERELY A PAWN.
WITHOUT ORDERS AND STRUCTURE, YOUR MIND BECOMES CHAOS. CHANGE, FOR YOU, IS INTOLER--
GRRKKK!
FILTHY DOG!
CHUDD
PHRRFF!
WHUMMP
KRAAK

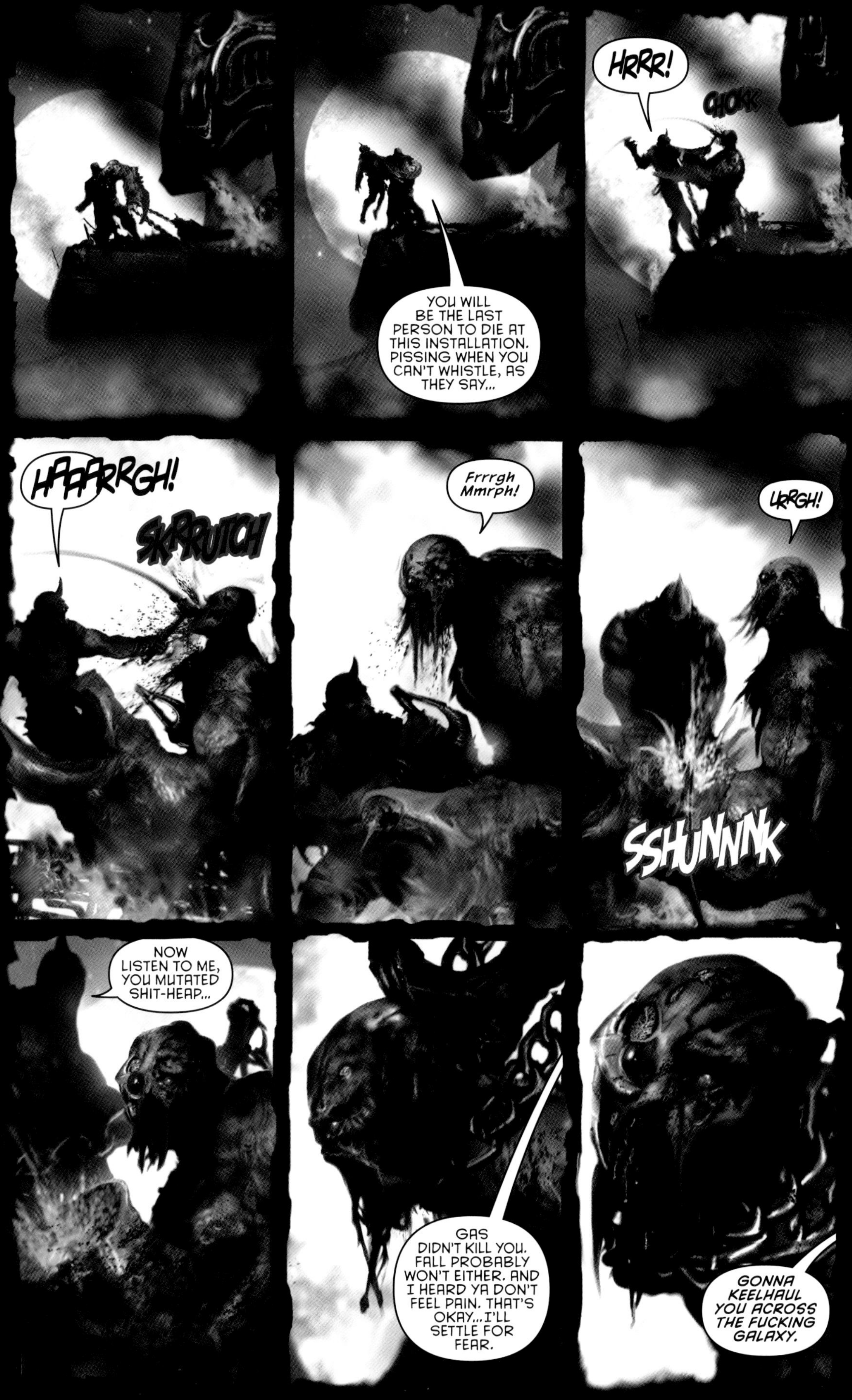
YOU WILL BE THE LAST PERSON TO DIE AT THIS INSTALLATION. PISSING WHEN YOU CAN'T WHISTLE, AS THEY SAY...
HRRR!
CHOKK
HAAARRGH!
SKRRUTCH
Frrrgh Mmrph!
URRGH!
SSHUNNNK
NOW LISTEN TO ME, YOU MUTATED SHIT-HEAP...
GAS DIDN'T KILL YOU. FALL PROBABLY WON'T EITHER. AND I HEARD YA DON'T FEEL PAIN. THAT'S OKAY...I'LL SETTLE FOR FEAR.
GONNA KEELHAUL YOU ACROSS THE FUCKING GALAXY.

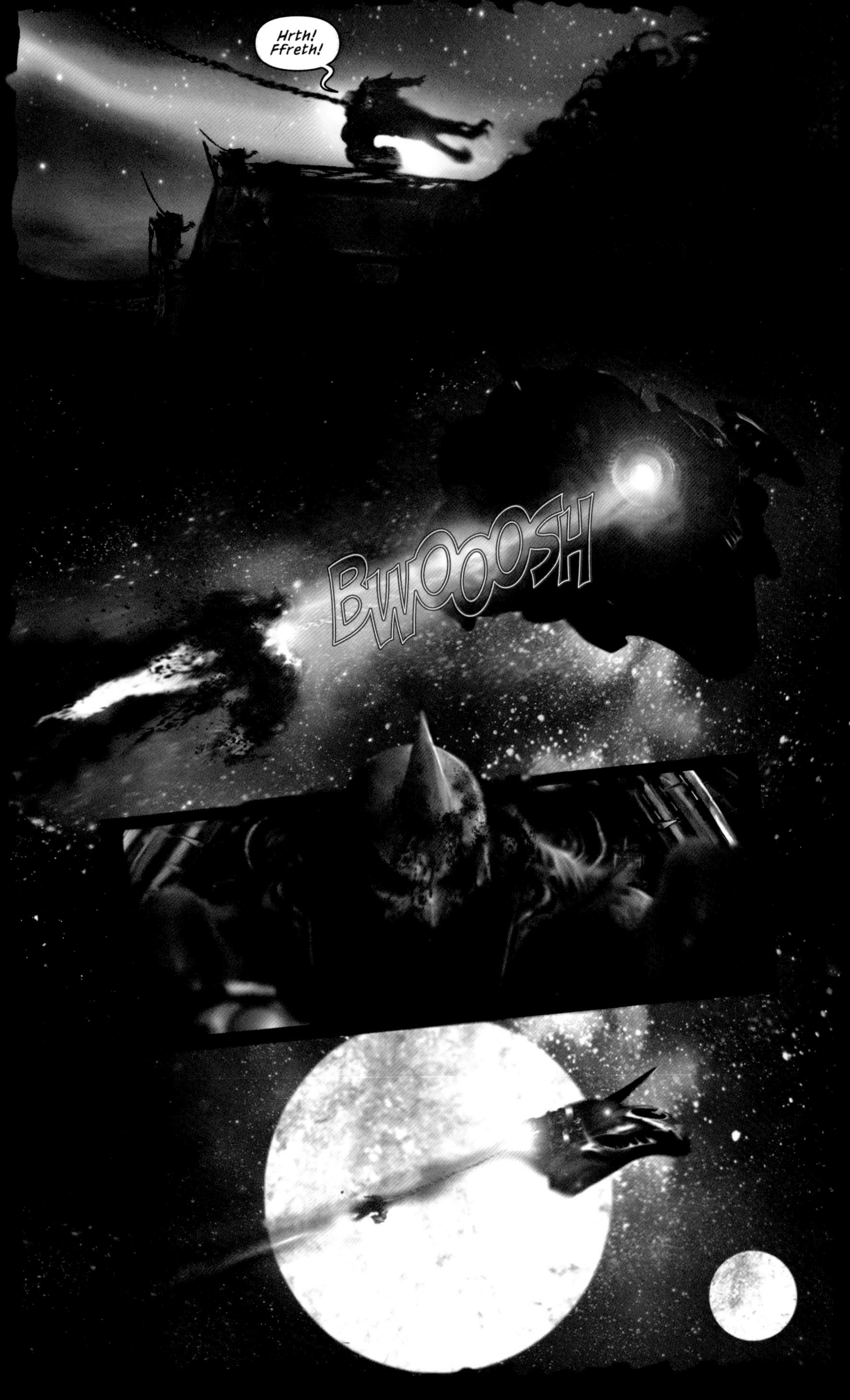
Hrth! Ffreth!
BWOOOSH

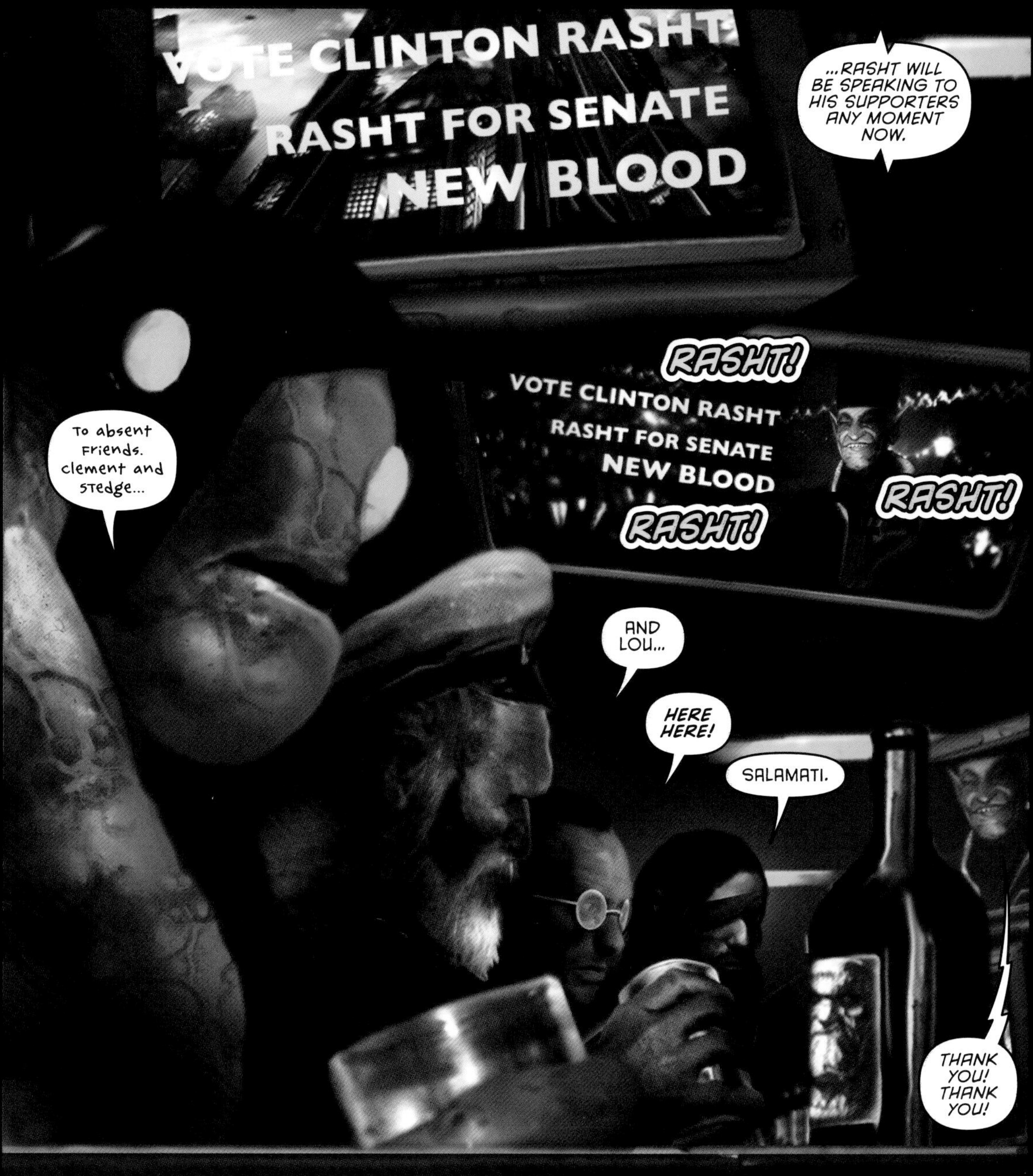
VOTE CLINTON RASHT
RASHT FOR SENATE
NEW BLOOD
...RASHT WILL BE SPEAKING TO HIS SUPPORTERS ANY MOMENT NOW.
RASHT!
VOTE CLINTON RASHT
RASHT FOR SENATE
NEW BLOOD
RASHT!
RASHT!
To absent Friends. clement and stedge...
AND LOU...
HERE HERE!
SALAMATI.
THANK YOU! THANK YOU!

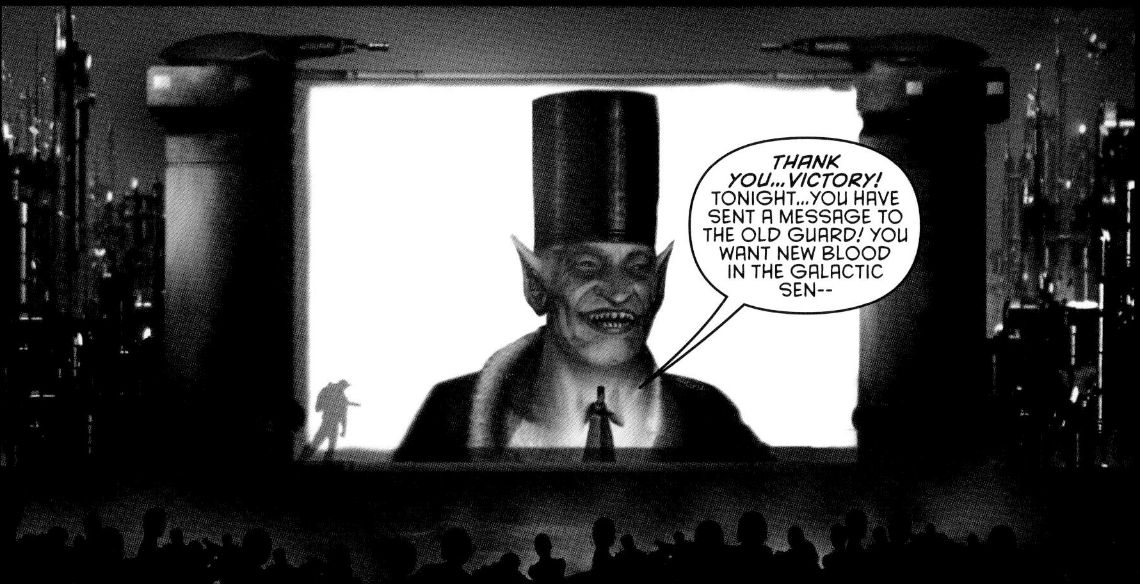
THANK YOU...VICTORY! TONIGHT...YOU HAVE SENT A MESSAGE TO THE OLD GUARD! YOU WANT NEW BLOOD IN THE GALACTIC SEN--

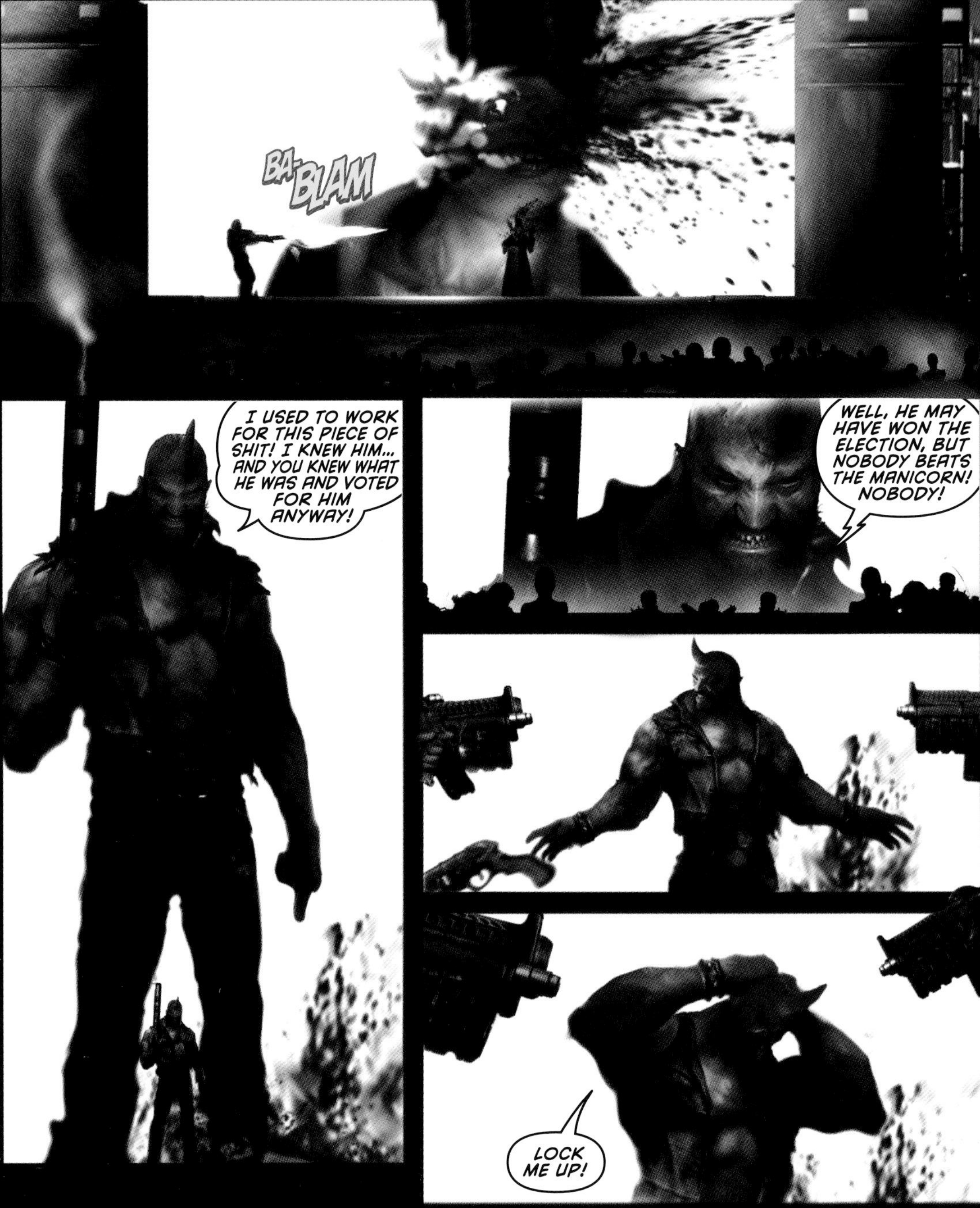
BA-BLAM
I USED TO WORK FOR THIS PIECE OF SHIT! I KNEW HIM... AND YOU KNEW WHAT HE WAS AND VOTED FOR HIM ANYWAY!
WELL, HE MAY HAVE WON THE ELECTION, BUT NOBODY BEATS THE MANICORN! NOBODY!
LOCK ME UP!

NOBODY BEATS THE MANICORN

written by ERIC PETERSON and JOE AUBREY
art and colors by CLINT LANGLEY lettering by TAYLOR ESPOSITO
created by ERIC PETERSON · JOE AUBREY · DARICK ROBERTSON

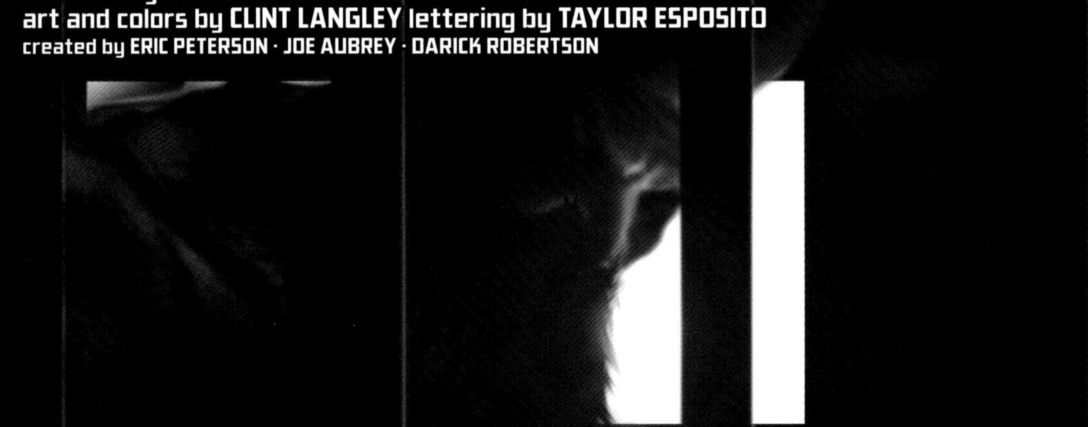

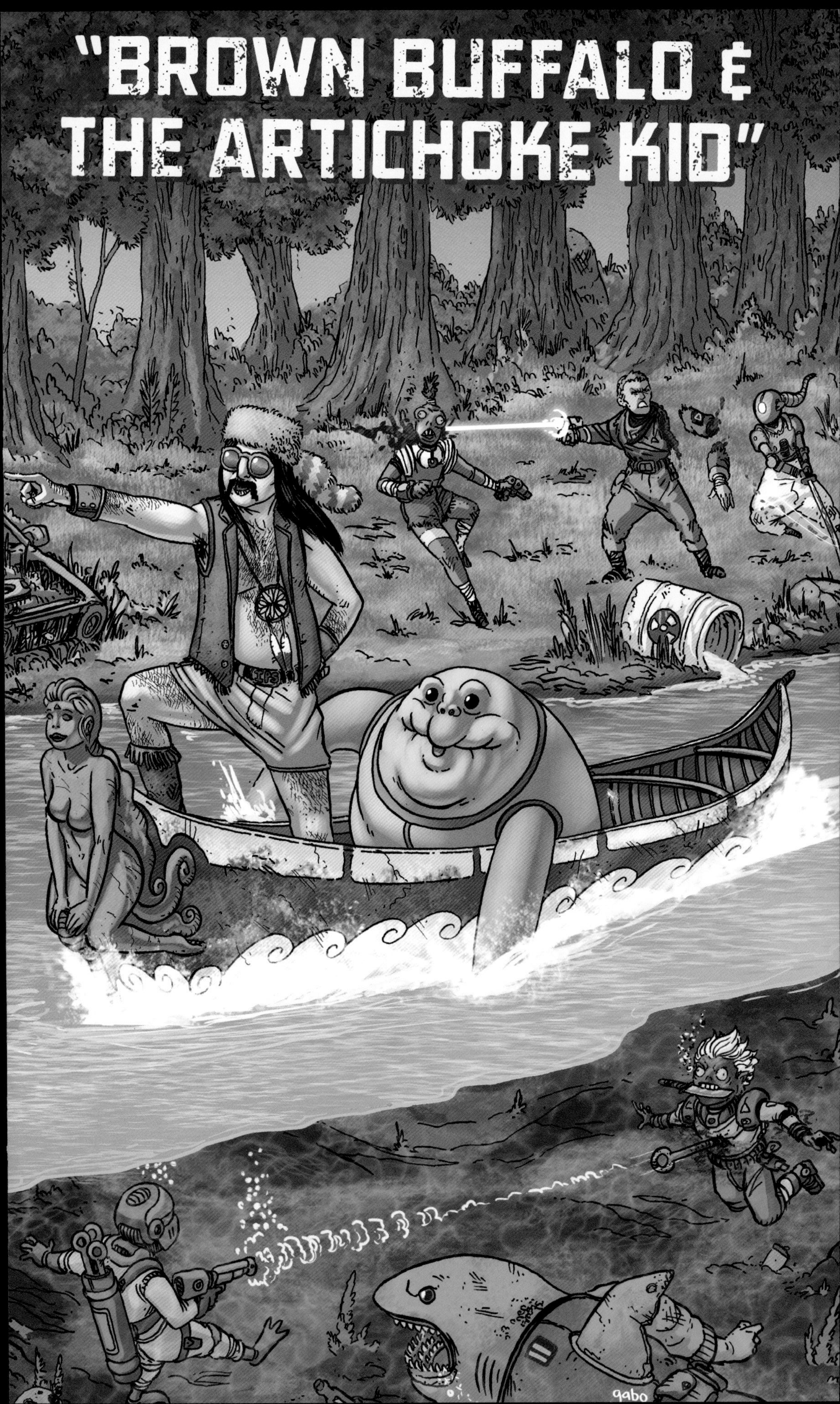
"BROWN BUFFALO &
THE ARTICHOKE KID"
gabo

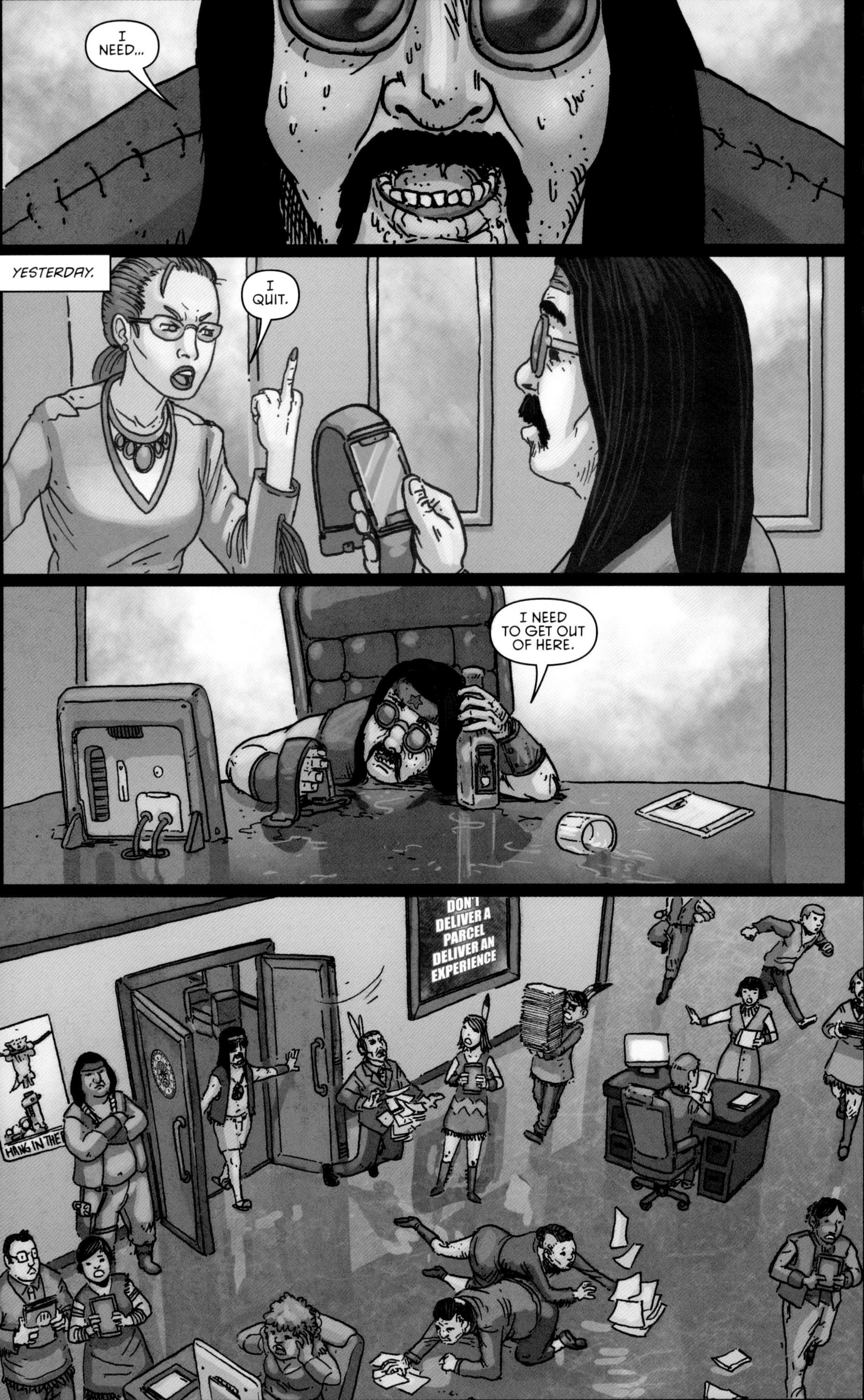
I NEED...
YESTERDAY.
I QUIT.
I NEED TO GET OUT OF HERE.
DON'T DELIVER A PARCEL DELIVER AN EXPERIENCE
HANG IN THE

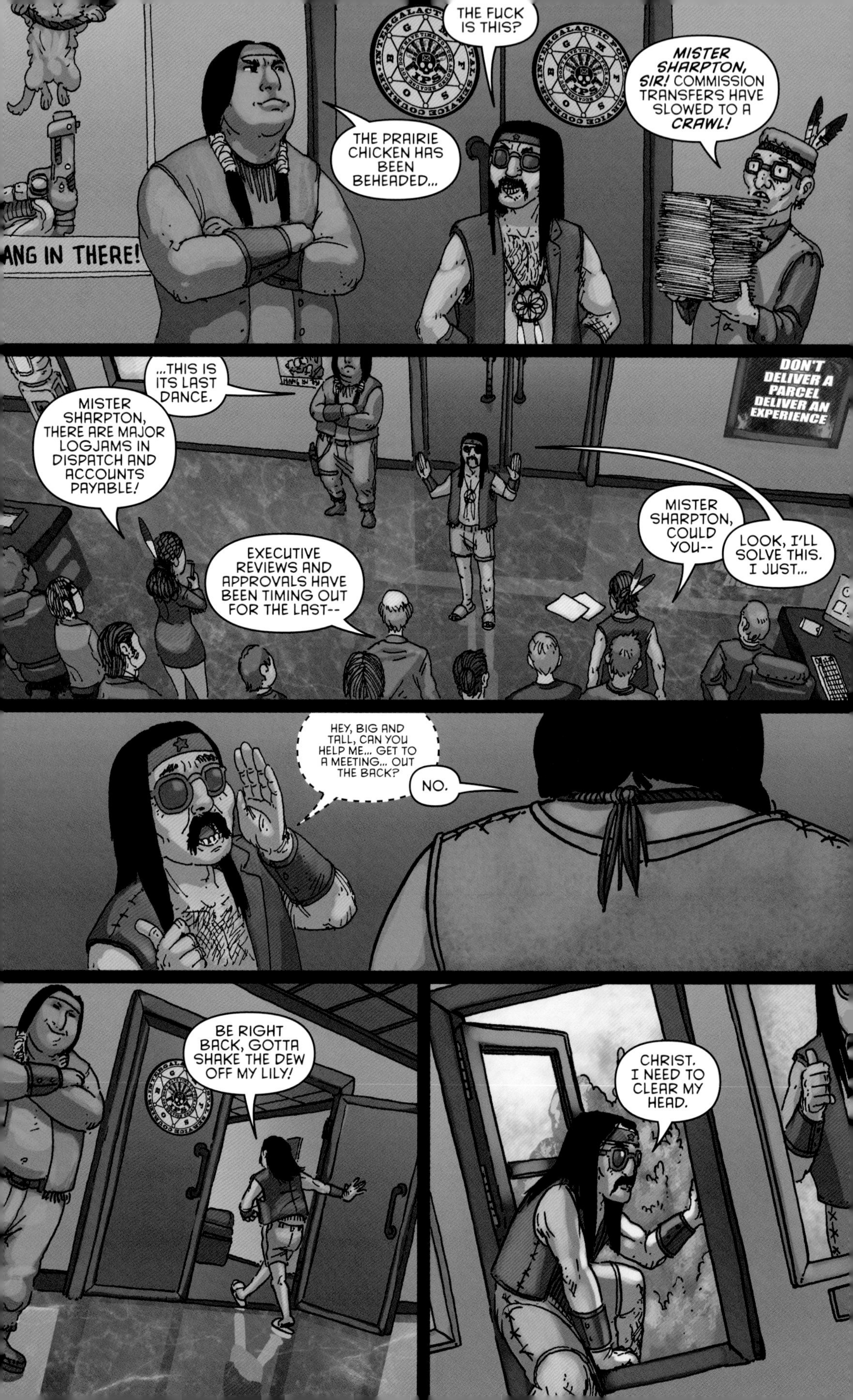
HANG IN THERE!
THE FUCK IS THIS?
THE PRAIRIE CHICKEN HAS BEEN BEHEADED...
MISTER SHARPTON, SIR! COMMISSION TRANSFERS HAVE SLOWED TO A CRAWL!
...THIS IS ITS LAST DANCE.
MISTER SHARPTON, THERE ARE MAJOR LOGJAMS IN DISPATCH AND ACCOUNTS PAYABLE!
DON'T DELIVER A PARCEL DELIVER AN EXPERIENCE
EXECUTIVE REVIEWS AND APPROVALS HAVE BEEN TIMING OUT FOR THE LAST--
MISTER SHARPTON, COULD YOU--
LOOK, I'LL SOLVE THIS. I JUST...
HEY, BIG AND TALL, CAN YOU HELP ME... GET TO A MEETING... OUT THE BACK?
NO.
BE RIGHT BACK, GOTTA SHAKE THE DEW OFF MY LILY!
CHRIST. I NEED TO CLEAR MY HEAD.

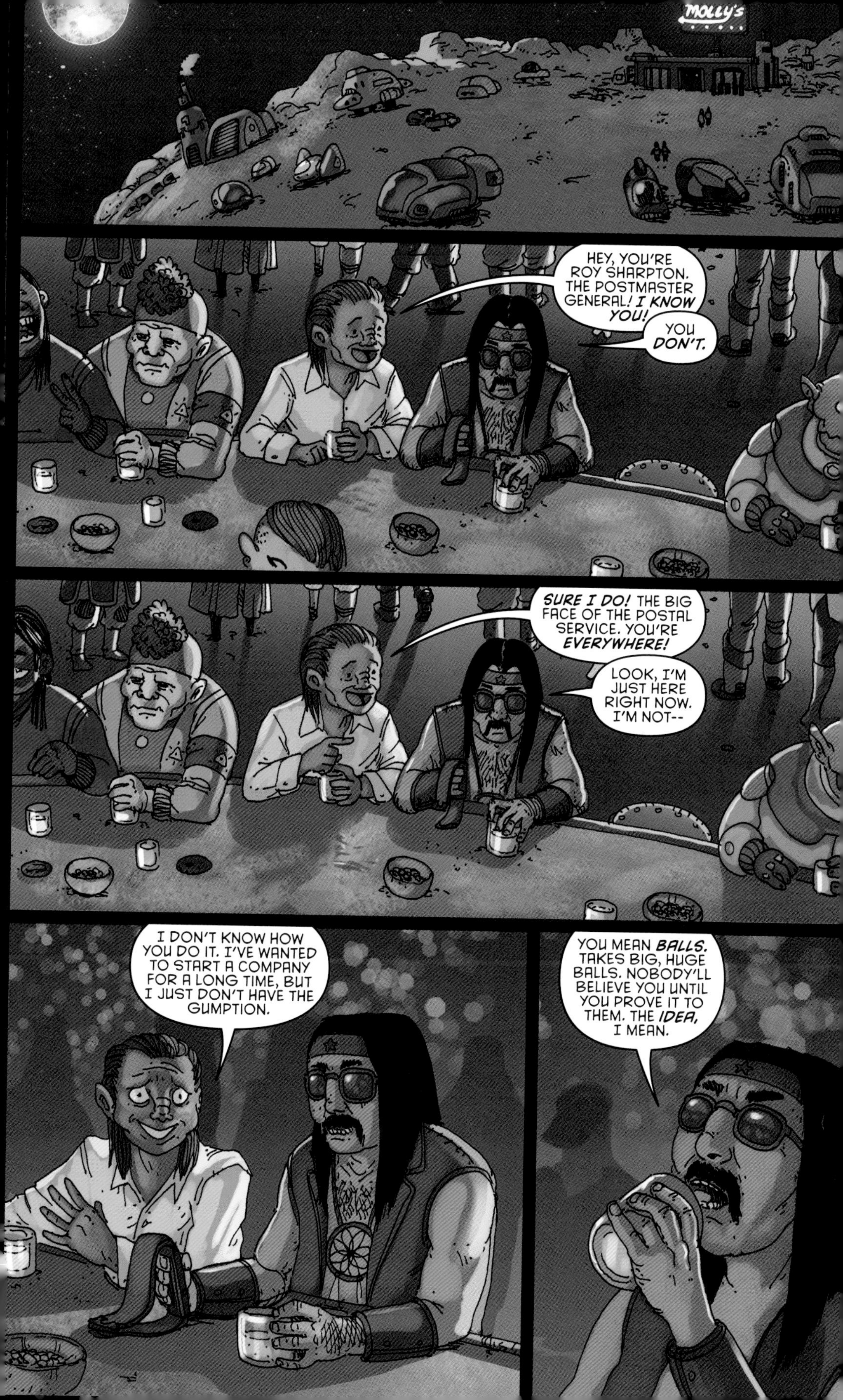
MOLLY'S
HEY, YOU'RE ROY SHARPTON. THE POSTMASTER GENERAL! I KNOW YOU!
YOU DON'T.
SURE I DO! THE BIG FACE OF THE POSTAL SERVICE. YOU'RE EVERYWHERE!
LOOK, I'M JUST HERE RIGHT NOW. I'M NOT--
I DON'T KNOW HOW YOU DO IT. I'VE WANTED TO START A COMPANY FOR A LONG TIME, BUT I JUST DON'T HAVE THE GUMPTION.
YOU MEAN BALLS. TAKES BIG, HUGE BALLS. NOBODY'LL BELIEVE YOU UNTIL YOU PROVE IT TO THEM. THE IDEA, I MEAN.

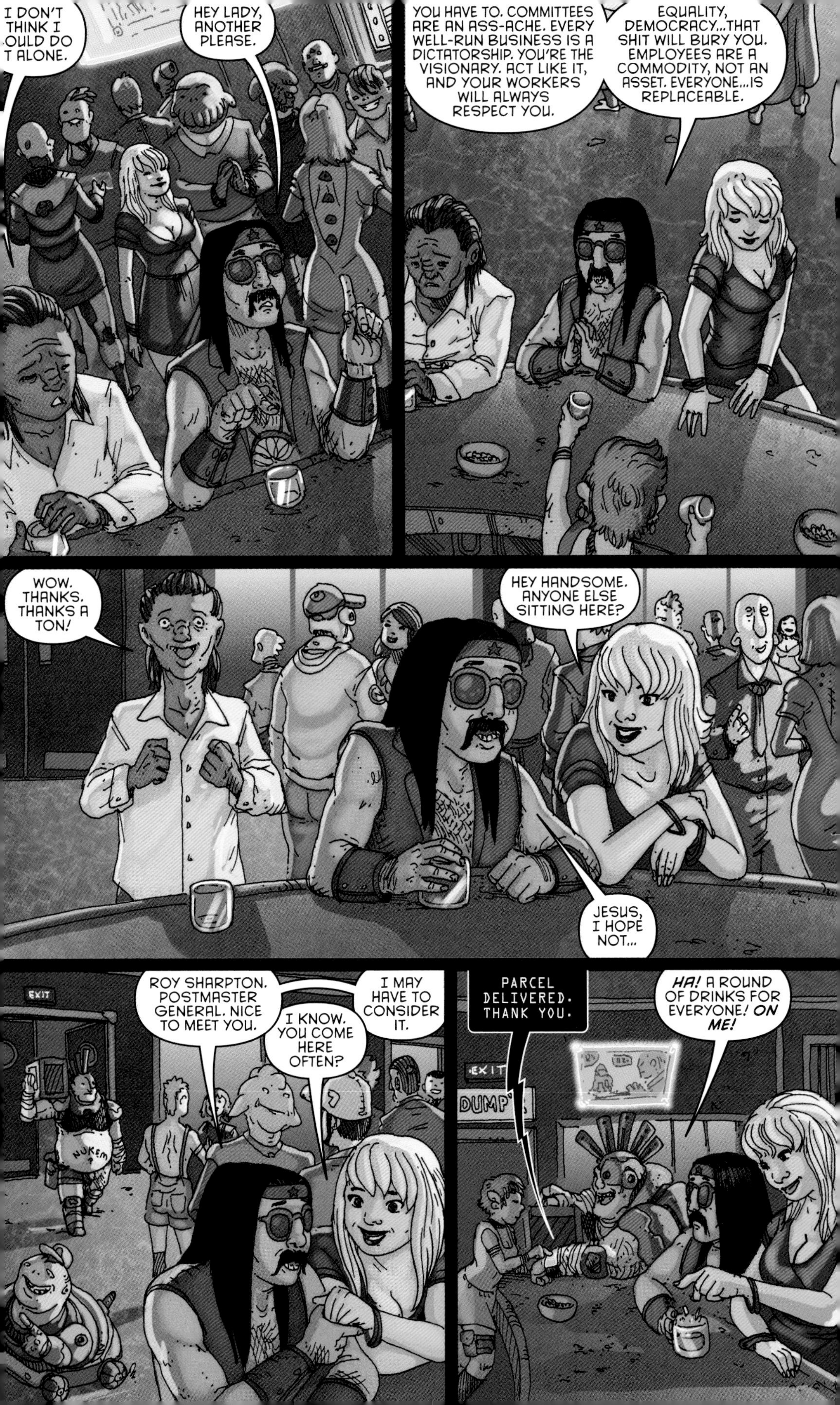

I DON'T THINK I OULD DO T ALONE.
HEY LADY, ANOTHER PLEASE.
YOU HAVE TO. COMMITTEES ARE AN ASS-ACHE. EVERY WELL-RUN BUSINESS IS A DICTATORSHIP. YOU'RE THE VISIONARY. ACT LIKE IT, AND YOUR WORKERS WILL ALWAYS RESPECT YOU.
EQUALITY, DEMOCRACY...THAT SHIT WILL BURY YOU. EMPLOYEES ARE A COMMODITY, NOT AN ASSET. EVERYONE...IS REPLACEABLE.
WOW. THANKS. THANKS A TON!
HEY HANDSOME. ANYONE ELSE SITTING HERE?
JESUS, I HOPE NOT...
EXIT
ROY SHARPTON. POSTMASTER GENERAL. NICE TO MEET YOU.
I MAY HAVE TO CONSIDER IT.
I KNOW. YOU COME HERE OFTEN?
NUKEM
PARCEL DELIVERED. THANK YOU.
EXIT
DUMP'S
HA! A ROUND OF DRINKS FOR EVERYONE! ON ME!

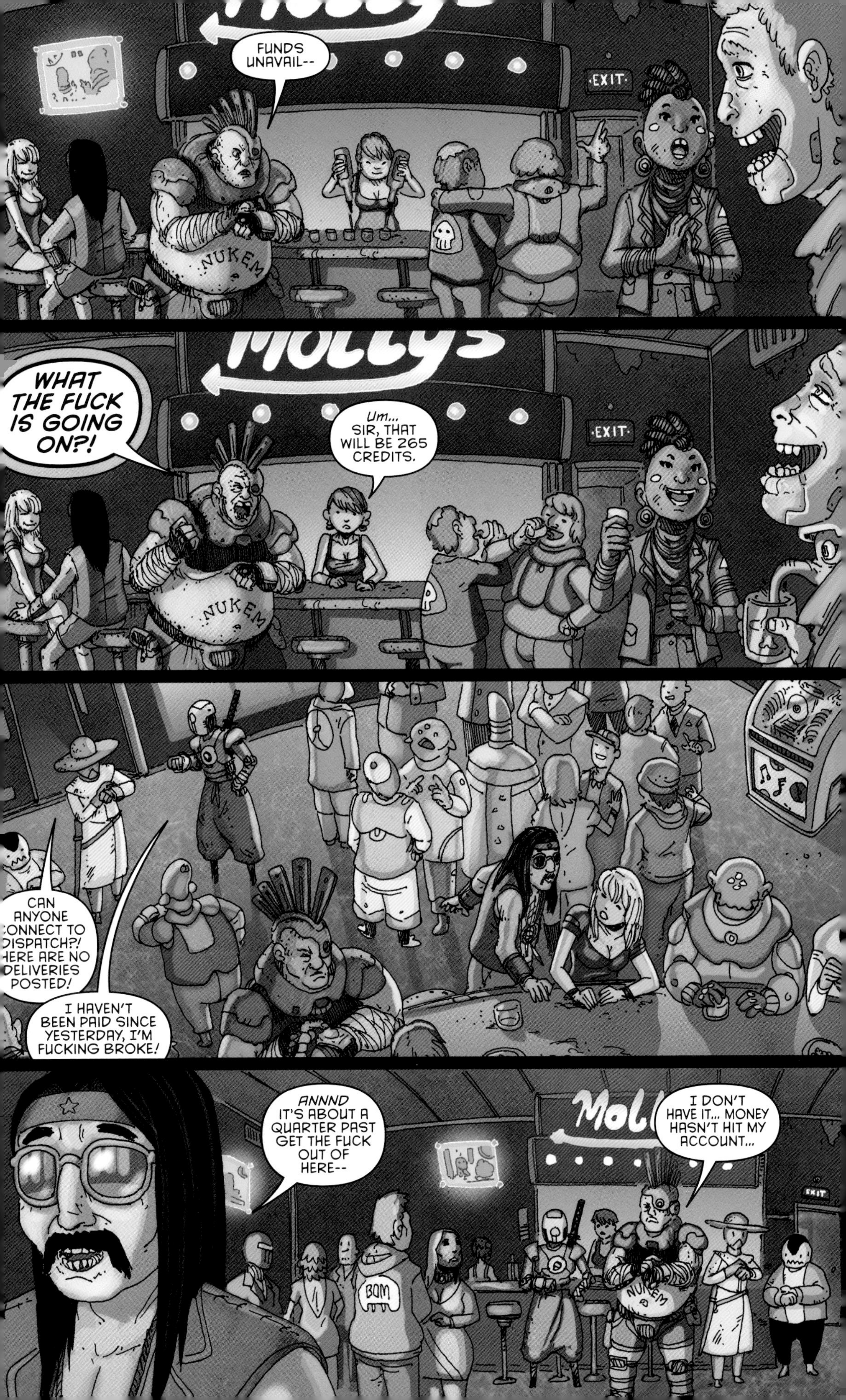
FUNDS UNAVAIL--
WHAT THE FUCK IS GOING ON?!
Um... SIR, THAT WILL BE 265 CREDITS.
CAN ANYONE CONNECT TO DISPATCH?! THERE ARE NO DELIVERIES POSTED!
I HAVEN'T BEEN PAID SINCE YESTERDAY, I'M FUCKING BROKE!
ANNND IT'S ABOUT A QUARTER PAST GET THE FUCK OUT OF HERE--
I DON'T HAVE IT... MONEY HASN'T HIT MY ACCOUNT...

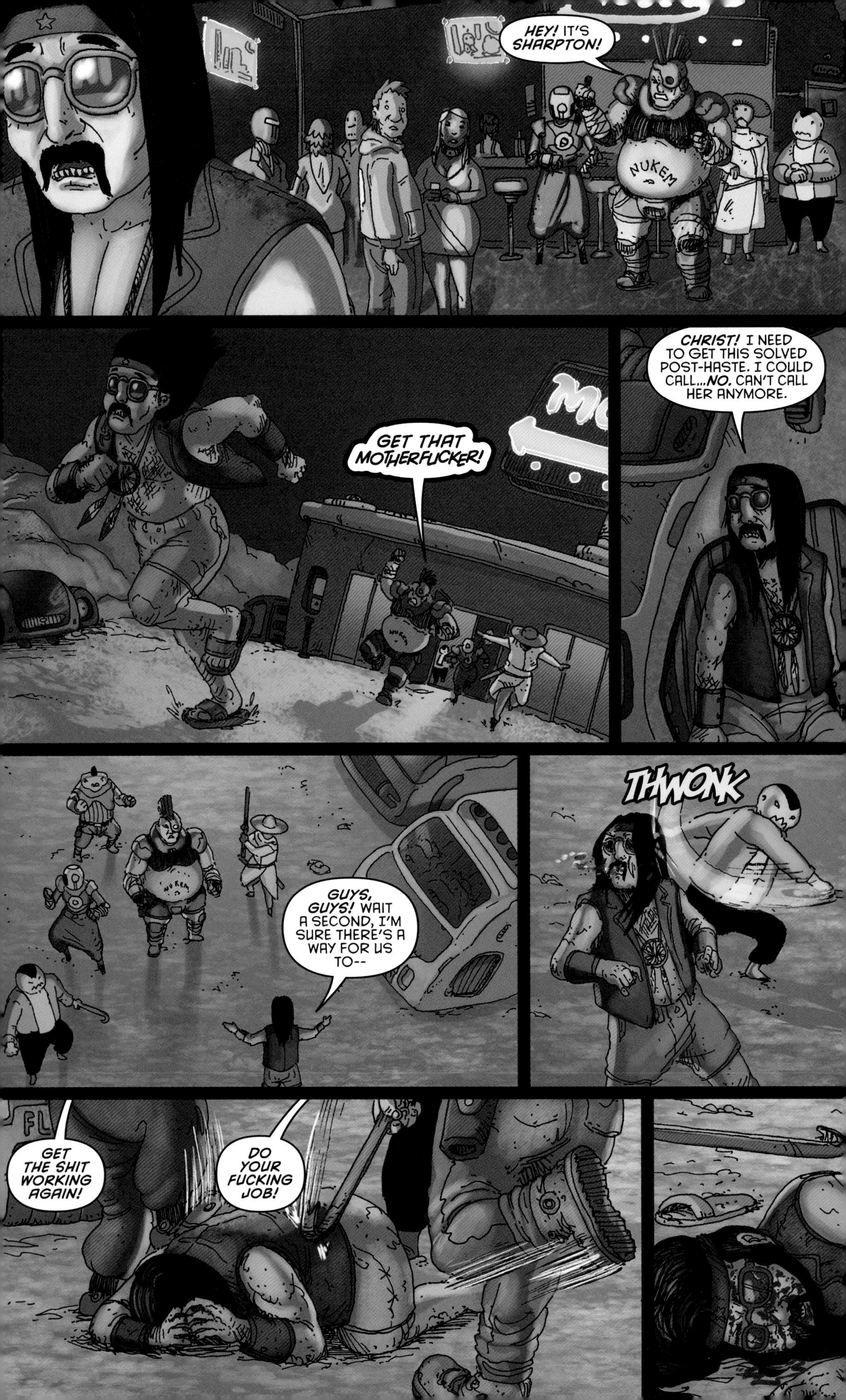
HEY! IT'S SHARPTON!
GET THAT MOTHERFUCKER!
CHRIST! I NEED TO GET THIS SOLVED POST-HASTE. I COULD CALL...NO. CAN'T CALL HER ANYMORE.
GUYS, GUYS! WAIT A SECOND, I'M SURE THERE'S A WAY FOR US TO--
THWONK
GET THE SHIT WORKING AGAIN!
DO YOUR FUCKING JOB!

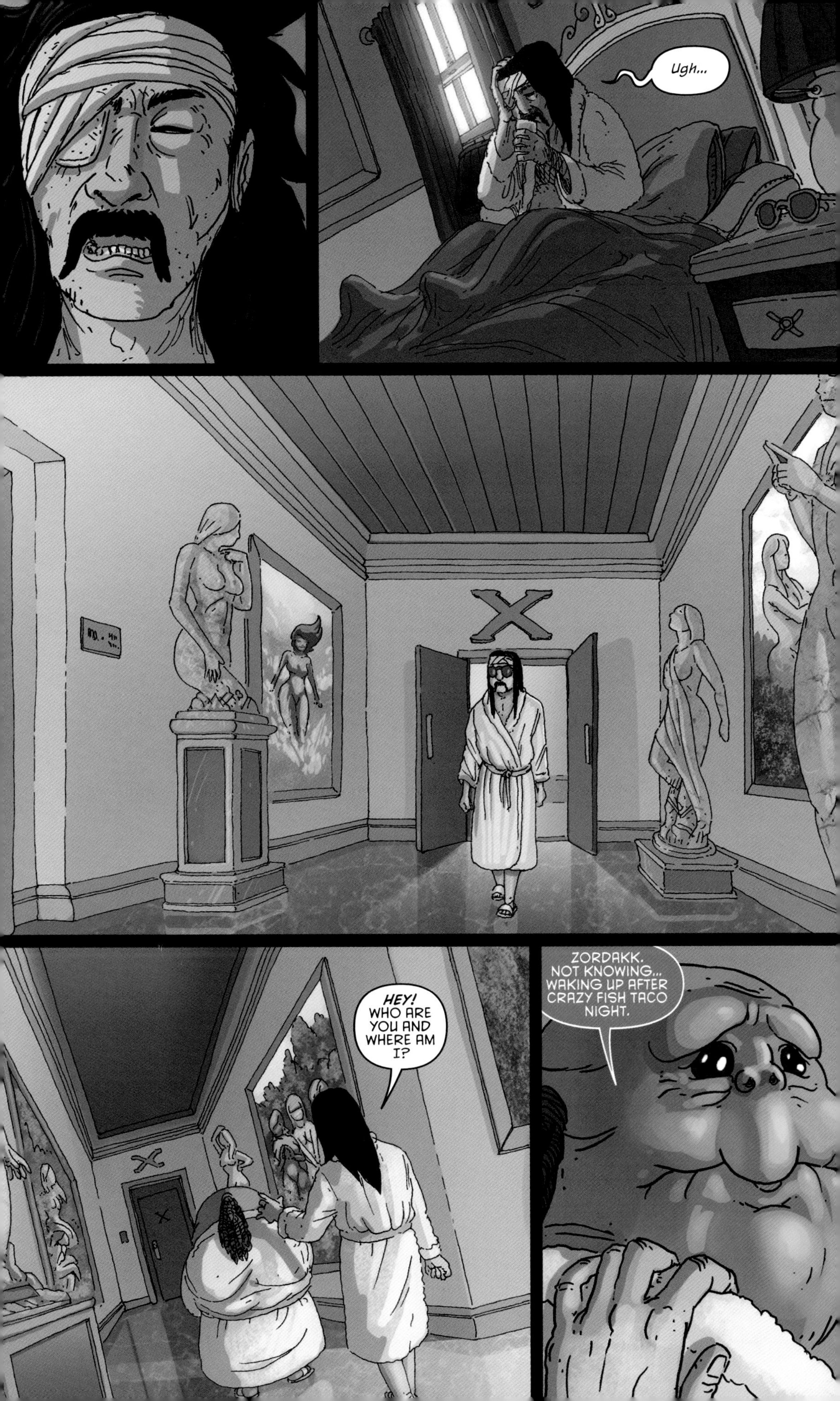
Ugh...
HEY! WHO ARE YOU AND WHERE AM I?
ZORDAKK. NOT KNOWING... WAKING UP AFTER CRAZY FISH TACO NIGHT.

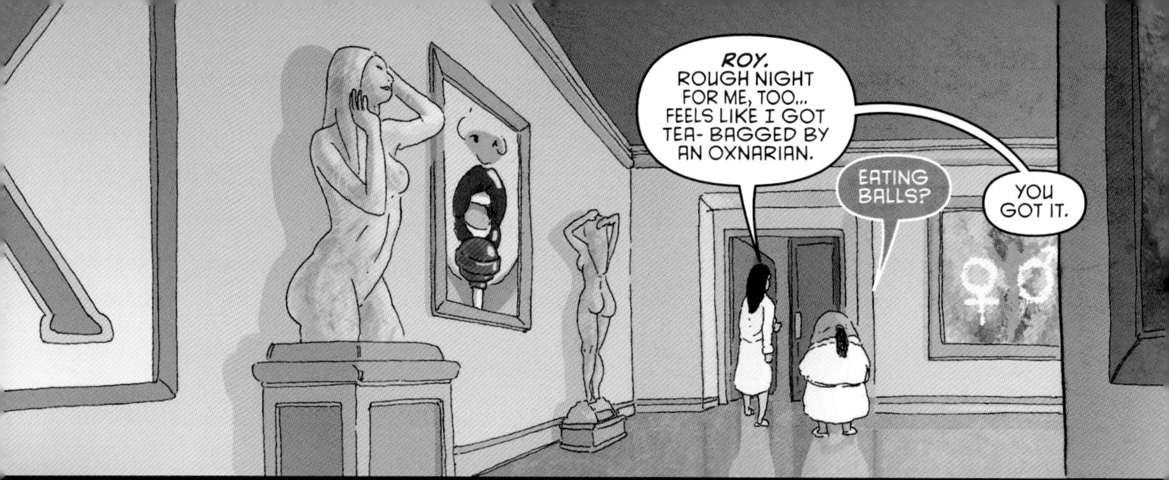
ROY.
ROUGH NIGHT FOR ME, TOO... FEELS LIKE I GOT TEA- BAGGED BY AN OXNARIAN.
EATING BALLS?
YOU GOT IT.

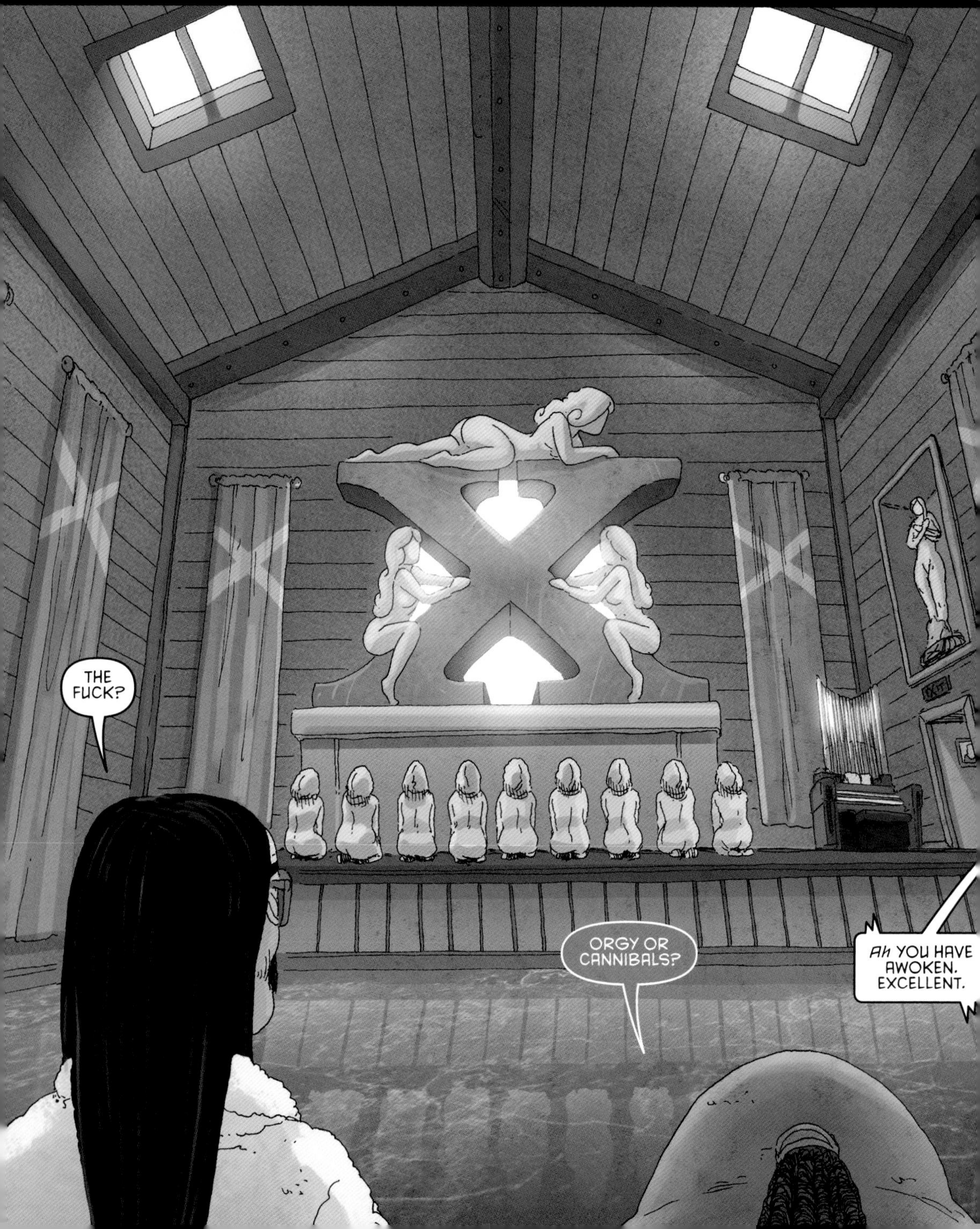
THE FUCK?
ORGY OR CANNIBALS?
Ah YOU HAVE AWOKEN. EXCELLENT.

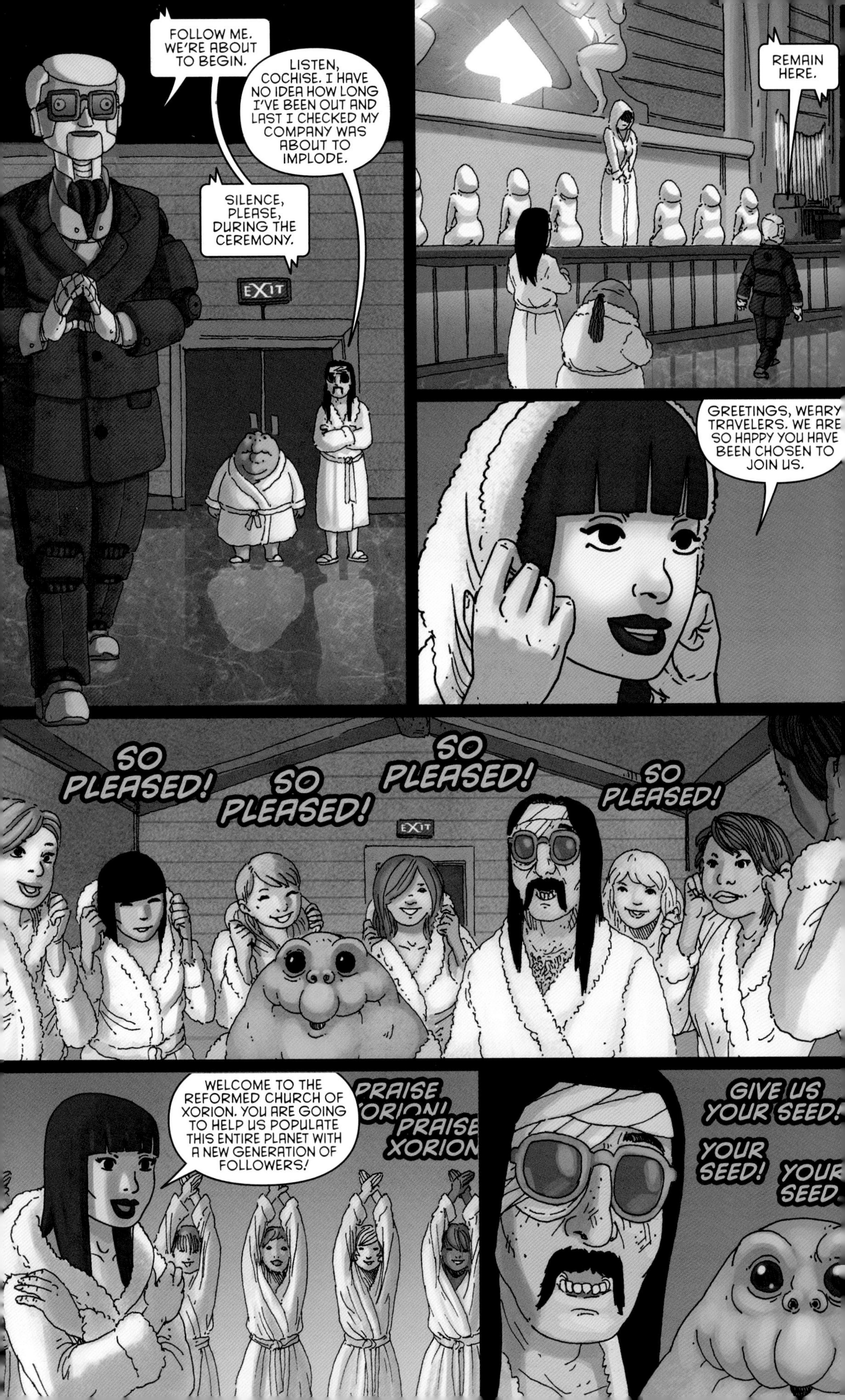
FOLLOW ME. WE'RE ABOUT TO BEGIN.
LISTEN, COCHISE. I HAVE NO IDEA HOW LONG I'VE BEEN OUT AND LAST I CHECKED MY COMPANY WAS ABOUT TO IMPLODE.
SILENCE, PLEASE, DURING THE CEREMONY.
EXIT
REMAIN HERE.
GREETINGS, WEARY TRAVELERS. WE ARE SO HAPPY YOU HAVE BEEN CHOSEN TO JOIN US.
SO PLEASED!
SO PLEASED!
SO PLEASED!
SO PLEASED!
EXIT
WELCOME TO THE REFORMED CHURCH OF XORION. YOU ARE GOING TO HELP US POPULATE THIS ENTIRE PLANET WITH A NEW GENERATION OF FOLLOWERS!
PRAISE XORION!
PRAISE XORION
GIVE US YOUR SEED!
YOUR SEED!
YOUR SEED

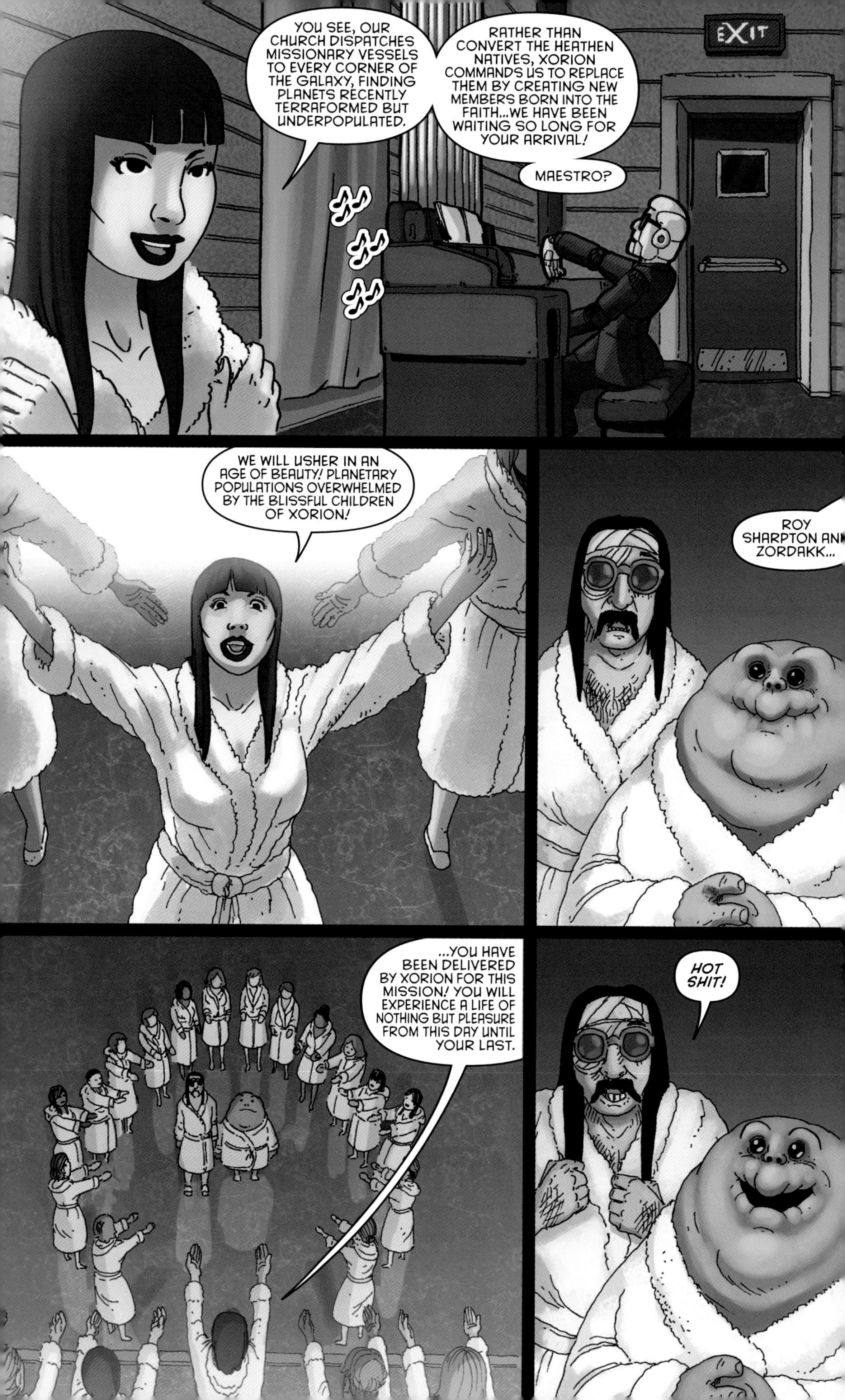

YOU SEE, OUR CHURCH DISPATCHES MISSIONARY VESSELS TO EVERY CORNER OF THE GALAXY, FINDING PLANETS RECENTLY TERRAFORMED BUT UNDERPOPULATED.
RATHER THAN CONVERT THE HEATHEN NATIVES, XORION COMMANDS US TO REPLACE THEM BY CREATING NEW MEMBERS BORN INTO THE FAITH...WE HAVE BEEN WAITING SO LONG FOR YOUR ARRIVAL!
MAESTRO?
EXIT
WE WILL USHER IN AN AGE OF BEAUTY! PLANETARY POPULATIONS OVERWHELMED BY THE BLISSFUL CHILDREN OF XORION!
ROY SHARPTON AN
ZORDAKK...
...YOU HAVE BEEN DELIVERED BY XORION FOR THIS MISSION! YOU WILL EXPERIENCE A LIFE OF NOTHING BUT PLEASURE FROM THIS DAY UNTIL YOUR LAST.
HOT SHIT!

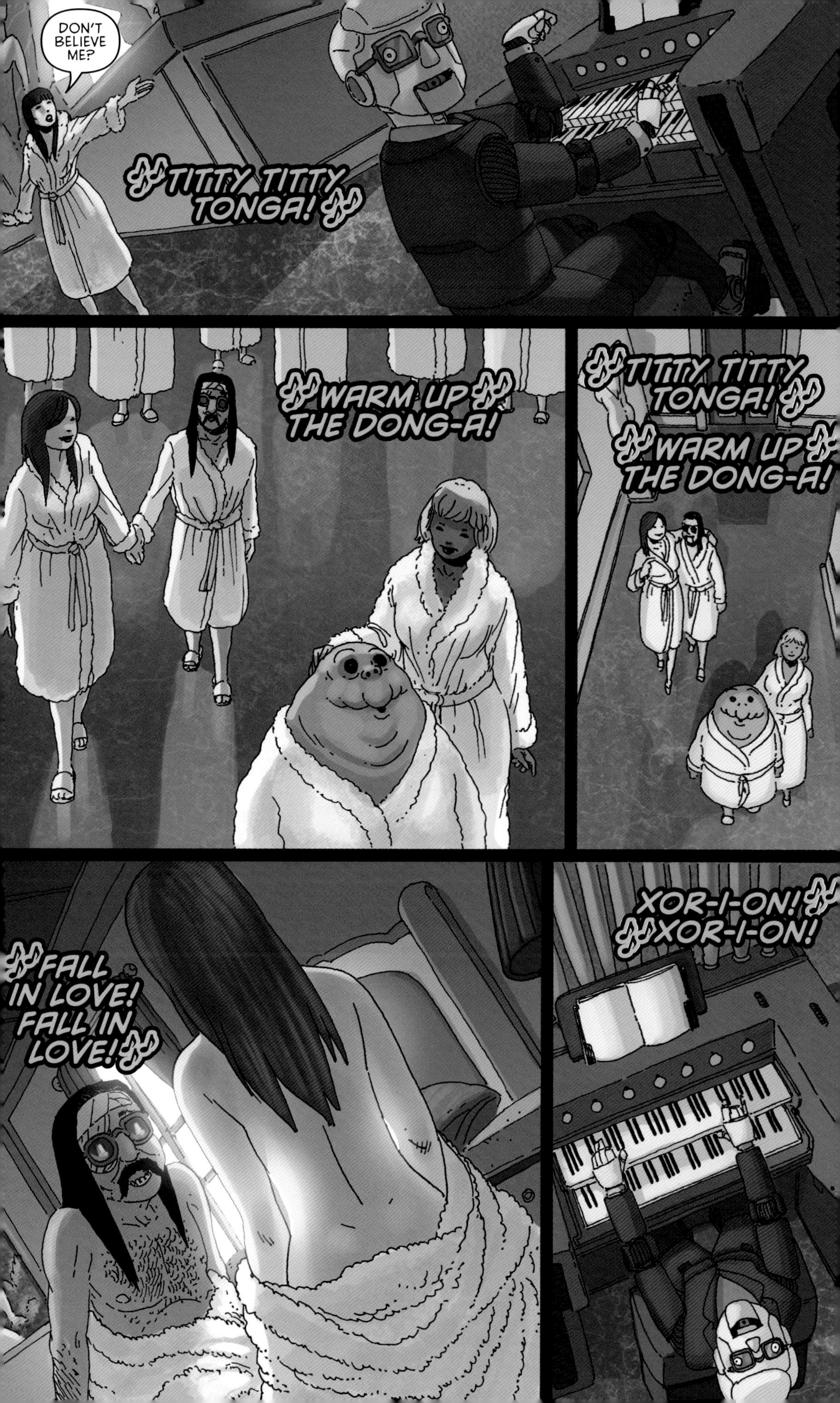

DON'T BELIEVE ME?
TITTY TITTY TONGA!
WARM UP THE DONG-A!
TITTY TITTY TONGA!
WARM UP THE DONG-A!
FALL IN LOVE! FALL IN LOVE!
XOR-I-ON! XOR-I-ON!

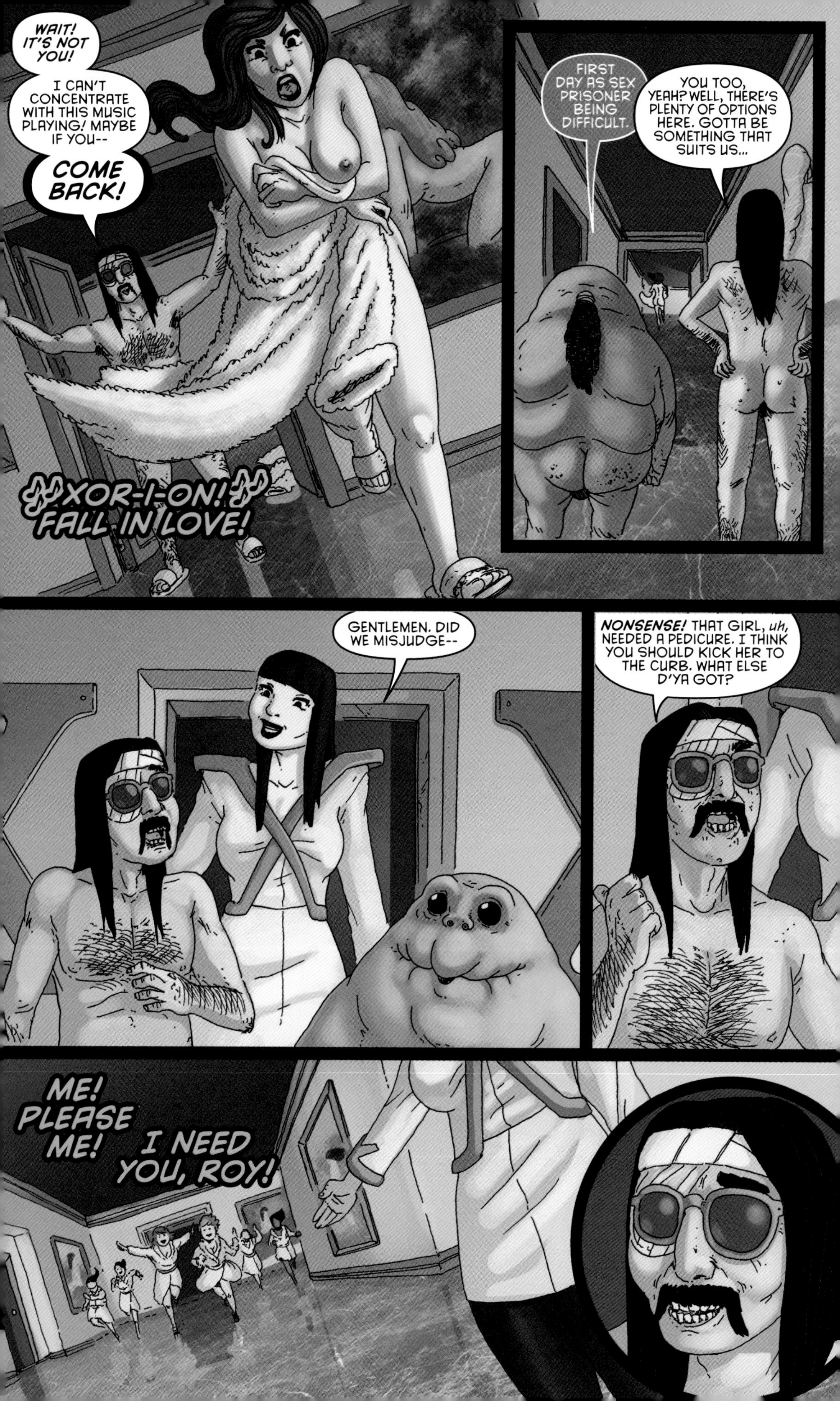
WAIT! IT'S NOT YOU!
I CAN'T CONCENTRATE WITH THIS MUSIC PLAYING! MAYBE IF YOU--
COME BACK!
XOR-I-ON! FALL IN LOVE!
FIRST DAY AS SEX PRISONER BEING DIFFICULT.
YOU TOO, YEAH? WELL, THERE'S PLENTY OF OPTIONS HERE. GOTTA BE SOMETHING THAT SUITS US...
GENTLEMEN. DID WE MISJUDGE--
NONSENSE! THAT GIRL, uh, NEEDED A PEDICURE. I THINK YOU SHOULD KICK HER TO THE CURB. WHAT ELSE D'YA GOT?
ME! PLEASE ME!
I NEED YOU, ROY!

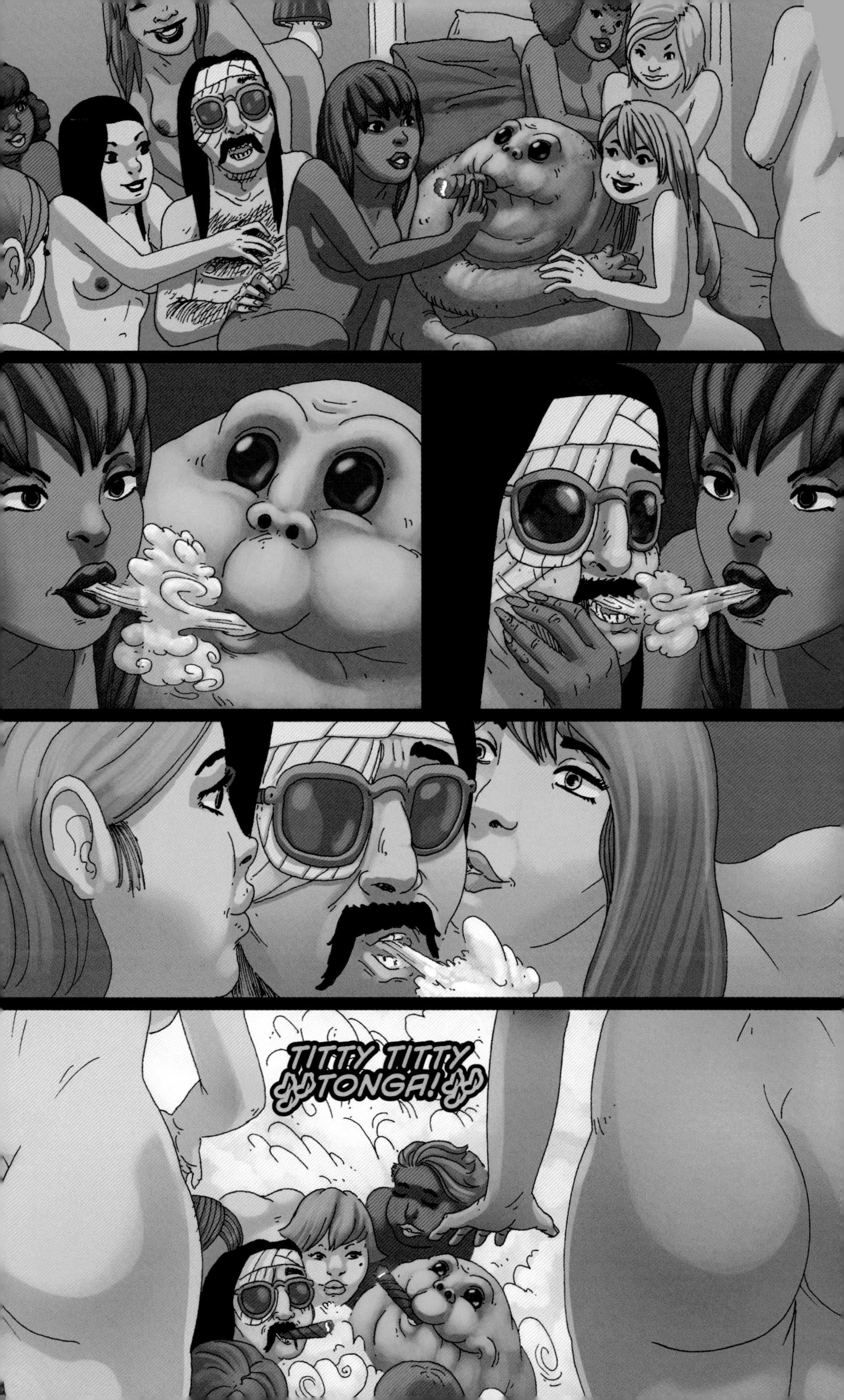
TITTY TITTY
♪TONGA!♪

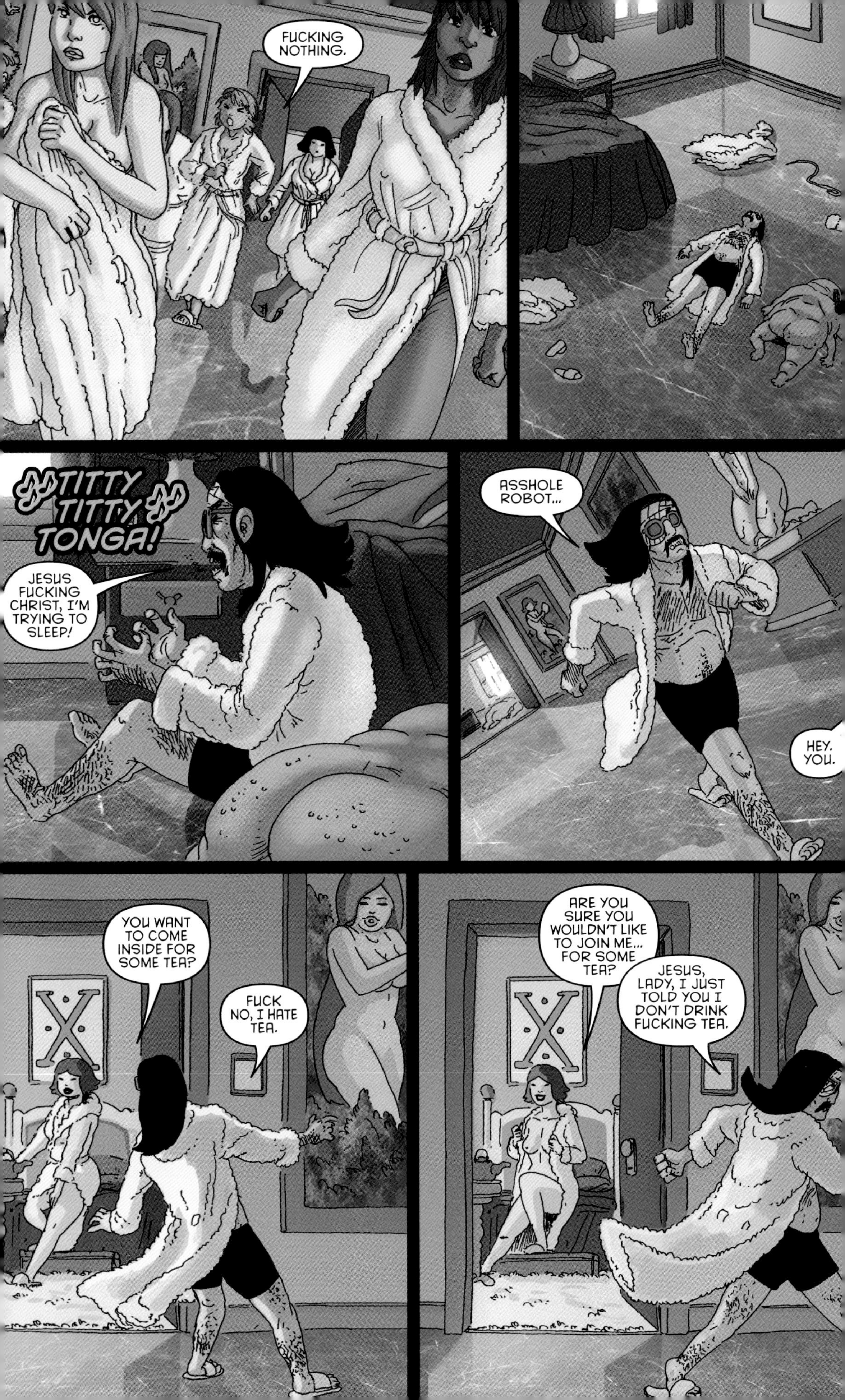
FUCKING NOTHING.
TITTY TITTY TONGA!
JESUS FUCKING CHRIST, I'M TRYING TO SLEEP!
ASSHOLE ROBOT...
HEY. YOU.
YOU WANT TO COME INSIDE FOR SOME TEA?
FUCK NO, I HATE TEA.
ARE YOU SURE YOU WOULDN'T LIKE TO JOIN ME... FOR SOME TEA?
JESUS, LADY, I JUST TOLD YOU I DON'T DRINK FUCKING TEA.

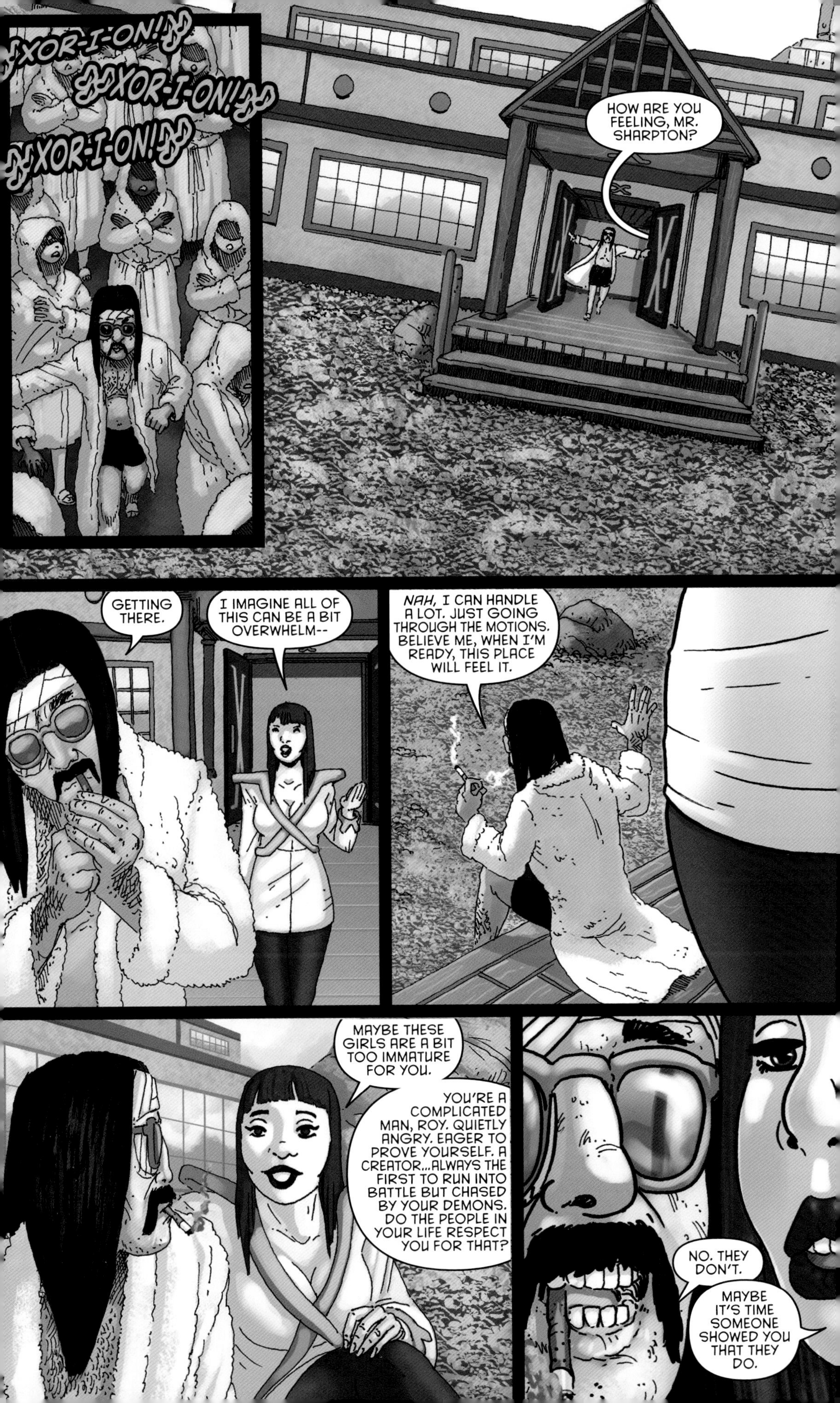
XOR-I-ON!
XOR-I-ON!
XOR-I-ON!
HOW ARE YOU FEELING, MR. SHARPTON?
GETTING THERE.
I IMAGINE ALL OF THIS CAN BE A BIT OVERWHELM--
NAH, I CAN HANDLE A LOT. JUST GOING THROUGH THE MOTIONS. BELIEVE ME, WHEN I'M READY, THIS PLACE WILL FEEL IT.
MAYBE THESE GIRLS ARE A BIT TOO IMMATURE FOR YOU.
YOU'RE A COMPLICATED MAN, ROY. QUIETLY ANGRY. EAGER TO PROVE YOURSELF. A CREATOR...ALWAYS THE FIRST TO RUN INTO BATTLE BUT CHASED BY YOUR DEMONS. DO THE PEOPLE IN YOUR LIFE RESPECT YOU FOR THAT?
NO. THEY DON'T.
MAYBE IT'S TIME SOMEONE SHOWED YOU THAT THEY DO.

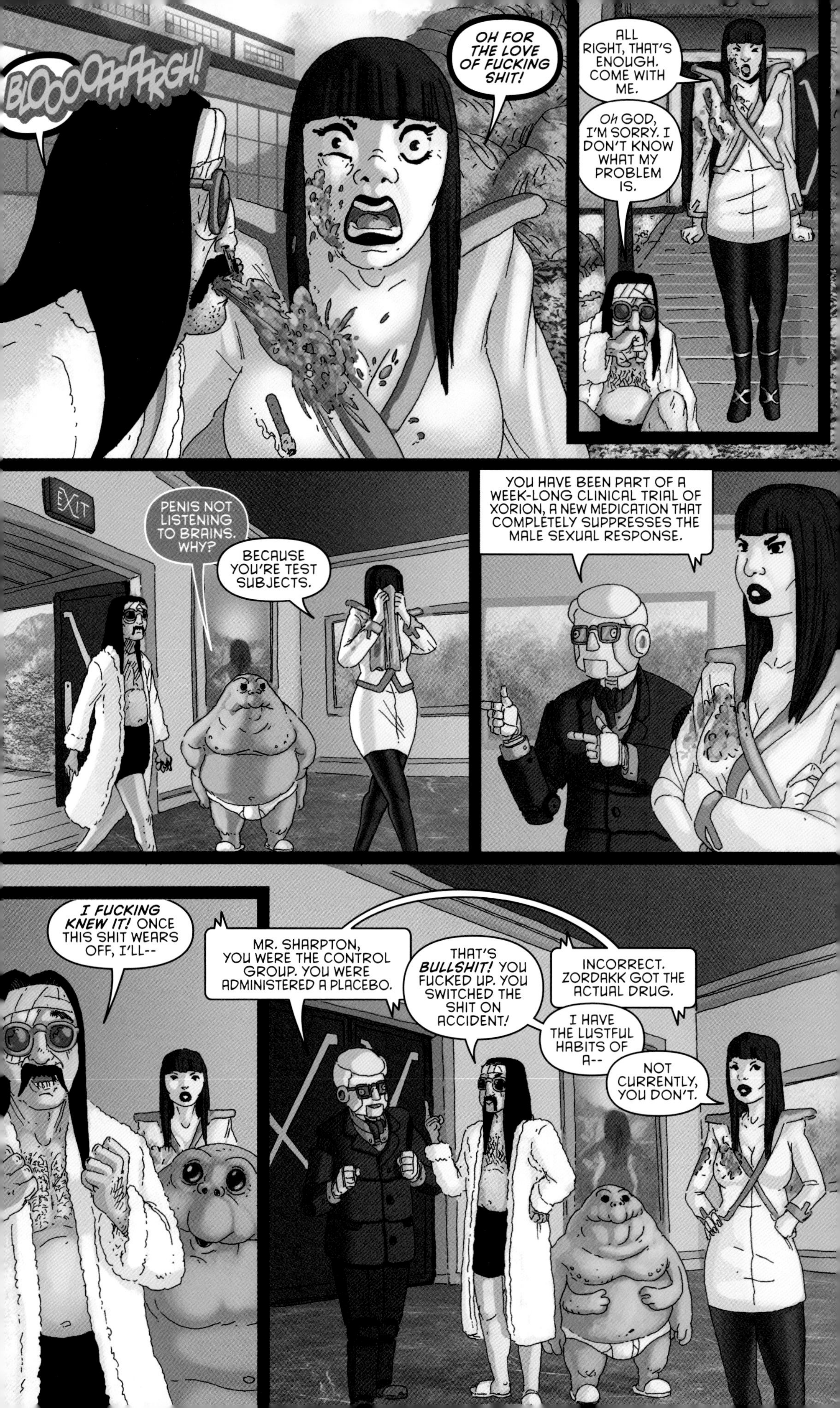
BLOOOOARRRGH!
OH FOR THE LOVE OF FUCKING SHIT!
ALL RIGHT, THAT'S ENOUGH. COME WITH ME.
Oh GOD, I'M SORRY. I DON'T KNOW WHAT MY PROBLEM IS.
EXIT
PENIS NOT LISTENING TO BRAINS. WHY?
BECAUSE YOU'RE TEST SUBJECTS.
YOU HAVE BEEN PART OF A WEEK-LONG CLINICAL TRIAL OF XORION, A NEW MEDICATION THAT COMPLETELY SUPPRESSES THE MALE SEXUAL RESPONSE.
I FUCKING KNEW IT! ONCE THIS SHIT WEARS OFF, I'LL--
MR. SHARPTON, YOU WERE THE CONTROL GROUP. YOU WERE ADMINISTERED A PLACEBO.
THAT'S BULLSHIT! YOU FUCKED UP. YOU SWITCHED THE SHIT ON ACCIDENT!
INCORRECT. ZORDAKK GOT THE ACTUAL DRUG.
I HAVE THE LUSTFUL HABITS OF A--
NOT CURRENTLY, YOU DON'T.

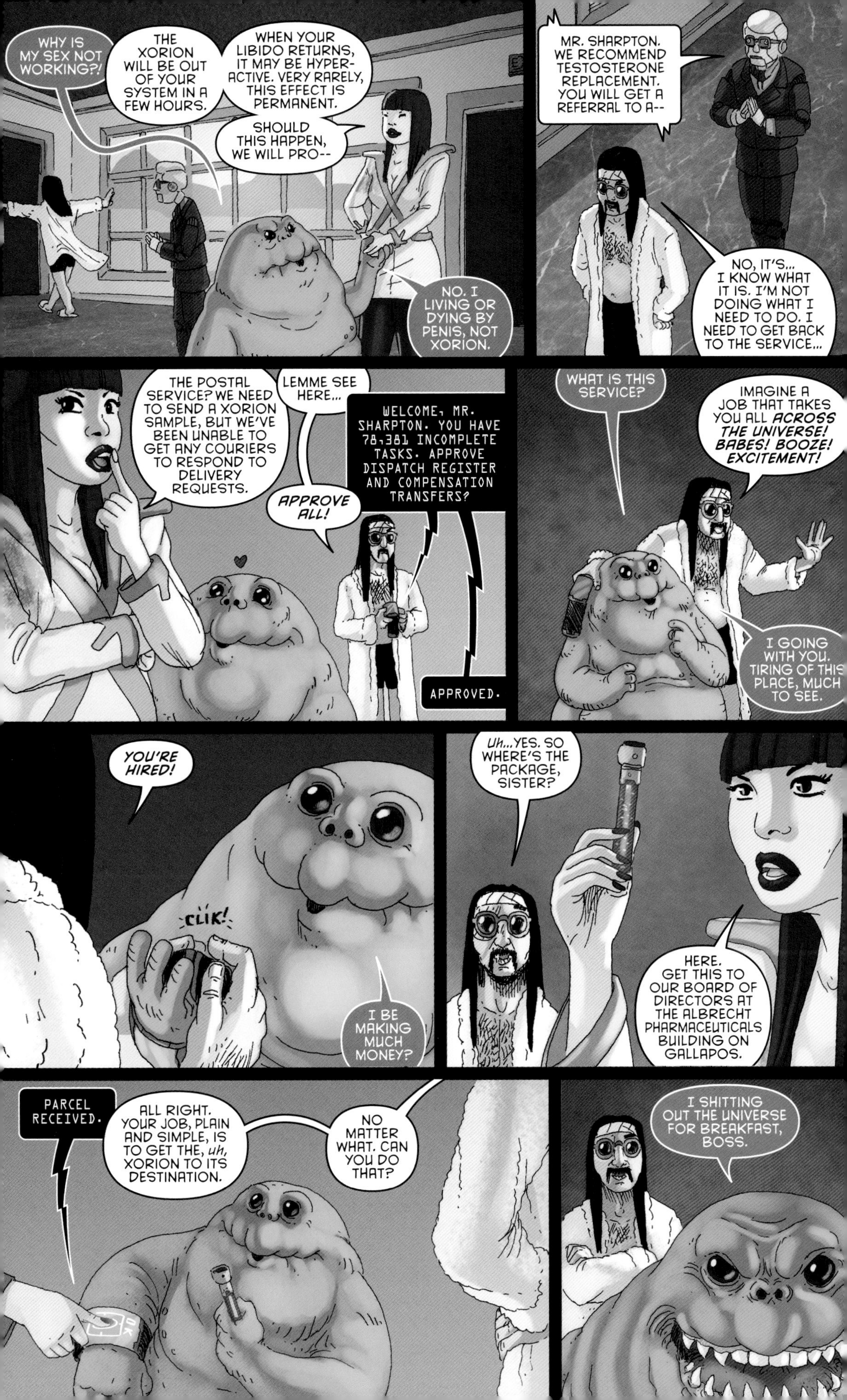
WHY IS MY SEX NOT WORKING?!
THE XORION WILL BE OUT OF YOUR SYSTEM IN A FEW HOURS.
WHEN YOUR LIBIDO RETURNS, IT MAY BE HYPER-ACTIVE. VERY RARELY, THIS EFFECT IS PERMANENT.
SHOULD THIS HAPPEN, WE WILL PRO--
NO. I LIVING OR DYING BY PENIS, NOT XORION.
MR. SHARPTON. WE RECOMMEND TESTOSTERONE REPLACEMENT. YOU WILL GET A REFERRAL TO A--
NO, IT'S... I KNOW WHAT IT IS. I'M NOT DOING WHAT I NEED TO DO. I NEED TO GET BACK TO THE SERVICE...
THE POSTAL SERVICE? WE NEED TO SEND A XORION SAMPLE, BUT WE'VE BEEN UNABLE TO GET ANY COURIERS TO RESPOND TO DELIVERY REQUESTS.
LEMME SEE HERE...
WELCOME, MR. SHARPTON. YOU HAVE 78,381 INCOMPLETE TASKS. APPROVE DISPATCH REGISTER AND COMPENSATION TRANSFERS?
APPROVE ALL!
APPROVED.
WHAT IS THIS SERVICE?
IMAGINE A JOB THAT TAKES YOU ALL ACROSS THE UNIVERSE! BABES! BOOZE! EXCITEMENT!
I GOING WITH YOU. TIRING OF THIS PLACE, MUCH TO SEE.
YOU'RE HIRED!
CLIK!
I BE MAKING MUCH MONEY?
Uh...YES. SO WHERE'S THE PACKAGE, SISTER?
HERE. GET THIS TO OUR BOARD OF DIRECTORS AT THE ALBRECHT PHARMACEUTICALS BUILDING ON GALLAPOS.
PARCEL RECEIVED.
ALL RIGHT. YOUR JOB, PLAIN AND SIMPLE, IS TO GET THE, uh, XORION TO ITS DESTINATION.
NO MATTER WHAT. CAN YOU DO THAT?
OK
I SHITTING OUT THE UNIVERSE FOR BREAKFAST, BOSS.

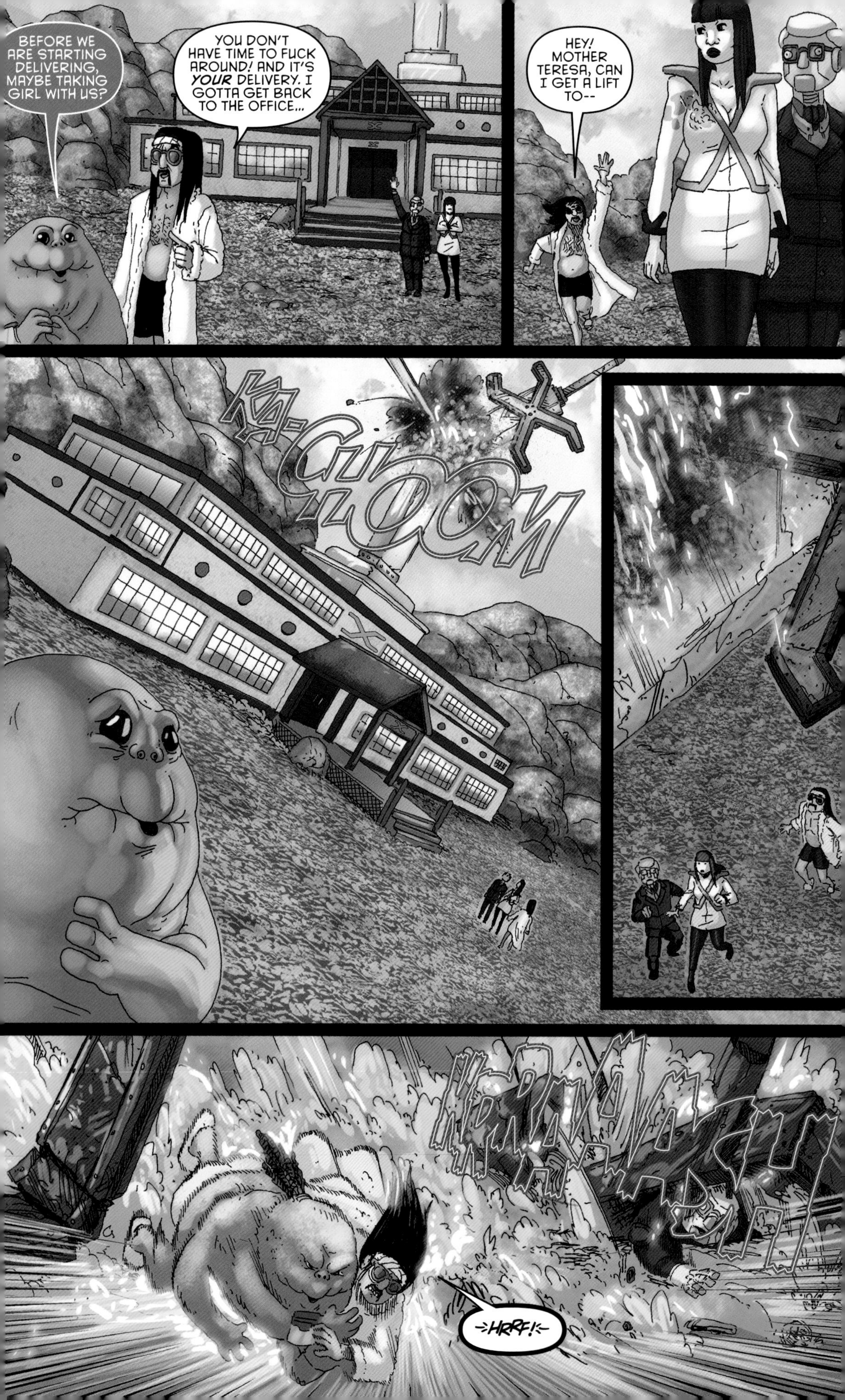
BEFORE WE ARE STARTING DELIVERING, MAYBE TAKING GIRL WITH US?
YOU DON'T HAVE TIME TO FUCK AROUND! AND IT'S *YOUR* DELIVERY. I GOTTA GET BACK TO THE OFFICE...
HEY! MOTHER TERESA, CAN I GET A LIFT TO--
KA-CHOOM
HRRF!

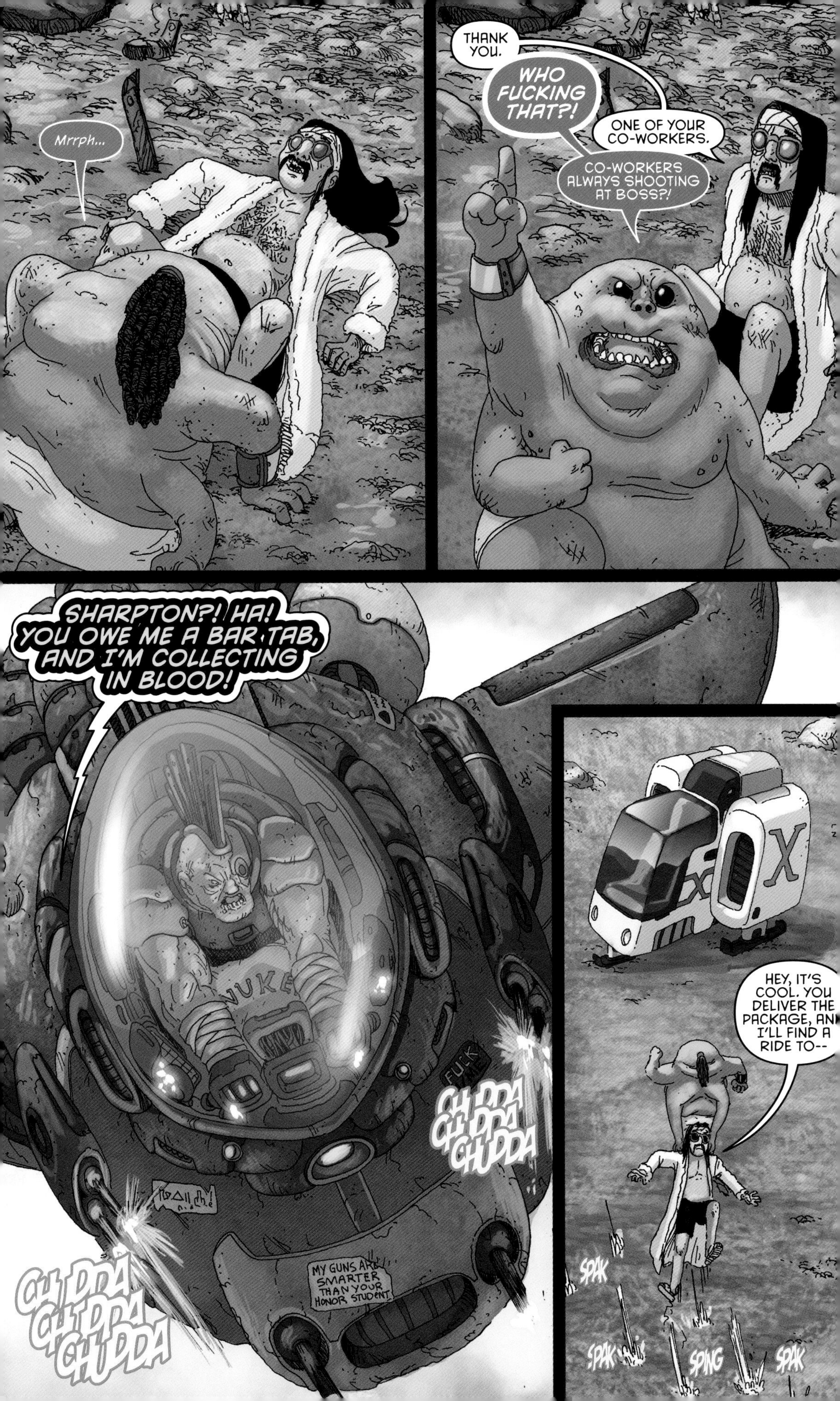
Mrrph...
THANK YOU.
WHO FUCKING THAT?!
ONE OF YOUR CO-WORKERS.
CO-WORKERS ALWAYS SHOOTING AT BOSS?!
SHARPTON?! HA! YOU OWE ME A BAR TAB, AND I'M COLLECTING IN BLOOD!
NUKE
FUCK
MY GUNS ARE SMARTER THAN YOUR HONOR STUDENT
CHUDDA CHUDDA CHUDDA
CHUDDA CHUDDA CHUDDA
X
HEY, IT'S COOL. YOU DELIVER THE PACKAGE, AN' I'LL FIND A RIDE TO--
SPAK
SPAK
SPING
SPAK

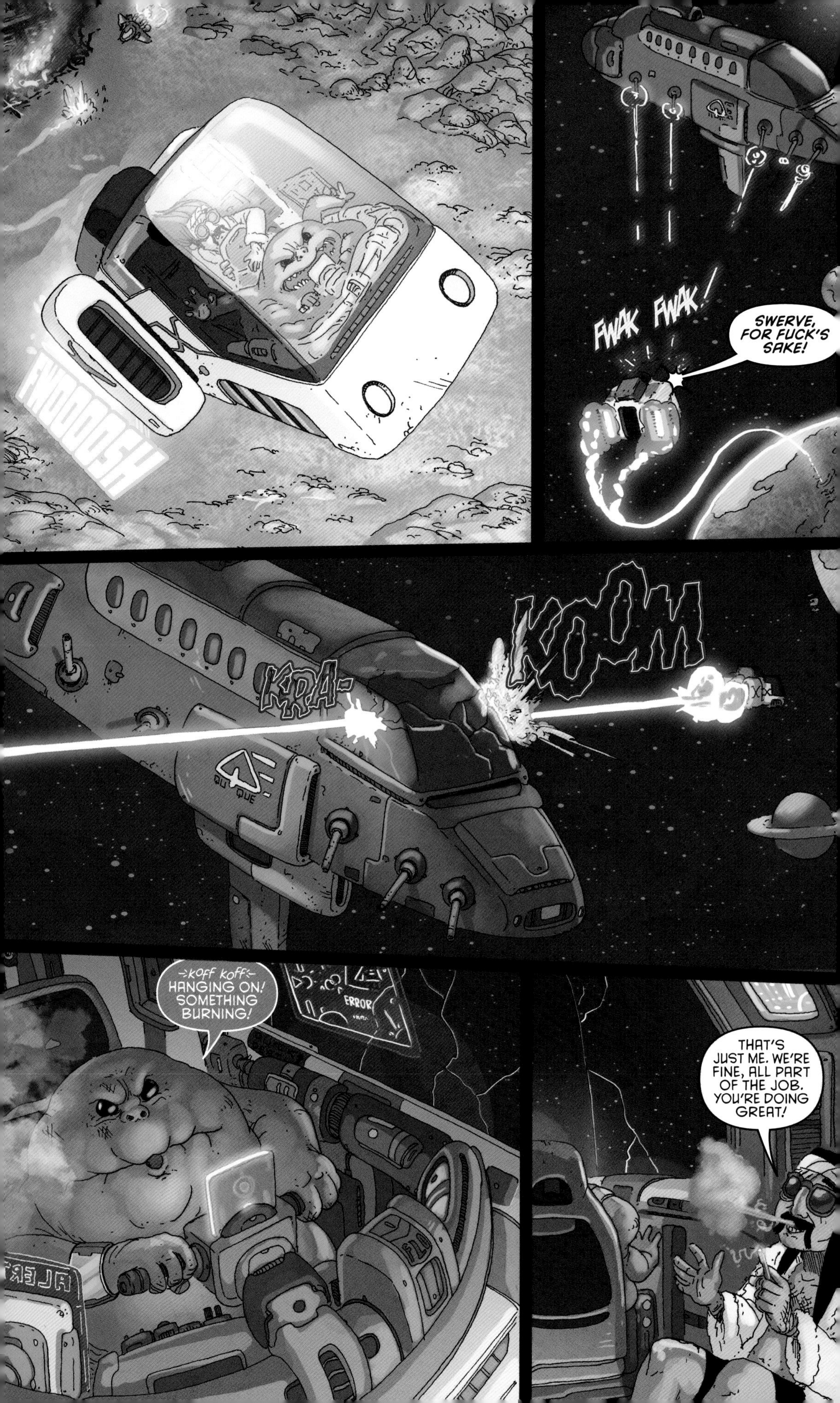
FWOOOSH
FWAK FWAK!
SWERVE, FOR FUCK'S SAKE!
KRA-
KOOM
-KOFF KOFF- HANGING ON! SOMETHING BURNING!
ERROR
THAT'S JUST ME. WE'RE FINE, ALL PART OF THE JOB. YOU'RE DOING GREAT!

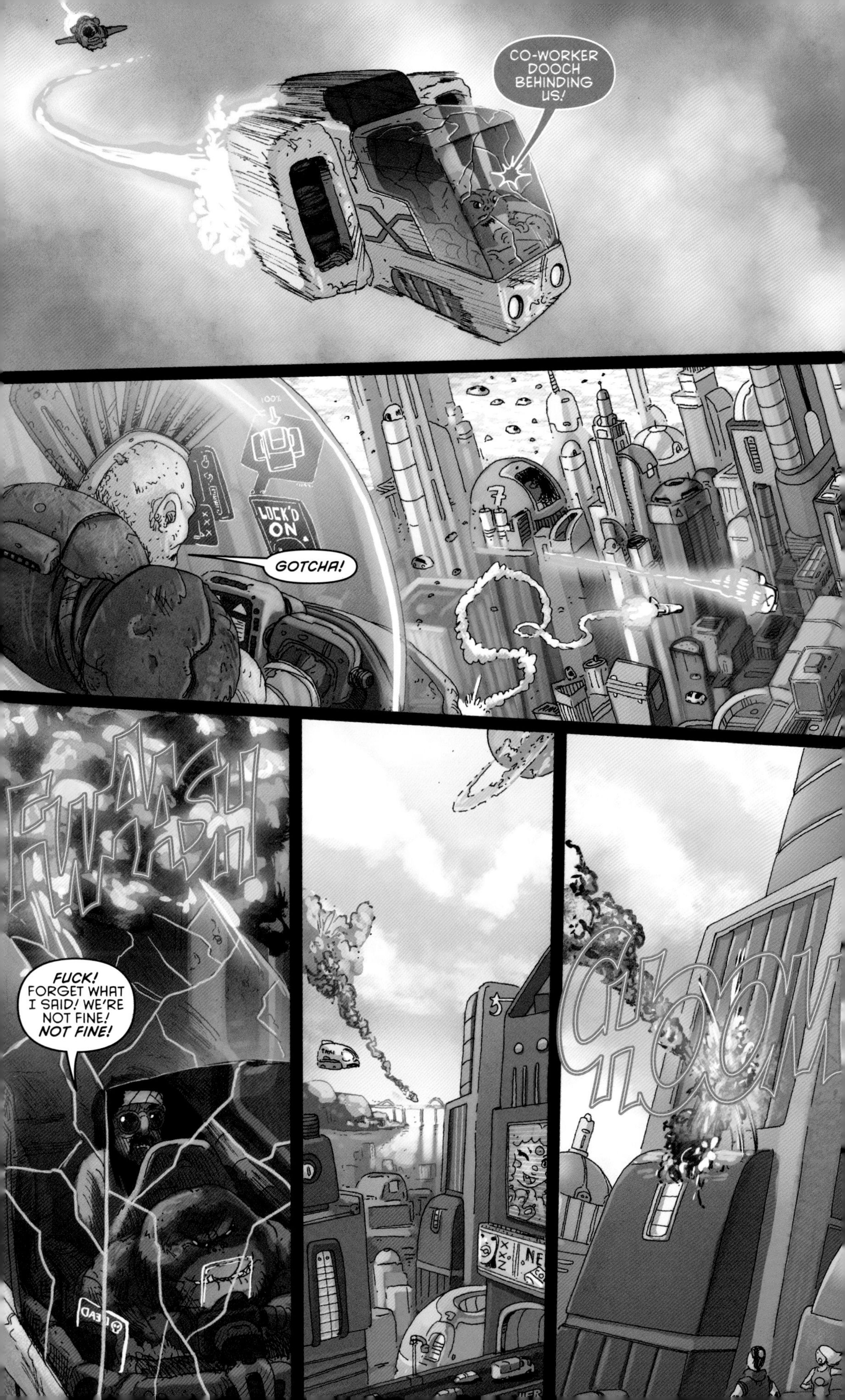
CO-WORKER DOOCH BEHINDING US!
LOCK'D ON
GOTCHA!
FUCK! FORGET WHAT I SAID! WE'RE NOT FINE! NOT FINE!

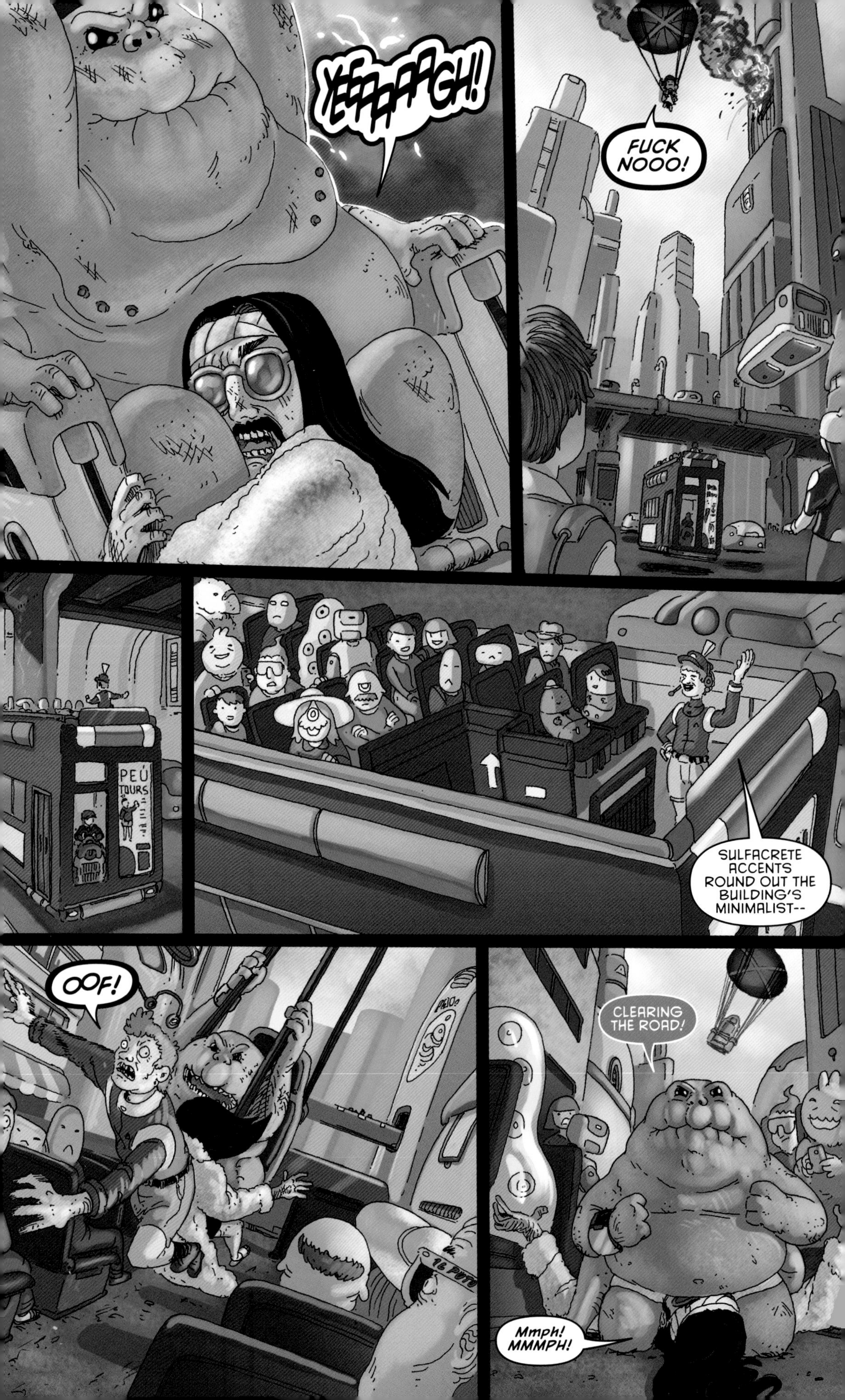
YEEAAAGH!
FUCK NOOO!
PEÚ TOURS
SULFACRETE ACCENTS ROUND OUT THE BUILDING'S MINIMALIST--
OOF!
CLEARING THE ROAD!
Mmph! MMMPH!

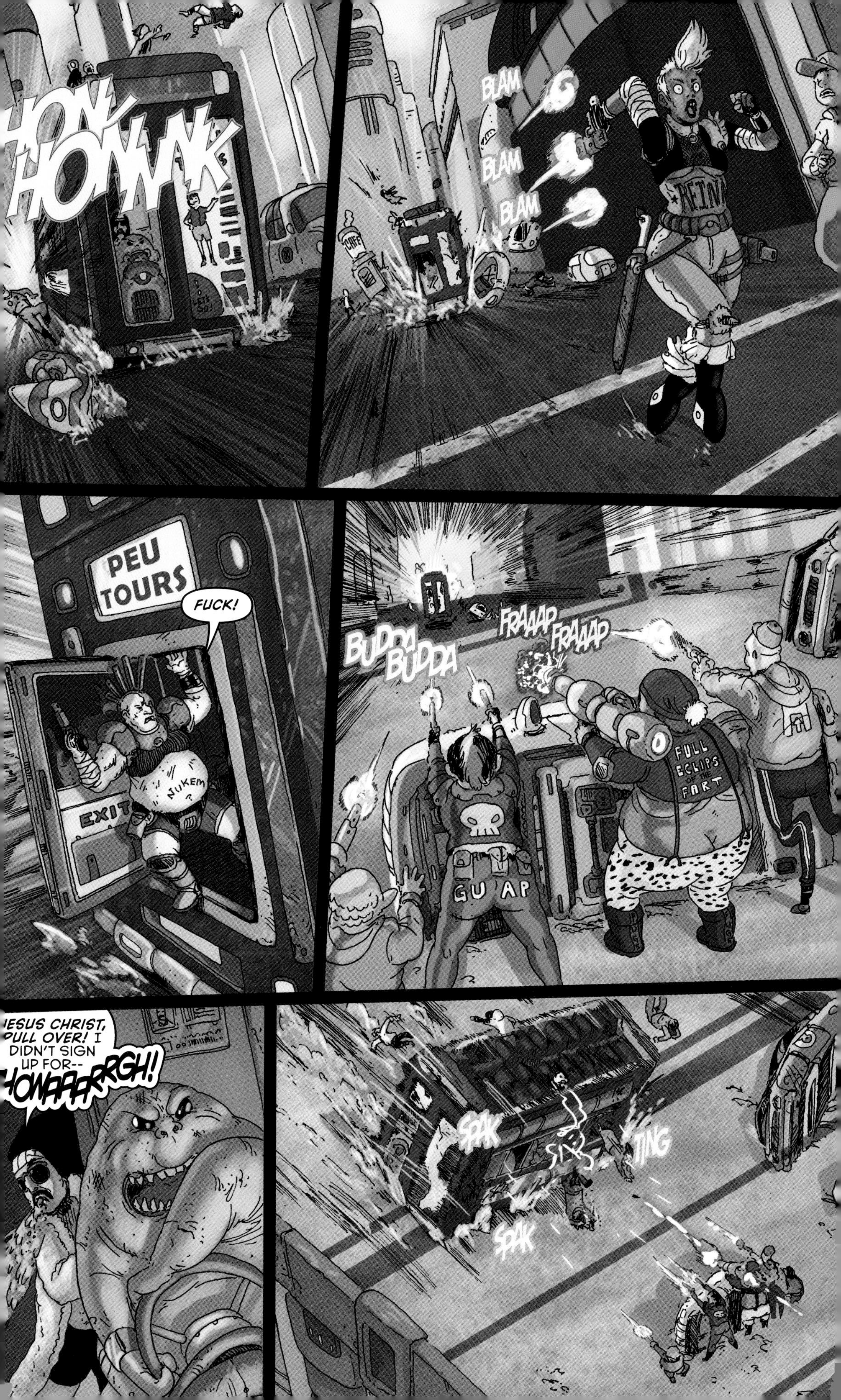

HON HONNK
BLAM
BLAM
BLAM
REINA
PEU TOURS
FUCK!
EXIT
NUKEM
BUDDA BUDDA
FRAAAP FRAAAP
FULL ECLIPS OF THE FART
GU AP
JESUS CHRIST, PULL OVER! I DIDN'T SIGN UP FOR--
HONAAARRGH!
SPAK
TING
SPAK

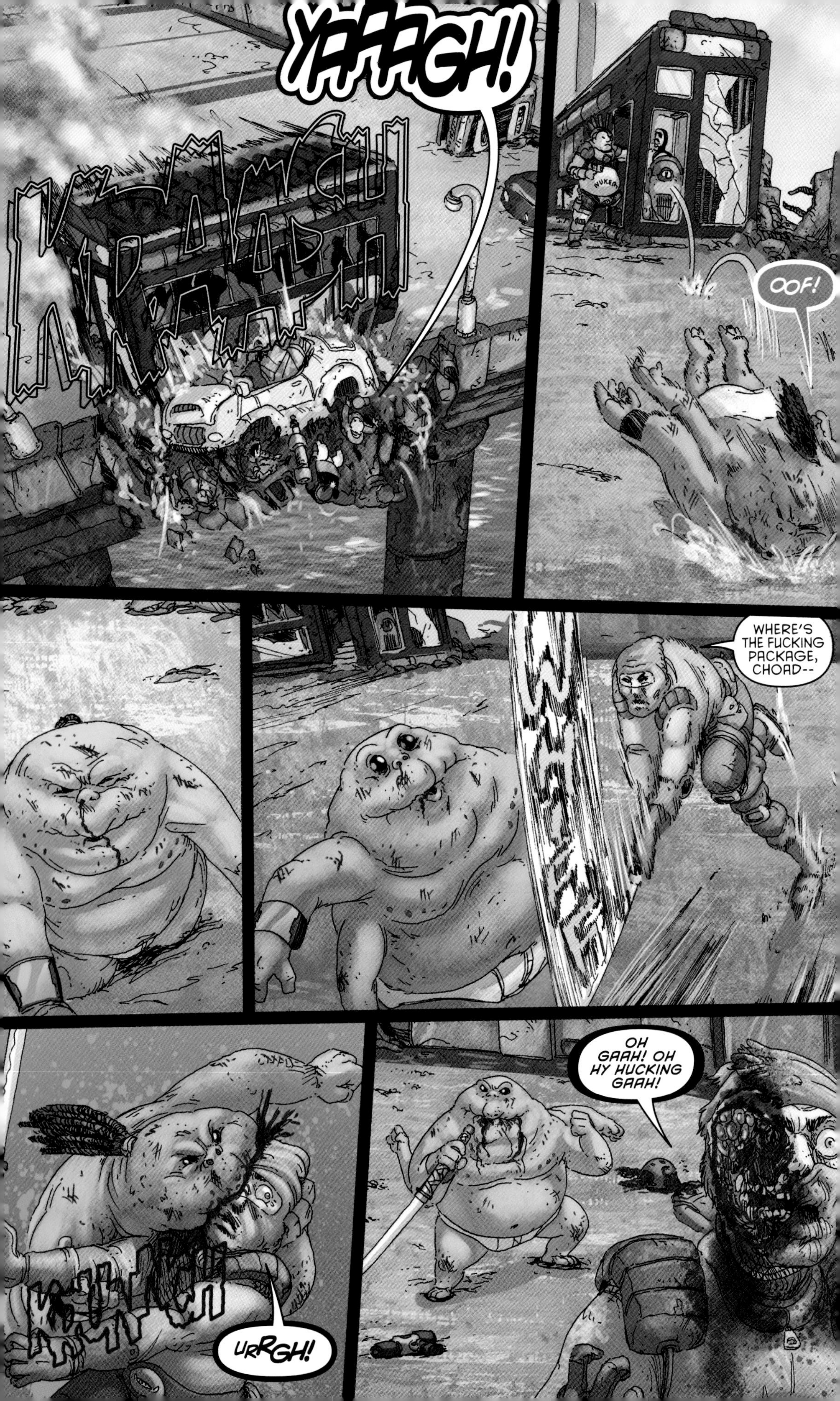
YAAAGH!
OOF!
WHERE'S THE FUCKING PACKAGE, CHOAD--
URRGH!
OH GAAH! OH HY HUCKING GAAH!

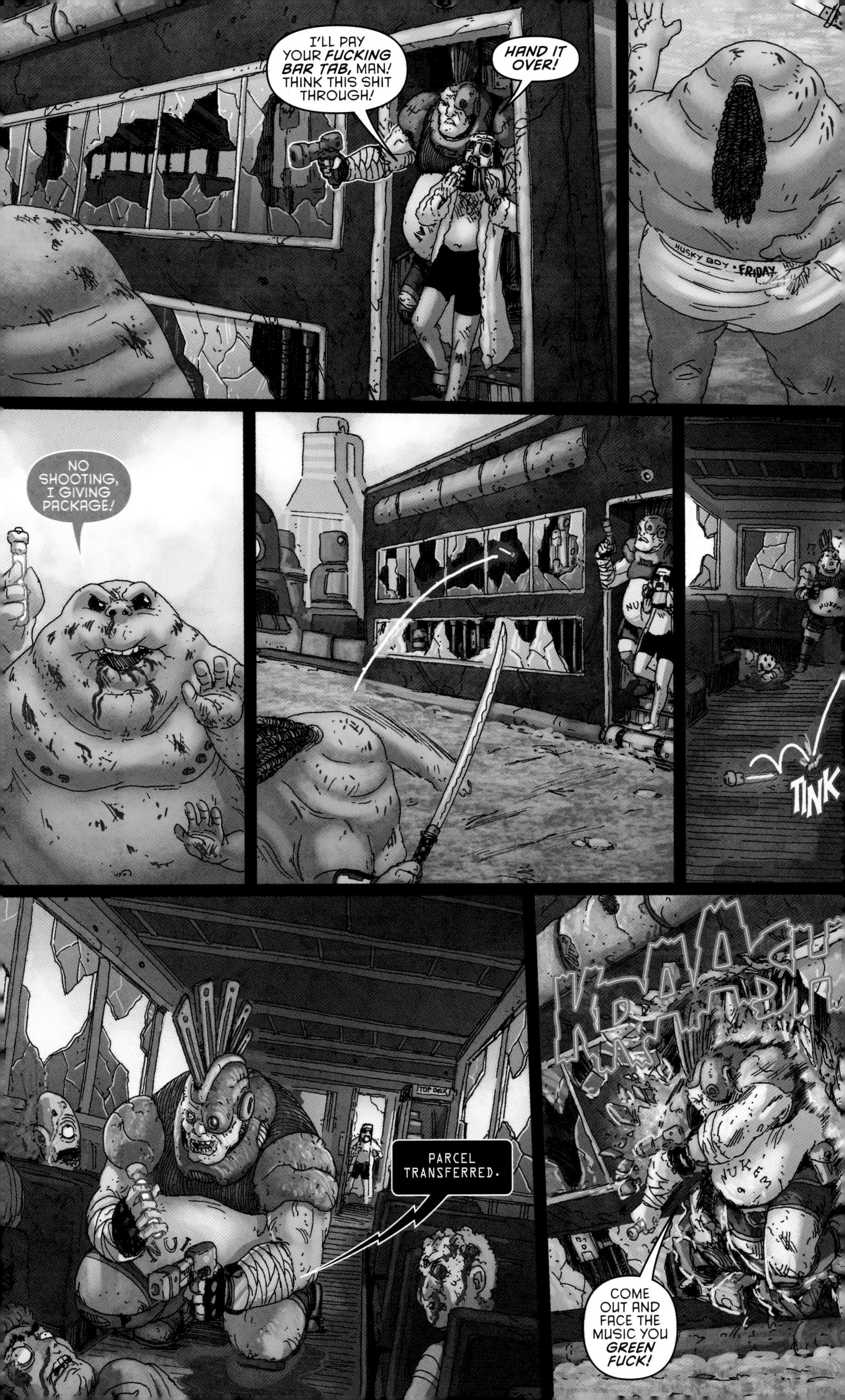
I'LL PAY YOUR FUCKING BAR TAB, MAN! THINK THIS SHIT THROUGH!
HAND IT OVER!
HUSKY BOY • FRIDAY
NO SHOOTING, I GIVING PACKAGE!
TINK
PARCEL TRANSFERRED.
TOP DECK
KRAAKABOOM
NUKEM
COME OUT AND FACE THE MUSIC YOU GREEN FUCK!

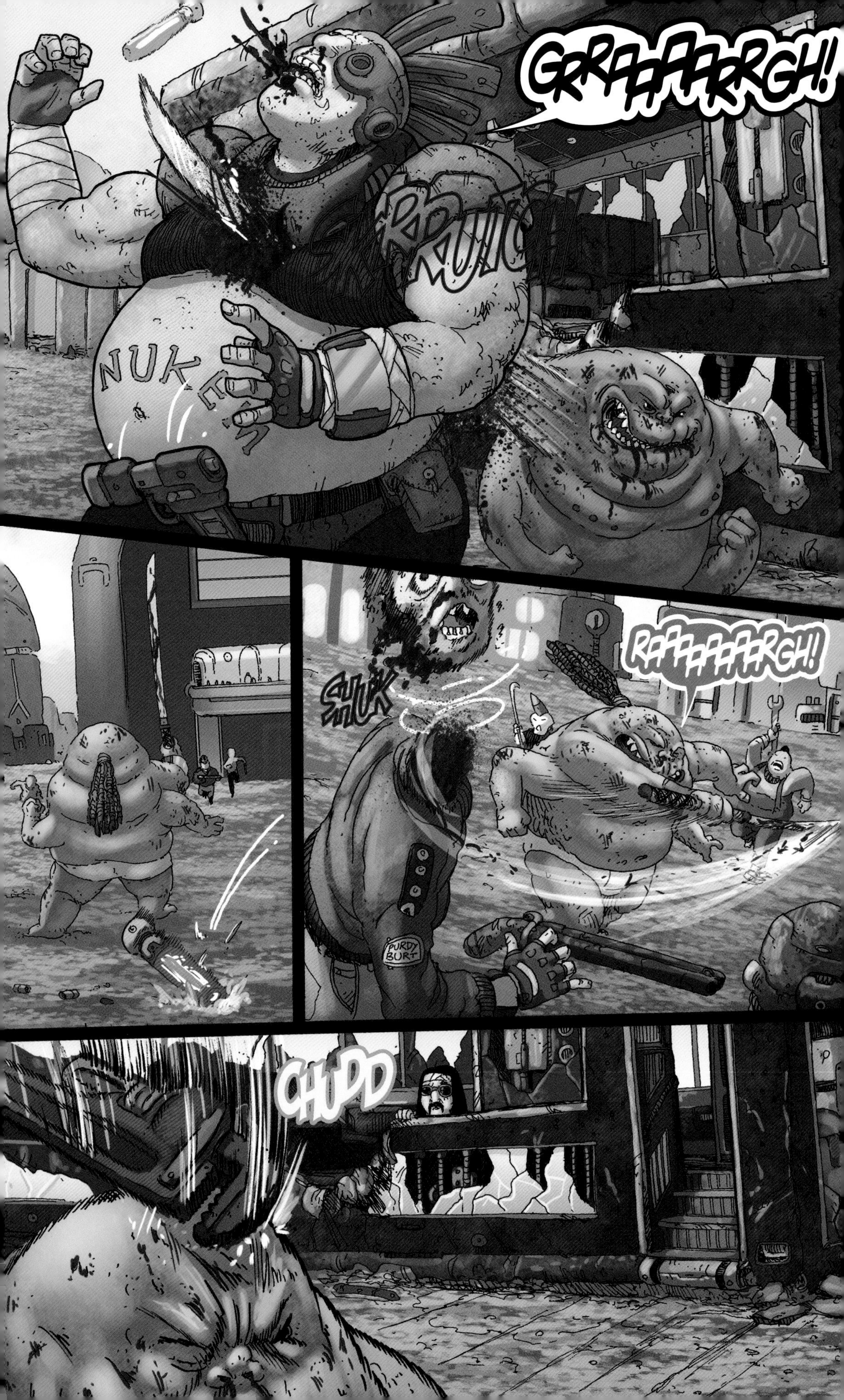
GRRAAARRGH!
SHRRUTCH!
NUKE 'EM
SHUK
RAAAAAARGH!
PURDY BURT
CHUDD

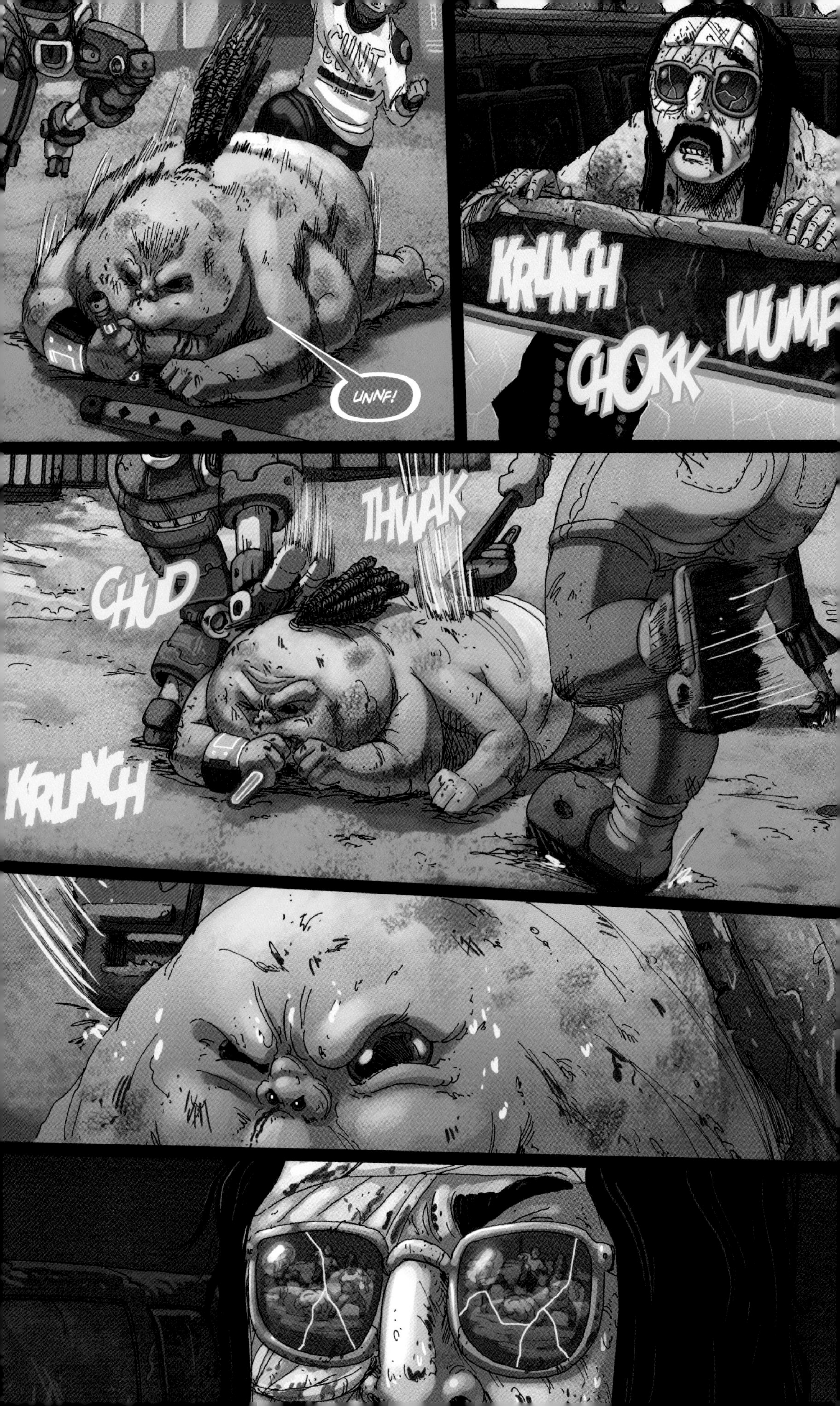
UNNF!
KRUNCH
CHOKK
WUMP
THWAK
CHUD
KRUNCH

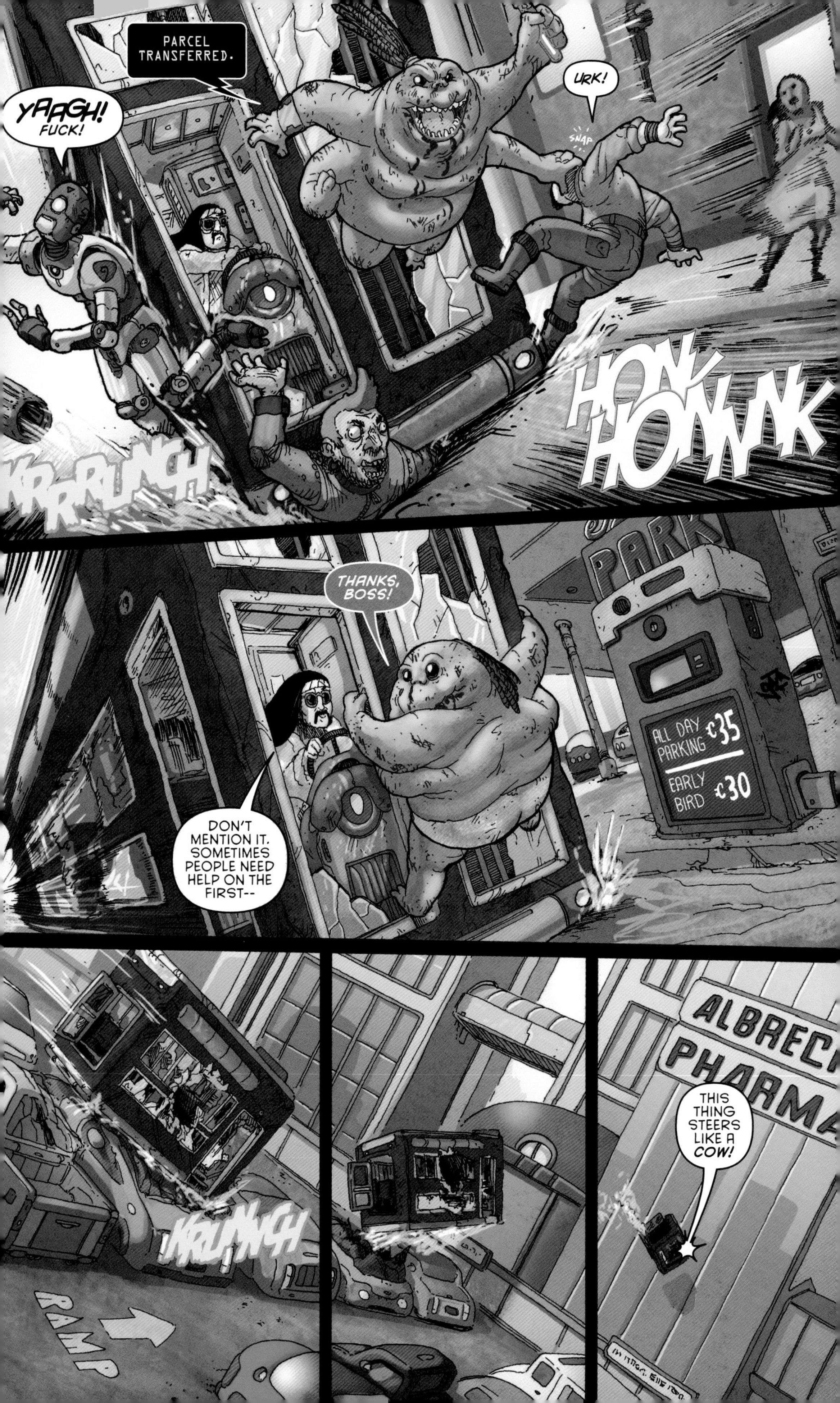

PARCEL TRANSFERRED.
YAAGH! FUCK!
URK!
SNAP
HONK HONNK
KRRRUNCH
PARK
THANKS, BOSS!
ALL DAY PARKING €35
EARLY BIRD €30
DON'T MENTION IT. SOMETIMES PEOPLE NEED HELP ON THE FIRST--
KRUNCH
RAMP
ALBRECH
PHARMA
THIS THING STEERS LIKE A COW!

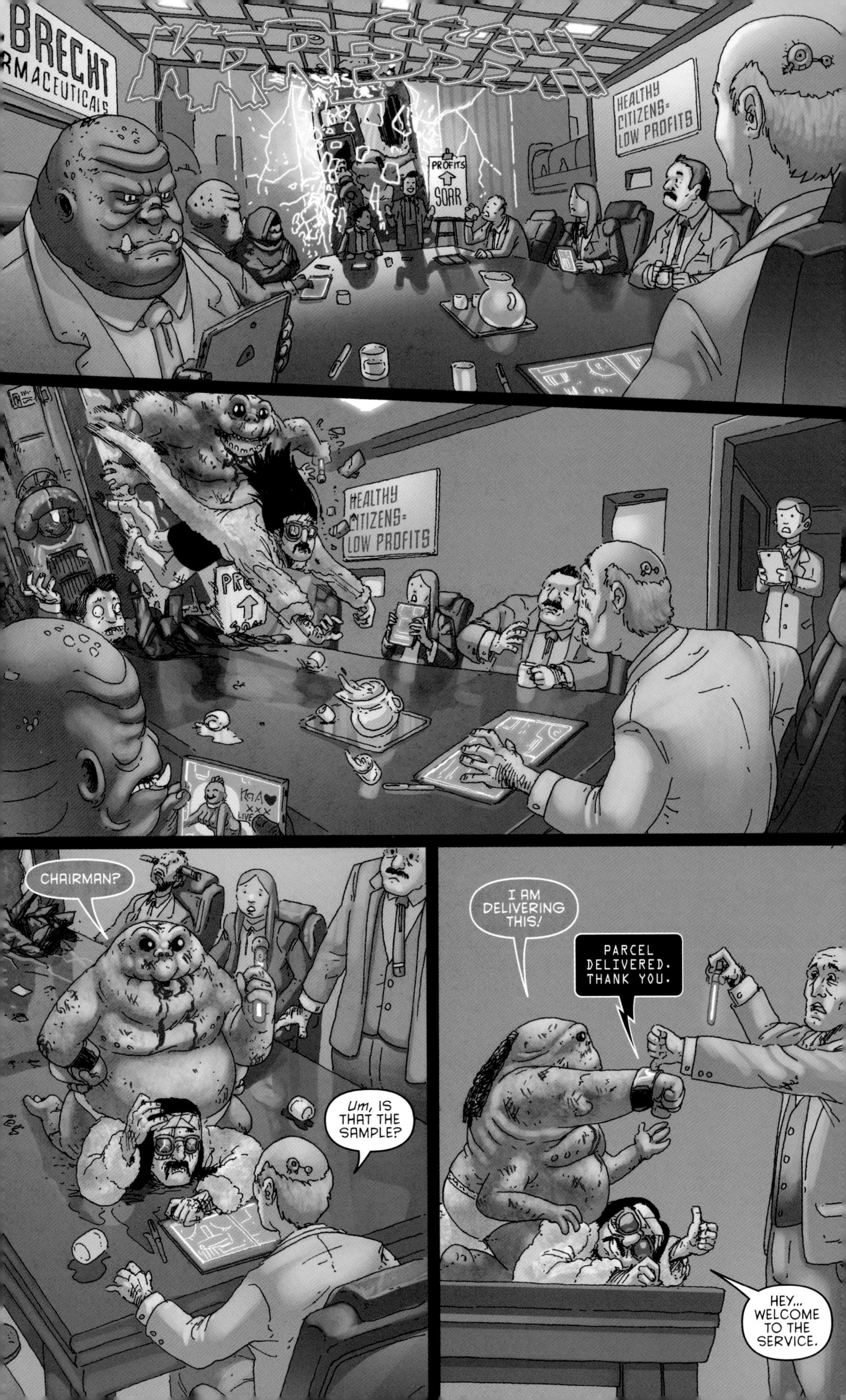
BRECHT
RMACEUTICALS
HEALTHY CITIZENS= LOW PROFITS
PROFITS SOAR
HEALTHY CITIZENS= LOW PROFITS
CHAIRMAN?
Um, IS THAT THE SAMPLE?
I AM DELIVERING THIS!
PARCEL DELIVERED. THANK YOU.
HEY... WELCOME TO THE SERVICE.

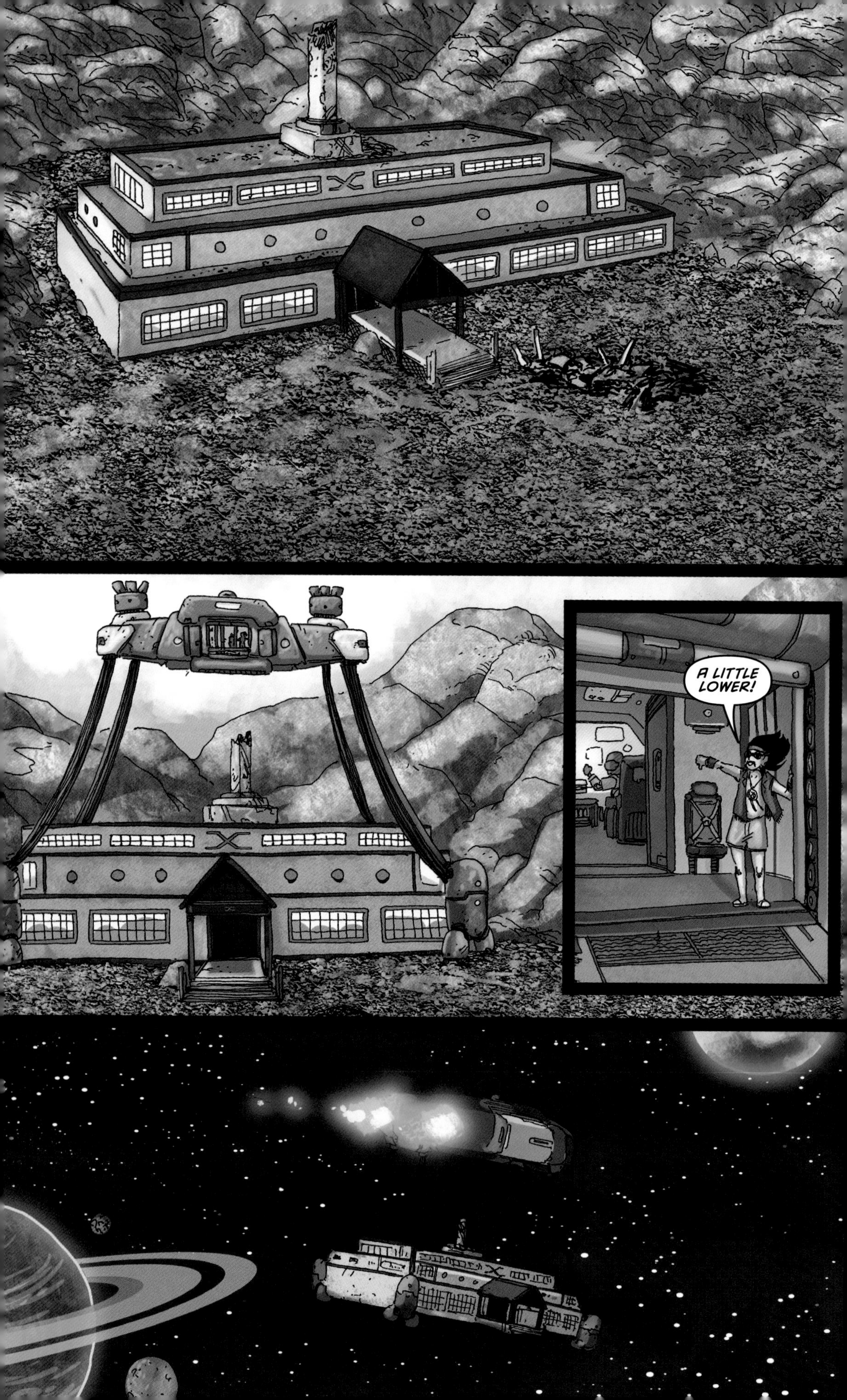
A LITTLE
LOWER!

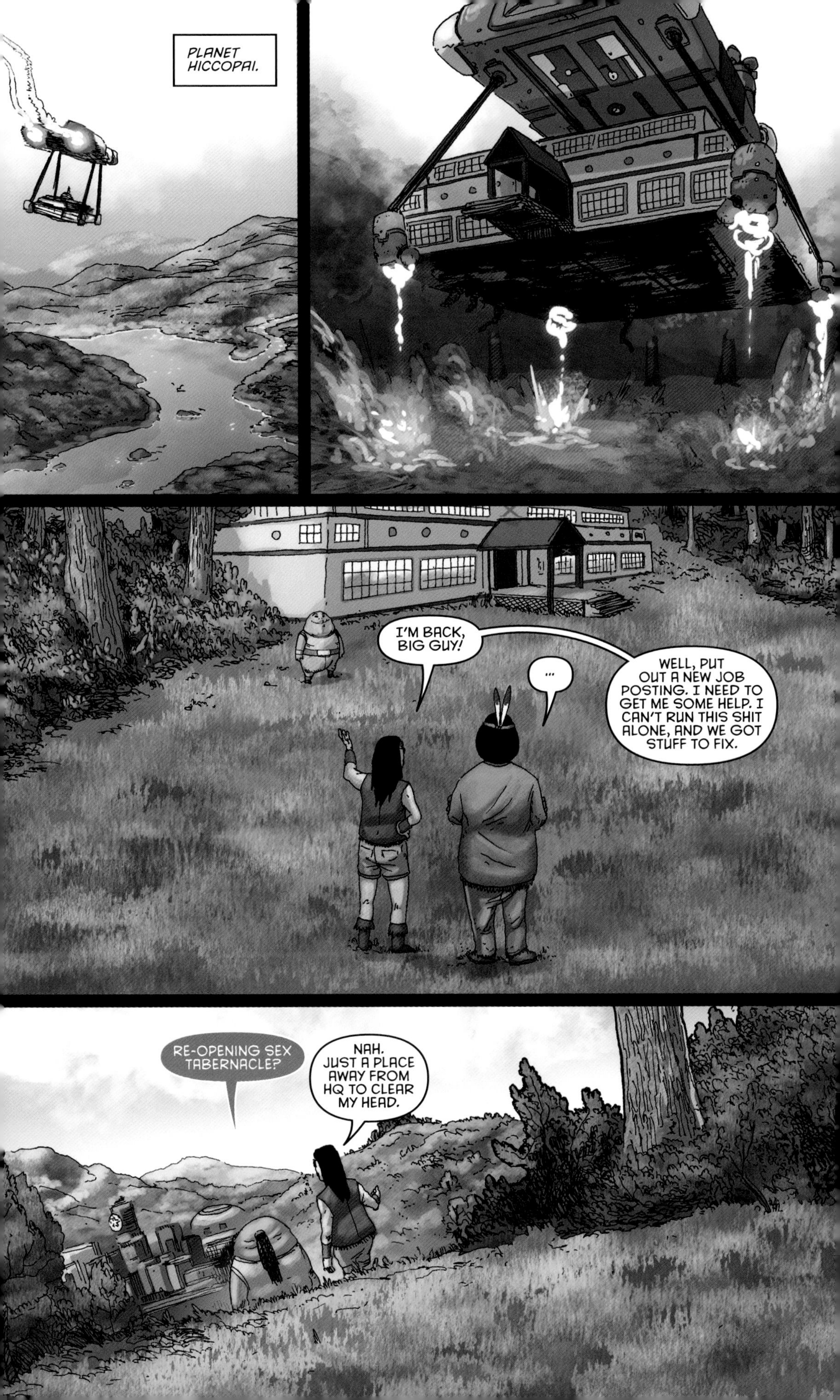
PLANET HICCOPAI.
I'M BACK, BIG GUY!
...
WELL, PUT OUT A NEW JOB POSTING. I NEED TO GET ME SOME HELP. I CAN'T RUN THIS SHIT ALONE, AND WE GOT STUFF TO FIX.
RE-OPENING SEX TABERNACLE?
NAH. JUST A PLACE AWAY FROM HQ TO CLEAR MY HEAD.

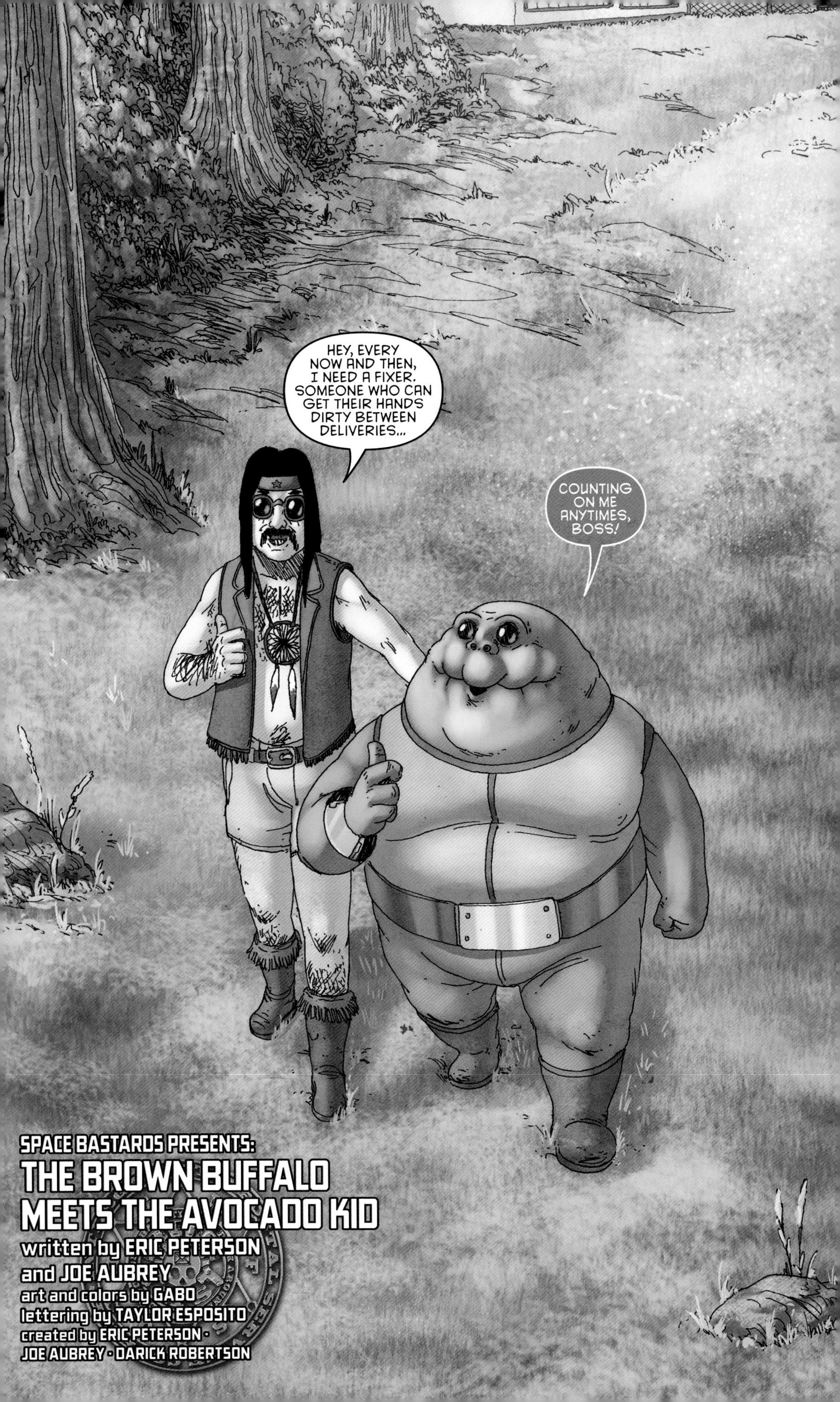
HEY, EVERY NOW AND THEN, I NEED A FIXER. SOMEONE WHO CAN GET THEIR HANDS DIRTY BETWEEN DELIVERIES...
COUNTING ON ME ANYTIMES, BOSS!

SPACE BASTARDS PRESENTS:

THE BROWN BUFFALO MEETS THE AVOCADO KID

written by ERIC PETERSON and JOE AUBREY
art and colors by GABO
lettering by TAYLOR ESPOSITO
created by ERIC PETERSON · JOE AUBREY · DARICK ROBERTSON

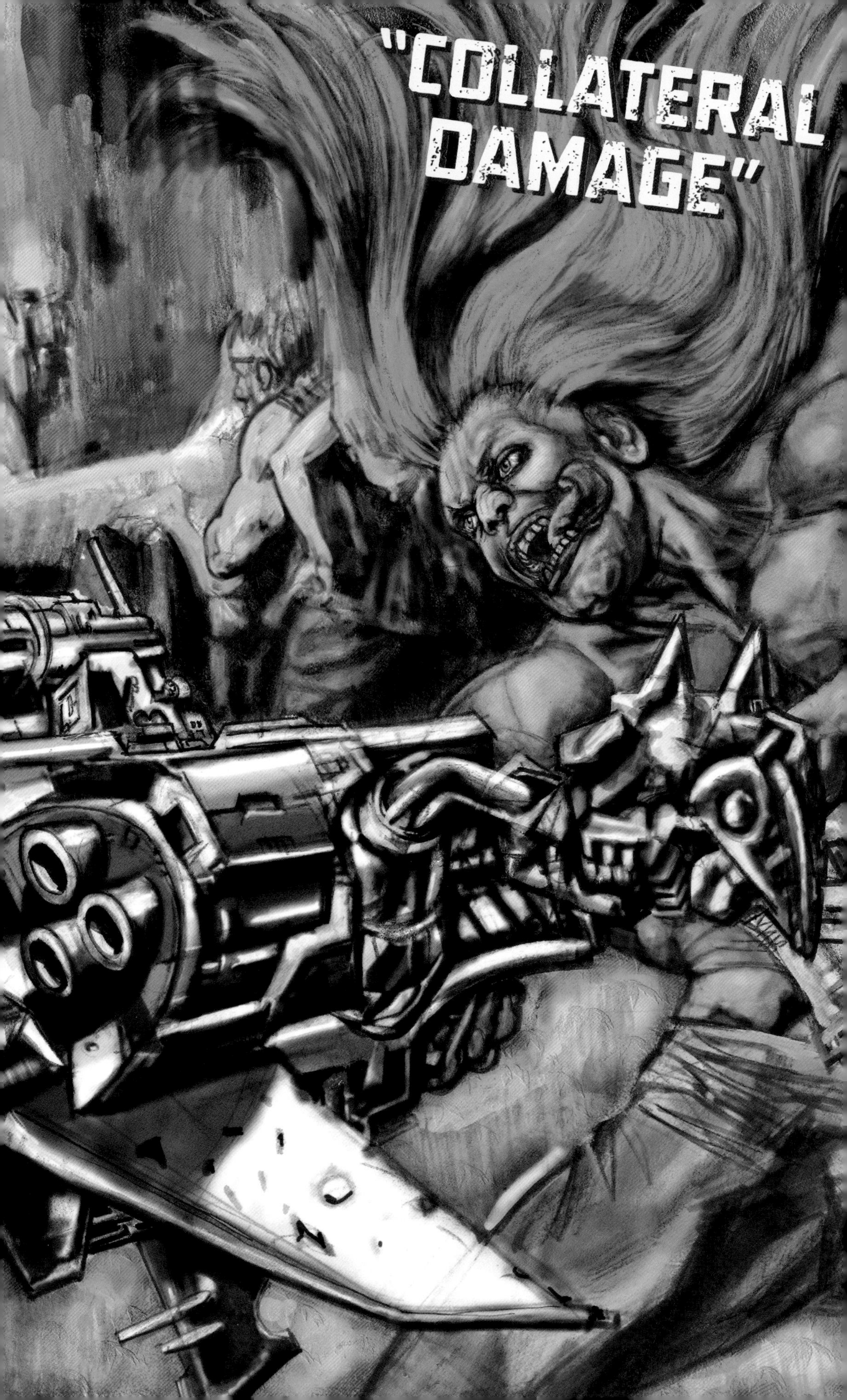
"COLLATERAL DAMAGE"

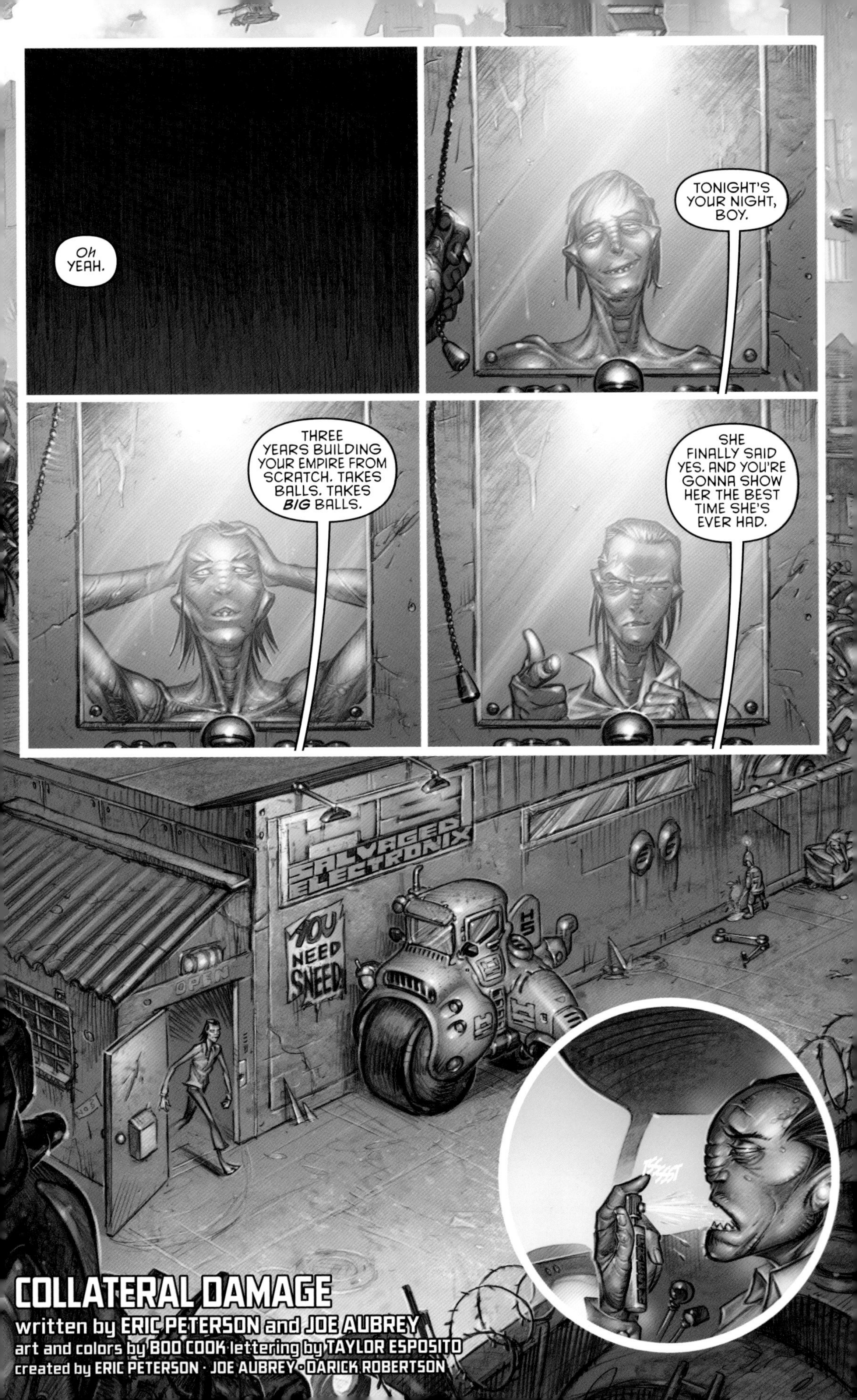

Oh YEAH.
TONIGHT'S YOUR NIGHT, BOY.
THREE YEARS BUILDING YOUR EMPIRE FROM SCRATCH. TAKES BALLS. TAKES *BIG* BALLS.
SHE FINALLY SAID YES. AND YOU'RE GONNA SHOW HER THE BEST TIME SHE'S EVER HAD.
HS SALVAGED ELECTRONIX
YOU NEED SNEED
OPEN

COLLATERAL DAMAGE

written by **ERIC PETERSON** and **JOE AUBREY**
art and colors by **BOO COOK** lettering by **TAYLOR ESPOSITO**
created by **ERIC PETERSON · JOE AUBREY · DARICK ROBERTSON**

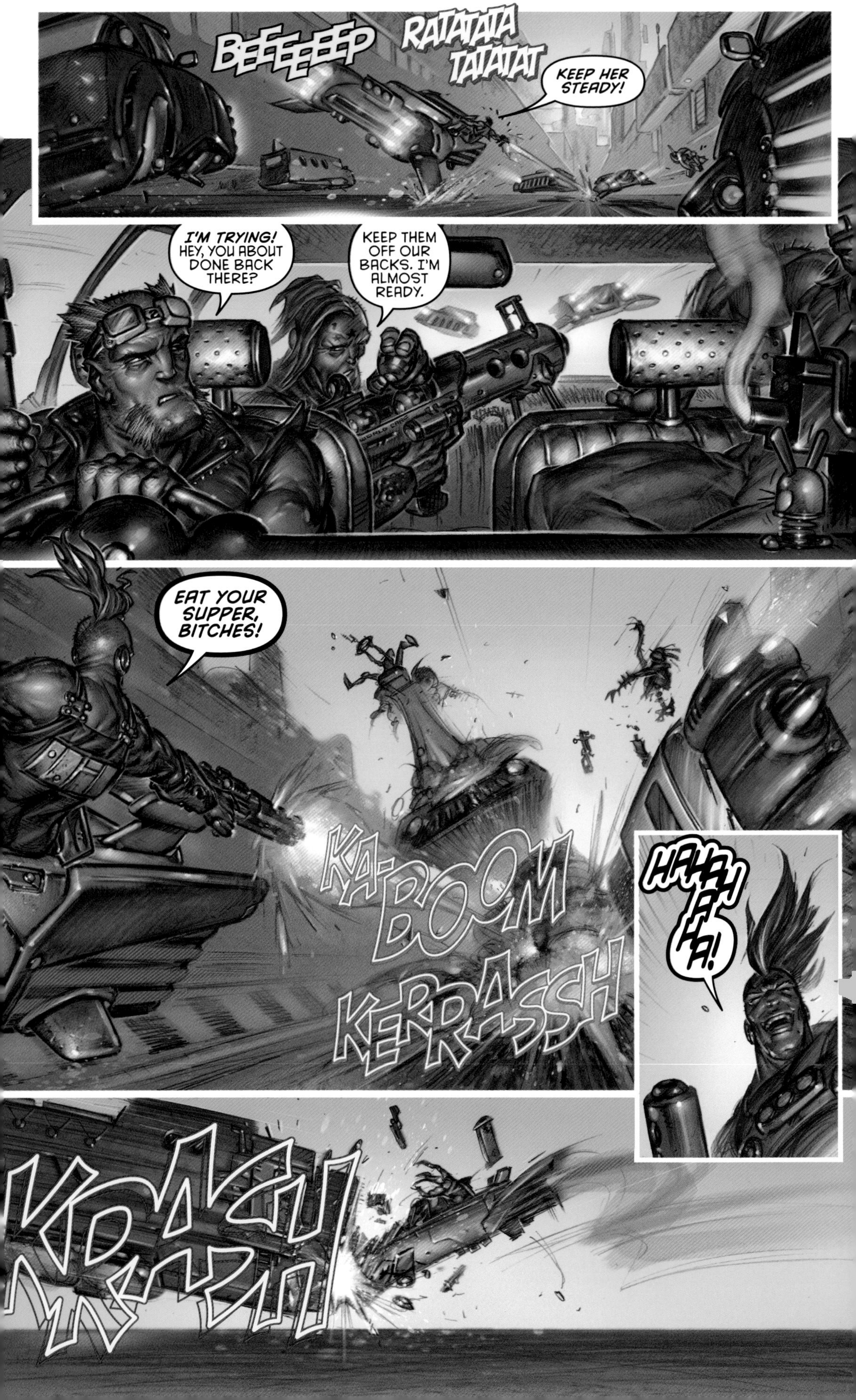
BEEEEEEP
RATATATA TATATAT
KEEP HER STEADY!
I'M TRYING! HEY, YOU ABOUT DONE BACK THERE?
KEEP THEM OFF OUR BACKS. I'M ALMOST READY.
EAT YOUR SUPPER, BITCHES!
KA-BOOM
KERRASSH
HAHAH HA HA!
KRAGH

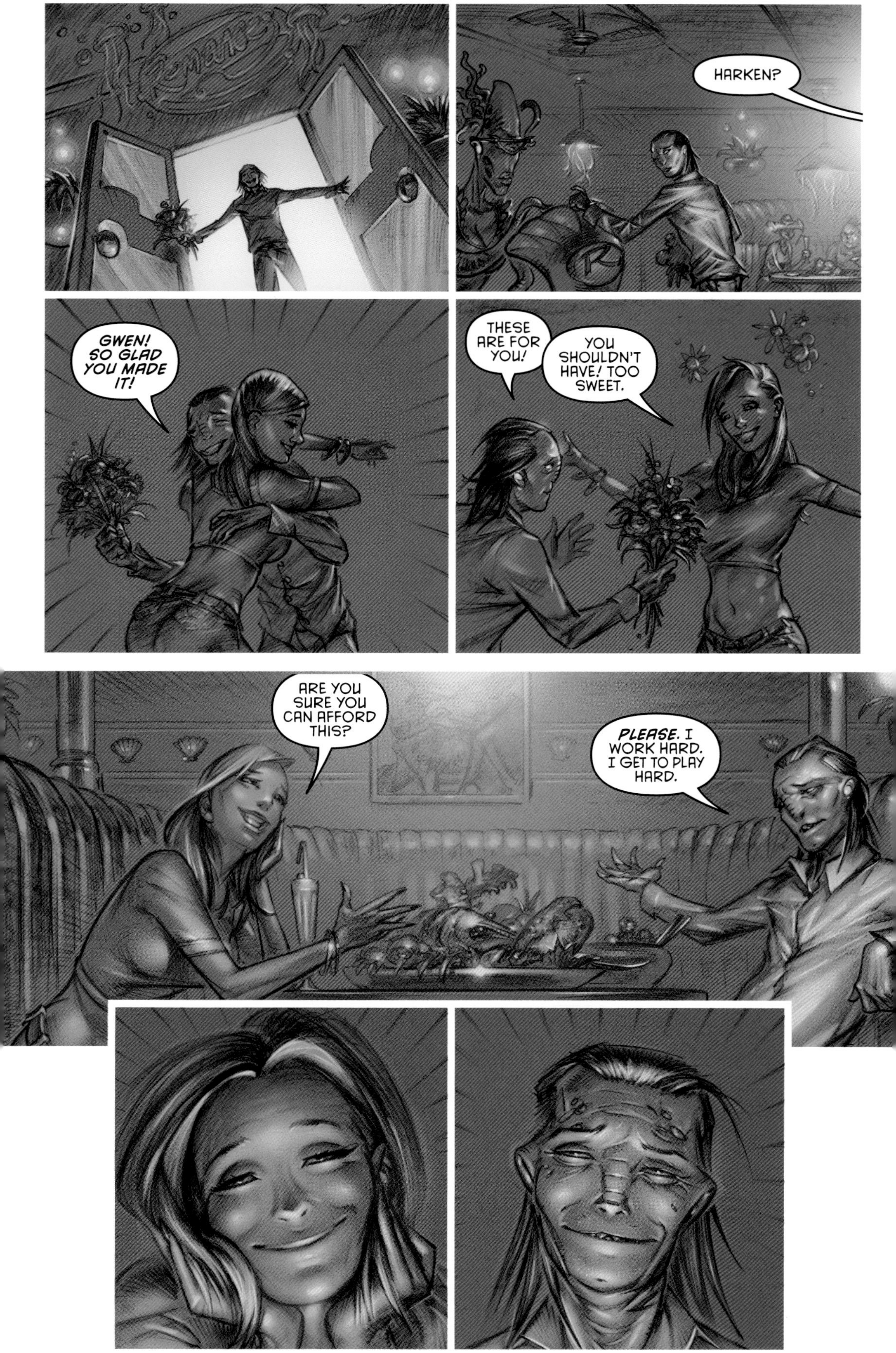
HARKEN?
GWEN! SO GLAD YOU MADE IT!
THESE ARE FOR YOU!
YOU SHOULDN'T HAVE! TOO SWEET.
ARE YOU SURE YOU CAN AFFORD THIS?
PLEASE. I WORK HARD. I GET TO PLAY HARD.

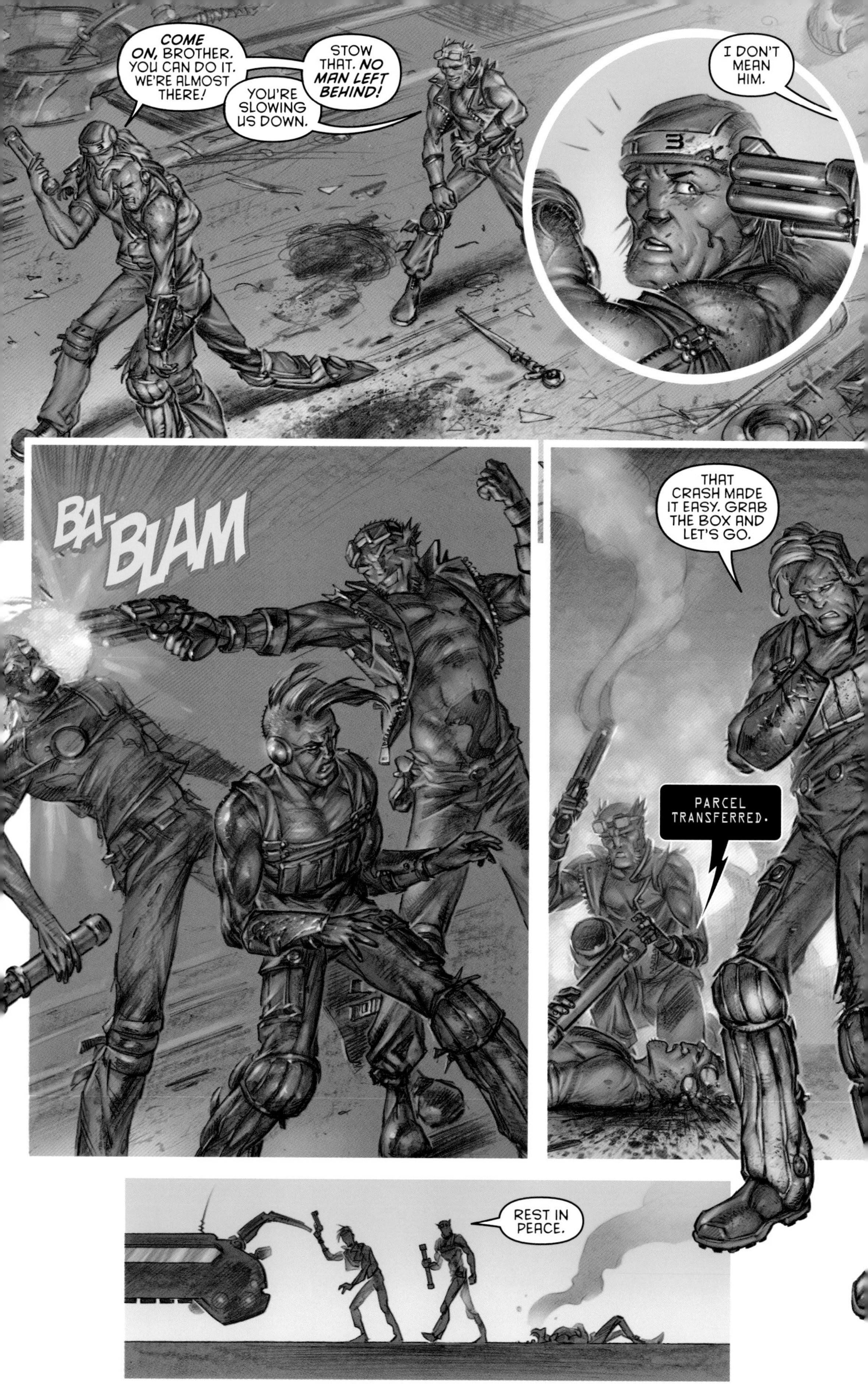
COME ON, BROTHER. YOU CAN DO IT. WE'RE ALMOST THERE!
YOU'RE SLOWING US DOWN.
STOW THAT. NO MAN LEFT BEHIND!
I DON'T MEAN HIM.
BA-BLAM
THAT CRASH MADE IT EASY. GRAB THE BOX AND LET'S GO.
PARCEL TRANSFERRED.
REST IN PEACE.

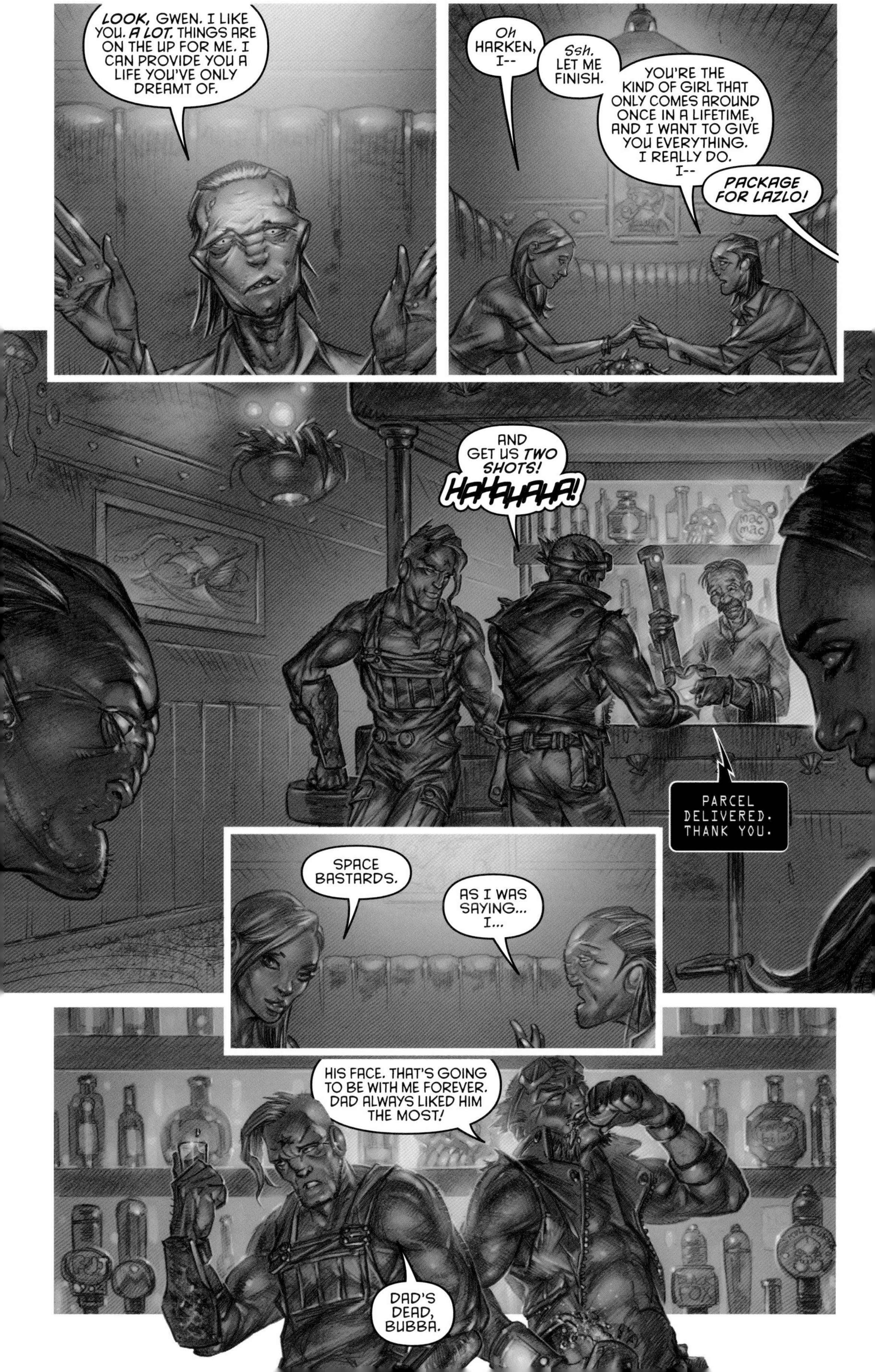

LOOK, GWEN. I LIKE YOU. A LOT. THINGS ARE ON THE UP FOR ME. I CAN PROVIDE YOU A LIFE YOU'VE ONLY DREAMT OF.
Oh HARKEN, I--
Ssh. LET ME FINISH.
YOU'RE THE KIND OF GIRL THAT ONLY COMES AROUND ONCE IN A LIFETIME, AND I WANT TO GIVE YOU EVERYTHING. I REALLY DO. I--
PACKAGE FOR LAZLO!
AND GET US TWO SHOTS!
HAHAHAHA!
PARCEL DELIVERED. THANK YOU.
SPACE BASTARDS.
AS I WAS SAYING... I...
HIS FACE. THAT'S GOING TO BE WITH ME FOREVER. DAD ALWAYS LIKED HIM THE MOST!
DAD'S DEAD, BUBBA.

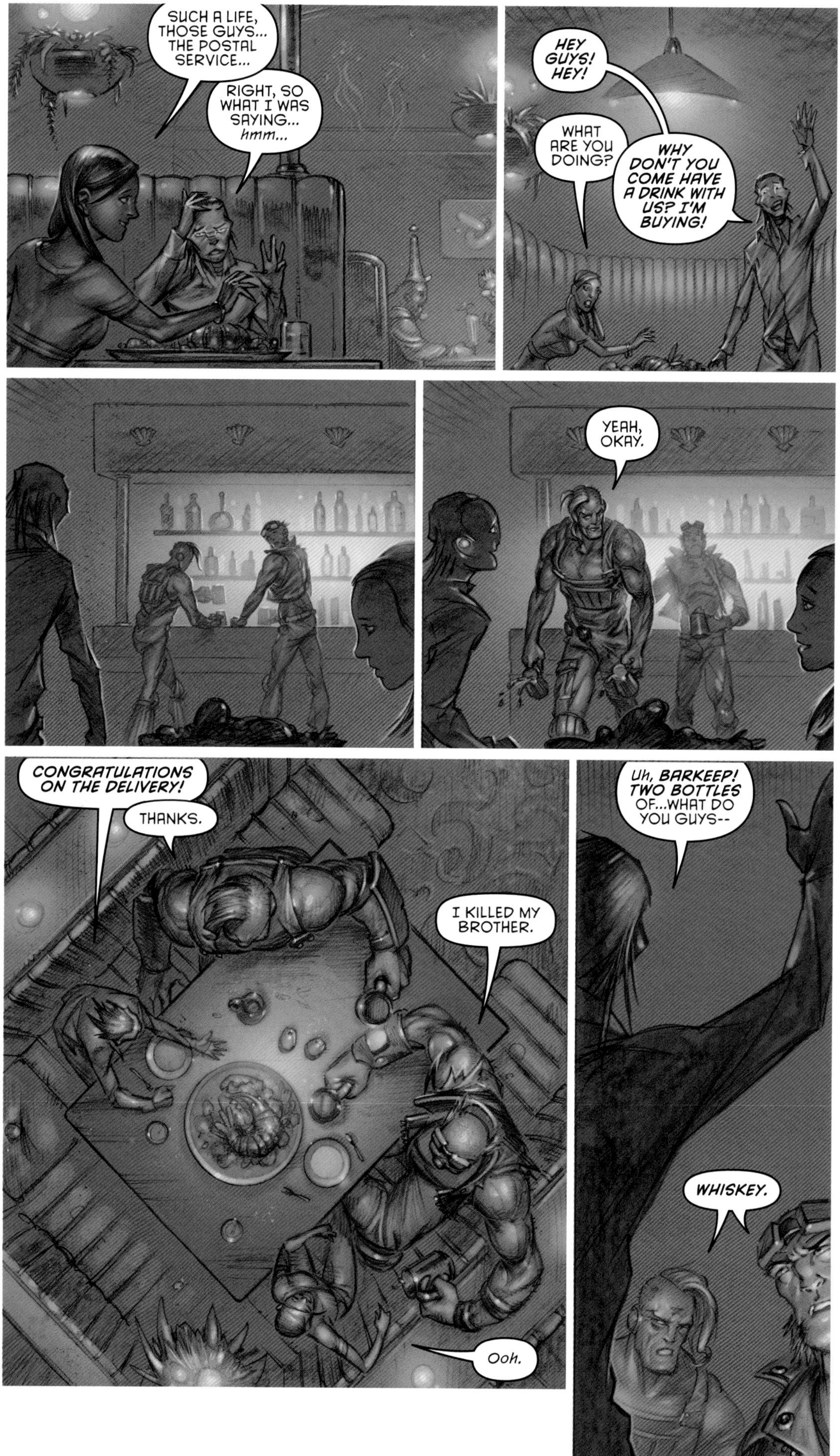
SUCH A LIFE, THOSE GUYS... THE POSTAL SERVICE...
RIGHT, SO WHAT I WAS SAYING... *hmm...*
HEY GUYS! HEY!
WHAT ARE YOU DOING?
WHY DON'T YOU COME HAVE A DRINK WITH US? I'M BUYING!
YEAH, OKAY.
CONGRATULATIONS ON THE DELIVERY!
THANKS.
I KILLED MY BROTHER.
Ooh.
Uh, BARKEEP! TWO BOTTLES OF...WHAT DO YOU GUYS--
WHISKEY.

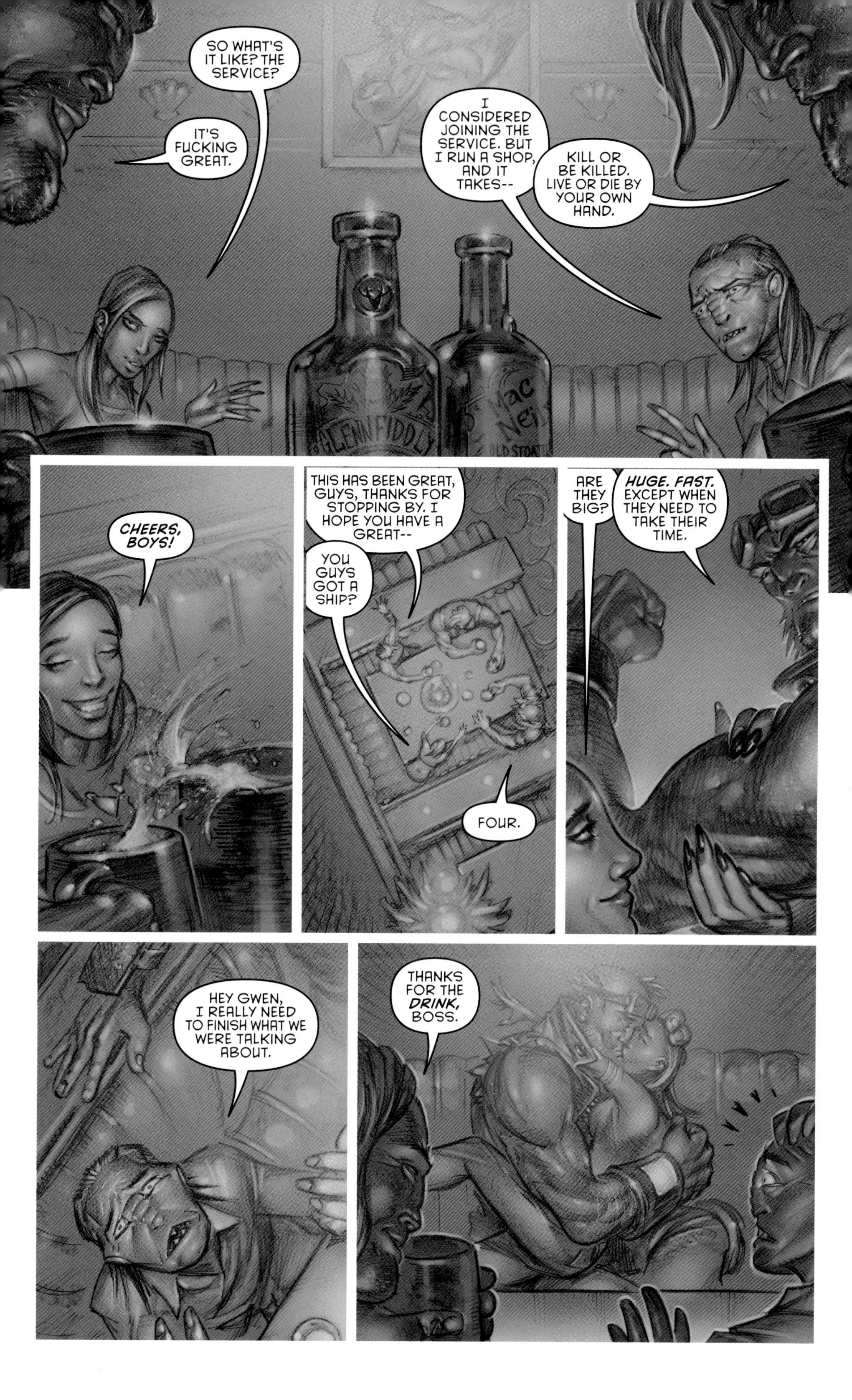
SO WHAT'S IT LIKE? THE SERVICE?
IT'S FUCKING GREAT.
I CONSIDERED JOINING THE SERVICE. BUT I RUN A SHOP, AND IT TAKES--
KILL OR BE KILLED. LIVE OR DIE BY YOUR OWN HAND.
CHEERS, BOYS!
THIS HAS BEEN GREAT, GUYS, THANKS FOR STOPPING BY. I HOPE YOU HAVE A GREAT--
YOU GUYS GOT A SHIP?
FOUR.
ARE THEY BIG?
HUGE. FAST. EXCEPT WHEN THEY NEED TO TAKE THEIR TIME.
HEY GWEN, I REALLY NEED TO FINISH WHAT WE WERE TALKING ABOUT.
THANKS FOR THE DRINK, BOSS.

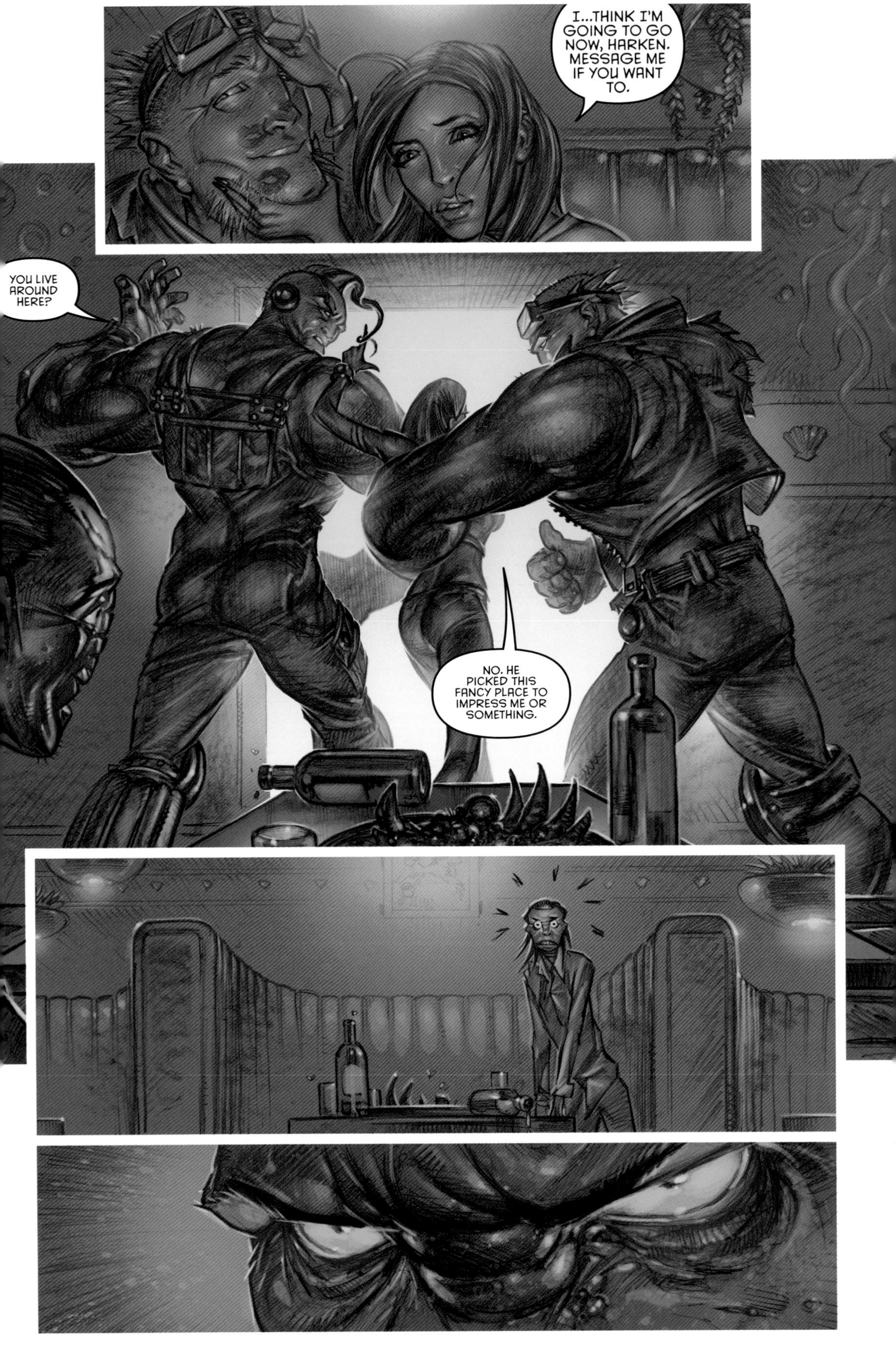
I...THINK I'M GOING TO GO NOW, HARKEN. MESSAGE ME IF YOU WANT TO.
YOU LIVE AROUND HERE?
NO. HE PICKED THIS FANCY PLACE TO IMPRESS ME OR SOMETHING.

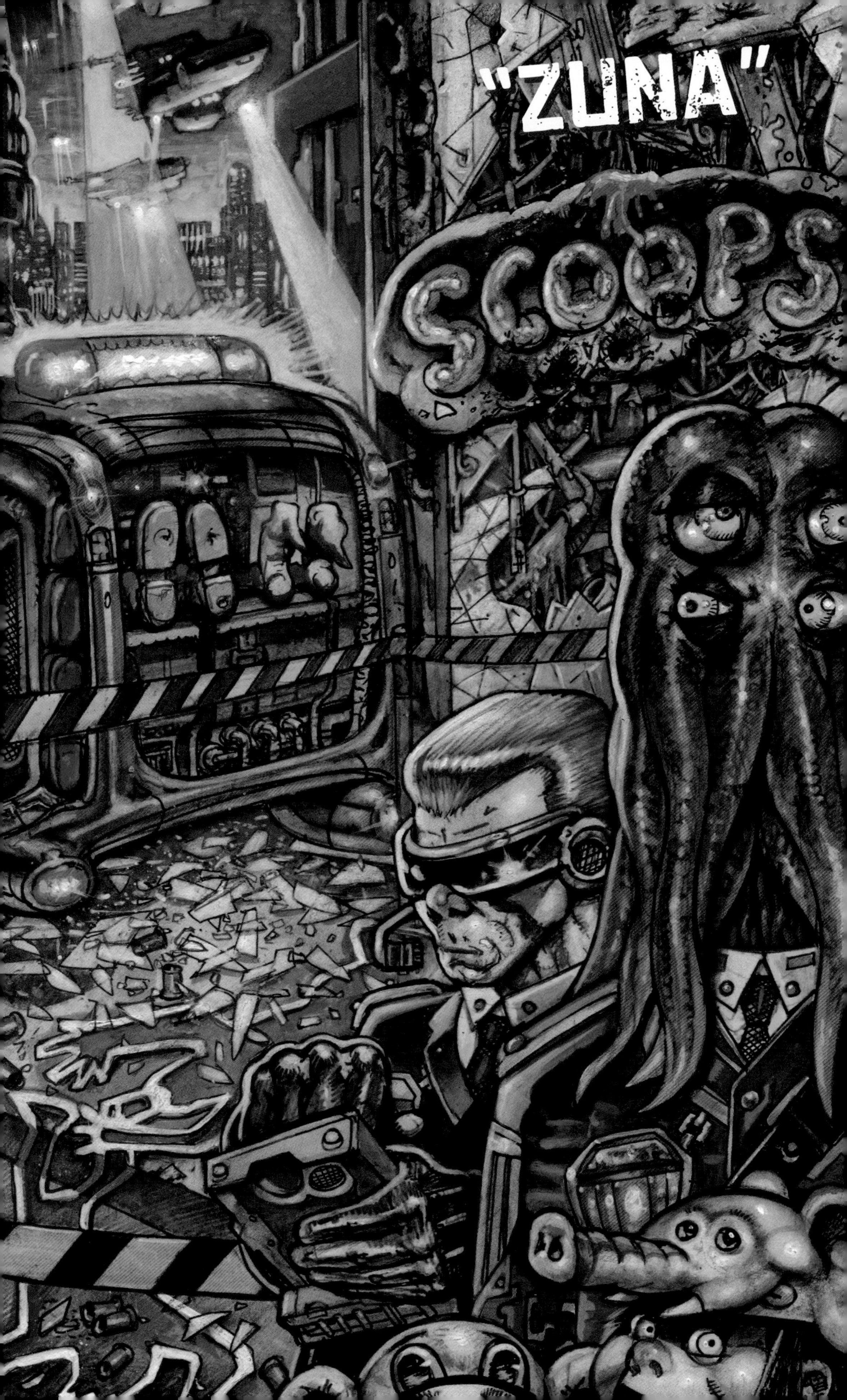
"ZUNA"
SCOOPS

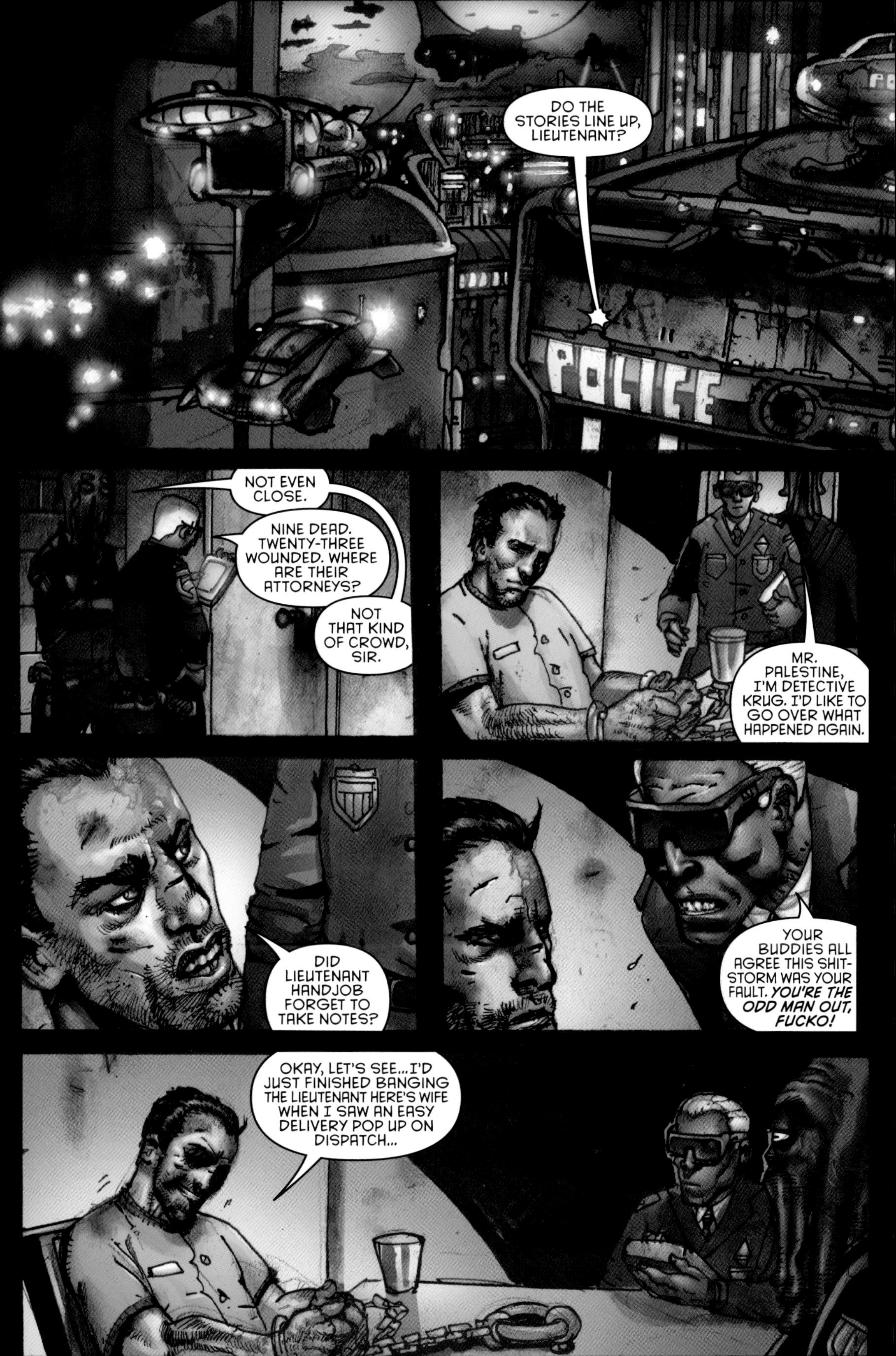

DO THE STORIES LINE UP, LIEUTENANT?
POLICE
NOT EVEN CLOSE.
NINE DEAD. TWENTY-THREE WOUNDED. WHERE ARE THEIR ATTORNEYS?
NOT THAT KIND OF CROWD, SIR.
MR. PALESTINE, I'M DETECTIVE KRUG. I'D LIKE TO GO OVER WHAT HAPPENED AGAIN.
DID LIEUTENANT HANDJOB FORGET TO TAKE NOTES?
YOUR BUDDIES ALL AGREE THIS SHIT-STORM WAS YOUR FAULT. *YOU'RE THE ODD MAN OUT, FUCKO!*
OKAY, LET'S SEE...I'D JUST FINISHED BANGING THE LIEUTENANT HERE'S WIFE WHEN I SAW AN EASY DELIVERY POP UP ON DISPATCH...

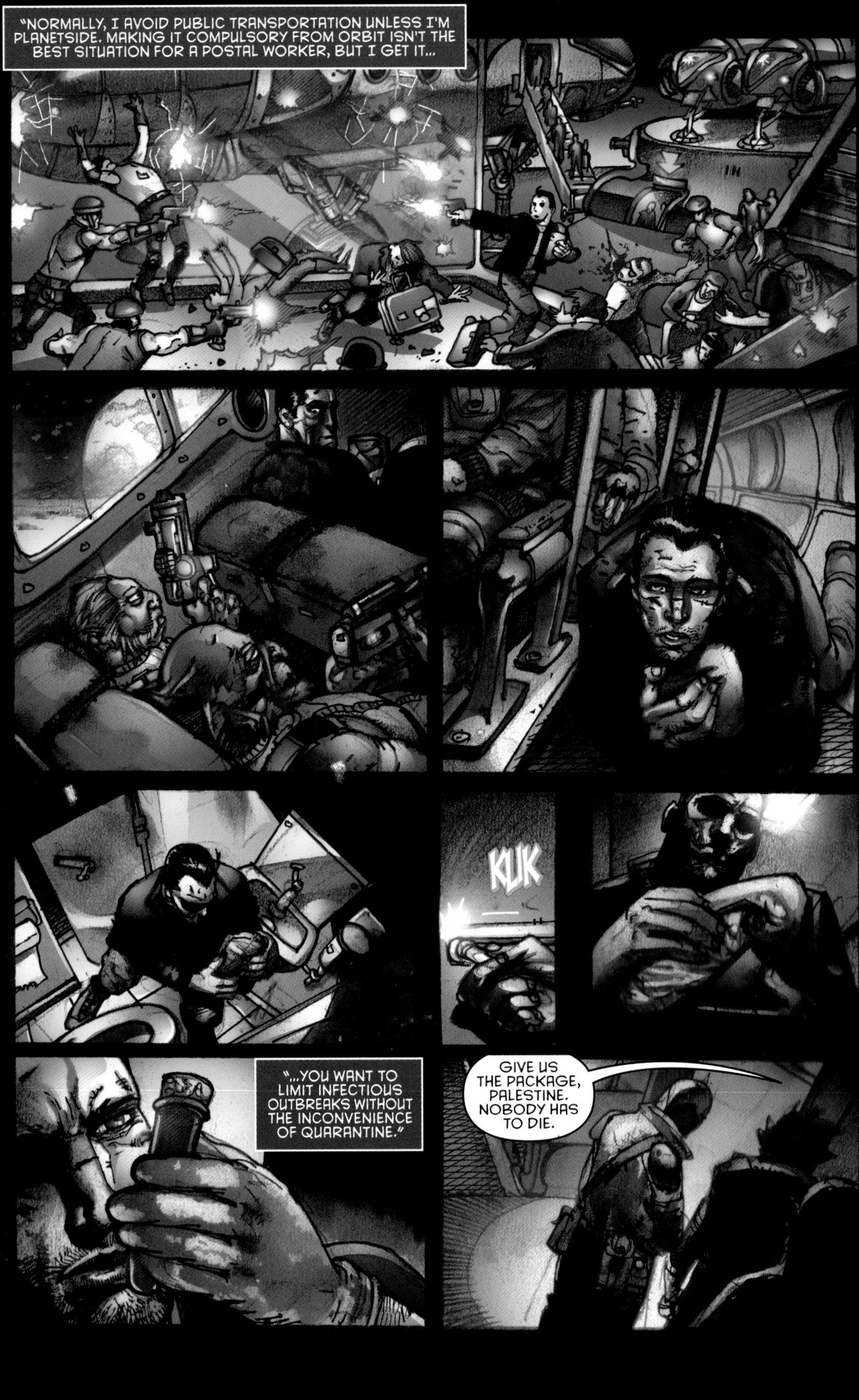
"NORMALLY, I AVOID PUBLIC TRANSPORTATION UNLESS I'M PLANETSIDE. MAKING IT COMPULSORY FROM ORBIT ISN'T THE BEST SITUATION FOR A POSTAL WORKER, BUT I GET IT...
KLIK
"...YOU WANT TO LIMIT INFECTIOUS OUTBREAKS WITHOUT THE INCONVENIENCE OF QUARANTINE."
GIVE US THE PACKAGE, PALESTINE. NOBODY HAS TO DIE.

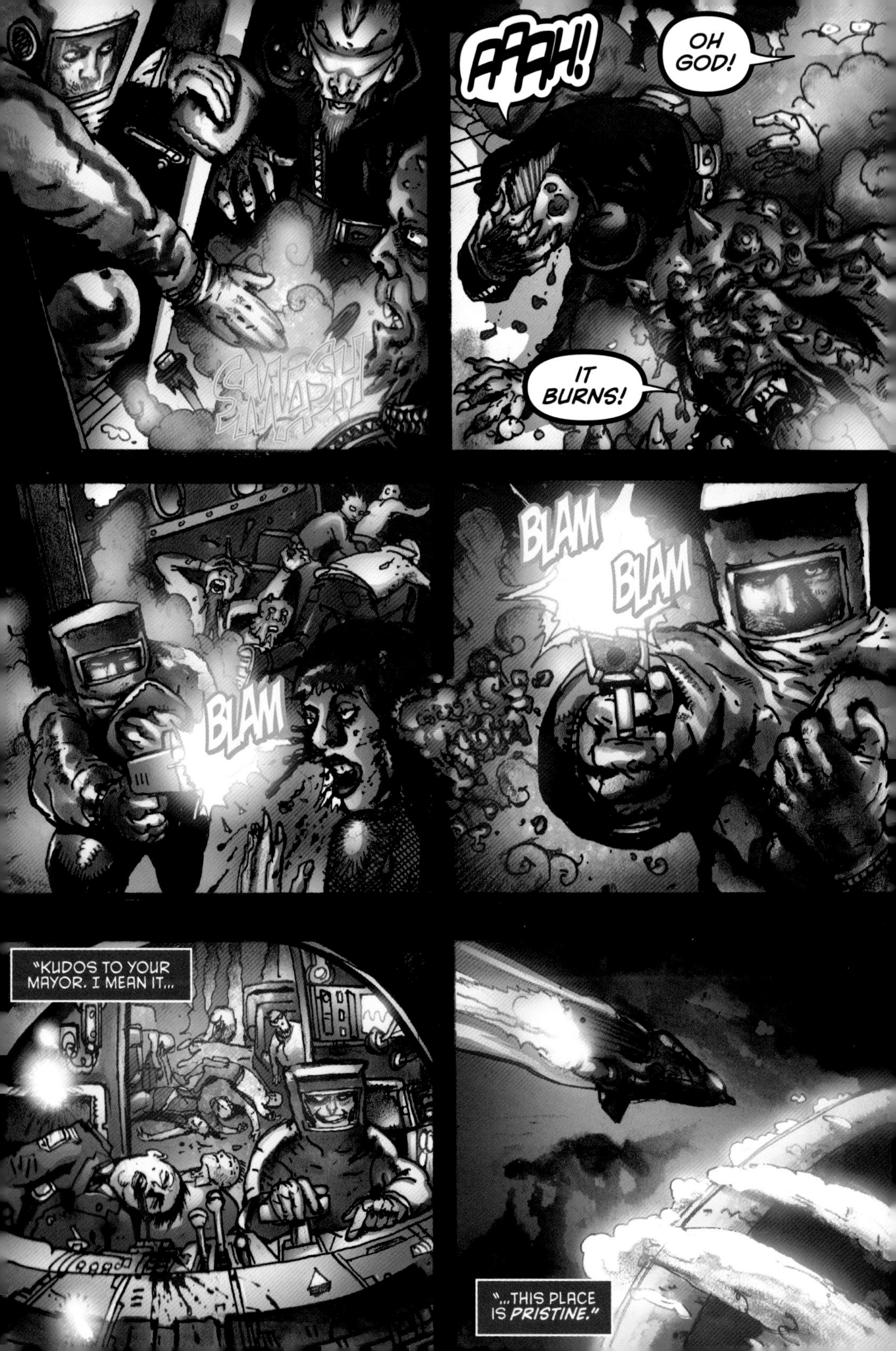
AAAH!
OH GOD!
IT BURNS!
BLAM
BLAM
BLAM
"KUDOS TO YOUR MAYOR. I MEAN IT...
"...THIS PLACE IS *PRISTINE.*"

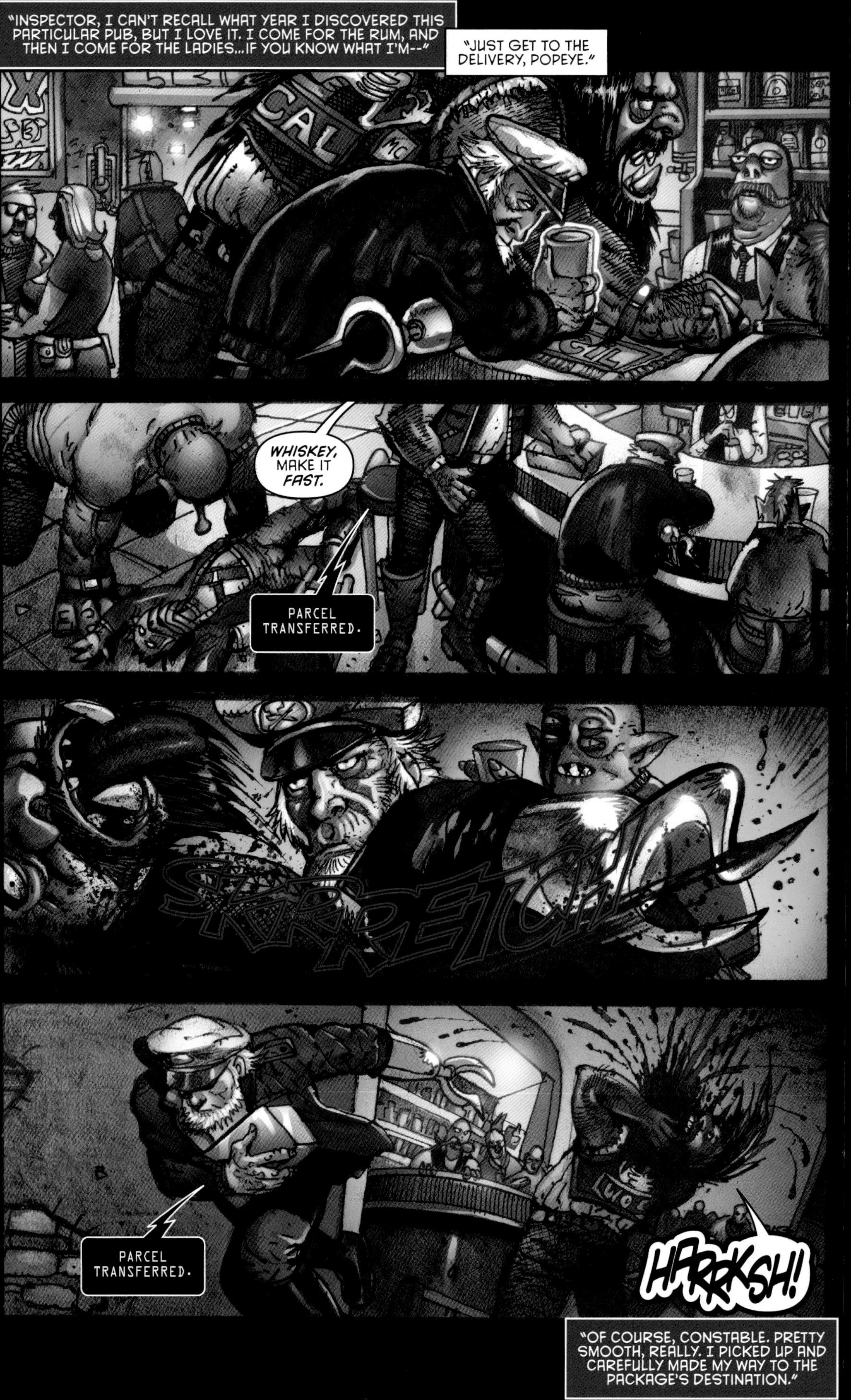
"INSPECTOR, I CAN'T RECALL WHAT YEAR I DISCOVERED THIS PARTICULAR PUB, BUT I LOVE IT. I COME FOR THE RUM, AND THEN I COME FOR THE LADIES...IF YOU KNOW WHAT I'M--"
"JUST GET TO THE DELIVERY, POPEYE."
WHISKEY, MAKE IT FAST.
PARCEL TRANSFERRED.
SKRRRETCH
PARCEL TRANSFERRED.
HRRKSH!
"OF COURSE, CONSTABLE. PRETTY SMOOTH, REALLY. I PICKED UP AND CAREFULLY MADE MY WAY TO THE PACKAGE'S DESTINATION."

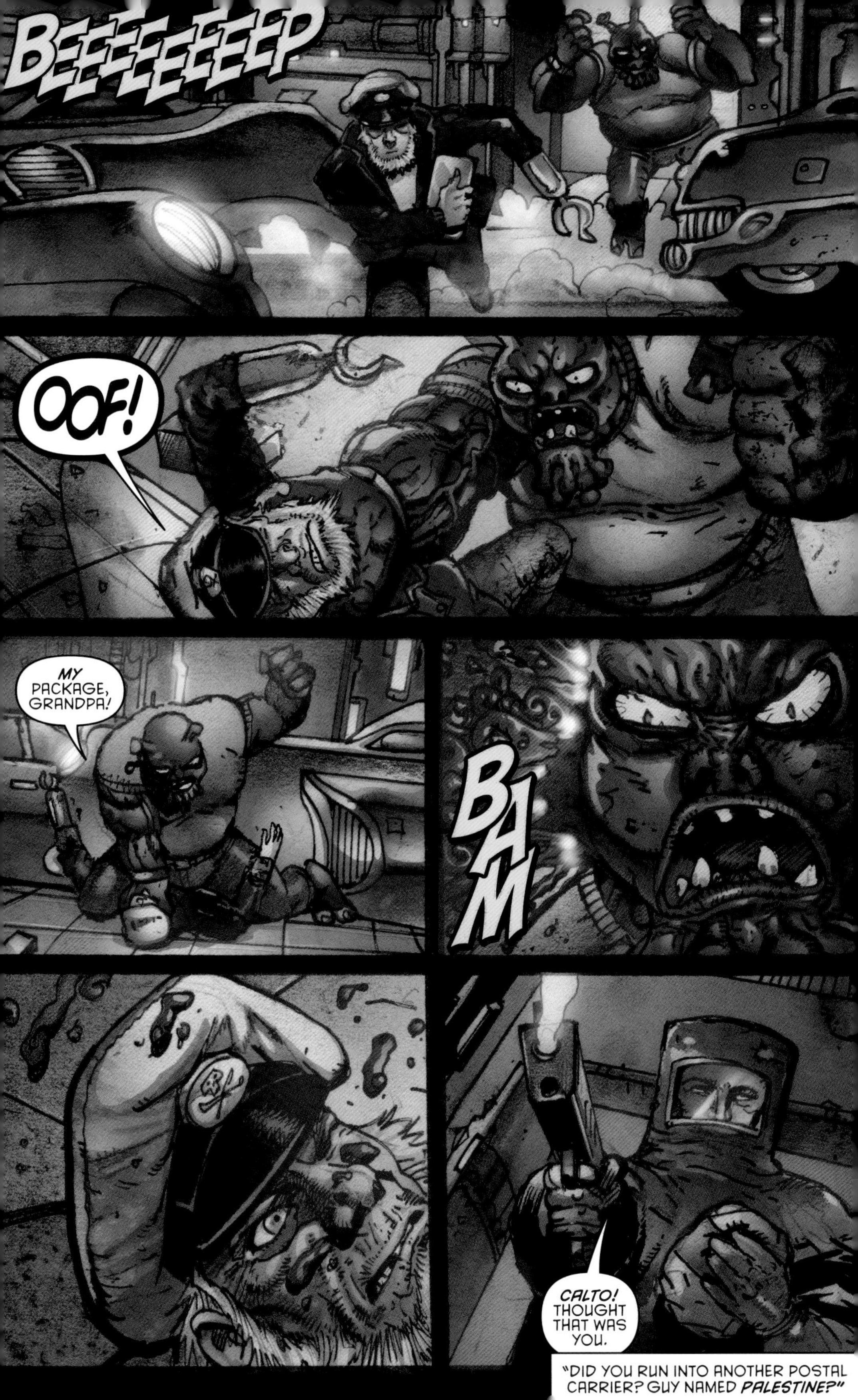
BEEEEEEEEP
OOF!
MY PACKAGE, GRANDPA!
BAM
CALTO! THOUGHT THAT WAS YOU.
"DID YOU RUN INTO ANOTHER POSTAL CARRIER? GUY NAMED PALESTINE?"

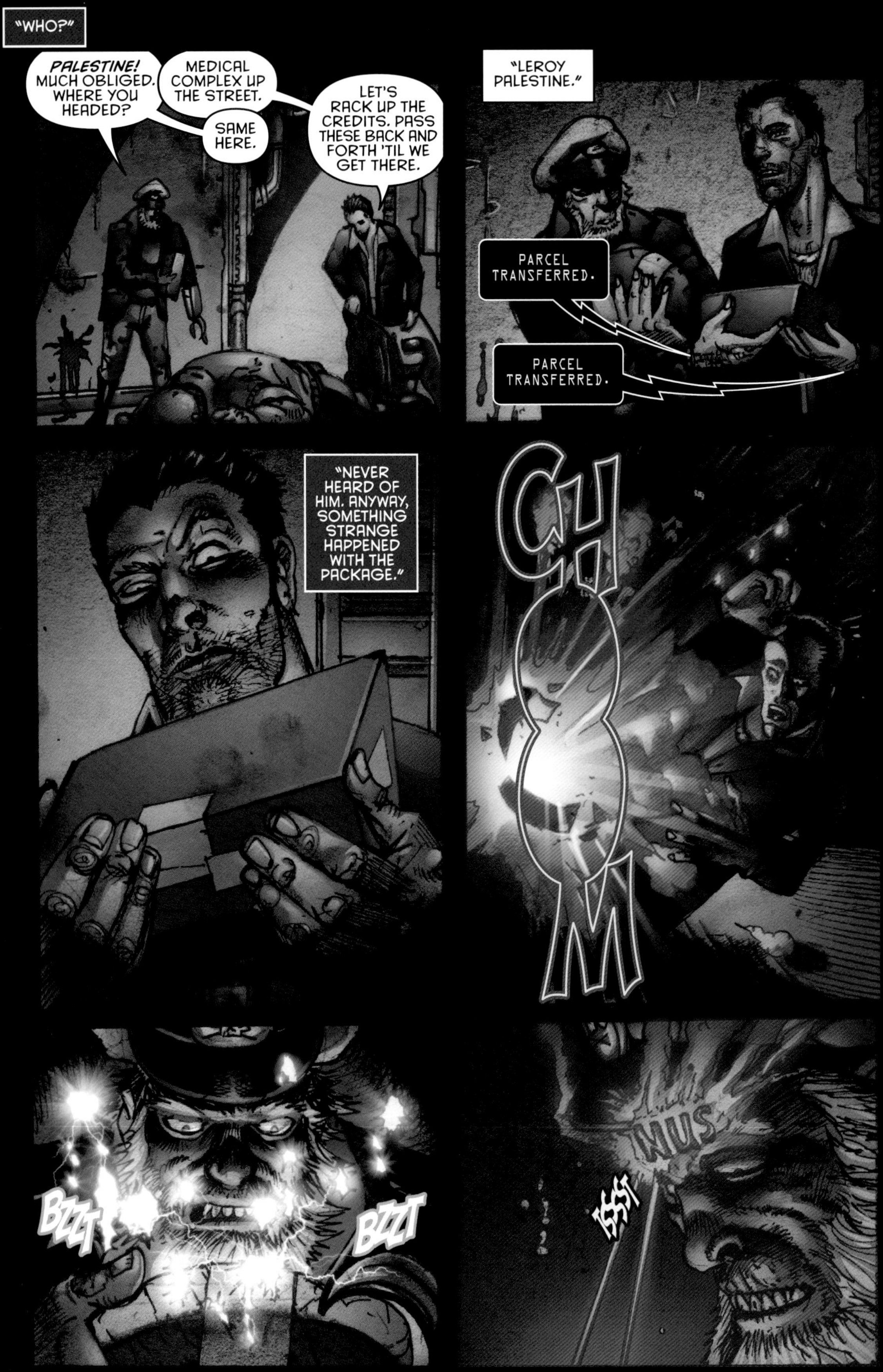
"WHO?"
PALESTINE! MUCH OBLIGED. WHERE YOU HEADED?
MEDICAL COMPLEX UP THE STREET.
SAME HERE.
LET'S RACK UP THE CREDITS. PASS THESE BACK AND FORTH 'TIL WE GET THERE.
"LEROY PALESTINE."
PARCEL TRANSFERRED.
PARCEL TRANSFERRED.
"NEVER HEARD OF HIM. ANYWAY, SOMETHING STRANGE HAPPENED WITH THE PACKAGE."
CHOOM
BZZT
BZZT
ISSST

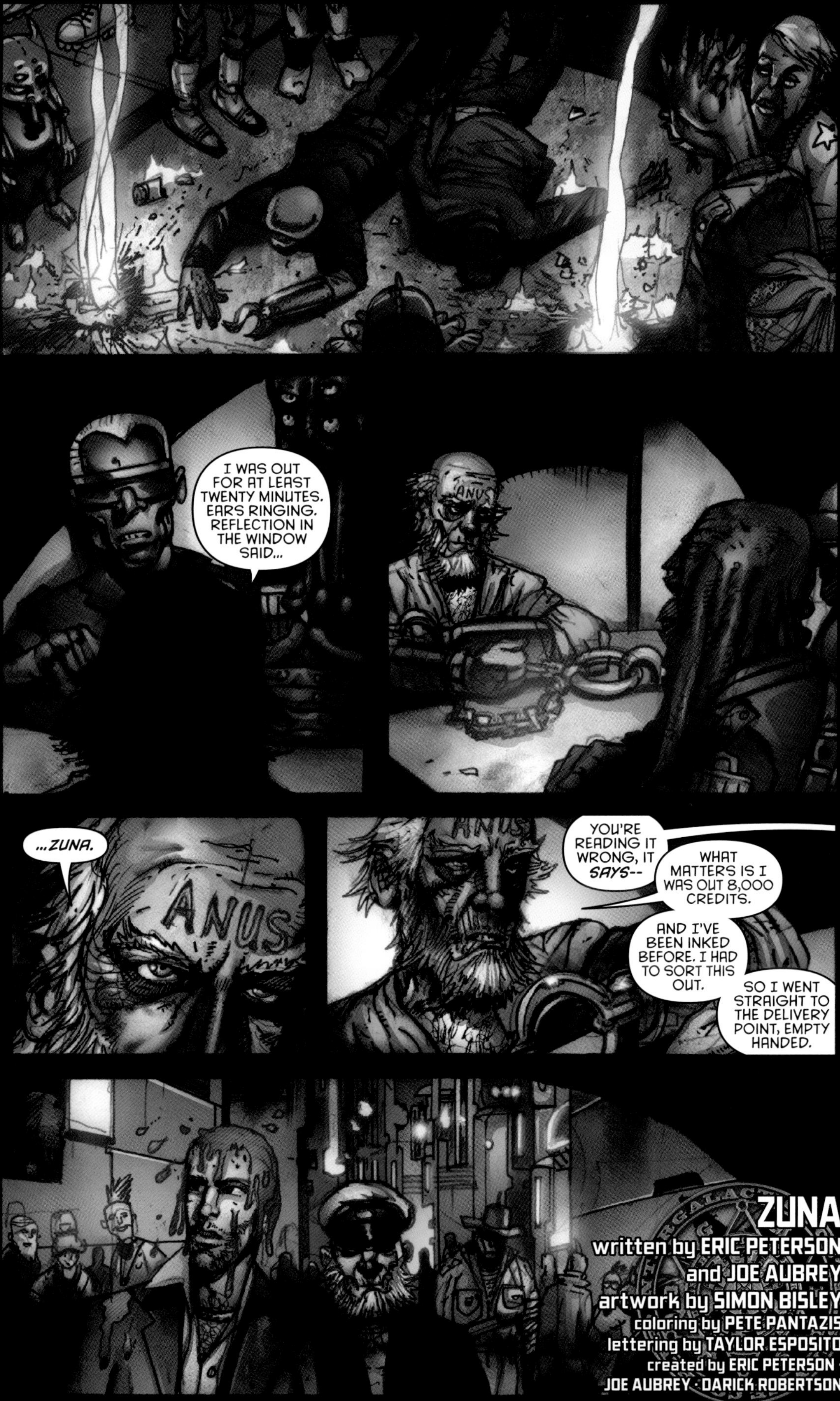
I WAS OUT FOR AT LEAST TWENTY MINUTES. EARS RINGING. REFLECTION IN THE WINDOW SAID...
...ZUNA.
YOU'RE READING IT WRONG, IT SAYS--
WHAT MATTERS IS I WAS OUT 8,000 CREDITS.
AND I'VE BEEN INKED BEFORE. I HAD TO SORT THIS OUT.
SO I WENT STRAIGHT TO THE DELIVERY POINT, EMPTY HANDED.
ZUNA
written by ERIC PETERSON
and JOE AUBREY
artwork by SIMON BISLEY
coloring by PETE PANTAZIS
lettering by TAYLOR ESPOSITO
created by ERIC PETERSON ·
JOE AUBREY · DARICK ROBERTSON

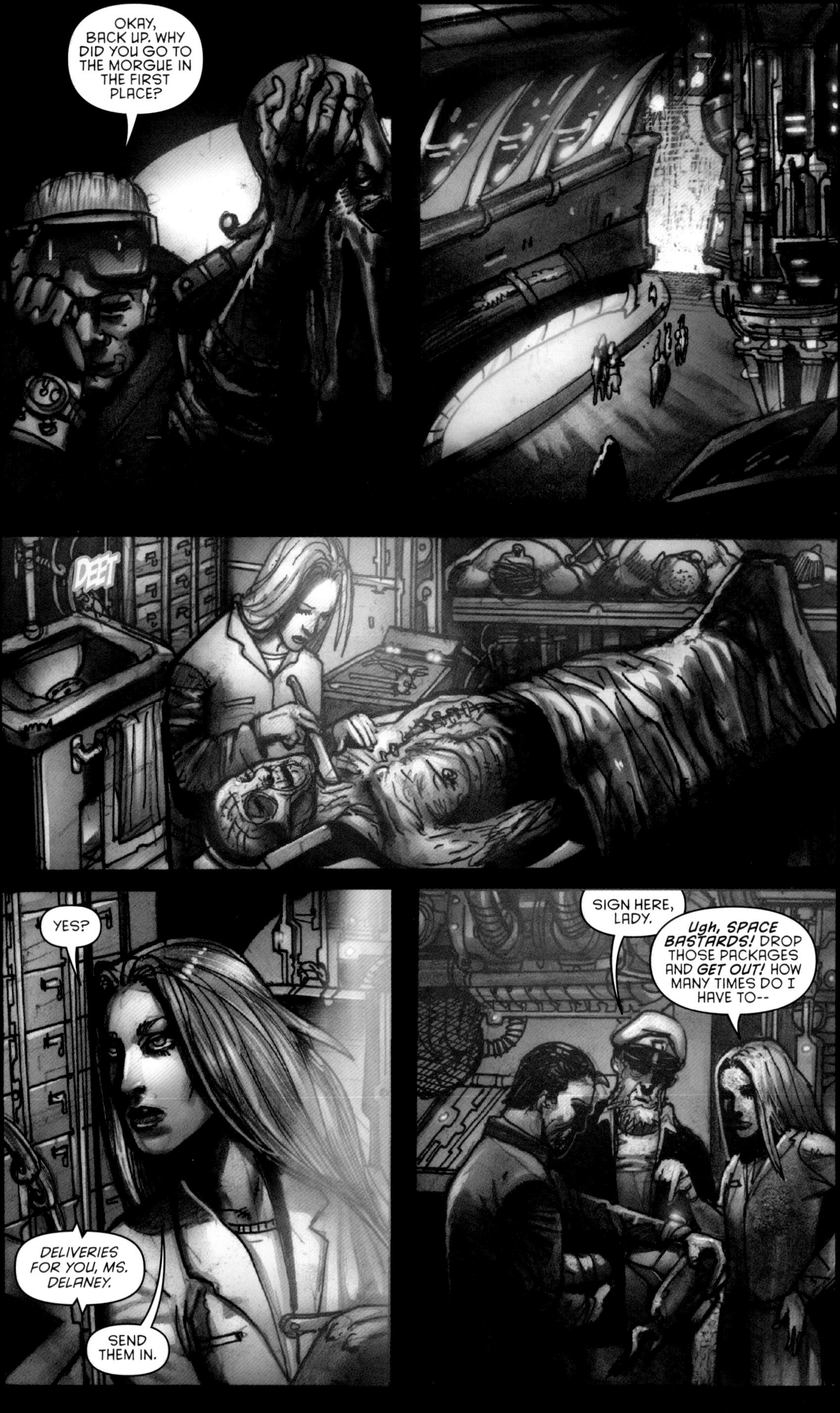

OKAY, BACK UP. WHY DID YOU GO TO THE MORGUE IN THE FIRST PLACE?
DEET
YES?
DELIVERIES FOR YOU, MS. DELANEY.
SEND THEM IN.
SIGN HERE, LADY.
Ugh, SPACE BASTARDS! DROP THOSE PACKAGES AND *GET OUT!* HOW MANY TIMES DO I HAVE TO--

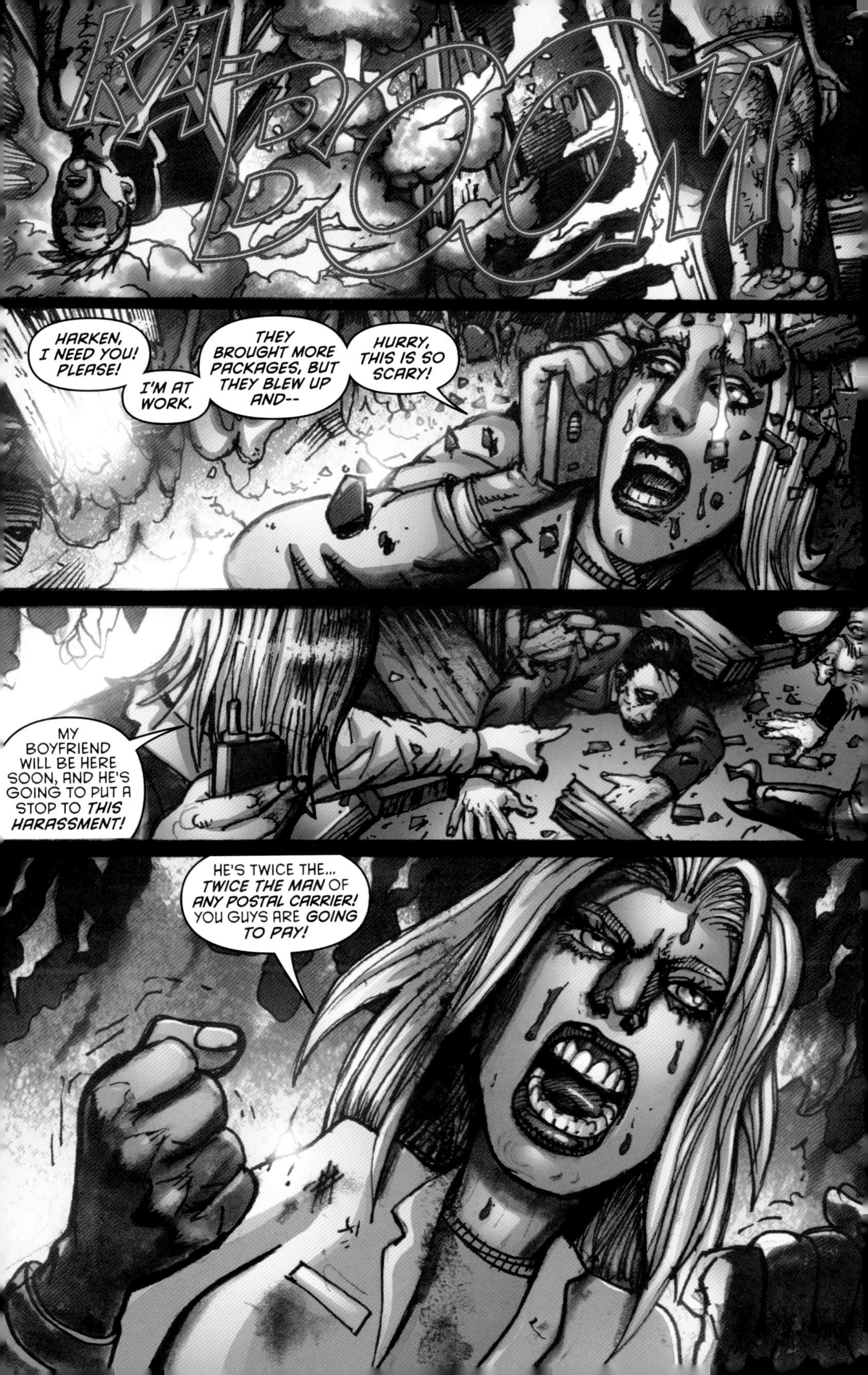
KA-BLOOM
BOOM
HARKEN, I NEED YOU! PLEASE!
I'M AT WORK.
THEY BROUGHT MORE PACKAGES, BUT THEY BLEW UP AND--
HURRY, THIS IS SO SCARY!
MY BOYFRIEND WILL BE HERE SOON, AND HE'S GOING TO PUT A STOP TO THIS HARASSMENT!
HE'S TWICE THE... TWICE THE MAN OF ANY POSTAL CARRIER! YOU GUYS ARE GOING TO PAY!

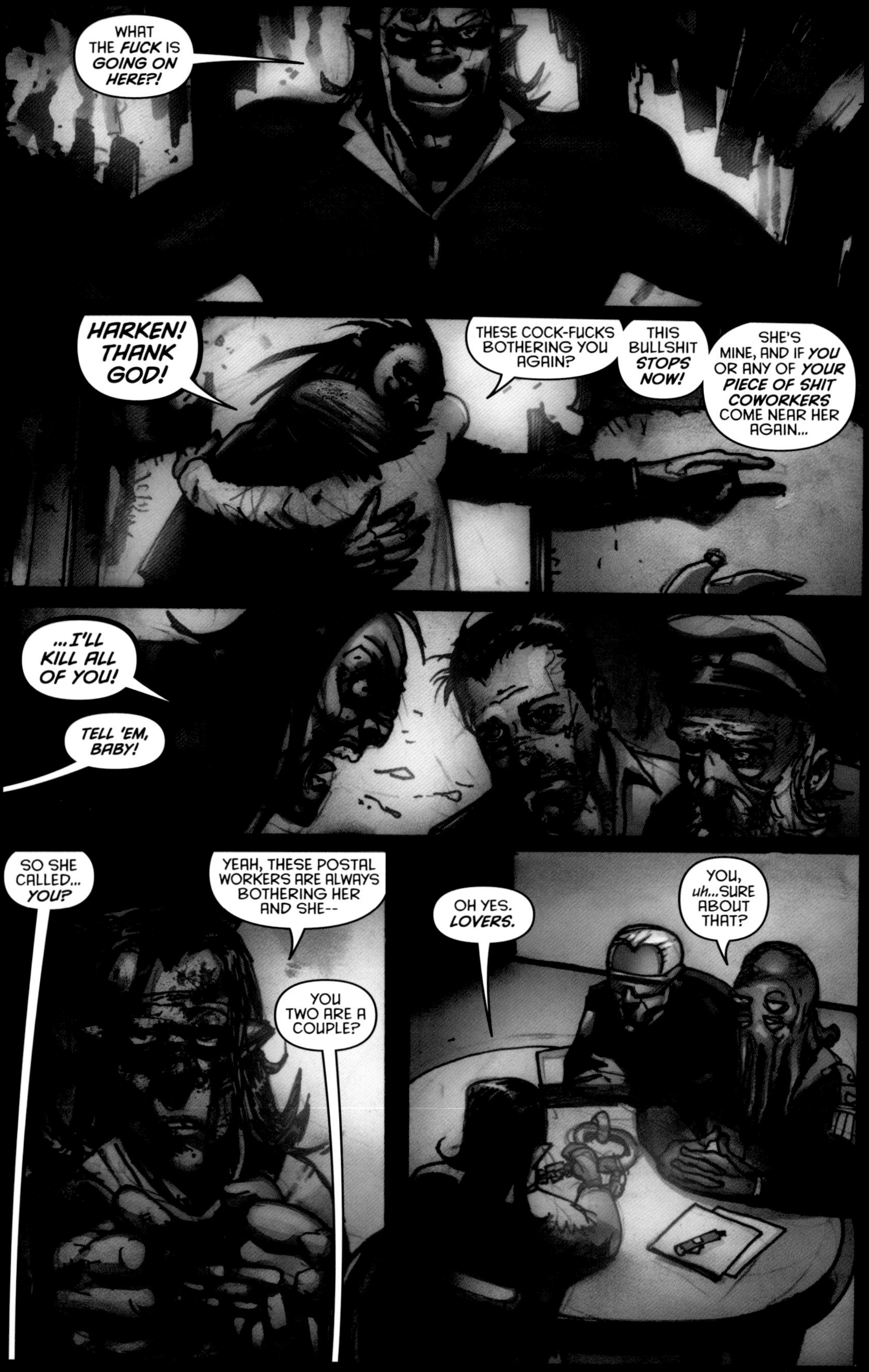
WHAT THE *FUCK* IS *GOING ON HERE?!*
HARKEN! THANK GOD!
THESE COCK-FUCKS BOTHERING YOU AGAIN?
THIS BULLSHIT *STOPS NOW!*
SHE'S MINE, AND IF *YOU* OR ANY OF *YOUR PIECE OF SHIT COWORKERS* COME NEAR HER AGAIN...
...I'LL KILL ALL OF YOU!
TELL 'EM, BABY!
SO SHE CALLED... *YOU?*
YEAH, THESE POSTAL WORKERS ARE ALWAYS BOTHERING HER AND SHE--
YOU TWO ARE A COUPLE?
OH YES. *LOVERS.*
YOU, *uh...*SURE ABOUT THAT?

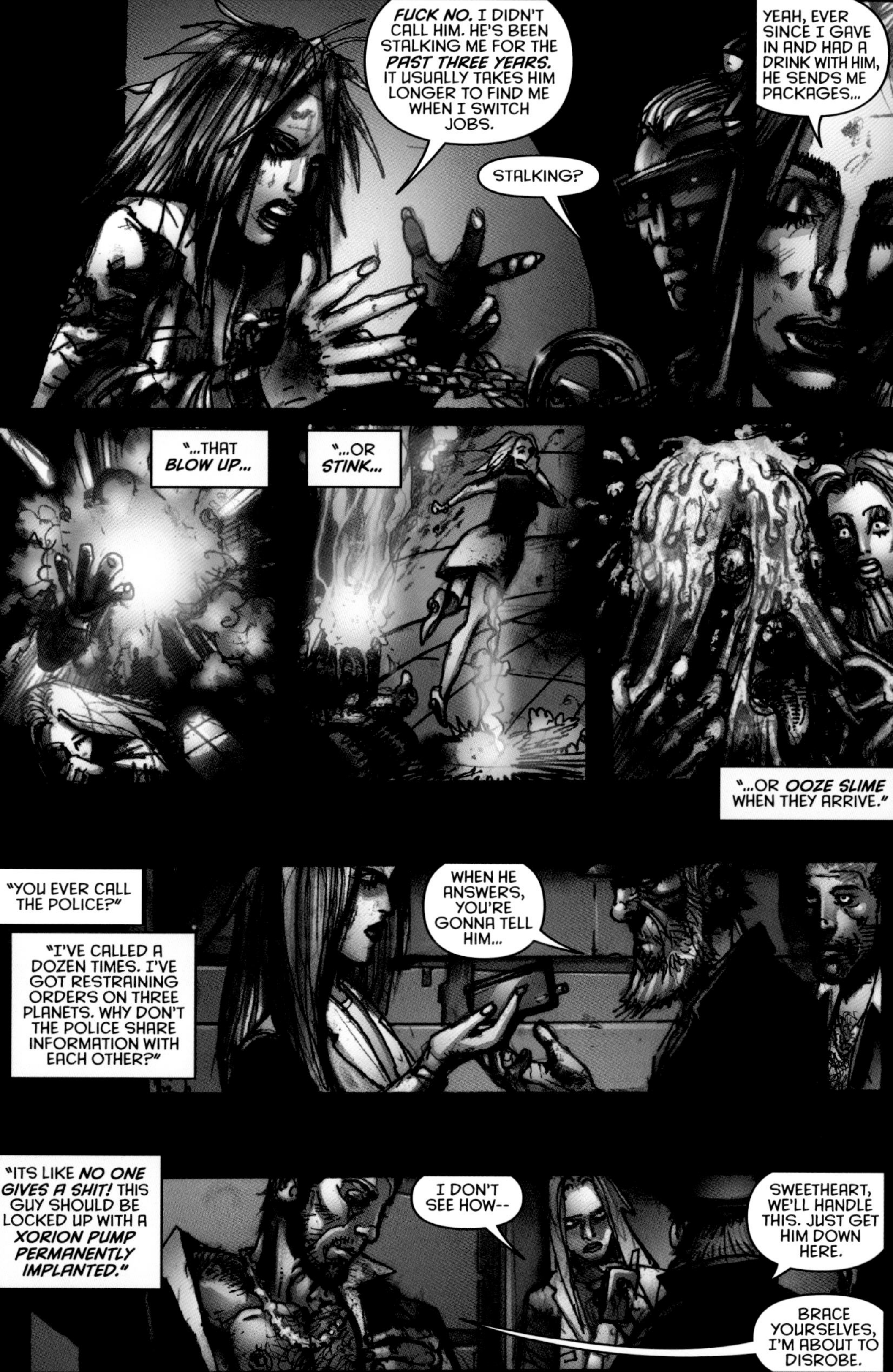
FUCK NO. I DIDN'T CALL HIM. HE'S BEEN STALKING ME FOR THE PAST THREE YEARS. IT USUALLY TAKES HIM LONGER TO FIND ME WHEN I SWITCH JOBS.
STALKING?
YEAH, EVER SINCE I GAVE IN AND HAD A DRINK WITH HIM, HE SENDS ME PACKAGES...
"...THAT BLOW UP...
"...OR STINK...
"...OR OOZE SLIME WHEN THEY ARRIVE."
"YOU EVER CALL THE POLICE?"
"I'VE CALLED A DOZEN TIMES. I'VE GOT RESTRAINING ORDERS ON THREE PLANETS. WHY DON'T THE POLICE SHARE INFORMATION WITH EACH OTHER?"
WHEN HE ANSWERS, YOU'RE GONNA TELL HIM...
"ITS LIKE NO ONE GIVES A SHIT! THIS GUY SHOULD BE LOCKED UP WITH A XORION PUMP PERMANENTLY IMPLANTED."
I DON'T SEE HOW--
SWEETHEART, WE'LL HANDLE THIS. JUST GET HIM DOWN HERE.
BRACE YOURSELVES, I'M ABOUT TO DISROBE.

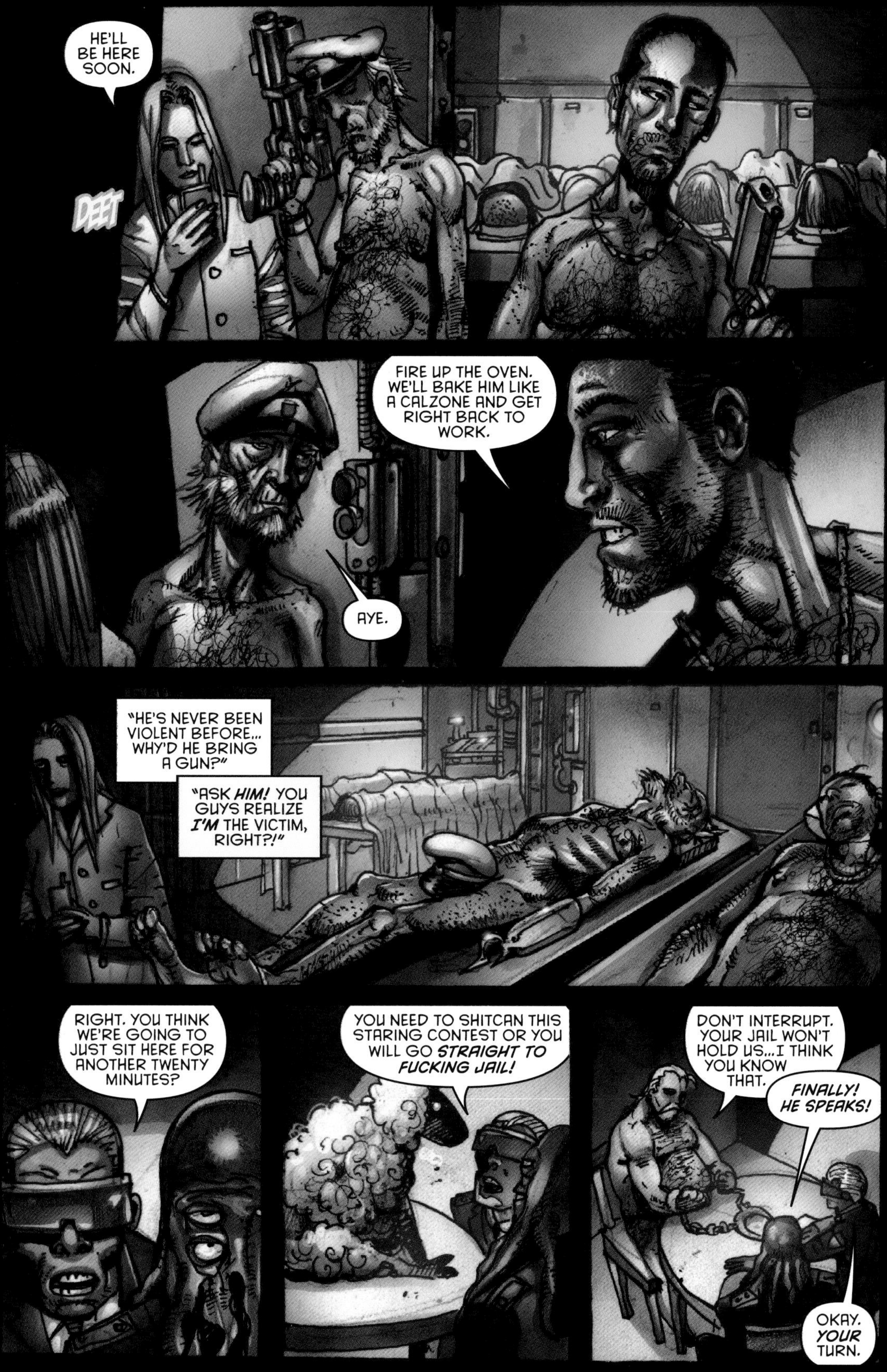

HE'LL BE HERE SOON.
DEET
FIRE UP THE OVEN. WE'LL BAKE HIM LIKE A CALZONE AND GET RIGHT BACK TO WORK.
AYE.
"HE'S NEVER BEEN VIOLENT BEFORE... WHY'D HE BRING A GUN?"
"ASK *HIM!* YOU GUYS REALIZE *I'M* THE VICTIM, RIGHT?!"
RIGHT. YOU THINK WE'RE GOING TO JUST SIT HERE FOR ANOTHER TWENTY MINUTES?
YOU NEED TO SHITCAN THIS STARING CONTEST OR YOU WILL GO *STRAIGHT TO FUCKING JAIL!*
DON'T INTERRUPT. YOUR JAIL WON'T HOLD US...I THINK YOU KNOW THAT.
FINALLY! HE SPEAKS!
OKAY. *YOUR* TURN.

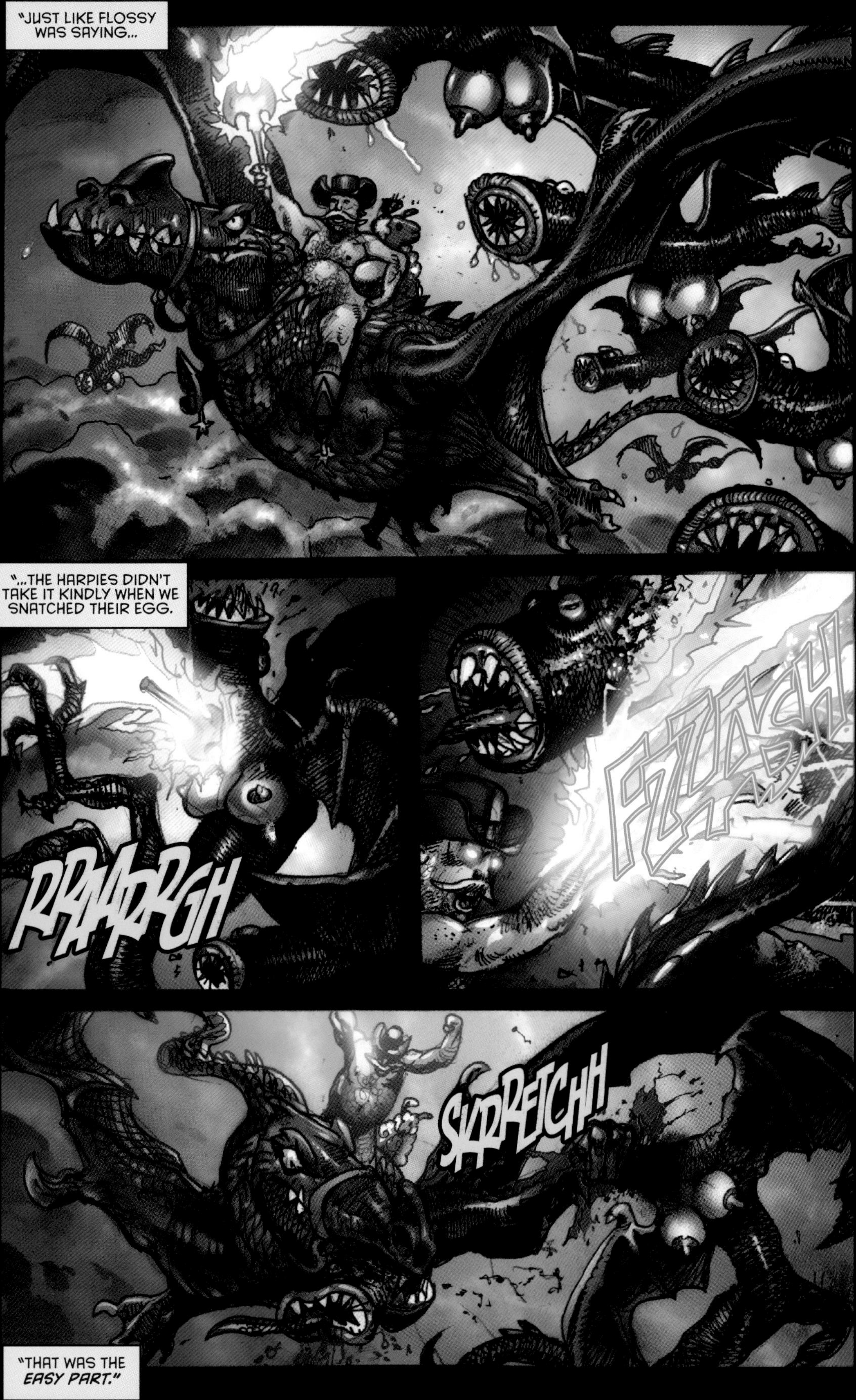
"JUST LIKE FLOSSY WAS SAYING...
"...THE HARPIES DIDN'T TAKE IT KINDLY WHEN WE SNATCHED THEIR EGG.
RRAARGH
FZZAASH
SKDRETCHH
"THAT WAS THE *EASY PART.*"

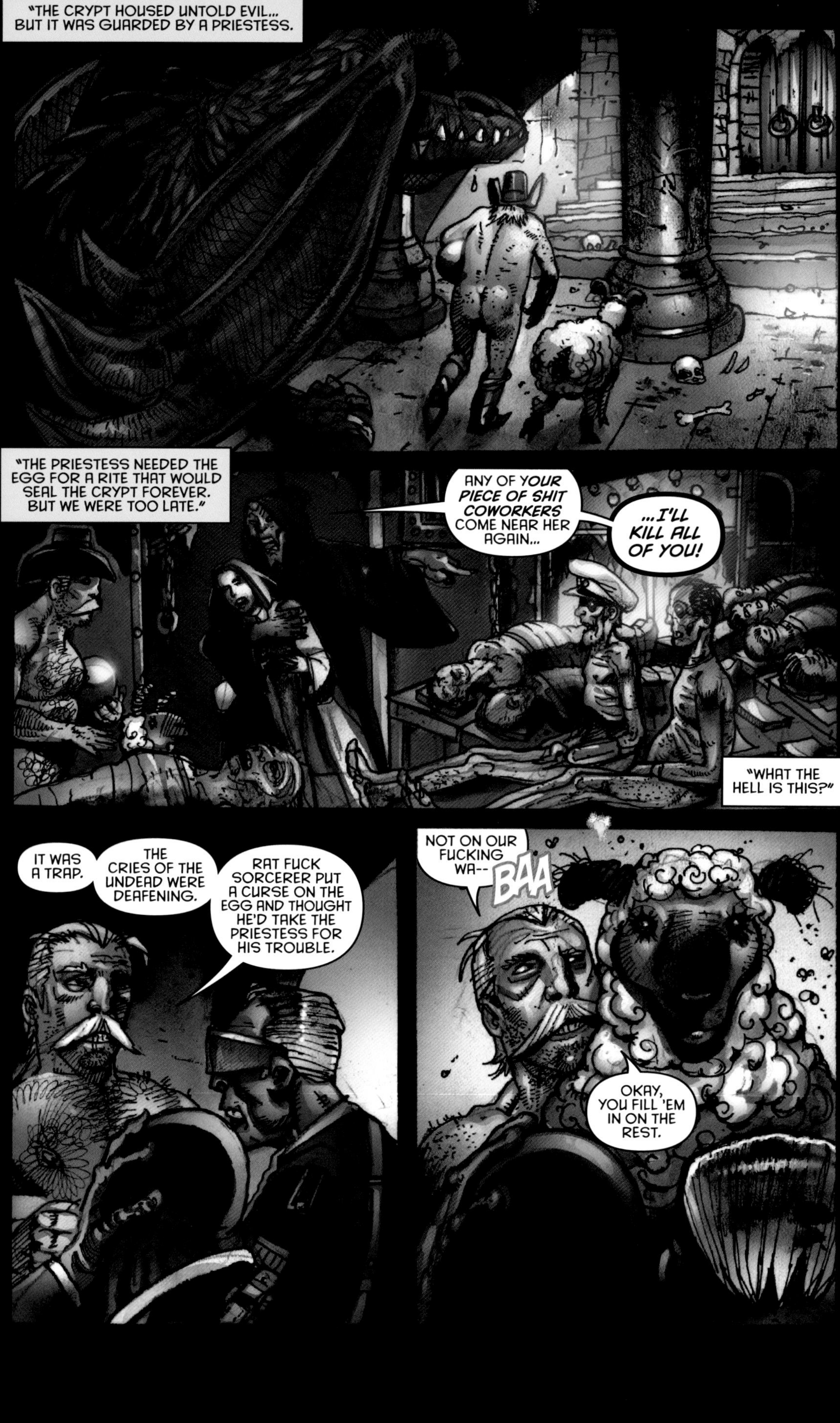
"THE CRYPT HOUSED UNTOLD EVIL... BUT IT WAS GUARDED BY A PRIESTESS.
"THE PRIESTESS NEEDED THE EGG FOR A RITE THAT WOULD SEAL THE CRYPT FOREVER. BUT WE WERE TOO LATE."
ANY OF YOUR PIECE OF SHIT COWORKERS COME NEAR HER AGAIN...
...I'LL KILL ALL OF YOU!
"WHAT THE HELL IS THIS?"
IT WAS A TRAP.
THE CRIES OF THE UNDEAD WERE DEAFENING.
RAT FUCK SORCERER PUT A CURSE ON THE EGG AND THOUGHT HE'D TAKE THE PRIESTESS FOR HIS TROUBLE.
NOT ON OUR FUCKING WA--
BAA
OKAY, YOU FILL 'EM IN ON THE REST.

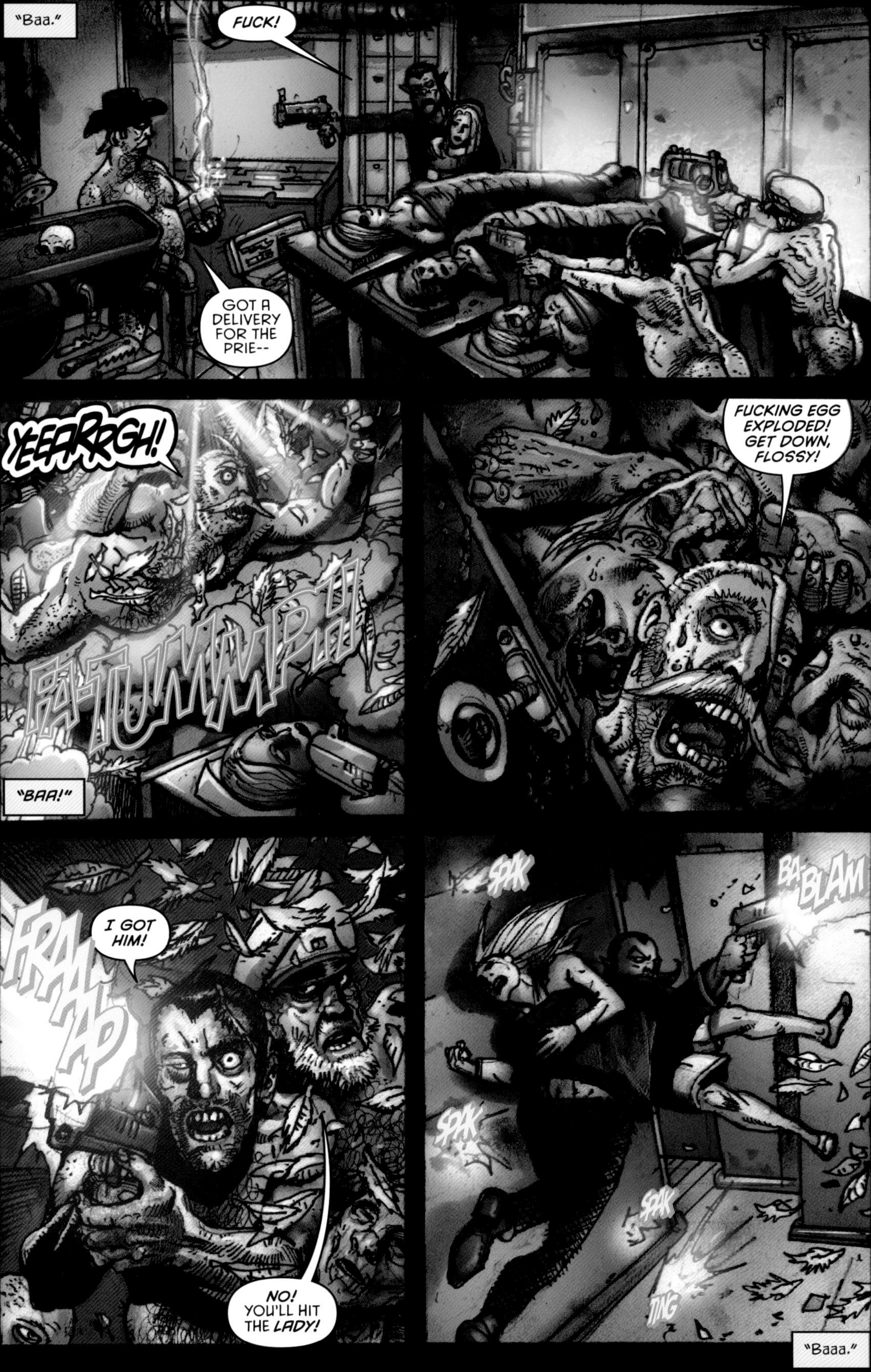
"Baa."
FUCK!
GOT A DELIVERY FOR THE PRIE--
YEEARRGH!
FA-TUMMPH
"BAA!"
FUCKING EGG EXPLODED! GET DOWN, FLOSSY!
FRAAAP
I GOT HIM!
NO! YOU'LL HIT THE LADY!
SPAK
BA-BLAM
SPAK
SPAK
TING
"Baaa."

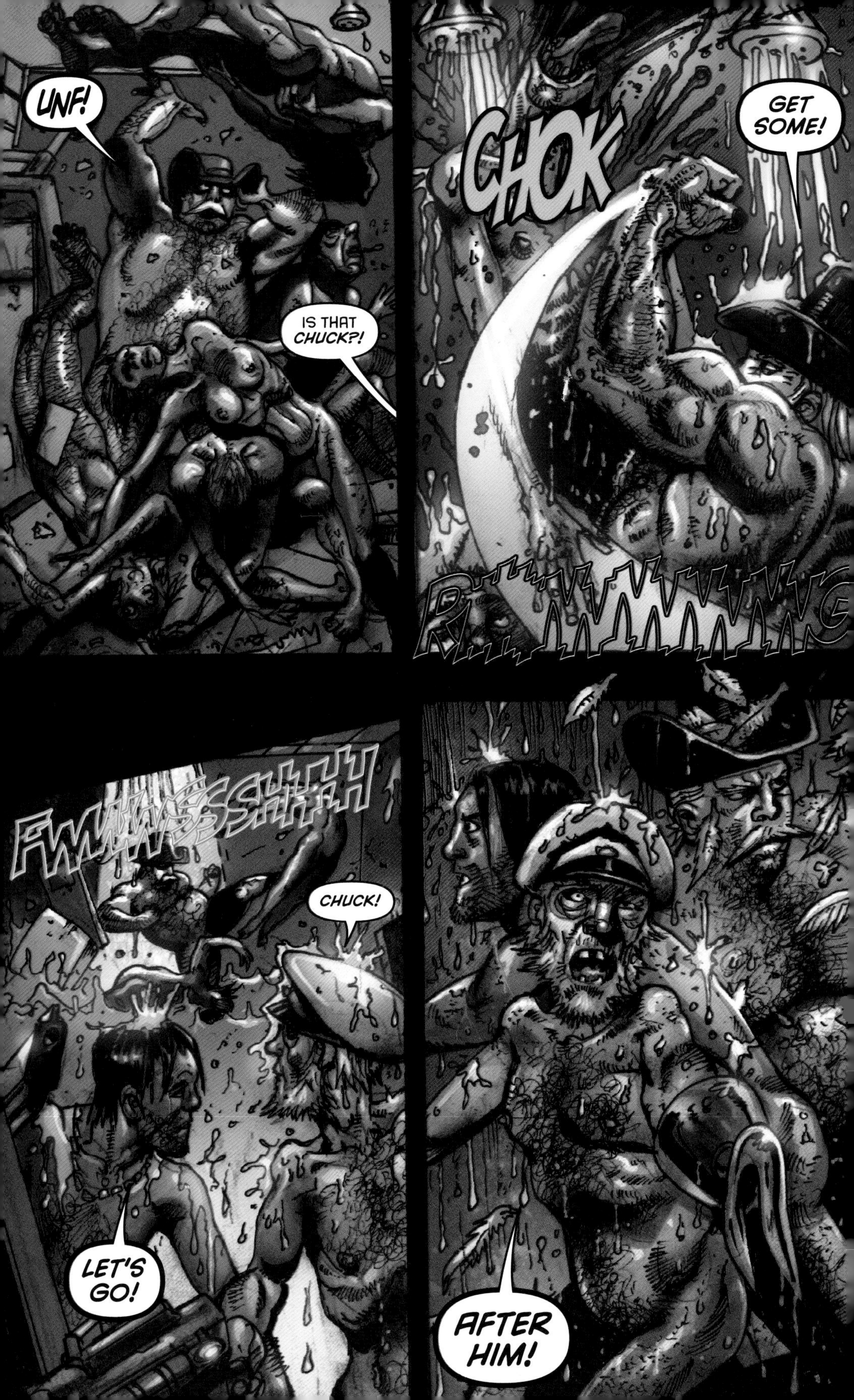
UNF!
IS THAT CHUCK?!
CHOK
GET SOME!
RNNNNNNNNNNNG
FWWWSSSHHHH
CHUCK!
LET'S GO!
AFTER HIM!

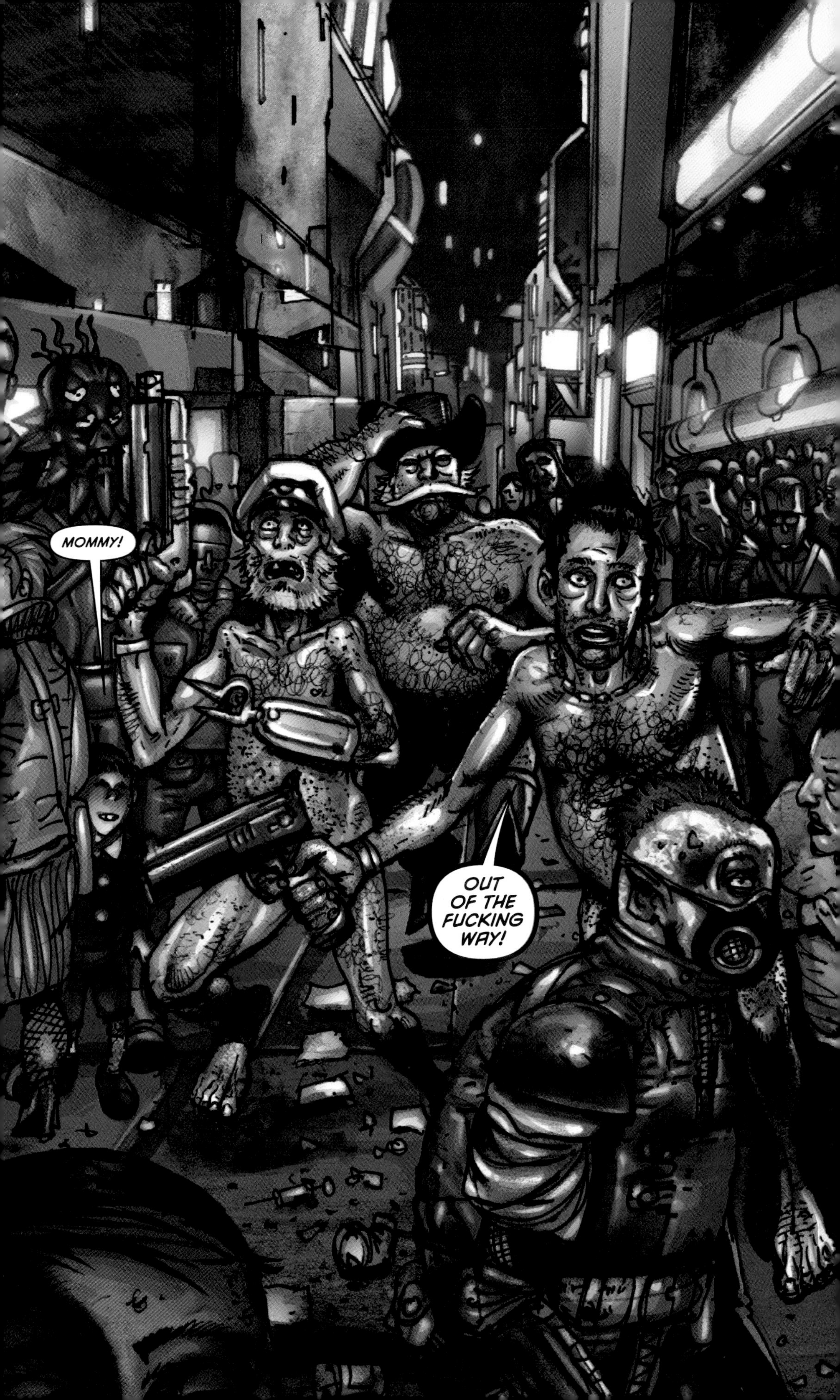
MOMMY!
OUT OF THE FUCKING WAY!

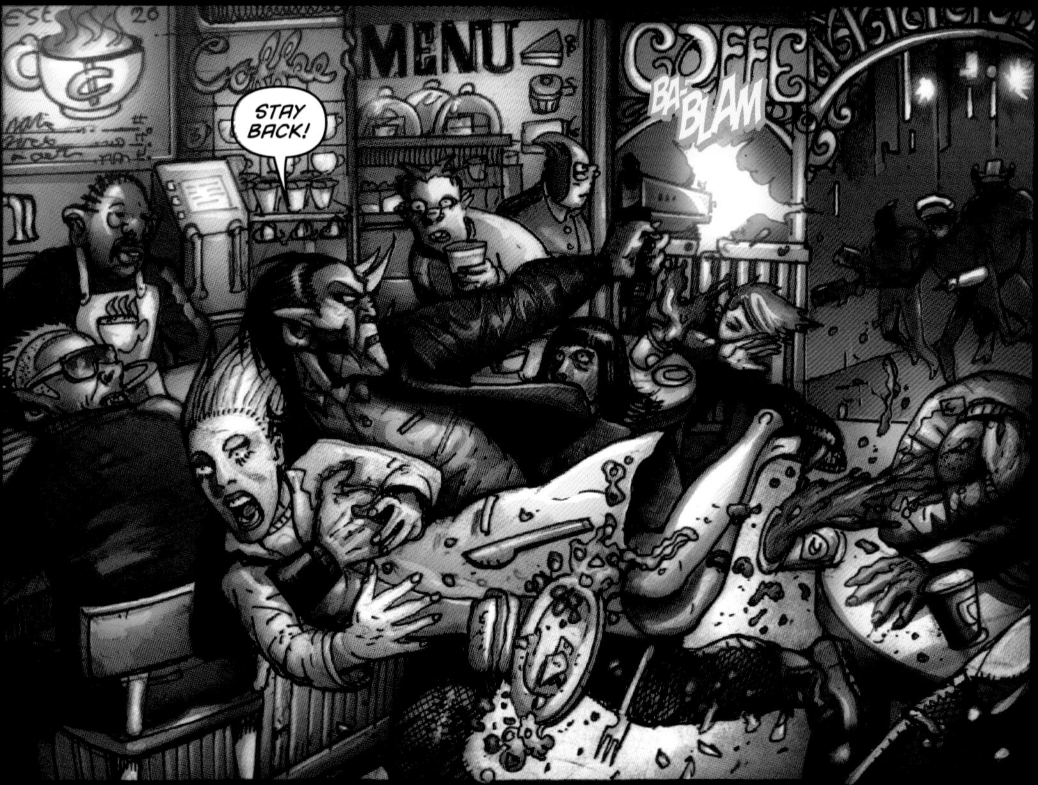
MENU
STAY BACK!
BA-BLAM

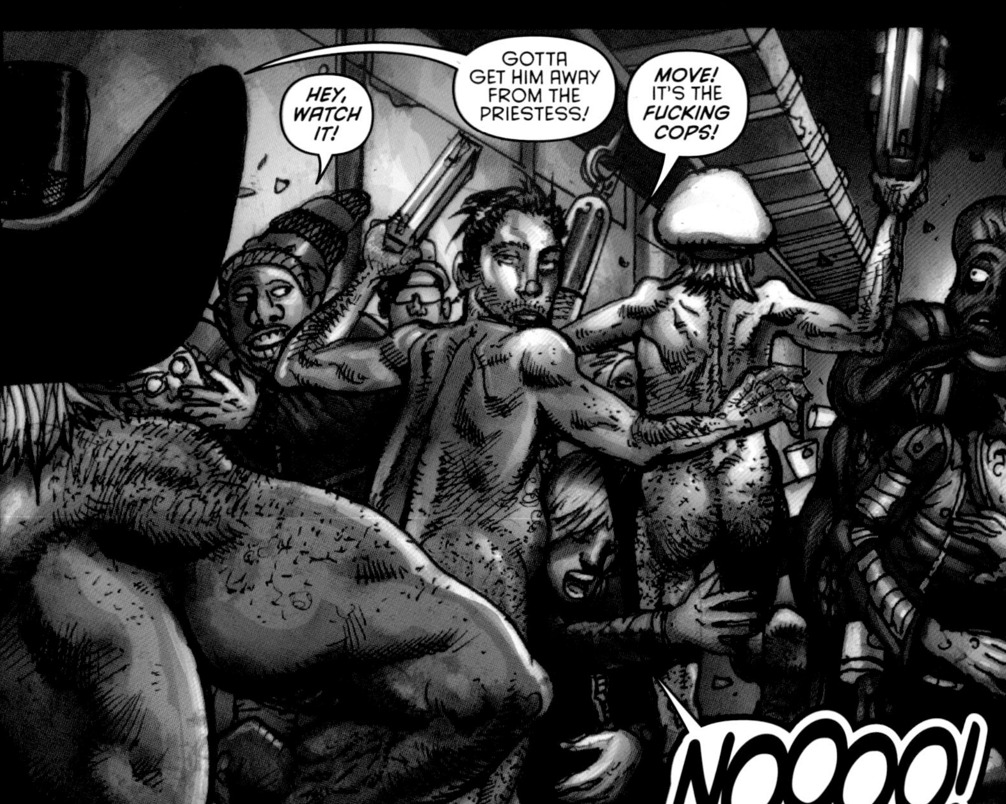
HEY, WATCH IT!
GOTTA GET HIM AWAY FROM THE PRIESTESS!
MOVE! IT'S THE FUCKING COPS!
NOOOO!

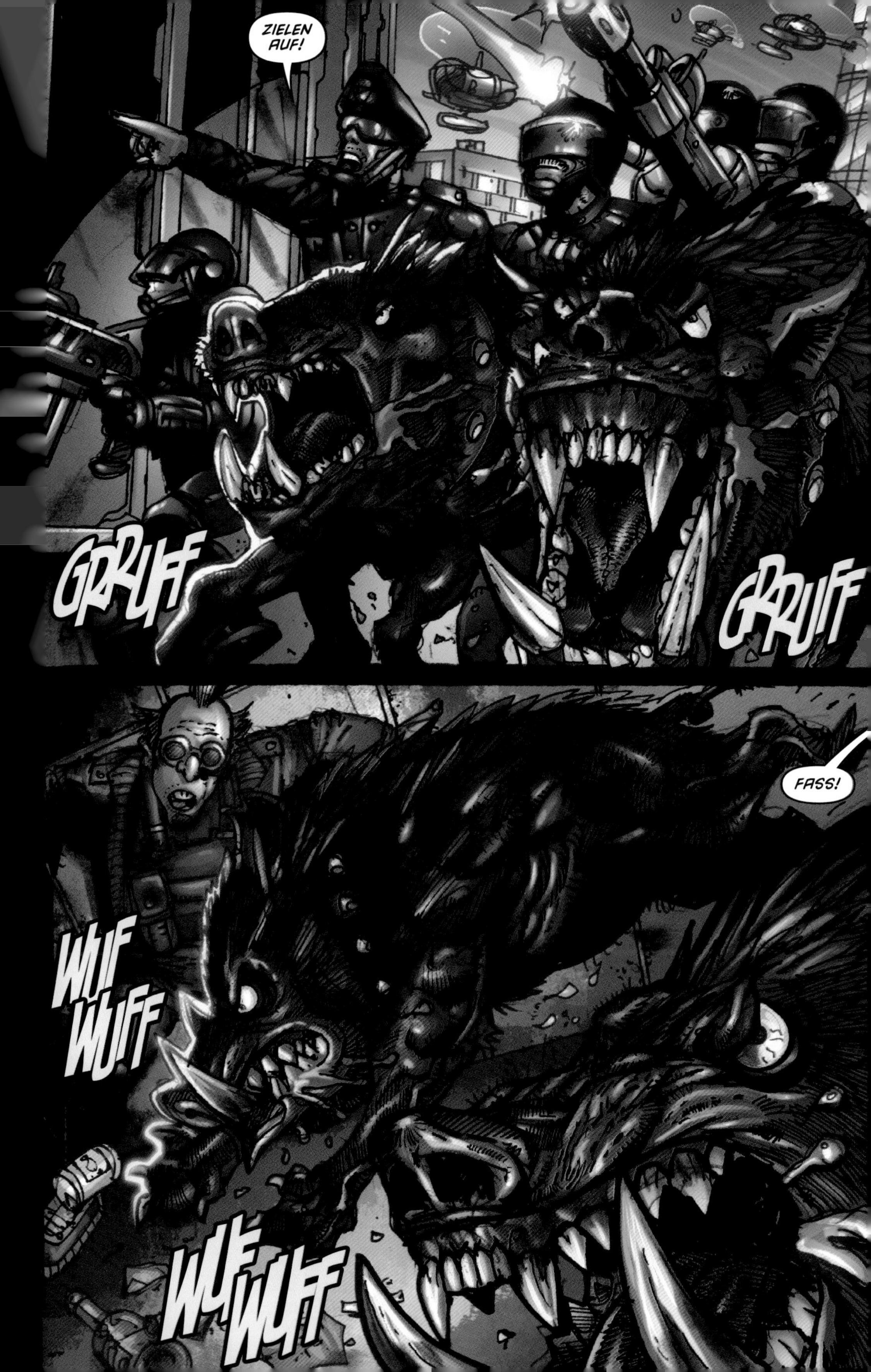
ZIELEN AUF!
GRRUFF
GRRUFF
FASS!
WUF WUFF
WUF WUFF

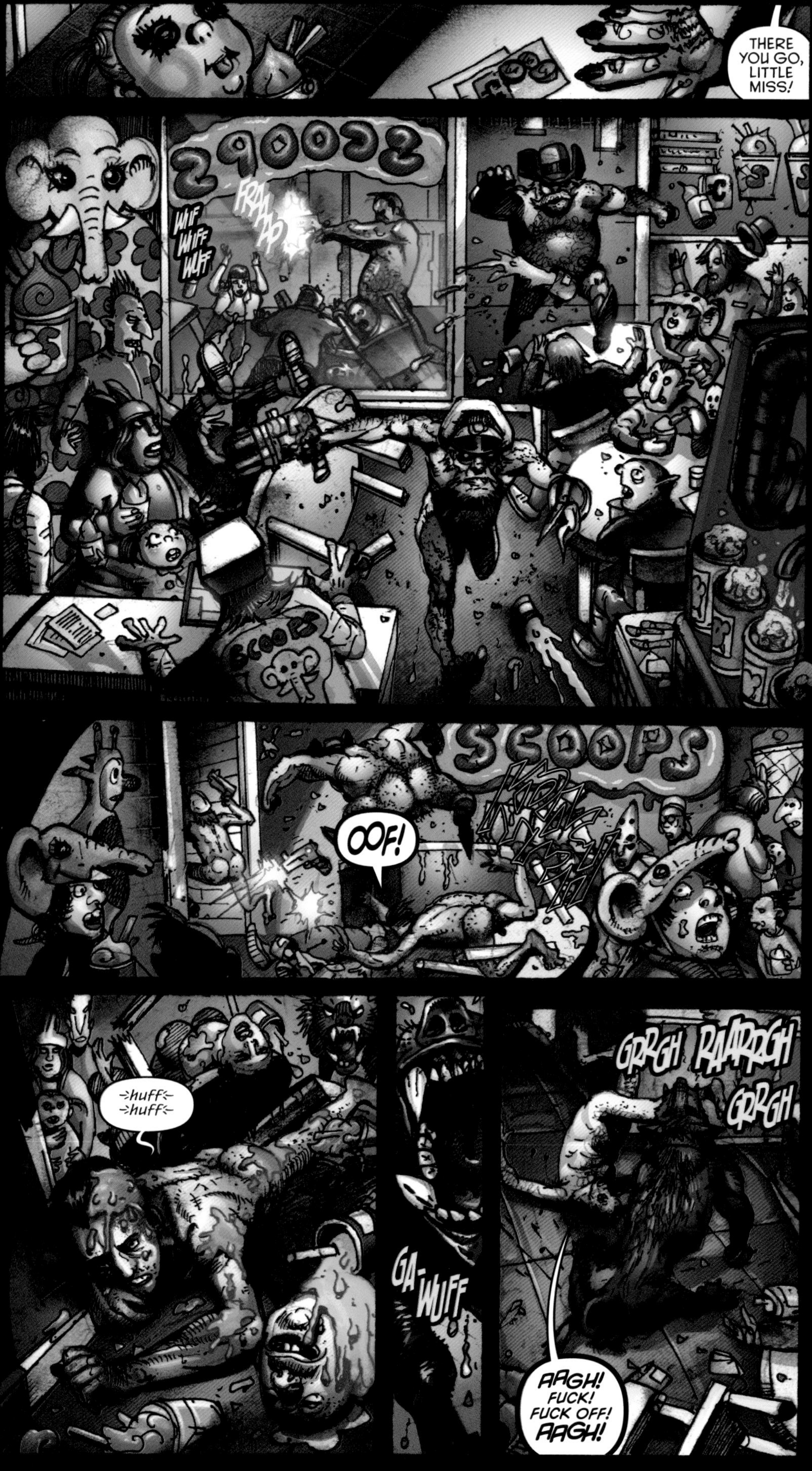
THERE YOU GO, LITTLE MISS!
WIF WIFF WUFF
FRAAAP
SCOOPS
OOF!
huff huff
GA-WUFF
GRRGH RAARRGH GRRGH
AAGH! FUCK! FUCK OFF! AAGH!

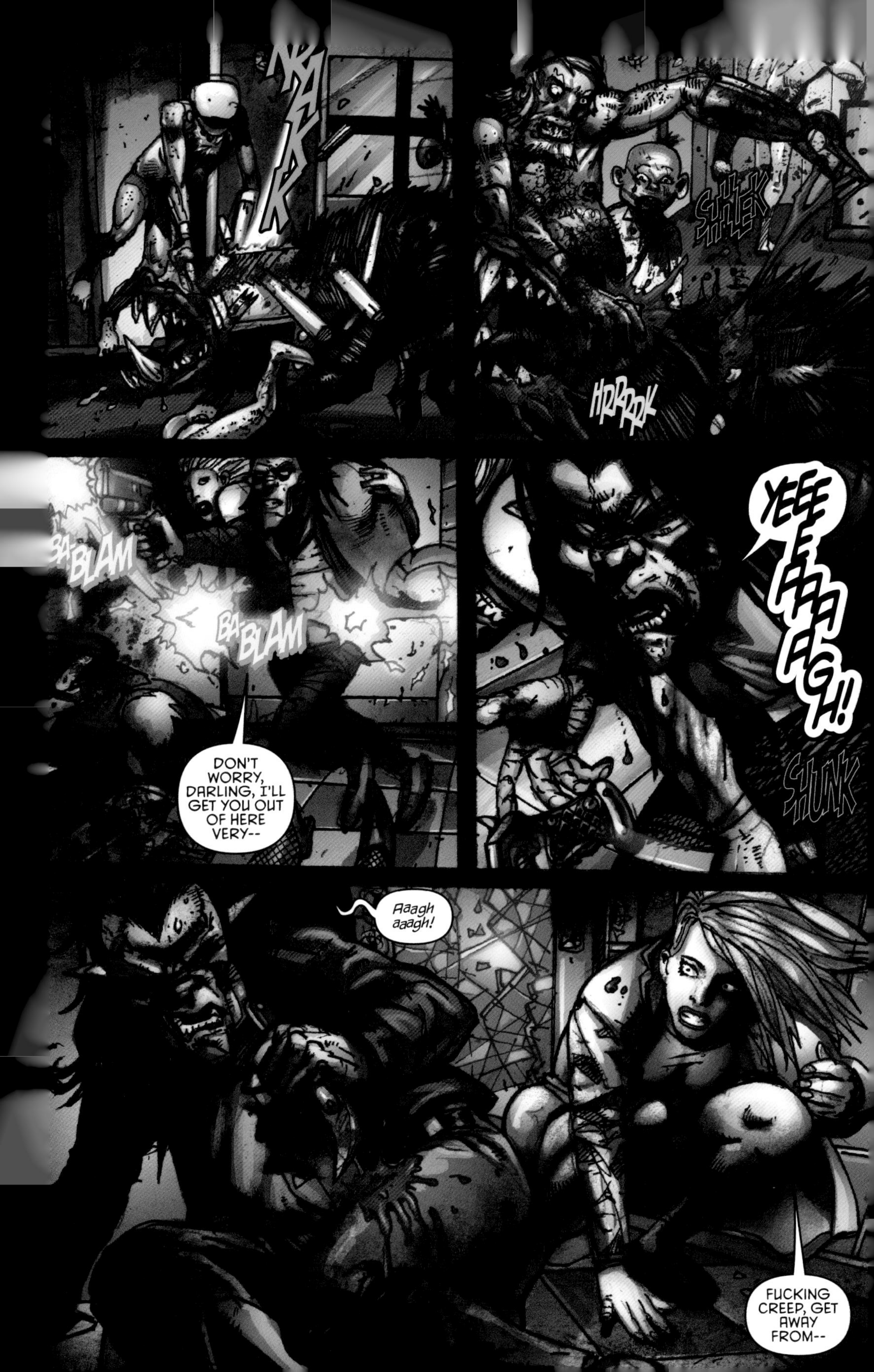
KRAKK
SHHLEK
HRRRRK
BA-BLAM
BA-BLAM
DON'T WORRY, DARLING, I'LL GET YOU OUT OF HERE VERY--
YEEEEAAAAAGH!
SHUNK
Aaagh aaagh!
FUCKING CREEP, GET AWAY FROM--

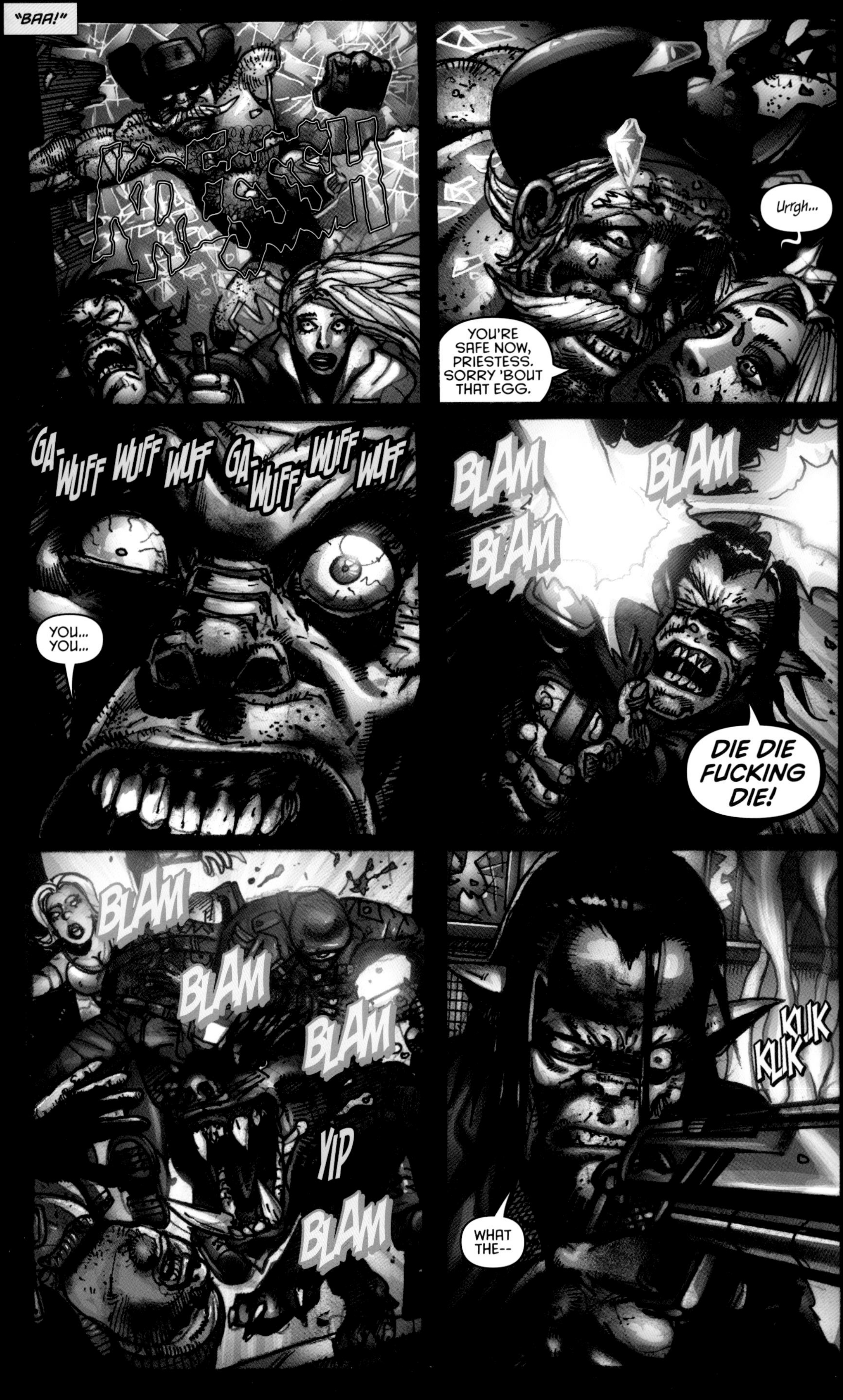
"BAA!"
Urrgh...
YOU'RE SAFE NOW, PRIESTESS. SORRY 'BOUT THAT EGG.
GA-WUFF WUFF WUFF GA-WUFF WUFF WUFF
YOU... YOU...
BLAM
BLAM
BLAM
DIE DIE FUCKING DIE!
BLAM
BLAM
BLAM
YIP
BLAM
KLIK KLIK
WHAT THE--

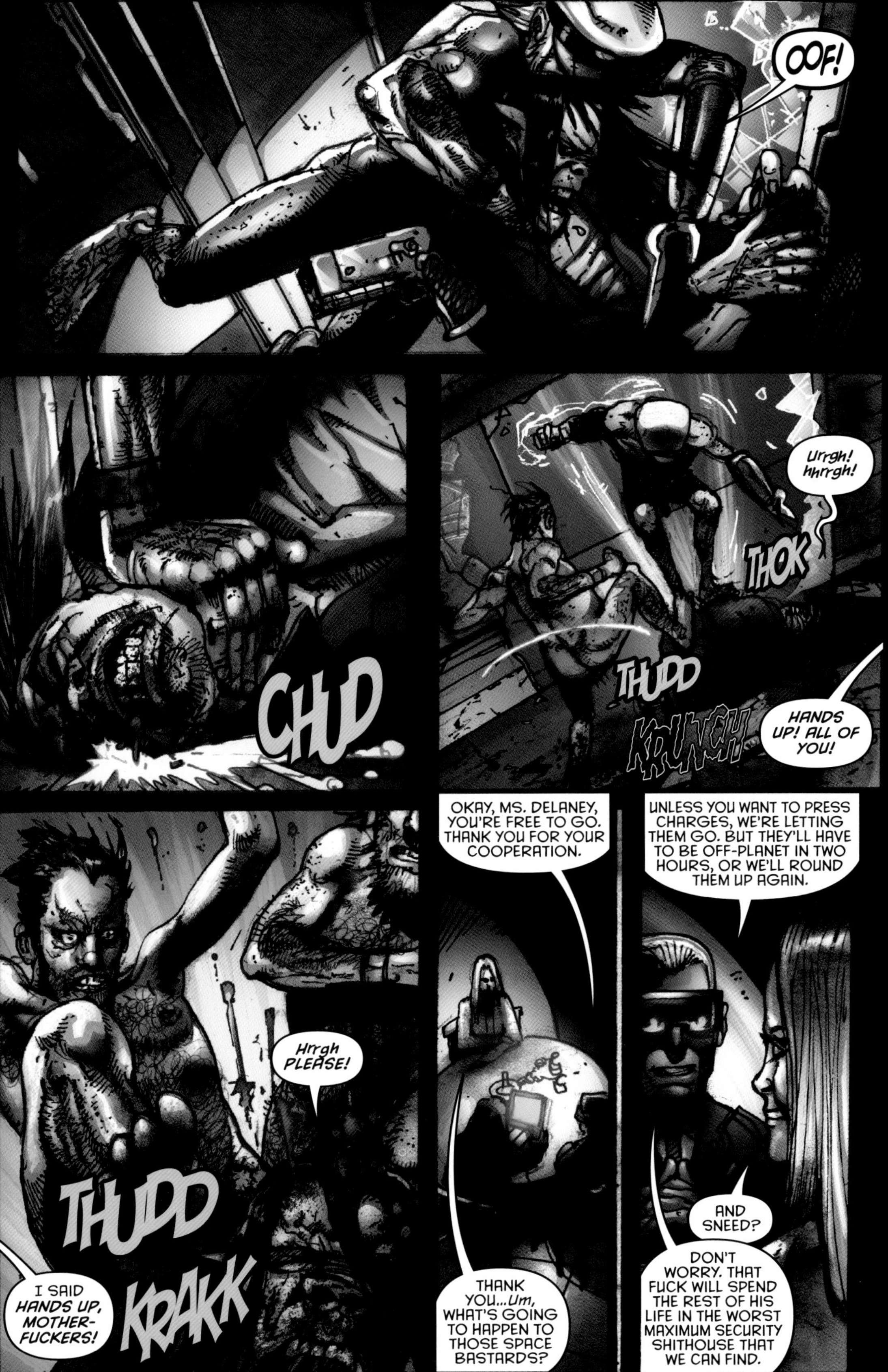
OOF!
CHUD
Urrgh! hhrrgh!
THOK
THUDD
KRUNCH
HANDS UP! ALL OF YOU!
Hrrgh PLEASE!
THUDD
I SAID HANDS UP, MOTHER-FUCKERS!
KRAKK
OKAY, MS. DELANEY, YOU'RE FREE TO GO. THANK YOU FOR YOUR COOPERATION.
THANK YOU...Um, WHAT'S GOING TO HAPPEN TO THOSE SPACE BASTARDS?
UNLESS YOU WANT TO PRESS CHARGES, WE'RE LETTING THEM GO. BUT THEY'LL HAVE TO BE OFF-PLANET IN TWO HOURS, OR WE'LL ROUND THEM UP AGAIN.
AND SNEED?
DON'T WORRY. THAT FUCK WILL SPEND THE REST OF HIS LIFE IN THE WORST MAXIMUM SECURITY SHITHOUSE THAT WE CAN FIND.

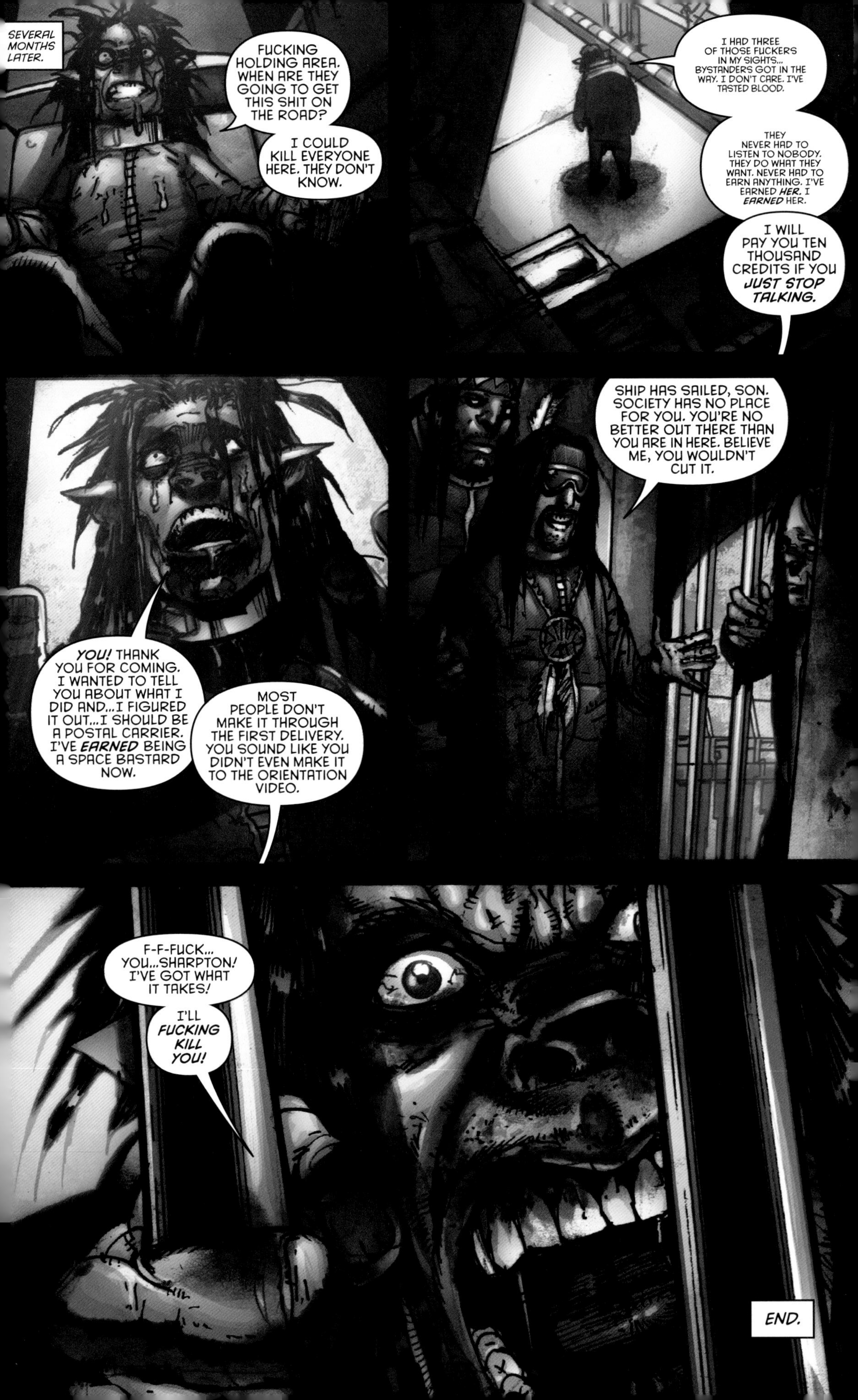
SEVERAL MONTHS LATER.
FUCKING HOLDING AREA. WHEN ARE THEY GOING TO GET THIS SHIT ON THE ROAD?
I COULD KILL EVERYONE HERE. THEY DON'T KNOW.
I HAD THREE OF THOSE FUCKERS IN MY SIGHTS... BYSTANDERS GOT IN THE WAY. I DON'T CARE. I'VE TASTED BLOOD.
THEY NEVER HAD TO LISTEN TO NOBODY. THEY DO WHAT THEY WANT. NEVER HAD TO EARN ANYTHING. I'VE EARNED HER. I EARNED HER.
I WILL PAY YOU TEN THOUSAND CREDITS IF YOU JUST STOP TALKING.
YOU! THANK YOU FOR COMING. I WANTED TO TELL YOU ABOUT WHAT I DID AND...I FIGURED IT OUT...I SHOULD BE A POSTAL CARRIER. I'VE EARNED BEING A SPACE BASTARD NOW.
MOST PEOPLE DON'T MAKE IT THROUGH THE FIRST DELIVERY. YOU SOUND LIKE YOU DIDN'T EVEN MAKE IT TO THE ORIENTATION VIDEO.
SHIP HAS SAILED, SON. SOCIETY HAS NO PLACE FOR YOU. YOU'RE NO BETTER OUT THERE THAN YOU ARE IN HERE. BELIEVE ME, YOU WOULDN'T CUT IT.
F-F-FUCK... YOU...SHARPTON! I'VE GOT WHAT IT TAKES!
I'LL FUCKING KILL YOU!
END.

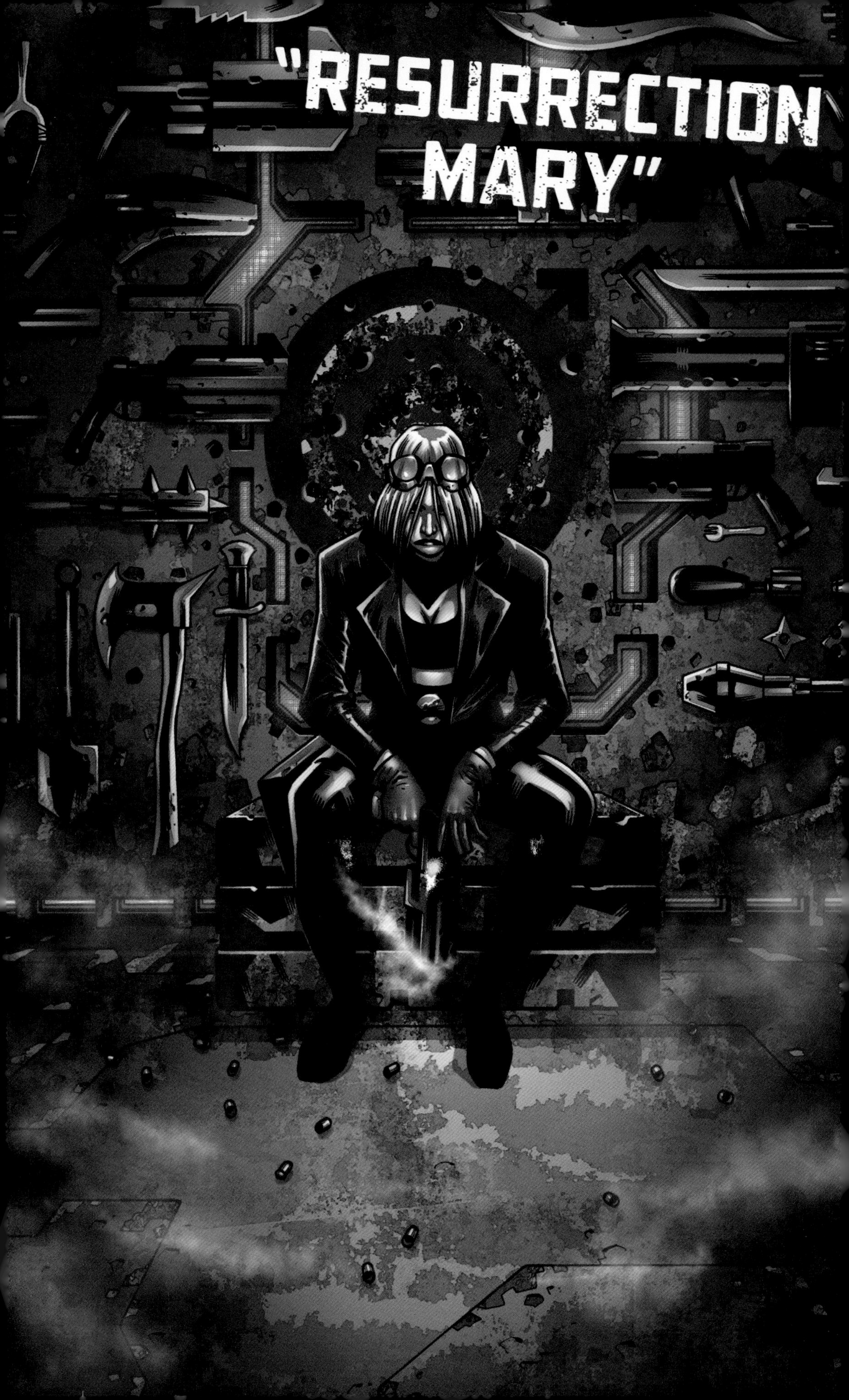
"RESURRECTION
MARY"

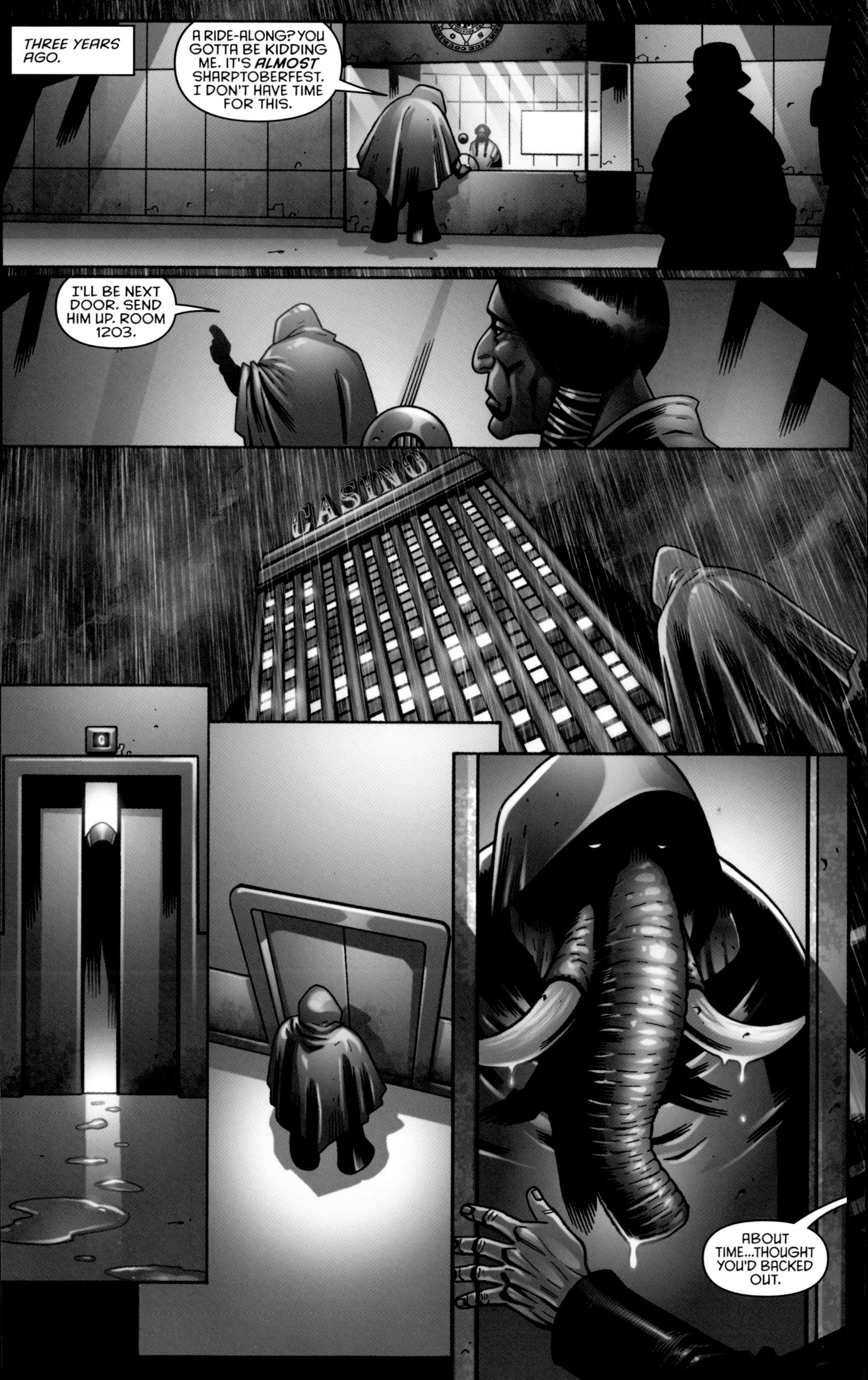
THREE YEARS AGO.
A RIDE-ALONG? YOU GOTTA BE KIDDING ME. IT'S ALMOST SHARPTOBERFEST. I DON'T HAVE TIME FOR THIS.
I'LL BE NEXT DOOR. SEND HIM UP. ROOM 1203.
CASINO
ABOUT TIME...THOUGHT YOU'D BACKED OUT.

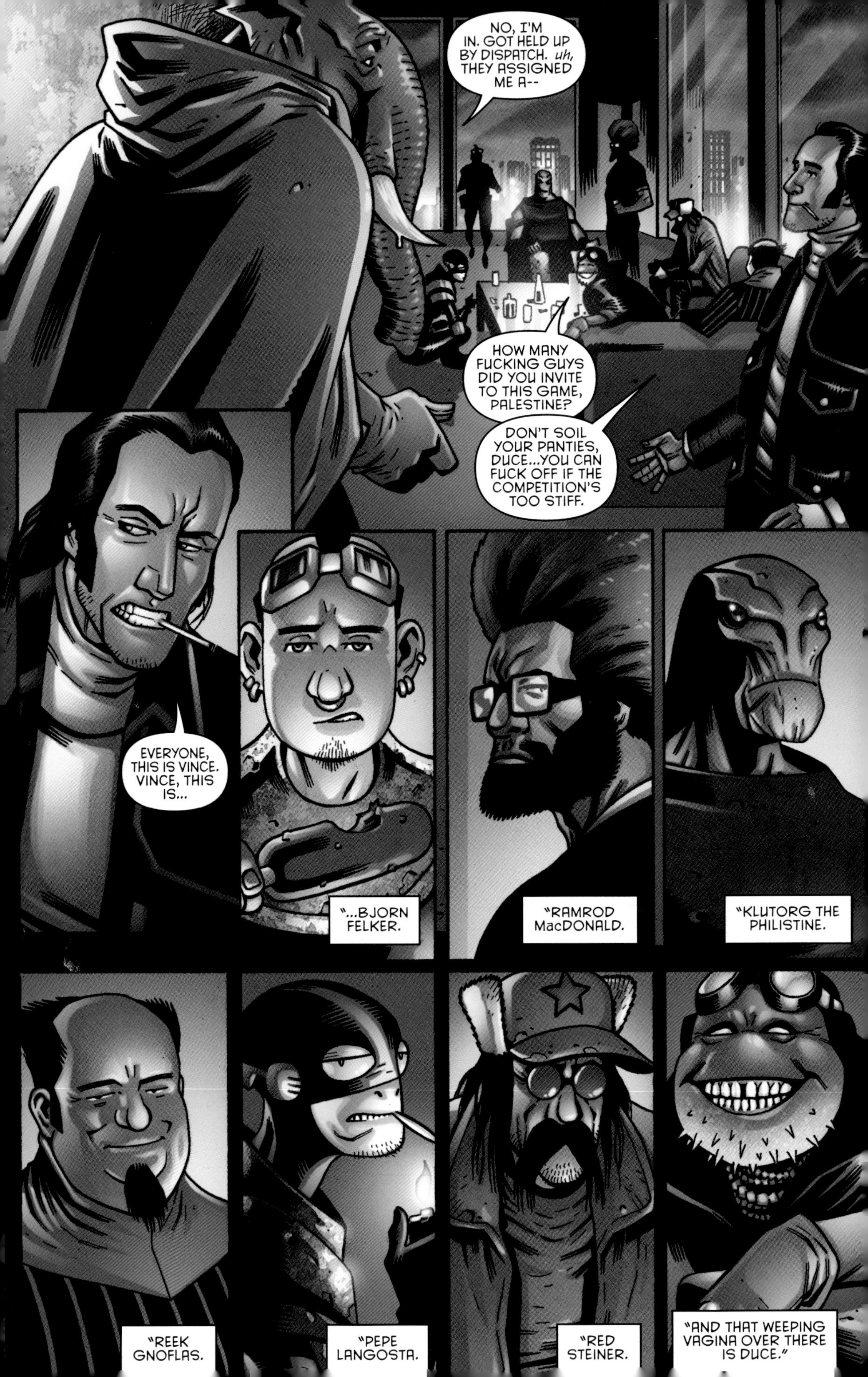

NO, I'M IN. GOT HELD UP BY DISPATCH. *uh,* THEY ASSIGNED ME A--
HOW MANY FUCKING GUYS DID YOU INVITE TO THIS GAME, PALESTINE?
DON'T SOIL YOUR PANTIES, DUCE...YOU CAN FUCK OFF IF THE COMPETITION'S TOO STIFF.
EVERYONE, THIS IS VINCE. VINCE, THIS IS...
"...BJORN FELKER.
"RAMROD MacDONALD.
"KLUTORG THE PHILISTINE.
"REEK GNOFLAS.
"PEPE LANGOSTA.
"RED STEINER.
"AND THAT WEEPING VAGINA OVER THERE IS DUCE."

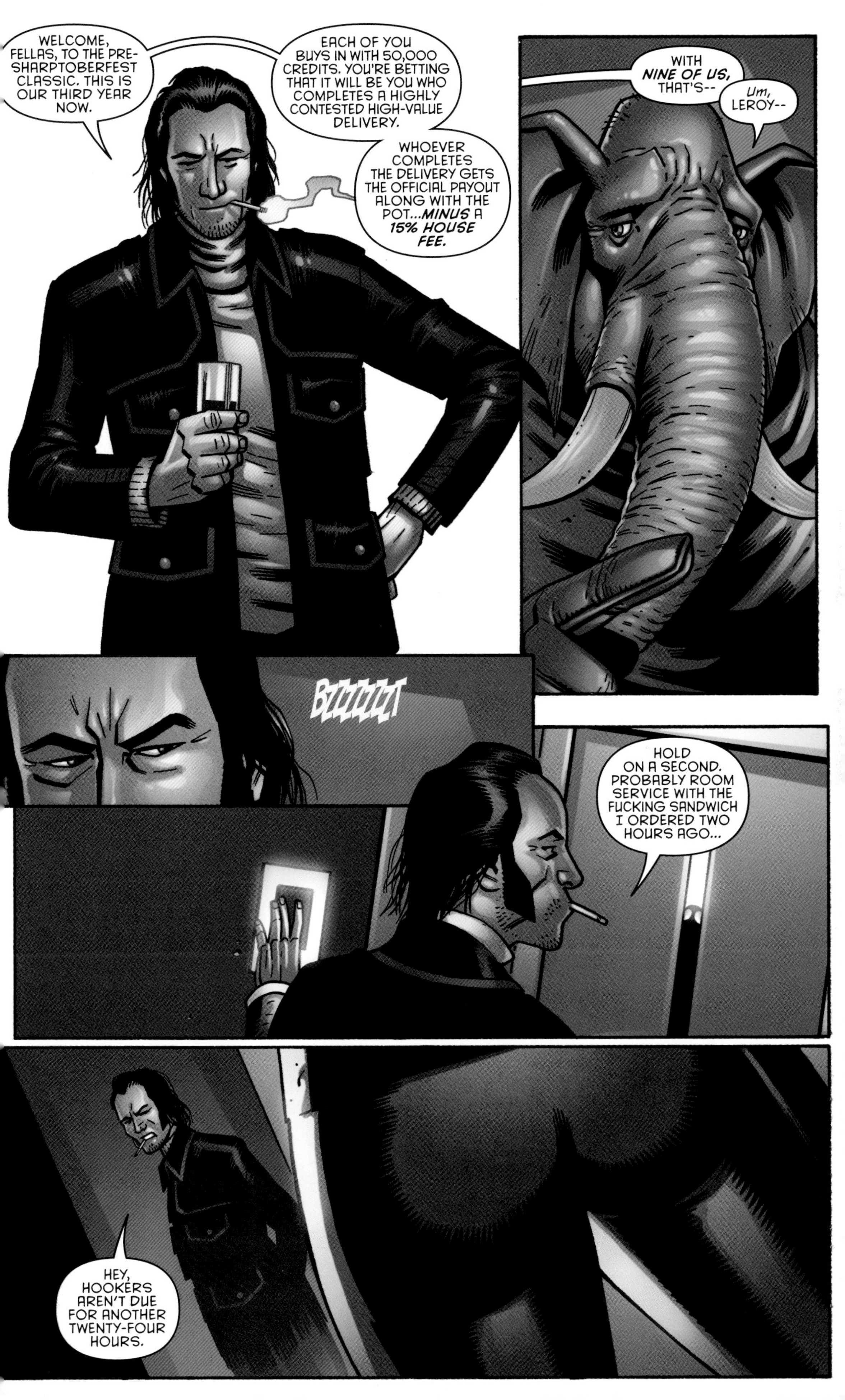
WELCOME, FELLAS, TO THE PRE-SHARPTOBERFEST CLASSIC. THIS IS OUR THIRD YEAR NOW.
EACH OF YOU BUYS IN WITH 50,000 CREDITS. YOU'RE BETTING THAT IT WILL BE YOU WHO COMPLETES A HIGHLY CONTESTED HIGH-VALUE DELIVERY.
WHOEVER COMPLETES THE DELIVERY GETS THE OFFICIAL PAYOUT ALONG WITH THE POT...*MINUS* A *15% HOUSE FEE.*
WITH *NINE OF US,* THAT'S--
Um, LEROY--
BZZZZZT
HOLD ON A SECOND. PROBABLY ROOM SERVICE WITH THE FUCKING SANDWICH I ORDERED TWO HOURS AGO...
HEY, HOOKERS AREN'T DUE FOR ANOTHER TWENTY-FOUR HOURS.

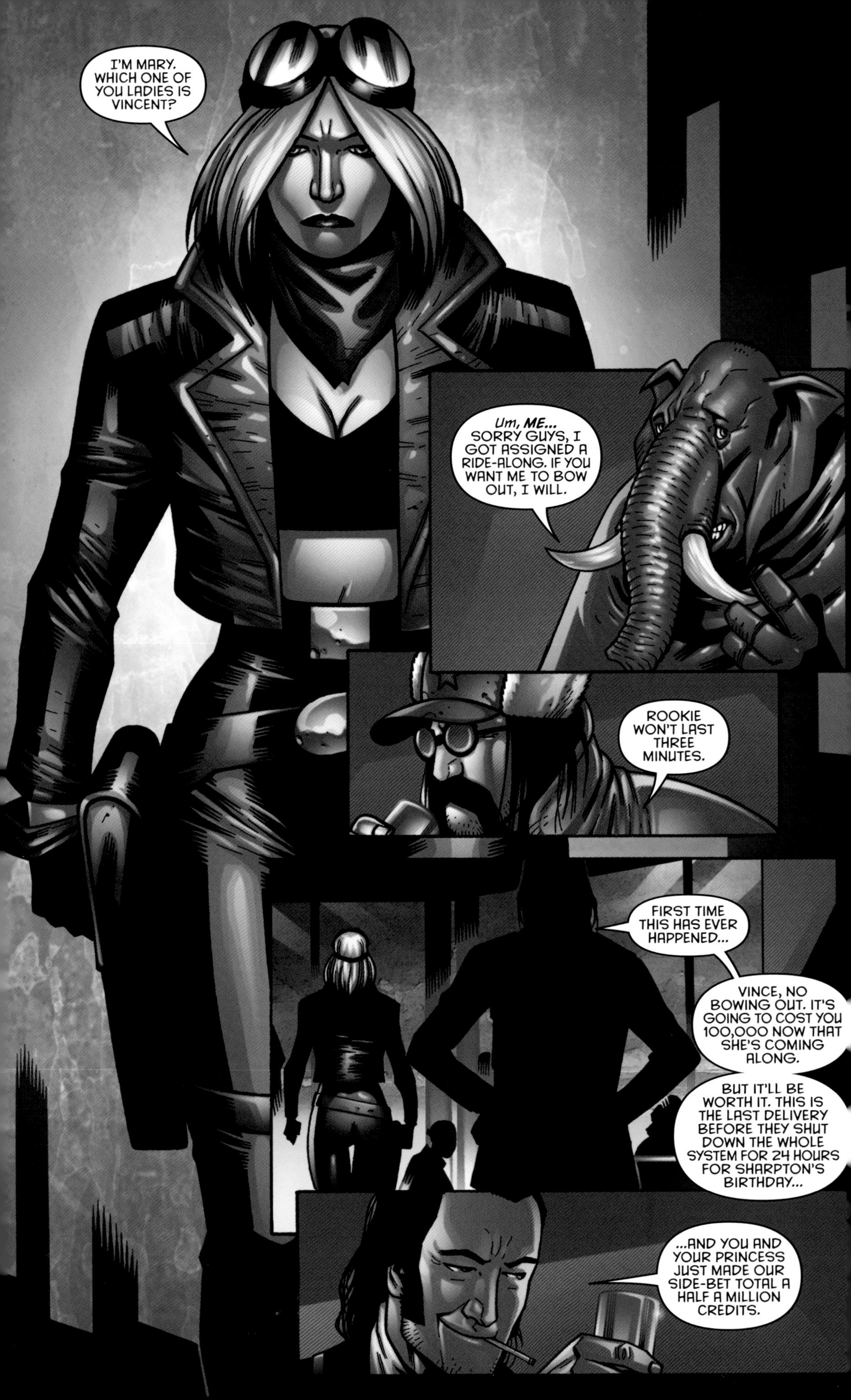
I'M MARY. WHICH ONE OF YOU LADIES IS VINCENT?
*Um, **ME...*** SORRY GUYS, I GOT ASSIGNED A RIDE-ALONG. IF YOU WANT ME TO BOW OUT, I WILL.
ROOKIE WON'T LAST THREE MINUTES.
FIRST TIME THIS HAS EVER HAPPENED...
VINCE, NO BOWING OUT. IT'S GOING TO COST YOU 100,000 NOW THAT SHE'S COMING ALONG.
BUT IT'LL BE WORTH IT. THIS IS THE LAST DELIVERY BEFORE THEY SHUT DOWN THE WHOLE SYSTEM FOR 24 HOURS FOR SHARPTON'S BIRTHDAY...
...AND YOU AND YOUR PRINCESS JUST MADE OUR SIDE-BET TOTAL A HALF A MILLION CREDITS.

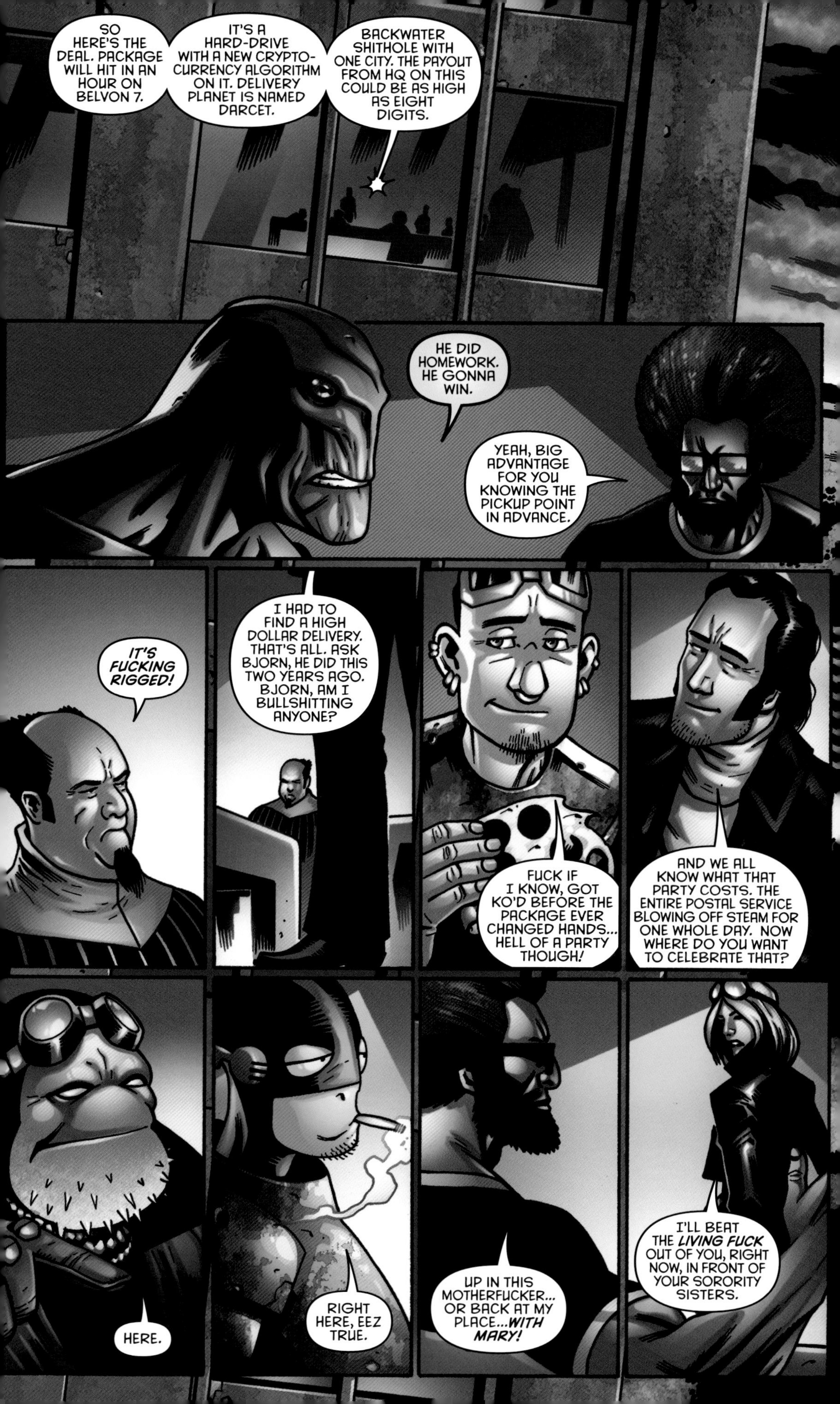

SO HERE'S THE DEAL. PACKAGE WILL HIT IN AN HOUR ON BELVON 7.
IT'S A HARD-DRIVE WITH A NEW CRYPTO-CURRENCY ALGORITHM ON IT. DELIVERY PLANET IS NAMED DARCET.
BACKWATER SHITHOLE WITH ONE CITY. THE PAYOUT FROM HQ ON THIS COULD BE AS HIGH AS EIGHT DIGITS.
HE DID HOMEWORK. HE GONNA WIN.
YEAH, BIG ADVANTAGE FOR YOU KNOWING THE PICKUP POINT IN ADVANCE.
IT'S FUCKING RIGGED!
I HAD TO FIND A HIGH DOLLAR DELIVERY. THAT'S ALL. ASK BJORN, HE DID THIS TWO YEARS AGO. BJORN, AM I BULLSHITTING ANYONE?
FUCK IF I KNOW, GOT KO'D BEFORE THE PACKAGE EVER CHANGED HANDS... HELL OF A PARTY THOUGH!
AND WE ALL KNOW WHAT THAT PARTY COSTS. THE ENTIRE POSTAL SERVICE BLOWING OFF STEAM FOR ONE WHOLE DAY. NOW WHERE DO YOU WANT TO CELEBRATE THAT?
HERE.
RIGHT HERE, EEZ TRUE.
UP IN THIS MOTHERFUCKER... OR BACK AT MY PLACE...WITH MARY!
I'LL BEAT THE LIVING FUCK OUT OF YOU, RIGHT NOW, IN FRONT OF YOUR SORORITY SISTERS.

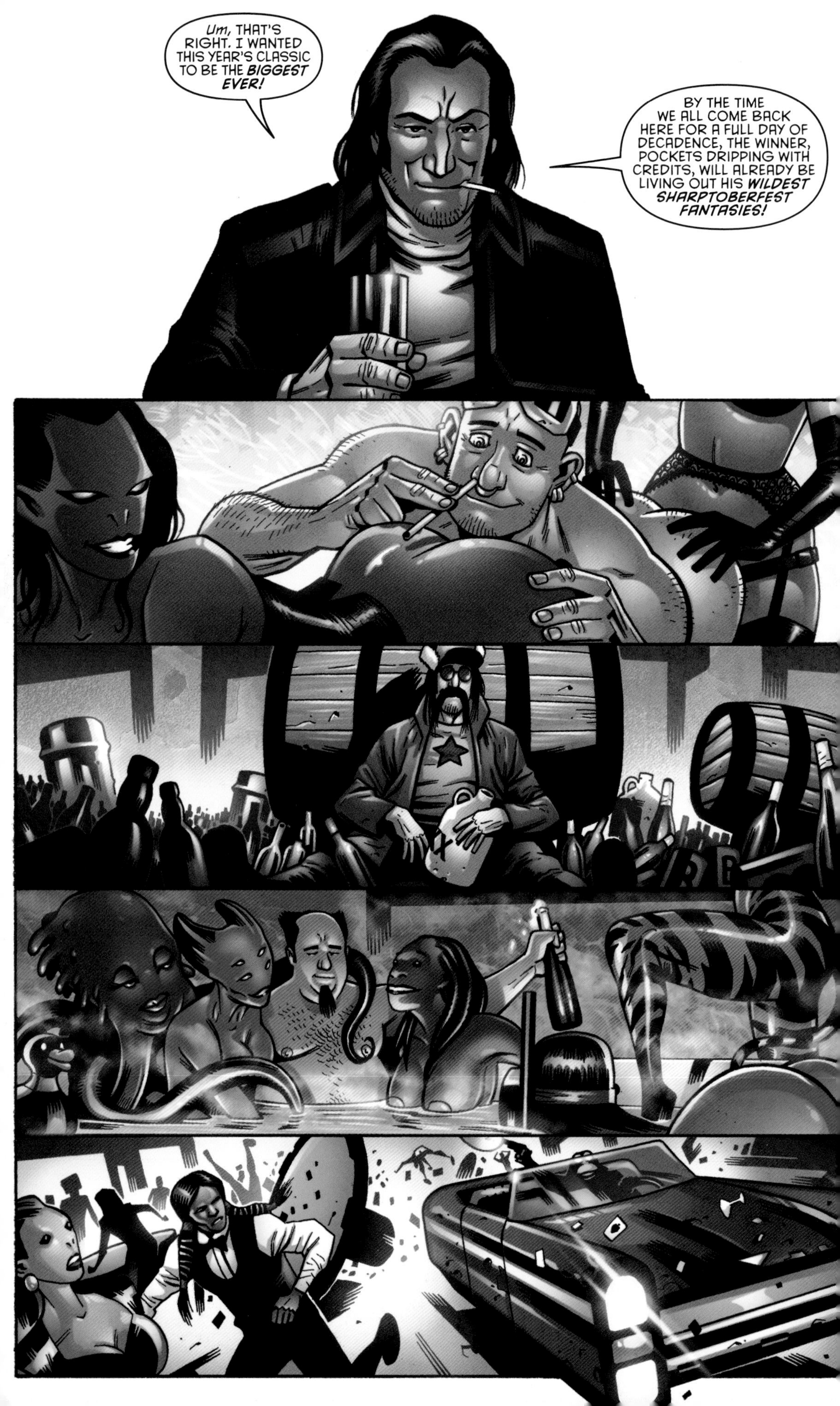

Um, THAT'S RIGHT. I WANTED THIS YEAR'S CLASSIC TO BE THE BIGGEST EVER!
BY THE TIME WE ALL COME BACK HERE FOR A FULL DAY OF DECADENCE, THE WINNER, POCKETS DRIPPING WITH CREDITS, WILL ALREADY BE LIVING OUT HIS WILDEST SHARPTOBERFEST FANTASIES!

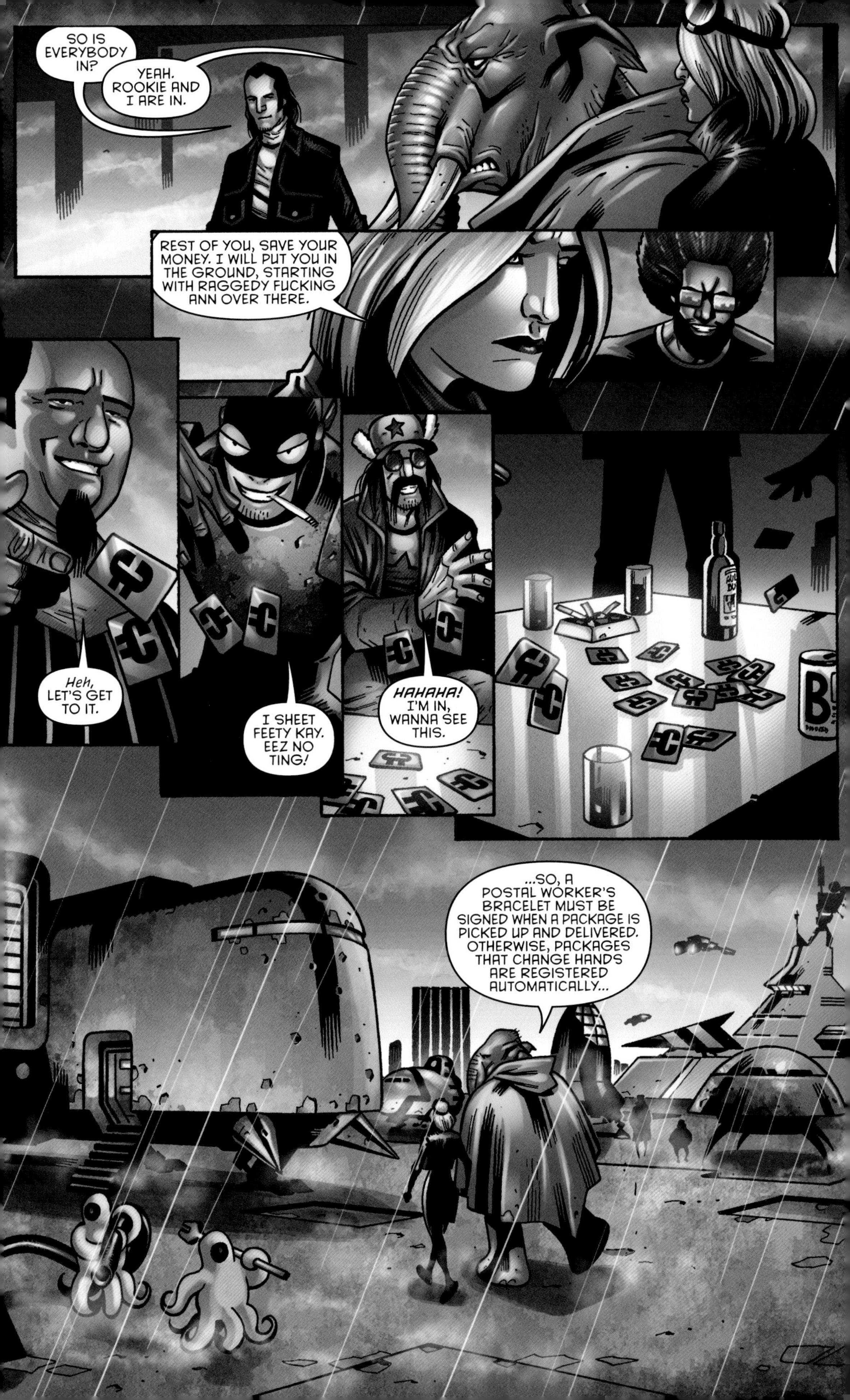
SO IS EVERYBODY IN?
YEAH. ROOKIE AND I ARE IN.
REST OF YOU, SAVE YOUR MONEY. I WILL PUT YOU IN THE GROUND, STARTING WITH RAGGEDY FUCKING ANN OVER THERE.
Heh, LET'S GET TO IT.
I SHEET FEETY KAY. EEZ NO TING!
HAHAHA! I'M IN, WANNA SEE THIS.
...SO, A POSTAL WORKER'S BRACELET MUST BE SIGNED WHEN A PACKAGE IS PICKED UP AND DELIVERED. OTHERWISE, PACKAGES THAT CHANGE HANDS ARE REGISTERED AUTOMATICALLY...

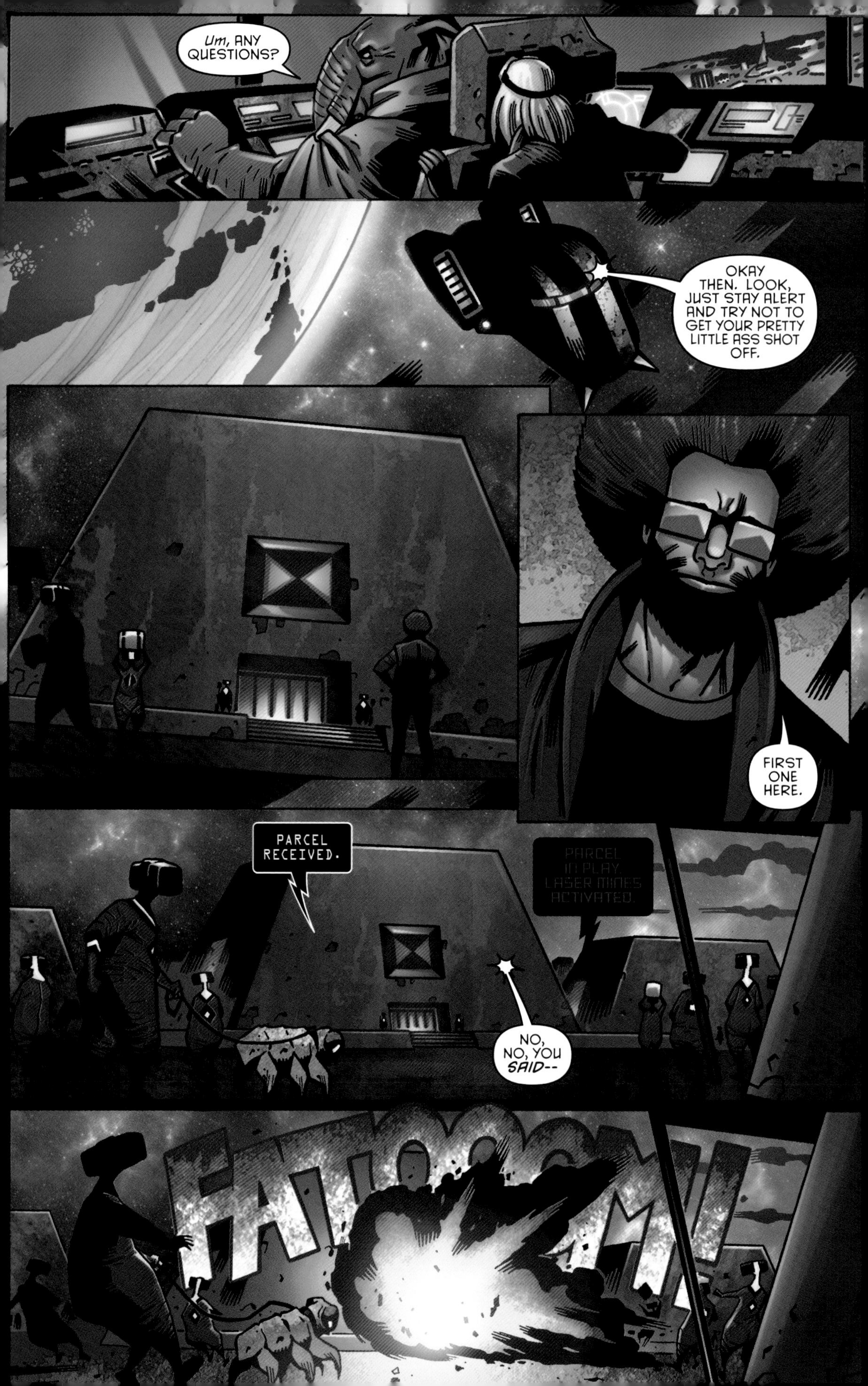

Um, ANY QUESTIONS?
OKAY THEN. LOOK, JUST STAY ALERT AND TRY NOT TO GET YOUR PRETTY LITTLE ASS SHOT OFF.
FIRST ONE HERE.
PARCEL RECEIVED.
PARCEL IN PLAY. LASER MINES ACTIVATED.
NO, NO, YOU SAID--

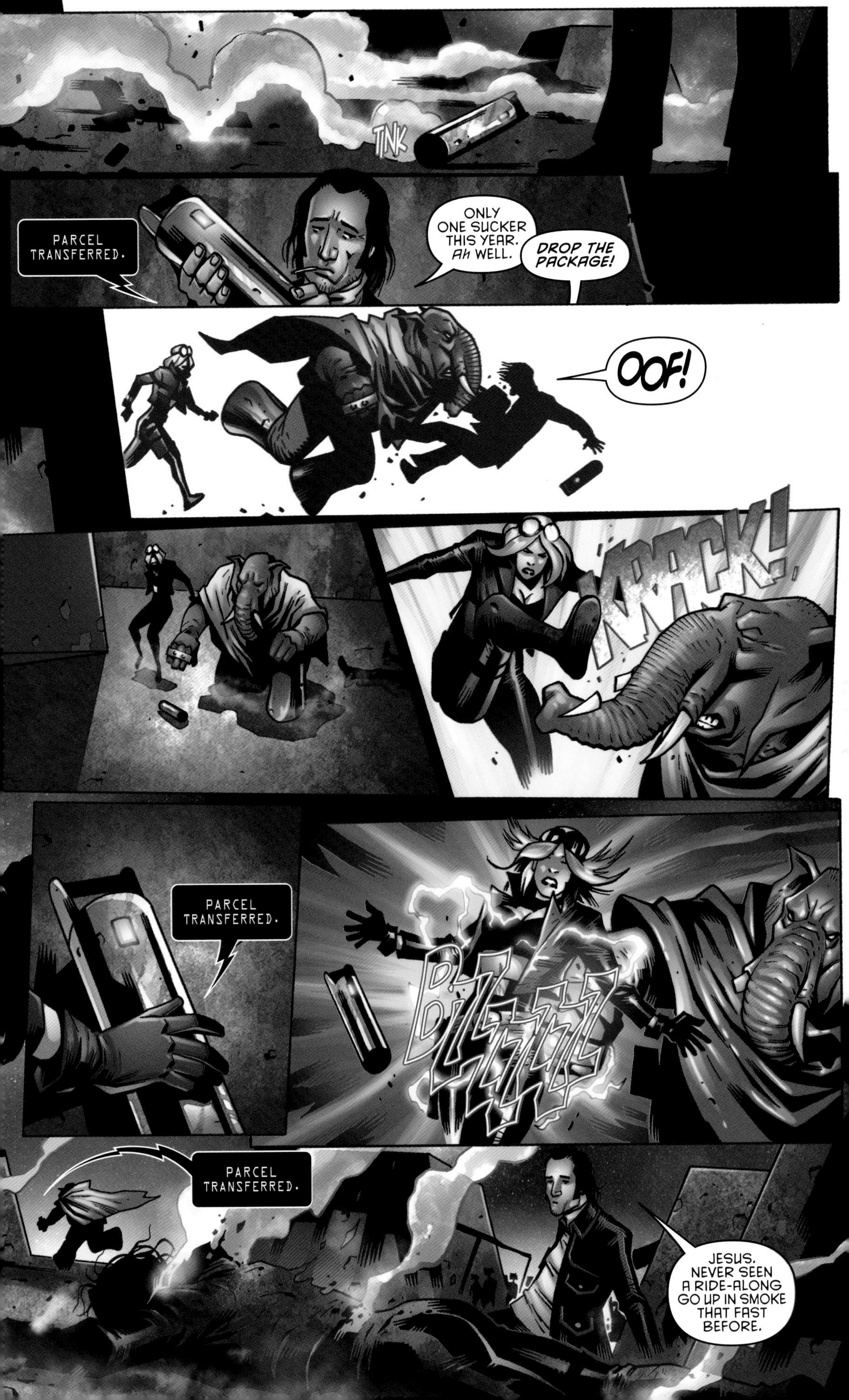
TNK
PARCEL TRANSFERRED.
ONLY ONE SUCKER THIS YEAR. AH WELL.
DROP THE PACKAGE!
OOF!
KRACK!
PARCEL TRANSFERRED.
BZZZZT
PARCEL TRANSFERRED.
JESUS. NEVER SEEN A RIDE-ALONG GO UP IN SMOKE THAT FAST BEFORE.

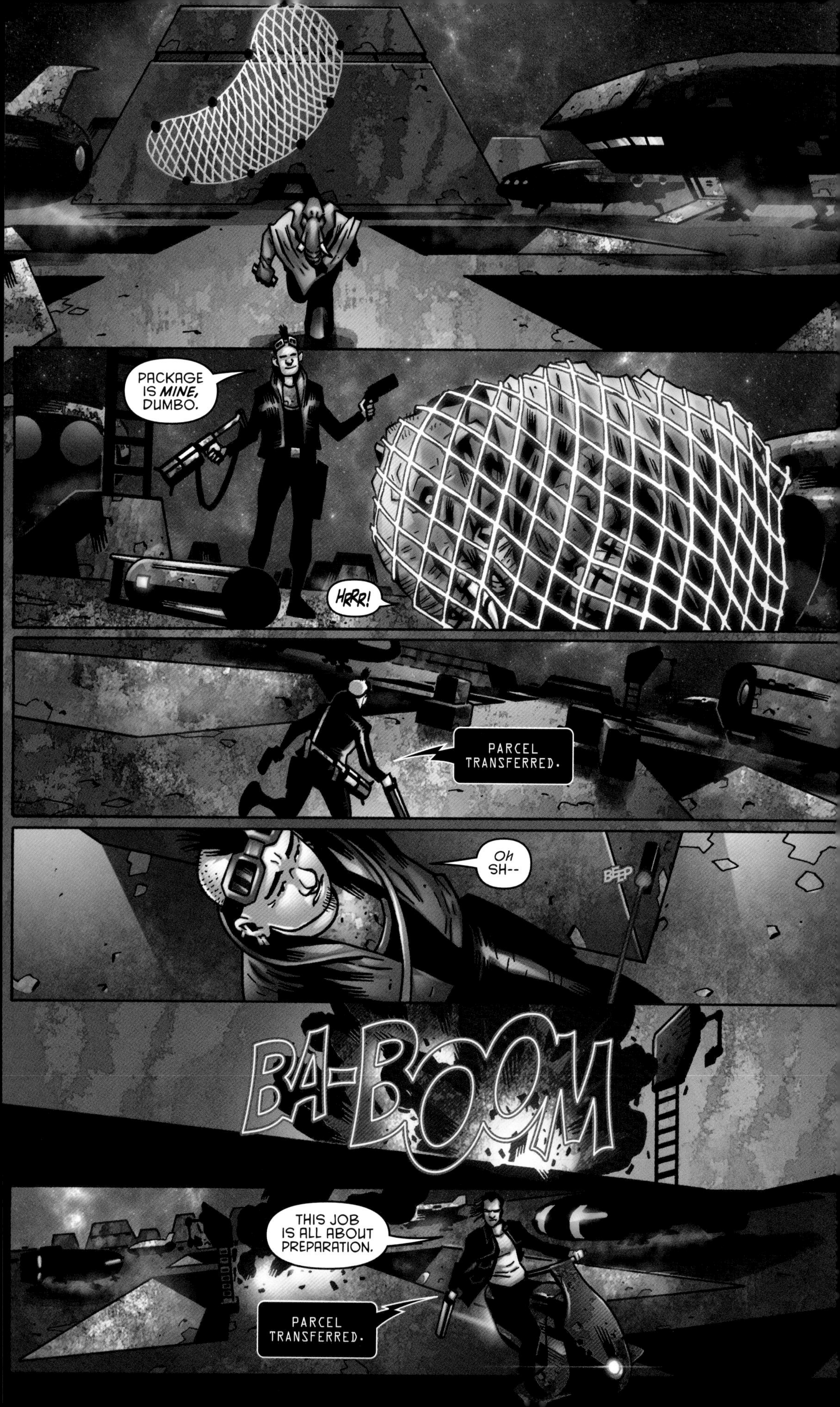
PACKAGE IS *MINE,* DUMBO.
HRRR!
PARCEL TRANSFERRED.
Oh SH--
BEEP
BA-BOOM
THIS JOB IS ALL ABOUT PREPARATION.
PARCEL TRANSFERRED.

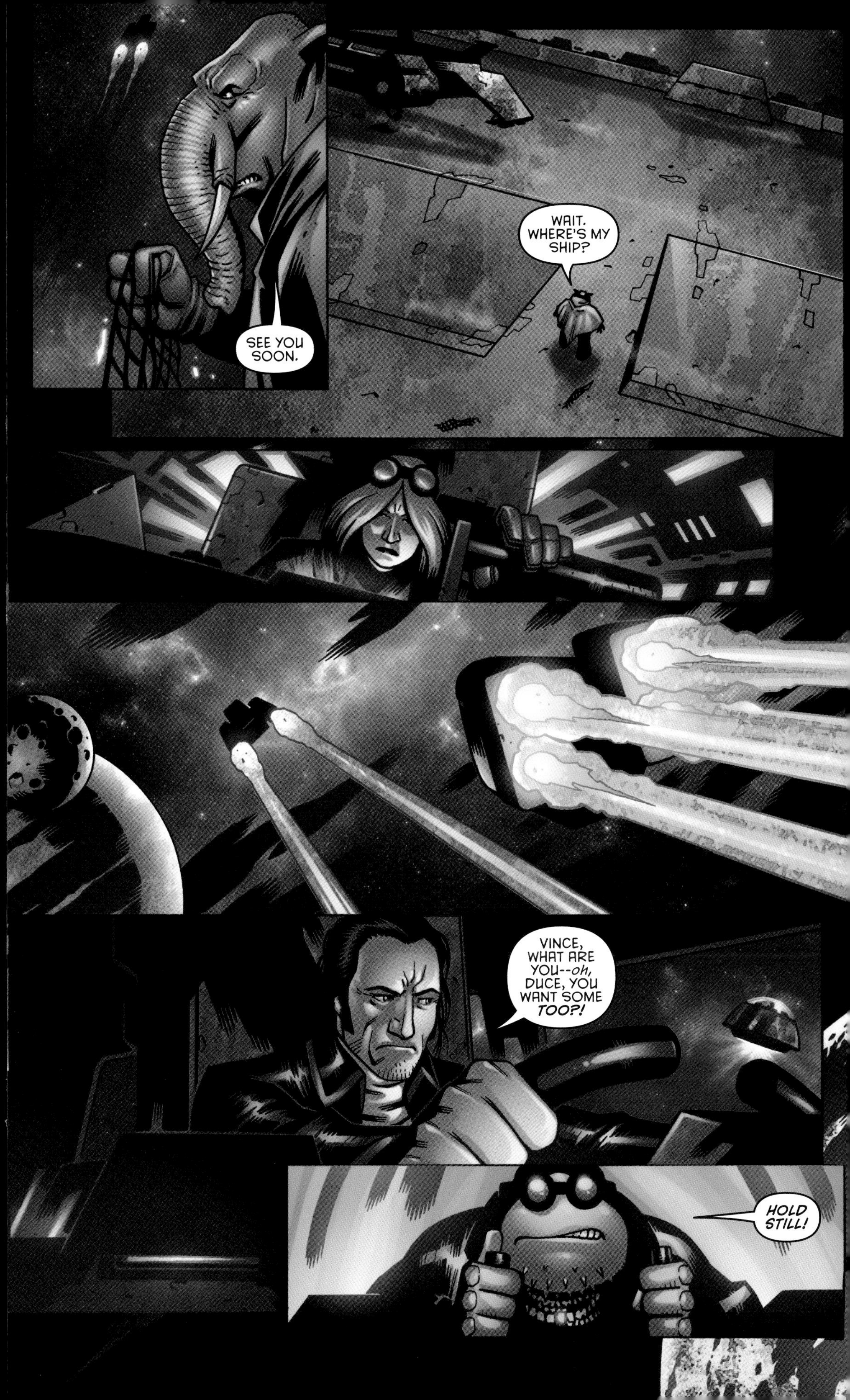
SEE YOU SOON.
WAIT. WHERE'S MY SHIP?
VINCE, WHAT ARE YOU--*oh,* DUCE, YOU WANT SOME *TOO?!*
HOLD STILL!

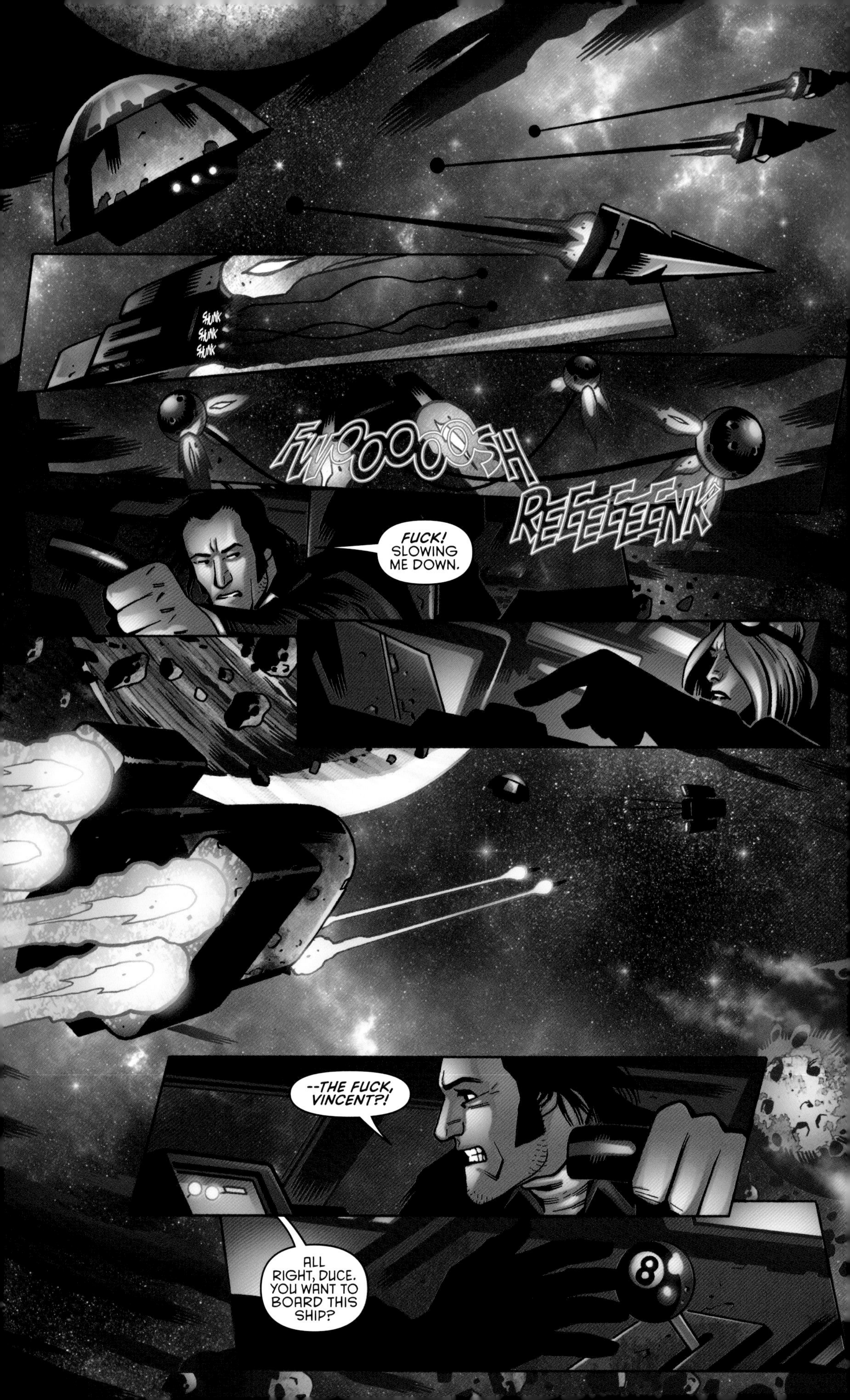
SHUNK
SHUNK
SHUNK
FWOOOOOOSH
REEEEEENK
FUCK! SLOWING ME DOWN.
--THE FUCK, VINCENT?!
ALL RIGHT, DUCE. YOU WANT TO BOARD THIS SHIP?

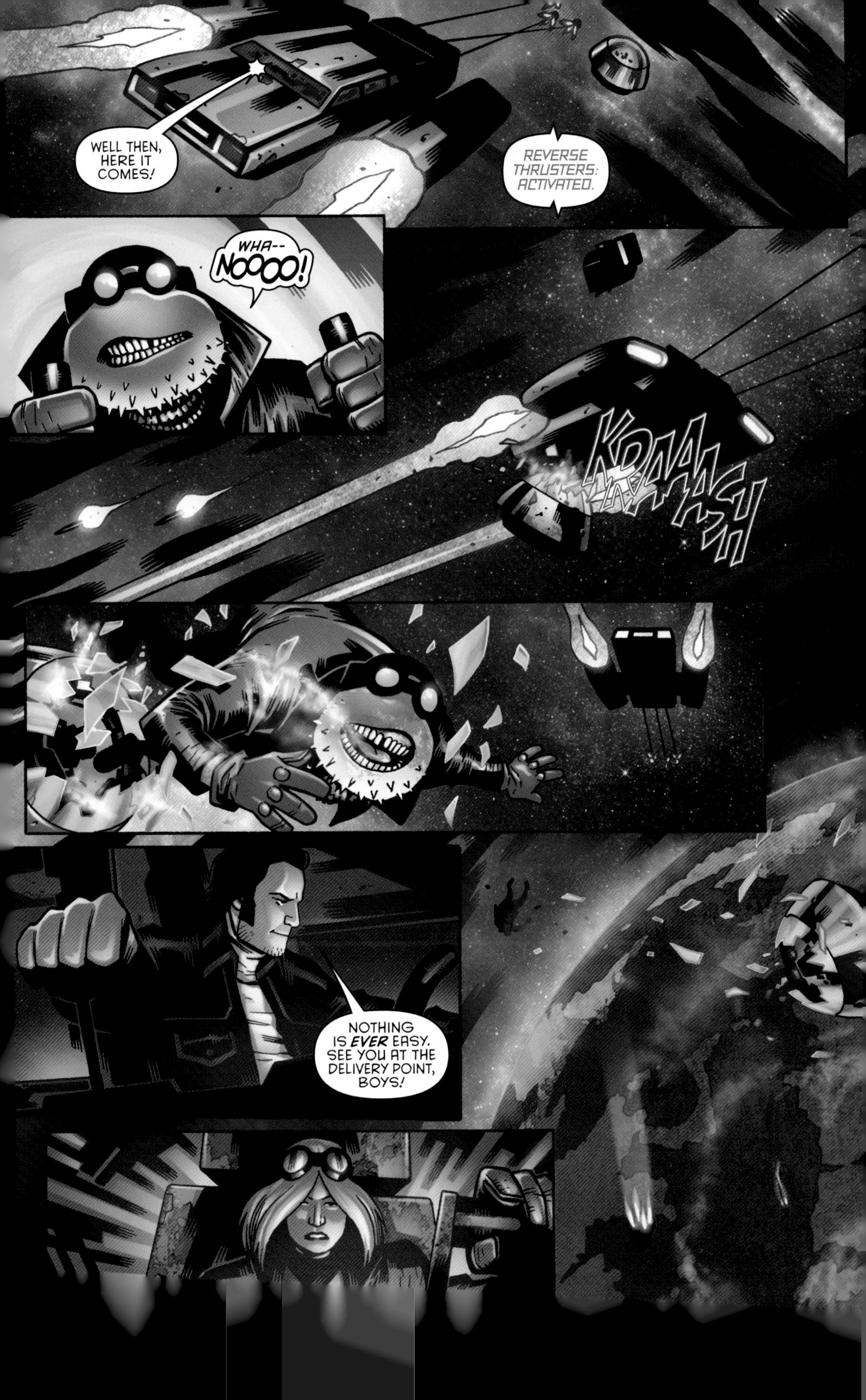
WELL THEN, HERE IT COMES!
REVERSE THRUSTERS: ACTIVATED.
WHA-- NOOOO!
KRAAANGH
NOTHING IS *EVER* EASY. SEE YOU AT THE DELIVERY POINT, BOYS!

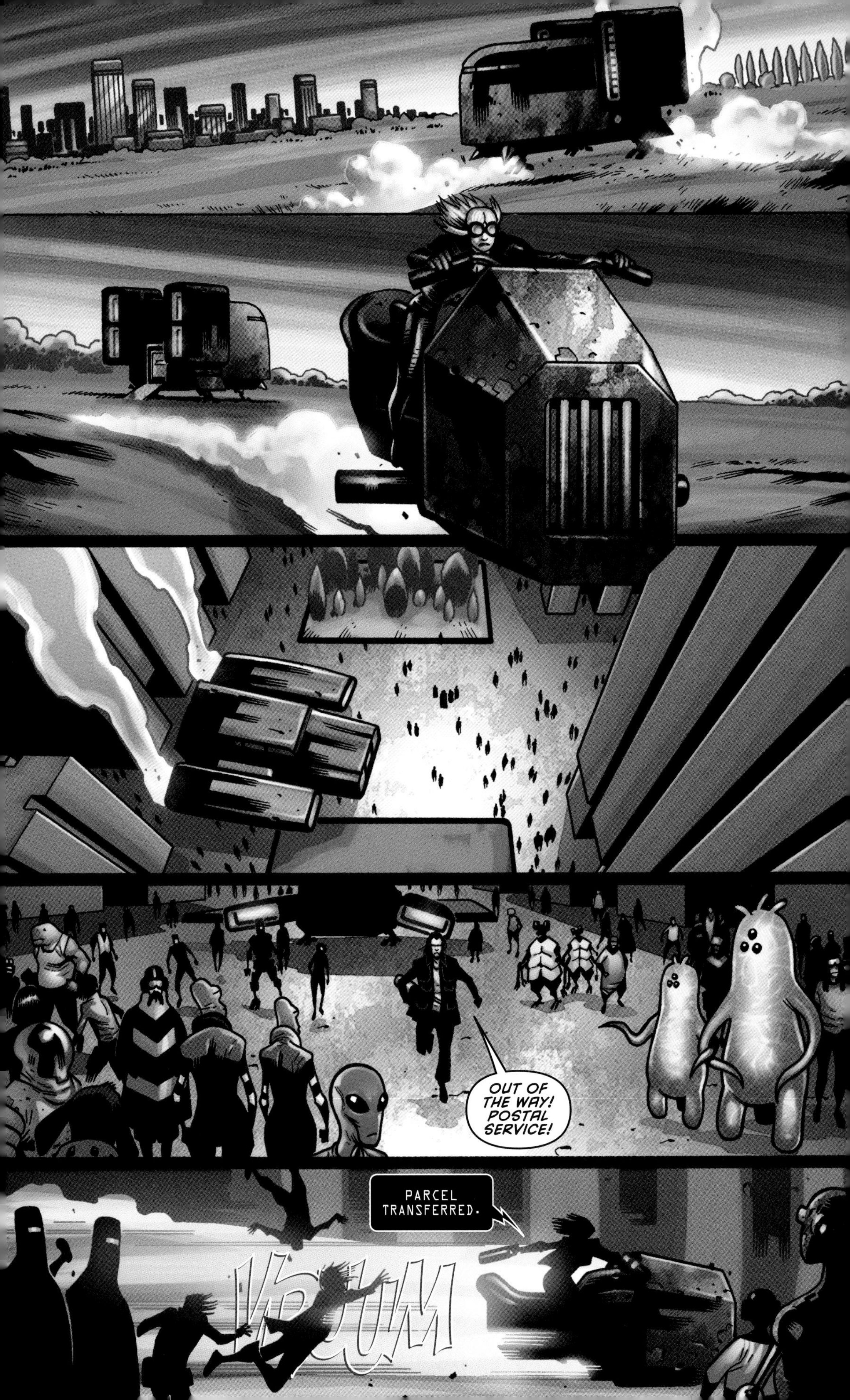
OUT OF THE WAY! POSTAL SERVICE!
PARCEL TRANSFERRED.
VROOM

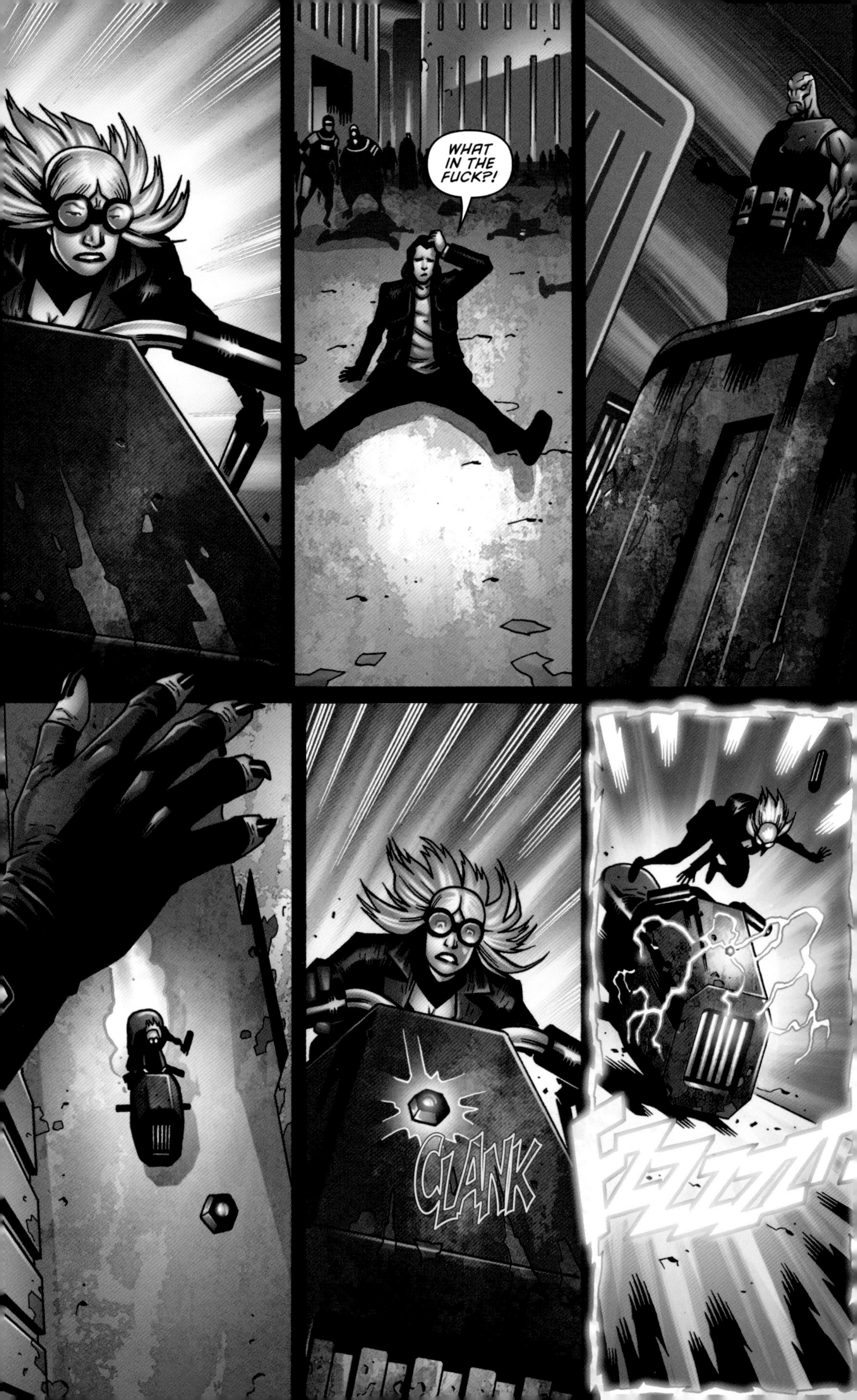
WHAT IN THE FUCK?!
CLANK

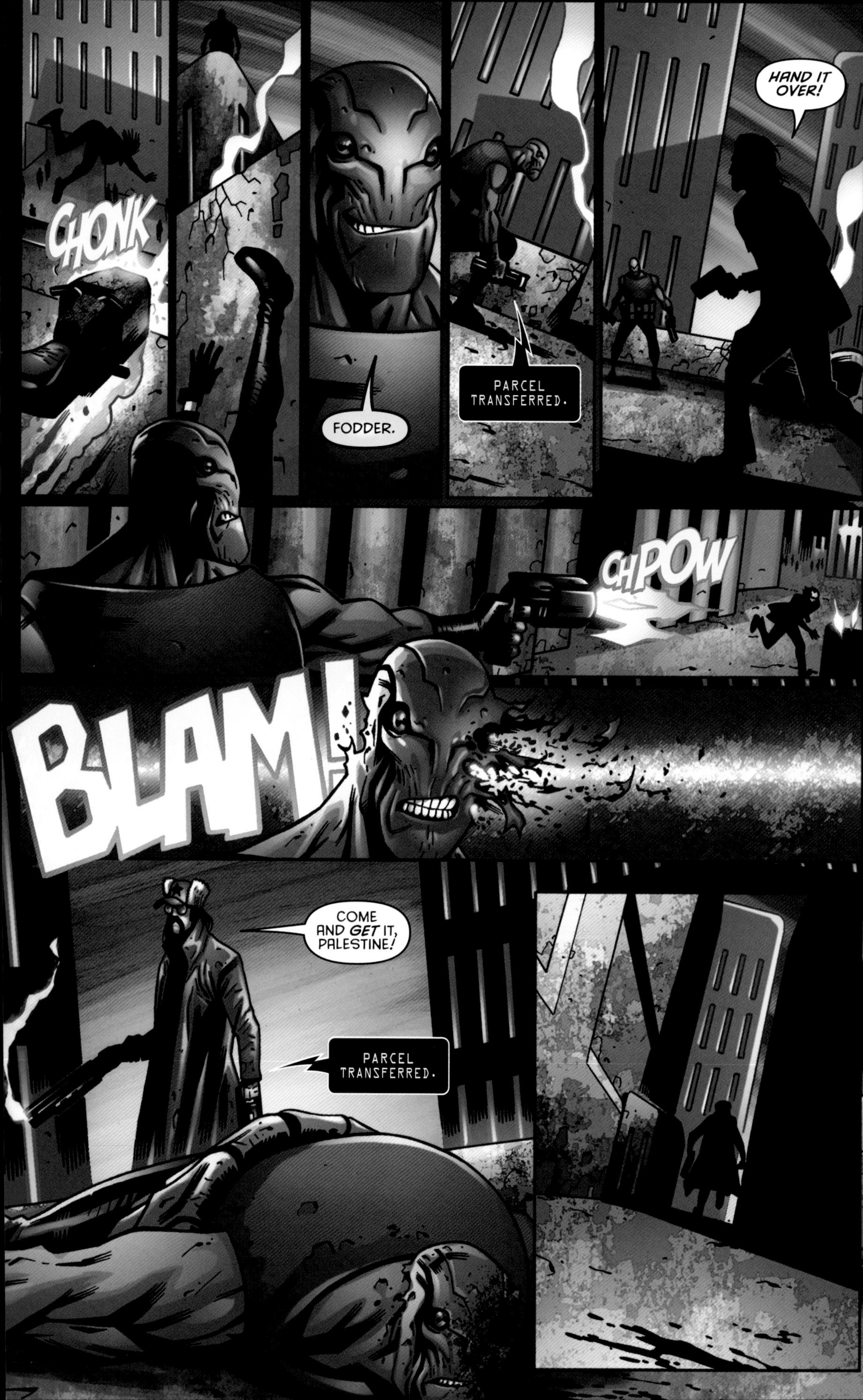
CHONK
FODDER.
PARCEL TRANSFERRED.
HAND IT OVER!
CHPOW
BLAM!
COME AND GET IT, PALESTINE!
PARCEL TRANSFERRED.

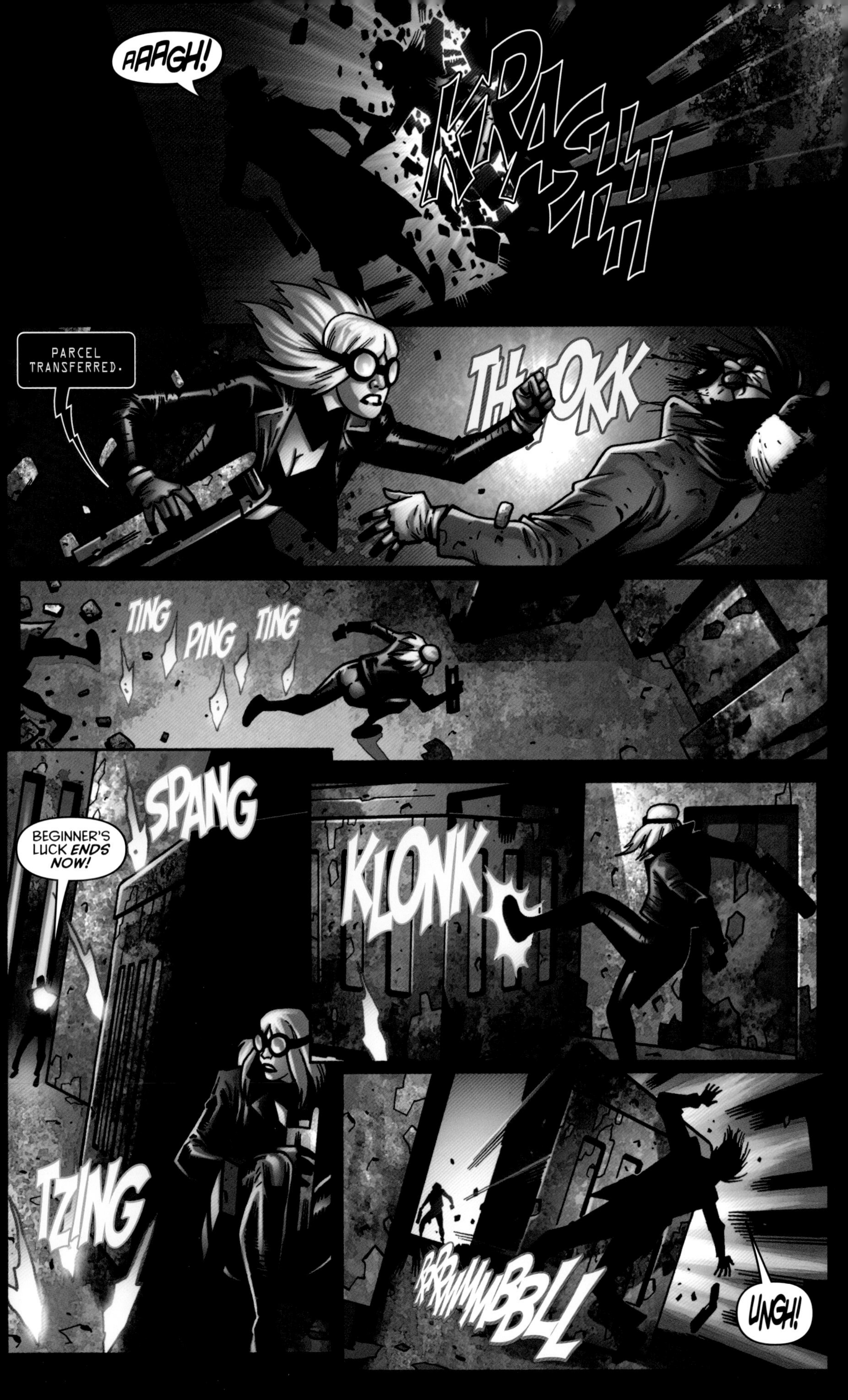
AAAGH!
KRASH
PARCEL TRANSFERRED.
THOKK
TING
PING
TING
SPANG
BEGINNER'S LUCK *ENDS* NOW!
KLONK
TZING
RRRUMMBBL
UNGH!

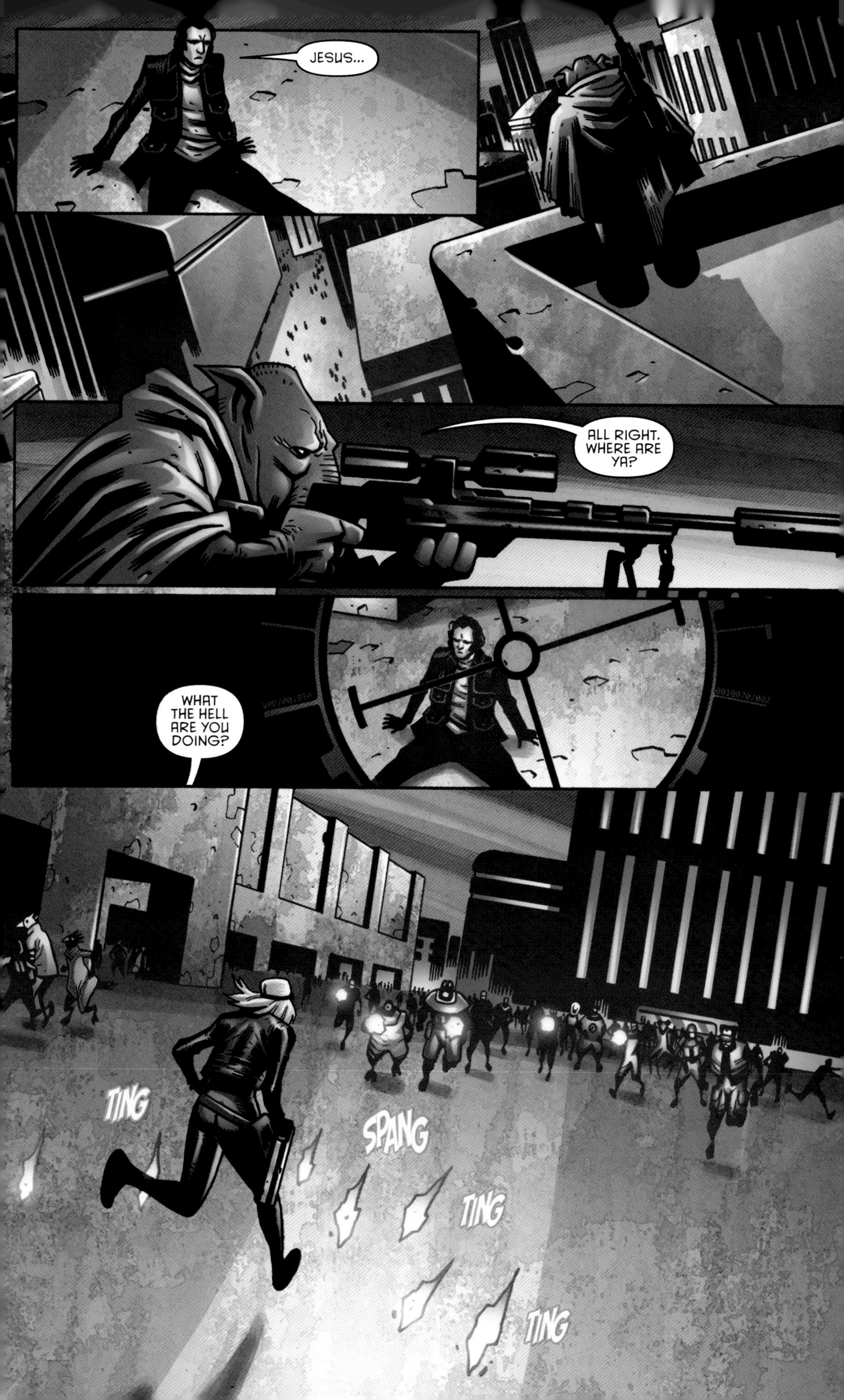
JESUS...
ALL RIGHT. WHERE ARE YA?
WHAT THE HELL ARE YOU DOING?
TING
SPANG
TING
TING

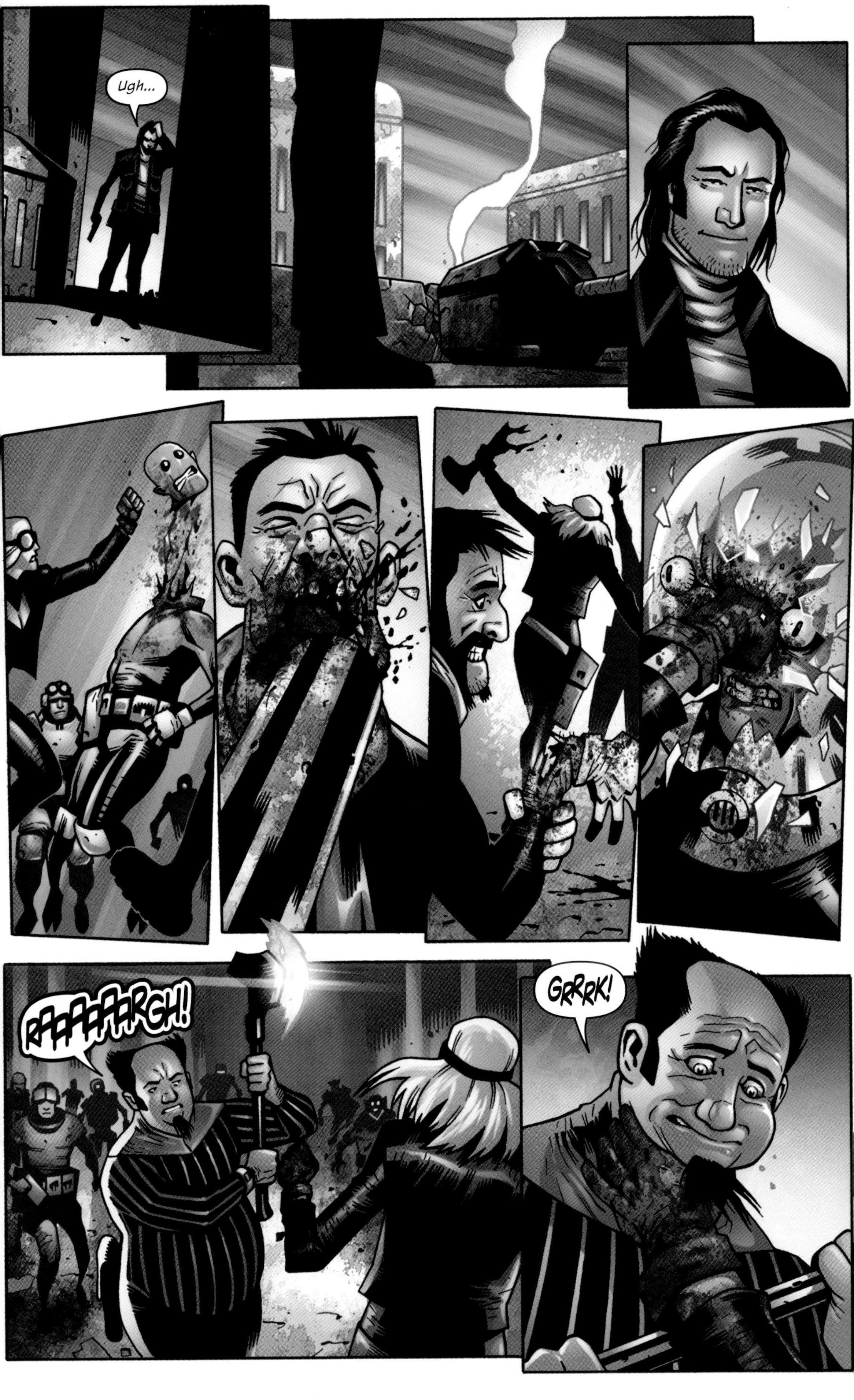
Ugh...
RAAAAAARGH!
GRRRK!

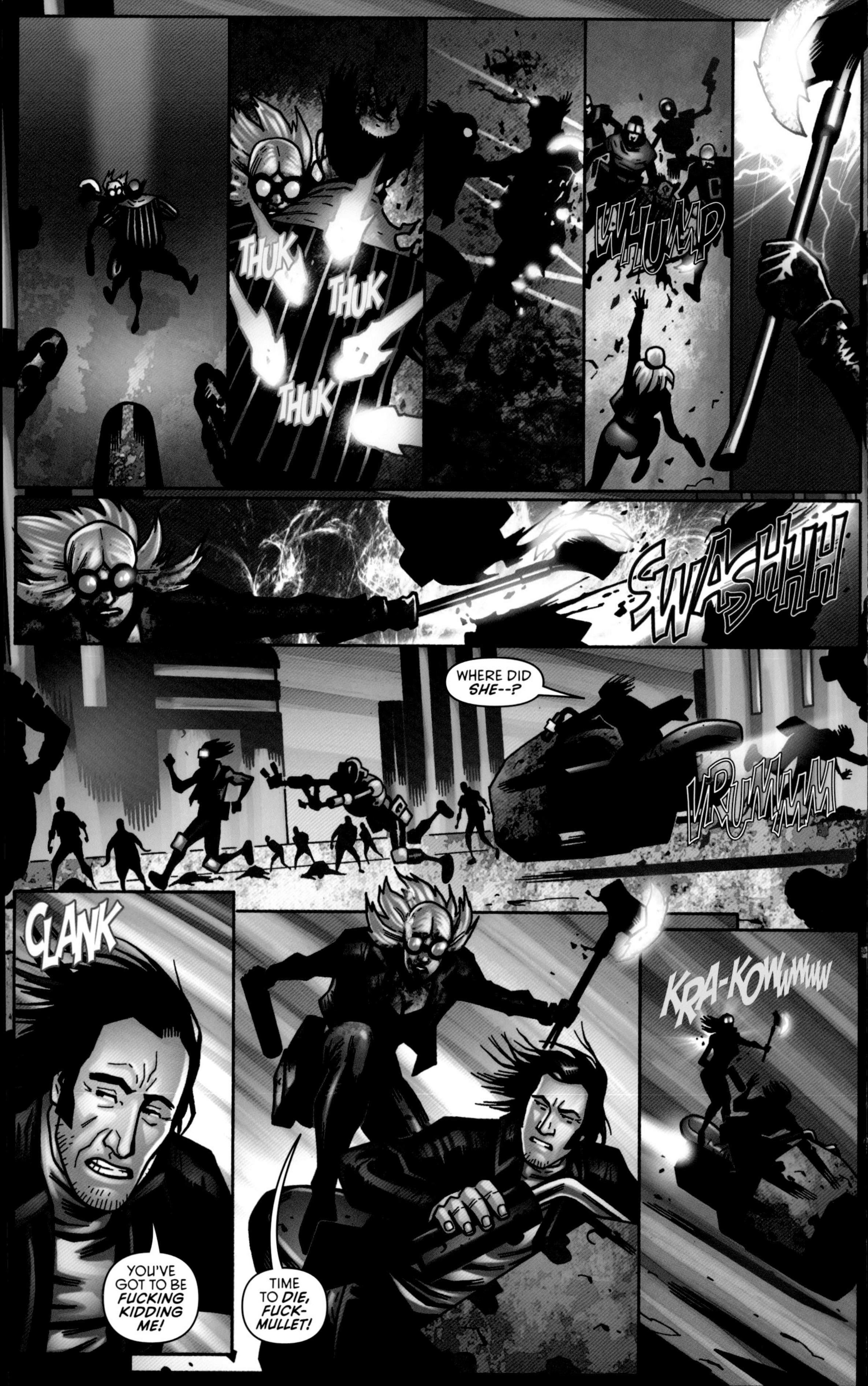
THUK
THUK
THUK
WHUMP
SWASHHH
WHERE DID SHE--?
VRUMMM
CLANK
YOU'VE GOT TO BE FUCKING KIDDING ME!
TIME TO DIE, FUCK-MULLET!
KRA-KOWWWW

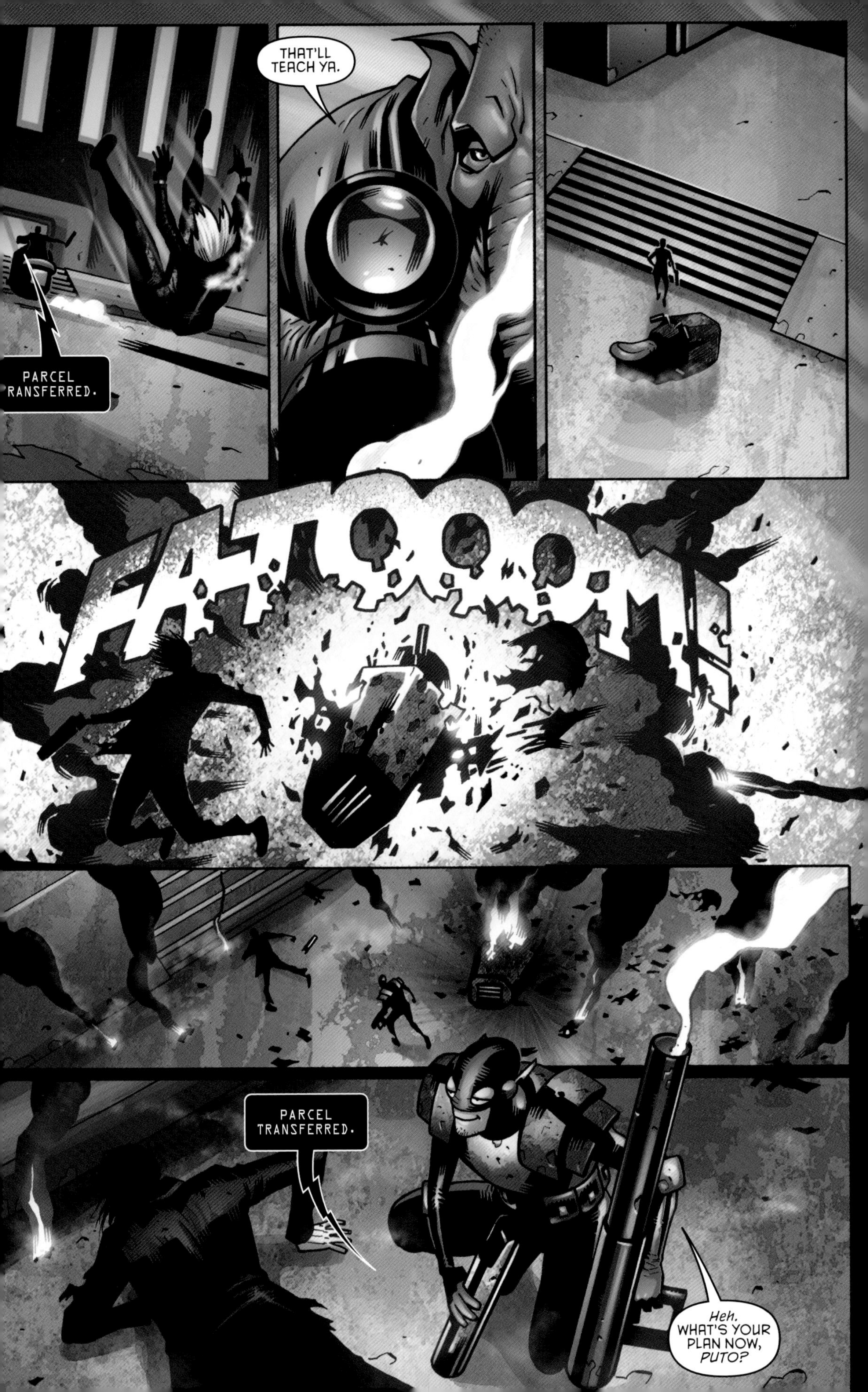
PARCEL RANSFERRED.
THAT'LL TEACH YA.
PARCEL TRANSFERRED.
Heh. WHAT'S YOUR PLAN NOW, *PUTO?*

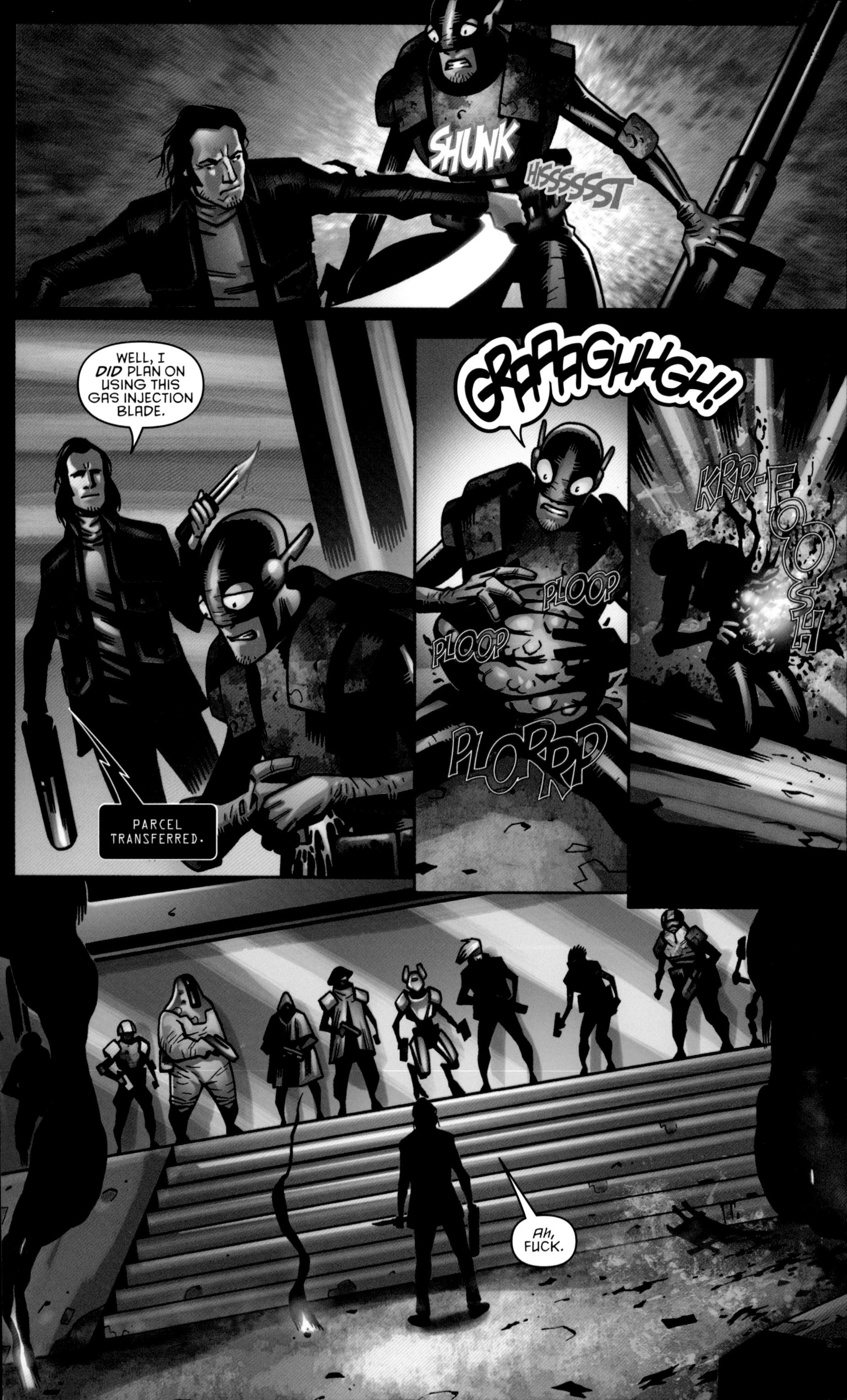
SHUNK
HISSSSST
WELL, I DID PLAN ON USING THIS GAS INJECTION BLADE.
PARCEL TRANSFERRED.
GRAAAGHHGH!
PLOOP
PLOOP
PLORRP
KRR-FOOOSH
Ah, FUCK.

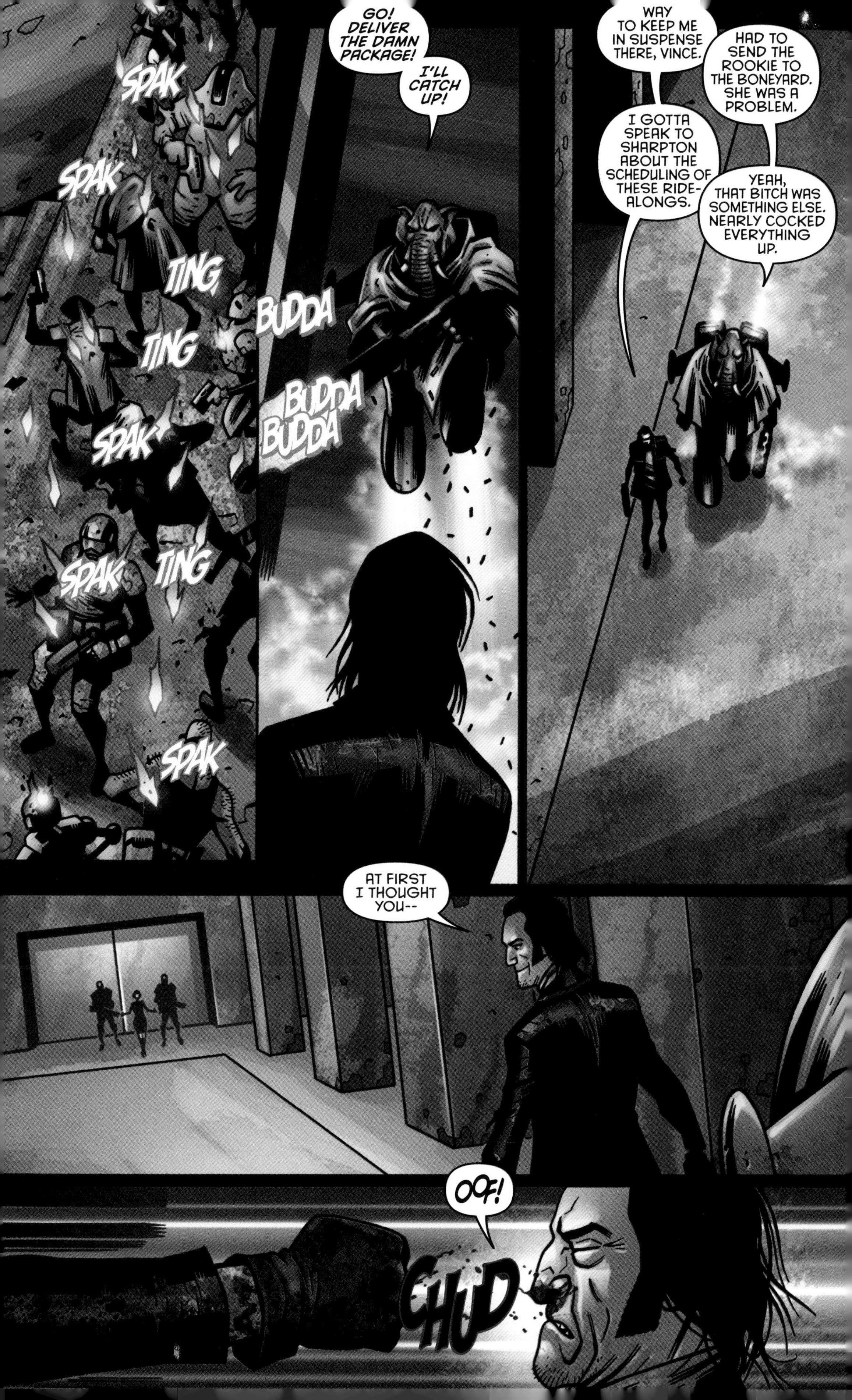
SPAK
SPAK
TING
TING
SPAK
SPAK
TING
SPAK
BUDDA
BUDDA
BUDDA
GO! DELIVER THE DAMN PACKAGE!
I'LL CATCH UP!
WAY TO KEEP ME IN SUSPENSE THERE, VINCE.
I GOTTA SPEAK TO SHARPTON ABOUT THE SCHEDULING OF THESE RIDE-ALONGS.
HAD TO SEND THE ROOKIE TO THE BONEYARD. SHE WAS A PROBLEM.
YEAH, THAT BITCH WAS SOMETHING ELSE. NEARLY COCKED EVERYTHING UP.
AT FIRST I THOUGHT YOU--
OOF!
CHUD

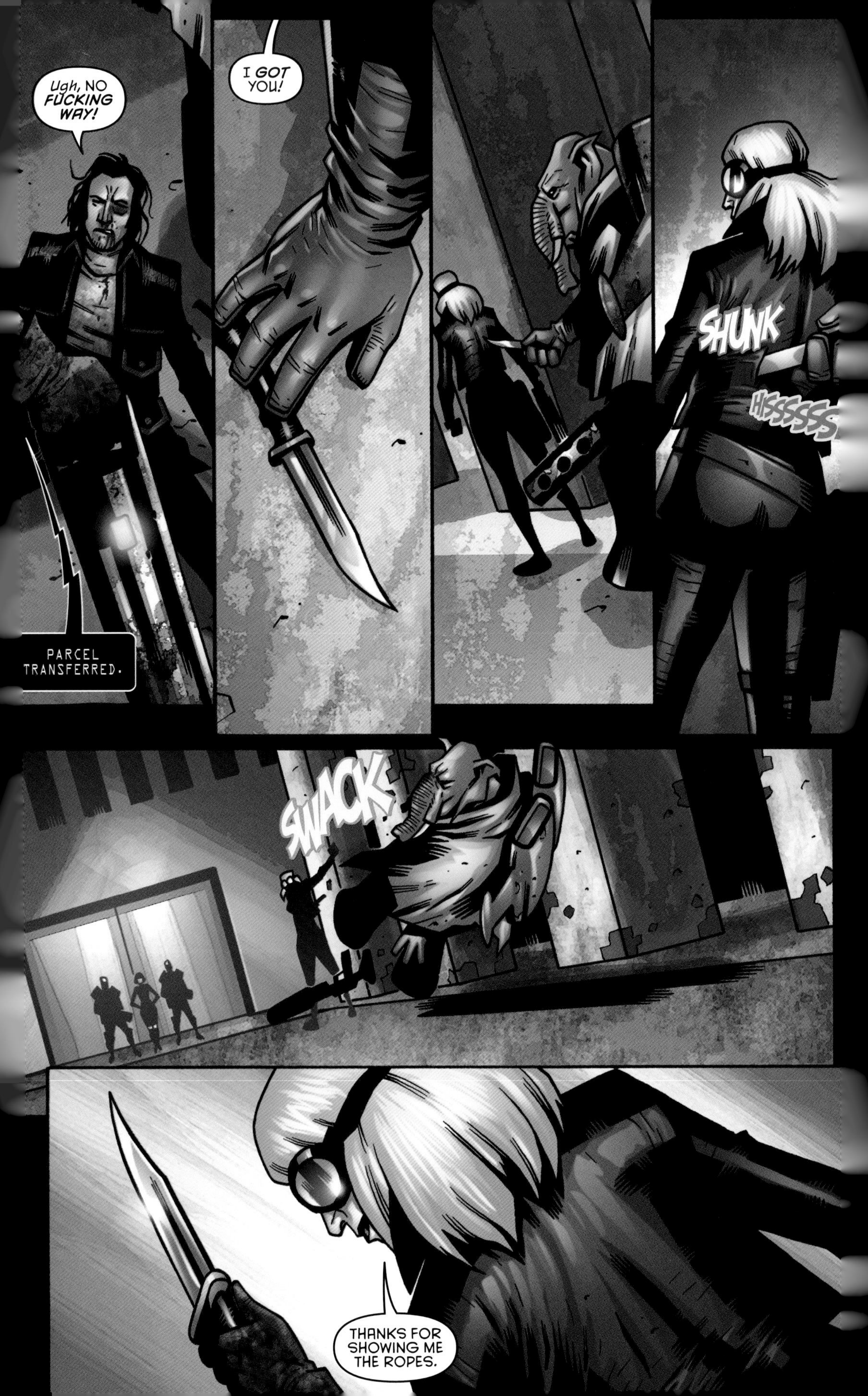
Ugh, NO FUCKING WAY!
PARCEL TRANSFERRED.
I GOT YOU!
SHUNK
HISSSSS
SWACK
THANKS FOR SHOWING ME THE ROPES.

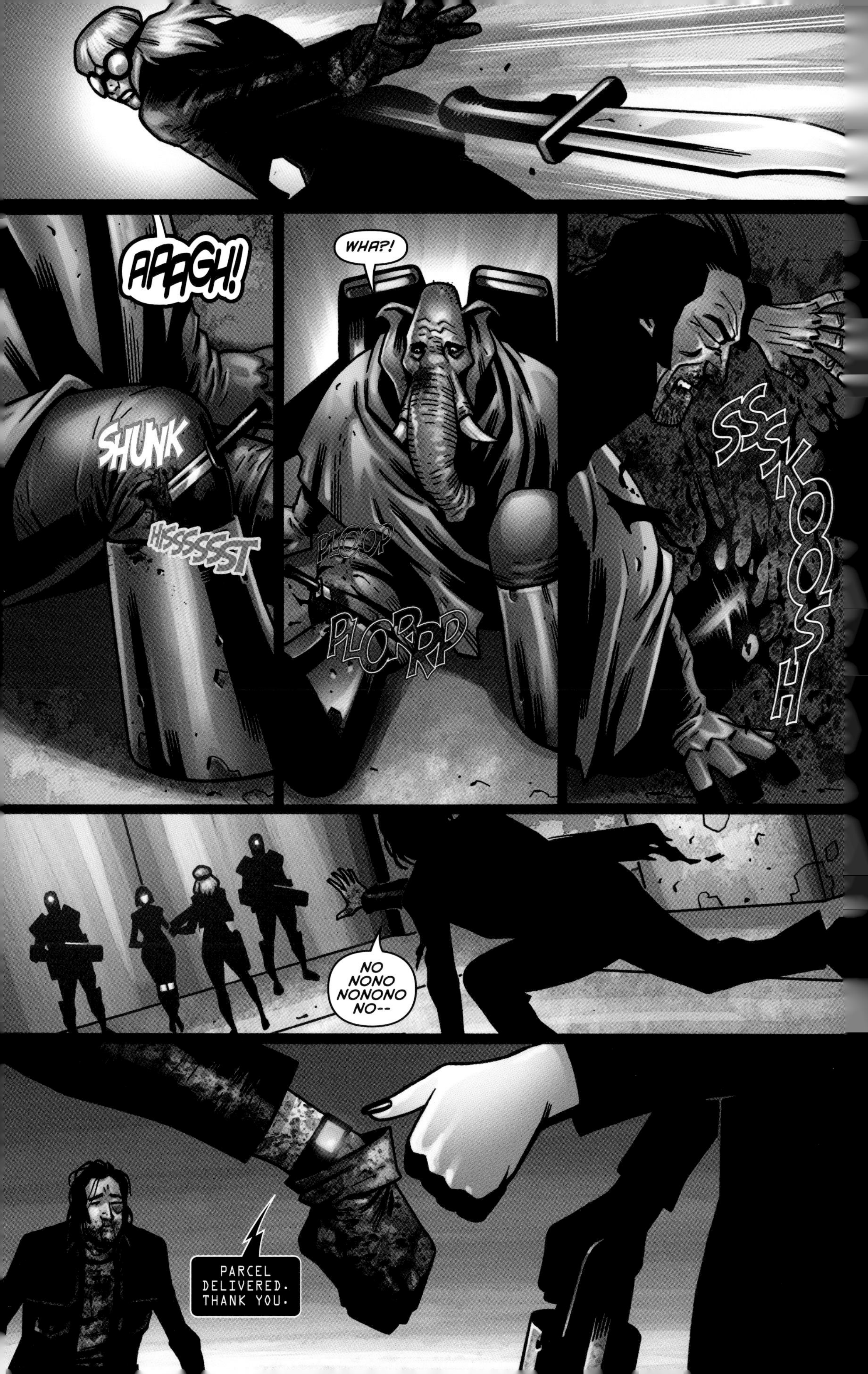
AAAGH!
SHUNK
HISSSSST
WHA?!
PLOOP
PLORRP
SSSKOOOSH
NO
NONO
NONONO
NO--
PARCEL
DELIVERED.
THANK YOU.

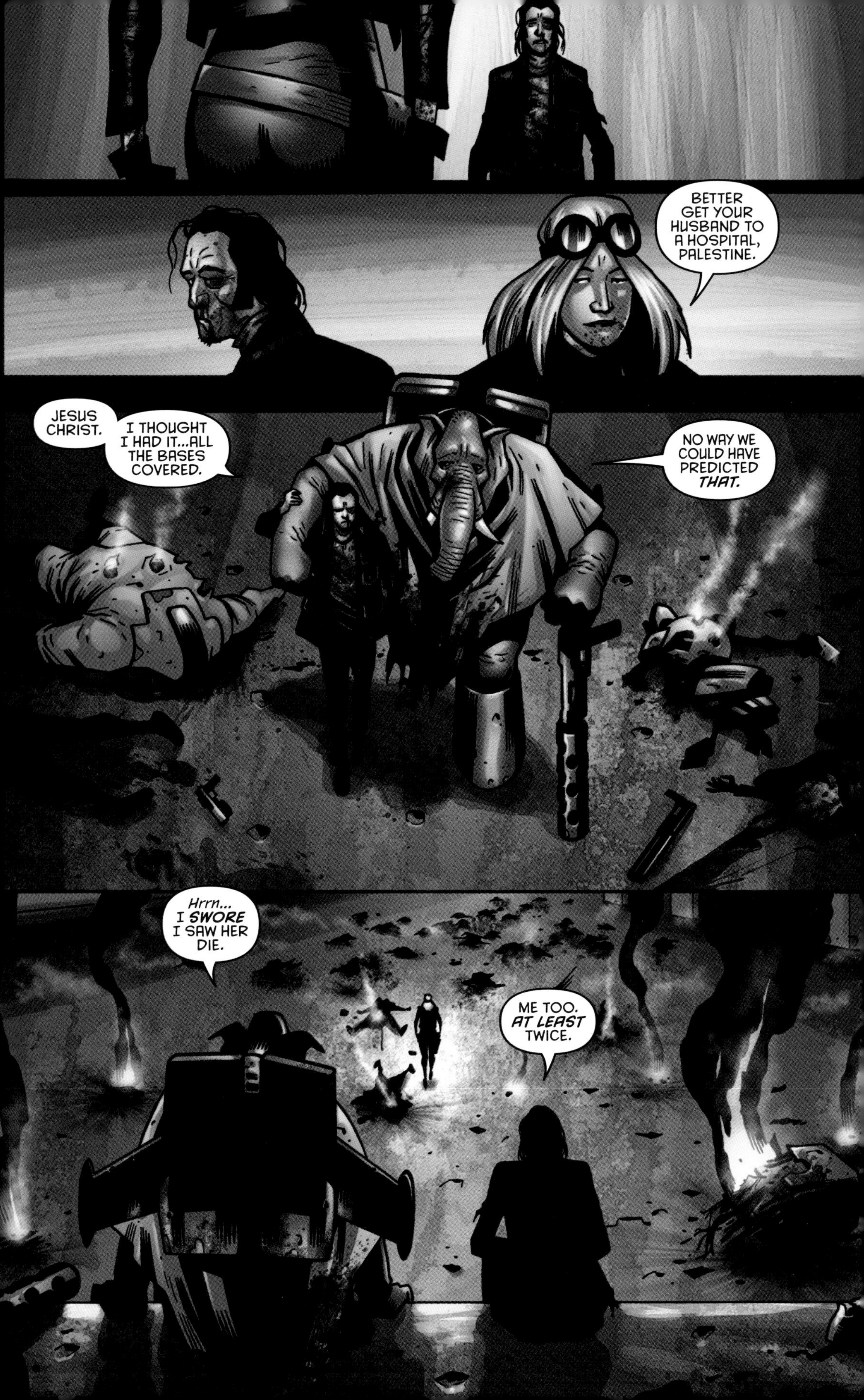
BETTER GET YOUR HUSBAND TO A HOSPITAL, PALESTINE.
JESUS CHRIST.
I THOUGHT I HAD IT...ALL THE BASES COVERED.
NO WAY WE COULD HAVE PREDICTED *THAT.*
Hrrn... I **SWORE** I SAW HER DIE.
ME TOO. *AT LEAST* TWICE.

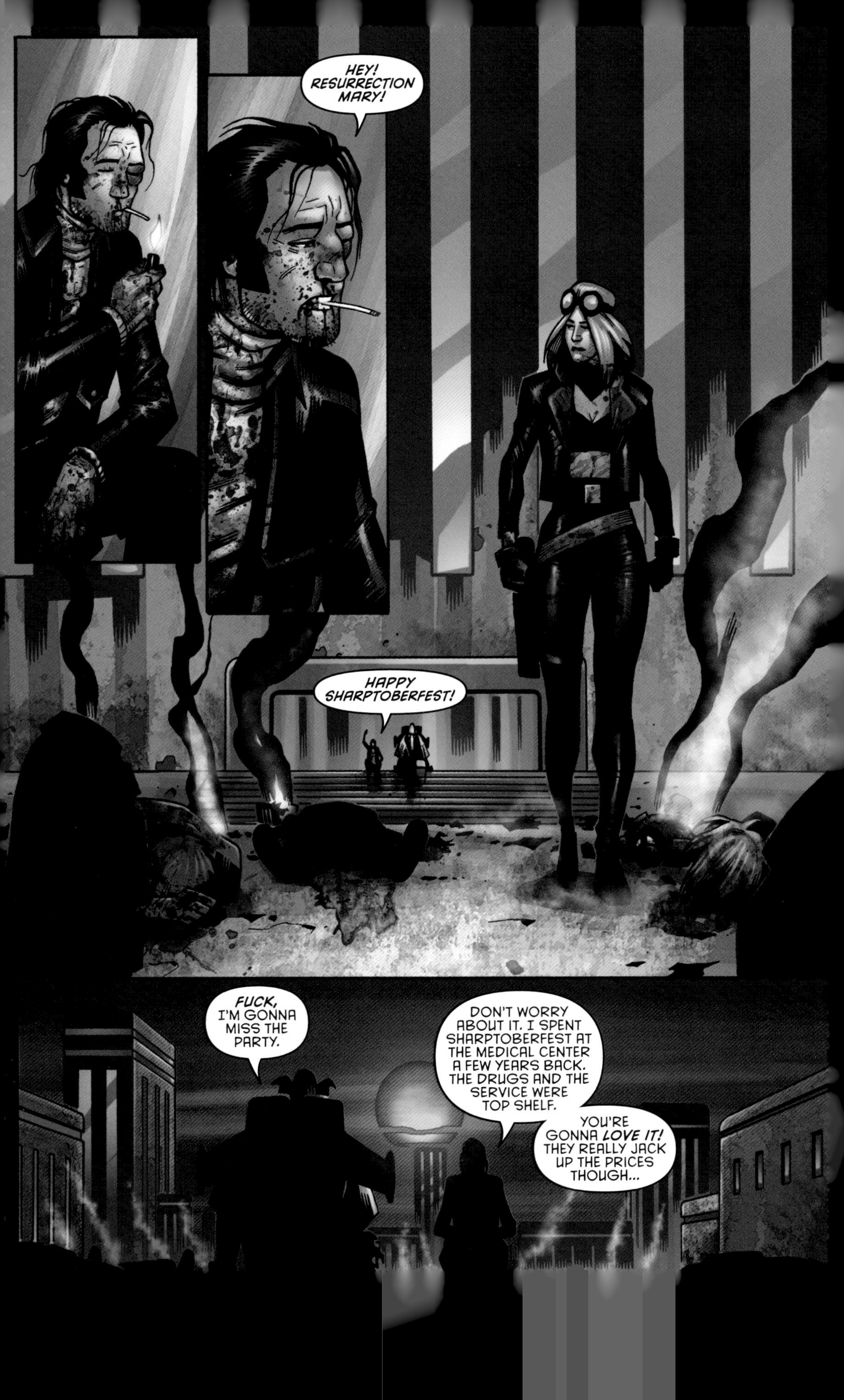
HEY! RESURRECTION MARY!
HAPPY SHARPTOBERFEST!
FUCK, I'M GONNA MISS THE PARTY.
DON'T WORRY ABOUT IT. I SPENT SHARPTOBERFEST AT THE MEDICAL CENTER A FEW YEARS BACK. THE DRUGS AND THE SERVICE WERE TOP SHELF.
YOU'RE GONNA LOVE IT! THEY REALLY JACK UP THE PRICES THOUGH...

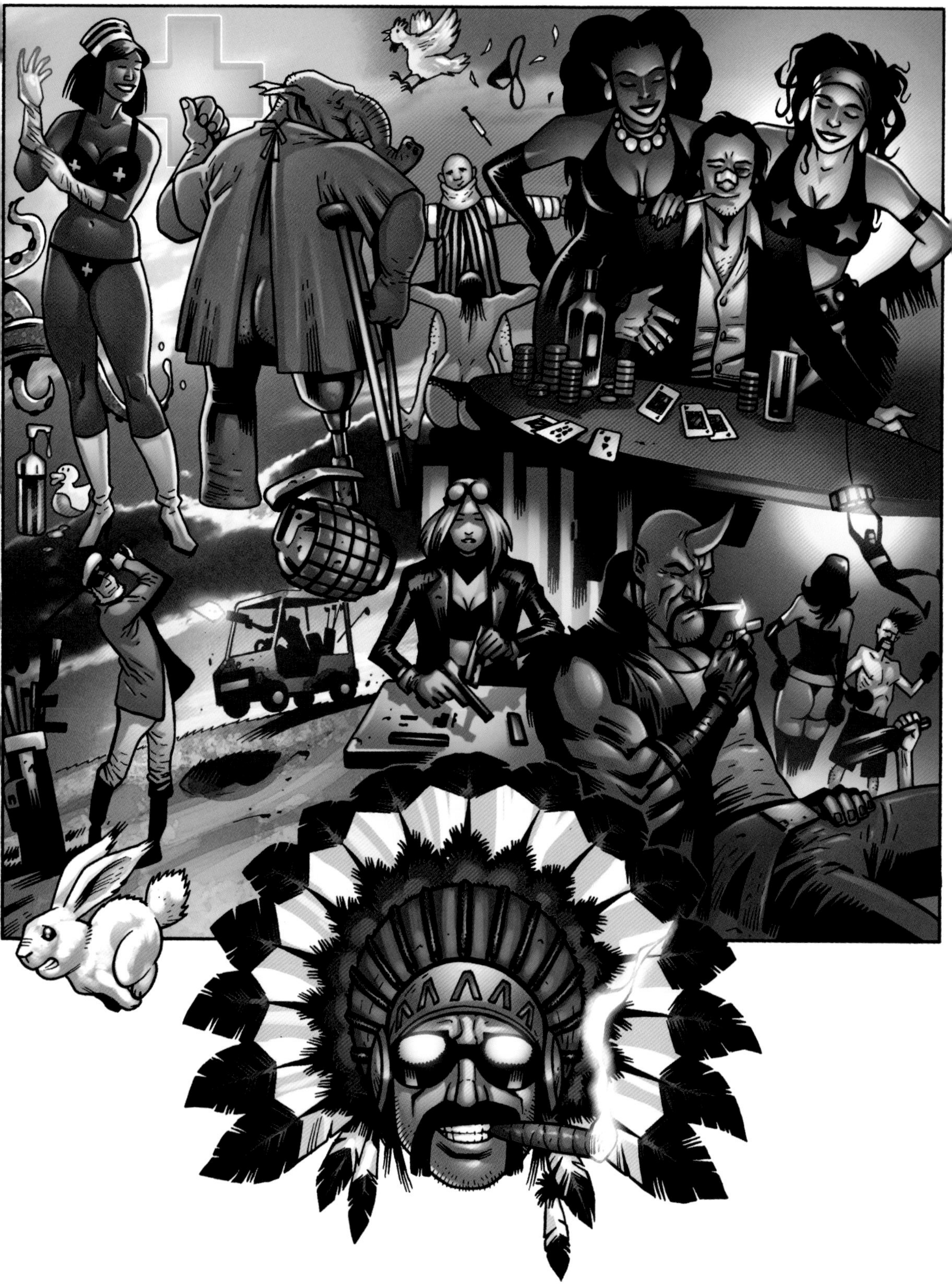

RESURRECTION MARY: SPACE BASTARD

written by ERIC PETERSON and JOE AUBREY artwork by COLIN MacNEIL
colors by PETER PANTAZIS lettering by TAYLOR ESPOSITO
created by ERIC PETERSON • JOE AUBREY • DARICK ROBERTSON

"FAILED FIRST DAYS"

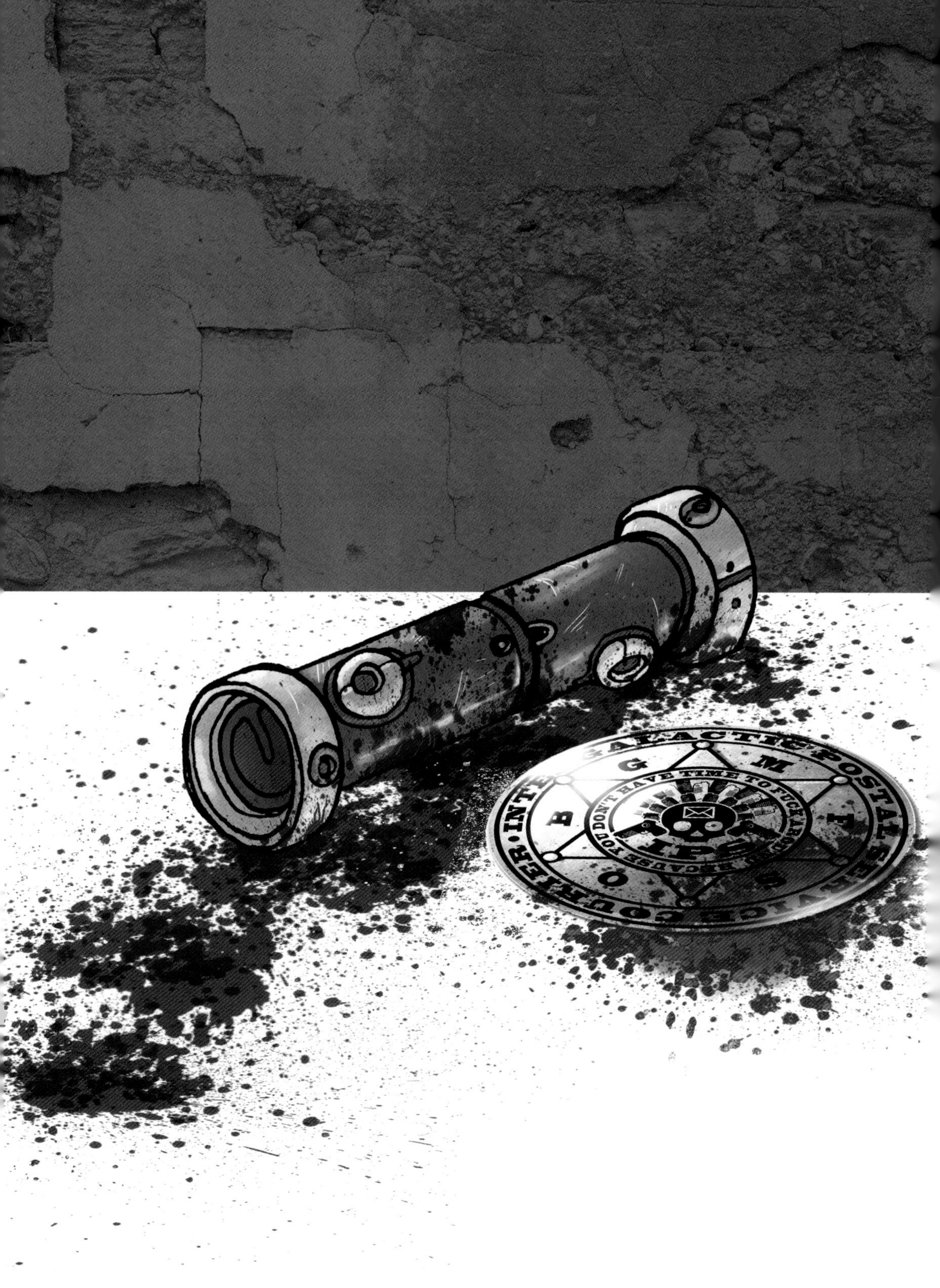

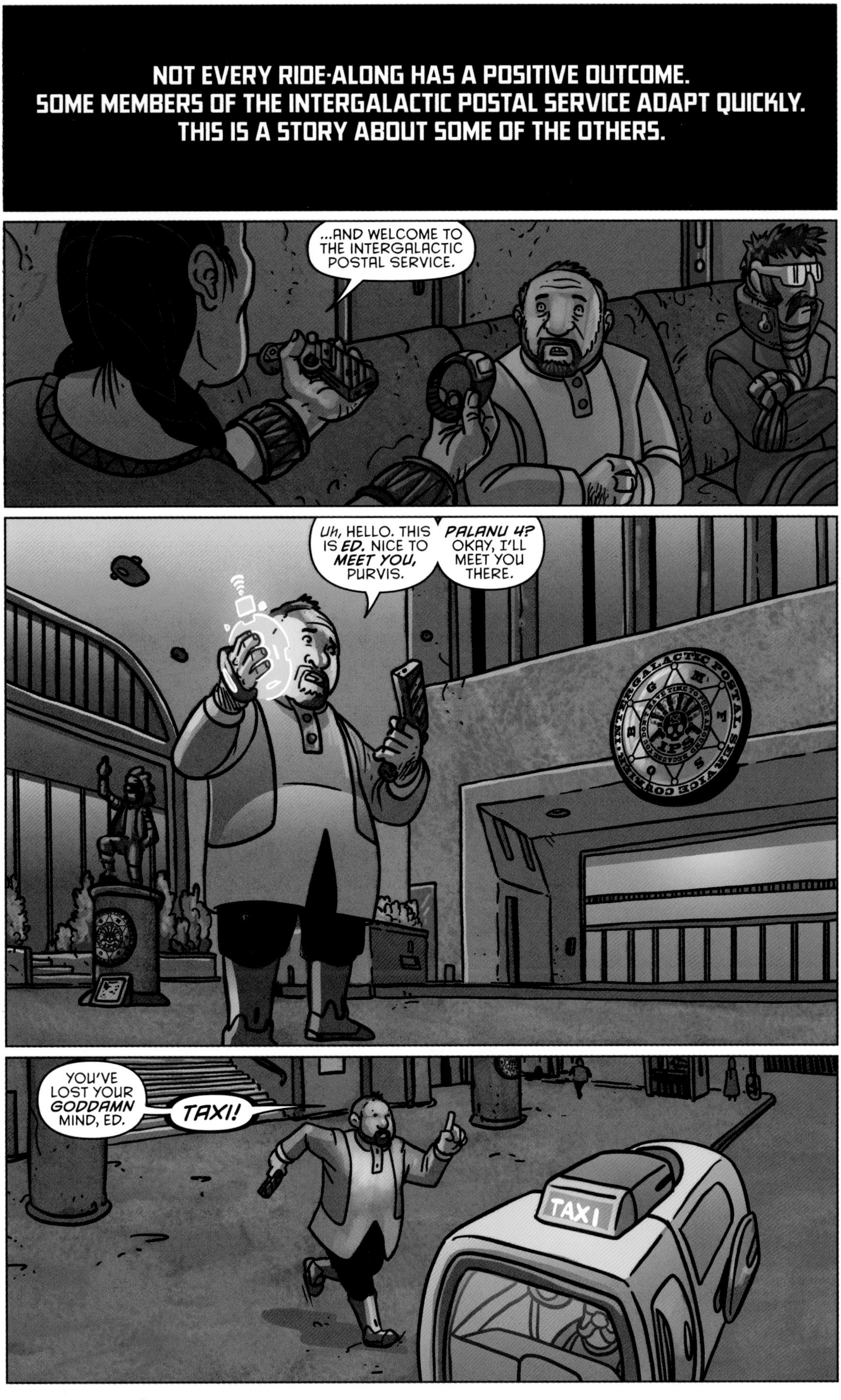
NOT EVERY RIDE-ALONG HAS A POSITIVE OUTCOME.
SOME MEMBERS OF THE INTERGALACTIC POSTAL SERVICE ADAPT QUICKLY.
THIS IS A STORY ABOUT SOME OF THE OTHERS.
...AND WELCOME TO THE INTERGALACTIC POSTAL SERVICE.
Uh, HELLO. THIS IS ***ED.*** NICE TO ***MEET YOU,*** PURVIS.
PALANU 4? OKAY, I'LL MEET YOU THERE.
YOU'VE LOST YOUR ***GODDAMN*** MIND, ED.
TAXI!
TAXI

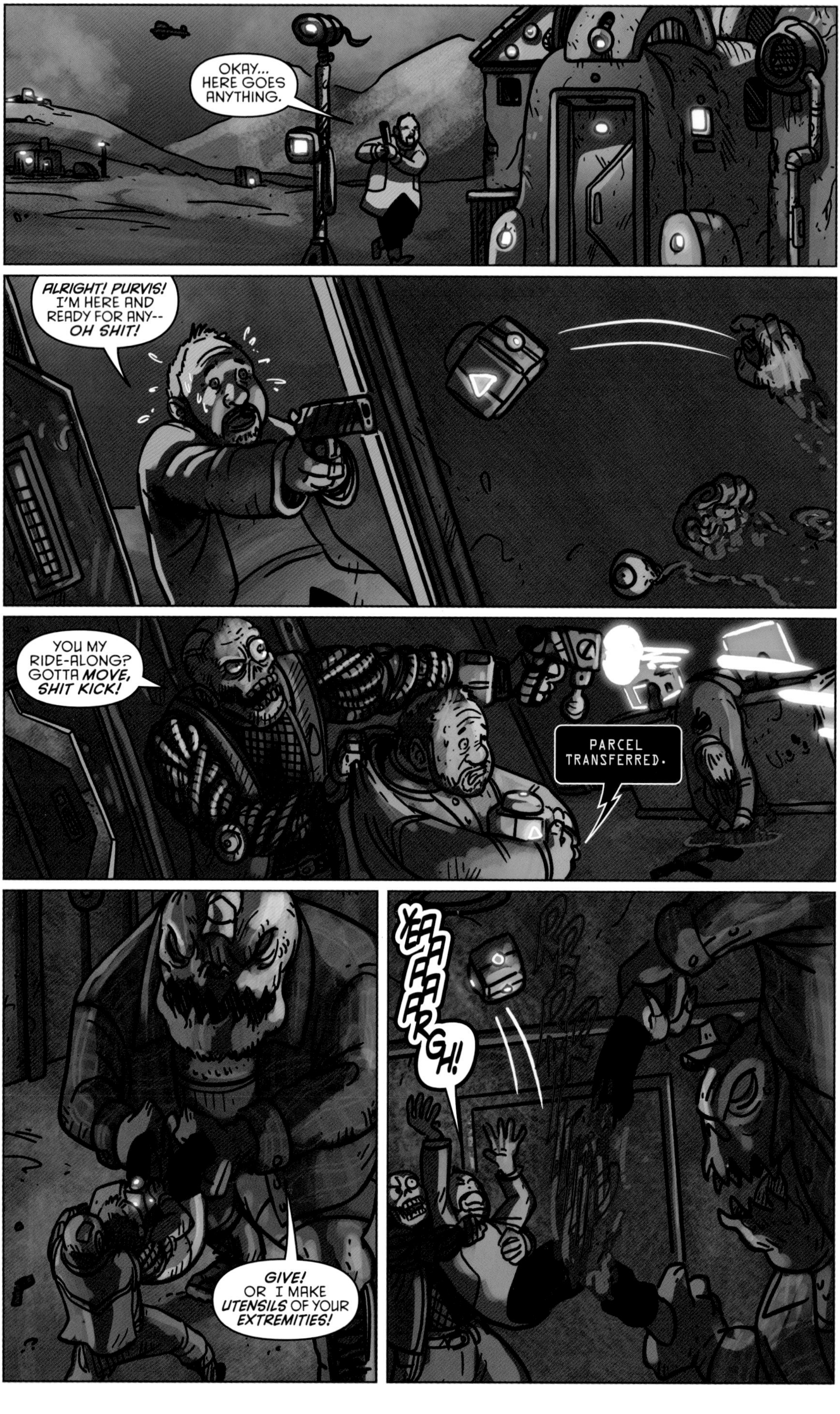
OKAY...
HERE GOES
ANYTHING.
ALRIGHT! PURVIS!
I'M HERE AND
READY FOR ANY--
OH SHIT!
YOU MY
RIDE-ALONG?
GOTTA MOVE,
SHIT KICK!
PARCEL
TRANSFERRED.
GIVE!
OR I MAKE
UTENSILS OF YOUR
EXTREMITIES!
YEAAAAARGH!

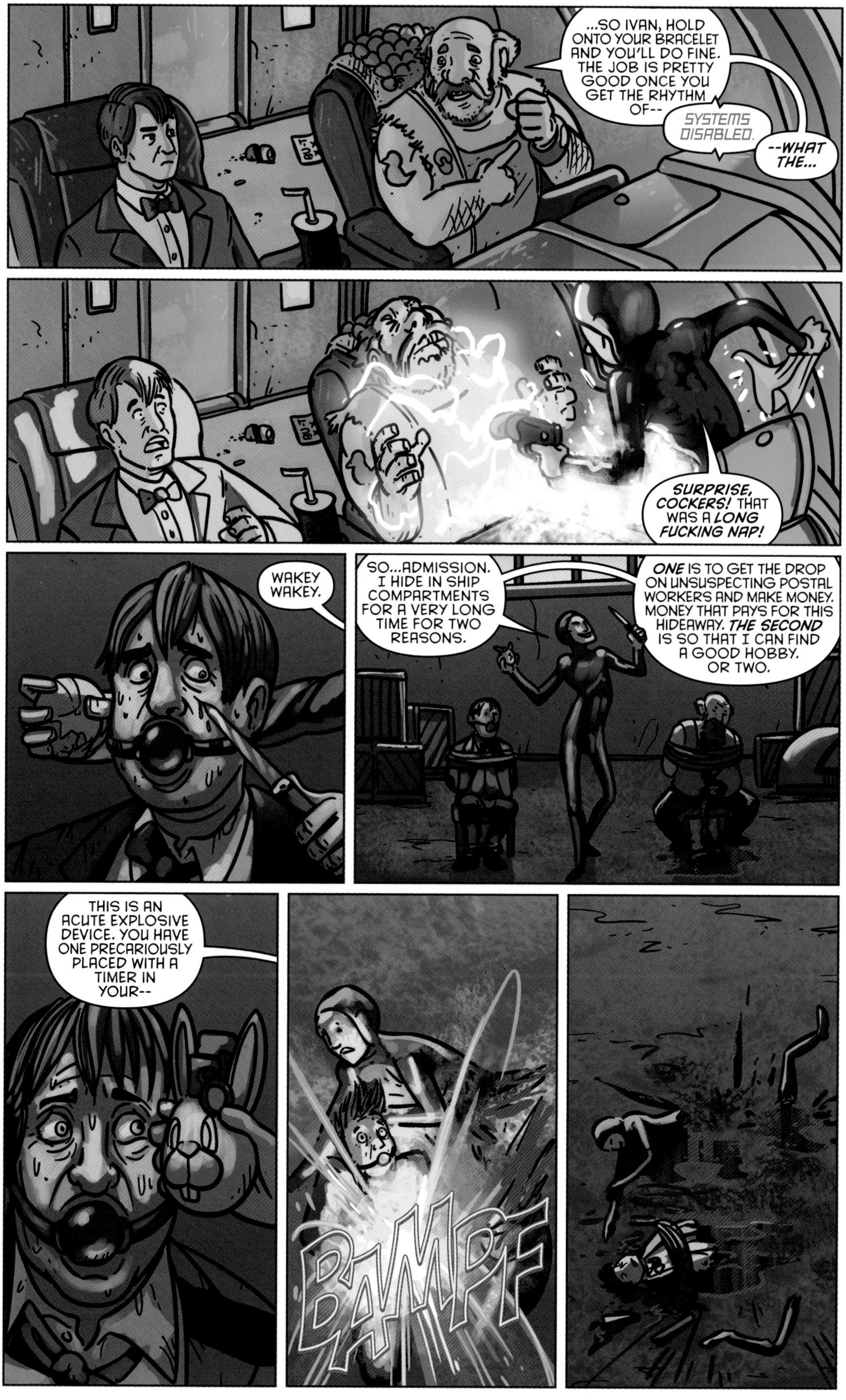
...SO IVAN, HOLD ONTO YOUR BRACELET AND YOU'LL DO FINE. THE JOB IS PRETTY GOOD ONCE YOU GET THE RHYTHM OF--
SYSTEMS DISABLED.
--WHAT THE...
SURPRISE, COCKERS! THAT WAS A LONG FUCKING NAP!
WAKEY WAKEY.
SO...ADMISSION. I HIDE IN SHIP COMPARTMENTS FOR A VERY LONG TIME FOR TWO REASONS.
ONE IS TO GET THE DROP ON UNSUSPECTING POSTAL WORKERS AND MAKE MONEY. MONEY THAT PAYS FOR THIS HIDEAWAY. THE SECOND IS SO THAT I CAN FIND A GOOD HOBBY. OR TWO.
THIS IS AN ACUTE EXPLOSIVE DEVICE. YOU HAVE ONE PRECARIOUSLY PLACED WITH A TIMER IN YOUR--
BAMPF

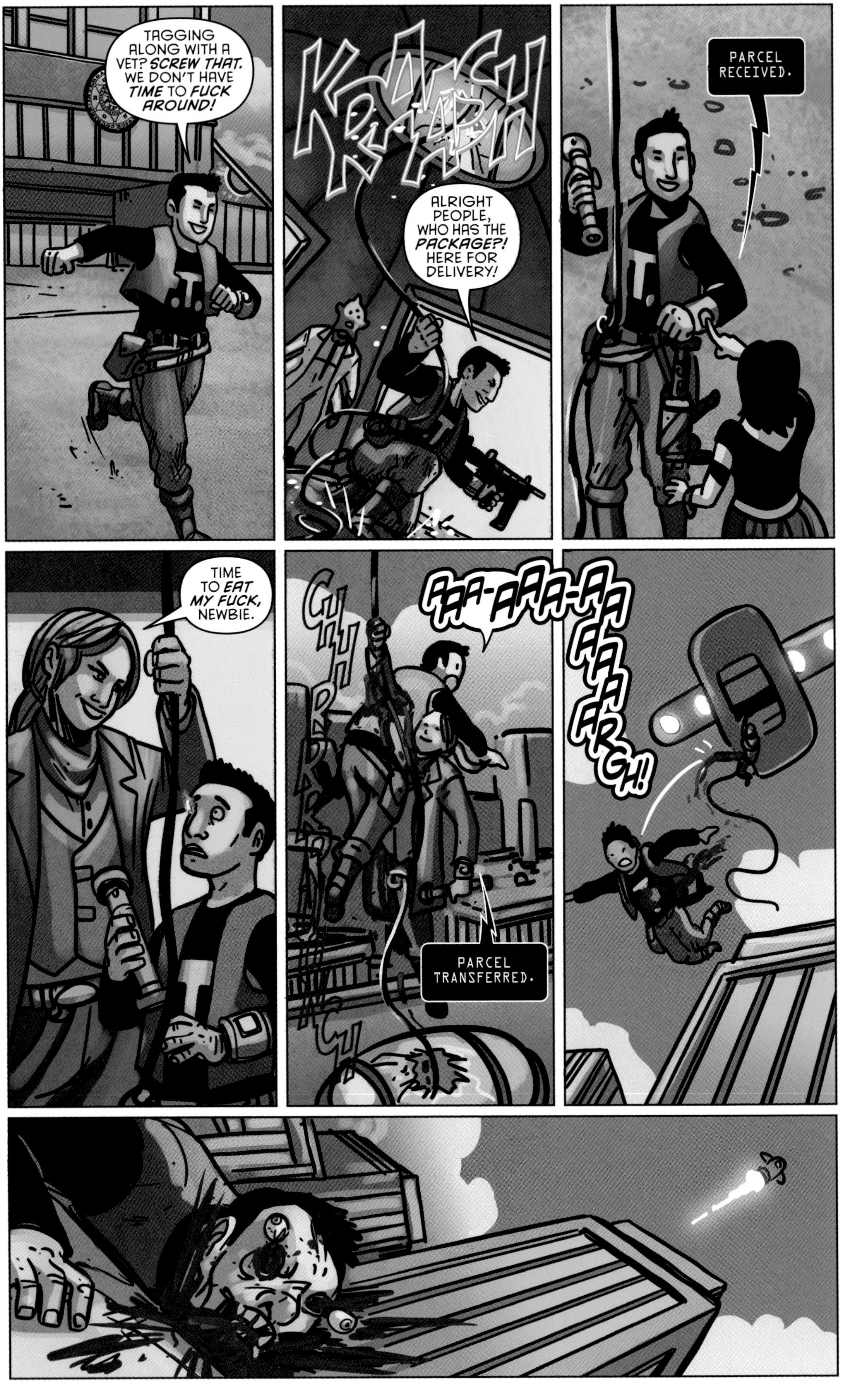
TAGGING ALONG WITH A VET? SCREW THAT. WE DON'T HAVE TIME TO FUCK AROUND!
ALRIGHT PEOPLE, WHO HAS THE PACKAGE?! HERE FOR DELIVERY!
PARCEL RECEIVED.
TIME TO EAT MY FUCK, NEWBIE.
AAA-AAAA-AAAAAAARGH!
PARCEL TRANSFERRED.

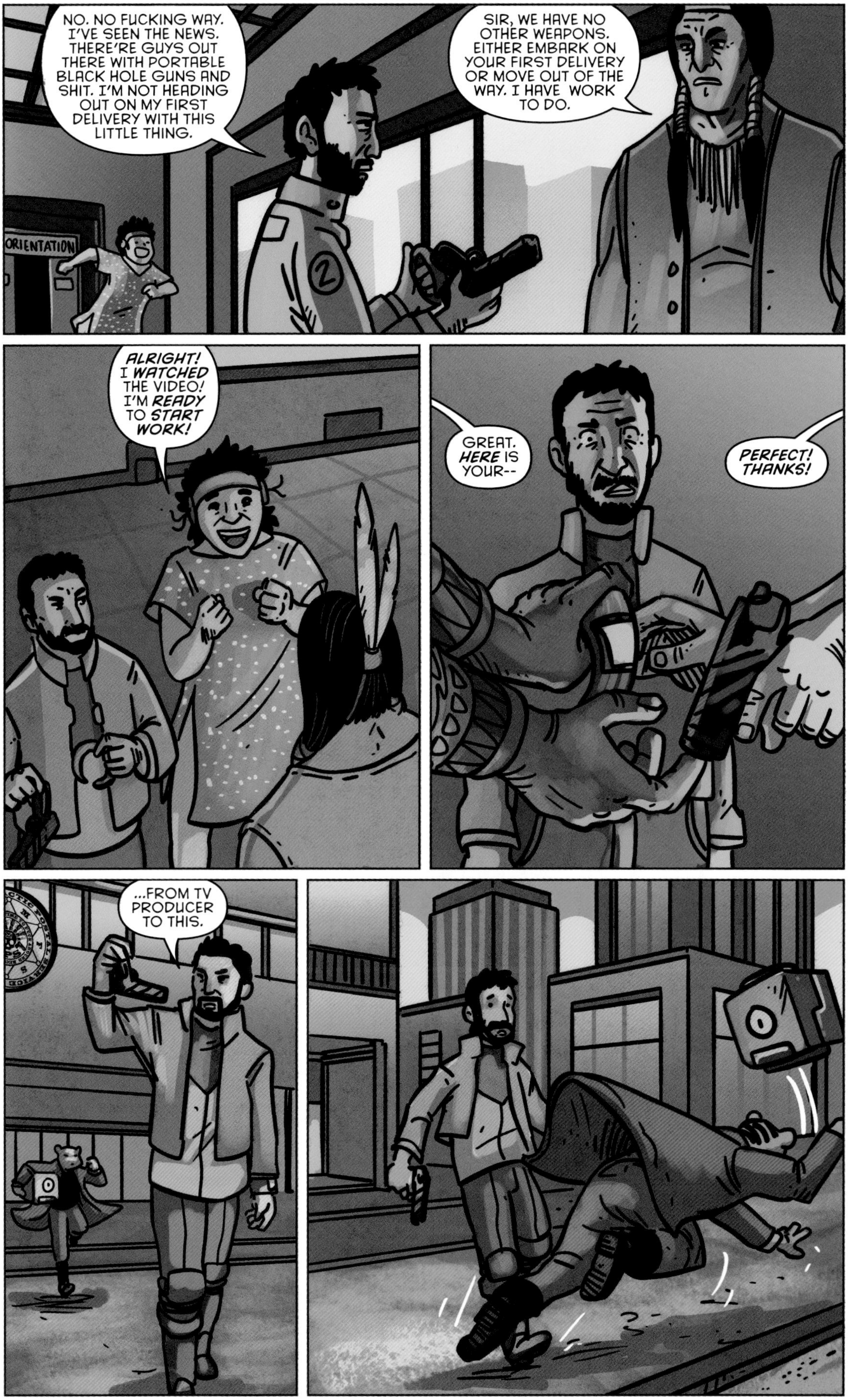
NO. NO FUCKING WAY. I'VE SEEN THE NEWS. THERE'RE GUYS OUT THERE WITH PORTABLE BLACK HOLE GUNS AND SHIT. I'M NOT HEADING OUT ON MY FIRST DELIVERY WITH THIS LITTLE THING.
SIR, WE HAVE NO OTHER WEAPONS. EITHER EMBARK ON YOUR FIRST DELIVERY OR MOVE OUT OF THE WAY. I HAVE WORK TO DO.
ORIENTATION
ALRIGHT! I WATCHED THE VIDEO! I'M READY TO START WORK!
GREAT. HERE IS YOUR--
PERFECT! THANKS!
...FROM TV PRODUCER TO THIS.

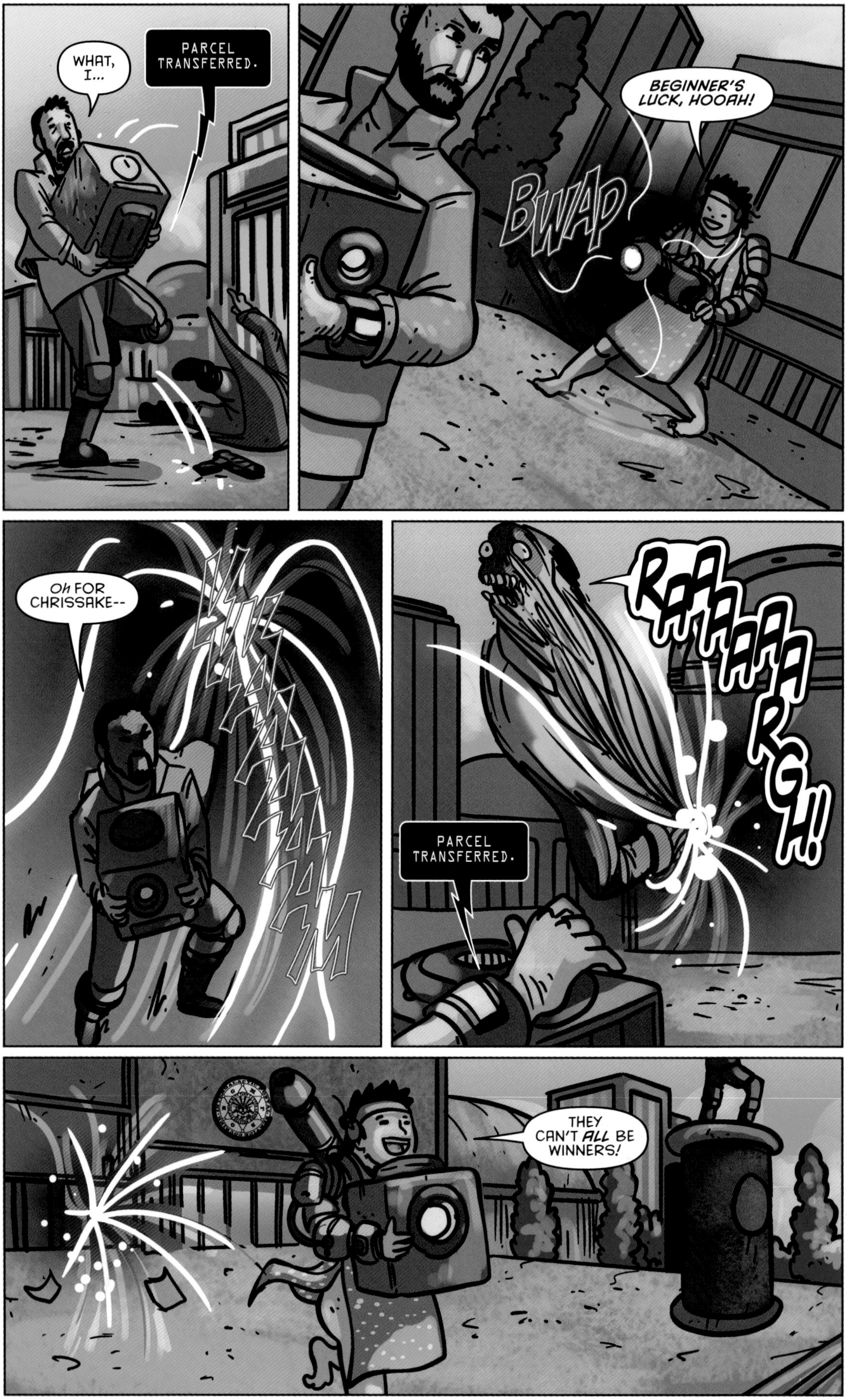
WHAT, I...
PARCEL TRANSFERRED.
BEGINNER'S LUCK, HOOAH!
BWAP
Oh FOR CHRISSAKE--
RAAAAAAARGH!
PARCEL TRANSFERRED.
THEY CAN'T ALL BE WINNERS!

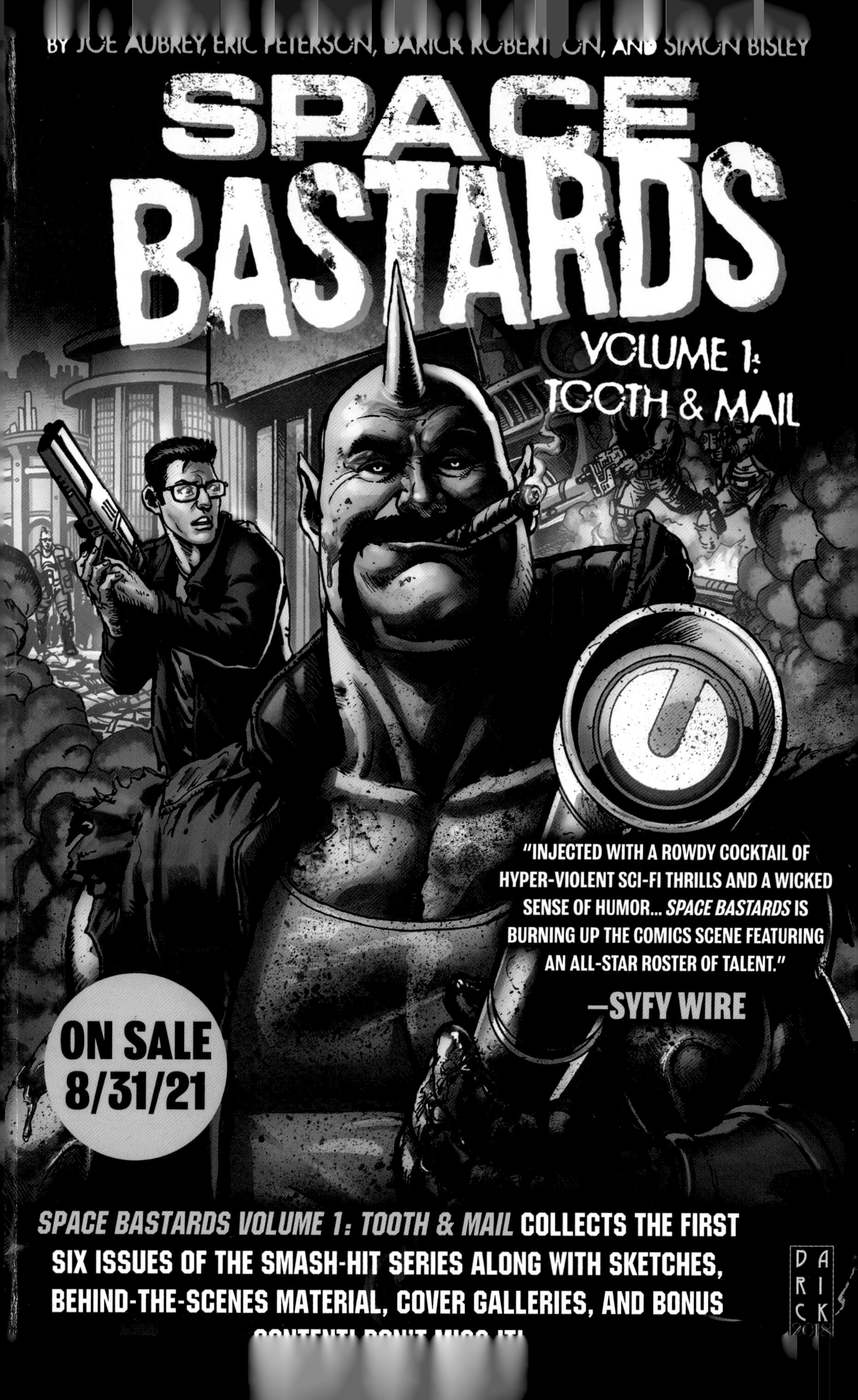

BY JOE AUBREY, ERIC PETERSON, DARICK ROBERTSON, AND SIMON BISLEY

SPACE BASTARDS

VOLUME 1: TOOTH & MAIL

"INJECTED WITH A ROWDY COCKTAIL OF HYPER-VIOLENT SCI-FI THRILLS AND A WICKED SENSE OF HUMOR... *SPACE BASTARDS* IS BURNING UP THE COMICS SCENE FEATURING AN ALL-STAR ROSTER OF TALENT."

—SYFY WIRE

ON SALE 8/31/21

SPACE BASTARDS VOLUME 1: TOOTH & MAIL COLLECTS THE FIRST SIX ISSUES OF THE SMASH-HIT SERIES ALONG WITH SKETCHES, BEHIND-THE-SCENES MATERIAL, COVER GALLERIES, AND BONUS CONTENT! DON'T MISS IT!

Want more?

JOIN THE INTERGALACTIC POSTAL SERVICE, EXPLORE THE *SPACE BASTARDS* WORLD
AND CHARACTERS, AND SNAG A PARCEL FEATURING EXCLUSIVE, LIMITED-EDITION
MERCH THAT ALLOWS YOU TO EXPERIENCE THE STORY IN A BRAND NEW WAY!

WWW.SPACEBASTARDS.COM!